PC Hardware Interfaces

A Developer's Reference

Michael Gook

D1210807

alist

PC Hardware Interfaces:
A Developer's Reference

A-LIST, LLC
295 East Swedesford Rd.
PMB #285
Wayne, PA 19087
702-977-5377 (FAX)
mail@alistpublishing.com
http://www.alistpublishing.com

This book is printed on acid-free paper.

Michael Gook. *PC Hardware Interfaces: A Developer's Reference*
ISBN 1-931769-29-X

Printed in the United States of America
04 7 6 5 4 3 2 1

A-LIST, LLC titles are available for site license or bulk purchase by institutions, user groups, corporations, etc.

Book Editor: Peter Morley

Contents

Chapter 7: Specialized Interfaces for Peripheral Devices _____ 373

Introduction to Interfaces

Informatics and data processing dictionaries define an *interface* as a common boundary shared by two systems, devices, or programs, as well as the elements of this connecting boundary and the auxiliary control circuits used for linking devices. This book deals mainly with interfaces that allow various peripheral devices and their controllers to be connected to personal (and not only personal) computers. Before starting a detailed discussion of specific PC interfaces, a series of general issues regarding the establishment of connections need to be considered.

General Computer Structure

PC compatible computers, like most computers, are built around the classic design of the von Neumann machine of 1945. According to this design, a computer consists of a central processing unit (CPU), memory, and input/output devices. The *processor* executes programs that are stored in the memory; the *memory* stores the programs and data available to the processor; the *input/output devices* provide a link to the external world. Over time, slight corrections have been made to the names of these three fundamental parts, and now devices that used to fall under the definition of input/output devices are called *peripheral devices*. The processor (one or more), memory, and the necessary elements linking them all each with another and with other devices are called the computer's *central part* or *core*.

Peripheral Devices

Peripheral devices are all computer components not pertaining to the core. They can be divided into several types:

❏ *Data storage* devices (external memory devices): disk (magnetic, optical, magneto-optical), tape (streamers), solid state (flash memory cards, modules, and USB devices). These devices are used for nonvolatile storage of information from the memory, and for loading this information back into the main memory. How this information is stored in these devices internally is not really important (the important thing is to correctly read out what has been stored).

❏ *Input/output* (I/O) devices convert information from its computer-internal representation form (bits and bytes) into a form understandable to man (and other creatures) and to various technical devices, and in the reverse direction. (It is not difficult to adapt a computer to control any equipment; all that is needed are sensors and actuating units.) To this category, displays (output devices), keyboards and mice (input devices), printers and scanners, plotters and digitizers, joysticks, acoustic systems and microphones, televisions and video cameras, remote control and telemetry devices belong. The form, into which these devices convert binary information, is determined by their functions.

❏ *Communications* devices are used to transfer information between computers and/or their parts. To this category, modems (wire, radio, infrared, etc.) and local and global network adapters belong. In this area, information needs to be converted from one form into another only so that it can be sent over some distance.

The main operation in the computer is execution of program code by the central processor, and the CPU must be able to interact with peripheral devices.

To access peripheral devices in the x86 processors that are used in the PC-compatible computers, the I/O address space allocated is separate from the memory address space. The size of the I/O space is 64 Kbytes; 1-, 2-, or 4-byte registers of peripheral devices can be mapped onto this space and accessed by several special processor instructions. Registers of peripheral devices can also be mapped onto the main memory space, onto the areas not taken by the system random-access (RAM) and read-only (ROM) memory. The I/O space is separated from the memory space in not all processor architectures. In any case, the addresses of different registers of different devices must not overlap in the address space onto which they are mapped: This is the requirement of conflict-free address resource allocation.

In terms of interaction with the rest of the computer's components, the processor cannot do anything other than access a location in memory or I/O space (to read or write a byte, a word, or a double word), and to react to the hardware interrupts. In this way, any peripheral device must present itself to the processor as a set of registers or memory cells, or be an interrupt source (the latter is not a mandatory requirement).

Hierarchy of Connections

The components of a computer system are connected with each other in a hierarchy, at the top of which the *system-level connection interfaces* are located. To these, the following belong:

❐ Front Side Bus (FSB) to which the central processor (processors in complex systems) is connected
❐ Memory Bus
❐ I/O buses providing communication between the computer core and the peripheral devices

This level of connections being of the system type means that physical memory and I/O addresses (if there are any) are used here.

The most representative specimens of the I/O buses in IBM PC are the ISA (rapidly becoming extinct) and PCI (evolving into PCI-X and further) buses. All processor accesses to the peripheral devices go through the I/O buses. *Controllers* and *adapters*[1] of peripheral devices or their interfaces are connected to I/O buses. Some peripheral devices are combined with their controllers (adapters) (e.g., Ethernet network adapters that are connected to the PCI bus). Other peripheral devices are connected to their controllers via intermediate *peripheral interfaces*, which make up the low level of the connection hierarchy.

Peripheral interfaces are the most varied of all hardware interfaces. Most storage devices (disk, tape type), I/O devices (displays, keyboards, mice, printers, plotters), and some communications devices (external modems) are peripheral devices that are connected via intermediate interfaces. To interact with a peripheral device, the processor accesses registers of the controller that represents the device connected to it.

In terms of the functions they perform, peripheral interfaces can be divided into specialized and universal, dedicated and shared:

❐ *Specialized* interfaces are oriented at connecting a certain narrow class of devices, and use very specific data transfer protocols. Examples of such protocols include the very popular VGA monitor interface, the floppy disk drive interface, the traditional

---

[1] A controller is more "intelligent" than an adapter.

keyboard and mouse interfaces, and the interface of the IDE/ATA hard disk controllers.

❐ *Universal* interfaces are more widely used; their protocols deliver all types of data. Examples include the communication port (COM), SCSI, USB, and FireWire protocols.

❐ *Dedicated* interfaces allow only one device to be connected to one port (connection point) of the adapter (controller); the number of devices that can be connected is limited by the number of ports. Examples are the COM port, VGA monitor interface, AGP, and Serial ATA.

❐ *Shared* interfaces allow multiple devices to be connected to one adapter port. Physical connections can take many forms: a bus (printed circuit like ISA or PCI; cable bus like SCSI or IDE/ATA), a daisy chain of devices (SCSI, IEEE 1284.3), a logical bus implemented with hubs (USB), or built-in repeaters (IEEE 1394 FireWire).

Interface Organization

The task of each of the interfaces considered here is to transfer information between some devices. To get the whole picture, the type of information that can be transmitted and the physical signals used to do this will be considered. Then, the types of relationships into which the interconnected devices can enter and the tasks various protocols need to accomplish will be looked into.

Types of Transferred Information

Information (data) that needs to be sent over interfaces can be of various natures. Some of the types of transmitted information are listed below:

❐ Analog information reflects a process continuous in time and magnitude (i.e., it can take on any of an indefinite number of values even within a definite interval). One example, sound (including speech) is continuous changes in (usually) air pressure. The task of how to transfer such information arises, for example, when a microphone (a device for converting air pressure changes to electric voltage changes) is connected to a computer.

❐ Discrete information depicts a process by a finite number of values. The elementary discrete information unit is a bit, which can take on one of two logical values: 1 (true, yes) or 0 (false, no). One bit can be used to reflect the state of a mouse button (whether it is pressed or not). Discrete binary information is natural to most computers as it is the easiest to obtain, process, store, and transmit. Discrete information can be not only binary; of interest is the ternary system, in which a tribit[1] can have three states — yes, no, and don't know.

❑ Digital information is a sequence (set) of values that have finite width (and, accordingly, finite number of possible values). An example is digitized sound, which is a sequence of samples of instantaneous pressure values taken at equal time intervals.

Discrete and digital information are often confused (although, it is not always necessary to tell them apart) because they look similar: in the binary number system, both of them are represented by collections of ones and zeroes. Digital information is a special case of discrete information. Concerning data transfer over different interfaces, the division of information into analog (continuous) and discrete is of importance.

In order to transmit data, they must be represented as a *signal*: a physical process (electric, optical, or electromagnetic, although others also are possible). Signals can be of different types: analog (continuous), discrete, or digital. The type of signal may not necessarily correspond to the type of the transferred data. So, for example, a telephone modem analog signal carries discrete (digital) data. The type and nature of the signal used is determined by the requirements of the interface: transmission range, data transfer rate, data reliability and validity, security, cost, connection ease, power consumption, and others.

Parallel and Serial Interfaces

For computers and devices connected to them, the most common task is transfer of, as a rule, significant amounts (more than one bit) of discrete data. The most common way to represent data by signals is the binary method: For example, logical one corresponds to the high (above the threshold) voltage level; logical zero corresponds to the low (below the threshold) voltage level. A reverse assignment is also possible. One binary signal transfers one bit of information within one unit of time. As already mentioned, the processor exchanges information with peripheral devices in bytes (8 bits), words (in the x86 world, one word is two bytes or 16 bits), or double words (32 bits). There are two approaches to organize the interface to transfer a group of bits:

❑ *Parallel interface*: A separate line (usually binary) is used for each transmitted bit of the group, and all bits of the group are transmitted simultaneously within one unit of time (i.e., they move over the interface lines in parallel). The 8-bit parallel printer port (LPT port), the 16-bit ATA/ATAPI interface, the 8- or 16-bit SCSI port, and the 32- or 64-bit PCI bus all are examples of the parallel interface.

---

[1] One of the ternary digit names.

❏ *Serial interface*: Only one signal line is used, and bits of the group are sent in turn one after another; each of them is assigned a unit of time (bit interval). The serial communications (COM) port, the serial USB and FireWire buses, and local and wide area network interfaces are all examples of the serial interface.

At first glance, the parallel interface seems to be easier and straightforward to organize, as there is no need to queue the bits for transmission and then assemble bytes from the received serial bits. Also, at first glance, the parallel interface is a faster way to transmit data, because bits are sent in packets. The obvious shortcoming of the parallel interface is the large number of wires and connector contacts in the connecting cable (at least one for each bit). For this reason, parallel interface cables and interface circuits of devices are cumbersome and expensive, which is tolerated for the sake of the desired transmission speed. The transceiver of the serial interface is more complex functionally, but its cables and connectors are much simpler and less expensive. Naturally, it is not wise (not to mention impossible) to lay multiple-wire parallel interface cables over long distances, the serial interface is much more suitable here. These considerations were decisive in selecting an interface until about the early 1990s. Then, the choice was simple: parallel interfaces were employed over short distances (a few or tens of meters maximum) where high speeds were required; over long distances, as well as when parallel cables were unacceptable, serial interfaces were used, sacrificing the transfer speed.

That the data transfer rate or speed is defined as the number of bits sent over a unit of time divided by the unit's duration. For simplicity, the interface *clock rate* or *frequency* — a unit that is the inverse of the unit's length (period) — can be used. This concept is natural for synchronous interfaces, which have a synchronization (clocking) signal that determines the allowable starting moments of all events (state changes). For asynchronous interfaces, the equivalent clock rate — a unit that is the inverse of the minimal length of one interface state — can be used. Using these definitions, it can be said that the maximum (peak) data transfer rate equals the product of the frequency and the interface width. The width of the serial interface is one bit; the width of the parallel interface equals the number of the signal lines used to transfer data bits. With the speed issue resolved, only the questions of maximum frequency and width remain. For both the parallel and the serial interfaces, the maximum frequency is determined by the attainable efficiency (at reasonable monetary and energy expenses) of the transceiver circuits of the devices and the cables' frequency characteristics. The advantages of the serial interface can already be seen here: Expenses for building high-speed elements do not have to be multiplied by the interface's width, as is to be done with the parallel interface.

There is a phenomenon in the *parallel* interface called *skew* that significantly affects the achievable frequency limit. In essence, skew means that signals sent simultaneously from one end of the interface do not arrive to the opposite end simultaneously because of the differences in the individual signal circuits' characteristics. The transit time is affected by the length of wires, insulation characteristics, connecting elements, etc. Obviously, the signal skew (difference in the arrival time) of different bits must be explicitly smaller than the time unit, otherwise the bits will be scrambled with the bits of the same name from previous and successive transfers. It is totally clear that the signal skew limits the allowable interface cable length: At the same relative signal propagation speed difference, as the transmission range increases, so does the skew.

The skew also hinders increasing the interface width: The more parallel circuits are used, the more difficult it is to make them identical. Because of this, wide interfaces even have to be broken down into several narrower groups, for each of which their own control signals are used. In the 1990s, frequencies of hundreds of megahertz and higher started to be employed (i.e., the time unit started to be measured in nanoseconds or fractions of nanoseconds). A proportionally small skew could be attained only within the confines of rigid compact constructions (like printed circuit boards), while to connect devices by cables tens of centimeters long, frequencies of up to tens of megahertz were the maximum. For the purposes of orientation among the numbers, in one nanosecond a signal travels 20–25 centimeters over electrical conductor.

In order to increase the bandwidth of parallel interfaces, Dual Data Rate (DDR) was employed in the mid-1990s. In essence, it consists of making the switching frequencies of the data signal lines and the clock signal lines equal. In the classical version, the data of the information lines were latched only at one transition (positive or negative) of the clock signal, which doubles the switching speed of the clock lines relative to the data lines. With double clocking, data are latched at both the positive and the negative transitions; therefore, the switching frequency for all lines becomes the same, which with the identical physical characteristics of cables and interface circuits makes it possible to double the bandwidth. This modernization wave started with the ATA interface (UltraDMA modes) and has already rolled over the SCSI (Ultra160 and higher) and the memory (DDR SDRAM) interfaces.

Moreover, *Source Synchronous transfer* is employed at high frequencies: The clocking signal, which determines the moments at which switching is done and the data are valid, is generated by the source of data itself. This makes it possible to align the data and clock signals more precisely in time, because they propagate over the interface in parallel and in one direction. The alternative — a common source clock — cannot handle high switching frequencies, because the time relations between data and clock signals at different (geographical) points will be different.

Increasing the interface signal switching frequency, as a rule, is accompanied by lowering the levels of the signals that are generated by the interface circuitry. This tendency is explained by power considerations: A frequency increase means that the time needed to switch a signal decreases. At higher signal amplitudes, a higher signal rise rate is required and, consequently, a higher transmitter current. Increasing output current (pulsing) is not desirable for various reasons: It causes great crosstalk interferences in the parallel interface, necessitates the use of powerful output signal drivers, and produces excessive heat. The tendency to lower signal voltages can be traced to the examples of the AGP interface (3.3 V — 1.5 V — 0.8 V), the PCI/PCI-X buses (5 V — 3.3 V — 1.5 V), the SCSI and other memory and processor buses.

The skew problem does not exist in serial interfaces; therefore, the frequency can be increased up to the capability limits of the transceiver circuits. Of course, cable frequency characteristics impose limitations, but it is much easier to fashion a good cable for one circuit than for several, and with high identity requirements to boot. And when the electric cable cannot handle the required frequency and range, a switch to optical cable can be made, whose undeveloped frequency reserves are huge. A parallel optical interface, on the other hand, is too much of a luxury[1].

The reasons stated above explain the tendency to switch to serial methods of data transfer. Table 1 lists the comparative characteristics of the parallel and serial interfaces presently employed to connect peripheral devices. To complete the picture of parallel data transfer method achievements, parallel buses used to connect processors to the memory must be mentioned. Their width reaches up to 128 bits and their data transfer rates can reach several gigabytes per second. However, these performance characteristics are obtained only over very short distances (some ten centimeters or even less). Serial network interfaces (Ethernet 10/100/1000/10000 Mbps, transfer technologies of global networks such as ATM, SONET, and SDH), with their impressive combination of gigabit speeds and communication range (hundreds of meters to tens and hundreds of kilometers) are not included in this table. There are some nuances when comparing parallel interface speeds, which are expressed in megabytes per second (MBps), and serial interface speeds, which are expressed in megabits per second (Mbps); they will be explained further on. For the time being, megabits per second can be divided by 10 (not by 8) to obtain an approximate value of megabytes per second.

Table 1. Parallel and Serial Interface Comparisons

Name, width	Use	Speed limits	Range	Prospects
Parallel interfaces and buses				
IEEE 1284 (LPT port), 8 bit	Connecting printers, plotters, scanners, and others.	2 MBps	1–10 m	Abandonment in favor of USB
SCSI, 8/16 bit	Connecting any internal and external devices	10-20-40-80-160-320 MBps	Up to 6-12-25 m	Move to the Serial SCSI

continues

---

[1] The 10-gigabyte Ethernet mode has a parallel/serial optical version.

Table 1 Continued

Name, width	Use	Speed limits	Range	Prospects
Parallel interfaces and buses				
ATA/ATAPI, 16 bit	Connecting internal data storage devices	16–33–66–10–133 MBps	Up to 0.5 m	Move to the Serial ATA
ISA, 8/16 bit	Connecting internal devices (expansion cards)	8–16 MBps	15–20 cm (within limits of the PCB with expansion slots)	Abandonment
PCI, 32/64 bit	Connecting internal devices (expansion cards)	66–133–266–533 MBps	10–15 cm (within limits of the PCB with expansion slots)	Move to PCI-X
PCI-X, 32/64/16 bit	Connecting internal devices (expansion cards)	533–4256 MBps	10–15 cm (within limits of the PCB with expansion slots)	
Serial interfaces				
RS-232C (COM port)	Connecting communications and other external devices	115200 bps (11.5 Kbps)	25 m	Abandonment in favor of USB
RS-422/485	Connecting industrial automation devices	10 Mbps	1,200 m	
USB 1.0-1.1	Connecting external devices	1.5–12 Mbps (up to1 MBps)	30 m	Move to USB 2.0
USB 2.0	Connecting external devices	1,5–12–480 Mbps (up to 24 MBps)	30 m	
IEEE 1394 (FireWire)	Connecting external devices, organizing multimedia device networks	100–200–400 Mbps	72 m	Moving to 800 Mbps and 1,600 Mbps.
Serial ATA	Connecting internal data storage devices	1.5 Gbps (150 MBps)	1 m	Moving to higher speeds

continues

Table 1 Continued

Name, width	Use	Speed limits	Range	Prospects
Serial interfaces				
Serial SCSI	Connecting internal and external devices	3 Gbps	6 m	Moving to 6 Gbps
Fibre Channel	Connecting external data storage devices	2 Gbps	15 m (copper cable) — 10 km (optical cable)	Moving to 4 Gbps
PCI Express	Connecting components on PCBs interblock connection	2,5–80 Gbps	Within the limits of the chassis	
Hyper Transport	Connecting components on PCBs	Up to 6.4 GBps (total of the two oncoming lines up to 12.8 GBps)	Within the limits of the PCB	
InfiniBand	Connecting components on PCBs; interblock and inter-computer connections (in clusters)	2.5, 10, and 30 Gbps	Up to 17 m over a copper cable; up to 10 km over optical cable.	

Signals and Transmission Medium

The most common physical process used to transmit interface signals is electromagnetic oscillations of various frequencies. The most usual electrical signals are electromagnetic oscillations of relatively low frequency range (up to tens or hundreds of megahertz) transmitted over electric wires. This type of transmitter places its signal in the form of certain voltage of current levels on one end of the electric communications line (cable) while the receiver on the other end of the line receives a signal that is like the signal sent to a greater or lesser extent. The degree of similarity (or dissimilarity) is determined by the cable's performance characteristics, its length, the frequency spectrum of the signal, and the amount of external interference. When high frequency is combined with great length (of interest is the LF factor: the product of the length L and the frequency F), wave characteristics of electromagnetic signals, such as propagation signal decay and reflections from the line's non-uniformities, must be taken into account.

Signal decay occurs not only because of electromagnetic losses (cable heating), but because of spurious radiation: electromagnetic signals emanating beyond the confines of the cable into the ether. Because of wave effects, electric cables employed to transmit the signal must be of special construction: coaxial cables, twisted pairs, and some others. The task of these constructions is to preserve the shape of the transmitted signal as faithfully as possible, not to allow it to escape the cable limits, and, as far as possible, not to let external interferences penetrate the cable. The last two items are especially important in providing information transmission security and confidentiality: preventing outside eavesdropping on and malicious damage to the information (or making it difficult). The overwhelming majority of peripheral device interfaces use wires to transmit electric signals, which provides transmission ranges of several, tens, and hundreds of meters at speeds of up to several gigabits per second; wire transmission also dominates in computer networks.

Electromagnetic oscillations in the hundreds of megahertz to tens of gigahertz range can also be employed for wireless radio transmission of signals. Frequencies lower than these require unacceptably large antennas for efficient emission and reception; with higher frequencies, difficulties exist so far in implementing transceivers, and moreover, signal propagation in this frequency range has some unattractive specifics (such as being absorbed by fog or rain). The first computer radio interface to have been widely used — Bluetooth — employs a microwave range frequency of 2.4 GHz. The radio waves propagate in a straight line in this range (there is no bending effect peculiar to low frequency radio waves) and, with some attenuation, can penetrate through walls. The unpleasant part is that the signal is reflected from various objects, so that the receiver receives not only the direct transmitter signal but also the bounced signals, which arrive with some delay relative to the original signal. Because of this multipath reception effect, communication on some frequencies is impossible at some points, but as soon as the receiver or transmitter is moved a little or the frequency is changed, the connection resumes.

Various methods are used to combat the problem of the signal decay due to the multipath reception effect; the Bluetooth technology employs the carrier hopping method. It uses omnidirectional antennas; the communication range, depending on how powerful the transmitter is, is limited to tens or hundreds of meters. Wireless interfaces are attractive because of the absence of cables and connectors, which have to be laid and connected to organize communications: In order to establish a radio connection, devices only have to be within the coverage area. However, they also have their demerit: The transmission medium is totally open to everyone including wrongdoers, who can intercept the signal to obtain information or introduce their own signals with malevolent purposes. The solution to this security problem lies beyond the scope of physical signal transmission. Another problem with radio interfaces is the high and constantly growing occupancy of the radio spectrum, which causes interference (unwanted interaction) of different equipment, including wireless and cellular phones, wireless local network equipment, microwave ovens, and other equipment.

Further up the electromagnetic oscillation frequency spectrum is, first, the infrared spectrum, which adjoins the visible optical range. These ranges are also used for optical transmission of signals both over wires (optical fiber) and without them.

The infrared port — the standard IrDA and its forerunners, HP-SIR and ASK IR — have been used for wireless connection of peripheral equipment (printers and other devices) to computers for many years. This type of connection looks especially effective with compact devices, whose size is proportionate to (or even smaller than) the cable and connectors of traditional interfaces. The IrDA port has directed emitters and receivers with a coverage angle of 15–30° and a range of about 1 meter, so to connect devices, they must be close enough to each other and properly oriented. The small coverage area (as compared to the radio interface) is not always a drawback: It is easier to control against unsanctioned connections, and users can be certain that no-one from behind the wall will tap into their line and eavesdrop on their traffic. The attainable maximum transfer speed is not high (4 Mbps); higher speeds are problematic because of the low signal strength that reaches the photoreceiver. Infrared communication also is employed in wireless local networks (IEEE 802.11 DFIR) where omnidirectional transceivers using the signal bounce off the walls and ceiling make it possible to provide a coverage area of about 10 meters; however, speeds are even lower here (1–2 Mbps).

The undisputed leader in terms of the LF factor is the fiber optic link, in which infrared light impulses are sent over glass or plastic optical fiber. Glass fiber is mostly used in telecommunications, where transmissions over long distances, from hundreds of meters to tens (or even hundreds) of kilometers, are required. For the right wavelengths, certain types of optic fibers pass the signal with acceptable attenuation and shape distortion, making speeds in the gigabit range over distances measured in kilometers possible. Optical lines have a throughput reserve in the form of wave multiplexing: Many optical signals of different frequencies can be sent over one fiber without interfering with each other. Similar signal multiplexing has far more modest possibilities in electric cables. The shortcoming of the glass optic is that its end devices (transceivers) and the connecting equipment are quite expensive; the cable itself can be even cheaper than copper cable. For interfaces that do not require signals to be transmitted over long distances (up to several tens of meters), plastic optic fiber can be used; its cables and connectors are significantly cheaper than for glass fiber. An example of an optic interface in modern personal computers is the Toslink interface, the optic version of the digital S/PDIF audio interface. The Fibre Channel (FCAL) interface can be encountered in servers; data storage devices that may be located kilometers away from the computer are connected using this interface, providing speeds of about 1 Gbps.

While on the subject of optic interfaces, it must be noted that they provide complete *galvanic decoupling* of connected devices. Moreover, optic interfaces are not sensitive to electromagnetic interference. In some cases, these characteristics play a decisive role, for example, when connecting equipment at power plants, on industrial premises with strong interferences, and the like. Fiber optic interfaces are most secure against unauthorized connection. Information cannot be taken off the channel without physically tapping into it, and should it be necessary, line state can be monitored and an unauthorized tapping attempt detected in due time.

Galvanic Decoupling of Connected Devices

Galvanic decoupling means that the circuit grounds of the connected devices do not electrically connect with each other over the interface circuits. Moreover, the devices can be under significantly different potentials.

Most electrical interfaces do not provide for galvanic decoupling. For example, the circuit grounds of the devices connected to a COM or LPT computer port are linked with the computer's circuit ground (and over the interface cables, their grounds are linked with each other). If there is a potential difference before the connection, then equalizing current will flow over the interface cable common wire, which is no good for several reasons. A voltage drop on the common wire due to this current flow causes signal levels to shift, and the flow of alternating current leads to the mixing of the useful signal with the variable component of interference. TTL interfaces are especially sensitive to this interference, whereas in the RS-232C interface the dead zone will absorb up to 2 V of interference or signal shift. If the common wire is broken or there is a bad connection, but much more often when devices are connected or disconnected under the power on, the potential difference is applied to the signal circuits and the equalizing current flowing through them often causes damages to the devices. In audio equipment, equalizing currents cause audible interference (background hum).

Interface signals are decoupled from the device's ground using optoelectronic devices (in the MIDI and current loop interfaces) or transformers (FireWire bus, Ethernet interfaces). Sometimes, direct current decoupling is achieved using decoupling capacitors (in cheap versions of the FireWire and PCI Express interface).

Potential difference between devices connected by a galvanically decoupled interface is limited by the maximum *dielectric breakdown voltage* for the given interface. For example, Ethernet adapters (for twisted pair) must be able to withstand voltages of up to 1.5 KV; decoupling implemented using optrons withstands 500–1,000 V; the capacitor decoupling used in FireWire provides up to a 60 V safety margin. Fiber optic interfaces provide galvanic decoupling for any voltages: thousands or even millions of volts. Any wireless interface also provides galvanic decoupling.

Device Interaction and Device Topology

The interfaces considered here are used to exchange information between connected devices; the exchange is conducted using transactions. An *interface transaction* is a finite operation of transferring a certain amount of information. Each transaction involves a *master device* (exchange initiator), which controls the interface during the given time period, and a *slave device* (target device), the second participant in the transaction that is selected by the master device and follows its commands.

A transaction can consist of a series of phases (states, steps) in each of which some elementary objective is accomplished. The set of phases depends on the complexity of the interface, and in the simplest case it comes down to simple data transfer phases. The *interface protocol* is a set of rules for interaction between master and slave devices for executing transactions. The complexity of the protocol depends on the potential number of involved devices, their interrelations, and the characteristics of the exchange that the protocol has to provide.

If the interface links more than two devices, then the protocol has to tackle the addressing issue: selecting the device that will respond to the given transaction. At the same time, the enumeration task needs to be addressed: assigning each device a unique address, at least within the limits of the given grouping. The user must play a minimal role in assigning addresses, or, even better, not to have any part in it at all: This is one of the principles of the Plug and Play system. Modern interfaces — the PCI, USB, FireWire — were from the beginning developed with the objective of totally automatic address assignment taken into account. Automatic address assignment capabilities were added to several old interfaces later on and they have remained in some (the Microsoft Plug and Play specification for the ISA bus, for example) but not in others (attempts to automate the SCSI were abandoned rather quickly).

While on the subject of the Plug and Play, one more objective needs to be mentioned: automatic detection of connected devices. Master devices must have a means to find out exactly what devices are connected to their interface, and must support configuration tables: lists of correspondences between device addresses and their identifiers. Solving the automatic device enumeration and detection issues allows the issue of automatic configuration, static or dynamic, to be discussed. *Static configuration* systems allow powered-down devices to be connected and disconnected; after all configuration changes have been made, these devices need to be reinitialized. This is the case with the PCI and SCSI buses, although special hot plug versions exist for them. *Dynamic configuration* systems allow devices to be connected on the fly, almost not affecting the operation of other devices. The USB, FireWire buses and, of course, the Bluetooth and IrDA wireless interfaces can be configured automatically.

Relations between connected devices can be *peer-to-peer* or *master/slave* types. In the case of peer-to-peer relations, any device (at least not only one) can attempt to become the master and in fact become it to carry out some transactions. This creates the *arbitration* objective: deciding which device becomes master for the next transaction. In the case of master/slave relations, only one of the devices connected by the interface can become master. The *host-centric* interface means that one central node, called the host, controls all transaction executions. The host role in the system-level interfaces is played by the computer's central part (the core with the closest surrounding); for peripheral level interfaces, the host role is played by a computer with an interface adapter (controller). The PCI, FireWire, and SCSI buses are examples of peer-to-peer interfaces; the USB and ATA are examples of host-centric interfaces.

The *topology* determines the configuration of connections between connected devices: point-to-point, bus, star, mixed, or daisy-chain.

The *point-to-point*, or dedicated, interface is the simplest connection, in which only two devices are present. Each of the devices knows that only one device can be on the opposite end and no addressing problem arises. If relations in this connection are of the master/slave type, then the arbitration issue does not exist either. A point-to-point interface with a slave device will have the simplest protocol. One example of such interface is the standard mode LPT port, to which only one device (printer) is connected.

Three possible exchange modes are distinguished for the point-to-point interface:

❒ The *duplex* mode allows information to be sent over one channel in both directions simultaneously. It may be asymmetrical, if the direct and reverse bandwidth are significantly different, or symmetrical. On the subject of the bandwidth, for duplex connections it often means the summary bandwidth of both the direct and reverse channels.

❒ The *half-duplex* mode allows information to be sent in the direct and reverse directions in turns; the interface is equipped with a means to switch the channel transfer direction.

❒ The *simplex* (unidirectional) mode provides only one data transfer direction (in the opposite direction, only auxiliary signals of the interface can be sent).

Bus type topology means connecting several devices to one bus. Bus in the given context means the collection of the signal lines connecting several devices. All devices use the same bus line to exchange information; they can all hear each other simultaneously. For an exchange transaction to be successful, only one device on the bus can be the master (initiator) at this moment; if more than one device on the bus is trying to become the master, than the arbitration protocol and mechanism — granting bus control rights — must also be implemented. The arbitration can be centralized, with one dedicated arbiter bus node doing it, or distributed, when the function is performed by all potential masters. Arbitration can be simple or prioritized, with various mechanisms to control node priority. Examples of buses with centralized arbitration are PCI and ISA; SCSI and FireWire employ distributed arbitration. Bus type topology is inexpensive and simple to implement, which is especially noticeable in parallel interfaces with a large number of signal lines. However, this is achieved at the expense of a more complex protocol and greater vulnerability, because the failure of one device (or a communications line) can paralyze the entire bus.

Star topology is a way to connect more than two devices in which each peripheral device is connected to the central device by its set of interface lines. As a rule, the central node is also the only master device, so the arbitration issue is excluded from the protocol. The addressing issue is solved exclusively by means of the central node (star topology can be considered as a collection of point-to-point connections), which also simplifies the protocol. Besides the simple protocol, star topology possesses a series of other benefits: high survivability (the failure of one of the peripheral devices or its communication lines does not affect the rest); the longest communication range (matching devices with the lines is easier to accomplish in point-to-point connections, in which the loads on the transmitters are minimal). However, when the number of signal lines is large, star interfaces turn out to be too expensive, so the star topology is mostly used for serial interfaces. An example of star topology is the new Serial ATA interface.

Daisy-chain topology connects one device to another in a chain in which each device has a pair of connectors and relays the interface signals from one connector to the other. Physical daisy-chain topology can have different logical organization. For example, in case of the SCSI, the chain provides bus connection but with the number of clients not set in advance (i.e., all the nodes are connected to one set of the signal lines at the same time). Another case is connecting a chain of devices to the LPT port; for example, a scanner, followed by an external hard disk drive, and finally a regular printer. In this case, the internal logic of the interface part of devices in the middle of the chain (the IEEE 1284.3 standard) relays signals from one connector to the other selectively, under the control of the special device selection protocol. As a result of the execution of this protocol, a point-to-point connection is established between the host and one of the chained devices, and the subsequent transfer is conducted as if there were only one device connected to the computer's port.

Some interfaces have hybrid topology; for example, in the PCI bus most of the signal lines have bus organization, but some signals are routed to each device (slot) radially from the central device (the bridge). The USB uses tree-like physical (external) topology (connection of stars with a USB hub at the center of each star), but logical hubs connect all devices in bus topology with the only master: the host controller.

Transfer Validity and Reliability and Flow Control

Data transfer integrity control involves detecting and sometimes correcting errors that occur during transfers. Far from all interfaces possess this control: In some of them, data integrity is not important, while in others the probability of errors is negligibly small. In new interfaces, transfer integrity is given serious attention as they, as a rule, are intended to work in extreme conditions (high frequencies, long distances, and interference).

A *parity check* is the simplest way to detect errors. In it, a parity bit is added to each transmitted information element (as a rule, a byte or a word) that supplements the number of one-value information bits to even (even parity) or odd (odd parity). The receiver checks the number of one-value bits, including the parity bit, for parity (odd or even, depending on what was agreed) and if it detects that the received parity does not match the parity that was sent, it considers the received data erroneous. It must inform the transmitting device about this in order to attempt to retransmit information that is distorted. A parity check is the most primitive and least effective way to control data integrity; with a noticeable overhead (usually one bit for each byte), this check does not catch all even parity errors (distortion of the even number of bits). Parity checking is employed in serial interfaces (COM port) and the SCSI bus; it used also to be employed for memory.

Information doubling is a more wasteful (but also more reliable) control method employed when small amounts of information are transferred. In it, each information element (usually a several-bit long bit field) is repeated twice; moreover, one of the copies can be sent inverted. If the two received copies differ, the reception is considered an error. This method is used to protect identifier packets in the USB interface. A development of this idea is repeating the block three times: If two of the three received copies match, they are considered the right ones (this can also be considered an error-correction method). This method is employed in the Bluetooth radio interface.

A more complex, but also more efficient, control version is calculating Cyclic Redundant Code (CRC) and adding it to the transmitted information. For example, using 16-bit CRC, errors in data blocks up to 4 KB can be detected with very high probability. CRC is practical to calculate with serial data transmission: for this, only simple hardware circuitry (feedback shift registers) is needed. Calculating CRC with parallel transmission (and by software utilizing the CPU) is resource-intensive. Nevertheless, CRC control is used in the parallel IDE/ATA interface, but only in the Ultra DMA mode (other transmission modes of this bus have no error control of any kind).

To correct transmission errors, Error Correction Codes (ECC) are employed. Here, the idea consists of calculating several control bits, each of which is calculated under the parity check rules for certain information group bits. Special division into groups (that partially overlap) makes use of the received information and control bits to detect and even correct errors. The number of control bits depends on the number of the information bits and the desired ratio of the corrected and detected errors. For example, to correct a single occurrence and to detect all double occurrence errors (and most errors of higher occurrence), four control bits are needed for every eight information bits, five for 16, six for 32, and seven for 64, respectively. The ECC control is widely used in memory operations (especially for cache) and in some interfaces (such as PCI-X).

Ensuring *transfer reliability* means informing the transaction's initiator whether or not it has been successfully executed, which in case of failure allows the initiator to undertake some corrective measures (an attempt to retransmit the data, for example). Some interfaces (and protocols) do not provide transfer reliability: For example, in the ISA bus even a non-existent device can be accessed. In this case, write operations are performed into nothing, while read operations usually return empty data (FFh), which the initiator cannot distinguish from real data. The PCI bus is reliable: the initiator always knows what has happened to its transactions; data transfer integrity is controlled (by parity check or ECC methods).

The issue of coordinating the work pace of devices connected by an interface is solved with the help of handshaking and/or flow control mechanisms.

Handshaking is mutual acknowledgement of individual protocol steps by both participants of the transaction, which makes it possible to match up the work pace of the initiator and target devices. Handshaking is widely employed in parallel interfaces (in the LPT port, expansion buses), where special interface lines are used for this purpose.

Flow control is the receiver's informing the data source (transmitter) of its capability to receive data: If the receiver cannot keep up servicing the incoming data, it requests the transmitter to suspend the transmission for a certain period of time or until special notification.

Interfaces that employ handshaking, as a rule, do not require a separate flow control mechanism (handshaking also takes care of the pace matching). In general, serial interfaces require some form of flow control; the COM port even has two versions of a flow control protocol.

Timing and Synchronization Concepts

In terms of requirements of timing and speed, data transfer transactions can be asynchronous, synchronous, and isochronous. It must be noted right away that there is no rigid correlation between the interface type and the type of transfers it conducts.

In *asynchronous* data transfers and interfaces, the participants do not have any particular responsibilities to each other in terms of timing: the initiator can begin a transaction at any time, while the target device, as a rule, can suspend it in case it is not ready to continue servicing it. Asynchronous transmission can be employed with all devices not working in real time: printers, scanners, data storage devices, etc.

In *synchronous interfaces*, the transaction parties are rigidly connected in terms of timing. They have a constant synchronization clocking signal to which all interface events are tied: bit transfer in serial and byte (word) transfer in parallel interfaces. As a rule, the clocking signal is of a precisely sustained and constant frequency, although there are some interfaces in which the clock signal period varies (the SPI, for example). Both the transmitter and the receiver have the synchronization signal; either a separate interface line is used to transmit the clocking signal, or it is packed into the common signal together with the transmitted data with the help of self-synchronizing codes. A separate clocking line makes an interface more expensive; moreover, at high speeds the old skew problem, limiting the parallel interface speed, appears. Modern serial interfaces (USB, FireWire), as in data transfer networks, use various synchronization coding methods, which makes it possible to achieve high speeds at long distances. Synchronous interfaces allow both synchronous and asynchronous data transfers; asynchronous interfaces cannot be used for synchronous transfers.

Synchronous data transfer is a *constant instantaneous speed* transfer. This type of transfer is needed, for example, for multimedia data transfers, in particular for transmitting digitized sound using pulse-code modulation (PCM): transmitting signal samplings at equal time intervals. In telephony, 8-bit samplings are transmitted at 8 KHz (overall speed 64 Kbps), while for transmitting high fidelity CD quality audio recording, 16-bit samplings are transmitted at 44.1 KHz over each stereo channel (overall speed 1.4 Mbps). Loss of synchronization causes data loss: distortion, interference, and temporary loss of sound altogether. A separate dedicated synchronous interface (or complex multiplexing schemes) is needed for each connected device for synchronous data transfers.

Isochronous data transfer transmits data with *constant average speed*: over a certain (fixed) time interval, a certain amount of data must be transferred, but the instantaneous data transfer speed is not specified. Of course, the instantaneous speed must be at least not lower than the average speed. Usually, an instantaneous speed (the throughput capacity or bandwidth of the interface) much higher than the necessary average speed is selected. This makes it possible to use one interface for connecting multiple devices and organize multiple concurrent isochronous transfer channels (their total speed will be somewhat lower than the throughput capacity (bandwidth) of the interface). Isochronous and asynchronous transfers can easily be conducted over the same interface. The issue of the interface bandwidth allocation is handled by the *isochronous resource controller*: a separate software support function.

Isochronous transfers are used by multimedia devices, such as audio and video equipment. Devices are equipped with buffer memory, into which the incoming isochronous transfer packets are stored; these data are used up (to reproduce sound, for example) by the device at constant instantaneous speed (the reverse transfer is done the same way). Isochronous transfers also are suitable for use in variable-speed multimedia applications (when data are compressed, their incoming speed may vary, but, of course, its upper limit is known). Isochronous transfers are supported by the USB, FireWire, Bluetooth, and the new interfaces AGP 3.0 and PCI Express. Regular data transfer networks with high enough speeds can also carry isochronous traffic. The ideal synchronization of isochronous devices has its peculiarities: Devices have to use their own (very precise) clock generators, because there is no direct synchronization between them (as in synchronous interfaces). One method used for solving the synchronization issue is feedback mechanisms, which make it possible for the devices to correct their clock drifts.

Peripheral Equipment Connection Evolution

Having considered the general issues of interface organization, it is time for a brief survey of the evolution of peripheral equipment.

System-Level Interfaces

A system-level interface is an interface that provides its clients with direct access to the computer's system resources: addressed memory and I/O spaces, as well as hardware interrupts. Clients of this interface type — controllers of proper peripheral devices, adapters and controllers of peripheral device interfaces — by the nature of their activity must have their I/O register and their local memory (if they have them) mapped onto the common memory and I/O space. This is required in order to provide efficient (high-speed and high-performance) software interaction with these devices by the central processor (CPU). The overall efficiency and productivity of the computer can be increased by relieving the CPU of routine I/O operations, which is achieved by the following two complementary approaches:

- ❏ Use specialized I/O coprocessors
- ❏ Allow controllers of the peripheral devices (or of their interfaces) to access system resources themselves

An *Input-Output Processor* is a processor with a reduced command set customized to perform I/O control operations. This processor can both work with the common address space or/and have its separate address space for the I/O subsystem it controls. The standard direct memory access (DMA) controller employed for the ISA bus and its successors' clients (of which, only COM and LPT ports and primitive audio adapters built into the motherboards have survived) can be considered, by a great stretch of imagination, to be a primitive processor of this type. Usage of I/O processors is also meant by the I2O (Intelligent Input-Output) abbreviation when talking about powerful computer server platforms.

Ordinary computers usually content themselves with *bus mastering*, which allows peripheral device controllers (or interface controllers) themselves to access the system resources, most often the main memory areas, when conducting data or control information exchanges. The peripheral device controller must temporarily assume the role of the exchange initiator on the interface that links the device with the computer core (mostly, with memory). Because traditionally this interface is of the bus type, such an active controller is called a bus master even if it connects to a dedicated two-point interface (such as AGP). The simplest bus master only exchanges data with memory in the direct access mode, although it makes the driver's job easier and more efficient than a standard DMA controller. For example, all modern IDE (ATA/ATAPI) controllers can do scatter write and gather read operations, which makes it possible to place a continuous data block into different physical memory pages. This in turn makes it possible to coordinate physical memory allocation used by the controller with logical memory allocation used by the CPU software that works in the virtual address space. More complex versions of memory interaction are used, for example, in communications controllers, such as LAN adapters and USB controllers. Here, the driver (a CPU program) forms control data structures in the memory that define the controller's job assignments (including the data location description that can be scattered over different pages). The controller works following these assignments, recording the execution results in these structures. Later, the driver relays the results of the work done to the concerned programs.

The history of system-level IBM PC interfaces began with the ISA bus, which was the central connecting interface in the IBM PC/XT: the CPU, the main memory, and the I/O devices all connected to this bus. Because of its central role in the PC/XT, the ISA bus was (and still mistakenly is) called a system bus[1]. With the IBM PC/AT, the ISA bus firmly took its present place in the bus hierarchy as an I/O expansion bus. The ISA bus provides an asynchronous parallel interface for connecting all kinds of peripheral adapters and controllers. Dedicated address, data, and control signal lines provide a very simple and inexpensive to implement device connection protocol. In the PC/XT, the ISA data bus was 8 bits wide and could address only 1 MB of memory with 20 address lines. With the aim of making the connected peripheral devices cheaper, only 10 bits out of the total available 16 I/O space address bits were actually used. The ISA bus has come to the present day in the 16-bit data and 24-bit address version. It now has bus-mastering capability, although only for no more than three devices. The issue of automatic configuration of ISA devices was acceptably solved with a more than 10-year delay when the ISA PnP specification came out in 1994.

---

[1] The current interpretation of the term "system bus" is an interface to connect processors.

The EISA bus was founded on more progressive ideas: It was a 32-bit synchronous bus supporting packet transfers, which allowed higher bandwidth. Moreover, the basis for automatic device configuration — the possibility to selectively access bus slots externally to the regular addressing and to define the standard configuration description structures (used addresses, interrupt requests, DMA channels, etc.) — was initially made in the EISA. A device in any EISA slot can request and receive direct bus control (become a bus master). The bus protocol provides fail-safe transfers (transactions into nothing are impossible in EISA). With all its progressive features, the EISA bus took root only in the powerful servers of its time: Both the motherboard and devices for EISA turned out to be too expensive. The EISA bus can be considered a second-generation I/O expansion bus.

There was also the Micro-Channel Architecture (MCA) bus with characteristics similar to EISA, but it passed into oblivion along with the poignantly famous IBM PS/2 computer series (of which only the PS/2 mouse and the small keyboard connector have been left). The VESA Local Bus (VLB), which disappeared almost as soon as it appeared, was only the system bus of the x486 processors routed to peripheral device slots: It was doomed by the low stability of this type of connection and the switch to Pentium and higher processors, which have entirely different interfaces. The idea of the VLB lay in bringing certain controllers (graphics and disk drive) closer to the memory and the processor in order to increase the throughput.

Connecting peripheral devices needs a bus with a long life span, because by nature, peripheral devices are more conservative than processors, which swiftly replace one another. Moreover, it must provide high bandwidth and bus mastering by an unlimited number of connected devices. The PCI bus with its modern versions has become such a long-life bus.

The main features of the PCI bus are as follows:

❐ *Parallel interfaces with a protocol that provide reliable exchange.* Address and data bus width is 32 bits with possible expansion to 64 bits. Data validity is achieved by parity checking, while the transfer reliability is provided by a mandatory acknowledgment from the target device, with the result that the transaction initiator always knows its outcome.

❐ *Synchronous interface and high-speed packet transfers.* 33 MHz at 32-bit data width allows bandwidth of 133 MBps to be achieved. The frequency can be raised to 66 MHz, which at 64-bit data width gives peak bandwidth of up to 532 MBps.

❐ *Automatic device configuration built into the bus specification.* The set of standard functions allows information about devices' needs in system resources (address space and interrupts) to be gathered as well as to control devices (enabling them as either transaction initiator or target devices).

❐ A *command set* to access resources of different address spaces, including the commands for optimized access to an entire cache memory line.

The declared high bus bandwidth is almost reached only by active bus devices (Bus Masters), as only they are capable of generating long packet transactions. Input/output over the PCI bus performed by the CPU gives much more modest real bandwidth values.

A distinctive feature of the PCI bus is that it can handle only a limited number of devices (no more than five or six) connected to the bus (earlier buses did not have such a rigid limitation). To connect more devices, *PCI bridges* are used, which form additional buses. However, the buffering mechanisms used in PCI bridges insert significant delays into transaction execution time across a bridge.

The PCI protocol's weak spot is read operations, especially if they are addressed to not very fast memory. These operations can tie the bus up for a long time by unproductive waiting for data.

The traditional way of signaling PCI interrupts also draws complaints: Only four interrupt lines for all devices on all buses condemn them to shared usage. Although there are no electrical contraindications for sharing interrupt lines in the PCI (as there are in the ISA), the absence of a unified interrupt request indicator makes identification of the device requesting interrupt difficult and response to this interrupt slow. This standardized interrupt request indicator appeared only in the PCI 2.3 after many years of active bus use. Although, starting from version 2.2, a new interrupt notification mechanism, the MSI, has been used, which takes care of all problems of the traditional notification.

The PCI specification was the starting point for creating a dedicated graphics accelerator interface, the *Accelerated Graphics Port* (AGP). This is a synchronous 32-bit parallel point-to-point interface. At a clock rate of 66 MHz, it can reach speeds of 264 MBps (mode 1x), 533 MBps (mode 2x, double synchronization), 1,066 MBps (4x, synchronization from data source), and in the latest version, AGP8x, speeds of 2,132 MBps are achieved. In addition to raising the peak speed, the AGP employs a more sophisticated protocol that allows memory request queuing. Thank to this feature, the bus does not idle while waiting for data, producing a positive effect on the efficiency. Another distinctive feature of AGP is hardware memory address translation, which makes it possible to coordinate the physical memory model that the accelerator employs with the virtual memory model, with which the graphics software of the central processor works. The AGP is a system-level specialized interface: Only the graphics accelerator (video card) is connected to it.

The PCI bus' use as a general-purpose bus was developed in the PCI-X standard, whose second version has already come out. In this standard, the peak speed has also been raised: The bus clock rate can be raised up to 133 MHz (PCI-X66, PC-X100, and PCI-X133). A new mode, Mode 2, appeared in version 2.0 with synchronization from the data source; memory write (and this operation only) speeds can increase two- or four-fold (PCI-X266 and PCI-X533, respectively). Consequently, the peak memory write speed in the 64-bit version of the bus can reach 4 GBps (reading speeds reach up to 1 GBps). Version 2.0 of the interface also defines a 16-bit version of the bus.

Bus protocol was changed in PCI-X: An additional transaction attribute transmission stage was added, in which the exchange initiator makes its identifier available (in PCI, the target device has no idea which device requests the transaction). Moreover, the number of bytes to be transmitted is also declared, allowing the exchange participants to plan their actions. The main change in the protocol is the split transaction capability: If the target device cannot respond quickly, it forces the initiator to release the bus and organizes data delivery later itself. Because of this, bus usage efficiency is significantly raised: bus idling while waiting for data is eliminated. Splitting transaction also raises efficiency of bridge operations: Their transaction costs become less wasteful.

A new way of interdevice communications was also introduced in PCI-X: Messages are addressed to device *identifiers* (bus, device, and function numbers) and not to resource (memory or I/O) addresses. In the previous versions of the bus, this capability was absent; this communication method helps to raise the intelligence level of the I/O subsystem.

Of interest is the fact that, with all its innovations, PCI-X remains compatible with PCI devices and buses: Each bus will work in the mode that the weakest participant can support, from the 33 MHz PCI to the PCI-X533. Bridges allow different system segments (PCI buses) to work in different modes, so it is possible to arrive to an effective configuration, in which new bandwidth-critical devices will get along with no problem with old devices.

Presently, third generation technology I/O interfaces, such as PCI Express and Hyper Transport, are beginning to be employed. A transition from bus to point-to-point serial link types is characteristic of third generation interfaces. As a matter of fact, third generation interfaces approach the characteristics of local networks (within the confines of the motherboard). Here, packets containing both the control information (commands) and the data proper are transferred between nodes. Each interface is made up of a pair of oncoming one-way links working independently of each other (no handshaking of any kind is provided for in transfers). Bandwidths of one interface can be different for different directions: a bandwidth is chosen taking into account the requirements of the given application. New capabilities appeared in the I/O architecture, including control over the quality of service (QoS), power consumption, and link resource budgets. Node connection topologies and link properties are different, but both the Hyper Transport and PCI Express, just like the previous generation buses, do not allow loops in the topology.

HyperTransport is a point-to-point connection between microchips within the card limits (connectors and expansion cards are not provided for). The topology's main version is a chain of device tunnels, each with two interfaces and transferring all packets through. Bridges and switches can also be employed for packet routing. Links can be 2, 4, 4, 16, or 32 bits wide; a clock rate of 200 MHz–800 MHz at double-edge latching provides a peak data transfer rate of up to 6.4 GBps (32-bit link). Because packets can be sent concurrently in both directions, the interface's bandwidth can be said to be 12.8 GBps. The common configuration principles and supported transaction types make PCI to PCI-X integration easy by using bridges.

PCI Express, or 3-Generation Input-Output (3GIO), is a point-to-point peripheral component interconnect on motherboards as well as on expansion cards. The 1-, 2-, 4-, 8-, 12-, 16-, or 32-bit interface provides transfer speeds of up to 8 GBps. It preserves the software features on the PCI bus (configuration, transaction types), which makes for a smooth migration from the PCI to PCI Express.

InfiniBand is a new server interconnect architecture based on the idea of constructing a centralized I/O fabric. InfiniBand nodes are connected with the help of the switching structure that allows redundant links. Link redundancy is welcomed: It allows the total throughput capacity to be raised. Redundancy is provided by both the internal elements of the switching structure and the presence of several interfaces and devices that allow connections to multiple points of the switching structure fabric. There are three levels on link throughput capacities in the InfiniBand: 0.25, 1, and 3 GBps. Each InfiniBand Link consists of one, four, or 12 oncoming one-way lanes working in half-duplex mode at transmission speeds of 2.5 Gbps each.

Links are made employing both intercard connectors and cable connections: copper up to 17 meters, and optical up 10 kilometers. In copper links, each lane is a differential signal wire pair; in optical links, each lane is a single fiber. The architecture allows up to tens of thousands of nodes to be linked into one subnet. Depending on the function, nodes are equipped with one of the two types of InfiniBand adapters: Host Channel Adapter (HCA) for the transaction initiating processor nodes, and Terminal Channel Adapter (TCA) for I/O nodes (storage device interface and network controllers, graphics controllers, I/O racks with traditional expansion buses, etc.).

Peripheral Interfaces

The traditional approach to organizing peripheral device connection consists of introducing a separate individualized interface for each type of device (for a group of similar type devices in the best case). This interface's controller (adapter) is connected to the I/O expansion bus and requires its resources: address ranges in the memory and I/O spaces, interrupt request lines, centralized DMA channels. Consequently, a computer with an extensive collection of peripheral devices has a great number of specific peripheral interface controllers that are not connected among themselves. Specific interfaces were introduced historically, but they often lost their technical justification as time went by.

The necessity for a special *monitor interface* is hard to argue against: Probably, no other device needs such a huge information stream to be output to it. However, tying the interface just to the CRT monitor turned out to be inconvenient for matrix LCD displays, and it began to change with time.

For the first *mass storage devices* (diskette drives), the individual interface allowed the actual peripheral device to be simplified to the highest degree. Inexpensive streamers also used this interface, but its capabilities are very limited. Even related devices — hard disk drives — required a new, albeit similar, interface to be introduced. Binding an interface to a specific type of hard disk drive caused the problem of controller/hard disk drive compatibility. Shortly afterward, the development of the mass storage devices required the utmost physical proximity of drive to its controller. For the sake of software compatibility, the traditional hard disk drive controller was placed onto the drive itself: The Integrated Drive Electronics (IDE) interface came into existence. A section of the ISA bus was used as the connection interface, with a ribbon cable connecting the controller to it via buffered transceivers. In this way, the specific ATA interface was born: still the most inexpensive and popular internal mass storage device interface, and not only of the disk drive type. It has been developing mainly in terms of increasing the data transfer speed: up to 133 MBps in the parallel version, and 150 MBps and up in the serial version (Serial ATA). Storage devices with an integrated controller do not need a specific interface: Only a fast means of data transport between the main memory and the device is needed.

The LPT port appeared as an adapter for the specialized Centronics Data Corporation *printer interface:* perhaps, the first affordable personal printer. The desire to connect different devices to the hardware on hand led to a chain of LPT port modernizations that culminated in adopting a standard for quite unified and symmetrical interface: the IEEE 1284, to which several devices can now be connected.

Connecting a *keyboard* (and PS/2 mouse) was done in an amazingly original way: To organize a serial bidirectional interface when a too high data transfer speed was not required, a separate microcontroller was installed on the PC/AT motherboard. The resulting interface was not compatible with any other standard interface and is held sacred to this time.

The *COM port* with its adapter was the first external PC interface not oriented at any specific device from the start: The subset of the RS-232C interface implemented in the COM port is used not only in telecommunications (where it originated), but also in many other peripheral devices. However, this interface is too slow, and only one device can be connected to it.

The first high efficiency universal shared peripheral interface in PCs was the *SCSI bus*, which was taken from mini-computers. Nominally, devices of the most varied type can be equipped with the SCSI bus: printers, scanners, mass storage devices, communications equipment, processing devices, etc. In practice, the SCSI is mainly used to connect mass storage devices and scanners: In other areas, it has more inexpensive (perhaps even specialized) alternatives. The SCSI bus has come a long way, from a slow 8-bit bus to the high-speed 16-bit Ultra-320 bus, and now the time of its serial version has arrived.

The destiny of the *Universal Serial Bus* (USB) was to revolutionize peripheral interconnections. The idea of its introduction lies in creating a practical, inexpensive, universal, efficient interface for connecting a large number of peripheral devices; the interface has a built-in hot swap and autoconfiguration support. Moreover, only one controller needs to transport data among all devices and the main memory buffers. This eliminates configuration problems when connecting multiple devices, it also means a multitude of controllers and adapters. A USB controller is a system to mass service exchanges among multiple devices. One-point service makes it possible to co-ordinate the pace of servicing different devices and, as far as possible, evenly to distribute the total bandwidth, leaving a guaranteed band for isochronous transfers. This task of mutual coordination is practically impossible to accomplish using isolated controllers. However, the totalitarian authority of the USB controller requires that it be sufficiently nimble. This was only partially achieved in the first version (USB 1.0): The throughput capacity that was to be shared out was too low (12 Mbps is the line speed, out of which $12:8 = 1.5$ MBps cannot be used because of the overhead expenses). For example, a USB 1.0 printer works slower than an LPT printer. However, the connection convenience is unarguable, and a great many USB devices have appeared. The second version (USB 2.0) with its 480 Mbps inspires more optimism.

Long before the USB appeared, in the "parallel world" of Macintosh computers, the no less universal serial FireWire bus, which was capable of carrying video data stream and used even for data storage devices right from the start, had taken root. Now, the FireWire (IEEE 1394) has also taken firm residence in PCs, supplementing the set of the external interfaces. The functional capabilities, practicality, and band-widths of the FireWire and USB 2.0 are quite close, but supporting both interfaces increases the range of equipment that can be connected.

Despite the USB and FireWire's strong positions, there are still a multitude of various interfaces. Take, for example, the swarm of flash memory device connection interfaces: CompactFlash, SmartMedia Card, MultiMedia Card, Secure Digital, Miniature Card, Memory Stick, etc. Each has its connector and individual protocol. A simple microcontroller with a USB interface makes it possible to bring them all to the common denominator, and to exchange data with PCs.

Interface Selection

When developing custom devices, the issue of choosing the appropriate connection interface arises. This issue should be decided based on the principle of reasonable sufficiency, giving preference to external interfaces as far as possible. It should be remembered that hardware development is closely connected with software support of the device: both the programs executed by the processor (software) and the programs executed by the embedded microcontroller (firmware), on the basis of which, as a rule, modern devices are built. There is a multitude of microcontrollers available with popular interfaces such as USB, RS-232, I2C, and others. However, in some cases, standard I/O expansion buses also have to be used.

These buses present wider possibilities for processor/equipment interaction, and are not constrained by the rigid limitations of the external interfaces. However, the versatility and efficiency of the internal expansion buses extracts the price of more intricate interface circuitry implementation and difficulties in providing compatibility with the other equipment installed in the computer. Mistakes here can cause computer malfunctions (it is luck if only temporarily). It is not without reason that respectable computer manufacturers guarantee their equipment's operability only if certified (by them or by independent laboratories) expansion cards are used with it. When external interfaces are used, troubles in case of errors most often only involve the connected device.

A significant issue to consider when selecting an interface is two aspects of hot swap capability: First of all, being able to connect/disconnect devices on the fly, without fear of damages to the devices themselves and their interface circuits, to the stored and transferred data, and, finally, to the user; secondly, being able to use the newly connected device without having to reload the system, as well as to be able to continue stable operation after disconnecting a device. Far from all external interfaces support the hot swap to the full extent; for example, a scanner with a SCSI interface must be connected to the computer and turned on prior to loading the operating system, otherwise, it will not be available to the system. Hot swap is not regularly used for internal interfaces: expansion buses, memory modules, and even most ATA and SCSI hard drives. Hot swap is supported by industrial computer expansion buses, and also in special array constructions of storage devices.

CAUTION   Expansion cards, memory modules, and processors can only be installed and pulled out with the computer's power supply turned off. Moreover, it is not enough only to turn an ATX computer off by its power switch, as the power supply continues to feed 3.3 volt to the motherboard. The power supply itself must be depowered by pulling the power cord out of the receptacle.

Chapter 1: Parallel Interface: The LPT Port

The parallel interface port was added to computers to allow users to connect a printer. Hence the name: the LPT port. (LPT stands for Line Printer Terminal.) The traditional LPT port, or Standard Parallel Port (SPP) is oriented toward data output; limited data input is also possible. Modifications of the LPT port include the Bidirectional port, the Enhanced Parallel Port (EPP), the Enhanced Capability Port (ECP), and others that expand its functional capabilities, increase productivity, and decrease the processor workload. At first, they were the in-shop solutions of individual manufacturers; later, the IEEE 1284 standard was adopted by the Institute of Electrical and Electronics Engineers.

On the hardware side, the port has an 8-bit data bus, a 5-bit status-monitoring signals bus, and a 4-bit control signals bus. These are brought into a DB-25S connector. TTL levels are used in the LPT port. The low noise tolerance of the TTL interface limits the cable length. There is no galvanic decoupling: The circuit ground of the attached device is connected to the computer's circuit ground. Because of this, the port is the computer's vulnerable spot, which can be damaged when the rules for connecting and grounding devices are not followed. The port is usually on the motherboard. Therefore, if it "burns out," its immediate surroundings often are damaged. The damage may extend to the entire motherboard.

The software side of the LPT port is a collection of registers, located in the input/output (I/O) addressing space. Port registers are addressed relative to the port's BASE address. The 3BCh, 378h, and 278h addresses are the standard values. The port may use the hardware interrupt line, usually IRQ7 or IRQ5. In enhanced operation modes, the Direct Memory Access (DMA) channel can be used.

The port is supported on the Basic Input/Output System (BIOS) level. It searches for the installed ports during the Power-On Self-Test (POST) routine. Through the Int17h print services (see *Section 7.3.3*), it provides for the character output (upon polling the readiness status without using hardware interrupts), the initialization of the interface and the printer, and the printer status poll.

More efficient are the services provided by the EPP BIOS, which most modern computers have. It contains advanced service functions to work with multiple devices connected to one port (under the IEEE 1284.3), as well as I/O functions allowing transmission and reception of not only single bytes but also blocks of data. This makes it possible to raise the exchange speed by reducing the overhead associated with calling a BIOS service.

Practically all modern motherboards (starting with Peripheral Component Interconnect (PCI) motherboards for *x*486 processors) have a built-in LPT port adapter. The LPT port also may be based on Industry Standard Architecture (ISA) expansion cards. On these, the LPT port typically neighbors a couple of communications (COM) ports and disk interface controllers (a Floppy Disk Controller and Integrated Drive Electronics, or FDC+IDE). Usually, there is an LPT port on the Monochrome Display Adapter (MDA) for monochrome text and the Hercules Graphics Card (HGC) for monochrome text and graphics. PCI cards that provide additional LPT ports also exist.

The LPT ports are used to connect printers, plotters, scanners, communications and data storage devices, electronic keys, programmers, and other equipment. Sometimes, the parallel interface is used to connect two computers in the LapLink network.

1.1. Traditional LPT Port

The traditional LPT port, called the Standard Parallel Port (SPP), is a unidirectional port for software implementation of the *Centronics* transfer protocol. (See *Section 7.3.1*). The names and the signal functions of the port connector conform to the Centronics interface (Table 1.1).

Table 1.1. Standard LPT Port Connector

DB-25S pin	Wire No. in the cable	I/O[1] function	Bit[2] function	Signal function
1	1	O/I	CR.0\	Strobe#
2	3	O (I)	DR.0	Data 0
3	5	O (I)	DR.1	Data 1

continues

Table 1.1 Continued

DB-25S pin	Wire No. in the cable	I/O[1] function	Bit[2] function	Signal function
4	7	O (I)	DR.2	Data 2
5	9	O (I)	DR.3	Data 3
6	11	O (I)	DR.4	Data 4
7	13	O (I)	DR.5	Data 5
8	15	O (I)	DR.6	Data 6
9	17	O (I)	DR.7	Data 7
10	19	I[3]	SR.6	Ack#
11	21	I	SR.7\	Busy
12	23	I	SR.5	PaperEnd (PE)
13	25	I	SR.4	Select
14	2	O/I	CR.1\	AutoLF# (AutoFeed#)
15	4	I	SR.3	Error#
16	6	O/I	CR.2	Init#
17	8	O/I	CR.3\	Select In#
18–25	10, 12, 14, 16, 18, 20, 22, 24, 26	N/A	N/A	N/A

[1] The I/O sets the direction of the port signal transmission (input/output). O/I denotes the output lines whose status is read when the output ports are read. O(I) denotes output lines whose status may be read only under special conditions.

[2] The \ character marks inverted signals. (Logical one in the register corresponds to the line's low level.)

[3] The Ack# input is connected by a 10 Kohm resistor to the +5 V power supply.

An SPP adapter has three 8-bit registers occupying adjacent addresses in the I/O addressing space, starting from the port's BASE address (3BCh, 378h, or 278h).

Data register (DR), address=BASE. Data written into this register are *output* to the Data[0:7] output lines. Data read out of this register, depending on the adapter circuit design, correspond either to previously written data or to the signals on the respective lines. These are not always the same.

Status register (SR) (read-only), address=BASE+1. This register represents the 5-bit input port of the printer status signals (bits SR.4–SR.7) and the interrupt flag. The SR.7 bit is inverted: The value of logical one in the bit corresponds to the low-level signal, and vice versa.

The functions of the status register bits are as follows (with the pin number of the port connector in parentheses):

❏ SR.7 — Busy — Inverted reflection of the Busy (11) line status. When the line's level is low, the bit is set to logical one, indicating permission to output the next byte.

❏ SR.6 — Ack *(Acknowledge)* — Indication of the Ack# (10) line status.

❏ SR.5 — PE *(Paper End)* — Indication of the PaperEnd (12) line status. The value of logical one corresponds to the line's high level: the signal that the printer is out of paper.

❏ SR.4 — Select — Indication of the Select (13) line status. The value of logical one corresponds to the line's high level: The printer is online.

❏ SR.3 — Error — Indication of the Error# (15) line status. The value of logical zero corresponds to the line's low level: the signal of any printer error.

❏ SR.2 — PIRQ — The Ack# interrupt flag (only for the PS/2 or Bi-Di port, see *Section 1.2*). It is set to logical zero if the Ack# signal causes a hardware interrupt. The value of logical one is set upon hardware reset and after reading the status register.

❏ SR[1:0] — Reserved.

Control register (CR), address=BASE+2. This register can be written into and read from. The register is connected with the 4-bit output port for control signals (bits 0–3), which also may be read. The output buffer is usually an "open collector." This allows this register's lines to be used properly for input when they are programmed to the high level. Bits 0, 1, and 3 are inverted.
The functions of the control register bits are as follows:

❏ CR[7:6] — Reserved.

❏ CR.5 — Direction — Transfer direction control bit (only for PS/2 or Bi-Di ports). A logical one written into the bit switches the port to the input mode. The bit status is undetermined during the register read operation.

❏ CR.4 — AckINTEN *(Acknowledge Interrupt Enable)* — A value of logical one allows interrupts at the Ack# line's trailing edge: the next-byte request signal.

❏ CR.3 — Select In — A value of logical one in this bit corresponds to the low level on Select In# (17), the signal that allows the printer to work pursuant to the Centronics interface mode.

❏ CR.2 — Init — The bit's zero value corresponds to the low level on the Init# (16) output: the hardware printer-reset signal.

❏ CR.1 — Auto LF *(Automatic Line Feed)* — A value of logical one in this bit corresponds to the low level on the Auto LF# (14) output: the automatic line-feed signal upon receiving the carriage-return byte. Sometimes the signal and the bit are called AutoLF or AutoFDXT.

❑   CR.0 — Strobe — A value of logical one in this bit corresponds to the low level on the Strobe# (1) output: the output-data strobe signal.

A *hardware-interrupt request* (usually IRQ7 or IRQ5) is generated upon the negative signal edge on pin 10 of the interface connector (Ack#) when CR.4=1. To avoid false interrupts, pin 10 is connected through a resistor to the +5 V line of the bus. Interrupts are generated when the printer confirms that it has received the previous byte. As previously mentioned, BIOS neither uses nor services this interrupt.

The following steps output a byte using the Centronics interface (and the necessary number of processor-bus operations):

1.   Write a byte to the data register (one IOWR# cycle).
2.   Read the status register and check the device readiness (bit SR.7, the busy signal). This step is repeated until either the ready signal is received or the software time-out is triggered (minimum one IORD# cycle).
3.   Upon receiving the ready signal, the data strobe is set by writing to the control register. The strobe is cleared by the next write operation. To switch only one bit (strobe), the control register usually is read beforehand, which adds an extra IORD# cycle to the two IOWR# cycles.

To output 1 byte, four or five I/O port register operations are needed. (This is in the best-case scenario, when the printer's readiness to receive a character is detected at the first reading of the status register.) This leads to the major shortcoming of using the standard port for output: low transfer rates accompanied by significant processor loading. Loading the processor to its capacity, the port can be accelerated to between 100 KBps and 150 KBps, not enough for output to a laser printer. The other shortcoming of the port is functional: the complexity of using it as an input port.

The standard port is asymmetrical. Twelve lines (and bits) usually output data; only five status lines input data. If a symmetrical bidirectional connection is needed, all standard ports are capable of working in the *nibble (transfer) mode*. In this mode, also called *Hewlett-Packard Bitronics*, 4 data bits are received simultaneously, and the fifth line is used for acknowledgement. This way, it takes two cycles to receive 1 byte, and every cycle requires at least five I/O operations.

The circuit design of the data output buffers of the LPT ports varies greatly. On many older adapters, the SPP data register also may be used to input data. If you write an all-ones byte into the port's data register and place code on the port's output lines using open-collector integrated circuits (or connect some lines to the circuit ground), this code can be read from the same data register. However, the output circuits of the information transmitter will have to "fight" the output current of logical ones from the output buffers of the adapter. TTL circuitry does not prohibit this approach because the electric current of an output contact that short-circuits to the ground usually does not exceed 30 milliamperes. However, if the external device is built on CMOS integrated circuits, these circuits may not have enough power to gain the upper hand in this struggle for the bus. Moreover, many modern adapters often have a matching resistor, up to 50 ohms, in their output circuits. A simple calculation shows that even if a pin short-circuits to the ground, during the output of a logical one, the voltage on this resistor will drop to 1.5 V. This means the receiver's input circuit will interpret it as a logical one, not as a logical zero. Therefore, do not assume that such an input method will work on all computers. On some older port adapters, the output buffer may be disconnected by a jumper on the card. Then, the port turns into a simple input port.

1.2. Parallel Port Enhancements

The standard port's shortcomings were partially eliminated by new kinds of ports that appeared in PS/2 computers.

Bidirectional Type 1 port (Type 1 parallel port). This interface was introduced in the PS/2. In addition to the standard mode, this kind of port can work in the input or bidirectional mode. The transfer protocol is software-generated, and to control the direction of the transfer, a special bit, CR.5, was added to the port's control register. When it is set to logical zero, the data buffer is used for output; this buffer is used for input when this bit is set to logical one. Do not confuse this port, also called *enhanced bidirectional*, with the EPP. The Type 1 port has taken root in conventional PCs; it is called *PS/2* or *Bi-Di* in SMOS Setup.

Direct memory access port (Type 3 DMA parallel port). This port was used in PS/2 models 57, 90, and 95. It was introduced to increase the data-transfer rate and to unload the processor during data output to the printer. Software working with this port only needed to define in the memory the data block to be printed. The output under the Centronics transfer protocol was conducted without the processor's participation.

Later, other LPT port adapters were developed with the hardware implementation of the Centronics transfer protocol, or *Fast Centronics*. Some of them used the First In, First Out (FIFO) data buffer, or *parallel port FIFO mode*. Being nonstandardized, such ports from different manufacturers needed their own special drivers. Software directly controlling the standard port registers could not use their expanded capabilities. Ports of this type were often a part of the VLB multicards. They also have been built on ISA bus cards and into motherboards.

1.3. IEEE 1284 Standard

The IEEE 1284 parallel interface standard, adopted in 1994, describes the SPP, EPP, and ECP. The standard defines five modes of data transfer, a method for the host and the peripheral to determine the supported modes and negotiate to the requested mode, and the physical and electrical interfaces. In accordance with the IEEE 1284 standard, the following parallel-port data-transfer modes are possible:

❐ *Compatibility mode* — A forward (output) unidirectional 8-bit channel with the Centronics protocol, software-controlled by the host. This is the port's default mode: The port assumes it at the initialization and between all mode changes.

❐ *Half-byte (nibble) mode* — A reverse (input) unidirectional, parallel-serial 4-bit channel, software-controlled by the host. It complements the compatibility mode but cannot work simultaneously with it. Switching is controlled by the host.

❐ *Byte mode* — A reverse (input) unidirectional 8-bit channel, software-controlled by the host. It complements the compatibility mode but cannot work simultaneously with it. The host controls the switching.

❐ *EPP mode* — A bidirectional 8-bit channel controlled by the processor, with hardware-implemented interlocked handshaking. Separate strobe lines distinguish between data and address transmissions.

❐ *ECP mode* — A bidirectional, symmetrical 8-bit channel with hardware-implemented interlocked handshaking. A control line distinguishes between data and address transmissions; commands can be used to compress data and to address channels.

The standard defines the method by which software may determine the mode available to the host (a PC) and the peripheral device (or another connected computer). Nonstandard port modes using the Centronics data-transfer protocol via hardware (Fast Centronics, parallel port FIFO mode) may not be IEEE 1284 modes, despite their EPP and ECP features.

On the computers with the LPT port built into the motherboard, the SPP, EPP, or ECP mode, or a combination, is set in BIOS Setup. The compatibility mode is fully compatible with the SPP. The other modes are considered in the sections that follow.

In the descriptions of the modes, the following terminology is used:

❐ *Host* — A computer with a parallel port
❐ *Ptr* — In the names of signals, it means the transmitting peripheral device
❐ *Forward channel* — A data-transfer channel from the host to a peripheral device
❐ *Reverse channel* — A data-transfer channel to the host from a peripheral device

1.3.1. Half-Byte (Nibble) Mode

The half-byte mode is intended for bidirectional data-transfer and can work on all standard ports. Ports have five status-input lines. The peripheral device can use these to send a byte to the host 4 bits at a time in two actions. (A "nibble" is half of a byte, or 4 bits.) The Ack# signal that produces the interrupt, which may be used in the given mode, corresponds to bit 6 of the status register. This complicates software manipulations with the bits when assembling the byte. The port signals are given in Table 1.2; the timing diagrams are in Fig. 1.1.

Table 1.2. LPT Port Signals in the Nibble Input Mode

Pin	SPP signal	I/O	Bit[1]	Description
14	AutoFeed#	O	CR.1\	*HostBusy handshaking signal:* Low level indicates the host is ready to receive a nibble; high level confirms receiving a nibble.
17	SelectIn#	O	CR.3\	High level indicates reception. (In the compatibility mode, the level is low.)
10	Ack#	I	SR.6	*PtrClk:* Low level indicates valid nibble data; high level is a response to the HostBusy level rising. A falling edge may trigger an interrupt.
11	Busy	I	SR.7	Data bit 3 is received, then bit 7, then the forward-channel busy status.
12	PE	I	SR.5	Data bit 2 is received, then bit 6.
13	Select	I	SR.4	Data bit 1 is received, then bit 5. After this, the low level indicates the peripheral device is ready to send data to the host.
15	Error#	I	SR.3	Data bit 0 is received, then bit 4.

[1] The \ character marks inverted signals. (Logical one in the register corresponds to the line's low level.)

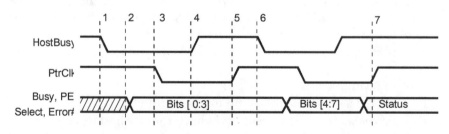

Fig. 1.1. Receiving data in the half-byte mode

Receiving 1 byte in the half-byte mode involves the following steps:

1. The host signals its readiness to receive data by setting the HostBusy line to low.
2. In response, the peripheral device places a nibble on the input status lines.
3. The peripheral device signals that a nibble is ready by setting the PtrClk line to low.
4. The host sets the HostBusy line to high, indicating it is receiving and processing the nibble.
5. The peripheral device responds by setting the PtrClk line to high.
6. Steps 1–5 are repeated for the second nibble, after which (at step 7) the peripheral device may signal that it has data for the host (Select) or that the forward channel is busy (Busy). It also may trigger interrupts (Ack) at this time.

The interlocked handshaking is processed by the host via software (using CR and SR). Therefore, the transfer rate cannot be raised above 50 KBps. Its unarguable advantage is that it works with *all* ports. It is used when the volume of the data stream is not large (such as for communicating with printers). When communicating with local area network (LAN) adapters, external disk-storage devices, or a CD-ROM, receiving voluminous data requires ample patience from the user.

1.3.2. Byte Input Mode

In this mode, data are received using the bidirectional port whose buffer may be turned off by setting the CR.5 bit to logical one. Like the preceding modes, it is software-controlled: all handshaking signals are analyzed and set by the driver. The port signals are described in Table 1.3; the timing diagram is given in Fig. 1.2.

Table 1.3. LPT Port Signals in the Byte Mode

Pin	SPP signal	Name in the byte mode	I/O[2]	Bit[3]	Description
1	Strobe#	HostClk	O	CR.0\	*Acknowledge signal:* The low-level strobe confirms a byte has been received at the end of each data-transfer cycle.
14	AutoFeed#	HostBusy	O	CR.1\	*Handshaking signal:* A low level indicates the host is ready to receive a byte. It is set to a high level upon receiving a byte.
17	SelectIn#	1284Active	O	CR.3\	*Data bus direction:* High level indicates input.
16	Init#	Init#	O	CR.2	Not used; set to high level.

continues

Table 1.3 Continued

Pin	SPP signal	Name in the byte mode	I/O[2]	Bit[3]	Description
10	Ack#	PtrClk	I	SR.6	Low level means that data have come from the peripheral device. In the idle phase (HostBusy=1), a negative impulse triggers an interrupt.
11	Busy	PtrBusy	I	SR.7\	Forward-channel busy status.
12	PE	AckDataReq[1]	I	SR.5	A request to transmit using the reverse channel.
13	Select	Xflag[1]	I	SR.4	Byte input mode acknowledgement.
15	Error#	DataAvail#[1]	I	SR.3	The reverse channel has data available.
2–9	Data[0:7]	Data[0:7]	I/O	DR[0:7]	Data channel.

[1] Signals follow the negotiation sequence.

[2] I/O sets the direction of the port signal transmission (input/output).

[3] The \ character marks inverted signals. (Logical one in the register corresponds to the line's low level.)

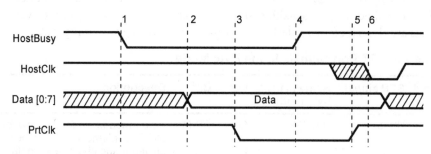

Fig. 1.2. Receiving data in the byte mode

The stages of receiving a byte are as follows:

1. The host signals its ability to receive data by setting the HostBusy line to low.
2. In response, the peripheral device places a byte of data on the Data [0:7] lines.
3. The peripheral device signals that the byte is valid by setting the PtrClk line to low.
4. The host sets the HostBusy line to high, indicating it is receiving and processing the byte.
5. The peripheral device responds by setting the PtrClk line to high.

6. The host acknowledges the byte has been received by pulsing the `HostClk` line. Steps 1–6 are repeated for each following byte. After the `HostBusy` line goes high (step 4), the peripheral device may signal that it has data for the host (`DataAvail#`), that the forward channel is busy (`PtrBusy`), and generate interrupts when the data is ready (`PtrClk`).

The interlocked handshaking implemented by the `HostBusy` and `PtrClk` signals is processed by the host using software (using the `CR` and `SR` registers). The peripheral device may not necessarily use the `HostClk` signal (this is an invitation to send another byte). Speeds on a par with those of the forward channel can be achieved (up to 150 KBps). However, this mode can only function in bidirectional ports, which early on used to be exploited mainly on rarely encountered PS/2 machines. Most modern ports can be configured into the bidirectional mode (using Bi-Di or PS/2 in BIOS Setup).

However, this mode can function only in bidirectional ports. Early on, these were used mainly on rare PS/2 machines. Most modern ports can be configured into the bidirectional mode (using Bi-Di or PS/2 in BIOS Setup).

1.3.3. EPP Mode

The Enhanced Parallel Port (EPP) protocol was developed by Intel, Xircom, and Zenith Data Systems long before the IEEE 1284 standard was accepted. This protocol is intended for increasing data-transfer efficiency of the parallel port. It was first implemented in the Intel 386SL chipset (IC 82360); later, it was adopted by many companies as an optional parallel-port data-transfer protocol. There are some deviations from EPPs before IEEE 1284 in the current IEEE 1284 EPP standard.

The EPP protocol provides four types of data-transfer cycles:

❏ Data Write Cycle
❏ Data Read Cycle
❏ Address Write Cycle
❏ Address Read Cycle

The data-exchange cycles differ from the address cycles in the strobe signals that they use. The purpose of the write and read cycles is obvious. Separating the address cycles makes it possible to connect devices with multiple registers by organizing a multiplexed address and data bus. Table 1.4 describes the EPP signals and their correlation with the SPP signals.

Table 1.4. LPT Port Signals in the EPP Mode

Pin	SPP signal	Name in EPP mode	I/O[2]	Description
1	Strobe#	Write#	O	The low level indicates a write cycle; the high level indicates a read cycle.
14	AutoLF#	DataStb#	O	*Data strobe:* set to low during data-transfer cycles
17	SelectIn#	AddrStb#	O	*Address strobe:* set to low during the address cycles
16	Init#	Reset#	O	*Reset:* The low-level signal switches the peripheral device into the compatibility mode.
10	Ack#	INTR#	I	*Peripheral interrupt:* used to generate an interrupt to the host
11	Busy	Wait#	I	*Handshake signal:* When low, it is OK to start a cycle; when high, it is OK to end the cycle.
2–9	Data[0:7]	AD[0:7]	I/O	Bidirectional address/data bus
12	PaperEnd	AckDataReq[1]	I	Used at the peripheral developer's discretion
13	Select	Xflag[1]	I	Used at the peripheral developer's discretion
15	Error#	DataAvail#[1]	I	Used at the peripheral developer's discretion

[1] Signals follow the negotiation sequence.

[2] I/O sets the direction of the port signal transmission (input/output).

The EPP has an *expanded register set* (Table 1.5) that occupies 5–8 contiguous bytes in the I/O addressing space.

Table 1.5. EPP Registers

Register name	Offset	Mode	Read/Write	Description
SPP Data Port	+0	SPP/EPP	W	*SPP data register*
SPP Status Port	+1	SPP/EPP	R	*SPP status register*
SPP Control Port	+2	SPP/EPP	W	*SPP control register*

continues

Table 1.5 Continued

Register name	Offset	Mode	Read/Write	Description
EPP Address Port	+3	EPP	R/W	*EPP address register:* reading (writing) creates an interlocked EPP address-reading (writing) cycle
EPP Data Port	+4	EPP	R/W	*EPP data register:* reading (writing) creates an interlocked EPP data-reading (writing) cycle
Not defined	+5...+7	EPP	N/A	May be used in some controllers for 16- or 32-bit I/O operations

Unlike in the software-controlled modes described previously, the external signals of the EPP are hardware-generated for each exchange cycle by a single CPU I/O instruction, addressed to the EPP data or address register. In the previously considered modes, the external exchange cycle was formed by a sequence of I/O operations. Fig. 1.3 shows a diagram of the data-write cycle. It illustrates an external exchange cycle, *embedded* in a processor system-bus write cycle. (These cycles sometimes are called *interlocked*.) The address-write cycle differs from the data-write cycle only in its external interface strobe.

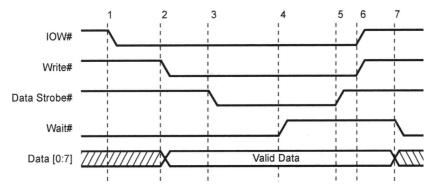

Fig. 1.3. EPP data-write cycle

The data-write cycle consists of the following phases:

1. The program executes an I/O write cycle (IOWR#) to port 4 (EPP Data Port).
2. The adapter sets the Write# signal (low level), and the data are placed onto the parallel-port output bus.

3. With the `Wait#` signal low, the data strobe is set.
4. The port waits for acknowledgement from the peripheral device (switching `Wait#` to high).
5. The data strobe is cleared, and the external EPP cycle ends.
6. The output cycle of the processor ends.
7. The peripheral device sets the `Wait#` signal to low to indicate that the next cycle may begin.

An example of an address-read cycle is given in Fig. 1.4. The data-read cycle differs only in that it uses a different strobe signal.

The distinguishing feature of the EPP is the entire data transfer occurs within one processor I/O cycle. This allows high transfer rates (from 500 KBps to 2 MBps) to be achieved. A peripheral device connected to the EPP can operate at the performance levels of a device connected via the ISA bus slot. The interlocked handshake protocol allows the automatic establishment of a transfer rate that both the host and the peripheral device support. The peripheral device can control the duration of all the data-exchange phases using only the `Wait#` signal. The protocol automatically adjusts to the cable length: Introduced delays will only lengthen the cycle. Cables that comply with the IEEE 1284 standard have the same wave characteristics for different types of lines; therefore, transmission breaks because of "competition" between the signals should not occur. An interesting phenomenon may be observed when network adapters or external drives are connected to the EPP: As the length of the interface cable increases, the productivity drops.

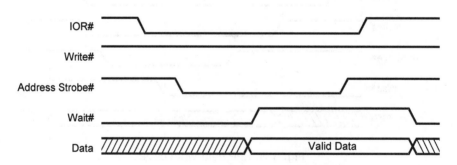

Fig. 1.4. EPP address-read cycle

Naturally, the peripheral device must not "hang" the processor during the bus cycle of the transfer. This is guaranteed by the computer's timeout mechanism, which ends any exchange cycle that lasts more than 15 microseconds (μsec). In a series of EPP implementations, the adapter watches the interface timeout: If the peripheral device does not answer in 5 μsec, the cycle terminates and the adapter's custom (non-standard) status register records an error.

EPP devices based on the pre-IEEE 1284 protocol deviate in the beginning of the cycle: The `DataStb#` or `AddrStb` strobe signals are set regardless of the state of the `Wait#` signal. This means that the peripheral device cannot hold off the beginning of the next cycle (although the device can extend it as necessary). This specification is called EPP 1.7. (It was proposed by Xircom.) This version was used in the 82360 controller. Peripheral devices compatible with the IEEE 1284 EPP will work normally with an EPP 1.7 controller, but an EPP 1.7 peripheral device may refuse to work with an IEEE 1284 EPP controller.

From the software standpoint, an EPP controller looks simple. (See Table 1.5.) To the three registers of the standard port, with the 0, 1, and 2 offsets relative to the base port address, two more registers have been added (`EPP Address Port` and `EPP Data Port`). Reading from and writing into these registers generates interlocked interface cycles.

The traditional roles of the standard port registers have been preserved for compatibility between the EPP and peripheral devices and software designed to use software-controlled data exchange. The handshaking signals are hardware-generated by the adapter; therefore, when initiaizing EPP to the control register (CR), bits 0, 1, and 3 (corresponding to the `Strobe#`, `AutoFeed#`, and `SelectIn#` signals) must be set to logical zero values. Software intervention could distort the handshake sequence. Some adapters have special protections (EPP Protect) that can be turned on to block software modification of these bits.

Using the EPP data register allows a block of data to be transferred with one `REP INSB` or `REP OUTSB` instruction. Some adapters allow 16- or 32-bit access to the EPP data register. Here, an ISA adapter simply decodes the address with an offset in the 4–7 range as the EPP data register address. However, it tells the bus controller the address is 8 bits wide. This leads I/O addressing of the 16- or 32-bit EPP data register to generate automatically two or four 8-bit bus cycles, addressed in an increasing sequence that begins from the offset 4. All four cycles will be executed in less time than the same number of single cycles, each triggered by a 1-byte I/O instruction. More advanced adapters have an "honest" 32-bit data register. For them, up to 4 bytes may be transferred by one processor instruction in one bus cycle. This way, transfer rates up to 2 MBps may be achieved, sufficient for LAN adapters, external disc drives, streamers, and CD-ROM drives. EPP address cycles are always executed in 1-byte mode.

An important feature of the EPP is that the processor accesses the peripheral device in real time: Data are not buffered. The peripheral driver is able to determine the state of and to control the communications. The read and write cycles may follow randomly or in blocks. This type of exchange is practical for *register-oriented* or *real-time* peripheral devices, such as data-collecting and -control devices. This mode of data transfer also is suitable for data storage devices, LAN adapters, printers, scanners, etc.

Unfortunately, not all ports support the EPP mode; several types of notebook PCs don't have it. Therefore, when developing custom devices, it is necessary to try using the ECP mode to achieve greater compatibility with computers.

1.3.4. ECP Mode

The ECP protocol was proposed by Hewlett-Packard and Microsoft to communicate with peripheral devices such as printers or scanners. Like the EPP protocol, this protocol provides high-performance bidirectional data exchange between a host and a peripheral device.

The ECP provides two forward and reverse cycles:

❑ Data-read and -write cycles
❑ Command cycles

The command cycles are subdivided into two types: channel-address transmission and Run-Length Count (RLC) transmission.

Unlike the EPP, the standard on the software (register) implementation of the ECP adapter was introduced with the ECP protocol. It is described in the Microsoft document *The IEEE 1284 Extended Capabilities Port Protocol and ISA Interface Standard*. This document defines protocol features not addressed by the IEEE 1284 protocol:

❑ Data compression by the host adapter using the Run-Length Encoding (RLE) method
❑ FIFO buffering for the forward and reverse channels
❑ DMA and programmed I/O usage

The real-time *RLE data-compression* feature enables compression ratios up to 64:1 when transmitting raster images that have long strings of identical data. The compression feature can be used only if both the host and the peripheral device support it.

ECP channel addressing is used to address multiple logical devices within a single physical device. For example, in a joint fax/printer/modem device with a single parallel port, it is possible to receive a fax and print simultaneously. In the SPP mode, if the printer sets the busy signal, the channel will be kept busy with data until the printer receives them. With the ECP mode, the software driver simply addresses another *logical channel* of the same port.

The ECP protocol redefines the SPP signals (Table 1.6).

Table 1.6. LPT Port Signals in the ECP Mode

Pin	SPP signal	ECP mode name	I/O[2]	Description
1	Strobe#	HostClk	O	*Data strobe:* paired with `PeriphAck` to transmit information in the forward direction (output).
14	AutoLF#	HostAck	O	Indication of the cycle type (command/data) in the forward-transmission mode; used as the acknowledgement signal with `PeriphClk` to transmit data in the reverse direction.
17	SelectIn#	1284Active	O	*ECP mode indicator:* The low level switches into the compatibility mode.
16	Init#	ReverseRequest#	O	*Reverse request:* The low level indicates the channel has been switched to the reverse-transmission mode.
10	Ack#	PeriphClk	I	*Data strobe:* paired with `HostAck` to transmit data in the reverse direction.
11	Busy	PeriphAck	I	Indication of the command/data status in the reverse direction; used as the acknowledgement signal with `HostClk` to transmit data in the forward direction.
12	PaperEnd	AckReverse#	I	*Reverse acknowledgement:* switched to low in response to `ReverseRequest#`.
13	Select	Xflag[1]	I	Acknowledgement of the ECP mode.
15	Error#	PeriphRequest#[1]	I	Call for the host's attention.
2–9	Data[0:7]	Data[0:7]	I/O	Bidirectional data channel.

[1] Signals follow the negotiation sequence.

[2] I/O sets the direction of the port signal transmission (input/output).

An ECP adapter also generates external handshaking signals using hardware, but it works differently from the EPP mode.

Fig. 1.5, *a*, shows two forward-transfer cycles: The data cycle is followed by the command cycle. The cycle type is set by the level on the `HostAck` line: high for data, low for a command. During the command cycle, the byte may contain the channel address or the RLE counter. The distinction is made by bit 7 (i.e., the topmost bit): If it is low, bits 0–6 contain the RLE counter (0–127); if it is high, they contain the channel address. Fig. 1.5, *b*, shows two reverse-transfer cycles.

Unlike the EPP mode transfer diagrams, Fig. 1.5 does not show the signals for the processor system-bus cycles. In this transfer mode, the driver-to-peripheral-device exchange is broken into two relatively independent processes, connected via the FIFO buffer. The driver-to-FIFO-buffer exchange may be performed using DMA and the software I/O. The peripheral-device-to-buffer exchange is accomplished using the ECP adapter. The driver in the ECP mode does not have the information about the exact state of the exchange process; however, the only thing that matters usually is whether or not it has been completed.

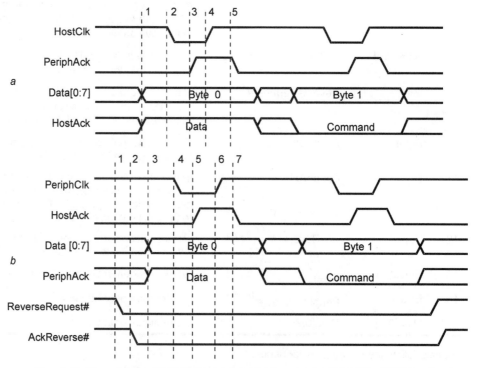

Fig. 1.5. Transferring data forward (*a*) and in reverse (*b*) in the ECP mode

Forward transmission of data on the external interface consists of the following steps:

1. The host places data on the data lines and indicates either a data cycle (high level) or a command cycle (low level) on the HostAck line.
2. The host sets the HostClk line to low, indicating valid data.
3. The peripheral device responds by setting the PeriphAck line to high.
4. The host sets the HostClk line to high. This edge may be used to clock the data into the peripheral device.

5. The peripheral device sets the `PeriphAck` line to low, indicating it is ready to receive the next byte.

Because ECP transfers are conducted via FIFO buffers, which may be present on both sides of the interface, it is important to understand at what stage data may be considered transferred. Data are considered transferred at Step 4, when the `HostClk` line goes to high. At this time, the counters of the sent and received bytes are updated. There are conditions in the ECP protocol that may cause the transfer of data to abort between Steps 3 and 4. In such a case, data should not be considered transferred.

Fig. 1.5 shows yet another difference between the ECP and EPP transfer modes. The EPP protocol allows the driver to intermix the forward- and reverse-transfer cycles without asking for acknowledgement to switch direction. With the ECP, *direction change* must be negotiated. The host must request the reverse channel-transfer by setting the `ReverseRequest#` line. Then, it must wait for the peripheral to acknowledge the request by setting the `AckReverse#` line. Because the previous transfer cycle may have been performed using DMA, the driver must either wait for DMA to complete or interrupt it, back-flush the FIFO buffer to determine the exact value of the transferred bytes counter, then request the reverse channel.

Reverse data-transfer consists of the following steps:

1. The host requests the channel direction change, setting the `ReverseRequest#` line to low.
2. The peripheral device allows the direction change by setting the `AckReverse#` line to low.
3. The peripheral device places data on the channel bus and indicates the nature of the cycle by setting the `PeriphAck` line to high (a data cycle) or low (a command cycle).
4. The peripheral device sets the `PeriphClk` line to high, indicating the data are valid.
5. The host responds by setting the `HostAck` line to high.
6. The peripheral device sets the `PeriphClk` line high; this edge may be used by the host to clock the data.
7. The host sets the `HostAck` line to low, indicating it is ready to receive the next byte.

1.3.5. ECP Modes and Registers

The software interface and ECP registers for IEEE 1284 adapters are defined by a Microsoft specification. The ECP can work in various modes, shown in Table 1.7. In this table, the code corresponds to the `Mode` field of the `ECR` register (bits [7:5]).

Table 1.7. ECP Modes

Code	Mode
000	*SPP mode:* the standard (traditional) mode
001	*Bidirectional mode:* a bidirectional port (Type 1 for PS/2)
010	*Fast Centronics:* unidirectional using FIFO and DMA
011	*ECP Parallel Port mode proper*
100	*EPP mode*[1]
101	Reserved
110	*Test mode:* FIFO and interrupts testing
111	*Configuration mode:* access to the configuration registers

[1] This mode is not included in the Microsoft specification, but it is treated as the EPP by many port adapters if the ECP+EPP mode is set in CMOS Setup.

The ECP adapter register model (Table 1.8) takes advantage of a peculiarity of the ISA for the bus and adapters: Only the ten low-order address bus lines are used to decode I/O port addresses. As a result, addressing `Port`, `Port+400h`, `Port+800h`, etc., will be interpreted as addressing `Port` in the 0–3FFh range. Modern PCs and adapters decode addresses consisting of numerous bits; therefore, addressing 0378h and 0778h will address two separate registers. Placing two additional ECP registers "behind" the standard port registers (offset 400h–402h) achieves two goals. First, these addresses have never been used by traditional adapters or their drivers, and their use in the ECP will not narrow the available I/O addressing space. Second, this provides compatibility with older adapters on the level of 000–001 modes and the possibility of determining whether an ECP adapter is present by trying to access its extended registers.

Every ECP mode has corresponding (and accessible) function registers. The mode is switched by a write into the ECR register. The "on-duty" modes, enabled by default, are 000 and 001. The half-byte input mode functions in either of them. It is always possible to switch from these modes into any other mode. However, from the higher modes (010–111), switching only is possible into the 000 or 001 mode. To ensure that the interface works correctly, it is necessary to wait until the DMA transfer has been concluded and the FIFO buffer has been cleared.

000 (SPP) mode. The port works as the unidirectional software-controlled SPP.

001 (Bi-Di PS/2) mode. The port works as bidirectional, Type 1 PS/2 port. The difference between this and the 000 mode is that the 001 mode can use the CR.5 bit to reverse the data channel.

010 (Fast Centronics) mode. This mode is intended only for high-efficiency output through the FIFO buffer using DMA. The handshake signals for the Centronics protocol are hardware-generated. The interrupt-request signal is based on the state of the FIFO buffer, not the Ack# signal. (The high-speed block-transfer driver is not "interested" in a request from a single byte.)

011 mode. This is actually the ECP mode described previously. The stream of data and commands transmitted into the peripheral device is placed into the FIFO buffer using the ECPDFIFO and ECPAFIFO buffers, respectively. They are output from the FIFO upon the corresponding indication of the cycle (i.e., the state of the HostAck line). The stream of data received from the peripheral device is extracted from the FIFO buffer using the ECPDFIFO register. Receiving address information from the peripheral device in the command cycle is not planned. Exchange with the ECPDFIFO register also can be conducted via the DMA channel.

100 mode (EPP). This is one method that enables the EPP mode (if it is supported by the adapter and enabled in CMOS Setup).

110 mode (test mode). This mode is intended for testing the interaction between the FIFO and interrupts. Data may be transmitted in and out of the TFIFO register using DMA or software. The exchange does not affect the external interface. The adapter executes dummy operations, without actual external cycles, working at the interface maximum speed (as if the handshake signals were coming through without delays). The adapter monitors the buffer state and generates interrupt-request signals as necessary. This way, the driver can determine the maximum throughput capacity of the channel.

111 mode (configuration mode). This mode is intended to provide access to the configuration registers. Making this a separate mode protects the adapter and the protocol from erroneous configuration changes during the exchange process.

RLE method compression in ECP mode. During the forward transfer, this compression is done by software. To transmit more than two identical bytes in a row, the ECPAFIFO register is loaded with a byte whose first seven low-order bits contain the RLC counter and whose topmost bit is set to logical zero. (The RLC value of 127 corresponds to 128 repeats.) Then, the byte is loaded into the ECPDFIFO register. The peripheral device performs decompression when it receives this pair of bytes (i.e., the command byte and the data byte). Receiving a stream of data from a peripheral device, an ECP adapter performs decompression using hardware and places into the FIFO buffer already decompressed data. This makes it obvious that it is impossible to output data using compression and DMA simultaneously.

As previously mentioned, each ECP mode has a corresponding function register (Table 1.8).

Table 1.8. ECP Registers

Offset	Name	Read/Write	ECP modes[1]	Definition
000	DR	R/W	000–001	Data register
000	ECPAFIFO	R/W	011	ECP address FIFO
001	SR	R/W	All	Status register
002	CR	R/W	All	Control register
400	SDFIFO	R/W	010	Parallel-port data FIFO
400	ECPDFIFO	R/W	011	ECP data FIFO
400	TFIFO	R/W	110	Test FIFO
400	ECPCFGA	R	111	Configuration register A
401	ECPCFGB	R/W	111	Configuration register B
402	ECR	R/W	All	Extended control register

[1] Registers are accessible only in these modes. The values of ECR bits 7–5 are shown.

The data register (DR) is used to transmit data only in the software-controlled modes (000 and 001).

The status register (SR) transmits the values of the signals on the corresponding lines (as in the SPP).

The function of the bits in the control register (CR) coincides with that of the SPP. In the 010 and 011 modes, writes into bits 0 and 1 (the AutoLF# and Strobe# signals) are ignored.

The ECPAFIFO register is used to place command cycle information (the channel address or RLE counter, depending on the value of bit 7) into the FIFO buffer. The information is output from the buffer during the command cycle of the output.

The SDFIFO register is used to transfer data in the 010 mode. Data that have been written into the register (or sent via the DMA channel) are sent through the FIFO buffer using the hardware-implemented Centronics protocol. The transfer direction should be set to forward in this mode (i.e., the CR.5 bit should be set to 0).

The DFIFO register is used to exchange data in the 011 mode (ECP). Data that have been written into or read from the register (or transmitted via the DMA channel) are transmitted through the FIFO buffer under the ECP protocol.

The TFIFO register provides the FIFO buffer testing mechanism in the 110 mode.

The ECPCFGA register allows information about the adapter to be read (i.e., the identification code in bits [7:4]).

The ECPCFGB register allows any information required by the driver to be saved. Writing into the register does not affect the port's functionality.

The ECR register is the main ECP control register. Its bits have the following functions:

- ❏ ECR[7:5] — ECP MODE — Sets the ECP mode.
- ❏ ECR.4 — ERRINTREN# *(Error Interrupt Disable)* — Disables interrupts at the Error# signal. (If this bit has the value of logical zero, the falling edge on the Error# line causes an interrupt to be generated).
- ❏ ECR.3 — DMAEN *(DMA Enable)* — Enables DMA channel exchange.
- ❏ ECR.2 — SERVICEINTR *(Service Interrupt)* — Disables service interrupts that were generated upon completion of the DMA cycle (if it is enabled), at the FIFO buffer filling or emptying threshold (if the DMA is not being used), and at the buffer overflow or underflow error.
- ❏ ECR.1 — FIFOFS *(FIFO Full Status)* — Signals that the buffer has been filled. When FIFOFS=1, the buffer has no free space.
- ❏ ECR.0 — FIFOES *(FIFO Empty Status)* — Indicates that the buffer is empty. The FIFOFS=FIFOES=1 combination indicates an FIFO error (underflow or overflow).

When the port is in the standard or bidirectional mode (000 or 001), the first three registers coincide with the standard port registers. This way, the compatibility of new drivers with old adapters and of old drivers with new adapters is ensured.

In its interface with the driver, the ECP resembles the EPP: After a mode has been set (i.e., a code written into the ECR register), data exchange with the device comes to reading from or writing to the appropriate registers. The FIFO buffer status is monitored by using the ECR register or by processing the service interrupts from the port. The entire handshake protocol is hardware-generated by the adapter. Data exchange with the ECP (except for software-implemented exchange) is possible through the DMA channel. This channel is effective when transmitting large blocks of data.

1.3.6. IEEE 1284 Negotiation

An IEEE 1284 standard peripheral device does not usually require the controller to implement all the modes provided by this standard. To determine the modes and methods used to control a device, the standard provides a *negotiation sequence*. The sequence's construction keeps older devices that do not support IEEE 1284 from responding to it; with these devices, the controller remains in the standard mode. Peripheral devices that support IEEE 1284 can provide information about their capabilities. The controller will set the mode acceptable to both the host and the peripheral device. All mode switching is conducted through negotiation.

During the negotiation phase, the controller places the *extensibility byte* on the data lines, requesting an acknowledgement to switch the interface into the required mode or asking for a peripheral device identifier (Table 1.9). The identifier is relayed to the controller in the requested mode (i.e., any reverse-channel mode, except the EPP mode). The peripheral device uses the Xflag signal (Select in SPP terminology) to confirm the requested reverse-channel mode. The exception is the half-byte mode, supported by all IEEE 1284 devices. The Extensibility Link request bit is intended for determining additional modes in future extensions of the standard.

Table 1.9. Bit Values of the Extensibility Byte

Bit	Description	Allowed combination of bit [7:0]
7	Request extensibility link (reserved)	1000 0000
6	EPP mode request	0100 0000
5	ECP mode with RLE request	0011 0000
4	ECP mode without RLE request	0001 0000
3	Reserved	0000 1000
2	Device identifier request in the following modes:	
	Half-byte	0000 0100
	Byte	0000 0101
	ECP without RLE	0001 0100
	ECP with RLE	0011 0100
1	Reserved	0000 0010
0	Byte mode request	0000 0001
None	Half-byte mode request	0000 0000

The negotiation sequence (Fig. 1.6) consists of the following steps:

1. The host places the extensibility byte on the data lines.
2. The host sets the SelectIn# line to high and the AutoFeed# line to low, starting the negotiation sequence.
3. The peripheral device responds by setting the Ack# line low and the Error#, PaperEnd, and Select lines high. A device that does not "understand" the IEEE 1284 standard will not respond, and further steps will not be carried out.

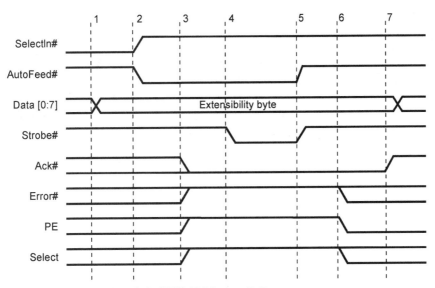

Fig. 1.6. IEEE 1284 negotiation sequence

4. The host sets the `Strobe#` signal to low to write the extensibility byte into the peripheral device.

5. The host sets the `Strobe#` and `AutoLF#` signals to high.

6. If the peripheral device has data for transmission by the reverse data-transfer channel, it responds by setting the `PaperEnd` and `Error#` signals to low. If the device supports the requested mode, the `Select` line is to set high; if it doesn't provide support, the line is set to low.

7. The peripheral device sets the `Ack#` line to high, indicating the end of the negotiation sequence. After this, the controller sets the required work mode.

1.3.7. Physical and Electrical Interfaces

The IEEE 1284 standard defines the physical characteristics of the receivers and transmitters of TTL level-compatible signals. The standard port specifications did not define the types of output circuits, the limit values of load resistors, or the capacities introduced by circuits and conductors. At relatively low transfer rates, this parameter spread did not cause compatibility problems. However, the extended modes (in functions as well as in transfer rate) demand explicit specifications. The IEEE 1284 standard defines two levels of interface compatibility. The *Level I* interface is defined for devices that operate at low transfer rates but use the reverse-channel capabilities. The *Level II* interface is defined for devices that operate in the extended mode at high transfer rates and are connected by long cables. The following requirements are set for the Level II transmitters:

❏ Open-circuit signal-voltage levels shall fall between –0.5 V and +5.5 V.
❏ Signal voltage levels at the steady load current of 14 milliamperes shall be no less than 2.4 V for the high level (V_{OH}) and no higher than 0.4 V for the low level (V_{OL}).
❏ The output impedance (R_O), measured at the connector, shall be 50±5 ohms at the V_{OH}–V_{OL} level. To provide the required impedance, resistors connected in series are used in the output circuits of the transmitter. Matching the impedances of the transmitter and the cable lowers the level of impulse distortions.
❏ The pulse rise (drop) rate shall be within 0.05 V/nsec and 0.40 V/nsec.

The requirements for the Level II receivers are as follows:

❏ Tolerable peak values of the signals shall be between –2 V and +7 V.
❏ Threshold voltages shall be no higher than 2.0 V (V_{IH}) for the high level and no lower than 0.8 V (V_{IL}) for the low level.
❏ A receiver shall have a hysteresis no lower than 0.2 V and no higher than 1.2 V. (Special integrated circuits known as Schmidt triggers have hysteresis.)
❏ The input current of an integrated circuit shall not exceed 20 microamperes. The input lines are connected to the +5 V power bus by a 1.2 K resistor.
❏ The output capacitance shall not exceed 50 picofarad (pF).

When the ECP specification was first introduced, Microsoft made a recommendation that dynamic terminators be used on each interface line. Nevertheless, an IEEE 1284 specification that does not call for dynamic terminators is followed today. Fig. 1.7 shows diagrams of some recommended schematics for the input, output, and bidirectional circuits.

The IEEE 1284 standard defines three types of connectors. *Types A (DB-25)* and *B (Centronics-36)* are characteristic of traditional printer-interface cables. *Type C* is a new, compact 36-contact connector.

Traditional interface cables have between 18 and 25 wires, depending on the number of GND (ground) circuit wires. These conductors may be twisted. No strict requirements were made for the cable shielding. It is unlikely that such cables will work reliably at a transfer rate of 2 MBps or at a length greater than 6.5 feet.

The IEEE 1284 standard regulates cable characteristics.

❏ All signal lines shall be twisted with separate return (common) lines.
❏ Each pair shall have an impedance of 62±6 ohms in the frequency range of 4 MHz to 16 MHz.

❏ The noise level of cross talk between the pairs shall not exceed 10%.
❏ The cable shall have a shield (foil) that covers no less than 85% of the outer surface. At each end, the cable shall be connected to the connector backshell using
a 360-degree concentric method.

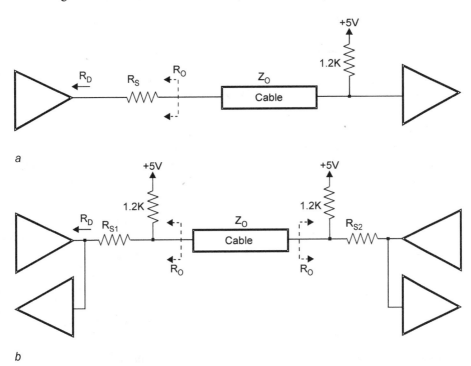

Fig. 1.7. Unidirectional (*a*) and bidirectional (*b*) circuits of the IEEE 1284 interface

Cables meeting these requirements are marked "IEEE Std 1284–1994 Compliant."
They may be as long as 32 feet. The available assembly types are listed in Table 1.10.

Table 1.10. IEEE 1284 Cable Types

Type	Description	Connector 1	Connector 2
AMAM	Type A Male – Type A Male	A (plug)	A (plug)
AMAF	Type A Male – Type A Female	A (plug)	A (socket)
AB	Type A Male – Type B Plug (standard printer cable)	A (plug)	B

continues

Table 1.10 Continued

Type	Description	Connector 1	Connector 2
AC	Type A Male – Type C Plug (new printer cable)	A (plug)	C
BC	Type B Plug – Type C Plug	B	C
CC	Type C Plug – Type C Plug	C	C

1.3.8. Development of the IEEE 1284 Standard

Additions to the main IEEE 1284 standard include the following:

❑ *IEEE P1284.1 (Standard for Information Technology for Transport-Independent Printer/System Interface (TIP/SI))* — Transport-independent host/printer interaction through a bidirectional interface based on the Network Printing Alliance Protocol (NPAP).

❑ *IEEE P1284.2* (Standard for Test, Measurement and Conformance to IEEE Std. 1284) — Testing devices, ports, and cables for compliance with IEEE1284.

❑ IEEE P1284.3 *(Standard for Interface and Protocol Extensions to IEEE Std. 1284 Compliant Peripheral and Host Adapter Ports)* — Interface and protocol port and 1284 device extensions for transparent work with multiple devices connected to the port in daisy chains and via multiplexers. Additional modes are Block ECP (BECP) and Channelized Nibble modes (using ECP channel addressing for half-byte mode).

❑ IEEE P1284.4 *(Standard for Data Delivery and Logical Channels for IEEE Std. 1284 Interfaces)* — A packet protocol for data transport and logical channel organization for 1284 devices. Corresponds to the transport and session layers of the OSI model; can work above the 1284.3 channel layer. Provides link establishment, configuration, flow control and data transfer, as well as service detection for port clients.

1.4. LPT Port System Support

System support of the LPT port includes a search for the installed ports and provides Int17h print services. (See *Section 7.3.3.*) During the initial POST testing, BIOS checks for parallel ports at the 3BCh, 378h, and 278h addresses. It places the BASE addresses of the ports it finds into the BIOS Data Area cells: 0:0408h, 0:040Ah, 0:040Ch, and 0:040Eh. These cells store the LPT1-LPT4 port addresses. The value of logical zero in these cells means there is no port with such a number. Cells 0:0478h, 0:479h, 0:47A, and 0:47Bh store the constants that set the timeouts for these ports.

Most port searches are conducted inefficiently: A test byte (AAh or 55h) is output to the BASE address (into the data register of the supposed port). Then, an input is made from the same address. If the written and the read bytes match, an assumption is made that the LPT port has been found. The address is placed into the BIOS Data Area cell. Subsequently, the port's BASE addresses may be modified by software. BIOS cannot determine the LPT4 port address on its own; the list of standard addresses only contains the three previously mentioned addresses.

Ports that have been found are initialized: Through a write operation into the control register, the Init# signal is activated and negated. Then, the value of 0Ch is written, which corresponds to the initial state of the interface signals. In some cases, the Init# signal is active from the moment the hardware is reset until port initialization during the loading of the operating system. This may be detected by the printer behavior during system reboot: Its online light goes and stays off for a long time. As a result, it becomes impossible to print screens (such as the BIOS Setup parameters) by pressing the <Print Screen> key before the operating system has been loaded.

EPP BIOS functions were introduced to provide support for the port modes defined in IEEE 1284. Before these functions can be used, the presence of EPP BIOS must be checked (not all BIOS versions have EPP functions). This Installation Check is done by using function 2 of Int 17h (querying the LPT status) with the keyword EPP loaded into the CH, BL, and BH registers. If the BIOS contains EPP functions, this call will return their entry point. EPP BIOS provides the following functions:

❒ *Query Config* — getting port address, interrupt number and port capabilities (version and modes available)

❒ *Get/Set Mode* — detecting and setting the current mode (SPP, BiDi, ECP, EPP, EPP 1.7)

❒ *Interrupt Control* — enabling and disabling interrupt use

❒ *EPP Reset* — resetting port

❒ Executing exchanges in the EPP mode: single address and data read/write cycles; data block input or output; combined operations (sending an address and inputting or outputting a byte or a data block)

❒ *Lock/Unlock Port* — selecting and Locking/Unlocking a device connected in chain or via a multiplexer

❒ *Device Interrupt* — installing interrupt handlers for the specified devices connected in chain or via a multiplexer.

❒ *Check INT Pending* — determining the device interrupt source

❒ *Multi-Port Extensions* — additional functions for working with multiplexers and chains: polling (version, current port selected, locking, interrupt); polling the selected port status; polling the chain (determining the selected device and its status); setting identifiers for devices that cannot communicate them themselves

1.5. Parallel Port and Plug-and-Play Functions

Most modern peripheral devices connected to the LPT port support the IEEE 1284 standard and plug-and-play functions. To support these functions, all the computer needs on the hardware side is an IEEE 1284-compliant interface controller. If the connected device supports plug-and-play, using the IEEE 1284 negotiation sequence, it can "arrange" possible exchange modes with the port that represents computer "interests." For plug and play to work, the connected device must present all the necessary information about itself to the operating system. At the minimum, there are the identifiers of the manufacturer, the model, and the set of supported commands. Detailed information about the device may contain the class identifier, a description and identifier of a brand-name device with which the given device is compatible. Based on the obtained information about the support for the specific device, the operating system may attempt to install the required software.

Devices supporting plug and play are recognized by the operating system during the boot stage — if they are connected to the port by the interface cable and powered up. If Windows detects a connected plug-and-play device that differs from the one recorded in its registry, it tries to install the drivers needed by the device from the OS distribution kit or from the new device's software-installation package. If Windows does not want to see the newly connected plug-and-play device, it may be an indication that the port or the cable is out of order. The plug-and-play system will not work if the device is connected by a cheap non-bidirectional cable that does not provide connection through the `SelectIn#` line (e.g., contact 17 on the LPT port and contact 36 on the Centronics connector).

1.6. Uses of the LPT Port

Usually, the LPT port is used to connect a printer. (See *Section 7.3.1.*) Its use is not limited to this.

To connect two computers employing the parallel interface, various cables are used, depending on the modes of the ports. The simplest and the slowest is the half-byte mode, which works in *all* ports. To use this mode, the cable only needs to have ten signal conductors and one common conductor. Table 1.11 shows the contact wiring for the cable connector. PC communication over this cable is supported by standard software, such as MS-DOS Interlink or Norton Commander. Note that a proprietary protocol is used, differing from the one described in Section 1.3.1.

Table 1.11. Computer-Computer Connection Cable (4 bits wide)[1]

X1 (computer No. 1) connector		X2 (computer No. 2) connector	
Bit	Contact	Contact	Bit
DR.0	2	15	SR.3
DR.1	3	13	SR.4
DR.2	4	12	SR.5
DR.3	5	10	SR.6
DR.4	6	11	SR.7
SR.6	10	5	DR.3
SR.7	11	6	DR.4
SR.5	12	4	DR.2
SR.4	13	3	DR.1
SR.3	15	2	DR.0
GND	18–25	18–25	GND

[1] X1 and X2 connectors are DB25-P type plugs.

Two computers can maintain a high rate of communication in the ECP mode. (The EPP mode is not convenient; it requires the bus I/O cycles of the computers to be synchronized).

Table 1.12 shows cable wiring for this mode. Of all the signals in the cable, only PeriphRequest# (contact 15) is not used. It is recommended that series resistors (0.5–1 Kohm) be put into the data-line circuits. They will prevent currents that are too strong from flowing through these lines when the ports of both computers are in the output mode. Such a situation can arise when the computer's communication software has not been launched yet. ECP mode communication is supported by Windows 9x; in its distribution kit, a PARALINK.VxD driver is included. However, because of a programming error, it does not work and needs to be patched. A patch for this driver, a test utility, and the necessary instructions can be found at the following Web sites: **http://www.lpt.com** and **http://www.lvr.com/parport.htm**.

Connecting a scanner to the LPT port is effective only if the port provides at least the bidirectional mode (Bi-Di), because the prevailing data stream is reverse. It is better to use the ECP, if the scanner supports this mode (or the EPP, which is unlikely).

Table 1.12. Computer-Computer 8-bit Communication Cable

X1 (computer No. 1) connector		X2 (computer No. 2) connector	
Contact	ECP mode name	ECP mode name	Contact
1	HostClk	PeriphClk	10
14	HostAck	PeriphAck	11
17	1284Active	Xflag	13
16	ReverseRequest#	AckReverse#	12
10	PeriphClk	HostClk	1
11	PeriphAck	HostAck	14
12	AckReverse#	ReverseRequest#	16
13	Xflag	1284Active	17
2–9	Data [0:7]	Data [0:7]	2–9

The connection of external data-storage devices (Iomega Zip drive, CD-ROM, etc.), LAN adapters, or other symmetrical I/O devices has its own peculiarities. In the SPP mode, such connections slow down the device performance. In addition, the fundamental asymmetry of this mode becomes noticeable: Data are input at *half the rate* of their output (which is slow enough). The bidirectional mode (Bi-Di or PS/2 Type 1) eliminates this asymmetry: The transfer rates become equal. Only by switching into the EPP or ECP mode can *normal* transfer rates be obtained. The LPT port connection in the EPP or ECP mode has almost the same connection speed as an ISA controller connection. This is also true when the standard bus interface devices are connected to the LPT ports using interface adapters (such as LPT-to-IDE, LPT-to-SCSI (Small Computer System Interface), or LPT-to-PCMCIA (Personal Computer Memory Card International Association)). Note that an IDE hard disk drive connected to the LPT port via an adapter can be presented to the system as an SCSI device. (This is more logical from the software standpoint.)

Table 1.13 gives a description of the LPT port connector contacts in different modes and their correspondence to the standard port register bits.

Table 1.13. Functions of the LPT Port Connector Contacts and Register Bits

Contact	I/O[1]	Bit[2]	SPP	ECP	EPP
1	O/I	CR.0\	Strobe#	HostClk	Write#
2	O/I	DR.0	Data 0	Data 0	Data 0

continues

Table 1.13 Continued

Contact	I/O[1]	Bit[2]	SPP	ECP	EPP
3	O/I	DR.1	Data 1	Data 1	Data 1
4	O/I	DR.2	Data 2	Data 2	Data 2
5	O/I	DR.3	Data 3	Data 3	Data 3
6	O/I	DR.4	Data 4	Data 4	Data 4
7	O/I	DR.5	Data 5	Data 5	Data 5
8	O/I	DR.6	Data 6	Data 6	Data 6
9	O/I	DR.7	Data 7	Data 7	Data 7
10	I	SR.6	Ack#	PeriphClk	INTR#
11	I	SR.7\	Busy	PeriphAck	Wait#
12	I	SR.5	PaperEnd	AckReverse#	$-$[3]
13	I	SR.4	Select	Xflag	$-$[3]
14	O/I	CR.1\	Auto LF#	HostAck	DataStb#
15	I	SR.3	Error#	PeriphRequest#	$-$[3]
16	O/I	CR.2	Init#	ReverseRequest#	Reset#
17	O/I	CR.3\	Select In#	1284Active	AddrStb#

[1] I/O sets the direction of the port signal transmission (input/output). O/I denotes the output lines whose status is read when the output ports are read.

[2] The \ character marks inverted signals. (Logical one in the register corresponds to the line's low level.)

[3] Defined by the user.

1.7. Configuring LPT Ports

Parallel port control is split into two stages: preliminary configuration (setup) of the port's hardware assets and extemporaneous switching (operational) of the operation modes by the application or system software. Operational switching is possible only within the limits of the modes enabled at the setup. It matches the equipment with the software and blocks false switches caused by incorrect program operations.

LPT port configuration depends on its physical implementation. A port located on an extension card (multicard) installed into an ISA or ISA+VLB bus is configured by jumpers on the card. A port built-in into the system board is configured by BIOS Setup.

The following port parameters are subject to configuration:

❏ *BASE address* — 3BCh, 378h, or 278h — During the initialization, BIOS checks for ports in this address order. Accordingly, it assigns the detected ports the following logical names: LPT1, LPT2, and LPT3. The 3BCh address is assigned to a port adapter located on an MDA or HGC. Most ports are configured by default to address 378h; they can be switched to 278h.

❏ *Interrupt request line* — IRQ7 for the LPT1, and IRQ5 for the LPT2 — Traditional printer-originated interrupts are not enabled, and this scarce resource can be spared. However, when working in a high transfer-rate ECP (or Fast Centronics) mode, interrupts can raise the transfer efficiency noticeably and decrease the processor workload.

❏ *DMA channel* — ECP and Fast Centronics modes — The DMA and its channel number are enabled.

❏ *Port work modes:*

- *SPP* — The port only works in the standard unidirectional software-controlled mode.
- *PS/2* (or *Bidirectional*) — This differs from the SPP in its capability to reverse the channel (by setting CR.5 bit to logical one).
- *Fast Centronics* — This hardware generation of the Centronics protocol uses the FIFO buffer and possibly DMA.
- *EPP* — Depending on how the registers are used, the port works in the SPP or EPP mode.
- *ECP* — By default, the SPP or PS/2 mode is enabled. Writing into the ECR can switch into any ECP mode, but writing code 100 into the ECR cannot guarantee a switch into the EPP mode.
- *ECP+EPP* — This is the same as the ECP, but writing code 100 into the ECR switches the port into the EPP mode.

Selecting the EPP, ECP, or Fast Centronics mode does not increase the data-transfer rate with the connected peripheral device; it only gives the driver and the peripheral device an opportunity to set the optimal mode within the limits of their "understanding." Most modern drivers and applications attempt to use efficient modes; therefore, there is no need to "clip their wings" without a valid reason.

Printers and scanners may desire the ECP mode. Windows (3.x, 9x, and NT) has system drivers for this mode. In the DOS environment, printing in the ECP mode is supported only by a separately loaded, custom ECP driver.

Network adapters, external disk drives, and a CD-ROM connected to the parallel port can use the EPP mode. No standard driver is available for this mode yet; its support is provided by the driver of the connected device.

1.8. Troubleshooting Parallel Port Malfunctions

It is sensible to begin troubleshooting parallel ports by *checking whether they are present* in the system. A list of installed port addresses is displayed on the monitor by BIOS before the operating system is loaded. The list may be inspected with the help of testing software or a debugger in the `BIOS Data Area`.

If BIOS detects fewer ports than are installed, two ports likely have been assigned the same address. When this happens, there is no guarantee that conflicting ports will work. When data are written into the registers, the conflicting ports will put out signals simultaneously. However, reading of the status register will cause a bus conflict. This conflict likely will lead to data corruption. Testing a port without a diagnostic loop-back plug will not show errors; during such testing, data from the output registers are read and will be identical for all conflicting ports that separately are in working order. This kind of test is done by BIOS when it checks for the presence of ports. To resolve such a situation, install ports one by one, monitoring the addresses that appear in the list.

If only one port is installed but BIOS does not detect it, then the port was disabled during the configuration process or it malfunctioned (probably because the equipment-connecting rules were not followed). If you are lucky, the malfunction may be fixed by "wiggling" the card up and down in its slot: Sometimes there are connection problems.

Even the following "miracle" can be observed: When warm-booting DOS after Windows 95, the port is not detected (and applications cannot print from MS-DOS). However, after DOS is rebooted, the port appears. This phenomenon is easier to live with than to fight.

Troubleshooting ports with the help of diagnostic software allows you to inspect the output register. With the help of special plugs, the input lines can be checked, too. Because the number of port output (12) and input (5) lines is different, thorough port testing with a passive loop-back plug is not possible. Different diagnostic programs require different loop-back plugs (Fig. 1.8).

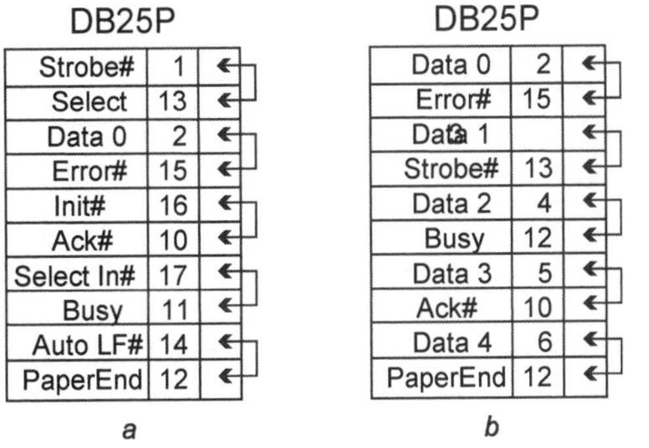

Fig. 1.8. Diagram of the loop-back plugs for CheckIt (*a*)
and Norton Diagnostics (*b*) used to test the LPT port

Most problems during work with the LPT port are caused by the connectors and cables. To check a port, a cable, or a printer, you may use special tests from some popular diagnostic programs (CheckIt, PC Check, etc.). Alternatively, you simply can try to print an ASCII file.

- ❑ If a file apparently can be printed from DOS (i.e., the file is copied on the device named LPTn or PRN quickly and without errors), but the printer has not issued a character, then there likely is a break (i.e., a bad contact in the connector) in the Strobe# circuit.
- ❑ If the printer is online, but a message says it is not ready, the problem should be sought in the Busy line.
- ❑ If the connection to the port printer works properly in the standard (SPP) mode, but starts malfunctioning when switched into the ECP mode, then the cable needs to be checked to ensure it meets the IEEE 1284 requirements. Cheap cables with untwisted wires usually work between 50 KBps and 100 KBps. However, between 1 MBps and 2MBps, available in the ECP mode, they may refuse to work, especially if the cable length exceeds 6.5 feet.
- ❑ During the installation of a plug-and-play printer driver, you may receive a message that says a "bidirectional cable" is required. In this situation, check for a connection between DB-25 connector pin 17 and Centronics connector contact 36. Although this connection was stipulated originally, it is absent in some cables.
- ❑ If the printer distorts the output, a break (or a short-circuit) in the data lines is possible. In this case, it will be handy to use a file that contains the code sequence of all printable characters. If certain characters or groups of characters are repeated when such a file is printed, the broken data-line wire can be easily determined by the period pattern of the repetition. It is practical to use the same file to check the hardware localization of the printer.

Hardware interrupts from the LPT port are not always used. Even the DOS background-printing program works with the port by status polling, and its servicing process is launched at the timer interrupt. Therefore, malfunctions of the port interrupt circuit rarely appear. However, a truly multitasking operating system (such as NetWare) attempts to work with the port via interrupts. The interrupt line can be tested only by connecting a peripheral device or a plug to the port. If a network adapter is connected to a port with an out-of-order interrupt channel, it probably will work — but at a low transfer rate. Any request will be answered with a delay of tens of seconds because the packet received from the adapter will be processed not at an interrupt (i.e., upon arrival), but at the external timeout.

Chapter 2: Serial Interface: The COM Port

The universal peripheral serial interface — the *COM port* (Communications Port) — has been present in PCs since the first models. This port provides *asynchronous*[1] data transfer employing the RS-232C standard. COM ports are implemented using Universal Asynchronous Receiver-Transmitter (*UART*) ICs compatible with the *i8250/16450/16550* software model. They each occupy eight adjacent 8-bit registers in the I/O addressing space and can have the standard *base addresses*: 3F8h (COM1), 2F8h (COM2), 3E8h (COM3), and 2E8h (COM4). Ports may generate *hardware interrupts* IRQ4 (usually used for COM1 and COM3) and IRQ3 (used for COM2 and COM4). On the hardware side, ports have lines for serial data transmission and receiving. They also have a set of lines for the control- and status-monitoring signals that comply with the RS-232C standard. COM ports have external connectors, *DB25P* or *DB9P male* plugs, on the computer back panel (see *Section 2.1*). A distinguishing feature of the interface is it uses "non-TTL" signals: all the external port signals are bipolar. There is no galvanic decoupling; the circuit ground of the attached device is connected to the computer's circuit ground. The data transmission rate may reach 115,200 bps.

Up to four COM1-COM4 serial ports can be supported at the BIOS level on a computer. (AT-class machines usually have two ports.) BIOS Int14h service provides port initialization, character input and output (without using interrupts), and status polling. Using Int14h standard calls, data transmission rate can be programmed to fall

---

[1] Only special adapters, such as SDLC or V.35, support synchronous transfer on a PC.

in the 110–9,600 bps range (less than the actual port capabilities). To increase the throughput, application software interaction with the port on the register level is widely used. For this, COM port hardware must be compatible with the i8250/1645/16550 software model.

The port's name indicates its main purpose: to connect equipment (such as a modem) that allows computer to communicate with other computers, networks, and peripheral devices. Peripheral devices with serial interfaces — printers, plotters, etc. — can be connected directly to the port. The COM port is widely used to connect a mouse and to directly link two computers. The COM port also is used to connect electronic keys to a computer.

Practically all modern motherboards (starting as far back as the PCI boards for the x486 processors) have two built-in adapters for the COM port. One of the ports also may be used for wireless infrared communications with peripheral devices (IrDA). ISA cards can have a couple of COM ports. On these, COM ports most frequently neighbor the LPT port and the disk interface controllers (FDC+IDE). If a greater number of interfaces is needed, additional special-purpose adapters, called multiplexors, may be installed. These are rather expensive cards; they usually have 4, 8, 12, or even 16 ports. Providing such a great number of connectors from the PC's back panel is problematic. Therefore, multiplexors are usually equipped with an external connector block, which also contains electronics, connected to the adapter through a cable with multicontact connectors. Multiplexors are not supported by BIOS.

The "classic" COM port only allowed software-controlled data transfer. The processor needed to execute several instructions to transfer each byte. Modern ports have several FIFO data buffers and allow transfers via the DMA channel. This significantly decreases the CPU workload, an especially important factor at high transfer rates.

2.1. The RS-232C Interface

The RS-232C interface is intended to connect data transmitting or receiving equipment (*DTE: Data Terminal Equipment*) to the terminal data channels equipment (*DCE: Data Communication Equipment*). The DTE role can be played by a computer, a printer, a plotter, or other peripheral equipment. The DCE role is usually played by a modem. The final purpose of the connection is to link two data transmitting devices. A complete schematic of the connection is shown in Fig. 2.1. The interface makes it possible to exclude the remote communications channel along with a pair of DCE devices by connecting two devices directly using a null-modem cable (Fig. 2.2).

The standard specifies the control signals of the interface, data transfer, electrical interface, and connector types. The standard provides for asynchronous and synchronous transfer modes, but the COM ports only support *asynchronous mode*. Functionally the RS-232C is equivalent to the CCITT/ITU V.24/V.28 standards, but has different signal names.

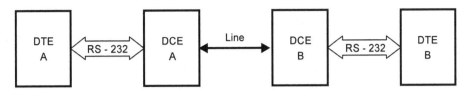

Fig. 2.1. A complete schematic of the RS-232C connection

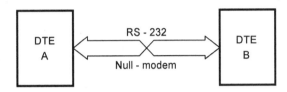

Fig. 2.2. An RS-232C connection using a null-modem cable

The *RS-232C* standard defines asymmetrical transmitters and receivers in which the signal is transmitted relative to the common wire: the circuit ground (symmetrical differential signals are used in other interfaces, such as *RS-422*). The interface *does not provide for the galvanic decoupling* of the devices. Voltages in the –12 V to –3 V range correspond to the logical one (*MARK* state) at the receiver *data input* (the RxD signal). Voltages in the +3 V to +12 V range correspond to the logical zero (*SPACE* state). For the *control signal inputs*, voltages in the +3 V to +12 V range correspond to the *ON* state, and in the –12 V to –3 V range, to the *OFF* state. The –3 V to +3 V range is the dead zone, providing receiver hysteresis: line state is considered to be changed only after crossing the threshold (Fig. 2.3). Signal levels on the transmitters' outputs shall be in the –12 V to –5 V and in the +5 V to +12 V ranges. The potential difference between the signal grounds (SG) of the connected devices shall be less than 2 V, a greater potential difference may cause erroneous signal reception. Make note that the TTL level signals (on the inputs and outputs of the UART ICs) are sent in the straight coding for the TxD and RxD lines and in inverted for all the others.

The interface supposes the connected devices to have *protective grounds* if they are both powered from AC line and have line filters.

Connecting and disconnecting interface cables of devices with individual power supplies must be done with their *power supplies turned off*. Otherwise, the difference of the devices' unbalanced voltages at the moment of establishing connection may be applied to the output or, which is more dangerous, to the input circuits of the interface and damage the ICs.

The RS-232C standard regulates the *types of connectors used.*

It is customary to have DTE devices (including the COM ports) equipped with *DB-25P* or with more compact *DB-9P* male plug connectors. The 9-pin connectors do not have contacts for the additional signals that are needed for the synchronous mode (in most of the 25-pin connectors, these contacts are not used).

DCE devices (modems) are equipped with female *DB-25S* or *DB-9S* connectors.

This rule assumes that the DCE connectors may be connected to the DTE connectors either directly or via "straight" adapter cables with a female plug on one end and a male on the other whose contacts are connected in the "one-to-one" fashion. There also are 9-pin connector to 25-pin connector adapter cables (Fig. 2.4).

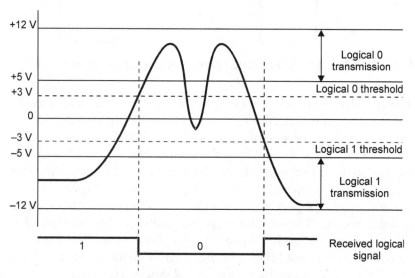

Fig. 2.3. Receiving RS-232C signals

	DB9S	DB25S			DB9P	DB25P	
TD	3	2	→ →	→	3	2	TD
RD	2	3	→ ←	→	2	3	RD
DTR	4	20	→ →	→	4	20	DTR
DSR	6	6	→ ←	→	6	6	DSR
RTS	7	4	→ →	→	7	4	RTS
CTS	8	5	→ ←	→	8	5	CTS
DCD	1	8	→ ←	→	1	8	DCD
RI	9	22	→ ←	→	9	22	RI
SG	5	7	→ →	→	5	7	SG

Fig. 2.4. Cables for connecting modems

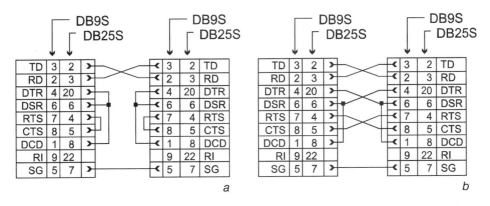

Fig. 2.5. Null-modem cables: *a* — minimal, *b* — complete

If DTE equipment is connected without using modems, then their connectors (males) are interconnected using a *null-modem cable* (Zero-modem, or Z-modem). Such cable has female plugs on both ends whose contacts are cross-wired as shown in one of the schematics in Fig. 2.5.

If a DTE piece of equipment has a female plug installed, it is almost 100 percent chance that it should be connected to another device by a straight cable, similar to one used to connect a modem. Female connectors are usually installed in those devices that are not intended to be connected via a modem.

Table 2.1 shows functions of the COM port (and of any other DTE type data transfer equipment) connector contacts. DB-25S connector contacts are defined by the EIA/TIA-232-E standard and DB-9S connector contacts are defined by the EIA/TIA-574 standard. Modems (DCE) have the same circuit and contact names, but the functions of their signals (input/output) are reversed.

Table 2.1. The RS-232C Connectors and Their Signals

Signal			Connector contact		PC external connector cable wire number				Direction In/Out
COM port	RS-232	V.24	DB-25P	DB-9P	1[1]	2[2]	3[3]	4[4]	
PG	AA	101	1	5	(10)	(10)	(10)	1	—
SG	AB	102	7	5	5	9	1	13	—
TD	BA	103	2	3	3	5	3	3	Out
RD	BB	104	3	2	2	3	4	5	In

continues

Table 2.1 Continued

Signal			Connector contact		PC external connector cable wire number				Direction In/Out
COM port	RS-232	V.24	DB-25P	DB-9P	1[1]	2[2]	3[3]	4[4]	
RTS	CA	105	4	7	7	4	8	7	Out
CTS	CB	106	5	8	8	6	7	9	In
DSR	CC	107	6	6	6	2	9	11	In
DTR	CD	108/2	20	4	4	7	2	14	Out
DCD	CF	109	8	1	1	1	5	15	In
RI	CE	125	22	9	9	8	6	18	In

[1] Ribbon cable for 8-bit multicards

[2] Ribbon cable for 16-bit multicards and for the built-in ports

[3] A version of a ribbon cable for the built-in ports

[4] Wide ribbon cable for the 25-contact connector

We will consider the asynchronous mode subset of the *RS-232C* signals from the standpoint of a PC COM port. For the sake of convenience, we will use the terminology mnemonics accepted in the descriptions of the COM ports and most of the equipment (it differs from the faceless RS-232 and V.24 cable notations). Remember that the active, ON, state of the control signals and the logical zero of the transmitted data are represented by the *positive potential* (above +3 V) of the interface, and the OFF state and logical one are represented by the *negative potential* (below −3 V). Table 2.2 shows the functions of the interface signals. Fig. 2.6 illustrates normal sequence of the control signals for the case of a modem connected to the COM port.

Table 2.2. Functions of the RS-232C Interface Signals

Signal	Function
PG	*Protected Ground.* It is connected to the device chassis and the cable shield.
SG	*Signal (Circuit) Ground* relevant to which signal levels operate
TD	*Transmit Data:* serial data, transmitter output
RD	*Receive Data:* serial data, receiver input

continues

Table 2.2 Continued

Signal	Function
RTS	*Request To Send.* The ON state informs the modem that the terminal has data for transmission. In half-duplex mode it is used to control the direction of the transfer: the ON state is the signal for the modem to switch into the transmit mode.
CTS	*Clear To Send:* permission to the terminal to send data. The OFF state disallows data transfer. The signal is used for hardware control of the data streams.
DSR	*Data Set Ready:* input of the signal indicating that the equipment is ready to transmit data (a modem in the operational mode is connected to the channel and has completed negotiation with the equipment on the opposite side of the channel)
DTR	*Data Terminal Ready:* output of the signal indicating that the terminal is ready to exchange data. The ON state maintains the commutated channel connected.
DCD	*Data Carrier Detected:* input of the signal indicating that the remote modem carrier signal has been detected.
RI	*Ring Indicator:* input of the call (ring) signal. In a commutated channel, this signal indicates that the modem is receiving a ringing signal.

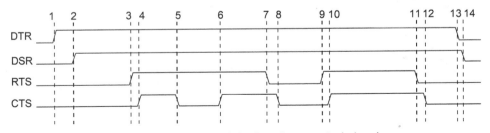

Fig. 2.6. Sequence of the interface control signals

1 — The PC indicates that it wants to use the modem by setting the DTR.

2 — The modem signals that it is ready and has established connection by setting the DSR signal.

3 — By setting the RTS signal, the computer asks a permission to transmit and informs the modem that it is ready to receive data.

4 — By setting the CTS signal, the modem informs that it is ready to receive data from the computer and to send them onto the line.

5 — By clearing the CTS signal, the modem indicates that it cannot continue to receive data (for example, its buffer is filled up) and that the computer has to suspend sending data.

6 — By the CTS signal, the modem gives the computer permission to resume transmitting data (room in the buffer has become available).

7 — Clearing of the RTS signal may mean either that the computer's buffer has filled up (the modem has to suspend sending data to the computer) or that the computer has no data to send to the modem. In such case, the modem usually stops transferring data to the computer.

8 — The modem acknowledges clearing of the RTS signal by clearing the CTS signal.

9 — To resume sending data, the computer sets the RTS signal again.

10 — The modem acknowledges its being ready.

11 — The computer indicates that the exchange has been competed.

12 — The modem answers by an acknowledgment.

13 — The computer clears the DTR signal, which usually is a signal to break the connection ("to hang up").

14 — By clearing the DSR signal, the modem indicates that the connection has been broken.

Examining this sequence, the purpose of the DTR/DSR and RTS/CTS connections in null-modem cables becomes clear.

2.2. Related Interfaces and Level Converters

Bipolar RS-232C signals are not always used in serial interface. Their use is inconvenient, e.g., because of having to use bipolar power supplies for transceivers. The ICs themselves of the above-described UART transceivers work with the TTL/CMOS logic signals. The same kinds of signals are used in the interfaces of various devices. For example, TTL/CMOS signals are used in the service ports of hard drives, mobile phones (but of very low levels) and in various other devices. Many devices (including pocket PCs and mobile phones) have low voltage level logic external serial interfaces. Of course, regular logic signals don't have such high noise resistance as the RS-232C, but neither is this always needed.

For interconversion between the RS-232C and CMOS logic levels, there are special buffer ICs for receivers (with hysteresis) and transmitters of bipolar signals. They are the first to become victims of the "pyrotechnical" effects when the rules for grounding and connecting equipment are not observed. Earlier they were often installed in sockets, which made their replacement easier. Fig. 2.7 shows pinouts of some popular RS-232C signal generating ICs. Often buffer circuits are included right into the interface LSI ICs. This lowers the price of the device, saves the card's real estate, but in case of an accident turns into great financial loses. Damaging interface ICs by short-circuiting them is unlikely: short circuit current of the transmitters usually does not exceed 20 mA.

Converters manufactured by companies Maxim and Sypex are often used in special adapter cables. They are practical in that they contain both receivers and transmitters. From the wide selection of these converters, it is easy to pick one that suits the number of receivers and transmitters needed, as well as the required power supply voltage characteristics (unipolar, bipolar, low-voltage).

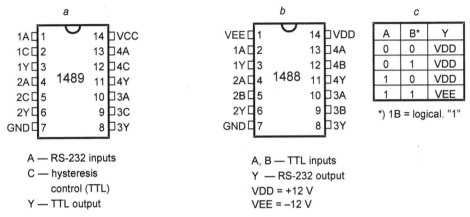

A — RS-232 inputs
C — hysteresis
    control (TTL)
Y — TTL output

A, B — TTL inputs
Y — RS-232 output
VDD = +12 V
VEE = −12 V

A	B*	Y
0	0	VDD
0	1	VDD
1	0	VDD
1	1	VEE

*) 1B = logical. "1"

Fig. 2.7. RS-232C signals generators:
a — a 1489 receiver; b — a 1488;
c — table of the transmitter output states
(*logical one is assumed on the missing output 1B)

When a great noise resistance is required (for high speed or long distance transmissions), different electrical versions of serial interface are used: *RS-422A (V.11, X.27)*, *RS-423A (V.10, X.26)*, and *RS-485*. Fig. 2.8 shows some schematics for connecting receivers and transmitters along with the line length limits (L) and the maximum transfer rate (V). Asymmetrical *RS-232C* and *RS-423A* interface lines have the lowest resistibility against the common-mode interference, although the differential input of an *RS-423A* receiver allows alleviating the situation to some degree. The best parameters have the *RS-422A* and *RS-485* interfaces working on symmetrical communication lines. They use differential transceivers with a separate (twisted) wire pair for each signal loop.

The *EIA-RS-422* (ITU-T V.11, X.27) and *EIA-RS-485* (ISO 8482) interfaces use symmetrical signal transmission and allow both point-to-point and bus topologies of connections. The information carrier in them is the potential difference between conductors A and B. Potential difference at the receiver's input $U_A - U_B > 0.2$ V (A is more positive than B) corresponds to the OFF (space) state, and $U_A - U_B < -0.2$ V (A is more negative than B) corresponds to the ON (mark) state. The $|U_A - U_B| \leq 0.2$ V range is the dead zone (hysteresis), providing protection from interferences. At the transmitter outputs, U_A and U_B signals usually switch between 0 V and +5 V levels (CMOS) or +1 V and +4 V (TTL). Differential output voltage must fall within the 1.5 V to 5 V range. The output resistance of transmitter is 100 ohm. The interfaces are electrically compatible, although there are some differences in their restrictions. The principal difference of the RS-485 transmitters is their capability to switch into the high impedance state. The RS-422/485 transmitters are compatible with the RS-423 receivers. Table 2.3 gives main parameters of the interfaces. Connection topologies are shown in Fig. 2.9.

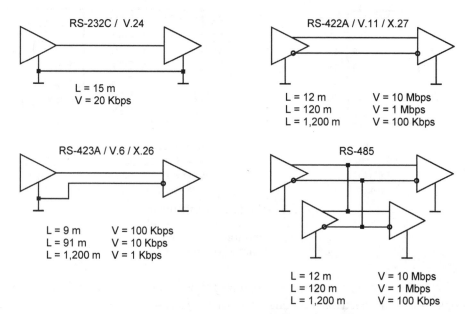

Fig. 2.8. Serial interface standards

Table 2.3. RS-422 and RS-485 Interface Parameters

Parameter	RS-422	RS-485
Operation threshold, $|U_A - U_B|$, V	0.2	0.2
Allowable level of common-mode interference, V[1]	−6.8...+6.8	−6.8...+11.8
Allowable input voltage, V[1]	−7...+7	−7...+12
Input resistance of the receiver, Kohm	4	12

continues

Table 2.3 Continued

Parameter	RS-422	RS-485
Minimal load resistance of the transmitter, ohm	100	60
Maximum number of nodes	One transmitter plus Ten receivers	32 (transmitters, receivers, or their combinations)
Maximum length, meters	1,200 (100 Kbps) 12 (10 Mbps)	1,200 (100 Kbps) 12 (10 Mbps)
Terminating plugs, R = 100 ohm	On the transmitter's far end	On both ends
Short circuit current, mA	< 150 to the bus GND	<250 to the bus with the −7 V − +12 V potential or between the A and B wires

[1] Voltage is measured relative to the node's "circuit ground."

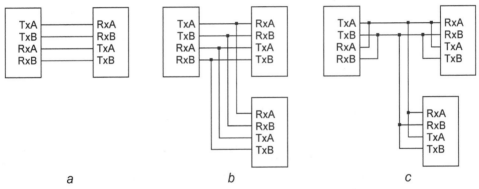

Fig. 2.9. Interface topology:
a — RS-422; *b* — RS-485 4-wire; *c* — RS-485 2-wire

To increase number of nodes, input resistance of receivers may be raised, but this leads to a drop in the permissible transmission rate or a decrease of the potential maximum transmission distance. The maximum transmission rate over the short distances (up to 10 meters) is limited by the transmitter's operating speed (frequencies of up to 25 MHz may be reached). Over the mid-distances the limitation is determined by the cable's capacitance (at 1,200 bps — 25 nF, at 9,600 bps — 30 nF, at 115 Kbps — 250 pF). The maximum distance is limited by the loop's DC resistance.

There are two types of the RS-485 interface: a 2-wire and a 4-wire. The 4-wire type (Fig. 2.9, *b*) sets out a master node whose transmitter services receivers of the rest of the nodes. The master node transmitter is always active: it does not need to switch into the high impedance state. Transmitters of the rest (slave) nodes must have tri-state outputs, they are connected by the common bus to the receiver of the master node. In the 2-wire type (Fig. 2.9, *c*), all nodes are equal.

In the simplest case — point-to-point connection — the RS-485 and RS-422 interfaces are equivalent and the high impedance state is not used.

To maintain the RS-485 bus quiescent state when there are no active transmitters present, active terminator plugs that "stretch" the potential of the conductors are placed on the line. In the quiescent state, wire B must have more positive potential than wire A.

With the multipoint connection, a method to access the transmission environment must be arranged. The most frequently method used is polling: one device designated master polls slave devices their readiness to transmit. Handing over the access right from one device to another is possible pursuant to the established protocol. Random access methods (analogous to Ethernet) are also sometimes used.

Differential input of the interfaces provides protection against interference, but here circuit grounds of the devices must be connected among themselves and to the ground bus. To interconnect the devices, a third wire of the interface is used (the cable shield may serve this purpose too). To prevent from flowing through the third wire too great a current equalizing the ground potentials, resistors are placed into its circuit (Fig. 2.10).

The RS-422 interface is often used to connect peripheral devices (such as printers). The RS-485 interface is a popular means of connecting industrial automation equipment.

To transmit a signal, the *"current loop" interface* instead of voltage uses current in the 2-wire line connecting receiver and transmitter. Current flow of 20 mA corresponds to logical one, and absence of current flow corresponds to logical zero. This kind of signal representation in the above-described format of asynchronous transmission allows detecting line breaks: the receiver will notice the missing stop-bit (line break acts as a constant logical zero).

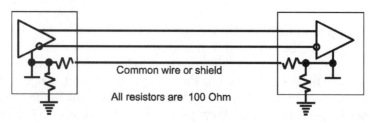

Fig. 2.10. Connection of the "circuit grounds" for the RS-422 and RS-485 interfaces

The current loop usually presupposes *galvanic decoupling* of the receiver's input circuits from the rest of the circuit. Here, the transmitter is the current source in the loop (this version is called active transmitter). Powering from the receiver also is possible (active receiver), here transmitter's output key may be galvanically decoupled from the rest of the transmitter's circuit. Simplified versions without galvanic decoupling also exist, but this is a degenerated case of the interface. Make note, the MIDI interface (see *Section 7.5.3*) is not compatible with the "classic" current loop.

Galvanically decoupled current loop allows transmitting signals over the distance of up to several kilometers, but at low transfer rates (rates over 19,200 bps are not used, and when the distance is measured in kilometers, the maximum speed is 9,600 bps and lower). The maximum distance is determined by the resistance of the wire pair and by the noise level. Because the interface requires one wire pair for each signal, usually only two signals of the serial interface are used (4-wire line). In the case of the bidirectional exchange, only signals to send and receive data are used; to flow control, the software XON/XOFF method is used. If there is no need for bidirectional exchange, then one wire pair is used to transmit data and the other to flow control with either the CTS signal (hardware protocol) or the reverse data line (software protocol). Using appropriate software, one current loop may be utilized to organize half-duplex bidirectional communication of two devices. Here each receiver "hears" both the opposite side transmitter's signals and the signals of its own transmitter. The communication protocols simply consider them as echo signals. For error-free reception, transmitters must operate in turns.

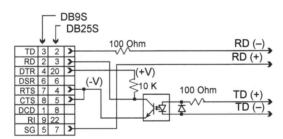

Fig 2.11. Converting RS-232C interface into the current loop

The current loop allows employment of dedicated physical (leased) lines without modems but at low transfer rates. Sometimes the current loop is used to connect RS-232C interface terminals if the design length of the interface is too short or galvanic decoupling is needed. It is not difficult to convert RS-232C signals into the current loop. Fig. 2.11 shows a very simple schematic diagram of a converter for connecting a terminal. The interface power supply is used to obtain the bipolar signal needed for the input circuits of the COM port. The schematics may be enhanced to provide overload protection for the optocouplers and to improve the shape of the voltage signals. The maximum transfer rate is determined by the operating speed of the used optocouplers (rate of 9,600 bps is achieved practically with any optocouplers).

2.3. The Asynchronous Mode

The asynchronous mode of serial transfer is byte-oriented (character-oriented): the minimal transferred unit of information is one byte (one character). Fig. 2.12 illustrates the format of the byte transmission. Transmission of each byte is set off by the *start bit*, which signals the start of the transmission to the receiver. It is followed by the *data bits* and, possibly, the *parity bit*. The transmission ends by the *stop bit*, which ensures there is a pause between transmissions. The start bit of the next byte is sent at any time after the previous byte's stop bit, i.e., it is possible to have pauses of any length between transmissions. The start bit, which always has strictly defined value (that of a logical zero), provides a simple method to synchronize the receiver by the signal from the transmitter. It is understood that both the receiver and the transmitter are working at the same transfer rate. The internal synchronizing generator of the receiver uses a reference frequency dividing counter, which is set to zero at the moment it receives the beginning of the start bit. This counter generates internal strobes by which the receiver latches in the following bits. Ideally, the strobe pulses are located in the center of the bit intervals, which allows receiving data even when the receiver and the transmitter transfer rates are slightly unmatched. It is obvious that when transmitting eight data bits, one parity bit, and one stop bit, the permissible frequency tolerance, at which data will be detected correctly, must not exceed five percent. Taking into account phase distortions and the quantized nature of the internal synchronization counter operation, in reality even smaller frequency tolerance is allowed. The smaller is the division factor of the internal reference frequency generator (the higher the transmission frequency), the higher is the inaccuracy of the strobe placement with respect to the center of the bit interval, thus necessitating stricter requirements to the frequency matching.

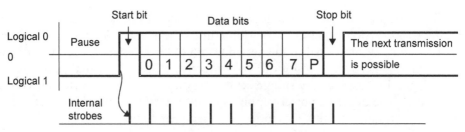

Fig. 2.12. Format of the RS-232C asynchronous transmission

The higher is the transmission frequency, the more distorted fronts affect the phase of the received signal. Combination of these factors results in heightening the requirements to the receiver and transmitter frequency matching as the transfer rate increases.

The format of the asynchronous transmission allows detecting potential *transmission errors*.

❑ If a logic transition signaling start of transmission has been received, but at the start bit strobe logical one has been latched, the start bit is considered false and the receiver returns into the wait state. The receiver does not have to report this error.

❑ If during time period allocated to the stop bit, logical zero (high) level is discovered, a stop bit error is recorded.

❑ If the parity check is employed, then after sending data bits, a *parity check bit* is sent. This bit complements the number of data bits logical ones to even or odd, depending on the prior agreement. An error is recorded if a byte with an erroneous parity bit value is received.

❑ The format check allows detecting line breaks: as a rule, the receiver "sees" logical zero if there is a line break. This logical zero is first treated as a start bit and data's zero bits, but then the stop bit check is triggered.

A set of *standard transfer rates* is adopted for the asynchronous mode: 50, 75, 110, 150, 300, 600, 1200, 2400, 4800, 9600, 19200, 38400, 57600, and 115200 bits per second (bps). Sometimes, term "baud" is used instead of the "bps", but when considering transmitting of binary data, this is incorrect. Bauds are used to measure the frequency of the line state changes, but when non-binary coding method is used (which is widely employed in modern modems) in the communication channel, the bit rate transfer (bps) and the frequency of the signal change (baudrate) may differ by several times.

The number of *data bits* can be 5, 6, 7, or 8 (5- and 6-bit formats are seldom used). The number of *stop bits* can be 1, 1.5, or 2 (one-and-a-half bit denotes only the length of the stop interval).

2.4. Data Flow Control

Two types of protocol may be used to control data flow: hardware and software. Sometimes, the flow control is confused with handshaking or acknowledgement. *Handshaking* means negotiating with the partner every elementary step of the protocol (a good example, signaling transmission protocols of the parallel port in the EPP and ECP modes). *Acknowledgement* is sending a notification of receiving a quantum of data (a byte, a frame, or a packet). *Flow control* assumes sending notifications as to whether or not the subsequent reception of data is possible. Quite often, flow control is based on the mechanism of handshaking or acknowledgement.

Hardware flow control protocol RTS/CTS uses the CTS signal that allows to stop sending data if the receiver is not ready to receive them (Fig. 2.13). Transmitter "lets go" the next byte only when the CTS line is set. It is impossible to stop the byte whose transmission has already been started by the CTS signal (this ensures the integrity of transmission). Hardware protocol provides the fastest transmitter reaction to the receiver state. ICs of asynchronous transceivers have at least two receiving registers: a shifting register to receive the next packet and a storage register from which the received byte is read. This makes it possible to implement hardware protocol based exchange without loosing data.

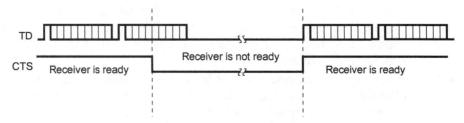

Fig. 2.13. Hardware flow control

The hardware protocol is practical when connecting printers and plotters, if they support it. When two computers are connected directly (without modems), the hardware protocol requires that the RTS and CTS lines were cross-connected.

With a direct connection, the transmitting terminal must have its CTS line switched into the ON state (by having its own RTS and CTS lines interconnected), otherwise the transmitter will not "talk."

The 8250/16450/16550 transceivers used in IBM PC do not process the CTS signal by the hardware means, but only reflect its state in the MSR register (see *Section 2.5*). It is left to the BIOS Int14h service to implement the RTS/CTS protocol, and it is not quite correct to call this service a hardware means. Should the program using a COM port interact with the UART on the register level (and not via BIOS), then to support this protocol, it handles the processing of the CTS signal by itself. Several communication programs allow ignoring the CTS signal (if a modem is not used), and they do not require that the CTS input should be connected with the output of even their own RTS signal. There are, however, different transceivers (such as 8251) in which the CTS signal is processed by the hardware means. For them, as well as for the "honest" programs, using the CTS signal at the connectors (and even in the cables) is mandatory.

The XON/XOFF software data flow control protocol assumes that a bidirectional data transfer channel is available. The protocol works as follows: if the receiving device discovers some reasons because of which it cannot continue to receive data, it sends an XOFF (13h) byte-symbol via the reverse serial channel. Having received this signal, the opposite device suspends the transmission. When the receiving device becomes ready to receive data again, it sends an XON (11h) character, having received which the opposite device resumes transmission. Comparing to the hardware implemented protocol, the transmitter's response time to the change in the receiver's state increases at least for the duration of the signal transmission (XON or XOFF) plus the time it takes the transmitter's program to react to receiving the character (Fig. 2.14). From this, it follows that only a receiver with an additional buffer for received data and which informs in advance of its inability to receive (still having room in its buffer) can work without data losses.

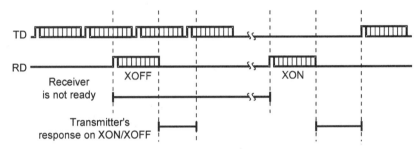

Fig. 2.14. XON/XOFF software flow control

The advantage of the software flow control consists in not having to transmit the interface control signals: the simplest cable for bidirectional exchange can have only three wires (see Fig. 2.5, *a*). A shortcoming, besides the necessity to have a buffer and the long response time (lowering the overall efficiency of the channel because of waiting for the XON signal), lies in its being difficult to implement the full-duplex exchange mode. In this case, it is necessary to extract flow control signals from the stream of the received data (as well as to process them), which limits the set of characters that can be transmitted.

Besides these two commonly used standard protocols, which are supported by OS and by most peripheral devices, there are custom protocols requiring special support.

2.5. Asynchronous Transceivers' ICs (UART)

In the COM ports, conversion of the parallel data into the serial for transmitting and the inverse conversion for receiving is done by dedicated UART (Universal Asynchronous Receiver-Transmitter) ICs. The same ICs generate and process the interface control signals. IBM PC XT/AT COM ports are based on the ICs compatible with the i8250 UART series on the register level: 8250/16450/16550A. This series is an improvement on the original model, intended for increasing the operating speed and lowering power consumption and the processor load during intensive exchange. Make a note that:

❐ 8250 has design flaws (appearance of false interrupts), which were taken into account in the XT BIOS.

❐ 8250A: The original design flaws are corrected, but the XT BIOS compatibility is lost as a result; this IC works in some AT models but it cannot be used for the 9,600 bps speeds.

❐ 8250B: 8250 and 8250A flaws corrected, the XT BIOS compatibility restored by restoring the original interrupt flaw; works in AT under DOS (except for the 9,600 bps speeds).

8250*x* ICs have low operating speeds with regard to requests from by the system bus. They do now allow their registers be referenced in the consecutive processor bus cycles and software delays must be inserted between the CPU references for these ICs to work correctly.

The following modifications of the UART ICs are used in the AT class computers:

❐ 16450: high-speed version of the 8250 for AT. It does not have the 8250 flaws, nor full compatibility with the XT BIOS.

❐ 16550: a development on the 16450. It can use the DMA channel to exchange data. It also has a FIFO buffer, which cannot be used because of the flawed operation.

❐ 16550A: has functional 16-byte input and output FIFO buffers and DMA capability. It is this chip that should be used in the AT class computers for the 9,600 bps and higher data exchange rates. Most of the modern chipset's I/O port controller ICs provide compatibility with this chip.

From the programming standpoint, 16550A UART ICs are sets of registers, access to which is determined by the address (offset of the address register relative to the port's base address) and the value of the DLAB bit (bit 7 of the LCR register). In the I/O addressing space, the IC occupies eight contiguous addresses. Table 2.4 lists the 16550A UART registers and their access methods. 8250 ICs differ in that they do not have FCR register and all of the FIFO and DMA capabilities.

Table 2.4. The 16550A UART Registers

Access		Register		Read/Write
Offset	DLAB	Name	Function	
0h	0	THR	Transmit Holding Register	WO
0h	0	RBR	Receiver Buffer Register	RO
0h	1	DLL	Divisor Latch LSB	R/W
1h	1	DLM	Divisor Latch MSB	R/W
1h	0	IER	Interrupt Enable Register	R/W
2h	x	IIR	Interrupt Identification Register	RO
2h	x	FCR	FIFO Control Register	WO
3h	x	LCR	Line Control Register	R/W
4h	x	MCR	Modem Control Register	R/W
5h	x	LSR	Line Status Register	R/W[1]
6h	x	MSR	Modem Status Register	R/W[1]
7h	x	SCR	Scratch Pad Register	R/W

[1] Some bits can only be read. Writing into the register may lead to protocol failure.

THR: *Transmitter Holding Register* (write only). Data written into the register are sent into the output transfer shift register (when it becomes available), from which they are placed onto the output TXD signal. Bit 0 (the lowest) is transmitted (and received) first. If a package is less than eight bits long, the high order bits are ignored.

RBR: *Receiver Buffer Register* (read only). Serial data (RXD) received by the receiver shift register are placed into the RBR register, from where the CPU can read them out. An overflow error occurs if the byte has not been read out of the register by the time the next byte is received. If a package is less than eight bits long, the high order bits have zero values.

DLL: *frequency Divisor Low byte register*

DLM: *frequency Divisor high byte register*. The divisor is calculated using the formula $D = 115200/V$, where V is the transfer rate in bps. The input synchronizing frequency of 1.8432 MHz is divided by the specified coefficient, which gives sixteen-fold data transfer frequency, used by UART.

IER: *Interrupt Enable Register*. A bit's value of logical one enables interrupts from the corresponding source.

IER register bits functions:

- Bits [7:4]=0: not used
- Bit 3 — Mod_IE: upon a modem status change (any of the CTS, DSR, RI, or DCD lines)
- Bit 2 — RxL_IE: upon a line break or error
- Bit 1 — TxD_IE: upon the end of transmission
- Bit 0 — RxD_IE: upon receiving a character (a timeout interrupt in the FIFO mode)

IIR: *Interrupt Identification and FIFO status indicator Register* (read only). To simplify software analysis, UART organizes internal interrupts in a four-level priority system. The order of priorities (in descending order) is: line status, receiving a character, emptying of the transmitter register, modem status. When an interrupt condition develops, UART points to the source with the highest priority until it is cleared by an appropriate operation. Only after this will it specify the next request source. Functions of the IIR register bits are described below.

- Bits [7:6] — FIFO mode status:
  - 11: 16550A FIFO mode
  - 10: 16550 FIFO mode
  - 00: regular mode
- Bits [5:4]: not used.
- Bit 3: reception timeout interrupt in the FIFO mode (buffer has data to read).
- Bits [2:1]: cause of the highest priority interrupt (in regular, non-FIFO mode):
  - 11: line error/break. Reset is done by reading the line status register.
  - 10: a character has been received. Reset is done by reading data.
  - 01: a character has been sent (THR register is empty). Reset is done by writing data.
  - 00: modem status has changed. Reset is done by reading modem status register.
- Bit 0: indication of a pending interrupt request (1: no interrupt pending, 0: interrupt pending).

In the FIFO mode, the interrupt cause is identified by the bits [3:1].

- 011: line error/break. Reset is done by reading line status register.
- 010: a character has been received. Reset is done by reading the receiver data register.
- 110: a timeout indicator (during time period four times the time it takes to send or receive a character no character has been transmitted or sent even though the buffer is holding at least one). Reset is done by reading the receiver data register.

❏ 001: the THR register is empty. Reset is done by writing data.
❏ 000: modem status change (CTS, DSR, RI, or DCD). Reset is done by reading the MSR register.

FCR: *FIFO Control Register* (read only). The function of its bits is described below.

❏ Bits [7:6] — ITL *(Interrupt Trigger Level)*: FIFO buffer saturation level interrupt threshold:
  • 00: 1 byte (by default)
  • 01: 4 bytes
  • 10: 8 bytes
  • 11: 14 bytes
❏ Bits [5:4]: reserved.
❏ Bit 3: DMA operations mode select.
❏ Bit 2 — RESETTF *(Reset Transmitter FIFO)*: reset transmitter FIFO counter (by writing a logical one; shift register is not reset).
❏ Bit 1 — RESETTRF *(Reset Receiver FIFO)*: reset receiver FIFO counter (by writing a logical one; shift register is not reset).
❏ Bit 0 — TRFIFOE *(Transmit and Receive FIFO Enable)*: enabling (by logical one) transmitter and receiver FIFO. Buffers are automatically cleared when modes are changed.

LCR: *Line Control Register* (setting channel parameters). Functions of the LCR register bits are described below.

❏ Bit 7 — DLAB *(Divisor Latch Access Bit)*: clock divisor access control.
❏ Bit 6 — BRCON *(Break Control)*: generating line break (sending zeros) at BRCON = 1.
❏ Bit 5 — STICPAR *(Sticky Parity)*: forced generation of the parity bit:
  • 0: parity check bit is generated according to the output character parity.
  • 1: constant parity check bit value: logical zero at EVENPAR = 1 and logical one at EVENPAR = 0.
❏ Bit 4 — EVENPAR *(Even Parity select)*: selecting parity control type: zero for odd parity, one for even parity.
❏ Bit 3 — PAREN *(Parity Enable)*, enabling parity check bit:
  • 1: parity check bit (parity or constant) is enabled.
  • 0: parity check bit is disabled.
❏ Bit 2 — STOPB *(Stop Bits)*: number of stop bits:
  • 0: 1 stop bit
  • 1: 2 stop bits (for 5-bit code, the stop bit is 1.5 bits long)

❑ Bits [1:0] — SERIALDB *(Serial Data Bits)*: number of data bits:
  - 00: 5 bits
  - 01: 6 bits
  - 10: 7 bits
  - 11: 8 bits

MCR: *Modem Control Register.* A description of the MCR register is given below.

❑ Bits [7:5]=0: reserved.
❑ Bit 4 — LME *(Loopback Mode Enable)*: diagnostics mode enable:
  - 0: normal mode
  - 1: diagnostics mode
❑ Bit 3 — IE *(Interrupt Enable)*: enabling interrupts (signaled by the external output OUT2):
  - 0: interrupts disabled
  - 1: interrupts enabled

  In the diagnostics mode, it is placed onto the MSR.7 input (DCD is emulated).
❑ Bit 2 — OUT1C *(OUT1 bit Control)*: control of the output signal 1 (not used); in the diagnostics mode, it is placed on the MSR.6 input (RI is emulated).
❑ Bit 1 — RTSC *(Request To Send Control)*: control of the RTS output; in the diagnostics mode, it is placed on the MSR.4 input (CTS is emulated):
  - 0: active (+V)
  - 1: inactive (–V)
❑ Bit 0 — DTRC *(Data Terminal Ready Control)*: control of the DTR output; in the diagnostics mode it is placed on the MSR.5 input (DSR is emulated):
  - 0: active (+V)
  - 1: inactive (–V)

LSR: *Line Status Register* (transceiver status, to be more exact). Functions of the LSR register bits are described below.

❑ Bit 7 — FIFOE *(FIFO Error status)*: FIFO mode received data error (buffer has at least one character received with a format, parity, or break error). In non-FIFO mode, it is always set to zero.
❑ Bit 6 — TEMPT *(Transmitter Empty Status)*: transmitter register is empty (neither the shift register nor the THR or FIFO buffer registers has data to transmit).
❑ Bit 5 — THRE *(Transmitter Holding Register Empty)*: transmitter register is ready to receive a byte to transmit. In the FIFO mode, indicates that the transmission FIFO buffer is empty. May generate interrupts.

❑ Bit 4 — BD *(Break Detected)*: line break indicator (the receiver input has been in the logical zero state for no shorter period than it takes to send a character).

❑ Bit 3 — FE *(Framing Error)*: frame error (incorrect stop bit).

❑ Bit 2 — PE *(Parity Error)*: parity check bit error (parity or fixed bit).

❑ Bit 1 — OE *(Overrun Error)*: overfilling (losing a character). If the reception of the next character begins before the previous one has been moved from the shifting register into the buffer or FIFO register, the first character is lost.

❑ Bit 0 — DR *(Receiver Data Ready)*: received data are ready (in the DHR or FIFO buffer). Reset is done by reading the receiver.

Error indicators — bits [4:1] — are cleared after the LSR register has been read. In the FIFO mode, error indicators are stored in the FIFO buffer together with each character. They are placed into the register (and generate interrupts) at the moment when the character that has been received with errors is at the top of the FIFO (first in line to be read out). In the case of a line break, only the "break" character is placed into the FIFO and the UART waits for the line to be restored and for the next start bit.

MSR: *Modem Status Register.* Functions of the MSR register bits are described below.

❑ Bit 7 — DCD *(Data Carrier Detect)*: DCD line status:
   - 0: active (+V)
   - 1: inactive (–V)

❑ Bit 6 — RI *(Ring Indicator)*: RI line status:
   - 0: active (+V)
   - 1: inactive (–V)

❑ Bit 5 — DSR *(Data Set Ready)*: DSR line status:
   - 0: active (+V)
   - 1: inactive (–V)

❑ Bit 4 — CTS *(Clear To Send)*: CTS line status:
   - 0: active (+V)
   - 1: inactive (–V)

❑ Bit 3 — DDCD *(Delta Data Carrier Detect)*: DCD status change

❑ Bit 2 — TERI *(Trailing Edge Of Ring Indicator)*: RI line envelope fall-off (end of ring)

❑ Bit 1 — DDSR *(Delta Data Set Ready)*: DSR state change

❑ Bit 0 — DCTS *(Delta Clear To Send)*: CTS state change

State change indicators (bits [3:0] are reset by reading the register.

SCR: *Scratch (work) Register* (8-bit wide). Does not affect the UART operation and is intended for temporary data storage (it is absent in the 8250 IC).

In the *diagnostics mode* (when LME = 1), an internal loopback "plug" is created inside UART:

❏ Transmitter's output is switched into the logical one state.
❏ Receiver's input is disconnected.
❏ Output of the transmitter's shift register is logically connected to the receiver's input.
❏ DSR, CTS, RI, and DCD inputs are disconnected from the input lines and are internally controlled by the DTRC, RTSC, OUT1C, and IE bits.
❏ Outputs of the modem control signals are switched into the passive state (logical zero).

Data transmitted serially are immediately received, which allows to diagnose the internal data channel of the port (including the shift registers) and interrupts servicing, and also to determine the UART's operational speed.

2.6. System Support of the COM Ports

The COM ports are supported by the BIOS Int14h service, which provides the following functions:

❏ *Initialization* (setting the exchange speed and the transmission format; disabling interrupt sources). It has no effect on the DTR and RTS signals (after hardware reset they are inactive).
❏ *Send character.* DTR and RTS signals are activated, and after the THR register is released, the character being output is placed into it.
❏ *Receive character.* Only the DTR signal is activated (the RTS signal goes into the inactive state), the driver is awaiting to receive a data character.
❏ *Status poll* of the modem and the line (reading the MSR and LSR registers).

Hardware interrupts are not used, input and output readiness wait is limited by the timeout. Readiness can be expeditiously checked by status polling, before an attempt is made to receive or send a character.

During the initial POST testing, BIOS checks for the serial port presence (UART 8250 or compatible registers) at the standard addresses and places the base addresses of the ports it discovers in BIOS Data Area cells 0:0400h, 0:0402h, 0:0404h, and 0:0406h. These cells store the addresses of the ports that have logical names of COM1 to COM4. Address value of zero means that no port with the given number exists. The constants setting timeouts for the ports are stored in the cells 0:47Ch, 0:47Dh, 0:473Eh, and 0:47Fh.

The discovered ports are initialized into the 2,400 bps exchange rate, seven data bits, even parity, one stop bit. The interface control signals DTR and RTS are switched into the initial state (OFF: negative line level).

2.7. Configuring COM Ports

There may be up to four serial COM1 to COM4 port on a computer; AT class machines typically have two ports. The process of controlling serial ports is split into two stages: initial configuring (Setup) of the port's hardware and the in-the-process (operational) changes of the work modes by application or system software. Configuring a COM port depends on how the port has been implemented. Ports physically located on an expansion card are configured by jumpers on the card itself. Ports built-in into motherboards are configured by BIOS Setup.

The following port parameters can be configured:

❑ *Base address,* which for the COM1–COM4 ports usually has the values of 3F8h, 2F8h, 3E8h, and 2E8h. During the initialization, BIOS checks the addresses for ports presence exactly in this order and assigns logical names COM1, COM2, COM3, and COM4 to the ports it detects. Ports COM3 and COM4 can have alternate addresses 3E0h, 338h and 2E0h, 238h, respectively. For PS/2, the standard COM3 to COM8 port addresses are 3220h, 3228h, 4220h, 4228h, 5220h, and 5228h, respectively.

❑ *Interrupt request line* used: for COM1 and COM3 lines, IRQ4 or IRQ11 are normally used, for COM2 and COM4: lines IRQ3 or IRQ10. Technically, interrupt numbers may be assigned to the base address (port number) in arbitrary order, but some programs and drivers (such as serial mouse drivers) are programmed to use the standard combinations. Each port that needs a hardware interrupt is assigned a separate line that does not coincide with the interrupt request lines used by the other devices. Interrupts are needed only for those ports to which input devices, UPS, or modems are connected. Only multitasking OSs (not always though) use interrupts for printer or plotter transfer and this scarce resource may be conserved. Also, interrupts are not used when two computers are connected with a null-modem cable. Whether one interrupt request line can be separately used by several ports (or shared with other devices) depends on the hardware connection implementation and the software used. With ports installed on the ISA bus, shared interrupts usually don't work.

❑ *DMA channel* (for 16450/16550 UART ICs located on the motherboard): enabling DMA and the channel number. DMA is rarely used with COM ports.

2.8. COM Port Applications

The COM port is widely used to connect various peripheral and communications equipment, to communicate with various technological equipment, control and monitoring equipment, programmers, in-circuit emulators, and other devices using RS-232C protocol.

Most frequently, COM ports are used to connect *pointer devices* (mouse, trackball). In this case, the port is used in the serial input mode. A mouse with the serial interface — *Serial Mouse* — can be connected to any functional port. To match the port and mouse connectors, DB-9S to DB25P or DB-25S to DB-9P adapters may be used. Mouse needs interrupt IRQ4 for COM1 and IRQ3 for COM2. The fact that in order to use mouse, COM1 port must use IRQ4 interrupt is a peculiarity of its driver, but for the user the important part is the fact of the limitation itself. Every event — mouse movement or pressing/releasing a button — is binary coded and sent through the RS-232C interface. Asynchronous transmission is used; bipolar power source is supplied by the interface control lines.

To connect *external modems*, a *DTE* to *DCE* cable with a complete set of wires (nine) is used. Its schematic diagram is given in Fig. 2.4. The same type of cable is used to match the connectors (by the number of contacts); for this, 9-to-25 mouse adapters also can be used. Communications software normally uses interrupts, but here there is a freedom of choice in selecting the port number (address) and the interrupt line. If operations at the transfer rates of 9,600 bps or higher are planned, then the COM port must be implemented using 16550A or a compatible UART IC. The extent to which the FIFO buffers and DMA channel operational features are available depends on the communications software used.

To connect *two computers* located a short distance apart from each other, their COM ports also can be directly connected with a null-modem cable. (See Fig. 2.5). Programs like Norton Commander or MS-DOS Interlink allow exchanging files at the transfer rates up to 115.2 Kbps without making use of the hardware interrupts. The same connection can also be used by the Lantastic net package, which offers more advanced features, as well as by the OS Windows services.

COM port allows connecting *electronic keys* (Security Devices) intended for protecting software from unlicensed use. These devices can be "transparent" (allowing to use the port to connect other equipment) as well as totally taking over the port.

Provided with a proper software support, COM port allows to turn a PC into a terminal, emulating the command set of the common specialized terminals (VT-52, VT-100, etc.) The simplest terminal can be obtained by interconnecting functions of BIOS COM port services (Int14h), teletype output (Int10h), and the keyboard input (Int16h). Such terminal, however, will only work at low exchange rates (if, of course, it is not done on a Pentium), since, although BIOS functions are universal, they are not very fast.

COM port also can be used as a bidirectional interface with three software-controlled output (TD, DTR, and RTS) and four input (CTS, DSR, DCD, and RI) lines utilizing bipolar signals. They may be used, for example, to programmatically implement synchronous serial interfaces (see *Section 10.5*). During the AT-286 times, there existed a schematic of a one-bit broad-impulse converter allowing to record an audio signal on the PC using an input line of the COM port. Playing this record back through the PC speaker made it possible to reproduce speech.

2.9. The COM Port and PnP

Modern peripheral devices connected to the COM port can support the PnP specification. The main task of the OS lies in identifying the device being connected. For this, a simple protocol that can be implemented on any COM port by purely software means has been developed. Fig. 2.15 illustrates this protocol.

1. *Check Port:* a check for the port being occupied by an application. If the port is free, it is initialized into the idle state with the line states being DTR=ON, RTS=OFF, TXD=Mark. If the port is busy, the further protocol steps are not carried out.

2. *Check Device:* a check for device presence. For a certain period of time (0.2 sec), the system waits for the DSR signal to appear, which would indicate that that there is device connected to the port. In the simplest case, the device will have a DTR-DSR jumper at the connector that provides the said response. If a device is detected, the subsequent protocol steps are carried out (the DTR and RTS control signals are manipulated in order to receive serial data information from the device). If there is no answer, the protocol switches into the Disconnect Idle state. In this case, operating systems that support dynamic configuring periodically execute the preceding sequence, trying to see if any new devices have been connected.

3. *Setup-1.* The port is programmed into the 1,200 bps, seven data bits, no parity, one stop-bit mode, and the DTR signal is held low for 0.2 sec. Then the DTR is set to logical one, and 0.2 sec later the RTS is also set to logical one.

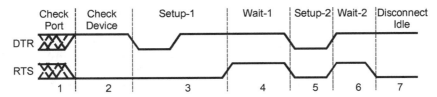

Fig. 2.15. Requesting a PnP device identifier

4. *Wait-1.* The operating system waits 0.2 seconds for the first character to arrive from the device. When it arrives, the system begins receiving the identifier. If during this time the character does not arrive, the operating system makes a second setup attempt (see 5), which differs somewhat from the first one.

5. *Setup-2.* Both the DTR and RTS, signals are set to logical zero for 0.2 seconds, after which they both are set to logical one.

6. *Wait-2.* The operating system waits for 0.2 seconds for the first character to arrive from the device, and when it arrives begins receiving the identifier. If the character does not come during this time, then depending on the status of the DSR signal, either the Verify Disconnect (if DSR=0) is performed or Connect Idle (if DSR=1) state is entered.

7. In the *Connect Idle* standby state, the DTR signal is set to logical one and the RTS signal to logical zero, the port is programmed to 300 bps, seven data bits, no parity, one stop bit mode. If during this state DSR=0 is discovered, the OS should inform that the device has been disconnected.

Receiving the device identifier one character at a time has timeout limitation of 0.2 sec per character as well as the overall time limit of 2.2 sec, which allows receiving a string up to 256 characters long. The PnP identifier string must have the start and end markers (28h or 08h and 29h or 09h, respectively), between which the body of the identifier in the standardized format is placed. Up to sixteen characters not related to the PnP identifier can go before the start marker. If during the first 0.2 sec of character wait (step 4 or 6) the start marker has not arrived, or the timeout has been triggered but the end marker has not been received, or a character has been received with errors, a switch into the *Connect Idle* state is made. If a valid identifier string has been received, it is handed over to the OS.

To *verify disconnection* (*Verify Disconnect*), the DTR is set to logical one, the RTS to logical zero, and every five seconds the state of the DSR signal is checked. When DSR=1, a switch into the *Connect Idle* state is performed (see list item 7), and when DSR=0, a switch into the *Disconnect Idle* state is done, in which the system can periodically poll the DSR signal to check if a device has been connected.

The described mechanism has been developed by Microsoft company with considerations for compatibility with devices not belonging to the PnP type: it ensures that it will be impossible to disable them and provides for the system stability to the messages which are not PnP identifiers. For example, a conventional Microsoft Mouse upon getting powered up from the interface will respond with the ASCII character "M" (a three-button mouse — with a string "M3").

2.10. COM Ports Malfunctions and Their Troubleshooting

COM port malfunctions occur (become apparent) during installation of new ports or unsuccessful connection of external devices.

2.10.1. Configuration Testing

Troubleshooting the serial ports (like the parallel ones) is started with checking whether the system identifies them. List of *addresses* of the installed ports usually appears in the table that BIOS displays before loading the OS. This list also can be viewed with the help of diagnostic programs or directly in the BIOS Data Area with the help of a debugger.

If BIOS detects fewer ports than are physically installed, it means that two ports have been assigned the same address or an incorrect address for one of the ports has been specified. Problems may turn up with the COM3 and COM4 port addresses: not all BIOS versions will look for ports at the alternative addresses 3E0h, 338h, 2E0h, and 238h; sometimes, the search is not done at the addresses 3E8h and 2E8h. The way in which the identified ports are shown in the list may be confusing: if two ports with addresses 3F8h and 3E8h are installed, in the list they will be referred to as COM1 and COM2 and these names can be used to reference them. However, the same ports may be referred to in the list as COM1 and COM3 (since 3E8h is the standard COM3 port address). But an attempt to reference COM3 port will be unsuccessful, since in this case 3E8h address will be in the BIOS Data Area memory cell 0:402h, which corresponds to the COM2 port, and in the COM3 port memory cell (0:404h) there will be a zero: indicator that no such port is present. You can "explain" to the system where what port is manually using any debugger by inserting correct values of the base addresses into the BIOS Data Area memory cells (you will have to do this every time after rebooting before using the "lost" port). There are diagnostic utilities allowing to find ports (such as PortFinder).

If two ports have been assigned the same address, a diagnostic program can discover port errors only when it is used with an *external loopback plug*. Software testing of the port without the plug will not show any errors, as in this case the diagnostic mode is activated (see the UART description) and the conflicting (but individually in order) ports will work in parallel, ensuring that the output information matches. In real life, normal functioning of the conflicting ports is not possible. In solving the address conflict you may find it helpful to install ports one by one while observing the addresses that appear in the list.

If only one physical port is installed and BIOS does not find it, the reasons for this are the same as in the case with the LPT port: either it was disabled during the configuration or has failed. The malfunction may be fixed by wiggling the adapter card in and out within the motherboard slot.

When using the COM port, corresponding *hardware interrupts* are involved: they are used when connecting a modem, a mouse, or other input devices. The reason for these devices not functioning may be incorrect interrupt request settings. Conflicts with other devices, as well as mismatches between the interrupt number and the port address, are possible here.

2.10.2. Functionality Testing

Initial testing of the COM port can be done with the help of a diagnostics program (CheckIt) without using loopback plugs. This testing mode allows checking the UART IC (internal diagnostic mode) and interrupt generation but not the input and output buffer ICs, which are more often the source of troubles. If the test fails, the cause needs to be looked for either in the address/interrupt conflict or in the UART IC itself.

For more reliable testing, it is recommended to use an external plug that is connected to the COM port connector (Fig. 2.16). Unlike in the case with the LPT port, the COM port has more input lines than output, which allows to fully test all the circuits. The plug connects receiver's input to the transmitter's output. The mandatory for all plug schematics RTS-CTS jumper allows the transmitter to operate: without it, characters may not be transmitted. The output DTR signal is normally used for checking input DSR, DCD, and RI lines.

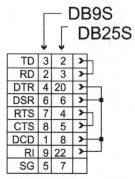

Fig. 2.16. Plug for checking COM ports (LoopBack for CheckIt and Norton Diagnostics)

If the test using external plug fails, the cause of the problem should be looked for in the external buffers, their power supplies, or the ribbon cables going to the external connectors. Here an oscilloscope or a voltmeter may be useful. The testing sequence may be as follows:

1. Check if the transmitter output circuits have their bipolar power supplies in order (this step is logically the first, but as technically it is the most difficult, it can be put off for the worst case scenario, when you get to feel like replacing the buffer ICs).

2. Check the voltages on the TD, RTS, and DTR outputs: After a hardware reset, there should be a negative potential of about –12 V (at least lower than –5 V) at the TD output. When a character output is attempted, positive voltage must appear on the RTS and DTR outputs and a bipolar pulse series issues from the TD output. If these signals do not appear, it is possible that there has been a mistake when connecting

the motherboard to the external connector using the ribbon cable. The most common possibilities are:

- The ribbon cable is not connected.
- The ribbon cable is connected incorrectly (the connector is reversed or inserted with a misalignment).
- Cable layout does not correspond to the motherboard's connector.

The first two possibilities are investigated by a careful inspection, but the third may require some extra efforts. Table 2.1 shows three known to the author versions of cable layout for 10-wire ribbon cable for COM port connectors; it is possible that for the COM ports built-in into motherboards, other versions exist. In theory, a ribbon cable fitting the connector is supposed to be supplied.

If the problem lies with the wrong cable layout, then these three output signals can be located on the other contacts of the connector (the voltage on the input contacts is very low). If there has been no success locating these signals, evidently the buffer gates have failed.

3. After connecting the contacts of the RTS and CTS lines (or having mounted a loopback plug), you should try to output a short file to the COM port (using COPY C:\AUTOEXEC.BAT COM1: command, for example). When the port is operative, this command is successfully executed in a few seconds with a message afterwards to that effect. At this, the voltages on the RTS and DTR outputs should change to negative and on the TD output should appear a packet of bipolar impulses with the amplitude greater than 5 V. If the voltages on the RTS and DTR lines have not changed, then there is a problem with the buffer gates. If negative voltage appears on the RTS output (and on the CTS input) and the COPY command terminates in error, most likely the CTS line receiver is faulty (or, once again, there are some problems with the ribbon cable). If the COPY command executes successfully but there are no changes on the TD output (they can be detected with an analog voltmeter, but their amplitude cannot be evaluated), then the buffer transmitter of the TD signal is at fault.

Replacing receiver and transmitter ICs is significantly easier if they are installed in sockets. Before changing an IC, you should ascertain, using an oscilloscope or voltmeter, that it is faulty.

If the buffering elements are included into the interface LSI IC (which is quite a commonplace nowadays), then such port cannot be repaired (not in the regular settings, anyway). You could try to disable a defective COM port built-in into the motherboard from the BIOS Setup, but the port may have burned out along with the circuitry controlling its disconnection: then it will be a "live corpse" in the I/O and interrupt map. Sometimes, the entire motherboard might be burnt.

Connectors and cables may be sources of malfunctions. Connectors happen to have bad contacts in them, and cables, besides possible breaks, may have inferior frequency characteristics. Cable frequency qualities usually manifest themselves at high transfer rates (56 Kbps or 115 Kbps). If it is necessary to use long cables at high transfer rates, then the data signal carrying wires should be twisted and have a separate circuit ground wire.

2.10.3. Powering Off the Interface, or Why the Mouse Does Not Work

When connecting devices with low power consumption to the COM port, one is tempted to power these devices off the output lines of the interface. If the DTR or TRS control lines are not being used in their direct capacity, they can be used as a power supply source providing about 12 V. Short circuit current to the circuit ground is limited to the 20 mA level by the buffer IC of the transmitter. At the initialization of the port, these lines go into the OFF state, that is, they provide *negative* voltage. The TD line in the quiescent state has the logical one on it, so it develops *negative* voltage on its output. The potentials of these lines can be controlled through the COM port registers (the TD output produces positive voltage if bit BRCON is set). Power also may be taken off the signal lines through rectifying diodes used with accumulating capacitors. Here you ought to take into consideration how long the output signal remains in the needed state (so that the accumulated energy were sufficient).

All manipulators (mice) connected to the COM ports take their bipolar power supplies off the interface lines (+V off the DTR or RTS, –V off the TD). Knowing this, in case your mouse does not function when connected to the port, you should check the voltages on the corresponding contacts of the connector. It happens sometimes that only a particular mouse (model or a piece of equipment) does not work with a particular port, even though other mice work without problems with this port and the same mouse work with other ports. Here the problem may lie in the voltage levels. The standard requires that the port provide no less than 5 V output voltage (absolute value), and if the particular port provides only this minimum, this power is not sufficient to power LEDs (the main energy consumers) on some mice.

The port receives its bipolar power supply through the motherboard from the computer's power supply. If +12 V is missing on the power supply's output, it usually will be manifested by the disks' being inoperative. Only the devices connected to the COM ports will "notice" the absence of the –12 V. In theory, the power supply monitors these voltages on its output (informing of problems by the Power Good signal, which triggers hardware reset). Simplified power supplies that do not control all their voltages can be encountered. Besides, there is a possibility of bad contacts in the motherboard power supply connector.

Chapter 3: Wireless Interfaces

Wireless interfaces free devices from the cables connecting them. This is especially attractive for compact peripheral devices, whose size and weight are comparable to the connecting cables. Wireless interfaces communicate using infrared (IrDA) and radio (Bluetooth). Besides these interfaces for peripheral devices, there are other wireless methods to connect to local area networks.

3.1. IrDA Infrared Interface

Using infrared emitters and receivers allows for wireless communication between two devices located up to several meters apart. *Infrared* is not hazardous to human health, does not interfere with radio signals, and provides confidential communication. Infrared rays cannot penetrate walls, so the reception area is restricted to a small, easily controlled space. Infrared is attractive for organizing communications between portable and stationary computers or docking stations. Some printers have an infrared interface, and many modern compact devices, including pocket computers, mobile telephones and digital cameras, are equipped with it.

Infrared systems are divided into low- (up to 115.2 Kbps), middle- (up to 1.152 Mbps), and high-speed (4 Mbps) categories. Low-speed systems are used to exchange short messages. High-speed systems are employed for exchanging files between computers, network connections, outputting data to a printer or a projector, etc. In the future, higher transfer rates are expected that will allow the transmission of video in real time. In 1993, the Infrared Data Association (IrDA), an association of infrared data-transmission systems developers, was formed, with the aim of making equipment from different manufacturers compatible. Currently, the IrDA 1.1 standard is in effect. Some companies have developed their own systems, such as Hewlett-Packard's Hewlett Packard Slow Infra Red *(HP-SIR)* and Sharp's Amplitude Shifted Keyed IR *(ASK-IR).*These interfaces provide the following transfer rates:

❏   IrDA Serial Infra Red (SIR), HP-SIR: 9.6 Kbps to 115.2 Kbps
❏   IrDA HDLC, or Middle Infra Red (MIR): 0.566 Mbps and 1.152 Mbps
❏   IrDA Fast Infra Red (FIR): 4 Mbps
❏   ASK IR: 9.6 Kbps to 57.6 Kbps

The emitter in infrared communication is a light-emitting diode with a characteristic power peak at 880 nm. The diode has an effective transmission cone of about 30 degrees. PIN diodes, which receive infrared within a 15-degree angle, are used as receivers. The IrDA specification defines the requirements for transmitter power output and receiver sensitivity, and specifies both the minimum and maximum strength of the infrared rays for the receiver. (The receiver can not pick up pulses of too low power, while those of too high power would merge into one pulse and effectively blind it.) Besides infrared, the receiver can be affected by outside factors, such as sunlight and incandescent lamps (constant optical power) and fluorescent lamps (variable, low-frequency). These interferences must be filtered out. The IrDA specification sets a bit error level (BER) of no more than 10^{-9} at 1 meter distance in daylight (illumination up to 10 Klux). Since the transmitter almost inevitably causes outside illumination of its own receiver saturating it, half-duplex communications with certain time intervals between transfer direction changes are necessary. Binary modulation (light on/off) and various coding schemes are used for transmission.

The IrDA specification defines a multilevel system of protocols, considered here in ascending order.

Options at the *IrDA physical level* are:

❏   IrDA SIR. For transfer rates from 2.4 Kbps to 115.2 Kbps, the standard asynchronous transmission — start bit (logical zero), 8 data bits, stop bit (logical one) — is used (as in COM ports). Logical zero is encoded by a signal 3/16th the duration of the bit interval (1.63 μsec at 115.2 Kbps). Logical one is encoded by an absence of pulses (IrDA SIR-A mode). Accordingly, the transmitter does not send during breaks between transmissions, and every transmission begins with a start-bit pulse.

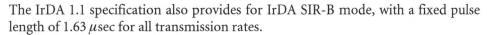

The IrDA 1.1 specification also provides for IrDA SIR-B mode, with a fixed pulse length of 1.63 μsec for all transmission rates.

❐ ASK IR. Asynchronous mode is also used for speeds between 9.6 Kbps and 57.6 Kbps, but with different encoding. Logical zero is encoded by sending pulses at 500 KHz, logical one is encoded by an absence of pulses.

❐ IrDA HDLC. Synchronous transmission mode is used for speeds between 0.576 Mbps and 1.152 Mbps, and the encoding is analogous to the SIR protocol (zero — pulsed, one — no pulse) but with pulses a quarter of the bit interval duration. The frame format complies with the HDLC protocol. The beginning and the end of a frame are marked by 01111110 flags; inside the frame, this combination is avoided by bit stuffing. A 16-bit CRC code is inserted into each frame to control data integrity.

❐ IrDA FIR (IrDA4PPM). Synchronous mode is also used for transmissions at 4 Mbps, but the encoding is somewhat more complicated. Every pair of adjacent bits is encoded by a positional pulse code: 00 —> 1000, 01 —> 0100, 10 —> 0010, 11 —> 0001 (in 4-character sequences, 1 sends a pulse at the corresponding quarter of the symbol interval). This encoding method makes it possible to reduce the frequency of switching on LED by half in comparison with the previous method. The consistency of the average frequency of the received impulses makes it easier for the receiver to adapt to external illumination. 32-bit CRC code is used to improve data integrity.

Above the physical level comes the *IrDA Infrared Link Access Protocol* (IrLAP). IrLAP is a modification of the HDLC protocol, reflecting the needs of infrared communication. This protocol encapsulates data into frames and prevents device conflicts. When more than two devices capable of "seeing" each other are present, one is designated as the master, all the rest as slaves. Communication always uses the half-duplex mode. The IrLAP describes the procedure for establishing, enumerating, and terminating connections. Connections are established at the speed of 9,600 bps, after which the transfer speed is negotiated to the maximum supported by both devices (9.6 Kbps, 19.2 Kbps, 38.4 Kbps, or 115.2 Kbps) and logical channels are established, each controlled by one master device.

Above the IrLAP protocol comes the *IrDA Infrared Link Management Protocol* (IrLMP). Using IrLMP, a device informs other devices about its presence in the coverage area. (IrDA devices can be configured dynamically by bringing a new device closer or moving it further away.) IrLMP allows detection of services offered by a device, control of data streams, and provision of multiplexer functions in a configuration in which multiple accessible devices are present. Using IrLMP, applications can determine whether the device they need is present in the coverage area. However, this protocol does not guarantee reliable data delivery.

The transport level is provided by the *IrDA Transport Protocol* (Tiny TP). Tiny TP, which resembles the TCP protocol, services the virtual channels between the devices, processes errors (lost packets, data errors, and the like), packages data into packets, and assembles the original data from packets. The transport level may also be serviced by the IrTP protocol.

The *IrCOMM protocol* allows an infrared connection to emulate a conventional wire connection:

❑ A 3-wire connection via an RS-232C interface (TXD, RXD, and GND)
❑ A 9-wire connection via an RS-232C interface (the complete COM port signal set)
❑ A Centronics connection (emulation of a parallel interface)

The *IrLAN protocol* provides access to local area networks, allowing transmission of Ethernet and Token Ring network frames. To connect to a local area network using an infrared connection, a server device with an IrDA interface and connected conventionally (i.e., by wires) to the network is needed, along with the appropriate software for the client device.

The *Object Exchange Protocol* (IrOBEX) is a simple protocol, implementing PUT and GET commands to exchange "useful" binary data between devices. This protocol is located above Tiny TP. IrOBEX has an extension for mobile communications that defines transmission of GSM-network information (notebook, calendar, call control, digital voice transmission, etc.) between a telephone and any sort of computer (from a desktop to a PDA).

This is not an exhaustive list of protocols related to infrared communications. The same frequency range (880 nm) is used for remote control of household appliances (televisions, video recorders, etc.) but different frequencies and physical encoding methods are employed.

An IrDA transceiver can be connected to a computer in various ways. In relation to the system block, it may be located either internally (on the computer's front panel) or externally, placed anywhere. The transceiver's location must be chosen taking into account the device's optical angle (30 degrees for the transmitter and 15 degrees for the receiver), as well as the distance to the device it controls (up to 1 meter).

Internal transceivers, with speeds of up to 115.2 Kbps (IrDA SIR, HP-SIR, ASK IR), are connected through regular 16450/16550-series compatible UART ICs using relatively simple modulator-demodulator circuits. In some modern motherboards, the COM2 port may be configured to use infrared communications at up to 115.2 Kbps. For this, in addition to the UART, the chipset includes modulator and demodulator circuits that support one or several infrared communication protocols. To use the COM2 port for infrared communication, the corresponding mode needs to be selected in CMOS Setup (disabling infrared communications means the COM2 port will be used conventionally). There are also internal adapters on expansion cards (for ISA, PCI, and PC Card buses) that the system sees as additional COM ports.

Specialized IrDA controller ICs are used for middle and high exchange rates. These are designed to support intensive software-controlled exchange or the DMA, and have direct bus-control capability. A regular UART transceiver is of no use, as it does not support synchronous transfer or high transfer rates. Physically, the FIR IrDA controller is implemented on an expansion card or is built in into the motherboard. As a rule, such a controller also supports SIR modes.

The transceiver is connected to the motherboard's infrared connector directly (if it is installed on the computer's front panel) or using a transitional connector (mini DIN) located on one of the blank covers on the computer's back panel. Unfortunately, there is no universal circuit layout for the internal connector, and for greater flexibility the transceiver (or transitional connector) is equipped with a cable and separate contacts for the connector. To assemble them in proper order is left to the user. Table 3.1 lists the functions of the infrared-transceiver connector contacts. Some transceivers supporting FIR and SIR modes have separate receiver outputs: IRRX for SIR and FIRRX for FIR. If the controller supports only one of the modes, one contact is left unconnected.

Table 3.1. Infrared Transceiver Connectors

Circuit	Function	Contact/option			
		1	2	3	4
IRRX (RX)	Input from receiver	1	3	3	3
FIRRX (RXH)	Input from FIR receiver	5	–	–	4
IRTX (TX)	Output to transmitter	3	5	1	1
GND	Common	2, 7	4	2	2
Vcc (+5V)	Power	4, 6	1	5	5
NC	Not used	–	2	4	–

External infrared adapters are factory-equipped with an RS-232C interface to connect to the COM port or the USB bus. USB carrying capacity is sufficient even for the FIR; the COM port is good only for the SIR. The external infrared IrDA SIR adapter for the COM port is not as simple as it may seem, as the operation of the modulator-demodulator requires a synchronization signal on the frequency equal to 16 times the frequency of the data transmission. This signal comes onto the synchronous input of the COM port's UART IC. There is no such signal on the output of the COM port, and it has to be extracted and reassembled from the asynchronous bit stream. The ASK infrared adapter is simpler in this respect. The transmitter must send high frequency pulses all the time while the TXD output remains in the high state; the receiver must form the envelope for the received pulses.

Use of the IrDA in applications requires the installation and setup of the corresponding drivers, as well as physical connection of the adapter and the transceiver. Windows 9*x*/ME/2000 place the IrDA controller into the Network Neighborhood group. Properly configured software allows connections with local area networks (for connection to the Internet or use of local network resources). It also allows data printout, synchronization of data between a PDA, a mobile phone, and a desktop computer, image upload from a digital camera to the computer, and a variety of other useful tasks without any worries about cable management.

3.2. Bluetooth Radio Interface

Bluetooth is the de facto standard for miniature, inexpensive means of short-range radio data exchange between mobile (and desktop) computers, mobile phones, and any other portable devices. The standard has been developed by a group of leading telecommunications, computer, and network companies — 3Com, Agere Systems, Ericsson, IBM, Intel, Microsoft, Motorola, Nokia and Toshiba — which formed the Bluetooth Special Interest Group to bring the technology onto the market. The Bluetooth specification is freely available on the web (**www.bluetooth.com**), although it is quite bulky (about 15 MB of PDF files). The openness of the specification is supposed to promote its rapid spread, a development that can already be observed. The name itself is the nickname of the Dutch king who united Denmark and Norway, an allusion to the technology's universal unifying role.

Every Bluetooth device has a radio transmitter and receiver working in the 2.4 GHz frequency range. In most countries, this frequency range is assigned to industrial, scientific, and medical use and does not require licensing, making the devices universally applicable. Bluetooth uses radio channels with discrete (binary) frequency modulation. The carrier frequency of the channels is $F = 2,402 + k$ (MHz), where $k = 0, ..., 78$. For some countries (such as France, where this frequency range is used by the military), a subset of this carrier frequency range is available with $F = 2,454 + k$, where $k = 0, ..., 22$. The coding is simple: logical one is represented by a positive frequency deviation, logical zero by a negative frequency deviation. Transmitters come in three power classes, with respective maximum power of 1 mW, 2.5 mW, and 100 mW. They must also have a low-power-consumption option for energy savings.

Transmission is accomplished by the carrier frequency hopping from one radio channel to another, which helps to combat interference and signal fading. The physical communications channel is assigned by a pseudorandom sequence of the available channels (79 or 23 available frequencies). A group of devices sharing one channel (i.e., with the same hopping sequence) form a *piconet*, which may consist of 2 to 8 devices. Each piconet has one master device and up to 7 active slave devices. Moreover, the coverage area of the master device's piconet may contain "parked" slave devices. They have the same hopping sequence and are synchronized on it with the master device, but cannot exchange data unless the master device allows them. Every active slave device in the piconet has a temporary number between 1 and 7. When a slave device is deactivated (parked), it releases its number to be used by the other devices. When next activated, it may receive a different number, which is why the number is temporary. Coverage areas of piconets may overlap, forming a scatternet. In this case, however, each piconet has only one master device, but a slave device may be a member of several piconets, using timesharing (i.e., working in different piconets at different times). Moreover, one piconet's master device may be a slave device in another piconet. These piconets are not synchronized in any way, and each uses its own channel (hopping sequence).

The master device organizes time multiplexing, dividing the airtime into sequentially numbered time slots, each 625 mcsec long, with a cyclicity of 2^{27}. The master and slave devices take turns to transmit: the master transmits in even slots; the slave addressed by the master transmits in odd slots (if it has anything to transmit). In the simplest case, each time slot corresponds to one carrier frequency in the hopping sequence (1,600 hops per second). The frequency sequence is determined by the address of the master device of the piconet. Data are transferred in packets, and each packet can take from 1 to 5 time slots. Because a radio receiver requires some time to settle into a new frequency, a substantial leading part of a time slot (about 250 μsec) cannot be used to transmit data. Out of the formal 625 bits in a time slot, only 366 are used; out of these, 166 bits are taken by the service information, and only 240 bits are left for useful data. When a long packet is sent, the carrier frequency does not change during its transmission (three or five time slots), which allows the overhead to be reduced (in a 5-slot packet, 2,781 bits are used out of the total $5 \times 625 = 3,125$ bits). Even though the carrier frequency does not change during a long packet transmission, the 625-μsec time slots continue to be counted, and the frequency following a long packet transmission will correspond to the next time slot (i.e., several carrier frequencies will be skipped).

Two types of physical links – synchronous and asynchronous – can be established between master and slave devices.

Synchronous Connection-Oriented (SCO) (or isochronous) links are used to transmit isochronous traffic (e.g., digital sound). In these point-to-point links, the master device and its associated slave devices are specified in advance, and each link is as-signed a time interval (in slots), during which slots are reserved for it. The result is symmetrical two-way links. Error packets are not retransmitted. The master device can establish up to three SCO links with one or several slave devices. A slave device may have up to three links with one master device or one link with each of two different slave devices. Under the network-classification criteria, SCO links fall into the circuit switching category.

Asynchronous Connection-Less (ACL) links perform packet switching using the "point-to-multipoint" scheme between the master unit and all the slave units of the piconet. The master device can connect any of the piconet's slave devices in the slots not used by SCO by sending it a packet and asking for a response. A slave device can transmit only when it is addressed by a master unit (having cor-rectly decoded its address). Most types of packets can be retransmitted in case of a reception error. A master unit also can send addressless broadcasting packets to all slave devices in its piconet. A master unit can establish only one ACL link with each of its slave units.

Information is sent in packets, whose data fields can be from 0 to 2,745 bits long. For ACL links, several types of CRC code-protection packages are provided (provi-sions are made for retransmitting data if an error is detected) and one without protec-tion (no retransmissions). In SCO links, data are not protected by the CRC code. Consequently, retransmissions are not provided for.

Data-distortion prevention and data-integrity control are performed in several ways. Data in some types of packets is protected by CRC code, and the recipient of information must acknowledge receiving a correct packet or report a reception error. To reduce the number of repeats, the Forward Error Correction (FEC) redundancy coding is employed. With FEC 1/3, every payload bit is sent three times, meaning the most plausible version can be chosen by majorization. The FEC 2/3 scheme is more complicated. It uses Hamming code, which allows the correction of all single er-ror instances and detect all double error instances in every 10-bit block.

Each voice channel provides 64 Kbits/sec transmission in both directions. Coding in the Pulse-Code Modulation (PCM) or Continuous Variable Slope Delta Modula-tion (CVSD; a version of adaptive delta impulse-code modulation) formats can be used in voice channels. PCM allows compression using the G.711 method. This provides only "telephone conversation" signal quality (meaning digital telephony with an 8-bit, 8 Kbps sample rate). CVSD provides higher quality, packing input PCM sig-nal at a sample rate of 64 Kbps. However, even here the spectral density of the signal in the frequency range 4 KHz to 32 KHz must be insignificant. Bluetooth voice (audio) channels are not suitable for transmission of high-quality audio signal, although a compressed signal (such as an MP3 stream) can be sent perfectly through an asyn-chronous data-transfer channel.

The asynchronous channel can provide a maximum transfer rate of 723.2 Kbps in asymmetrical configuration (leaving the 57.6 Kbps band for the reverse channel) or 433.9 Kbps each way in the symmetrical configuration.

To provide security, Bluetooth uses data authentication and encryption on the link level. These may be complemented at the upper protocol level.

An important part of Bluetooth is the Service Discovery Protocol (SDP), which allows a device to find out about services on other Bluetooth devices. Having established a connection, the device can avail itself of the services it needs (e.g., to output documents to printer, connect to the web, etc.).

The RFCOMM protocol provides serial port emulation (9-wire RS232) via L2CAP. Traditional cable connections of the devices (including the null-modem) can be easily replaced by radio connection, without any modifications to the upper level software. The protocol also allows multiple connections (one device with many), and the radio connection will replace the cumbersome and expensive multiplexers and cables. The OBEX protocol, used in the infrared wireless connections (in the IrDA protocol hierarchy) can work through the RFCOMM protocol. The PPP protocol, which is located below the TCP/IP protocol stack, can also work through RFCOMM, opening the way to all Internet applications. The AT commands, which control telephone connections and fax transmission services (the same commands are used by the modems for dial-up lines), also work through RFCOMM.

The special bit-oriented binary Telephony Control Protocol (TCS BIN), which defines Bluetooth device connection call paging (for voice communications and data exchange) also works through L2CAP. Means to control groups of TCS devices also are available in this protocol.

Host-Controller Interface (HCI) is a uniform method to access low-level Bluetooth hardware and software resources. It consists of a set of commands for controlling radio communications, receiving status information, and data transmission itself. Through this interface, the L2CAP protocol interacts with Bluetooth equipment. The physical Bluetooth equipment can be connected to various interfaces, such as an expansion bus (e.g., a PC Card), a USB bus, or a COM port. For each of these connections, there is a corresponding transport-level HCI protocol and interlayer providing HCI's independence from the connection method.

Chapter 4: Serial Buses: USB and FireWire

Serial buses make it possible to connect many devices using only one or two pairs of wires. The functional capabilities of these buses are much broader than traditional local network interfaces: USB and FireWire can transfer isochronous audio and video traffic. Serial buses differ fundamentally in their organization from parallel buses. Serial buses have no separate lines for address, control, and data signals: All protocol functions have to be carried out using one or two (in the case of FireWire) pairs of signal wires. This affects how the bus protocol is built, which in serial buses is based on sending packets, or chains of bits ordered in a particular way. In USB technology, the concept of packets and frames has a somewhat different interpretation than in data transfer networks.

The most popular serial buses are USB and FireWire, although the latter is not yet widely used in PC-compatible computers. FireWire and USB, while having much in common, are nevertheless significantly different technologies. Both buses provide easy connection of a large number of peripheral devices (127 for USB, 63 for FireWire) and allow hot plugging and connection and disconnection. The topological structures of both buses are relatively similar, but FireWire allows greater connection structure freedom and connection lengths. Many devices are equipped with USB hubs, which users often even do not notice. Both buses have lines to supply power to the devices, but the maximum power rating of the FireWire is considerably higher. Both buses support the Plug and Play technology (automatic configuration upon power up or re-set) and solve the problem of a shortage of addresses, DMA channels, and interrupt lines. Bandwidth and bus control are different in each bus.

The USB is oriented at peripheral devices connected to PCs. Isochronous USB transfers make it possible to transfer digital audio signals, while the USB 2.0 is capable of carrying video data. All transmissions are centrally controlled, and the PC is the required controlling center located at the root of the tree-like bus structure. Purchasers of modern PCs get a USB controller almost for free as it is built into the chipsets of all contemporary mother-boards. Older USB 1.0 motherboards can be provided with USB 2.0 capability by installing a USB 2.0 controller into a PCI slot. The On The Go (OTG) extension allows some periph-eral devices (a digital camera, for example) to function as hosts and have devices connected to them (a printer, for example). Several PCs can be directly connected by USB only with the help of auxiliary devices (sometimes, transparently to the user).

The FireWire bus is oriented at consumer electronics devices, which can be joined into a unified home network using it. One or several computers can be connected to this network. The fundamental advantage of the 1394 bus is that is does not require a special bus controller (a computer). Any transmitting device can be assigned a por-tion of the isochronous traffic bandwidth and begin transmitting upon a signal from an autonomous or remote controller: Receivers will hear its message. If a controller is present, appropriate software can control devices, and implement, for example, a non-linear video editing studio or provide the necessary multimedia data to all information consumers requiring it.

4.1. Universal Serial Bus: USB

The Universal Serial Bus (USB) is an industry standard of a PC architecture extension that is oriented at integration with telephone and consumer electronics equipment. Version 1.0 was published at the beginning of 1996; most devices support Version 1.1, which came out in the fall of 1998 and fixed the problems that were discovered in the first version. In spring 2000, USB Version 2.0, which expanded the original bandwidth by a factor of 40, was published. Versions 1.0 and 1.1 of the bus provided two data transmission speeds: Full Speed (FS) of 12 Mbps and Low Speed (LS) of 1.5 Mbps. Version 2.0 defines an additional transfer rate: High Speed (HS) of 480 Mbps, which makes it possible to substantially widen the range of devices that can be connected to the bus. Devices supporting all three speeds can be connected and work simultane-ously on the same high-speed bus. Employing a repeating hubs bus makes it possible to connect devices up to 25 meters away from the computer. Detailed and up-to-date information on the USB can be found on the Internet at **www.usb.org**. The USB Implementers Forum, Inc. (USB-IF) coordinates USB device development, classifica-tion, and standardization.

4.1.1. USB Architecture

USB provides data exchange between a host-computer and multiple peripheral devices. It is a unified centralized hardware and software system for servicing of multiple devices and multiple application software processes. A host-controller with multiple-level software support links software processes with all devices. This is what makes the USB fundamentally different from traditional peripheral interfaces (LPT, COM, GAME, keyboard, and mouse ports). These interfaces are compared in Table 4.1.

Table 4.1. Comparison of USB and Traditional Interfaces

Traditional interfaces (COM, LPT, Game, etc.)	USB
In general, each connected device requires its own controller (adapter).[1]	All devices are connected via one Host Controller.
Each controller needs to have system resources allocated to it (memory and I/O area ranges, as well as interrupt requests).	Only the Host Controller needs system resources to be allocated.
Only few devices can be connected to the computer.	Up to 127 devices can be connected.
Device drivers can communicate directly with the controllers of their devices independently of each other.	Device drivers communicate only with the common driver of the Host Controller.
Because of the drivers' independence, results of simultaneous operation of multiple devices cannot be predicted and there are no quality of service (delays and transfer rates) guarantees for different devices.	Centralized planned exchange guarantees quality of service (QoS), which allows multimedia data to be transferred, along with regular asynchronous exchange.
Vast variety of interfaces, connectors, and cables specific to each type of interface.	A single convenient and inexpensive interface to connect various types of devices. Possibility of selecting device operation speed (1.5–12–480 Mbps).
No built-in means for detecting device connection and disconnection and device identification; difficulty supporting Plug and Plug.	Hot-plugging is possible; Plug and Play is fully supported; dynamic configuration available.
No error control means.	Built-in means of ensuring data integrity.
No default power supply for devices.	Devices are bus-powered; power consumption can be controlled.

---

[1] The SCSI also allows multiple devices to be connected via one controller, but compared with the USB, its parallel interface is too expensive, bulky, and has more limited topology.

The USB architecture allows four basic data flow types between the host and peripheral devices:

❐ *Isochronous transfers* — are real-time flow transfers conducted over a dedicated portion of the bus bandwidth and guaranteed to be delivered within a specified time period. At full speed, one 1.023 MBps channel (or two 0.5 MBps channels) can be organized, taking up 70% of the available bus bandwidth (the rest can be filled by less bulky channels). At high speed, one channel of up to 24 MBps (192 Mbps) can be obtained. Data are not guaranteed to be delivered intact: Corrupted data are not retransmitted, invalid packets are ignored. The USB interface allows establishment of synchronous connections between devices and application programs using isochronous transfers. Isochronous transfers are used for data stream devices such as video cameras, digital audio devices (USB speakers, microphone), and devices to record and playback audio and video (CD and DVD). The USB interface can transmit noncompressed video data streams only at high speed.

❐ *Interrupts* — transfers of spontaneous messages that must be executed with no larger delay than the device allows. The time limits for servicing interrupts are set in the 10–255 msec range for low speed, 1–255 msec for full speed, while at high speed, even 125 μsec can be allowed. Delivery is guaranteed; in case of accidental exchange errors, data are retransmitted, although this increases the processing time. Interrupts are used, for example, to input data from a keyboard or to transmit information about mouse movements. Interrupts can also be used to deliver data to devices (a device signals that it requires data and the host delivers them in time). Message length can be 0–8 bytes for low speed, 0–64 bytes for full speed, and 0–1,024 bytes for high speed.

❐ *Bulk data transfers* — carried out without any requirements in terms of delivery deadlines and speed. Bulk transfers can take up the entire bandwidth left over from other types of transfers. They have the lowest priority and can be suspended during high bus load. Delivery is guaranteed: In case of an error, data are retransmitted. Bulk transfers are suitable for exchanging data with printers, scanners, mass data storage devices, etc.

❐ *Control transfers* — used to configure devices when they are first connected to the bus, and to control them afterward. The protocol provides guaranteed data delivery and acknowledgement by the device of successful execution of the control command. Control transfers can be used to send a command to a device (a request, possibly accompanied by data) and to receive a reply from it (an acknowledgement or rejection of the request and optional data). Only control transfers synchronize requests with responses in USB; other types of transfers do not explicitly synchronize input flow with the output flow.

The hardware portion of the USB consists of:

❏ Peripheral USB devices, named *USB functions*, which carry out useful functions.
❏ *Host Controller*, which links the bus with the computer's center joined to the Root Hub, which provides connection points for USB devices. There are two types of USB 1.x Host Controllers: Universal Host Controller (UHC) and Open Host Controller (OHC) support full speed and low speed; Enhanced Host Controller (EHC) only supports the high speed of the USB 2.0.
❏ *USB hubs*, which provide additional connection points.
❏ *USB cables*, which connect devices to the hubs.

The software portion of the USB consists of:

❏ *Client software*: USB device drivers that provide application software access to the devices. These drivers interact with the devices proper only via the software interface of the USB common driver (USBD). USB device drivers do not access any USB device hardware registers directly.
❏ *USB Driver* (USBD), which is responsible for all USB devices, their enumeration, configuration, making services available, bus bandwidth and power supply distribution, etc.
❏ *Host Controller Driver* (HCD), which converts input/output requests into data structures used by the Host Controller to execute physical transactions, accessing the host-controller's registers and the communications area of the system memory.

The USBD and the HCD comprise the host part of the USB software. The USB specification delineates the range of their tasks, but does not describe the interface between them.

A physical USB device must be equipped with USB interface that provides complete support for the USB protocol, standard operation execution (configuration and reset), and information describing the device. Physical USB devices can be *compound devices*, which consist of several function devices connected to the internal hub and providing additional external connection points to its internal hub.

The *Host Controller*, which is a software/hardware subsystem of the host computer, manages the whole USB system. The Host Controller is either an intelligent PCI bus device or a part of the south bridge of the motherboard that actively interacts with the system memory.

The physical USB interface is as simple as it is elegant. The USB cable and connector system make it impossible to connect devices incorrectly (Fig. 4.1, *a* and *b*). The device's USB connector is labeled by a standard symbol (Fig. 4.1, *c*) to make it easily identifiable. Type A sockets are installed only on the downstream hub ports; type A plugs are installed on the peripheral device cables or upstream hub port cables.

Type B sockets and plugs are used only on cable ends connected to peripheral devices or upstream hub ports (small devices usually have cables permanently wired into them). Compact devices use mini B connectors, while for the OTG (see *Section 4.1.9*) mini A plugs and mini AB sockets are used. Hubs and devices provide dynamic connecting and disconnecting, and inform the host of these events.

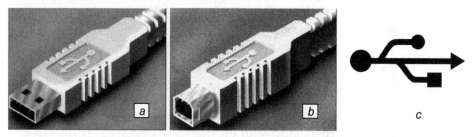

Fig. 4.1. USB connectors: *a* — type A plug; *b* — type B plug; *c* — icon

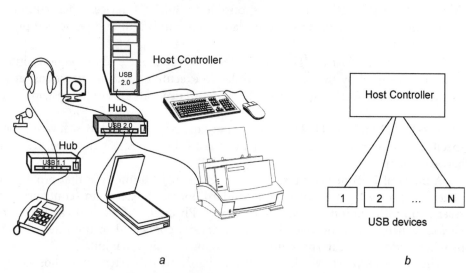

Fig. 4.2. Different viewpoints on the USB:
a — physical topology, *b* — logical topology

How the devices are to be powered must be taken into consideration when planning connections: As a rule, bus-powered devices are connected to the self-powered hubs. Only low power devices are connected to the bus-powered hubs: Thus, only devices like a USB mouse and other position indicators (a trackball, a touch pad) can be connected to a USB keyboard with an internal USB hub.

The *physical topology* of the USB is a multi-tiered star (Fig. 4.2, *a*). At its apex is the Host Controller connected to the root hub. The hub is a device that provides additional connection points and can also be used to power devices connected to it. A peripheral device or an intermediate hub can be directly connected to each hub's port; the bus allows up to five levels (not counting the root) of hub chaining. Because compound devices already have an internal hub, they cannot be connected to the fifth level hub. Each intermediate hub has several *downstream ports* for connecting peripheral devices or lower level hubs, and one *upstream port* for connecting to the root hub or to a downstream port of a higher-level hub.

The *logical USB topology* is a simple star: Hubs (including the root hub) create an illusion of each logical device being connected directly to the Host Controller (Fig. 4.2, *b*). Device interactions in the star are solely subordinate, based on the polling/response system: the Host Controller sends to or receives data from the device it selects. A device cannot send data at its own initiative; direct transfers between devices are not possible. At its own initiative, a device can only send a signal of its wakeup, which is done by means of special physical signaling system (not by transmitting data).

A *logical USB device* is a set of independent *endpoints* (EP) with which the Host Controller (and the client software) exchanges information. Each logical USB device (function as well as hub) is assigned a unique address on the particular USB bus (1–127) by the host's software configuration facility. Each endpoint of a logical device is identified by its number (0–15) and the direction of transmission (IN — transmission towards the host, OUT — transmission away from the host). Points IN4 and OUT4, for example, are two different endpoints, with which even different modules of the client software can communicate. The particular set of the endpoints depends on the device, but every USB device necessarily has a bidirectional endpoint 0 (EP0), through which general control over the device is exercised. Endpoints with numbers 1 through 15 (1 to 2 for low-speed devices) are used for application purposes. Device address and number and direction of the endpoint uniquely identify the information sink or source during information exchange between the Host Controller and USB devices. Each endpoint has a set of characteristics that describe the type of data transmission supported (isochronous, bulk, interrupts, control), packet size, and requirements to how often it requires to be serviced.

A device can perform several different functional tasks: For example, a CD-ROM drive can play audio disks and function as a mass data storage device. To perform each task, an *interface* is defined in a device: a set of endpoints designed to carry out the preset task and the rules for their use. In this way, each device must provide one or more interfaces. Having several interfaces allows several drivers to work with one device, each of the drivers accessing only its interface (which is a part of the USB device). Each interface can have one or more *alternate settings*, of which only one can be active at any one time. The alternate interfaces have different sets of endpoints (and possibly different characteristics).

A set of interfaces that can be supported simultaneously makes up the *device configuration*. A device can have one or more possible configurations, out of which the host selects one as active during the configuration process. The available functionality of the device and quite often the power it consumes depend on the configuration selected. Until a device has been assigned a configuration number, it cannot function as an application and its current consumption must not exceed 100 mA. The host selects the configuration on the basis of which of the total resources requested by the current configuration are available, including the current drawn off the bus.

4.1.2. Data Transfer Model

Each unit of the client software (usually, represented by the driver) communicates exclusively and independently with one interface of its device (function) (Fig. 4.3). In this figure, links represent communications pipes that are established between device drivers and their endpoints. Pipes are established only with the sets of the device endpoints of the selected alternative interfaces from the active configuration. The other endpoints are not available.

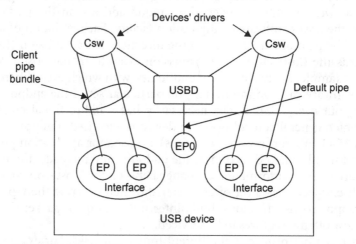

Fig. 4.3. Client software interaction with USB device interfaces

Requests, Packets, and Transactions

To transmit and receive data, client software sends an Input-Output Request (IRP) packet and awaits an acknowledgement that it has been processed. The IRP format is determined by how the USB driver is implemented in the particular operating system. The IRP only carries information about the request: Where the buffer of the transferred data is located in the main memory and the length of the transmission. The device driver is disengaged from the parameters of the specific current connection (speed, permissible packet size). The USB driver handles the request as USB transactions: If necessary, it can break long requests into packets that can be sent in one transaction. A USB *transaction* is a sequence of packet exchanges between the host and peripheral device, in the process of which one data packet can be sent or received (transactions, in which data are not transferred, are also possible). A request is considered to have been processed when all its associated transactions have been successfully completed. The client driver is not informed of the temporary difficulties that may be encountered during transaction execution: It must wait until all the exchanges have been completed (or until a time-out termination). However, the device can signal of fatal errors by a stall reply, which causes the request to be terminated abnormally; the client's driver is informed of this event. In this case, all subsequent requests over this channel are cancelled. Operations over the given channel can only be resumed after explicit notification that the device driver has handled the error condition with the special request (also a USB driver call).

Long requests are split into transactions in such a way that maximum packet length can be used. The last packet with the final piece of the request can be shorter than the maximum packet length. When data are input, the Host Controller can interpret receiving a packet shorter than expected (the maximum packet size for the given endpoint) in one of two ways:

❏ As the end of data block indicator. In this case, the IRP terminates normally and the following requests to the given channel are executed.
❏ As an error indicator, upon which the given request is terminated, an error message is issued, and the channel is deactivated (all its awaiting requests are cleared).

An indicator by which the Host Controller determines how it is to process the given request must be sent in every IRP. When bulk transfers are performed, the most standard practice is to use short packets as end of block indicators. In this way, for example, in one version of the data storage device protocols, short packets of a known length are used for controlling purposes.

Pipes

There are two types of USB communications pipes:

❏ *Stream pipes* deliver data from one end of the pipe to another; they are always one way. The same endpoint number can be used for two different stream pipes: input and output. Data transmissions in different stream pipes are not synchronized with each other. This means that client drivers' requests for different pipes submitted in a certain order relative to each other may be executed in a different order. Requests for one pipe are executed strictly in the order of their arrival. If a major error is encountered (such that causes a Stall signal to be generated), the stream will be stopped. Bulk, isochronous, and interrupt data can be transferred in streams. Streams carry data of arbitrary format, which is determined by the developer of the device (but not by the USB specification).

❏ *Message pipes* are bidirectional. Message transfers in opposite directions are synchronized with each other and are strictly ordered. The opposite side must acknowledge having received and processed each message. Normally, the next message cannot be sent until the previous message has been processed; however, during error handling, unprocessed messages may be cleared. Message formats are defined by a USB specification: There is a set of standard messages (requests and replies) and reserved message indicators; the format of the latter is determined by the device or interface manufacturer.

Pipe characteristics are associated with the characteristics of the endpoint (bandwidth, service type, buffer size, etc.). Pipes are organized when the USB devices are configured. The bus bandwidth is divided among all established channels. The allocated portion of the bandwidth is reserved for the pipe, and if establishing a new pipe requires a portion that does not correspond to the already existing allocation, the pipe allocation request is denied.

Pipes also differ in their purpose:

❏ The *Default Pipe,* or Control Pipe 0, whose owner is the USB driver, is used to access configuration information of all devices. This pipe is established with Endpoint Zero, which always only supports control transfers in all devices.

❏ *Client Pipes* belong to device drivers. Streams, as well as messages, can be sent over these pipes, which support any type of USB transfers (isochronous, interrupts, bulk, and control).

The device interface, with which the client driver works, is a pipe bundle. For these pipes, the device driver is the only source and sink of all transferred data.

The owner of all devices' default pipes is the USB driver; it uses them to transfer configuration, control, and status information. The default message pipe may be used by a client driver to perform current device control tasks and to read its status, but it can do this only via the USB driver. For example, a USB printer driver sends messages over the default pipe to poll the printer's current status (three indicators in the format of the LPT port status register are sent: I/O error, printer selected, end of paper).

Frames and Microframes

The host organizes exchanges with devices according to its resource allocation plan. For this, every 1 μsec, the host controller generates frames, into which all the planned transactions are packed. Each frame begins with a Start-of-Frame (SOF) packet, which serves as a synchronizing signal for isochronous devices, as well as for hubs. Frames are sequentially numbered; the 11 lowest bits of the frame number are sent in the SOF marker. In the High Speed mode, each frame is divided into eight microframes, and SOF packets are sent at the start of each microframe (every 125 μsec). The SOF packet carries the same frame number in all eight microframes; the new value of the frame number is sent in microframe zero. Several transactions can be carried out in each frame (microframe); their maximum number depends on the speed, length of the data field of each of them, and the delays introduced by the cables, hubs, and devices. All frame transactions must be completed before the End-Of-(micro)Frame interval. The period (frequency), with which (micro)frames are generated, can be varied somewhat with the help of the special `host controller` register, which allows the frequency to be adjusted for isochronous transfers (see *Section 4.1.5*).

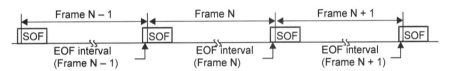

Fig. 4.4. USB frames

Framing is also used to provide bus robustness. At the end of each (micro)frame an End-Of-Frame (EOF) time interval is allocated, during which hubs are prohibited from transferring data toward the controller. If a hub detects that a data transfer is being conducted from a port toward the controller during this time, the port is disconnected, thus isolating the talkative device, and the USB driver is informed of this.

The Host Controller's (micro)frame counter is used as the index source when accessing the frame descriptor table. Usually, the USB driver builds a descriptor table for 1,024 sequential frames (see details on planning for UHC, OHC, and EHC in *Section 4.1.9*) that it periodically accesses. Using these descriptors, the host plans frame loading in such a way that, in addition to the scheduled isochronous transactions and interrupts, there is always a room in them for control transactions. Any free frame time can be filled by bulk data transfers. The USB specification allows up to 90% of the bus bandwidth (i.e., (micro)frame time) to be taken by periodic transactions (isochronous and interrupt).

4.1.3. Bus Transactions

Traffic — a flow of packets with transmitted information — is conducted via USB using transactions. Each transaction only allows data exchange between the host and the addressed device (its endpoint). All transactions (exchanges) with USB devices consist of two or three packets; a typical transaction packet sequence is shown in Fig. 4.5. Each transaction is scheduled and is started at the initiative of the Host Controller by sending a token packet. A *transaction token* describes the transaction type and direction, the address of the selected USB device, and the endpoint number. The device addressed by the token recognizes its address and prepares for the exchange. The data source defined by the marker sends a data packet. Isochronous transfer transactions terminate at this stage: Packet reception is not acknowledged here. The acknowledgement mechanism is employed for other types of transactions, which guarantees data delivery. Fig. 4.6 shows packet formats; Table 4.2 lists the packet types. Data are sent with the least significant bit (depicted on the left in the timing diagrams) first in all packet fields, with the exception of the CRC field. The Sync and EOP field lengths are shown for fast-speed and low-speed transfers; for high-speed transfers, the Sync field is increased to 32 bit intervals and the EOP field is increased to 8 (in SOF packets, the EOP field is 40 bits long; see *Section 4.1.6*).

```
┌──────────────┐       ┌──────────┐       ┌──────────────┐
│ OUT / SETUP  │       │   Data   │       │  Handshake   │
└──────────────┘       └──────────┘       └──────────────┘
   ├──────────┤           ├────────┤
  Device is waiting       Host is wating

┌──────────────┐       ┌──────────┐       ┌──────────────┐
│     IN       │       │   Data   │       │  Handshake   │
└──────────────┘       └──────────┘       └──────────────┘
   ├──────────┤           ├────────┤
  Host is wating        Device is waiting
```

Fig. 4.5. USB transaction packet sequence: *a* — data output, *b* — data input

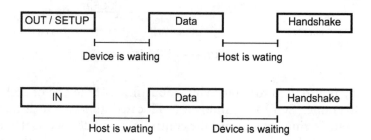

Field	Sync	PID	Check	Addr	Endd r	CRC C	EOP		Sync	PID	Check	Data	CRC C	EOP		Sync	PID	Check	EOP
Length (bits)	8	4	4	7	4	5	2		8	4	4	8×n	16	2		8	4	4	2
			Token								Data						Acknowledgement		

Fig. 4.6. USB packet formats

Table 4.2. Packet Types and Their PIDs

Name	PID Code	Contents and function
		Token packets
OUT	0001	Output transaction token; carries the endpoint identifier (device address and endpoint number; endpoint direction is determined by the PID code).
IN	1001	Input transaction token; carries the endpoint identifier (device address and endpoint number; endpoint direction is determined by the PID code).
SETUP	1101	Control transaction token; carries endpoint identifier (device address and endpoint number).
SOF	0101	Start-of-(micro)frame token; carries 11-bit frame number (instead of the Addr and EndP fields).
PING	0100	Flow control probe token (in USB 2.0).
		Data packets
Data0	0011	Data packets; PID sequencing allows even and odd packets to
Data1	1011	be determined for correct acknowledgement.
Data2	0111	Extra types of data packets used in transactions with high-
Mdata	1111	bandwidth isochronous endpoints (in USB 2.0 for HS).
		Handshake packets
ACK	0010	Errorless packet reception acknowledgement.
NAK	1010	Busy indicator (endpoint is not ready for data exchange; control transaction has not been completed).
STALL	1110	Host intervention request by an endpoint.
NYET		Errorless reception acknowledgement but indicating that there is no more room to receive the next maximum size packet (in USB 2.0).
		Special purpose packets
PRE	1100	Low-speed transfer preamble (enables data traffic's translation to a low-speed hub port).
ERR	1100	Split transaction error indicator (in USB 2.0).
SPLIT (SS and CS)	1000	Split transaction token (in USB 2.0). Depending on the function, it is marked either as SS (start token) or as CS (end token); the function is determined by the SC bit in the token body.

Transfer-Error-Handling Mechanisms

All received packets are checked for errors. This is made possible by the formats of the received packets and some conventions:

❏ A packet starts with a synchronization sequence followed by its Packet Identifier (PID). The identifier is followed by its inverted copy — Check. The two copies not matching is an indication of an error.

❏ The body of the packet (all packet fields, excluding the PID and EOP) are protected by a CRC code: 5 bit for token packets and 16 bit for data packets. The CRC's value being different from the expected value is indication of an error.

❏ A packet is completed with a special EOP signal; if there is incomplete byte in the packet, the packet is considered invalid. A false EOP, even on the byte boundary, will not allow the packet to be received because of the CRC control error, practically unavoidable in the given situation.

❏ Packet data are relayed to the physical level by using bit stuffing (after six logical one bits, a logical zero bit is inserted), which prevents losing bit synchronization when a monotonous signal is sent. Reception of more than six logical one bits is considered an error (in the high-speed mode, this serves as the end of frame indicator).

Detecting any of the errors listed above makes the receiver consider that packet invalid. Neither the device nor the Host Controller responds to the packets that have been received with errors. In isochronous transfers, data in invalid packets are simply ignored (lost); means to reliable packet delivery are used in other types of transfers.

To detect that its partner does not acknowledge a packet, each device has a *timeout counter*, which breaks off waiting for the answer after a certain amount of time has elapsed. The USB has a set *packet roundtrip time*: the interval from when the transmitter completes sending a packet (marked by EOP) until it begins receiving response. The *response time* for end devices (and the Host Controller) is the interval from when a device senses EOP to the moment it begins sending a response packet. For hubs, a packet-delay time is specified, and for cables a signal-propagation delay time is also specified. The timeout counter must take into consideration the maximum delay allowable for the permissible bus configuration: up to 5 intermediate hubs, each cable up to 5 meters long. The permissible time-out value, expressed in bit intervals, depends on the speed:

❏ For full speed and low speed, the delay inserted by one cable segment is small in comparison with one bit time (bt). Based on this, the following model for calculating the maximum allowable delays is employed in USB 1.0. For each cable segment, the maximum allowable delay is set at 30 nanoseconds (nsec); for each hub, it is 40 nsec. Consequently, five intermediate hubs together with their cables introduce a delay of 700 nsec for a double turnaround, which in the full-speed mode corresponds to approximately 8.5 bt. For a full-speed device, the response delay must not exceed 6.5 bt (7.5 bt, taking its cable into consideration). Based on this, the specification directs that a high-speed transmitter's timeout counter be set to 16–18 bt.

❑ For high speed, the cable segment delay is much larger than a bit time, and the calculations are somewhat different in USB 2.0. Here, each cable segment is allotted 26 nsec, while each hub gets 4 nsec plus 36 bit times. Consequently, double passage through six cable segments ($2 \times 6 \times 26 = 312$ nsec or 150 bit times) and five hubs ($2 \times 5 \times 4 = 40$ nsec or 19 bit times plus $2 \times 5 \times 36 = 360$ bit times) takes up to 529 bit times. A device response delay of up to 192 bit times is allowed, and the overall delay due to cables and hubs is up to 721 bit times. Based on these calculations, the specification directs that at high speed the timeout counter be set to 736–816 bit times.

The Host Controller has an error counter for each endpoint of every device, which is zeroed out when each transaction with this endpoint is scheduled. This counter records all protocol errors (including timeout errors), and if the number of errors exceeds the threshold of three, then the channel with the given endpoint is stopped and its owner (the device driver of the USB driver) is informed of this. Until the threshold is reached, the host handles non-isochronous transfer errors by attempting to repeat the transactions without notifying the client software. Isochronous transfer errors are not retransmitted and the host informs the client about the errors right away.

Acknowledgements, Flow Control, and Device Error Reporting

Handshake packets are used to acknowledge reception, flow control, and report errors. The Host Controller can send only the ACK packet to a device, confirming by this that a data packet has been received without errors. A device sends the host the following handshake packets:

❑ ACK: positive acknowledgment of a successful output or control transaction execution.

❑ NAK: negative acknowledgement. It is sign that a device is not ready to execute the given transaction (no data to send to the host, no room in the buffer, or a control operation has not been completed). This is a normal response, of which only the Host Controller — which will have to repeat this transaction later — is informed. In input transactions, a device sends a NAK response instead of the data packet if the data are not ready.

❑ STALL: a severe error message that means that the work with the given endpoint cannot continue without some sort of software intervention. This response is relayed both to the USB driver, which cancels further transactions with the given endpoint, and to the client drive, which is supposed to provide the said software intervention.

Output data flow control based only on the NAK answer in case the device is not ready makes very inefficient use of the bus bandwidth: In order to find out that a device is not ready, a large data packet is sent over the bus for nothing. In the Bulk-OUT and Control transactions in USB 2.0, this wastefulness is avoided by using the *Ping Protocol*. The host can query device readiness to receive a maximum size packet by sending it a Ping probe token. The device can answer this token with either ACK (if it is ready) or NAK (if it is not ready to receive a maximum size packet). A negative response will make the host repeat the attempt later; a positive response will allow it to execute a data output transaction. The device's reaction to the output transaction following a positive reply to the probe token is more diverse:

❐ ACK means a successful reception and readiness to receive the next full-size packet.
❐ NYET means a successful reception but not being ready to receive the next packet.
❐ NAK is an unexpected answer as it contradicts the positive reply to the probe, but it is possible if the device suddenly became not ready.

A high-speed device indicates the potential intensity of the NAK messages in the endpoint descriptors: For the endpoints of the Bulk and Control types, the bInterval field indicates the number of microframes per each NAK (0 means that the device will never give an NAK response to an output transaction).

Providing Reliable Delivery

Bulk, interrupt, and control transfers are performed with reliable data delivery. After a receiver successfully receives a packet, it confirms it by sending an ACK acknowledgement packet. If a receiver detects an error, it ignores the packet and sends no confirmation of its reception. The data source considers the next packet to have been successfully transmitted if it receives an ACK confirmation from the receiver. If no confirmation comes, then the source tries to retransmit the same packet in the next transaction. However, the confirmation packet can be lost because of some interference; in such case, data packets are numbered so that the receiver does not consider the repeated packet as a new portion of data. The numbering is done modulo 2 (1-bit number): Packets are divided into odd (with the DATA1 identifier) and even (with the DATA0 identifier). For each endpoint (except isochronous), the host and the devices have Toggle Bits whose initial states are synchronized. In IN and OUT transactions, data packets are sent and expected with DATA0 or DATA1 identifiers that correspond to the current state of these bits. The data receiver switches its bit when it successfully receives a data packet with the expected identifier; the data source switches its bit when it receives a confirmation of successful reception from the receiver. If the receiver gets an errorless packet with an unexpected identifier, it confirms it with an ACK but ignores its data because this packet is a repeated transmission of already received data.

Transaction Protocols for Different Types of Transfers

Transactions for different types of transfers have protocol differences due to several factors: whether or not the bandwidth, response time, reliable delivery, and input/output synchronization are guaranteed. Depending on these characteristics, one or other of the above-described protocol mechanisms are used in transactions. Error detection is employed in all types of transactions, so the corrupted data are ignored. Exactly what type of protocol mechanism is being used in the current transaction is known to both the Host Controller (by the previously received endpoint descriptor) and the USB device, to which this end point pertains.

Isochronous Transfer Transactions

Isochronous transactions provide guaranteed exchange speed but not reliable delivery. Because of this, their protocol does not include acknowledgements, as resending a packet will cause a breakdown in the data delivery schedule. Flow control based on acknowledgements is absent: A device must keep up with the exchange rate declared in the descriptor of the isochronous endpoint. Isochronous data transmitters and receiver synchronization are considered in more detail in *Section 4.1.5*.

Isochronous output transactions are made up of two packets sent by the Host Controller: an OUT token and a DATA packet. In the input transactions, the host sends an IN token, to which the device answers with a data packet (whose data field may be of zero length if the device has no ready data). Any other response is considered by the host as an error, and it stops the given channel.

In isochronous transfers, data are checked for validity (detecting and discarding packets with errors) and integrity (detecting missing packets). The integrity check is based on the exchange rate being strictly determinate: In compliance with its descriptor, the endpoint awaits a transactions with a period of $2^{bInterval-1}$ (micro)frames. Only one transaction in a (micro)frame is possible for a regular isochronous endpoint, and a packet reception error is expressed by the absence of data in the (micro)frame in which they are expected. Consequently, packet numbering (Toggle Bit) is not needed. Full-speed devices and Host Controllers must send packets only of the DATA0[1] type. Up to three data packets can be sent in each (micro)frame for high-bandwidth isochronous endpoints (USB 2.0). Any of these packets can get lost, and in order to detect such a situation packet enumeration inside a microframe is needed. For this purpose,

---

[1] Although pursuant to the specification, they must receive the DATA0 as well as DATA1.

two new data packet types — DATA2 and MDATA — have been introduced. In addition to enumeration, the diversity of packet types allows the communication partner to be informed of the plans for the given microframe. In IN transactions, the device indicates by the packet identifier how many more packets it intends to send in the same microframe, which allows the host not to attempt unnecessary input operations. Thus, if only one packet is sent in the microframe, it will be of the DATA0 type; if two packets are sent, their sequence will be DATA1, DATA0; if three packets are sent, they will follow in the order DATA2, DATA1, DATA0. In OUT transactions, for outputting a packet that is not the last one, the MDATA (More Data) packet type is used in the microframe, and the last packet identifier indicates how many packets preceded it. Thus, the DATA0 packet is used for one output transaction; the sequence MDATA, DATA1 is used for two; and the sequence MDATA, MDATA, DATA2 for three. Other types of transactions can wedge in between the high-bandwidth transactions in a microframe. Maximum size packets must be used in all microframe transactions apart from the last one.

Interrupt and Bulk Transfer Transactions

Interrupt and bulk transfer transactions look the same on the bus. Here, all the flow control, reliable delivery, and error-reporting mechanisms described above are employed. The toggle bits in the device and the endpoint of the packet sequence control are initialized as follows:

❑ For the endpoints of the bulk transfers, any event associated with the transfer configuration (configuration or interface setting, error handling) sets the bits into the DATA0 state. Sending a new transfer request packet (IRP) does not initialize the bits.

❑ Only DATA0 packets are used for the regular endpoints in interrupt transactions, because only one packet per transaction can be sent here and the query period is unknown.

❑ For high-bandwidth endpoint interrupt transactions, the DATA0 packet goes first in a microframe; the following packets in the same microframe follow in the alternation sequence DATA1-DATA0.

Pursuant to the USB specifications, interrupt transactions can be used both to input data and to output them upon a request. However, interrupt outputs are not considered in such detail as the more conventional input transactions. Using the interrupt transaction for input/output operations is attractive because of the possibility of obtaining both almost guaranteed speed (without taking transmission errors into consideration), as well as guaranteed delivery.

Control Transfer Transactions

The function of the control transfers is to issue a command (Write Control) or a request (Read Control) to a device, and indicate the execution results. Transfers consist of two or three stages, and are executed with the help of several transactions:

☐ The *Setup Stage* is intended for sending a control message from the host to a device. This message describes the command (request) that the device has to execute. The command may be used to transmit or receive data.

☐ The *Data Stage* is intended for sending additional control information (Write Control) or receiving information from a device (Read Control). This stage may be skipped if no information needs to be input and the information being output fits into the Setup Stage message.

☐ The *Status Stage* is intended for notifying the host of the fact and results (success or failure) of a command execution completion.

The *setup stage* is performed as one transaction beginning with a Setup token. Further, the host sends an 8-byte data packet (DATA0) with a standard structure request message (see *Section 4.1.10*). The device confirms successful receipt of this packet with an ACK response and begins to service the command request. If the host does not receive the acknowledgement, it has to repeat the request.

The host executes the *data transfer stage* (only for the three-stage transfers) using one or several IN (Read Control transfer) or OUT (Write Control) transactions, providing flow control and reliable delivery with the help of repeated transactions and number alternation. The first transaction of the data phase begins with a DATA1 packet.

The host signals the transition to the *Status Stage* by a transaction, in which the direction of the data transfer is opposite to the previous phase (Setup or Data). If there was no data phase, or a Write Control transfer was executed, the host executes an IN transaction. If the previously executed transfer was a Read Control, the host performs an OUT transaction (outputs a zero length DATA1 packet) or sends a PING probe token (in USB 2.0). At this stage only the response from the peripheral device is of any interest:

☐ If the device has not completed executing the command, it answers with an NAK packet. The host must repeat the transaction until it receives a different answer.

☐ If the device has successfully executed the command, it answers an IN transaction with a zero length DATA1 packet, and an OUT (or PING) transaction with an ACK confirmation.

☐ If the device has completed command execution but did so with an error, then it will respond with a STALL packet.

Until the host receives a response indicating successful command execution, it has no right to access the given endpoint with another command. In this way, command execution serialization is provided: A device will not drown in a stream of commands that it cannot handle; the data being input will correspond to the state the device was in at the moment the request command — which might be preceded by control writes — was issued. This synchronization of USB device input and output streams is not directly supported by any other transfer type. Control transfers for all USB devices are supported by zero endpoints (EP0); client endpoint control transfers are supported in far from all cases.

4.1.4. Bus and Device Bandwidth

The serial transfer speed (1.5, 12, and 480 Mbps for LS, FS, and HS, respectively) is only a starting point for determining the real exchange throughput of a specific device on the bus and of all devices on the bus together. The bus bandwidth as a whole is also determined by the ratio of overheads to the transmitted useful data. Overhead expenditure sources, the ratio of overheads to overall traffic, and bus loading by different types of transactions with different data block sizes are considered in the following pages. To evaluate the possible data exchange speed with a specific device connected to the USB, a few aspects need to be mentioned:

❑ Only one transaction, defined by the bInterval descriptor of the endpoint, is conducted with a regular endpoint of periodic transfers (isochronous and interrupts) in each nth (micro)frame. Up to three transactions can be conducted in a microframe with a high-bandwidth endpoint. In Table 4.6, high-bandwidth endpoints are represented by a data field size of 1,024–3,072 bytes, and the bus load they produce pertains to all of their transactions in the microframe (from 1 to 3). The bandwidth *Vmax* of a periodic transfer endpoint is determined by dividing the size of a maximum length data packet *Dmax* by the length of the service period *T*: $Vmax = Dmax/T$. The service period *T* is determined the following way:

- For isochronous endpoints, $T = Tk \times 2^{bInterval-1}$, where *Tk* is the period the SOF markers are sent with (1 msec for full speed and 125 μsec for high speed); *bInterval* lies in the 1–16 range. Consequently, the service period for FS can be from 1–32,768 msec; for HS, the service period is 0.125–4,096 msec.

- For FS/LS interrupt endpoints, $T = 1 \times bInterval$ (msec); *bInterval* lies in the range 1–255; the service period can be between 1–255 msec.

- For HS interrupt endpoints, $T = 0.125 \times 2^{bInterval-1}$ (msec); *bInterval* lies in the range 1–16; the service period can be between 0.125–4,096 msec.

❑ When conducting *bulk transfers*, the number of transactions with one endpoint in one microframe is not defined, but its maximum does not exceed the value indicated in the tables. The USB driver can also use the simple policy of queue servicing, under which no more than one transaction is done for each endpoint in the microframe. Each microframe has room for one or two bulk transfer transactions, no matter how heavy the isochronous traffic may be; but when multiple devices request such transactions, the average transmission speed for each of them will obviously not be high.

Bus Overhead and Load

The following pertain to the overhead expenses of serial bus transfer:

❑ Service information expenses (token and acknowledge packet, service fields of the data packets).
❑ Bit stuffing expenses: Six consecutive logical ones in any field of the frame cause one additional bit to be transmitted over the bus. The share of these overhead expenses can be from 0% to 15% of the volume of the useful data. Because of this share being indeterminate, the given expenses are not taken into account in the tables given below.
❑ Signal propagation delays in cables and hubs expenses.
❑ Expenses of the internal device response to transaction delay.
❑ Expenses for repeating transactions in case of reception errors or the device not being ready.

Overhead expenses for each transaction depend on the transaction type: The most efficient are isochronous transactions (no acknowledgements); the most resource-intensive are three-stage control transactions. The number of overhead expenditure bytes for each full- and high-speed transaction is given in Table 4.3 (low speed is not considered). High overhead at high speed is explained by the strong effect of the propagation delays: At full speed, the turnaround time (see *Section 4.1.3*) takes up to two bytes, while at high speed, up to 90 bytes are devoured (because the bit time of about 2 nsec is much smaller than the permissible propagation delay).

Table 4.3. Overhead Expenses for One Transaction and Maximum Bus Use Efficiency

Transfer type	Overhead/data length — efficiency	
	FS	**HS**
Isochronous	9/1,023 — 99%	38/1,024 — 96%
Interrupt	13/64 — 83%	55/1,024 — 95%
Bulk data	13/64 — 83%	55/512 — 90%
Control (3 stage)	45/64 — 59%	173/64 — 27%

It is obvious that, with the view toward decreasing the portion of the bus overhead, it is practical to use maximum length packets. However, this type of transaction takes up too much time in the (micro)frame, leaving little time for other transactions. Theoretically, 12,000 bits (including the stuffed bits), or 1.5 KB, can be transferred over the bus in each frame (1 msec) at full speed (12 Mbps), although in reality this number is smaller due to the propagation and response delays. At high speed (480 Mbps), 60,000 bits, or 7.5 KB, are sent in each microframe (125 μsec). Tables 4.4, 4.5, and 4.6 list the throughput capacity parameters for different type of transactions depending on the data field length. Whether different types of transactions can be combined in one (micro)frame can be evaluated by adding up the portions of the frame they take (the result may not exceed 100%). The tables show that low-speed devices at low bandwidth use up a significant part of the bus time. This is tolerated in USB 1.x for the sake of simplicity, while in USB 2.0 the high bandwidth is saved by using split transactions (which require substantially more complex hubs).

Table 4.4. Low-Speed Transaction Bandwidth

Data field size	Maximum endpoint bandwidth (KBps)	Part of frame taken	Maximum number of transactions in a frame	Maximum bus bandwidth (KBps)	Maximum endpoint bandwidth (KBps)	Part of frame taken	Maximum number of transactions in a frame	Maximum bus bandwidth (KBps)
	Control transfers				Interrupts			
1	1	26%	3	3	1	11%	9	9
2	2	27%	3	6	2	11%	8	16
4	4	28%	3	12	4	12%	8	32
8	8	30%	3	24	8	14%	6	48

Table 4.5. Full-Speed Transaction Bandwidth

Data field size	Maximum endpoint bandwidth (KBps)	Part of frame taken	Maximum number of transactions in a frame	Maximum bus bandwidth (KBps)	Maximum endpoint bandwidth (KBps)	Part of frame taken	Maximum number of transactions in a frame	Maximum bus bandwidth (KBps)
	Isochronous transfers				Bulk and interrupt transfers			
1	1	1%	150	150	1	1%	107	107
2	2	1%	136	272	2	1%	100	200
4	4	1%	115	460	4	1%	88	352
8	8	1%	88	704	8	1%	71	568
16	16	2%	60	960	16	2%	51	816
32	32	3%	36	1,152	32	3%	33	1,056
64	64	5%	20	1,280	64	5%	19	1,216
128	128	9%	10	1,280				
256	256	18%	5	1,280		Not available		
512	512	35%	2	1,024				
1,023	1,023	69%	1	1,023				

Table 4.6. High-Speed Transaction Bandwidth

Data field size	Maximum end-point bandwidth (KBps)	Part of frame taken	Maximum number of transactions in a microframe	Maximum bus bandwidth (KBps)	Maximum end-point bandwidth (KBps)	Part of frame taken	Maximum number of transactions in a microframe	Maximum bus bandwidth (KBps)
	Isochronous transfers				Bulk and interrupt transfers			
1	8	1%	192	1,536	8	1%	133	1,064
2	16	1%	187	2,992	16	1%	131	2,096

continues

Table 4.6 Continued

Data field size	Maximum end-point bandwidth (KBps)	Part of frame taken	Maximum number of transactions in a microframe	Maximum bus bandwidth (KBps)	Maximum end-point bandwidth (KBps)	Part of frame taken	Maximum number of transactions in a microframe	Maximum bus bandwidth (KBps)
	Isochronous transfers				*Bulk and interrupt transfers*			
4	32	1%	178	5,696	32	1%	127	4,064
8	64	1%	163	10,432	64	1%	119	7,616
16	128	1%	138	17,664	128	1%	105	1,3440
32	256	1%	107	27,392	256	1%	86	22,016
64	512	1%	73	37,376	512	2%	63	32,256
128	1,024	2%	45	46,080	1,024	2%	40	40,960
256	2,048	4%	25	51,200	2,048	4%	24	49,152
512	4,096	7%	13	53,248	4,096	8%	13	53,248
	Isochronous transfers				*Interrupt transfers*			
1,024	8,192	14%	7	57,344	8,192	14%	6	49,152
2,048[1]	16,384	28%	3	49,152	16,384	28%	3	49,152
3,072[1]	24,576	41%	2	49,152	24,576	42%	2	49,152

[1] For a high-bandwidth endpoint, the rows pertain to two or three transactions in a microframe, in each of which the data field length does not exceed 1,024 bytes.

Bus Sharing by Different-Speed Devices

The USB specification allows devices with significantly different transfer speeds to be connected to one bus. For them to share the bus without conflicts in terms of (micro)frame time allocations, corresponding limitations on the maximum data field length have been adopted for each speed mode.

☐ *Low speed* (LS, 1.5 Mbps): up to 8 bytes; moreover, a two-stage control transaction takes up 30% of a frame, while an interrupt transaction takes up 14%.
☐ *Full speed* (FS, 12 Mbps): up to 1,023 bytes for isochronous exchanges (69% of a frame) and 64 bytes for the other exchange types (5% of a frame).

❐ *High speed* (HS, 480 Mbps): up to 1,024 bytes for the interrupt and isochronous transfers (14% of a microframe); up to 512 bytres for bulk and control transfers (7–8% of a microframe).

Transceivers (as well as the connecting cables) of low-speed devices are not capable of working with full-speed signals, with which all SOF tokens and all exchange packets of full-speed devices are transferred. Because of this, a USB hub does not relay traffic to its downstream ports to which low-speed devices are connected unless the Host Controller transmits a special packet: a low-speed transfer preamble (PRE). All devices except the hubs ignore this packet. By issuing a preamble packet, the Host Controller guarantees that it will send the next packet at low speed. This packet will be a token that defines the type of transaction to be conducted with a LS device, while in output transactions this will be a data packet (which requires a separate preamble). A hub allows only one packet following the preamble to be sent to its downstream port with an LS device; when the hub detects the packet end (an EOP at low speed), it disables relaying again. In order for the hub to have sufficient time to switch the operating modes of its transceiver, a gap of four FS bit times is inserted between the preamble and the following packet. For a LS device to reply, no preambles are needed: Hubs can transparently relay the upstream traffic at both speeds (LS and FS). Naturally, the Host Controller must be able to receive both FS and LS packets. It is obvious that low-speed transactions make very inefficient use of the frame time, but this circumstance is tolerated in USB 1.x for the sake of being able to use inexpensive devices and unsophisticated hubs, which are simple repeaters. SOF tokens are not relayed to the low-speed ports, so LS devices cannot and do not support isochronous traffic, for which use of this token is necessary.

The effective coexistence of three speeds in USB 2.0 is more complex to implement and costs more. First of all, practically, a USB 2.0 Host Controller has two controllers: an EHC operating only at high speed and a USB 1.x companion controller (perhaps more than one) for the full and low speeds (UHC or OHC). The ports of the root hub have equal rights, but each port is connected to the corresponding controller during the autoconfiguration process, depending on the characteristics of the device (or hub) connected to it.

Second, USB 2.0 hubs are more complex: In addition to a repeater, they also have a transaction translator. When both the upstream and downstream ports of a hub are working at the same speed (FS or HS), the hub works in the repeater mode. In this case, a transaction with a device connected to the hub takes the entire channel from the Host Controller to the device for the entire duration of its execution. But when a USB 1.1 device or hub are connected to a port of a USB 2.0 hub working in the HS mode, then *split transactions* are used. In this type of transaction, the transfer is conducted at HS over the segment of the channel between the host and the hub (its transaction translator), while between the transaction translator and the USB 1.x device (or a hub), the exchange is conducted in the device's FS or LS mode. These exchanges are separated in time; any high-speed transactions, including split ones, can intrude in between them. Consequently, split transactions allow the high bandwidth capacity not to be wasted: Transactions with a hub at high speed take 1/40th (for FS) and even 1/320th (for LS) of the bus time of transactions with the target device itself[1]. All the intricacies of the split transactions are hidden from old (USB 1.x) devices and hubs, which provides backward compatibility.

Hub ports can determine by hardware the speed that the connected device supports. All HS devices work in FS mode when first connected, and only after mutual negotiation with the hub's port will they switch to the HS mode. If an HS device is connected to a USB 1.x hub, which does not support such negotiation, the device will remain in the FS mode, perhaps with reduced functionality. In the USB 2.0 system, a device can be asked (by requesting its descriptors, see *Section 4.1.10*) what will change in its functionality if it is connected at a different speed (by changing the connection topology).

It is quite understood that a USB 2.0 device can make use of the high-speed mode if there are only USB 2.0 hubs on the way to the Host Controller (also a USB 2.0). If this rule is violated and there happens to be an old hub between them, then the communications can only be established in the FS mode. If this speed suits the device and the client software (for example, for a printer or a scanner, this will only result in the user having to wait longer), then the connected device will work, but the user will be informed of the configuration being non-optimal. As far as possible, the configuration should be corrected, since USB cables can be connected and disconnected on the fly. Devices and software critical to the bus bandwidth will refuse to operate in incorrect configurations, and request to be reconfigured. In the case of an old Host Controller, none of the advantages of the USB 2.0 will be available to the user. In this event, the Host Controller will have to be replaced (either the motherboard should be replaced or a PCI card USB 2.0 controller should be installed).

A USB 2.0 Host Controller and hubs allow the total bus bandwidth to be also increased for old devices. If FS devices are connected to different ports of USB 2.0 hubs (including the root hub), their total USB bus bandwidth can be increased in comparison with 12 Mbps by as many times as there are HS hub ports used. Of course, the total bandwidth of all devices, including HS devices, cannot be higher than the total bandwidth of the HS bus (overhead expenses also need to be taken into account). Moreover, the architectural singularities of the Host Controller and hubs need to be taken into account. The Host Controller can multiply the FS/LS bus bandwidth by the number of its built-in USB 1.x controllers. The effect of the hub's bus bandwidth multiplication depends on how its transaction translator is implemented (see *Section 4.1.8*).

---

[1] The actual ratios are lower because of the somewhat higher overhead for HS in general than for transaction splitting.

4.1.5. Synchronization During Isochronous Transfers

In isochronous data transfers, devices that are interconnected into one system need to be synchronized. Let's consider an example of USB use. A USB microphone (data source) and USB speakers (data sink) are connected to a computer and interconnected via the software mixer (client software). Each of these components may have its own understanding of time and synchronization: Let's say the microphone has a sampling frequency of 8 KHz and data width of 1 byte (producing a 64 Kbps stream), the speakers have a sampling frequency of 44.1 KHz and data width of 2 × 2 bytes (176.4 Kbps), while the mixer works at a sampling frequency of 32 KHz. In this system, the mixer is the connecting unit, and its clock is considered to be the master clock. The software mixer services data in packets, the service sessions are carried out at certain regular time intervals (let's say every 20 msec, or at a frequency of 50 Hz). The mixer must have *sample rate converters*, which convert n input samples into m output samples using the interpolation method (i.e., making up intermediate samples). These converters allow the mixer to receive data from the microphone at its frequency (8,000 samples per second, in our case) and send them to the speakers at another frequency (44,100 samples per second). The natural solution to the task of providing interaction among these components would be to establish synchronous interconnection among them, taking care of the data stream transfer as well as of the synchronization signal. USB, which provides concurrent connection of multiple devices, does not provide synchronous interface to devices. Synchronous links in USB are based on isochronous transfers. In this case, the following frequencies are involved:

❑ F_s (sample rate): data source and sink clocks.
❑ F_b (bus clock): the USB clock frequency — FS frame frequency (1 KHz) and HS microframe frequency (8 KHz). All USB devices can see SOF tokens at this frequency.
❑ Service frequency: frequency with which client software accesses the USB drivers to send and receive isochronous data.

In a system without a common synchronization source, the following deviations are possible between pairs of sync signals:

❑ Drift: deviation of formally identical frequencies from the nominal values (there are no absolutely identical clock generators).
❑ Jitter: frequency fluctuation relative to the nominal.
❑ Phase shift if the signals are not tied together by the Phase Locked Loop (PLL) system.

In a digital data transfer system, these deviations result in potential data excess or shortage at the source or sink, fluctuating or progressing in time. Speed negotiation is performed using the *feed-forward* or *feedback* mechanisms. Which of these two mechanisms is used depends on the type of synchronization supported by the isochronous endpoint of a given device.

In terms of the type of data source or data sinks synchronization with the system, there are asynchronous, synchronous, and adaptive types of endpoints in USB, each of which has its corresponding USB channel type. The synchronization type is set by bits [3:2] of the attribute byte (see *Section 4.1.10*) in the isochronous endpoint's descriptor.

❑ 00 — no synchronization.

❑ 01 — *asynchronous endpoint* of a device that has no capabilities to synchronize its sampling rate with SOF tokens or with other USB system frequencies. Data transfer frequency is either fixed or programmed. The number of data bytes received during each (micro)frame is not constant. An example of an asynchronous source device is a CD player clocked by a quartz generator or a satellite TV receiver. An example of a sink device would be cheap speakers clocked by an internal clock generator.

  • An asynchronous data source declares its transmission speed implicitly by the number of samples it sends in one (micro)frame: The client software will process as much data as have actually come in.

  • An asynchronous data sink must provide *explicit feedback* to the adaptive driver of the client's software in order to synchronize the stream delivery rate.

❑ 11 — *synchronous endpoint* of a device with an internal clock generator synchronized with the SOF (micro)frame markers (1 or 8 KHz). During one (micro)frame, sources and sinks generate (use up) the same number of data bytes set at the channel programming stage. An example of a synchronous data source would be a digital microphone with its sample rate synthesized by SOF tokens. While maintaining a constant frequency, the frequency synthesizer must take into account the possibility of one or two tokens going missing (because of possible transmission errors). These endpoints use *implicit feedback* to adjust to the bus frequency. In software terms, organizing channels with this type of device is the simplest.

❑ 10 — *adaptive endpoint* of a device capable of adjusting its internal frequency to the necessary data stream (within reasonable limits). An example of an adaptive data source would be a CD player with a built-in sample rate converter; an example of a data sink is high-fidelity USB speakers or headphones.

  • An adaptive source allows the speed to be changed under control of the sink that provides *explicit feedback*.

  • An adaptive sink determines the instantaneous frequency value by the amount of data received over a certain averaging interval. In this way, *implicit feed-forward* frequency declaration is performed.

The feedback, which allows the device frequency to be synchronized with the bus frequency, can be explicit or implicit. The feedback mechanism will be considered using an asynchronous sink as an example; it works similarly for an adaptive source. An asynchronous sink must explicitly inform the Host Controller of the frequency, at which the data are to be sent relative to the (micro)frame frequency: F_s/F_b. It is assumed that one sample is represented by one data byte; for a different sample size, a corresponding recalculation needs to be done (for the device and its client software) so that the F_s/F_b ratio is the number of bytes transferred during one (micro)frame. The F_s/F_b ratio may turn out not to be an integer number; in this case, its entier determines the constant volume of transfer (data field size) with the given endpoint in each (micro)frame, while the fractional part is the accumulating remainder that will cause periodic transfer increase in some (micro)frames. In the given case, the sink must calculate the F_s/F_b ratio with an averaging interval of no less than 1 sec. This ratio can change over time (even if only because of the rounding error), so the host must periodically request the F_s/F_b ratio from the device, which is what is called explicit feedback data.

The F_s frequency is set precisely to 1 Hz. Taking into account the maximum transfer size in a frame (1,023 bytes) and the frame frequency (1 KHz), 10 bits is enough at full speed for both the integer and the fractional parts of the F_s/F_b ratio. At high speed, up to 3,072 bytes can be transferred in a microframe, so 12 bits are needed for the integer part. A microframe frequency of 8 KHz requires a 13-bit fractional part. Based on this, the feedback data are represented as follows:

- ❐ By a three-byte number in FS; bits [23:14] are the integer part, bits [13:4] are the fractional part, the rest of the bits are reserved (zeroes).
- ❐ By a four-byte number in HS; bits [28:17] are the integer part, bits [14:4] are the fractional part, the rest of the bits are reserved (zeroes).

The feedback information stream is always one way, opposing the data flow it controls (hence being called feed*back*). The explicit feedback data of the device are taken off the endpoint with the same number as the endpoint used for the main data transfer operation. This endpoint also is isochronous: Bits [5:4] = 0 1 in its attribute byte indicate that this endpoint is used for feedback (in an endpoint used for transferring data, these bits will be zeroed out). The value of the polling interval (bInterval), with which the Host Controller must request the feedback data, is also set in the descriptor. This will allow the Host Controller constantly to adjust the number of bytes sent during each (micro)frame without data buffer overflow or underflow. If there have been no changes since the last poll, the endpoint can reply to the poll with a zero length data packet.

An adaptive source must analogously receive the feedback information from the host so that it can generate exactly the amount of data per each frame as is needed for the Host Controller. Here, the data stream and the feedback stream go in opposite directions, so the endpoint with the same number as the data source is also used for the explicit feedback.

In some cases, allocating a special feedback endpoint in a device for endpoints requiring feedback can be avoided by using implicit feedback. This can be done if the device has a group of functionally linked isochronous endpoints working off a common clock and if there is an endpoint among them with a direction opposite to the endpoint that requires feedback. If feedback is needed for an asynchronous sink, then the implicit feedback information is taken from the data transfer speed of the source synchronized with it. For an adaptive source, the implicit feedback information is analogously taken from the speed of the sink synchronized with it. Bits [5:4] of the attribute byte of the data endpoint, which can be used as a source of the implicit feedback, have value 10. Links by synchronization are created in the group based on the endpoint numbers. To find a source of implicit feedback for a point, an isochronous point of the opposite direction with the same or lower number and whose attribute byte bits [5:4] = 10 must be used.

USB allows both the device and the host to place time markers in the continuous isochronous transfer stream for any endpoint. To do this, the host sends a special control request, *Synch Frame*, to the device in which it indicates the number of the frame expected to come in the near future and the number of the endpoint to which the given time marker pertains. The device and the host have the same time reference point, based on the frame number sent in the SOF token. Synchronization by the zero microframe of the given frame is presupposed for HS devices. The time marker can be used, for example, to indicate the starting moment for an isochronous transfer (for an Open Host Controller, the number of the starting frame is shown in the isochronous transfer descriptor; for a Universal Host Controller, the driver itself places the isochronous transaction descriptors in the frame list). Consequently, the device can get ready for the start of an isochronous exchange in advance.

A USB Host Controller can adjust frame frequency. For example, the Universal Host Controller has an SOF_Modify register, using which software can change the division factor used to divide 12 MHz frequency to obtain 1 KHz frame frequency within ±0,5%. Naturally, the Host Controller can adjust its clock to the internal clock of only one device.

4.1.6. Physical Interface

The USB physical interface is defined by the mechanical and physical specifications of the bus. The information signals and 5 V voltage supply are sent over four-wire cable. To make hot swapping possible, the connectors are constructed in such a way that the supply circuits connect earlier and disconnect later than the signal circuits; moreover, a protocol for signaling device connection and disconnection is provided. In addition to the standard connectors shown in Fig. 4.1, miniature connectors are also used. The functions of the USB connector contacts are listed in Table 4.7; Fig. 4.7 shows contact numbering. All USB cables are straight: they connect like contacts (except the ID circuit; see *Section 4.1.9*).

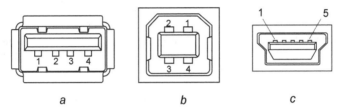

Fig 4.7. USB connectors: *a* — series A receptacle, *b* — series B receptacle, *c* — series mini B receptacle

Table 4.7. USB Connector Contact Functions

Circuit	Contact (standard connector)	Contact (mini connector)
VBus (+5 V)	1	1
D−	2	2
D+	3	3
GND	4	5
ID (connected to GND on series A mini plug)	−	4

A USB cable comprises a shielded twisted pair with 90 ohm impedance for the signal circuit and one non-shielded pair of wires for the voltage supply (+5 V); the maximum segment length (cable length from a device to the hub) is up to 5 meters. For low-speed mode, non-shielded non-twisted pair up to 3 meters long can be used for the signal circuit (it is cheaper). Limitations on the segment length are dictated by the signal decay and the introduced delays. The signal propagation delay in one cable segment must not exceed 26 nsec, so at large linear delay, the maximum cable length can get shorter. The maximum device distance from the Host Controller is determined by the delay introduced by the cables, intermediate hubs, and the devices themselves (see *Section 4.1.3*).

Two wires — D+ and D– — are used to transmit signals. There are the following devices on each side of the interface (hub port side and the connected device side; Fig. 4.8):

❏ Differential receiver, whose output is used when receiving data.
❏ Controlled (switchable) differential FS/LS driver: A voltage source that in addition to a differential signal can also generate a single-ended 0 (SE0) signal, as well as disconnect itself from the line to provide half-duplex exchange.
❏ Single-ended receivers, indicating the current state of each signal wire.

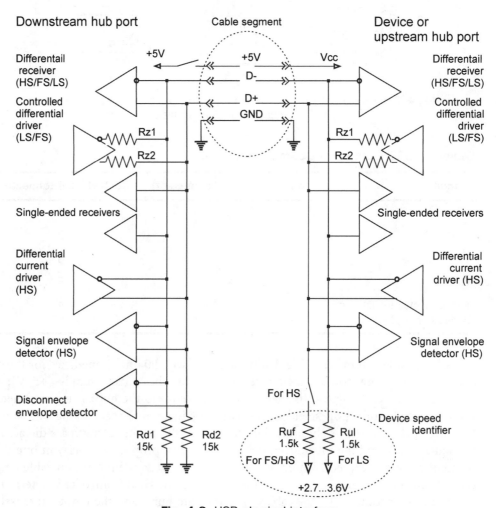

Fig. 4.8. USB physical interface

❏ Resistors that pull signal levels for detecting device connection:
  ● Rd1, Rd2 (15 K) on the hub side
  ● Ruf (for an FS/HS device) or Rul (for an LS device)
❏ Additional components for high-speed operations (for HS devices only):
  ● A switch that disconnects the Ruf resistor when the high-speed mode is se-
    lected
  ● Series resistors Rz1 and Rz2 on the outputs of the differential driver that pro-
    vide line matching and load
  ● Controllable differential current driver
  ● Signal envelope detector
  ● Disconnect envelope detector (only on the downstream hub ports)

The static output signal levels of FS/LS drivers must be no lower than 0.3 V (low
level) or higher than 2.8 V (high level). Receivers must withstand input voltages between −0.5 V and +3.8 V. The sensitivity of differential receivers must be 200 mV with
common mode range 0.8 V — 2.5 V. Linear receivers must have hysteresis: they must
be able to sense as the low level signal anything up to a threshold of 0.8 V, and as the
high level signal anything down to a threshold of 2 V.

HS Mode Signal Specifics

The high-speed mode (480 Mbps, or half as fast as Gigabit Ethernet) requires that the
transceivers be meticulously matched with the communications line. Only cables with
a shielded twisted pair for the signal lines can work at this speed. USB equipment must
have additional special transceivers for high-speed operation. Stringent demands regarding maximum trace length, signal trace lengths being equal, proximity of other
signal lines, copper pour, and other factors, are placed on the conductor layout
from the USB interface microchip to the connector (or to the place where the cable
is soldered in).

Unlike the potential drivers for the FS and LS modes, the HS transmitters are current drivers, requiring terminating resistors on both signal lines. Resistors Rz1 and Rz2
serve as terminators (shown in Fig. 4.8): When working in the HS mode, the differential driver FS/LS generates an SE0 signal (i.e., both of its outputs are grounded and
these resistors become loads for the D+ and D− lines). Their resistance (taking into
account the driver's output impedance) is 2×45 ohm, which provides the required
matching with the line's impedance. The device and the hub turn on their HS terminators (and disconnect Ruf) after both have successfully confirmed the HS mode
in the process of resetting the device.

The differential current drivers generate current impulses with a nominal value of
17.78 milliamperes that flow through a load of 22.5 ohms (two load resistors at both

ends of each signal line are connected in parallel). When the J signal is being transmitted, current is passed to the D+ line; when the K signal is transmitted, the current flows through the D− line. In this way, a differential transmission signal of about ±400 mV is obtained[1].

The signal arrives weakened to the input of the differential receiver; in order to eliminate the noise influence on the signal, a signal envelope detector with a 100–150 mV threshold is introduced into the device schematics. The signal from the differential receiver is squelched until the signal envelope detector is triggered. The delay from the moment the envelope detector is triggered to when the differential receiver turns on may be up four bit times, but it will only result in a shorter Sync pattern received at the beginning of the packet.

Stringent requirements are made to the static (levels) and dynamic (duration and the raise and fall times) signal characteristics in the HS mode, and there are special templates called Eye Patterns that the signals must match. Wideband (no lower than 1 GHz) differential oscilloscopes and signal generators can be used for testing; specialized testers for USB 2.0 equipment are also produced. For testing HS devices (hubs included), the USB 2.0 specification defines special control requests that switch the selected port into the test mode.

Data Transfer

Transfers over two USB wires are not limited to differential signals. Receivers and transmitters use many line states and commands to organize the hardware interface. Moreover, not only electrical signal levels, but also their duration in one or another state, are taken into consideration. In terms of signal levels at the receiver input, the following signals are distinguished:

☐ Diff0: (D+)−(D−) > 200 mV at (D+) > 2 V
☐ Diff1: (D−)−(D+) > 200 mV at (D−) > 2 V
☐ SE0 (single-ended zero): (D+) < 0.8 V and (D−) < 0.8 V.

For transmitting data, the Diff0 and Diff1 signals are used; they encode the J (Data J State) and K (Data K State) states. At full and high speeds, the J state corresponds to the Diff1 signal, and the K state corresponds to the Diff0 signal. At low speed, the situation is reversed: J corresponds to Diff0, and K corresponds to Diff1. The infor-

---

[1] With this type of signal generation method, a linear (in-phase) signal component also appears in a two-wire line; this signal's amplitude equals half the amplitude of the differential signal. In order to generate a purely differential signal, current impulses of different polarity need to be simultaneously sent into the D+ and D− lines, which is what has to be done when the signal needs to be sent over long distances. The simplification of differential signaling adopted in USB allows an inexpensive solution to be used within the given distance limitation boundaries (5-meter long cable segment).

mation is transmitted serially using the NRZI encoding (Fig. 4.9): When a zero bit is sent, the signal state (J or K) at the beginning of the bit time is changed to the opposite; when a one bit is sent, the signal state does not change. The duration of the bit time is determined by the nominal transfer speed: 0.666 μsec for the low-speed mode (LS, 1.5 Mbps); 83.3... nsec for the full-speed mode (FS, 12 MBps); and 2.0833... nsec for the high-speed mode (HS, 480, Mbps).

The Bus Idle state in the FS/LS corresponds to the long J state; in the HS mode, it corresponds to the SE0 state.

The *start of the packet indicator* is a transition from the idle state into the K state, which is the first bit of the *Sync pattern*: a sequence of zeroes that in the NRZI is coded by switching the states (J and K) in the beginning of each bit time. The Sync pattern allows the receiver to adjust to the necessary synchronization frequency and phase. The Sync pattern is concluded with a value one bit (no state change); the bits that follow it pertain to the identifier and the packet body. In the HS mode, the beginning part of the Sync pattern can be lost by the hub (because of the signal envelope detector delay). Taking this into account, the Sync pattern for the HS is increased to 32 bits (including the last value one bit). Going through five hubs, each of which can lose up to 4 sync bits, the arriving Sync pattern may be reduced to 12 bits.

To prevent losing synchronization when sending a long sequence of ones, the *bit-stuffing* technique is used: After each six consecutive ones, the transmitter inserts a zero into the data stream; the receiver deletes these ones. Receiving more than six value one bits in a row is considered a bit-stuffing error.

The end of packet (EOP) is marked by an SE0 signal that lasts 2 bit times and is followed by a switch into the bus idle state. In the HS mode, a violation of the bit-stuffing rule is used for the EOP marker: sending the sequence 01111111 without bit-stuffing serves as the EOP. Receiving the seventh value one bit will produce a bit-stuffing error that in the HS mode is the end of packet indicator. A correct packet is distinguished from a bad one by an integer number of received bytes and the correct CRC value. The starting zero (causing the state switch) in the EOP makes it easier to determine the boundaries of the packet body precisely. In SOF packets, the EOP field is lengthened to 40 bits for detecting device disconnection.

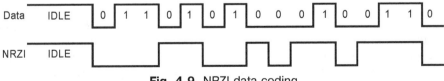

Fig. 4.9. NRZI data coding

Special Signaling: Dynamic Attach and Detach Detection, Device Reset, Suspend, and Resume

A hub detects device attach by the voltage levels of the D+ and D− lines in the following ways:

❑ When there is no device connected, the signal levels in the D+ and D− lines are low (in the SE0 state), which is caused by the hub's Rd1 and Rd2 resistors.
❑ When an LS device is connected, the signal level of the D− line goes up pulled by the device's Rul resistor (switch into the LS-Idle state).
❑ When an FS/HS device is connected, the signal level in the D+ line goes up pulled by the device's Rul (switch into the LS-Idle state).

The connection detection and reset sequence for an FS/LS device is depicted in Fig. 4.10. The hub monitors the signals from the downstream port and signals when they change. After it detects a state change, the system software waits about 100 msec (signal settle time) and then checks the port's status. Having detected the fact of connection and the device type (LS or FS/HS), the software issues a bus reset command to this port.

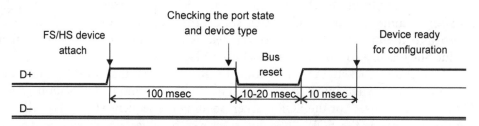

Fig. 4.10. Device connection and reset detection

To execute the Bus Reset command, the hub drops the level of the signal that was set high by the device (D+ or D−) for 10–20 msec (i.e., sends an SE0 signal for 10–20 msec). It is assumed that after this the device should be ready for configuration (i.e., respond only to the accesses to EP0 at the zero device's address).

Bus reset for HS devices starts up the speed negotiation protocol. Upon connection, as well as at the reset signal, an HS device places its circuitry into the FS state (disconnects the terminators and connects the Ruf resistor). Thus, at first, an HS device looks to the hub like an FS device. The so-called chirp sequence is used to negotiate the speed: In response to the SE0 issued by the hub to perform the reset (grounding the D+ line), an HS device places its transmitters into a chirp K state (i.e., sends a current pulse into the D− line). An HS hub will respond to this pulse with a pulse into the D+ line, which results in a chirp J state. This pulse exchange is performed twice more; after the negotiation has been successfully completed, both the device and the hub switch into the HS operation mode (and the Ruf resistor disconnects). All this chirping lasts 10–20 msec, after which the bus switches into the HS-Idle state (a prolonged SE0 signal). Now the host needs to query the hub's status again to ascertain the mode of the connected device. If an HS device is connected to an FS port, the hub will not respond the device's chirps.

A hub detects an *FS/LS device detach* simply by more prolonged SE0 state. The hub conveys this fact to the USB driver so that the device is struck out of all work lists. An HS device detach cannot be detected in this way, because an HS device detach does not change the bus state (SE0). The effect of signal reflection at the loss of the line match is employed to detect an *HS device detach*. Especially for this purpose, an extra disconnect envelope detector circuit is added to the hub circuitry and the EOP indicator in the (micro)frame marker (0111 ... 111) is lengthened to 40 bit times. When relaying an SOF on an HS port, the detector monitors the level of the J signal, and if it exceeds the 625-mV differential signal threshold, it means that there is no load at the other end (i.e., the device is disconnected). Lengthening the EOP is necessary because a device can disconnect internally, and because of the cable delay (2×26 nsec), the reflected signal may be delayed up to 25 nsec. In order to reduce the overhead, the EOP is only lengthened for the SOF packets, which only appear once every 125 μsec.

The hub signals the *device suspend command* by a prolonged Bus-Idle state. It must stop relaying all the frames, including (micro)frame tokens, to the ports to which this command is issued. Frame tokens are not relayed to the LS ports; so that LS devices do not go into the suspend state when there is not useful traffic, the hub sends the LS-EOP indicator (SE0 during 1.33... μsec) with the same period instead of SOF tokens. The suspend state is entered into for no less than 20 μsec: During this time, the device must manage to enter the suspend state and get ready to receive the resume signal.

A hub signals the suspend command for an HS port by a 3 msec bus idle state (SE0), after which it switches its circuits into the FS mode (disconnects the terminators) but remembers that the port is in the HS mode. At the beginning, there is no difference between the reset and suspend commands for an HS device. In order to distinguish them, after 3–3.125 msec of the continuous SE0 state, the HS device switches its circuits into the FS mode (disconnects the terminators and connects the Ruf resistors). Next, after 100–875 μsec, the device checks the state of the lines. If both the D+ and D− lines are in the low-level state, it means that the hub issued a reset command (and the device must execute the chirp sequence). If the level of the D+ line is high and of the D− low (FS-Idle), then it is a suspend signal. Consequently, in terms of the bus signal states, the suspend state looks like the LF/FS mode bus idle state: i.e., the J state.

The *resume command* is executed by switching the bus into the K state for long enough to wake up the device (20 msec), after which the hub sends the LS-EOP indicator

(SE0 for 1.33 μsec). Afterward, the bus is switched into the bus idle state for the corresponding speed and traffic begins to be sent. Both the hub and the suspended device (remote wakeup) can issue a resume signal. Upon the resume signal, an HS device and its hub port switch their circuits into the HS mode without going through the speed negotiations (they remember their modes).

Remote Wakeup is the only case in USB in which a device, not a host, initiates signaling. Only that suspended device for which the bus is in the FS/LS J state (either the D+ or D– line is pulled up by the resistors) can issue a resume signal. To issue a resume signal, the device generates a K state for 900 μsec, which is sensed by the hub and relayed by it to the upstream port as well as to all enabled downstream ports, including the port from which the given resume signal has come.

Power Supply

USB provides power to the devices over the V_{bus} line, which has the nominal voltage of +5 V relative to the GND line. Power is supplied to the downstream hub ports; function devices can only draw power (the same as hub with its upstream port). Of course, devices can provide their own power supplies. Bus power is allocated in 100-milliampere units; a device can draw a maximum of five units (0.5 A). When the device is just connected to the bus (before it is configured), it may draw no more than one power unit (100 mA). A port that supplies five power units is called a *high-power* port; a *low-power* port supplies only one power unit. In terms of drawing bus-powered devices, they are categorized as follows:

❐ *Root hubs* obtain power from the same source as the Host Controller. When external sources are used, hubs must have a high-power port; when autonomous (off batteries) power is used, ports can be either high or low power.

❐ *Bus-powered hubs* can have only low-power ports (and no more than four of those, because the hub controller draws one power unit). This type of hub supplies power to its downstream ports only after it has been configured (because until then, it can only draw one power unit).

❐ *Self-powered hubs* can draw only one power unit. This type of hub provides power to its downware ports from another source; the ports can be either high power or low power (in battery-powered hubs).

❐ *Low-power bus-powered functions* can draw no more than one power unit.

❐ *High-power bus-powered functions* can draw up to five power units.

❐ *Self-powered functions* can draw no more than one power unit, even if they lose their own power supply. The rest of the power they need to work must be drawn from other sources.

The device or hub power mode and the maximum current from the bus (accurate to within 2 mA) are described in the device configuration descriptor. With a self-powered hub, a situation in which it loses its power supply during work is possible. In this case, the hub must disconnect from the bus and then reconnect, but indicate in its descriptor that now it is powered from the bus. In this case, all the devices downstream also disconnect and upon reconnection are reconfigured based on the new power supply budget.

Hub ports must provide over-current protection on the basis of 5 A per port (this does not abolish the consumption rates). Triggering of the over-current protection is indicated, for example, by a system speaker beep. The hub's port power supply control may be common (to all ports at the same time) or selective: These capabilities are described in the descriptor of the port's zero endpoint.

When a device is bus-powered, it gets less power than the hub provides, because of the losses due to the resistance of the feed lines and the connector contacts. The potential on each cable (between the A and B plugs) in each of the GND and V_{bus} lines can drop up to 0.125 V. The worst case in terms of power supply is when there is one bus-powered hub between the power supply (a self-powered hub) and the device and that bus-powered hub introduces its voltage drop (up to 350 mV). A high-power hub port must supply 4.75–5.25 V under load; a low-powered hub must supply 4.4–5.25 V. A bus-powered device must be able to make its configuration information available at the 4.4 V on its cable's A plug; a low-powered device should also work normally with such voltages. At least 4.75 V are needed at the plug of a high-powered device for it to work normally.

Power-Consumption Management: Suspend, Resume, and Remote Wake-up

The USB has a highly developed power-consumption management system. The host computer can have its own power-management system, to which the same name USB system is logically connected. The USB software interacts with the computer power managment system supporting such system events as suspend and resume. Moreover, USB devices can themselves be sources of the events that are handled by the host's power management system.

All USB devices must support the *suspend mode*, in which the average current drawn off the bus does not exceed 500 microamperes (μA). High-power devices that can initiate remote wakeup are allowed to draw up to 2.5 mA. A device must automatically enter the suspend mode when there is no activity on the bus. The suspend mode is always initiated by the host, and can be both global and selective. The resume can be performed for various reasons and under various scenarios.

The *global suspend* is performed via the root hub: A special control command disables it from relaying all downstream traffic, which is what causes the general signaling suspension. This causes all devices and hubs of the bus to switch into the suspend state. Resume after global suspend can be performed in several ways:

❏ At the host's initiative: by a command to the root hub, which will produce a resume signal for all connected to it segments.

❏ At a device's initiative: by a remote wakeup command. The resume signal can be issued by any device that has been enabled by a control request to do this. This signal is sensed by the hub port to which the wakeup device is connected, after which it is spread by the hub to all enabled hubs (reflecting on the port source of the signal) and to the upstream port. Propagating in this way, the resume signal reaches the root hub, which continues to relay this signal to the downstream ports for 20 msec longer, after which it terminates the resume signaling by an LS-EOP indicator.

❏ Upon a port event (a device attach or detach) of a hub that has been enabled by a control request to generate remote wakeup.

❏ By a bus reset, which causes reconfiguration of all devices.

The *selective suspend* involves a bus segment or even a single device. To perform a selective suspend, a setting control signal `Set_Port_Suspend` is sent to the hub to which the bus segment or the device to be suspended is connected, which will disable downstream transfers for the selected port. Resuming after a selective suspend is performed somewhat differently:

❏ At the host's initiative: by sending a cancellation control request `Port_Suspend` to the hub. This will cause resume signaling to the given port during 20 msec concluded with a LS-EOP indicator. Afterward, the hub resumes transferring downstream traffic to this port, and after 3 msec sets a resume procedure conclusion indicator in its status register for the given port.

❏ At a device's initiative: by remote wakeup. Here, the hub that performed the suspend acts differently: It does not propagate the resume signal to the other ports (there may be active devices and traffic transferred there). Having sensed the resume signal, the hub itself sends it to the same port for 20 msec, then sends an LS-EOP indicator, and 3 msec later clears port-suspend indicator for this port.

❏ Upon a port event (a device attach or detach) of the hub, which has been enabled by a control request to generate remote wakeup.

❏ By a bus reset, which causes all devices to be reconfigured.

If device attach/detach events transpire on a selectively suspended hub port, then this port will switch into either connected or disconnected state from the suspended state, depending on the status of the current connection.

Following a selective suspend of some of the hub's ports, the hub itself may be placed into the suspend state (global or also selective). This will not hinder the propagation of the remote wakeup signal upstream. When the resume signal comes to the port from above, the suspend state of its selectively suspended ports will be preserved: The host must remove the suspend state itself by corresponding requests. A remote wakeup signal automatically takes the port to which it arrives out of the suspend state.

4.1.7. USB Devices

A peripheral device with the USB interface can be divided into two parts: the interface and the functional part. Physically, they may share the same microchip, but logically their functions are distinctly separate.

All USB protocol and signal functions are executed by the Serial Interface Engine (SIE). The SIE faces the USB by its USB port (a set of transceivers considered in *Section 4.1.6*). The SIE receives and transmits packets serially, calculating and checking the CRC, stuffing bits, performing NRZI encoding, checking formats, handling acknowledgements, and controlling the correct packet sequence in the process. With the functional part of the device, the SIE exchanges only pure user data. The SIE signals about the next packet arriving to one or another endpoint, accepts data for output (input at the host's request) and informs of executing this operation. The number and type of the supported endpoint depends on how the SIE is implemented. The most complex in terms of support are endpoints of the control type; for this reason, many USB devices support only one control endpoint: EP0. For each supported endpoint, the SIE has buffer memory allocated, the amount of which must correspond to the maximum packet size declared in the endpoint's descriptor. The SIE block is in charge of all descriptors (they are located in its local memory), relays them to the host upon requests, performs configuration and alternative settings. The SIE also handles all host's requests, both standard and the specific (controlling endpoints, handling suspend and resume operations).

A USB device must support all the states defined in the specification:

□ *Attached*: A device is connected to a hub but the power from the bus is not applied; the device cannot declare its presence in any way, and is not controlled by the host. If the bus power is not used (even for SIE), then this state is absent.

□ *Powered*: A device is connected to a port and power is applied; the device can declare itself by pulling the D+ or D− line by a resistor to the power rail. This is a transitory step to the default state.

□ *Default*: Entered into when a device is initially powered, connected to the bus, or when reset from the bus is received. The device has the zero address (the USB default address) and responds only to the accesses to EP0. Draws only one bus-powered unit.

□ *Addressed*: The device is assigned its unique bus address (1–127) by a `Set_Address`, but responds only to accesses to EP0; draws no more than one power unit off the bus.

❐ *Configured*: A device is configured by a `Set_Configuration` request, responds to accesses to all endpoints described in the given configuration, and can draw the declared current from the bus. If necessary, the interface alternative settings can be modified by a `Set_Interface` request.

❐ *Suspended*: A device is connected, powered (at least minimally), but suspended (no activity at the port to which it is connected). It may be assigned an address and configured prior to being suspended, but the host cannot use this device's functions until a resume operation is executed, which will return the device to the state it had been prior to suspension. If the device has remote wakeup capability and has been enabled by the host, it can generate remote wakeup signals while in the suspend state.

A USB device must be able to be physically connected at full, low, or high speed, depending on the data transfer speed needed and based on technical and economical considerations. Low-speed devices (and their cables) are somewhat cheaper, but it is not advantageous to use them in terms of overall bus efficiency (see *Section 4.1.4*). A high-speed USB port is used only when the device's functional part is efficient enough; equipping a device with it makes the device somewhat more expensive (although, against the background of the cost of the functional part, it is not that important).

As a rule, peripheral USB devices have a built-in microcontroller that is the source and sink of the information sent via the endpoints. The microcontroller must follow the directives from the bus, perform reset and suspend upon signals from the port, and conform to the configuration and interface settings. Requests to control the standard properties (disabling or enabling endpoints, enabling remote wakeup capability) arrive to the controller indirectly: The SIE services them first.

The interface between the SIE and the microcontroller provides data transfer with the necessary control signals. It also transfers interrupts (or other signaling) to the microcontroller upon an event such as packet arrival, buffer release by the transmitting endpoint, timeout triggering (for isochronous endpoints), and unrecoverable protocol errors blocking endpoints.

4.1.8. USB Hubs

A hub is the key Plug-and-Play system element in the USB architecture. A hub performs many functions:

❐ Provides physical connection of devices, generating and sensing signals at each of its ports according to the bus specification, and relaying the traffic from the upstream ports to the downstream ports and vice versa.

❐ Provides controlled informational link of the bus segments, including segments that operate at different speeds. Each downstream port can be selectively enabled or disabled to relay traffic.

❒ Monitors the state of the devices connected to it, informing the host of changes such as device attachment and detachment.

❒ Detects bus errors, carries out the recovery procedure, and isolates faulty bus segments. Thanks to the hubs' watchfulness, a faulty device cannot block the entire bus.

❒ Manages power consumption, supplies power to the downstream ports; selectively generates port suspend signals and relays these signals to various directions (see *Section 4.1.6*).

The structure of a USB 2.0 hub is shown in Fig. 4.11. A hub comprises a set of ports, a hub controller (a USB function connected to an internal port), a repeater, a transaction translator, a port routing logic, and the power supply control circuits. A USB 1.x hub is simpler: It does not have the transaction translator and a downstream port router, which are both connected to the repeater.

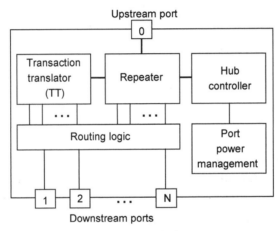

Fig. 4.11. USB 2.0 hub structure

Ports

From the upstream port side, a hub looks like any USB device (see Fig. 4.8, *right*). This port is always powered and enabled; for USB 1.x, it always operates in the full-speed mode, while for USB 2.0, the upstream port always is high-speed, although it can also work in the full-speed mode.

Downstream hub ports have a set of transceivers, shown on the *left* of Fig. 4.8. The host controls the downstream ports and determines their status by sending requests to the hub controller. Each of these ports can determine whether a device is connected to it and, if so, what its operating speed is. A port can be selectively enabled or disabled upon a command from the host; it can also be disabled using hardware.

Using hardware, a port is disabled upon an attach or detach, and also upon an error detected by the hub. A hub ignores signals from the disabled ports and does not relay traffic to them. A reset command can be sent to the port that generates corresponding signaling and device type ascertainment (the device's HS indicator is checked). Also any port can be selectively suspended, after which a resume command with corresponding signaling can be sent to it. In terms of power supply, a port can be powered or not. Power management can be either selective or common for all ports. A port may happen to be not powered because of the current protection mechanism being actuated; moreover, this protection can also be either selective or common for all ports. In the latter case, a port may turn out to be not powered because of another port's overload. An HS port can also have a test command sent to it.

Each downstream port can be in one of states listed below; these states are monitored and controlled by requests to the hub (see *Section 4.1.10*). Transitions from one state to another are initiated by signals from devices (attach, detach, remote wakeup) or by control requests from the host or the hub (when serious errors are detected).

❐ *Not powered.* Port is depowered by either a `Clear_Port_Power` request or by a power supply malfunction (current protection having been actuated or the external power loss). A nonpowered port cannot be used for any interface operations. Only after it is powered can a port recognize a device attach and interact with the device. Power to the port is turned on by the `Set_Port_Power` command.

❐ *Disconnected.* A port is capable only of detecting a device attach. A port switches into this state from any other state when it detects that its device has been disconnected.

❐ *Disabled.* A port has a device connected, but it does not relay traffic and resume signals. A port switches into this state from any other state upon a `Port_Disable` command, upon a reset signal on the upstream port, or if the hub detects a grave error that requires the given port should be isolated.

❐ *Enabled.* A device is connected and can support fully functional data and signal traffic. A port switches into this state from any other (powered) state by a `Port_Reset` command; from the disabled state, a port is switched into the enabled state by a `Set_Port_Enable` command, and from the suspend state by a `Clear_Port_Suspend`.

❐ *Suspended.* A port sends a suspend signal, the traffic is not relayed, and only the resume and device detach signals are accepted from it. The port is switched into this state by the `Set_Port_Suspend` command. It can return to the enabled state upon a remote wakeup signal or a `Clear_Port_Suspend` or `Port_Reset` command.

Hubs can have downstream port state light indicators (a pair of light emitting diodes or one two-colored one) controlled either by the hub's hardware logic or by the host-controller's software. Their signals have the following meanings:

❑ *Not lit:* The port is not being used.
❑ *Green:* The port is functioning properly.
❑ *Yellow:* A connected device error or power overload (port is automatically discon-nected).
❑ *Blinking green:* Software requires user's attention.
❑ *Blinking yellow:* Hardware requires user's attention; for example, a high-power de-vice is connected to a low-power port.

Hub Controller

A hub controller is a program-accessible USB function that the host interacts with to control device configuration and the connections on the bus. Like any other USB de-vice, a hub controller has a set of descriptors describing it (see *Section 4.1.10*). Hubs belong to class 09, subclass 00 devices. In addition to the mandatory zero endpoint, the hub interface has an endpoint of the Interrupt-IN type serving to inform the host about the hub's state change. A hub is controlled in general and its ports in particular by using special requests to EP0 described further. Tables 4.8 and 4.9 give the complete idea about hub's controllability and observability.

Repeater

A hub repeater provides a dynamic link between ports to transfer packets and resume signals. In the bus idle state, all ports operate in the receive mode and await the SOF indicator or a resume signal. Based on these events, a port connection of a certain type is established (Fig. 4.12).

Only enabled ports can transfer packets (the upstream port is always enabled). If an enabled port detects a packet start, then a link is established according to Fig. 4.12, *b* or *c,* and the repeater transfers the packet until it encounters the EOP. Having finished transferring the packet, the repeater again enters the bus idle state. It can be see from the illustrations that the downstream traffic is transmitted using the broadcast method. The upstream traffic is transmitted in such a way that only hubs lo-cated in the chain between the device and the host can see it but not any other devices.

A resume signal is transferred somewhat differently. From an upstream port, a resume signal is transmitted to all downstream ports, except those that are disabled or selectively suspended. A resume signal detected on a downstream enabled port is picked up by the hub and is translated to the upstream port and to all downstream ports (including the port signal source) except those that are disabled or selectively suspended. From a selectively suspended port, a resume signal is picked up by the hub and transmitted only to the same port, after which the hub concludes the resume signaling (LS-EOP) and switches the port into the enabled state.

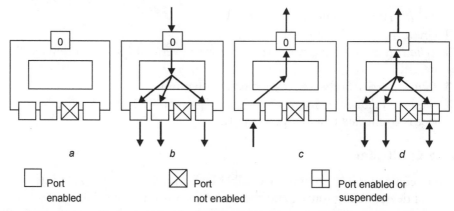

<table>
<tr><td>☐ Port
enabled</td><td>☒ Port
not enabled</td><td>⊞ Port enabled or
suspended</td></tr>
</table>

Fig. 4.12. Connections provided by hub repeater: *a* — bus idle, *b* — relaying a packet from an upstream port, *c* — relaying a packet from a downstream port, *d* — relaying an upstream resume from an enabled port.

Faulty Device Location and Isolation

Hubs ensure USB bus robustness by automatically disabling downstream ports that threaten bus operability. A malfunctioning device connected to a port may become inactive at the wrong time or, on the other hand, generate senseless babble instead of valid data. The hub nearest to the device is on a lookout for this type of situation and disables upcoming transfers from faulty devices no later than at the boundary of a (micro)frame. The hub makes sure that upstream packets do not cross the boundary of a (micro)frame. For this, the hub is equipped with a counter that determines the following instances in (micro)frames (shown in Fig. 4.4):

❏ EOF1: After this moment, a packet from a device cannot start.
❏ EOF2: Since this moment, the hub awaits a start of packet (SOF) only from the upstream port.

During upstream packet transfer (while the repeater is awaiting the EOP), the following special situations are possible:

❏ A start of packet indicator is detected on another enabled port; this is a collision, and the hub can react to the situation in one of two ways:
  • To trash the transaction by sending to the host a constant K or J state instead of the packet body. The Host Controller will understand this situation, although at the cost of losing the other packet.

- To ignore this SOF indicator until the completion of the current packet transfer. Here, the host will not find out about the problem.

❏ The EOP is not detected in the current transfer and the time in the (micro)frame has already approached EOF2: This talkativeness is considered an error in the downstream port, from which the transfer is being made. Upon this error, the hub automatically disables the given port and records this state change. Another reason for automatic disabling of an enabled port is its being in a different than the bus idle state from the EOF2 moment to the end of the (micro)frame.

If the upstream link is established after the EOF1, then the repeater transfers the FS-EOP instead of a frame, so that the upstream hub will not disable the port of the connected hub. If an EOP does not arrive before EOF2 from the downstream port that caused this situation, the port will be automatically disabled.

The repeater inverts signals when transferring packets for LS ports, because they represent J and K signals differently (see *Section 4.1.6*). Moreover, downstream traffic is not transferred to the LS ports until a special PRE packet arrives. After the PRE packet, only one packet is transferred down to the LS port. Instead of SOF tokens, an LS-EOP is sent to the LS port, so that the device will not be suspended.

The repeater is more complex functionally for HS ports, as reclocking is needed. Signal and power line noises affect the receiver's output state transition moment during the rise and fall of the input signal, causing jitter (undesirable phase fluctuations). At low speeds (LS, FS), the jitter is not serious because the signal rise/fall time is significantly shorter than one bit time. At the speed of 480 Mbps, this ratio is different and the jitter accumulated in the chain of repeaters (hubs) will lead to loss of bit synchronization. Reclocking is done with the help of the elasticity buffer; a small FIFO memory area that stores the bit sequence of the transferred signals. The information in the buffer is the bits extracted from the NRZI signal, and comes from the port's receiver at the frequency of the input signal (the frequency is adjusted by the Sync field). From the buffer, the information goes to the transmitters but is now clocked by the internal hub clock generator. Because the frequencies of the input signal and the internal clock generator cannot match perfectly, the rate at which the buffer is filled differs from the rate it is emptied. To compensate for this difference, at the start of the packet reception, its transfer is delayed until half of the buffer fills up; during the transmission of the packet, the filling of the buffer may change. The elasticity buffer introduces its share into the hub's delay. The depth of the buffer is calculated based on the permissible speed difference: Under the specification, the clock frequency must be maintained accurate to $\pm0.05\%$; therefore, the maximum speed discrepancy may reach $\pm0.1\%$. With a maximum length packet (9,644) a discrepancy up to $9,644 \times 0.1\% \approx 10$ bits can be reached; with a little bit to spare, the half-length of the elasticity buffer was set at 12 bits. An analogous technology is employed in high-speed local networks (Fast Ethernet, FDDI).

When going through the hub's repeater, an HS packet can not only lose up to four bits of the beginning part of the sync pattern, but also pick up up to 4 additional bits (dribble bits) after the EOP. This bit acquisition, like the initial loss, is due to the delay introduced by the signal envelope detector of the HS receiver. After going through five hubs, the number of extra bits may reach 20, but it is not a cause for concern: The information receiver will be able to determine the end of packet by the EOP indicator. The maximum packet length of 9,644 bits includes these extra bits.

Transaction Translator

A *transaction translator*, which is part of a USB 2.0 hub, converts bus exchange speeds: the HS on the upstream port side into the FS or LS on the side of the downstream ports to which USB 1.x devices are connected. The translator executes split input/output transactions and translates microframe tokens into FS port frame tokens.

Transactions are split by the host, which knows the current bus topology (what USB 1.x devices or hubs are connected to what ports of what USB 2.0 hubs). Transaction splitting is done in two or three stages, depending on the type and direction of the transfer:

❐ A special Start Split (SS) transaction is executed between the host and the translator. This transaction carries all the information necessary to start the transaction with the target device. At this stage, the translator plays the role of a specifically addressed USB device.

❐ A regular USB 1.0 transaction is executed between the translator and the target device (the hub), in which the translator plays the role of the Host Controller.

❐ A special Complete Split (CS) transaction is executed between the host and the translator, which carries to the host the results of executing the transaction with the target device. Here, the translator plays the role of a specifically addressed USB device. This stage is absent in an isochronous output.

In all of these transactions, the regular silent reaction to the reception of damaged packets and the timeout mechanism are used.

The hub translates each zero microframe token to a full-speed SOF indicator. On the FS/LS side, split transactions are executed inside of these frames. The host schedules a split transaction to start in the zero microframe, so that by the end of the last (seventh) microframe, the split transaction can be completed and data transferred (so as not to accumulate carry forward remainders). Timing relations between the transactions at the both ends of the translator are illustrated in Fig. 4.13.

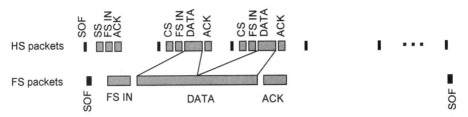

Fig. 4.13. Transaction translation

The general structure of the transaction translator is shown in Fig. 4.14. The HS Handler places the information from the split starts into its buffers, picks out the results from the buffers upon completion requests and sends them as packets to the host. This handler services all regular USB protocol functions, including CRC calculation and checking, sending acknowledgements to the host, etc. Based on the start requests picked up from the buffers, the FS/LS Handler generates regular USB transactions starting with IN, OUT, SETUP tokens (and for LS ports, also with a PRE preamble). The handler places the results of these transactions (data and acknowledgements) into the buffer. The transaction translator has buffers, into which all necessary data about split transactions currently being executed are placed. When a transaction is completed (on both sides), the buffer is cleared for servicing the next split transaction.

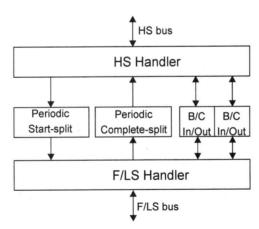

Fig 4.14. Transaction translator structure

Periodic transactions (isochronous and interrupts), for which timing is crucial, are handled by the translator in a pipeline fashion. Split transaction start data are placed into the SS buffer, from where they are picked out by the FS/LS handler (the buffer is of the FIFO type) and are launched as transactions on the secondary bus. The results of these transactions are placed in the CS buffer (also of the FIFO type), from where they are extracted by the host. The host is responsible for the filling and emptying of these buffers, as it schedules SS and CS transactions.

Nonperiodic transactions (control and bulk transfers) are handled differently: The translator has two or more buffers, each of which services one transaction from the beginning till the end. Here, start transactions are acknowledged by the translator: an NAK answer means that a transaction cannot be accepted for execution (no room in the buffers, i.e., the host needs to repeat the start attempt). An ACK response means that the transaction has been accepted for execution and the result should be picked up some time later by performing a completion transaction.

The specification defines the following two versions of translator implementations (which one is being used can be found out from the hub interface protocol code):

❑ Each downstream port has a translator (protocol code 2). This is the most efficient option to increase the bus bandwidth for FS/LS devices.

❑ One translator for all ports (protocol code 1). Here, the potential for increasing the bandwidth depends on the buffer size of the periodic transactions and the number of buffers for nonperiodic transactions.

Specific Hub Descriptors and Requests

USB hubs are standard devices of subclass 00 of class 09. The protocol code defines the transaction translator (for USB 2.0 hubs); it depends on the type, current work speed, and structure of the hub, and can have the following values:

❑ 00: an FS hub or HS hub working in FS (without a transaction translator)
❑ 01: an HS hub with one transaction translator
❑ 02: an HS hub with several transaction translators

The hub maintains these codes in both its device and interface descriptors.

In addition to the standard descriptors, the hub has a special hub class descriptor.

The hub has only one interface, in which only one endpoint (besides the zero endpoint) of the Interrupt-IN type — Status Change Endpoint — is employed for polling the status change of the ports with the maximum possible polling period (bInterval = FFh). From this endpoint, the host receives information as a bit map whose size in bytes depends on how many ports the hub has. The least significant bit of the map (bit 0) carries the hub's status change indicator (1 = changed), bit 1 carries the status change of port one, bit 2 carries the status change of port two and so on. Usually, these are one-byte messages, because more than 7-port hubs are seldom encountered. If there has been no change in the status of the ports, the hub answers the polling with an NAK (sends no data). When there has been a change in the hub status indicator bit, the host executes a hub status read operation, GetHubStatus. When there has been a change in the port status indicator, the host executes a port status read operation for this port: GetPortStatus.

The hub supports all standard requests to devices, with the exception of the interface control request (there is only one such command) and the time marker (a hub has no isochronous points). Moreover, a hub must support all hub class requests.

The special class requests GetHubStatus and GetPortStatus (wLength=4) are used to query the status of a hub and of each of its downstream ports. The GetHubStatus request returns a wHubStatus word followed by a wHubChange word. In the GetPortStatus request, the wIndex word indicates the port's number. This request returns a wPortStatus word, followed by a wPortChange word. The formats of these words are given in Table 4.8.

Table 4.8. Hub and Port Status and Status Change Word Formats

Bit	Field name	Function
Hub status word wHubStatus		
0	Hub_Local_Power	Indicates the state of the hub's power local source: 0 — local power supply normal, 1— local power supply lost.
1	Hub_Over_Current	Current overload (only for hubs with common current protection for all ports): 1 — protection was activated, 0 — otherwise.
[2:15]	Reserved	(0)
Hub status change word wHubChange		
0	C_Hub_Local_Power	Local power supply status change indicator: 1 — local power status has changed, 0 — there has been no change.
1	C_Hub_Over_Current	Common overload status change indicator: 1 — there has been a change, 0 — there has been no change.
[2:15]	Reserved	(0)
Port status word wPortStatus		
0	Port_Connection	Current port connection status: 1 — a device is connected, 0 — no device is connected.
1	Port_Enable	Current port enable status: 0 — disabled, 1 — enabled. Software set only by the host; reset by software or by hardware on a device error.

continues

Table 4.8 Continued

Bit	Field name	Function
Port status word wPortStatus		
2	Port_Suspend	Port suspend state: 0 — not suspended, 1 — suspended or in the process of resuming. Software set only; reset by software or by a remote wakeup signal from this port.
3	Port_Over_Current	Port current overload (only with selective port protection): 1 — protection was activated, 0 — otherwise.
4	Port_Reset	Port reset: 1— Reset signal is activated, 0 — reset signal is not activated. Software set; hardware reset by the hub after completion of the signalling.
[5:7]	Reserved	(0)
8	Port_Power	Port power supply status (reflects the actual situation only when the power supply is selectively controlled): 0 — port is not powered; 1 — port is not selectively depowered.
9	Port_Low_Speed	Low-speed indicator: 1 — LS device attached to the port; 0 — HS or FS device attached to this port (determined by bit 10).
10	Port_High_Speed	High-speed indicator: 1 — high speed has been negotiated with the device; 0 — no high speed has been negotiated with the device.
11	Port_Test	Port testing status: 1 — port is in the testing mode; 0 — port is not in the testing mode. (Software set.)
12	Port_Indicator	Port indicator control: 0 — hardware controlled; 1 — software controlled.
[13:15]	Reserved	(0)
Port status change word wPortChange		
0	C_Port_Connection	Device connect status change: 1 — no change to current status has occurred; 0 — current status has changed.
1	C_Port_Enable	Port enable status change. Set to one when port has been automatically disabled because of a detected error.
2	C_Port_Suspend	Device suspend status change. Set to one when resume operation is complete.

continues

Table 4.8 Continued

Bit	Field name	Function
Port status change word wPortChange		
3	C_Port_Over_Current	Selective port over-current protection status change: 1 — status has changed; 0 — status has not changed (or no selective protection).
4	C_Port_Reset	Port reset status change: 0 — no change has occurred; 1 — reset completed
[5:15]	Reserved	(0)

Setting a hub or port feature with a SetHubFeature or SetPortFeature command, respectively, enables that particular hub or port feature. The features are disabled using the ClearHubFeature and ClearPortFeature commands. The hub and port features are given in Table 4.9.

Table 4.9. Controlling Hub and Port Features

Feature	Number (wValue)	Enable	Disable
Hub feature		SetHubFeature	ClearHubFeature
C_Hub_Local_Power	0	Setting (for diagnostics purposes) of the same name indicator in the hub status change word.	Clearing the same name indicator in the hub status change indicator (acknowledgement that the host has received it).
C_Hub_Over_Current	1	As above.	As above.
Port feature		SetPortFeature.	ClearPortFeature.
Port_Connection	0	Not used; no operations performed by the hub.	
Port_Enable	1	Switching a powered port into the Enabled state.	Switching a port into the Disabled state.
Port_Suspend	2	Port suspend.	Resuming a suspended port.
Port_Over_Current	3	Not used; no operations performed by the hub.	
Port_Reset	4	Reset and switching a powered port into the Enabled state.	Not used; no operations performed by the hub.

continues

Table 4.9 Continued

Feature	Number (wValue)	Enable	Disable
Port_Power	8	Powering port.	Depowering port.
Port_Low_Speed	9	Not used; no operations performed by the hub.	
C_Port_Connection	16	Not allowed.	Clearing the same name indicator in the port status change indicator (acknowledgement that the host has received it).
C_Port_Enable	17	Not allowed.	As above.
C_Port_Suspend	18	Not allowed.	As above.
C_Port_Over_Current	19	Not allowed.	As above.
C_Port_Reset	20	Not allowed.	As above.
Port_Test	21	Switching the port into the test mode (only for the ports in the Disabled, Disconnected, or Suspended mode)	Absent. The testing mode is exited only by resetting hub.
Port_Indicator	22	Software control of the port indicator.	Disabling software control of the port indicator.

The port number is set in the wIndex field of the least significant byte of the testing mode set request; in the most significant byte, the selector determining the test to be executed is set (see *Section 4.1.6*).

In the indicator control setting request, the port number is set in the wIndex field of the least significant byte; in the most significant byte, the selector defining the indicator mode is set: 0 — indicator operates automatically, 1 — forced amber, 2 — forced green, 3 — forcibly turned off, 4=FFh — reserved.

A hub with the protocol type 1 or 2 has transaction translator control requests, which are generally used for debugging purposes. They are as follows:

❐ GetTTState: querying translator's status (for diagnostics).
❐ StopTT: halting translator (if there are several translators, then the particular port's translator).

❐ ResetTT: resetting translator to the initial state (if there are several translators, then the particular port's translator).

❐ ClearTTBuffer: clearing the nonperiodic transaction buffer. The device, endpoint, and hub port address are indicated (if there is only one translator for all ports, then port 1 is indicated).

4.1.9. Host

Each USB must have one (and only one) host: a computer with a USB controller. The host is divided into three main levels:

❐ *USB bus interface* provides physical interface and bus protocol. The bus interface is implemented by the Host Controller, which has a built-in root hub that provides physical bus connection points (series A USB receptacles). The host computer is responsible for generation of (micro)frames. On the hardware level, the Host Controller exchanges information with the main memory using bus mastering in order to minimize the load on the central processor.

❐ *USB system* using Host Controllers translates the client's model of data exchange with devices — I/O request packets (IRP) — into transactions that are carried out with the actual bus devices. The system is responsible for allocation of USB resourses, such as the bandwidth and the power supply (for bus-powered devices). The system consists of three main parts:

  ● *Host Controller Driver* (HCD) is a module associated with a specific controller model that abstracts the USB driver and allows different type controllers to be in integrated into one system.

  ● *USB Driver* provides the main interface between clients and USB devices. The Host Controller Driver Interface (HCDI) between the USBD and HCD is not regulated by the USB specification. It is defined by the developers of operating systems, and must be supported by developers of Host Controllers if they want their devices to be supported by specific operating systems. Clients cannot use the HCD interface; they have to use the USBD interface. The USBD provides the exchange mechanism in the form of I/O Request Packets (IRP) that are comprised of requests to transport data over the specified channel. Additionally, the USBD abstracts the device to the USB client to a certain extent, which makes it possible to configure the device and to control its status (including standard control through the zero endpoint). Specific USBD interface implementation is defined by the operating system; the USB specification only presents general concepts.

  ● *Host software* implements the functions necessary for the USB system operation as a whole: detecting device attach and detach and taking corresponding steps upon these events (loading proper drivers), device enumeration, allocating bandwidth and power resources, etc.

❏ *USB clients* are software elements (applications or system components) that interact with the USB devices. Clients can interact with any device (or sets of the available endpoints that belong to the selected interfaces) that is connected to the USB system. However, the USB system isolates clients from direct exchange with any ports (in the I/O space) or memory cells that represent the interface part of the USB controller.

All of the combined host's levels have the following capabilities:

❏ Detecting USB device attach and detach
❏ Manipulating control streams between devices and the host
❏ Manipulating data streams
❏ Collecting statistics of device activity and status
❏ Controlling electrical interface between the Host Controller and USB devices, including control of the power supply

The full scope of the software part of the host is implemented by the operating system. Until the operating system has been loaded, only a truncated portion of the USB software can function, supporting only the devices needed for loading the operating system. Thus, modern motherboards' BIOS supports a USB keyboard using the functions of the Int 9h service. After the whole USB system has been loaded, this preload support is ignored: The system begins to work with the controller from the scratch (i.e., resets and reinitializes all connected devices). After the operating system terminates its work, the state of the USB system is not handed back to the preload support; therefore, operating system termination is considered as an initial turning on by the USB preload support. The PC 2001 specification requires USB BIOS support to the extent that an operating system can be loaded from USB devices.

The Host Controller is a hardware intermediary between USB devices and the host. Currently, there are three specifications for Host Controllers, each of which has its own set of drivers for the host part:

❏ Universal Host Controller (UHC): USB 1.x controller developed by Intel
❏ Open Host Controller (OHC): USB 1.x controller developed by Compaq, Microsoft, and National Semiconductor
❏ Enhanced Host Controller (EHC): controller providing support for the USB 2.0 bus high-speed mode

All these controller versions accomplish the same task — carrying out physical transactions with devices over USB according to the descriptors of these transactions that are placed into the system main memory by the Host Controller driver. Moreover, different transaction types are serviced differently. In terms of error handling, isochronous transactions are the simplest because their errors do not require transaction to be repeated. In case of errors, transactions of guaranteed delivery transfers require to be repeated until successful termination or until defeat is admitted. In terms of scheduling, periodic transactions have to be executed strictly on schedule; all other transactions are executed as the schedule allows, and are placed into queues. Because of the peculiarities in the scheduling and possible transaction repeats, the order in which transaction descriptors are serviced is different from that in which they are placed into the memory, which adds more work to the Host Controller and its driver. Each of the three versions of the Host Controller solves these tasks in its own way, and uses different transaction scheduling strategies, as illustrated in Fig. 4.15.

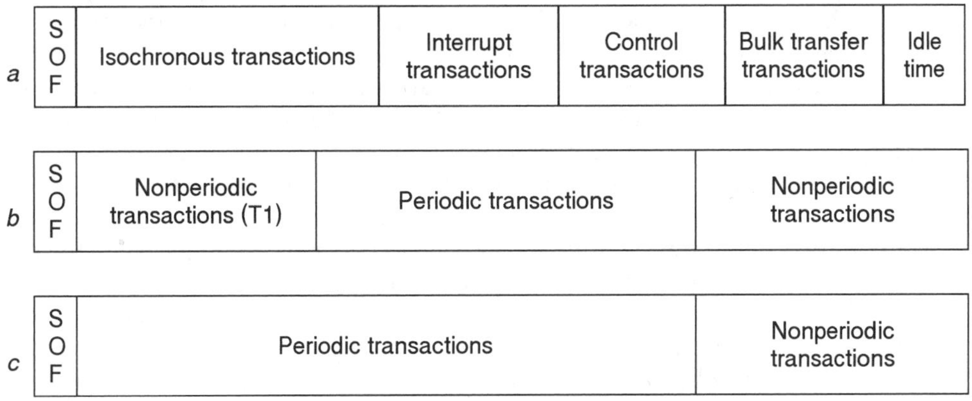

	S O F	Isochronous transactions	Interrupt transactions	Control transactions	Bulk transfer transactions	Idle time
a						

	S O F	Nonperiodic transactions (T1)	Periodic transactions	Nonperiodic transactions
b				

	S O F	Periodic transactions	Nonperiodic transactions
c			

Fig. 4.15. Time division in a frame: *a* — UHC, *b* — OHC, *c* — EHC (in a microframe)

Universal Host Controller: UHC

The Intel UHC made its appearance in the PIIX3 microchip (a PCI-ISA bridge) of the chipsets for the Pentium motherboards, and has been used in many successive Intel products. It is an FS/LS Host Controller that delegates the greater share of the transaction planning work to the software (i.e., the UCH driver). The UHC controller interface is described in the Universal Host Controller Interface (UHCI) Design Guide, version 1.1 of which came out in 1996.

The UHC driver builds descriptors for the host-controller, which are called *transfer descriptors* (TD) in UHCI; however, the name is deceptive, for they actually describe each bus transaction. In USB terms, one transfer can consist of several transactions, while the control transfers use an additional transaction type of their own for each phase (see *Section 4.1.3*). For all guaranteed delivery transfer transactions, the transaction descriptors have to be organized in queues. These transfers need queues, because it is not known in advance how many times they will have to be repeated.

The queue can be advanced only upon successful completion of the transaction at the head of the queue: This rule provides guaranteed packet deliver sequence. Each queue has its header (QH). Isochronous transfers are always executed just once, which makes their scheduling easier. The driver places the transaction descriptors and queue headers into the memory, and links them according to the transaction execution schedule in each frame. The UHC driver has to compose a detailed schedule for each frame to be transferred, for which a 1,204-frame Frame List is used.

The Host Controller makes rounds of the descriptor lists, starting from the point indicated by the Frame List for the current frame, and carries out the corresponding transactions. The results of executing a transaction are placed into its descriptor, the executed transaction is marked as inactive and, in its next round, the controller simply skips it and goes to the following transaction. The driver must periodically examine the descriptors, extract the already executed descriptor, and hand the execution results to the client's driver. The controller's logic presupposes that each queue corresponds to one I/O request (IRP) from the client's driver. The UHC driver breaks a request into transactions, places the descriptors for these transactions into the corresponding queue, and then includes the queue in the nearest schedule. The driver is responsible for the balanced bus loading in each frame, and in particular for guaranteeing no less than 10% of the bandwidth for the control transfer transaction. The necessary access frequency to the periodic transfer points is also provided by transaction scheduling.

The UHC is an active PCI device (Bus Master). The main interaction of the driver with the Host Controller is carried out with the help of the descriptors located in the memory. The controller has registers (in the I/O space), using which its behavior can be handled: to perform a reset, global suspend, and wakeup, to adjust frame frequency, to control interrupt requests, and to control the ports of the built-in root hub. The controller allows debugging mode operation, halting after executing each transaction.

In the process of executing the scheduled transaction, the controller reads the descriptors and data necessary to start the transaction from the memory. As soon as enough information to start a transaction arrives from the memory to the controller's FIFO buffer, the controller starts a transaction on the USB bus. In the process of executing it, the necessary data exchanges with the memory are executed; after completing the transaction, the controller modifies the descriptors in the memory according to the conditions of the transaction completion. During a transaction, FIFO buffer overflow or underflow errors may arise, caused by an overload of the system memory controller or the PCI bus. These severe errors generate hardware interrupts.

Interrupts from the UHC can be caused by various events, such as execution of selected transactions, detection of an undersize packet, reception of a resume signal, or errors. The controller does not generate interrupts upon device attach or detach.

The UHC provides special support of the traditional keyboard and mouse interfaces via the 8042 controller, by interrupting accesses to ports 60h and 64h. When old software accesses these ports, the UHC calls the System Management Interrupt (SMI), which in x86 PCs is handled transparently for the usual programs. The SMI handler, which intercepts these accesses, generates a sequence of actions necessary to execute these accesses with the help of a USB keyboard and/or mouse. The only exception is made for the command that controls GateA20 — instead of generating a SMI, this gate is manipulated by hardware (as has been done in 8042 for a long time). This hardware support is enabled by corresponding options in the SMOS Setup.

A great inconvenience when working with UHC is created by the necessity to examine by software all the transfer descriptors to separate the already completed transfers. Their descriptors have to be extracted from the chains by software, maintaining the interconnection of the entries. Transaction scheduling (composing lists of descriptors and headers) is also a rather labor-intensive task for the processor. Obviously, the aim of simplification of the Host Controller hardware was pursued in its design. However, this can turn into the efficiency of the USB being dependent on how powerful and loaded the central processor is. This approach to organizing input and output can hardly be considered "intelligent."

Open Host Controller: OHC

The specification for the Open Host Controller Interface (OHCI) was developed by Compaq, Microsoft, and National Semiconductor, and published in the Open Host Controller Interface Specification for USB, version 1.0a of which was released in 1999. The OH controller, like the UH controller, is intended to support full and low speeds. However, the hardware facilities of the OHC take upon themselves the larger part of the scheduling task, removing the central processor of the load of the constant descriptor handling routine. The OHC works with the endpoint and transfer descriptors.

Endpoint Descriptors (ED) are created for all configured endpoints of the attached devices. These descriptors are placed into the memory and are interconnected; the configuration of the interconnections sets the order, in which they are serviced by the Host Controller. An endpoint descriptor describes its full address and direction, type, allowed packet size, speed, the status of the endpoint and the descriptor, pointers to the transfer queues linked with the given endpoint, and the pointer to the descriptor of the next endpoint. Separate chains of endpoint descriptors are created for all control and bulk transfer endpoints; special registers of the OHC point to the beginning of these chains. The endpoints of periodic transfers are organized into a binary tree (Fig. 4.16), in whose branches the interrupt point descriptors are located; the descriptors of the interrupt points with the minimal servicing interval and all isochronous transfer descriptors are located in the trunk of the tree. The tree has 32 end branches; it is parsed from the end branches toward the trunk. In each of the 32 adjacent frames, the entrance is made from its own branch. For this purpose, the OHC has a Host Controller communication area (HCCA) *base address register,* which points to the zero branch, and a frame counter, the lower five bits of which set the entrance branch for the next frame. Thus, the descriptor handler goes over each branch of the fifth level once every 32 frames ($T=32$ msec), of the fourth level once every 16 frames ($T=16$ msec), of the third level once every eight frames ($T=8$ msec), of the second level once every four frames ($T=4$ msec), and of the first level once every two frames ($T=2$ msec); for the zero level (the trunk), $T=1$ msec.

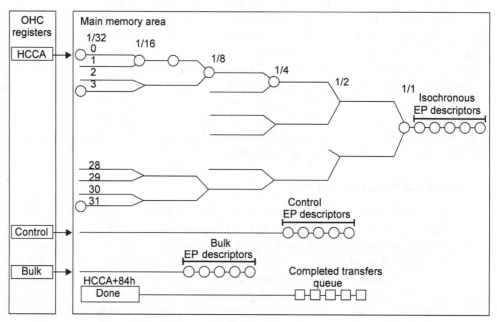

Fig. 4.16. OHC endpoint descriptor link configurations

The *UHC Transfer Descriptors* actually describe USB transfers. Each transfer can be broken into several transactions by the Host Controller, based on the packet size set in the endpoint descriptor. The transfer data buffer can be located on one or two physical memory pages, which can be disjointed. In the virtual logical address space, the buffer must be a contiguous area. The transfer size can reach up to eight kilobytes, but if the buffer does not begin from the start of the page, then the maximum transfer size decreases (down to 4,097 bytes in the worst case). Transfer descriptors are organized into queues, which are attached to the endpoint descriptors.

The *OHC* has timers, using which it schedules transactions in a frame as shown in Fig. 4.15. After an SOF indicator, the controller begins sequential examining of the chain of the control transfer endpoint descriptors, and executes as many of them as it manages within T1 time. Then it begins examining the periodic transfer tree, starting with the nth end branch and going towards the trunk until it passes through all endpoint descriptors on its way. If it still has time remaining in the frame, it goes back to the non-periodic transfers (*Bulk and Control*). The controller gathers the descriptors that it has already serviced into a special Done Queue, from which they can be easily extracted by the driver. Upon completion of processing a transfer descriptor, the controller can generate or not generate an interrupt; in the former case, it can do this with a delay specified for each transfer descriptor.

The OHC has a register for adjusting frame frequency. A root hub with two or more ports is a part of the controller.

The OHC, like the UHC, is a PCI Bus Master device; but compared with the UHC, it is more intelligent.

Enhanced Host Controller: EHC

The Enhanced Host Controller was introduced by Intel to provide high-speed support in USB 2.0. Its interface is described in the Enhanced Host Controller Interface Specification for Universal Serial Bus, version 1.0 of which was published in 2002. The EHC controller is designed to work only with high-speed connections to the root hub; the EHC works with FS/LS speed devices connected via an intermediate USB 2.0 hub by using split transactions (see *Section 4.1.8*). Those ports of the root hub, to which USB 1.x hubs and devices are connected directly, are serviced by a companion-controller (UHC or OHC). Ports and controllers are switched by routing logic that is a part of the USB 2.0 root hub. Detecting device attach to the root hub is done by the EHC driver using its registers. Having detected an FS/LS device attach, the driver switches the given port to the companion controller, and from this moment, the port is run by the companion controller and its driver. The companion controller and its driver may even not know that they are a part of the USB controller team. For the ports that remain in charge of the OHC, an external hub is emulated: The software manipulates ports using standard requests to the USB hubs.

The EHC has the PCI configuration register and the memory-mapped operational I/O registers and uses the system memory to interact with the driver.

In terms of interaction with the driver, the EHC partially resembles the UHC, but the high transfer speed (480 Mbps) requires the controller's intellect to be boosted in order to decrease the number of the exchanges between the driver, the memory, and the controller. Many OHC concepts can be seen in the EHC. Data structures are designed so as to minimize memory accesses. All structures must be located in the memory in such a way so as not to cross the 4-KB memory page boundaries: This makes it possible to optimize OHC coexistence with the virtual memory, which is based on page readdressing of the x86 processors.

In terms of transaction scheduling, transfers in the EHCI are divided into periodic (isochronous and interrupts) and asynchronous (control and bulk transfers). Each of these scheduling types is implemented in its own way, and can be turned on to work and turned off. The controller starts each microframe by executing periodic transfers (if they are enabled); the time left over after the periodic transfers is given to executing asynchronous transfers (analogous to the UHC; Fig. 4.15, *a*). The driver is responsible for ensuring that time for asynchronous transfers is left in the microframe. The Host Controller's hardware only watches that the transactions do not cross the microframe boundary: If the controller sees that the transaction may not terminate by the EOF1 moment, it will not start it. The controller may even take some extra insurance here, as it does not know exactly how long it will take it to execute a transaction (it does not know how many bits it will have to stuff or what the delays in the cables, hubs, and devices are).

For all guaranteed delivery transfers (interrupt, control, and bulk transfers), Queue Element Transfer Descriptors (qTD) are used. They describe buffer queues that provide automatic ordering of the executions of the transfer streams. In EHC, a "transfer" is a sequence of same type transactions; only the total size of the transferred blocks is limited (to 20 KB). A host control transfer is scheduled as a sequence of two or three EHC transfers. The driver can dynamically add new transfers to the queue (during execution of the schedule). Using hardware, the controller supports the end of block signaling by short packets: Having received a short packet, the controller may switch to the alternative transfer sequence for the given queue (a conditional jump is made). Special data structures are used for isochronous transfers: Isochronous Transaction Descriptors (iTD) for HS and Split-Transaction Isochronous Transfer Descriptors (siTD) for splitting transactions for FS devices. For HS, isochronous transfers the descriptor can describe a transaction of up to 24 KB of data; for FS, the length is up to 1,023 bytes.

The basis of the *periodic transaction scheduling* is the *Frame List* for 1,024, 512, or 256 entries. The base address and list length are set by software; the current list item is selected by the frame counter. The schedule begins executing in each microframe; accordingly, each current item in the list is selected eight times consecutively, after which the controller moves on to the next item. A list item may point to an iTD, siTD, or to the head of the interrupt queue (QH). Besides, it can point to the special Frame Span Traversal Nodes (FSTN) structures that are used to provide proper servicing of split transactions near the frame boundary. In addition to the pointer itself, a list item contains the identifier (Typ) of the type of the structure that the pointer references (iTD, siTD, QH, or FSTN), as well as terminator mark T. All isochronous transfer descriptors and queue headers have a horizontal pointer to the next structure; in this pointer, the type of this structure (Typ), as well as the terminator mark T, are given. The chain of the descriptors and queue headers, beginning with the frame list, must terminate with a descriptor (or a header) that has the terminator T set. Only after it has completed servicing this descriptor (or the header) does the controller starts executing the asynchronous transfer schedule. To simplify split transaction scheduling (they must not cross frame boundaries), the controller performs a phase shift between the bus frames (B-Frame), which the hubs and devices can see by the frame number change in the SOF marker, and the host frames (H-Frame) with which the driver operates when building schedules, and using which periodic transactions are selected from the frame list. The bus frames lag one microframe behind the host frames. A more detailed description (but not the motives) is given in the EHCI specification. For servicing split periodic transactions, there is a special FSTN structure that contains a pair of pointers: a regular pointer, which provides transition to the next structure (iTD, siTD, QH, or FSTN), and a reverse pointer, which can only point to the queue header. The nuances of split transaction scheduling will not be given here; they can be found in the EHCI specification.

The basis of the *nonperiodic transaction scheduling* is the *Asynchronous List*, which is a ring made up out of queue headers. In the OHC, the AsyncListAddr register points to the current list entry; the controller sets about processing this entry after completing processing the periodic transfers in the given microframe (or right away, if periodic transactions are disabled or absent). Further, as the controller is processing the queues, it enters the addresses of the next pointers into this register. Thus, all asynchronous queues are serviced in circle, without attachment to specific frames or microframes.

The *iTD descriptor* describes an isochronous transfer, which can be executed in 1–8 phases (microframes in which the given descriptor is accessed). Each phase in the descriptor has a transaction record that controls the execution and reflects the status of the transaction (activity, execution errors, whether an interrupt needs to be generated after execution, the real length) and contains a pointer to the data buffer. Each phase can be executed in 1–3 microframe transactions (the endpoint may be high-bandwidth). The descriptor also contains the endpoint description: the address of the device and the endpoint, direction, and packet size. The controller forms the transaction based on the indicated packet size. Data buffers can be located in different physical memory pages, but logically they have to be a contiguous virtual memory area. For storing data (maximum eight phases of three transactions of 1,024 bytes: 24,576 bytes), up to seven 4-KB pages may be needed; all these pages have corresponding pointers in the descriptor.

The *siTD descriptor* describes one split transaction. The address part contains the number and direction of the endpoint, device address, and also the address and number of the hub port that carries out the transfer of the given transaction. The descriptor has μFrame_S-mask and μFrame_C-mask bit mask fields that determine, in which microframes of the given frame the SS and CS transactions, respectively, are to be executed (see *Section 4.1.8*). In the descriptor, the controller marks off the microframes, in which the CS transactions have actually been executed. The descriptor has a regular set of fields that controls the execution and reflects the status of the transaction (activity, execution errors, whether an interrupt needs to be generated after execution, real length). Additionally, the siTD has specific fields that control the current phase

(SS or CS), as well as an indicator of the specific split transaction error: a skipping of the microframe, in which the next CS transaction has to be executed. This skipping may occur if the controller does not issue the current transaction because of time shortage in the microframe. The block of transferred data (up to 1,023 bytes) may be located in one or two physical memory pages, and there are the necessary pointers for them in the descriptor. The siTD has a specific element: a Back Pointer to the siTD of the previous frame, which is used when planning IN transactions that terminate close to the frame boundary.

A *descriptor that is an entry of the qTD queue* describes one transfer up to 20,480 bytes in size. The descriptor is linked to its queue header; it contains a pair of pointers to the next entries of the given queue:

❐ The main pointer refers to the descriptor of the next transfer that has to be executed after the current transfer has normally terminated.
❐ The alternative pointer refers to the descriptor of the transfer that has to be executed if the current transfer is terminated by a short packet.

The descriptor has a regular set of fields that control and reflect the status of the transaction: the activity, execution errors, whether an interrupt needs to be generated after execution, the marker used (IN, OUT, or SETUP). The total length of the transfer is shown in the descriptor. The buffer for the data to be transferred has to be located in a contiguous virtual memory area; the maximum transfer length buffer is described by an array of five physical memory pointers.

A *queue head* (QH) is created for each configured non-isochronous endpoint of each USB device. Queue heads of nonperiodic endpoints are interconnected horizontally into a ring, for which each head has a corresponding pointer. A queue head carries an exhaustive description of the endpoint: its number and direction, the maximum packet length, number of packets in a microframe (for high bandwidth endpoints), the device address and its speed. For FS/LS devices, it also contains information for executing split transactions: the numbers of the hub and port that splits transactions, and microframe masks for SS and CS transactions. The queue head has an overlay area into which the controller places the qTD fields of the current transaction.

The EHC controller generates interrupts for different event categories that can be selectively masked:

❐ Upon completion of the transmission whose descriptor has a corresponding marker, and also upon receiving a short ending packet. These interrupts can be delayed until a certain programmed time threshold, which allows the ECH interrupt frequency to be lowered. Without the delay, the interrupt request frequency may reach the frequency of microframes; with the delay, they cannot be generated more often than the time threshold value.

❏ Upon a Host Controller event: a frame list cycle, status change or overload of the hub's ports, special enabling of the queue header sequence change by software, system connection error (the FIFO buffer overflow or underflow due to the PCI bus' being busy).

Placing transfers into queues, like including isochronous transfers into the schedule, as well as adding and deleting queues, can be done by the driver dynamically in the process of the Host Controller's operation. However, in order to preserve the integrity and coherence of the structures, the software must observe certain interaction rules so as not to try to change the structures that at the current moment are being processed by the controller. To implement this synchronization, the controller uses special indicator bits in its status register and in the data structures. To find the processed transfers, the driver has to examine the activity indicators in all transfer descriptors. The EHC does not provide the service of queueing executed transfers like the OHC does. But in comparison with the UHC, the EHC driver, of course, has less work to do, because it works with transfers, not transactions. However, an additional, quite difficult task of split transaction planning has been added to the EHC driver workload.

USB with No PC: On-The-Go Extension

The USB protocol is oriented at exclusively subordinate relationship: All transactions with all connected devices are controlled by the host — as a rule, a computer (a PC) with a USB controller. There can be no equality of any kind on the USB; however, it is desirable to be able to manage without a computer in some cases. For example, it would be convenient to connect a digital camera to a photo printer directly, to be able to print photographs without a PC. Practically all USB devices have built-in microcontrollers, and the functional capabilities of these controllers are growing steadily. A peripheral device equipped with at least the most primitive means of conducting a dialog with the user (at least a one-line display and a few control buttons) is quite capable of taking upon itself the control functions in terms of organizing USB transactions. The task of this mini-host can be simplified if implementing a point-to-point connection of two devices without intermediate hubs. In this case, the host has to only identify one connected device and, if it knows how the device can be used, to configure it. The task of transaction planning with one device is much simpler than the general task of the full-scale host and its controller. Creating this type of simplified links of a pair of devices is exactly what the On-The-Go USB extension is aimed at.

The On-The-Go Supplement to USB 2.0 (version 1.0a of which came out in June 2003) defines supplements to USB 2.0 necessary to implement field linking of two devices. The most part of the specification is devoted to describing connectors, and OTG terminology is also tied to the connector types (simply, the user sees connectors on the devices and just tries to connect using available cables). The OTG divides devices into the following groups:

❏ A-Device: a device into whose socket a *Standard-A* (or Mini-A) plug is inserted. This device supplies power (V_{bus}) to the bus and plays the role of the host, at least at first after connecting to the other device. In the course of the communications session, the A-device may hand over the host functions to its partner and itself become a peripheral device (in USB terminology).

❏ B-Device: a device into whose socket a Standard-B (or Mini-B) plug is inserted. When connected to another device, a B-Device plays the role of a peripheral (slave) USB device. If this is a dual-role device, then in the course of the communications session the host functions can be handed over to it.

❏ Dual-role device: a device with a sole Mini-AB receptacle that supplies no less than 8 mA current to the bus and supports FS (can additionally support HS, and as a peripheral device can also support LS). This device has reduced host capabilities, a list of supported peripheral devices, and the means of conducting a dialog with the user. For controlling communications, the device supports just the Session Request Protocol (SRP) and the Host Negotiation Protocol (HNP).

A dual-role device may also support hubs (this complicates its tasks); however, standard USB hubs do not allow operation of the SRP and HNP protocols.

In the main USB specification, there are thee connector types (plugs and sockets): standard four-contact A and B (shown in Fig. 4.1) and a five-contact Mini-B connector. Here, cables with a Standard-A plug on one end and a Standard-B (Mini-B) at the other end can be used as well as soldered into devices cables with a Standard-A plug on the other end. The OTG introduces five-contact Mini-A plugs and a universal five-contact Mini-AB receptacle (Fig. 4.17). Inside the Mini-A plug, contacts 4 and 5 are electrically connected; in the Mini-B plug, contact 4 is unattached. Color coding is used to make distinguishing different type connectors easier: Mini-A connectors must be white, Mini-B connectors must be black, and Mini-AB receptacles must be gray.

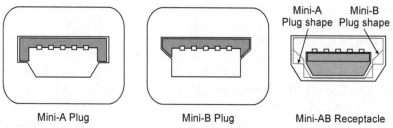

Mini-A Plug   Mini-B Plug   Mini-AB Receptacle

Fig. 4.17. New OTG connectors: *a* — Mini-A plug, *b* — Mini-AB receptacle

Both Mini-A or Mini-B plugs can be inserted into the Mini-AB receptacle of a dual-role device. Contact 4 (ID) is used for identifying the connected device.

❑ If contact 4 (ID) is connected to the GND line (resistance < 10 ohm), then a Mini-A plug is inserted meaning that a B-Device is connected; consequently, the dual-role device must become the host.

❑ If contract 4 (ID) is not connected to the GND line (resistance >10 ohm), then a Mini-B plug is inserted meaning that an A-Device is connected; consequently, the dual-role device must become the peripheral device.

The Session Request Protocol (SRP) is designed to provide additional power savings: when an A-Device does not need to conduct bus exchange, it can remove the V_{bus} power. But when this happens, the B-Device can still request attention (i.e., request a communications session). Here, a session is called a time interval, during which a dual-role device supplies the power needed for work. A request can be executed by sending positive pulses either over the V_{bus} line or over the signal lines (D+ or D–). A B-Device must use both methods of issuing the request; an A-Device can recognize any of them (whichever is more convenient for its developer).

The Host Negotiation Protocol (HNP) allows an A-Device and a B-Device to switch roles during the communications session (if they are both dual-role devices). The protocol can only be initiated if the A-Device sends a special enabling request to the B-Device, having ascertained prior to it that the B-Device does support the HNP protocol. Support capability for the HNP and SRP protocols is communicated by the B-Device in the special descriptor of an OTG device.

The B-Device can request bus control (to become the host for a while) when the A-Device ceases activity (places the bus into the idle state). For this, the B-Device disconnects from the bus by disconnecting its pull up resistor from the D+ line. The A-Device considers this as role change request, and connects its pull up resistor to the D+ line. Now, the B-Device can begin transactions having control over the bus. When it wants to relinquish bus control, it ceases the activity and connects its pull up resistor to the D+ line. The A-Device considers this as the return of control, and disconnects its pull up resistor form the D+ line: The initial roles determined by the connector type are restored.

The OTG descriptor (length 3, type 9) must be present in all configuration of the OTG device; it is read out by a regular Get_Descriptor request. The OTG descriptor contains only one attribute byte, in which bit 0 indicates SRP support and bit 1 indicates HNP support (the rest of the bits have zero values).

Having ascertained that the HNP protocol is supported, the A-Device must indicate its relation to the HNP before the configuration of the B-Device is selected.

This is done by the Set_Feature requests (bmRequestType=00000000b to the device, bRequest=3):

❏ By a Set b_hnp_enable (wValue=3) request, the A-Device enables the B-Device to request the host role.
❏ By a Set a_hnp_support (wValue=4) request, the A-Device only informs the B-Device that it is connected to a port that supports HNP and that the host role request can be enabled later.
❏ By a Set a_alt_hnp_support (wValue=5) request, the A-Device informs the B-Device that it is connected to a port that does not support HNP, but that the A-Device has another port that does support HNP.

4.1.10. Device Configuration and Control

USB supports dynamic configuration by monitoring device attach and detach. It allows the attached devices to be identified, their resource needs (bandwidth and bus power supply) determined, correct configuration selected, and devices controlled; all of this provides full Plug-and-Play support. For these purposes, the rules for connected device behavior, a descriptor system, and standard control requests to devices are defined. The key role in the Plug-and-Play system is played by hubs, which allow the work of devices connected to them to be selectively controlled, which is needed during the configuration stage. In the process of bus operation, the device enumeration process is constantly performed, monitoring changes in the physical topology.

Automatic Configuration

All devices are connected via hub ports. Hubs detect device attach and detach to their ports (see *Section 4.1.9*) and inform of their port status upon a request from the controller. The host performs a reset by a control request to the hub (Port_Reset) and enables operation of the port (one!) at which the new connection was detected. Upon the initial connection and after a reset a device is in the Default State: It responds only to zero endpoint messages and has zero address (USB Default Address). Subsequently, accessing a device at zero address, the host interacts only with one newly connected device. The host reads off the descriptors of this device using standard requests, and assigns it a unique bus address (1–127). In this way, the host populates its list of the connected devices. After it has been assigned a unique number, the device switches into the Addressed State, but its application functionality is not yet enabled. The device is capable of fully fledged operation (application exchange with the host, drawing the full current load off the bus, etc.) only after the host selects its configuration out of those available by a control request (Set_Configuration); the device then switches into the Configured State.

If the new device is a hub, having configured it the host determines devices connected to it, identifies them, assigns them numbers, and configures them in the same way. If the new device is a function, the notification of the connection is sent to the appropriate software and, if necessary, client drivers are loaded for it.

When a device is disconnected, the hub automatically disables the corresponding port and informs the host of this disconnection; the host removes information about the given device from all its data structures. If a function device is disconnected, the notification is sent to the interested software. If a hub is disconnected, the removal process is performed for all devices connected to it.

Device Identification and Classification

Having detected connection of a device (by a message from the hub), the USB system reads off its descriptors in order to determine what software components to load and whom to inform about the appearance of the new device. The device descriptor has two-byte fields that identify the device:

- ❑ `idVendor`: assigned by the USB-IF
- ❑ `IdProduct` and `bcdDevice`: determined by the vendor

In addition, the device can have alphanumerical string descriptors containing the names of the vendor and the device, and its serial number. These alphanumeric descriptions can be of any length and format (but coded in UNICODE); pointers in the `iManufacturer`, `iProduct`, and `iSerialNumber` fields refer to these string descriptors.

For determining the device's purpose, capabilities, and protocols supported by the device and its individual interfaces, the device descriptor contains class, subclass, and protocol codes. The regular codes in the 1–FEh range are assigned by the USB-IF, but only for already standardized devices. (A value of zero means there is no definition; a value of FEh is assigned specific meanings by device developers and manufacturers.) These identifiers are directly related to interfaces: Using them, a suitable driver and client application can be picked automatically by the operating system. Presenting a regular code obliges the device to comply with the standard requirements demanded of the interfaces with the indicated protocol for the given class and subclass; this includes having to execute all specific requests and to make available the specific descriptors if there are any. At the same time, the device can have expanded capabilities.

The class, subclass, and protocol codes are contained not only in the interface descriptors, but also in the device descriptors. A zero device class code means that the device comprises a set of independent interfaces, each of which can be assigned its own class, subclass, and protocol code. Moreover, the device subclass and protocol are also zeroes (i.e., the device as a whole cannot be described in the standard way). A regular device class code means that its interfaces are not independent (aggregated interfaces).

Moreover, the subclass code (also assigned by the USB-IF) is a supplementary modifier. A regular protocol code means that the device supports all protocols required of a device of its class and subclass. The zero device protocol code means that protocols can be defined only for individual interfaces.

USB device classification pertains not to the application functions performed by devices, but to the methods of communication between the host and the devices. The classification allows the interface characteristics to be generalized; in this, as a rule, the protocol code sets the type of the endpoints and their use rules, while the subclass code defines the format of data transferred via particular endpoints. The classification allows the variety of drivers needed to different devices to be reduced: The driver can abstract itself from a concrete function device that it services. The operating system links the client drivers that it has at its disposal with the concrete device interfaces using class, subclass and protocol codes, as well as the vendor, product, and product version identifiers.

Examples of classes, subclasses, protocols are listed in Table 4.10; complete information about the classification's state and the requirements to the already defined classes, subclasses, and protocols can be found on the site **www.usb.org**. Some of these classes are considered in more detail in *Section 4.1.11*.

Table 4.10. Some Standard Device Classes and Protocols

Subclass	Protocol (endpoints used by the interface)
Class 01: audio devices	
01: AUDIOCONTROL, controlled audio processing module (regulator, filter, mixer, reverberator, etc.)	00: protocol is not defined
02: AUDIOSTREAMING, a receiving device or an audio stream source	
03: MIDISTREAMING, a receiving device or a MIDI message stream source	
Class 03: human/machine interface devices	
01: devices used during operating system loading	01: keyboard
	02: mouse
Class 07: printers	
01: sending data to printer using printer control languages (PCL) used in printers with traditional interfaces and receiving status information	01: unidirectional (EP0, Bulk-OUT)

continues

Table 4.10 Continued

Subclass	Protocol (endpoints used by the interface)
Class 07: printers	
01: sending data to printer using printer control languages (PCL) used in printers with traditional interfaces and receiving status information	02: bidirectional (EP0, Bulk-OUT, Bulk-IN)
	03: bidirectional IEEE 1284.4 (EP0, Bulk-OUT, Bulk-IN)
Class 08: mass storage devices	
01: Reduced Block Commands (RBC), typically for flash memory devices, but any storage devices can use this command set	00: CBI Transport with interrupts (EP0, Bulk-OUT, Bulk-IN, Interrupt-IN), only for FS
02: SFF8020i, MMC-2 (ATAPI), typically for CD/DVD	01: CBI Transport without interrupts (EP0, Bulk-OUT, Bulk-IN, Interrupt-IN), only for FS
03: QIC-157 (tape devices)	
04: UFI, typically for FDD.	50h — BO Transport (Bulk-OUT, Bulk-IN, EP0)
05: SFF8070i, typically for FDD.	
06: transparent SCSI command transfer	
Class 09h: hubs	
00: no division into subclasses	00: USB 1.x hub
	01: USB 2.0 hub with one transaction translator
	02: USB 2.0 hub with many transaction translators
Class 0Eh: video devices	
01: VIDEOCONTROL, a controlled video processing device	00: protocol not defined
02: VIDEOSTREAMING, a receiving device or a video stream source	
03: VIDEO_INTERFACE_COLLECTION, a set or interconnected video device interfaces	

Descriptors

USB adopted a hierarchy of descriptors that describe all device properties. Standard USB descriptors start with the descriptor length byte, followed by the descriptor type byte.

❏ The *Device Descriptor* (type 1) describes the device as a whole (USB version, class, vendor, model, protocol, number of possible configurations). For HS devices, the general description is supplemented by a *Device Qualifier Descriptor* (type 6) that describes the number of configurations, which the device will have when operating at a different speed (the device descriptor pertains to the speed, at which the device is working at any given moment).

❏ The *Configuration Descriptors* (type 2) describe the number of interfaces, attributes (power supply type and remote wakeup generation capability) and power drawn off the bus in each configuration for the current speed. There are also *Other Speed Configuration Descriptors* for HS devices (type 7) that describe the same parameters with the same formats.

❏ The *Interface Descriptors* (type 4) describe the number of application endpoint, class, and interface protocol for each of the interfaces available in the specific configuration. There can be several different settings of the given interface in the configuration, each of which has its corresponding interface descriptor. The zero setting is the primary interface.

❏ The *Endpoint Descriptors* (type 5) define the number and direction of the endpoint, attributes (transfer types), maximum data field length, and servicing interval (for periodic transfer endpoints).

❏ The *String Descriptors* (type 3) are optional text information strings that can be displayed by the host. References (one-byte offsets) to string descriptors contain device, configuration, and interface descriptors. A zero value offset means that the given structure has no string descriptors. Strings are composed of UNICODE characters without an explicit end of string indicator: This is determined by the length declared in the descriptor header. String descriptors can be given multiple languages; when selecting the necessary descriptor, a 16-bit LanguageID identifier is indicated in the request in addition to the offset. A string descriptor called from the zero offset contains the list of the supported language identifiers in its body.

❏ A *Class-Specific Descriptors* can be used in a certain type of devices: For example, there is an Interface Power Descriptor (type 8) for hubs. The specific descriptors also must begin with the length and type fields.

Descriptors are obtained from devices using `Get_Descriptor` request, indicating the descriptor type. In this way, the device descriptor (and qualifier), configuration descriptor (for the given or other speed), and string descriptor (and also an OTG descriptor; see *Section 4.1.9*) can be explicitly requested. Interface and endpoint descriptors are not individually addressed; their addresses are appended to the end of the configuration descriptor address. All devices are required to be able to read all existing descriptors; descriptor writing capability (by the Set_Descriptor request) can be implemented as an option. A positive device response to a descriptor write request transaction means that it has been accepted and that the device will obey its properties.

Upon a configuration descriptor request, the device presents a whole series of descriptors, starting with the configuration descriptor proper. It is followed by the descriptor of the primary interface and its endpoints for each available interface, followed by all alternative versions with their endpoints. The total length of the whole configuration description is not known in advance; it is indicated in the wTotalLength field of the configuration descriptor. Therefore, in order to obtain the configuration, a request is first made, in which the length of the configuration descriptor proper is stated (9 bytes, although 4 bytes is sufficient), and then the request is repeated using the length value obtained from this field.

Requests to USB Devices (Control Transfers)

Requests to a device are made using control transactions addressed to its Control type endpoints. The specification defines the packet format at the Setup stage, allowing various types of requests to be constructed. Requests can be addressed to a device as a whole, to its interface, to a specific endpoint, or other parts of the device. The packet format makes it possible to determine the presence, direction, and length of the message at the data phase; the meaning of these data depends on the request. The request set includes:

❏ Standard requests for all devices. The list of requests and the data format are defined by the USB specification.
❏ Requests for a class. The list of requests and the data formats are defined by the standard for the given device class.
❏ Specific requests, defined by the designer of the specific device.

All USB devices have the main control channel, endpoint zero (EP0), from which all main standardized requests are made. A device can also have other endpoints of the Control type; they will have their own specific requests, but the format of their Setup phase must be the same, so that the continuation of the control transaction can be determined by it in the same standard way. However, additional endpoints of the Control type are not often encountered in devices that can be explained by the difficulty of their implementation (in most cases, EP0 alone is sufficient for control purposes).

A device must reject the request if it is not supported, or has wrong parameters. The specification sets limits on the request execution time (from the time a command is issued to the time an acknowledgement or rejection is received): The overall limit is up to 5 seconds, but the address-assignement request must take no more that 50 msec to execute (otherwise, the device enumeration process will be too protracted).

During the Setup stage, the request itself is sent to the device in the 8-bit data field; the request also indicates the direction, in which the transfer will be conducted in the Data stage. The request is identified by the mandatory bmRequestType and bRequest fields. The contents of the wValue, wIndex, and wLength fields are used not in all requests; non-used fields must be zeroed out. The Data stage is used not in all requests (wLength=0 when it is absent). During the Status stage, the device confirms successful request execution (by an ACK packet) or rejects it (by a STALL packet). Receiving a STALL packet from a control endpoint is a normal response and does not require the given endpoint to be unblocked.

Standard Device Requests

Standard requests are defined for all USB devices, although there are exceptions for some devices: No alternative interface setting control is needed if there are no alternative settings; time marker settings are needed (and possible) only for isochronous endpoint devices. Standard requests are addressed to EP0.

The Set_Address request is addressed to the entire device; the address assigned to the device is sent in the wValue field.

The Get_Descriptor and Set_Descriptor requests are addressed only to the whole device. Here, the wValue field contains the descriptor type (1, 2, 3, 6, or 7 for Get and only 1, 2, or 3 for Set) in the most significant byte; the least significant byte contains the string offset (for type 3 descriptors) or the configuration number (for type 2 or 7 descriptors). The wIndex field is used only for string descriptors to specify the language (Language ID). The wLength field sets the descriptor's length. If the actual length of the descriptor being read is larger than the requested descriptor, then only its beginning is read; if it is greater, then the device returns only the actual number of bytes.

The *configuration control requests* Get_Configuration and Set_Configuration are also addressed only to a device. In the Set request, only the wValue field is used: In its least significant byte, the number of the configuration being setup is sent. In the Get request, only the wLength field (=1) is used: A one-byte reply containing the number of the current configuration is expected.

The *alternative setting control requests* Get_Interface and Set_Interface are addressed to the interface whose number is indicated in the wIndex field. In the Set request, in the least significant byte of the wValue field, the number of the alternative setting is sent. In the Get request, the wLength field (=1) indicates that a one-byte reply containing the number of the current alternative setting for the given interface is expected.

The *time marker setting request* Synch_Frame is addressed to a device. In its wIndex field, it contains the number of the endpoint to which the given marker pertains.

The wLength field (=2) points to two bytes of the transferred data: the frame number for the given marker.

The *status read request* Get_Status can be addressed to a device, interface, or endpoint. Here, the wIndex field specifies the target number (an interface or an endpoint; it equals zero for a device). The wLength field indicates the number of status bytes expected. The meaning of the status data depends on to whom they are addressed:

❐ In the standard device status request (wLength=2), only the lower bits of the word are defined: D0 (Self Powered): self powered indicator (0 — device is powered from the bus); D1 (Remote Wakeup): device can generate Remote Wakeup signal; D2 (Port Test): port is in the testing mode.

❐ Reading the interface status does not return any information in a standard request (zeroes are returned). However, it can be used in a class request; for example, for printers, this request (wLength=1) returns a status byte analogous to the LPT port status (printer selected, error, end of paper, etc.).

❐ In a standard endpoint status request (wLength=2), only the least significant bit of the word is defined: D0 (Halt): endpoint halt indicator (a device answers with a STALL packet to transactions to this endpoint).

The *feature control requests* Set_Feature and Clear_Feature can also be addressed to a device, interface, or endpoint. Here, the wIndex field defines the target number (interface or an endpoint; for a device, it equals zero); the wValue field sets the feature number. The set of the standard controlled features is not large:

❐ Device_Remote_Wakeup feature control. The addressee is a device, wValue=1.

❐ Endpoint_Halt control. The addressee is an endpoint, wValue=0. The halted endpoint answers all transactions with a STALL packet. Resetting the halt indicator unblocks and initializes the endpoint, including setting the initial value of the Toggle Bit.

❐ Test_Mode control. The addressee is a device, wValue=2. Here, the wIndex field is also used to define the test to conduct: 01 — Test_J; 02 — Test_K; 03 — Test_SE0_Nack; 04 — Test_Packet; 05 — Test_Force_Enable. The values 06–3Fh are reserved for standard tests; the values C0–FFh are given over to the device developers. This request can only turn the test on; in order to turn the test off, the device has to be de-powered and then powered up again, as it no longer perceives control requests while in the test mode.

4.1.11. USB Applications

Thanks to its versatility and ability to transfer copious amounts of traffic efficiently, the USB is used to connect PCs to extremely diverse devices. It is destined to replace the traditional PC ports, such as COM and LPT, as well as the games adapter and

MIDI interface port. The USB 2.0 specification allows connection of traditional ATA and SCSI bus clients to be considered, as well as taking over a part of the FireWire bus' application niche. What makes the USB attractive is the possibility of dynamic device connection and disconnection and using devices practically right away, without having to reboot the operating system. Also practical is the possibility of connecting a large number of devices (up to 127) to one bus, albeit using hubs. The Host Controller is integrated into most modern motherboards. Expansion USB controller cards (usually for the PCI bus) are also available. However, the universal use of the USB is being delayed by insufficient activity on the part of device manufacturers: from lists of supported operating systems, it can be seen that all devices are supported by Windows 98/SE/ME, while N/A is often found in the Linux, MacOS, Unix, and even Windows 2000 columns.

In order for the USB system to become operational, it is necessary for the Host Controller's (or controllers' if there is more than one) drivers to be loaded. When a device is connected to USB, Windows issues a "New device detected" message and, if it is the first time the device has been connected, offers to load the drivers for it. The system is already familiar with many device models and includes their drivers in the distributive. However, the device manufacturer's driver can also become necessary; as a rule, it is included into the device distribution kit, or can be found on the Internet. Unfortunately, not all drivers work properly: A raw driver of an initial version may have to be replaced with a more polished one in order for the device to be identified and work properly. But this is a problem common to all devices, not just USB ones.

The USB's main application areas are as follows:

❐ *Input devices*: keyboard, mice, trackballs, tablet pointers, etc. Here, the USB provides single interface for different devices. The suitability of using USB for keyboards is not obvious, although it reduces the number of cables snaking from the system block onto the user's desk when used in pair with a USB mouse (connected to the hub built into the keyboard).

❐ *Printers*: USB 1.1 provides almost the same speed as the LPT port in the ECP mode, but there is no problem with the cable length and connecting more than one printer when using USB (additional hubs are needed for this, however). USB 2.0 allows high resolution printing speed to be increased by reducing time for large bulk data transfers. However, there is a problem with the old software that works with the LPT port on the register level: it will not be able to work with a USB printer.

❐ *Scanners*: Using USB makes it possible to dispense with SCSI controllers and with taking up the LPT port. Moreover, USB 2.0 allows the data transfer rate to be increased.

❐ *Audio devices*: speakers, microphones, headphones. USB allows audio data streams sufficient to provide the highest quality sound to be transferred. Transferring data in digital form from the very signal source (a microphone with a built-in converter and adapter) to the receiver and digital signal processing in the host computer makes it possible to get rid of noise pickup intrinsic to the analog audio transfers. Using these audio components makes it possible in many cases to dispense with the computer's audio card: The audio codecs (ADC and DAC) are taken outside of the computer and all signal processing functions (mixer, equalizer) are implemented by the central processor purely by software. Audio devices may even have no speakers or microphone proper, but limit themselves to the converters and standard jacks for connecting regular analog devices.

❏ *Music synthesizers and MIDI controllers with the USB interface:* USB allows a computer to process streams of many MIDI channels (the bandwidth of the traditional MIDI interface is significantly lower than a computer's capabilities).

❏ *Video and photo cameras:* USB 1.1 allows static images of any resolution to be transmitted in acceptable time. Live video streams with acceptable frame frequency (25–30 Kbps) can be sent only at low resolutions or with data compression, which, of course, reduces image quality. USB 2.0 allows live video streams to be sent at high resolutions and without data compression (and the corresponding quality loss). Cameras, as well as TV signal image capture devices and TV tuners with the USB interface are also produced.

❏ *Communications:* Various types of USB interface modems are produced, including cable and xDSL modems and high-speed infrared communications (IrDA FIR) adapters. The bus makes it possible to get over the COM port speed limit (115.2 Kbps) without increasing the central processor's workload. Ethernet LAN adapters connected to the computer via the USB are also produced. But even two computers cannot be directly interconnected by USB ports without using additional devices: The bus can have only one host computer (see previous discussions). A special device for linking two computers looks like a button cut into a USB cable with two Standard-A plugs at the ends. A linking device — USB Link — can also be located on the motherboard with an output to an external connector; in this case, the two computers are connected by a regular cable, which is connected to a regular USB port on one computer and to the USB Link port on the other. The USB Link software even makes it possible to build a network on the basis of a chain of USB connections. For connecting several computers into a local network, special devices are produced that perform packet switching among the computers. Connecting more than two computers is also complicated by the topological limitations of the USB: the length of one cable segment must not exceed 5 meters, whereas using hubs to extend the range is not efficient (each hub gives only 5 meters of extra range).

❏ *Interface converters* allow devices with most various interfaces to be connected via the USB port, which practically all computers now have. These interfaces include

Centronics and IEEE 1284 (LPT ports), RS-232C (UART 16550A emulation — the basis of the COM ports), other serial interfaces (RS-422, RS-485, etc.), the keyboard port and even Games port emulators, ATA, ISA, PC Card bus adapters, and any other type of interfaces for which there is enough bandwidth. In this respect, the USB becomes a magic wand when it comes to connecting a device to a port that is not there, such as an LPT or a COM port in a notebook PC or some other situation. In this regard, the converter's software can emulate the classic version of the standard IBM PC port hardware, but only under the control of a protected mode operating system. MS-DOS applications can communicate with devices via the I/O or memory addresses, interrupts, and DMA channels, but only from an MS-DOS session opened in the USB capable operating system (most often, Windows). When a bare MS-DOS is loaded, the magic wand does not work anymore. Interface converters have extended the life of traditional interface devices being pushed out of PC by the PC'99 and PC'2001 specifications. The data transfer rate over a USB/LPT converter may turn out to be even higher than in a real LPT port working in the SPP mode.

❑ *Mass storage devices:* The data transfer speed of hard disk drives, CD and DVD drives, streamers, etc. connected using USB 1.1 is comparable to the speed obtained using an LPT port; however, the interface — in terms of both hardware and software — is more convenient using USB. When these devices are connected using USB 2.0, the data transfer speed becomes comparable with the ATA and SCSI, while the limit on the connected devices is quite high. Of special interest is using USB in nonvolatile (flash) memory electronic storage devices: A storage device of this type can be very compact (the size of a key trinket) but high capacity (storing from tens of megabytes up to a gigabyte or more). There are devices for connecting ATA/ATAPI interface devices externally: In essence, these are just interface converters placed into a 5-inch or 3.5-inch form factor external box bay and sometimes implemented right in the case of a 36-contact ATA connector. Devices for reading and writing SmartMedia Cards and CompactFlash Cards also exist.

❑ *Gaming devices:* Joysticks of all kinds (from sticks to steering wheels), consoles with various sensors (analogous and discrete) and actuating mechanisms (e.g., vibrating and rocking car-racer seats) can be connected in the regular way. The resource-devouring interface of the old gaming adapter (abolished way back in the PC'99 specification) is not used here.

❑ *Analog and digital (ISDN) telephones:* Connecting a telephone turns the computer into a secretary with autodial, auto-answering, security, and other capabilities.

❑ *Monitors:* Here, the USB bus is used to control the monitor parameters. The monitor informs the system of its type and capabilities (synchronization parameters). This does not require the USB and has been done over the DDC bus; however, USB monitors can be controlled by the system: Brightness, contrast, color temperature, etc. now can be regulated by software and not only by the monitor's front panel button. Monitors, as a rule, usually have hubs built in. This is practical, as it is not always convenient to connect peripheral devices to the system block.

❑ *Electronic keys:* These devices can be made with any intellectuality level of protection and can be implemented in USB plug cases. They are much more compact and portable than the analogous devices for the COM and LPT ports.

Of course, the areas in which the USB is used are not limited to the above-listed classes of devices.

USB hubs are produced both as separate devices and built into peripheral devices (keyboards, monitors). As a rule, hubs draw power from the mains (they must supply power to the devices that are connected to them). Hubs that are installed inside the system block and draw power from its power supply are also produced. This type of hub is cheaper than external hubs and does not need an extra power supply socket. One of the implementation versions involves placing a hub on a bracket, which is then installed into the cutout on the computer's back panel. Access to these hub's connectors from the back of the system block is not very convenient for users. Another alternative is a hub that is installed into a 3.5-inch bay. Its connectors are easily accessible, and the port status indicators are clearly visible; however, the cables coming from the front of the system block are inconvenient, not to mention unaesthetic. On the other hand, for connecting electronic keys (if they are changed often) or miniature storage devices, this method is the most convenient.

Supplementary USB devices may be used to extend the communications range. The simplest version of such a "distance extender" is a 5-meter USB cable with a regular type A plug on one end and a miniature one-port hub with a type B receptacle on the other (far) end. Should it be needed, a chain of up to 5 of such distance extenders can be used between a USB device and the root hub, which together with the device's cable gives the range of up to 30 meters. Another version of an extender is two devices interconnected by a regular twisted pair Category 5 cable (or even by a fiber optic cable) and placed between the peripheral device and the root hub. The far-end part of the extender may be a hub with several ports on the peripheral side. Unfortunately, range extension is limited to 60 meters, because of the signal delay time inherent to the USB protocol. It is impossible to use additional hubs even with a 50-meter extender, because the signal delay in the cable consumes the time limits allowed hubs by the USB specification. But even a range this long allows the USB application area to be expanded, to implement remote video surveillance, for example. Claims of some manufacturers that ranges of up to 100 meters (up to 500 meters using optic fibers) can be obtained sound somewhat doubtful, because the response wait timeouts in the USB specification put stringent limits on the range, and signals in cables cannot be accelerated to speeds greater than the speed of light.

The details of how to implement interaction of certain classes of devices on the USB are considered below. These examples make it possible to grasp the application possibilities of the USB, and can be used as the starting points for developing custom devices, including functionally quite original ones.

USB Printers

The classes and protocols of USB interface printers are defined in the Universal Serial Bus Device Class Definition for Printing Devices, the first version of which came out in 1997; Version 1.1 came out in 2000. The protocols are defined with the aim of providing easy transition from traditional printer interfaces, both serial (RS-232, RS-422) and parallel (unidirectional Centronics or bidirectional IEEE 1284). Connecting a USB printer emulates its connection to the LPT port in the SPP or bidirectional (IEEE 1284) mode. The class definition of a USB printer does not affect the data sent to the printer; it can be any page descriptor language (PDL). Printers can work only at full and high speeds (there are no bulk data transfers at low speed in USB).

A printer has all of a USB device's standard descriptors; it has no specific class descriptors. In the device descriptor, a printer presents zero class, subclass, and device codes. A printer has at least one configuration; a configuration has one interface. At the interface level, class 07 (subclass 01) is defined for printers. The protocol code is defined by the selected alternative interface setting:

❏ Unidirectional interface: Data are sent to the printer via an endpoint of the Bulk-OUT type; printer status data are sent upon a class-specific request `Get_Port_Status` via EP0 in the format adopted for the parallel port (three significant bits of the LPT port status register).

❏ Bidirectional interface: Data are sent to the printer via an endpoint of the Bulk-OUT type; printer status data are sent via an endpoint of the Bulk-IN type. Here, the printer status (the three bits) can also be obtained using a `Get_Port_Status` request via EP0.

❏ Bidirectional interface with data delivered over logical channels in compliance with the IEEE 1284.4 (IEEE 1284.4 compatible bidirectional interface), introduced in Version 1.1. The exchange model is the same as in the previous interface. Protocol code 3 corresponds to this interface version.

Only one endpoint (not counting the zero endpoint) is used in a printer to output data (Bulk-OUT); for bidirectional interfaces, a Bulk-IN is also used to obtain the reverse channel status data.

A printer supports standard requests to USB devices, except the time marker setting request (a printer has no isochronous endpoints). Additionally, it must support class requests (Table 4.11).

Table 4.11. Class Request to Printers

Request	bmRequestType	bRequest
Get_Device_Id	10100001b	0
Get_Port_Status	10100001b	1
Soft_Reset	00100011b	2

Upon a Get_Device_Id request, the printer returns a Capabilities string that describes it using the format and syntax defined in the IEEE-1284. In the wValue field of the request, the number of the wanted configuration is indicated; the most significant byte of the wIndex sets the interface number (0), the least significant byte sets the number of the alternative setting. The returned string starts with a two-byte string length field (the MSB comes first), which is followed by the identifier proper.

Upon a Get_Port_Status request, the printer returns a status byte analogous to the LPT port status byte. Here, only three bits are significant (the rest are zeroed out).

❏ Bit 3 (Not Error). Error indicator: 1 — no error, 0 — error.

❏ Bit 4 (Select). Printer-selected indicator: 1 — printer selected (available), 0 — printer not available.

❏ Bit 5 (Paper Empty). Out-of-paper indicator: 1 — out of paper, 0 — not out of paper.

Upon a Soft_Reset request, the printer flushes its data buffer, switches into the initial state, switches the endpoints into the initial state, and enables them (if they had been disabled). In terms of the USB interface, this reset does not affect the printer status (addressed, configured).

To work with a USB printer, the device descriptor and the descriptors of all possible configurations must be read and a configuration and the necessary alternative interface settings selected. When working with a bidirectional interface, the type of the reverse channel endpoint — Bulk — causes some inconveniences: If the printer has nothing to "say," the printer status data request made by the driver will hang until a driver timeout. The formal definition of the results of the Get_Port_Status request (at least according to the specification's Version 1.1) does not make it possible to judge whether there are data in the reverse channel. However, remembering how the LPT port operates, which is what the USB connection emulates, it can be supposed that the indicator of data presence in the reverse channel is bit 3 (Not Error). In the LPT port, this bit reflects the current state of the Error# signal, which in all IEEE 1284 modes (except the SPP compatibility mode) is used to signal data presence in the reverse channel.

Mass Data Storage Devices

The task of a USB data storage device comes down to sending commands to the device defining the transactions being executed, receiving information from the device that the command has been executed, and, finally, transferring the stored data. The USB specification defines several subclasses and protocols. A subclass defines the contents of a command block; a protocol defines the method of transporting commands, status, and data. Subclasses and protocols are independent: Any block format can be delivered by any transport. Storage devices have no special class descriptors, but they do have two class requests (Table 4.12).

Table 4.12. Class Request to Storage Devices

Request	bmRequestType	bRequest	Applicability to protocols
Get_Max_Lun	10100001b	FEh	50h
Bulk-Only_Mass_Storage_Reset	00100001b	FFh	50h
ADSC	00100001b	00	00, 01

The *Bulk-Only transfer protocol* (code 50h) is used in storage devices at any speed (FS or HS); it is recommended for all new developments. This protocol provides mutual synchronization of the host and the device, using the nonsynchronized (by the USB system) streams of the independent Bulk-IN and Bulk-OUT channels via a pair of corresponding endpoints. Additionally, two class requests for determining available logical devices and interface resetting are used.

Upon a Get_Max_LUN request, the device returns a byte containing the maximum possible number of a logical device (LUN, numbering starts from zero). In the wIndex field of the request, the interface number is indicated, wLength=1.

By a Bulk-Only_Mass_Storage_Reset request, the interface indicated in the wIndex field is reset: the Bulk-IN and Bulk-OUT endpoints are enabled, the Toggle Bit is switched into the DATA0 state, the interface is switched into the wait-for-command state, and all previous requests are flushed.

Command and status blocks are recognized in the sequence of packets by fixed packet length (they always fit exactly into one packet), signatures, and the correspondence of the fields' contents to the predetermined values (zeroes in the reserved fields are checked). A command block up to 16 bytes long makes it possible to transport any set of commands used in the mass storage devices with traditional interfaces (ATA/ATAPI, SCSI, etc). The command and data transfer protocol works as follows:

❒ The host sends a Command Block Wrapper (CBW), a fixed length packet (31 byte) that includes:
  - A four-byte signature (dCBWSignature=43425355h)
  - A four-byte tag (dCBWTag) that serves to mark and identify the status block in the response

- A four-byte transferred data length field (dCBWDataTransferLength)
- Flag byte (bmCBWFlags), in which only bit 7 is used to indicate data transfer direction (the rest of the bits are zeroed out)
- A byte with a 4-bit number of the logical device that the given command block is accessing (bCBWLUN in bits [3:0]; the rest of the bits are set to zeroes)
- The command block length byte (bCBWCBLength in bits [4:0], allowable values 1–16; the rest of the bits have zero values)
- The command block proper (CBWCB) 1 to 16 bytes long and a filler bringing the length of this field to 16 bytes

❏ The device confirms successful reception by an ACK, analyzes the packet, and, if the wrapper is correct and the command block is valid, executes reception or transmission of the requested data block. The host initiates data exchange in accordance with the sent command (data may also not be sent, in which case zero data length is indicated).

❏ The device answers each command block (after a successful execution or a rejection) with a CSW status block in the analogous wrapper, which is a 13-byte packet containing:

- A four-byte signature (dCSWSignature=53425355h)
- A four-byte tag (dCSWTag), tying this reply to the specific command block
- A four-byte field (dCSWDataResidue), in which the difference between the requested (and transferred) data amount and the amount actually processed by the device is indicated
- A command execution status byte (bCSWStatus): 00 — successful, 01 — failed, 02 — a phase error (desequencing of the command and data)

If the device receives an invalid command packet, it rejects it by a corresponding CSW (with the status byte = 01). For each command packet issued, the host must receive a reply: a status block with the same tag (tags are assigned by the host, the device only uses them to mark its replies). A phase error (the command/reply sequence getting out of order) is handled by an interface-reset class request, which is sent over EP0: The interface switches into the initial state (ready to receive a command block). By the same reset, the endpoints that may have been disabled are enabled.

The *Control-Block-Interrupt protocol* (CBI, codes 00 and 01) is intended only for FS devices (there are no Bulk-IN/OUT endpoints in the LS). It is not recommended for new developments; its use in the HS is not allowed. Commands are delivered by the Access_Device_Specific_Command (ADCS) request sent via EP0 (the main message pipe). Data are delivered via the Bulk-IN and Bulk-OUT endpoints. The command completion status information is sent via the same endpoints (including the EP0). In the protocol with code 00, an additional Interrupt-IN endpoint with a two-byte packet length is allocated for transferring status data.

A command block is sent in the data phase of a control transaction that carries out the ADSC request. In the wIndex field of the request, the interface number is indicated; the wLength field shows the command block length. A positive acknowledgement (ACK) of the status phase means that the command has been successfully received (this reply may be delayed for an indeterminate period by the device sending NACKs).

Command execution status can be sent in several ways:

❑ By an interrupt: When a device has something to inform about the command execution status, it returns two bytes in a transaction with the Interrupt-IN endpoint; the meaning of these bytes depends on the subclass of the device.

❑ Over the main message pipe: In the completion phase, the device can reply with a STALL packet, which means that the command has been rejected. The status can be ascertained by sending a corresponding command that presupposes receiving status in the data phase via the Bulk-IN endpoint.

❑ Over the data transfer channel: Having detected an error in the process of executing a command, the device answers with a STALL packet to the next Bulk-IN/OUT transaction. The status can be ascertained by sending the next command block (having enabled the endpoints by a Clear_EP_Half request prior to this).

Data are sent in packets via the Bulk-IN and Bulk-OUT endpoints; a short packet serves as the end of data block indicator. The host and the device monitor the correspondence of the volume of the transmitted data to the volume requested in the command. If a discrepancy is detected, the device can signal about this by sending status via the Interrupt-IN endpoint or via a STALL response in data transfer transactions.

A device can be reset by sending an ADSC request with a special command block whose contents are 1D, 04, FF, FF, FF... Upon this command, the device attempts to terminate the current operations safely and flushes all buffers and queues. Afterward, the host must execute Clear_EP_Halt requests in order to enable the endpoint and place the ToggleBit switch into the initial state. Resetting a device via a USB port (by a request to the hub) while a command is being executed is fraught with the danger of losing the data.

The Interrupt-IN is used only for protocol 00. The host expects an interrupt for each ADSC it sends; if the device answers the ADSC with a STALL, an interrupt for this command is no longer expected. If the host sends the next ADSC while the device has an interrupt request that has not been sent yet, the device cancels this interrupt.

Human Interface Devices (HID)

Devices that provide an interface between users and computers belong to the Human Interface Device (HID) class; they include:

❑ Keyboards, mice, trackballs, other pointing devices, joysticks
❑ Controls on the computer front panel, such as buttons, switches, regulators, etc.

❏ Controls specific to remote audio and video controls, telephones, various game simulators (steering wheels, pedals, control columns, etc.)

These devices typically transfer small volumes of asynchronous data and are not very demanding to service timing. Other devices with data of a similar nature (bar code readers, thermometers, voltmeters, etc.) also belong to this class. This class is described in detail in the Device Class Definition for Human Interface Device (HID) document, Version 1.11 of which came out in 2001. The HID can work at any USB speed.

HID are divided into subclasses only with respect to the necessity of a given device to be supported during operating system loading. The special protocol code singles out only the keyboard and mouse, which are the standard input devices.

The host exchanges report messages with HID; there are three Report Types:

❏ Type 1: Input from a device
❏ Type 2: Output into a device
❏ Type 3: Feature control

If a device is capable of exchanging different (not by type but by purpose) reports, then each report starts with a Report ID byte. For example, a keyboard/pointing device combination can issue key press reports as well as pointing device reports.

HID interfaces provide bidirectional report exchange between the device and the driver. It contains:

❏ The mandatory bidirectional channel (via EP0) to output reports and input polling data.
❏ The mandatory unidirectional channel for asynchronous report input upon interrupts (from the device to its driver via an Interrupt-IN endpoint).
❏ An optional channel for output upon interrupts; if the device has an Interrupt-OUT endpoint, then output reports are sent via this endpoint.

Human interface devices have a special HID class descriptor referencing the report descriptor and a set of physical descriptors (the type and length of these descriptors are shown, which allows them to be received by a Get_Descriptor request).

The report descriptor is a complex structure that describes the transferred data in terms of its function (input, output, or feature control), use, legitimate values range, size, etc. This information is needed for HIDs that parse and assemble reports. The driver has an Item Parser module, which determines the application, to which a specific report needs to be sent.

The set of physical descriptors describes the part of the body, with which humans use a specific control. These descriptors are optional and are reported by few devices; they introduce additional complexity into the description, although they allow applications to use specific controls more precisely.

HIDs support all standard device requests and the specific requests listed in Table 4.13.

Table 4.13. Human Interface Device Class Requests

Request	bmRequestType	bRequest
Get_Report	10100001	01
Get_Idle	10100001	02
Get_Protocol	10100001	03
Set_Report	00100001	09
Set_Idle	00100001	0A
Set_Protocol	00100001	0B

The Get_Report and Set_Report requests are used to receive and send reports via EP0. Here, the upper byte of the wValue field defines the report type, while the lower byte contains its identifier. The wIndex field contains the interface number; the wLength field sets the report length, which is sent in the data phase.

The Set_Idle request allows reports to be sent over the interrupt channel if there have been no changes in the status of the values reported on. The upper byte in the wValue field sets the idle duration; the lower byte contains the report identifier. The wIndex field sets the interface number, wLength=0 (no data phase). If the duration is set to zero, the device will send reports only if there have been status changes (needed for a keyboard, for example). Nonzero duration is interpreted as the duration of the interval (in 4-msec units), during which the Interrupt-IN point answers with NAKs if there has been no status change. For example, the frequency of nonproductive polling of pointing devices (a mouse or joystick) can be limited without losing the event response efficiency (the duration set here and the bInterval that sets the polling frequency of the Interrupt-IN point are independent of each other).

The Get_Idle request allows the current duration value to be read for a report whose identifier is given in the lower byte of the wValue field. In the wIndex field, the interface number is set, wLength=1 (one data byte is received).

The Set_Protocol request (only for devices that are involved in initial operating system loading) allows the device operation protocol to be switched. The protocol type is set in the wValue field: 0 — the protocol (simplified) used during the loading (Boot Protocol); 1 — the regular Report Protocol. The interface number is set in the wIndex field, wLength=0.

The Get_Protocol request determines the current protocol. The interface number is set in the wIndex field, wLength=1 (one data byte is received).

Audio Devices

In USB terms, audio devices are, as a rule, combination devices consisting of a set of independent interfaces. Any audio signal starts out at the *Input Terminal* and finishes up at the *Output Terminal*. Between the terminals, various *Units* can be located that perform some types of conversions and connections.

There are various terminal types:

❏ A *USB terminal* is a USB connection that delivers audio data streams from the host to the device (input terminal) or from a device to the host (output terminal); as a rule, data are delivered via isochronous endpoints. For USB terminal interfaces, there is subclass 02 — AUDIOSTREAMING that has its own specific descriptors describing the delivery and synchronization methods and the stream format.

❏ *Input (end) terminals* are devices for sound recording, such as built-in or externally connected microphones of various types, and microphone sets for spatial sound recording (each variety has its own type code assigned).

❏ *Output (end) terminals* are devices for reproducing sound, such as various types of speakers, and headphones.

❏ *Bidirectional (end) terminals* are phone receivers and headsets, with and without echo suppression.

❏ *Telephone terminals* are devices for connecting to a telephone network or a mini ATS.

❏ *External terminals* are analog and digital inputs and outputs of various standards and formats, including the S/PDIF interfaces and audio data streams transferred over the IEEE 1394 bus.

❏ *Built-in terminals* are record, CD, and DVD players, devices to provide accompanying sound for TVs and video recorders, receivers (radio, television, satellite), analog and digital sound recording devices, radio transmitters, synthesizers, and test signal generators, etc.

All these terminals need to be controlled over the USB bus; they all have descriptors that describe their controllable properties.

The Units that are in the audio signal path can perform highly diverse functions: switching, level regulating, mixing, panning, filtering, reverberation, and all the sound effects that have become easily realizable using digital signal processing. These modules are assigned subclass 01 — AUDIOCONTROL, which also has its own specific descriptors and requests.

Closely related to the audio devices are MIDI devices, which are sinks and sources of MIDI messages. For them, subclass 03 — MIDISTREAMING was introduced; it has its own specific descriptors and requests. A USB MIDI device can play the role of a simple interface converter (deliver messages between the host and MIDI connectors on a device), as well as a role of a MIDI synthesizer converting MIDI messages into audio streams. Here, messages from both the external connectors and the USB can be processed. In terms of an audio device, a MIDI synthesizer is a built-in input terminal. It provides an audio stream whose further destination is determined by the audio device (using subclass 01 and 02 interfaces.)

Development of USB Device

Despite the quite complex exchange protocol, self-designed USB devices also can be outfitted with a USB interface. A wide assortment of microchips is produced for this purpose, with various USB speeds (LS, FS, or HS) and endpoint number and capabilities (transfer type, buffer size). These microchips can be used for various functional purposes.

Microcontrollers with a USB port are produced around the MCS51, M68HC05, and M68HC11 kernel or based on the RISC architecture. They differ in their memory sizes (main and nonvolatile), efficiency, power supply, and power consumption. Microcontrollers may have built-in ADC/DAC, discrete general-purpose I/O lines, and serial and parallel ports of various types. They can be used to connect devices with any type of interface, signal processors, etc. From this assortment, a suitable microchip can be selected, on the basis of which the device being developed can be implemented with a minimal number of additional parts. Microcontrollers come with the means for developing their firmware, which is the most complex part of these devices. There are USB microcontrollers that can work without programming their nonvolatile memory. For example, some microcontrollers from Cypress Semiconductor allow small size EEPROM to be used only to store the identifier in it. When such device has been powered up, it does not have any application microcode software, and the device is functionally dead until this software has been loaded from the computer. However, when a device is connected to the USB bus, it presents the descriptors with its identifiers (idVendor, idProduct, and bcdDevice). Moreover, the device knows how to use the specific host request Firmware_Load to load a microprogram from the host computer into its local memory via USB and to launch the program. In the process of executing the program, the device can acquire new properties and descriptors. In order for the host to see the device in its new role, the so-called ReNumeration is performed, in which the microprogram disconnects and then reconnects the USB port. The host interprets this as a new device attach, reads its new descriptors, and then configures the device. Of course, this kind of flexibility is not always needed, but this is especially handy when developing and doing joint debugging of a device's hardware and software components, including its firmware support.

There also are peripheral USB microchips — USB ports — that are connected to microcontrollers using an 8/16-bit data bus with the regular control signal set (CS#, RD#, WR#, etc.), an interrupt request line, and, possibly, a DMA channel line. Specialized converters of USB interfaces into serial (RS-232, RS-422/485) or parallel are also produced;

they do not have to be programmed, and only the device identifier needs to be written into the EEPROM. USB microchips combining both functions and hubs also exist. It is impossible to enumerate all the versions, especially given that new microchips come out all the time. Information about them can be found on the Internet (**www.cypress.com, www.devasys.com, www.iged.com, www.microchip.com, www.netchip.com, www.motorola.com, www.semiconductor.philips.com, www.natsemi.com, www.intel.com, www.ftdichip.com, www.gigatechnology.com**).

An important part of developing own devices is the software support for the host computer that carries all the benefits of the device to the user. In some cases, already existing drivers can be used (for example, a virtual COM port driver for an interface converter). In other cases, the software has to be designed from scratch, and it is good luck if the USB microchip's manufacturer takes care to provide instrumental means for developing all parts of the firmware. For example, for its USB microchips (micro-controllers and peripheral ICs), Cypress supplies a universal driver that supports access to endpoints of all types (control over EP0, bulk, and isochronous and interrupts endpoints). When this driver is installed, a predefined list of vendor and device codes (`idVendor` and `idProduct`), with which the given driver is going to be associated, is automatically entered into the Windows registry. The developer of the device must place one of the identifier combination options into the device descriptor, and when this device is connected to a USB, the operating system will automatically load its driver. If the developer created a text device descriptor, its contents will be displayed by the operating system when the device is connected. The application software associated with the given device must access it through its driver (directly or via intermediary library functions).

When developing custom USB devices (and, naturally, their software), consideration must be given to the principal differences in the program/device interaction capabilities between USB connections and traditional connections to regular ports or expansion buses:

❑ Traditional connections allow real-time device control (with respect to the program code being executed). In this way, for example, software-controlled exchange via an LPT port is performed in the compatibility mode. Even though this mode is inefficient (it places a great load on the CPU), in most cases it nevertheless allows data transmission or control action issuance speeds sufficient to control a device be achieved. For example, data transmission speeds of up to 100–150 KBps can be achieved using the Centronics protocol. The same LPT port can also be used to generate serial interface (I2C, SPI, JTAG, etc.) signals by software. Moreover, signals measured in microseconds (and even shorter, if the device response does not need to be analyzed) can be generated by software.

❑ USB connections separate the moments when the data are physically exchanged with a device (actual device control) from the moments these data (control actions) are generated by the program. The time interval between these events is indeterminate and quite noticeable: The USB driver cannot (and will not) hand over a newly-arrived I/O request packet (IRP) to the host controller immediately. First of all, the driver needs to put the request into the proper form by converting it to a transfer descriptor (and for a universal host controller, it also needs to be broken into transactions), which takes time. Second, the driver must coordinate the moment when it issues a new descriptor with the controller's operating cycle, which is tied to the USB frames. Third, the request is placed into the queue, which may not be empty by this time; therefore, it is not known in advance exactly when the controller will get to the given transfer. Consequently, the delay from the moment the output data are generated to the moment they arrive to the target device can be from units to tens of milliseconds in a best case, and even larger in worse situations (i.e., when the bus is heavily loaded). If an application requires two-way information exchange with the device, then the mutual asynchronism of the exchanges with different endpoints of the device needs also to be taken into account. Only Control-type endpoints provide input/output synchronization, but they are seldom given to application developers (synchronization of isochronous endpoints is a somewhat different and quite a complicated subject).

Even from this perfunctory description of the particular features of USB connections, it is clear that software-controlled interfaces (analogous to the parallel port examples given earlier) will be too slow. If the next step of the interface protocol (output) is executed based on the results of the input of the current device status, then resolution in milliseconds is too optimistic an evaluation of its response speed even for HS devices (USB 2.0). Endpoints of the Interrupt-IN or Interrupt-OUT can be used for time-sensitive dialogs, which is in fact done in human interface devices, for example. However, these endpoints have high bandwidth only in the high-speed mode in USB 2.0. USB provides rather high bandwidth for stream exchanges, which should be kept in mind when designing device interaction principles. The interaction is efficient when it is performed using packet exchanges and not single-byte read/write operations. When deciding on the number of the endpoints to be used in the interface, their mutual asynchronism needs to be kept in mind. A practical example of solving the synchronization problem — the Bulk Only Transport protocol for mass storage devices — was described earlier.

4.2. IEEE 1394 Bus: FireWire

The High Performance Serial Bus standard, which has received the official name IEEE 1394, was adopted in 1995. The objective was to create a bus with characteristics as good as a parallel bus, but to which it is significantly cheaper and easier to attach devices (thanks to switching over to a serial interface). The standard is based on the FireWire bus used by Apple as an inexpensive alternative to the SCSI in its Macintosh and PowerMac computers. The name FireWire is now also applied to the IEEE 1394 implementations; it coexists with the short name 1394. Another name of the same interface — iLink, sometimes Digital Link — is used by Sony in its consumer electronics products. MultiMedia Connection is the name used in the logotype of the 1394 High Performance Serial Bus Trade Association (1394TA).

The 1394 standard defines three possible speeds to transmit signals over cables: 98.404 Mbps, 196.608 Mbps, and 393.216 Mbps, which are rounded up to 100 Mbps, 200 Mbps, and 400 Mbps. In the standard, the speeds are designated as S100, S200, and S400, respectively. In the last approved version of the standard, P394-2000, no new speeds (S800, S1600, and S3200) were introduced, and now the 1394 coexists with USB, for which a speed of 480 Mbps has already been defined by specification 2.0.

The main characteristics of the FireWire bus are as follows:

❏ *Multifunctionality.* The bus provides a digital link for 63 devices without using additional equipment (hubs). Consumer electronics devices, such as digital camcorders, video conference cameras, photo cameras, cable and satellite TV receivers, digital video players (CD and DVD), acoustic systems, and digital musical instruments, as well as peripheral computer devices (printers, scanners, disk mass storage devices) and computers themselves can be connected into a single network.
❏ *High exchange speed and isochronous transfers.* Even at its starting level (S100), the bus is capable of simultaneously transmitting two broadcast-quality video channels (at 30 frames per second) and a CD-quality stereo audio signal.
❏ *Low component and cable prices.*
❏ *Ease of installation and usage.* FireWire expands the Plug and Play technology. The system allows dynamic device attach and detach (hot swapping). Bus powering (current of up to 1.5 A can be supplied) lets the connected devices communicate with the system even when their own power supply fails. Not only PCs but also other intelligent consumer electronics devices can control the bus and other devices.

At VESA's initiative, the FireWire bus is being positioned as a home network bus, interconnecting all domestic and computer equipment into a unified complex. This is a peer-to-peer bus, in which it significantly differs from the USB.

4.2.1. Network Physical Layer

A 1394 cable network is built under simple rules: All devices are interconnected by cables using any type of topology (tree, chain, or star). Each full-size device (a network node) usually has three equitable connectors. Some compact devices have only one connector, which limits the possible options of where they can be placed. The standard also allows up to 27 connectors on one device, which will function as a cable concentrator. There are many allowable ways in which devices can be connected, but the following restrictions apply:

❏ No more that 16 cable segments can be between any pair of nodes.
❏ The cable segment length must not exceed 4.5 m.
❏ The total cable length must not exceed 72 m (using higher quality cables allows this restriction to be relaxed).
❏ The topology must have no loops, although automatic loop elimination in pathological configuration is planned in future versions.

Standard 1394 cable has six wires enclosed within the common shield, and same type six-contact connectors at the ends (Fig. 4.18, *a*). Two twisted pairs are used to transmit signals (TPA and TPD) separately for the receiver and the transmitter; two wires are used to supply power to the devices (8–40 V, up to 1.5 A). The standard makes provisions for galvanic device decoupling using transformers (decoupling voltage of up to 500 V) or capacitors (in cheap devices with a decoupling voltage of up to 60 V relative to the common wire.) Some domestic devices have only one four-contact connector or smaller (Fig. 4.18, *b*) that has only signal circuits. These devices are connected to the bus using a special adapting cable only as the end devices (although special splitting adapters can be used). The signal pairs in the FireWire cables are cross connected (Table 4.14), since all ports have equal rights.

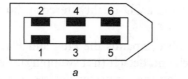 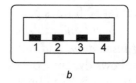

a   *b*

Fig. 4.18. FireWire connectors: *a* — six-pin receptacle,
b — four-pin receptacle

Table 4.14. FireWire Connecting Cables

Connector A			Wire	Connector B		
4-pin	6-pin	Circuit		Circuit	6-pin	4-pin
–	1	Power	White	Power	1	
–	2	GND	Black	GND	2	
1	3	TPB–	Red	TPA–	5	3

continues

Table 4.14 Continued

Connector A			Wire	Connector B		
4-pin	**6-pin**	**Circuit**		**Circuit**	**6-pin**	**4-pin**
2	4	TPB+	Green	TPA+	6	4
3	5	TPA−	Orange	TPB−	3	1
4	6	TPA+	Blue	TPB+	4	2
Shield	Shield	Shield	Shield	Shield	Shield	Shield

In the impending version, which is currently called P1394b, new transmission media versions are provided for:

❏ Category 5 UTP cable with standard RJ-45 connectors (two wire pairs are used); the length of segment is up to 100 m. Positioned as an inexpensive option for S100.
❏ Plastic optical fiber (two POF fibers for short distances and HPCF for long distances); positioned as an inexpensive option for S200.
❏ Multimode optical fiber (two 50 mcm fibers). A more expensive option for the future speeds of up to S3200.

Any device that has more than one 1394 connector is a repeater. The signal detected on the receiver input of any connector is resynchronized by the internal clock generator, and is placed on the transmitters of the rest of the connectors. In this way, signals are delivered from each device to all the others, and the signal jitter causing loss of synchronization is eliminated.

The 1394 standard defines two bus categories: cable buses and backplane buses. Backplane buses usually are parallel interfaces interconnecting the internal subsystems of devices connected to a 1394 cable. A network may contain multiple buses connected by bridges: special devices transferring packets among the buses and filtering traffic. For connecting buses of different types, interface conversions are needed. An interface FireWire bus card for PC is a PCI/1394 bridge. Connections of the 1394 cable bus with backplanes of peripheral devices are also bridges. Bridges can also connect cable buses, which expands the topological potential for connecting devices.

4.2.2. IEEE 1394 Protocol

The 1394 protocol is implemented in three layers (Fig. 4.19).

❏ The *Transaction Layer* converts packets into data sent to applications and vice versa. It implements the request/reply protocol complying with the ISO/IEC

13213:1994 (ANSI/IEEE 1212, 1994 edition) standard on the control and status register architecture for microcomputer buses (reading, writing, blocking). This makes linking the 1394 bus with standard parallel buses easier.

❏ The *Link Layer* forms packets from physical layer data and performs the reverse conversion. It is used by the nodes to exchange datagrams with acknowledgements. The layer is responsible for packet transfer and the isochronous transfer control.

❏ The *Physical Layer* sources and receives bus signals. It provides the initialization and arbitration, assuming that only one transmitter is working at any given moment. The layer delivers data streams and signal levels of the serial bus to the layer above. These two layers may be galvanically decoupled, with the microchips of the physical layer powered from the bus. Galvanic decoupling is necessary in order to prevent sneak common-wire circuits that may develop through the protective grounding of the power supply blocks.

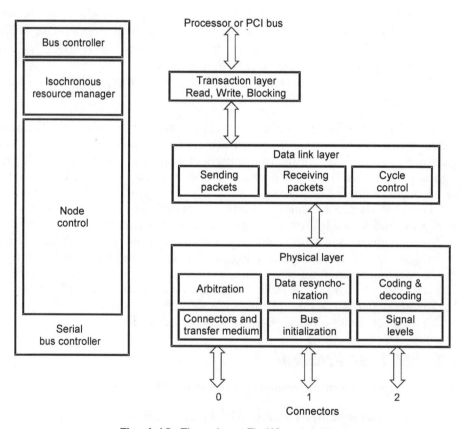

Fig. 4.19. Three-layer FireWire structure

The hardware part of FireWire usually consists of two specialized microchips: the physical level PHY Transceiver and the bus link bridge LINK Chip. They can communicate using, for example, the ABM/Apple interface LINK/PHY. The microchips of the link layer carry out all the functions of their layer and some functions of the transaction layer; the rest of the functions are done by software.

Asynchronous messages are transferred using 64-bit 1394 device register addressing. Sixteen bits of the address are allocated to address network nodes: The 6-bit node identifier field allows up to 63 devices on each bus; the 1-bit bus identifier field allows up to 1,023 buses of various types (including internal) connected by bridges to be used in the system. The bus protocol allows device memory and registers be addressed in the DMA mode. The address space of each device has configuration registers containing all information necessary for other devices to interact with it. Data are sent in packets; arbitration status bits are sent at the start of each packet. A device can send data only if it wins the arbitration. There are two main data transfer types: isochronous, for which the bus was actually built, and asynchronous. Isochronous transfers provide guaranteed bandwidth and delay time; asynchronous transfers provided guaranteed delivery.

Asynchronous messages are sent between two devices. The initiator sends a request to the target device, on which the latter immediately (actually, after a short bus idle interval) issues either a positive (ACK) or, if a data error has been detected, negative (NACK) reception acknowledgements. A meaningful reply to the request (if required) will be sent back in the analogous way (the receiver must acknowledge it). If no ACK is received, the transmission is repeated several times until it succeeds or an error is recorded.

Isochronous transfers are broadcast. Up to 64 isochronous channels can be organized in the network, and each isochronous transfer packet, in addition to the data proper, carries the channel number. Data integrity is ensured by a CRC code. All bus devices hear isochronous transfers of all channels, but they receive only data from the channels in which they are interested. During the configuration stage, a device's isochronous data source (camera, receiver, player) receives the number and parameters of its allocated channel.

The bus supports dynamic reconfiguration (hot swapping capability). When a device is connected to the bus, it broadcasts a short asynchronous self-identifying packet. Upon receiving this packet, all devices already connected record a new device appearance and execute the bus reset procedure. During this process, the bus structure is determined, each node is assigned a physical address, and the arbitration process for the roles of the cycle master, isochronous resource controller, and the bus controller is performed. One second after the reset, all devices are available for further use, and each device has complete information about all other connected devices and their capabilities. All devices also detect a device being disconnected from the bus. Owing to the power supply lines, the interface part of the device can remain connected to the bus even when its functional part has been depowered.

A *cycle master* is a device that broadcasts start-of-cycle packets every 125 ms. In each of these packets, the cycle master sends the value of the 32-bit time counter, incremented at 24.576 MHz, to each node that supports isochronous exchange. In each cycle, one packet for each active isochronous channel is sent first, and then the bus remains in the idle state for some time. Afterward, the part of the cycle allocated to the asynchronous packet transfer starts. Each device that needs asynchronous transfer sends one packet in this part of the cycle. Devices that have no packets to transfer accordingly do not occupy the bus. After all devices have each sent one packet, they can send additional packets during the remaining cycle time.

An *isochronous resource controller* is a device that distributes channel numbers and allocates bus bandwidth for isochronous transfers. The controller is needed when there is at least one device on the bus that is capable of isochronous transfers. The controller is selected by arbitration from the devices that support isochronous exchange. After a reset, devices that require an isochronous transfer request the bandwidth they need. The bandwidth is measured in the special allocation units, of which there are 6,144 in a 125-μsec cycle. A unit takes about 20 nsec, which corresponds to the transmission time of one quadlet (a 32-bit word) at a speed of 1,600 Mbps. This method of measuring bandwidth makes it possible for different speed devices to use the bus simultaneously: In one cycle, adjacent packets can be sent at different speeds. At least 25 ms of the cycle is reserved for asynchronous traffic, so the total distributed isochronous traffic bandwidth is 4,915 units. Digital video requires bandwidth of 30 Mbps (25 Mbps for the video data and 3–4 Mbps for the audio data, clock, and packet headers). In the S100, digital video devices request about 1,800 units; in the S200, they request about 900 units. If the necessary bandwidth is not available, the controller will refuse the device's request and will not allocate it a channel number. A device that has not been allocated a channel will periodically repeat its request. When a node no longer needs isochronous exchange, it must release the bandwidth and the channel number it had been allocated so that other devices can avail themselves of these resources.

A *bus controller* is an optional element of a 1394 network that controls device features. This role can be played by a computer, a digital recording editing device, or a specialized intelligent control console. A bus master implementing `Topology_Map` and `Speed_Map` allows several frequencies to be used on one bus, according to the capabilities of the specific pair of devices taking part in the exchange. Otherwise, when different speed devices are connected, all transfers will be conducted at the speed that is available to all active devices.

4.2.3. 1394 Devices and Adapters

Unlike in Macintoshes, the 1394 interface is not as widely used in PC compatible computers as the already mandatory USB. FireWire adapters most often come as expansion cards, but they are already being built into some motherboard models.

A 1394 adapter for PC is a PCI/1394 bridge, because only the PCI bus is capable of letting through the full FireWire data stream.

The 1394 interface is becoming generally accepted for modern digital consumer audio, video, and photo equipment, which does not need a computer to use it. In addition to digital devices with built-in 1394 adapters, traditional analog and digital devices (players, cameras, monitors) can be connected to a FireWire bus using external interface and signal converting adapters.

Mass storage devices with the 1394 interface are also produced, including CD, DVD and AV drives (hard disk drives optimized for writing and reading multimedia data). 1394/IDE interface converters are also produced; these are designed as bays for standard IDE devices of 5 inch or 3.5 inch form factors. Regular hard drives, and CD and DVD drives can be placed into these bays, becoming mobile mass storage devices.

4.2.4. Use of the 1394

The main advantage of the 1394 bus is that it needs no controller. Any transmitting device can receive isochronous traffic bandwidth and start transmitting upon an autonomous or remote control signal: The receiver will "hear" the information it transmits. When there is a controller, appropriate software can control device operation, implementing, for example, a digital non-linear video editing studio or supplying the required multimedia data to all interested information users.

The biggest attraction of the 1394 bus is the possibility of interconnecting consumer electronics devices into a home network, with or without a PC. Moreover, the motley of different types of consumer electronics connectors are replaced with same type 1394 cables and connectors. Different types of digital signals (compressed video, digital audio, MIDI commands, device control signals, data) are multiplexed into one bus that traverses all premises. Using the same data sources (broadcast receivers, storage devices, video cameras, etc.), various applications can be viewed or listened to simultaneously in different places with the high quality provided by the digital technologies. Using a computer equipped with a 1394 adapter and the appropriate software significantly expands this network's capabilities. The computer becomes a virtual switch of the home audio/video studio. Applications for audio and video devices use logical plugs and sockets analogous to the connectors used in the conventional physical equipment. Plugs correspond to the outputs, and sockets to the inputs of the corresponding devices. By inserting these plugs into sockets, a required system can be assembled. Of course, in order for it to work, the Digital Interface for Consumer Electronics Audio/Video Equipment specification, an IEEE-1394 standard extension introduced by the Digital Video Consortium (DVC), must be implemented in the devices. Eventually, this specification is going to become an ISO/IEC standard.

The 1394 is supported by several operating systems, including Windows 98, Windows 95 OSR 2.1, and more recent ones. Audio-video files (AVI) can be edited using packages such as Adobe Premiere, Asymetrix Digital Video Producer, Ulead MediaStudio, and MGI VideWave. A codec converter of digital video data transferred over the 1394 bus into AVI files is produced by Adaptec.

One of the problems of digital transfer of multimedia information is copyright protection. Users must have the option of reproducing received programs or purchased disks, but their authors (manufacturers) must be able to protect their rights using restrictions on digital copying at their discretion. For the purposes of digital information copyright protection, the 5C consortium (comprising Sony, Matsushita, Intel, Hitachi, and Toshiba) are developing a data enciphering specification.

Chapter 5: SCSI Bus

The Small Computer System Interface (SCSI) bus is used to attach various small devices to a computer. Devices that can be attached include data-storage devices with random access (hard disks) and sequential access (streamers), CD-ROM and CD-R/RW drives, automatic media changers, printers, scanners, communications devices, and processors. A SCSI device can be either a *host-adapter*, which connects the SCSI bus with an internal computer bus, or a *target controller*, which connects a device to the SCSI bus. There can be more than one host-adapter on a bus: This allows peripheral sharing by several computers connected to one SCSI bus.

The bus treats all devices as peers that can function as both exchange initiators and target devices. In most cases, however, the host-adapter is the initiator. Each target device can have up to eight independently addressed logical devices that have their own logical unit numbers (LUN) representing peripheral devices or their parts. The exchange initiator sends a command-containing message to the target device. Commands are used to control devices and, of course, to exchange data. Data exchange is controlled by the target device that receives a command. During this process, it occupies the bus only during the active data transfer, relinquishing it while it searches for the data. During this time, other devices can use the bus to exchange data, which makes the SCSI bus highly practical for working with a large number of devices under the control of multitask or multithread operating systems.

The SCSI command system has been meticulously standardized, which makes for a high level of compatibility between devices of the same class from different vendors or of different models. Devices are classified according to their functional purpose and the commands needed to interact with them. Every device must support commands mandatory for its class. There are also commands mandatory for devices of all classes. In mass storage devices of different classes (random access magnetic discs, serial access tapes, optical discs, etc.), SCSI uses only one type of addressing, Logical Block Addressing (LBA): This makes it possible for devices of different classes or storage capacity to interact in a uniform way. Moreover, this allows blocks of data to be copied from one SCSI device to another directly, without the intermediate step of placing them into the computer's main memory. There also are keyword data search commands for mass data storage devices. SCSI supports command chains up to 256 commands long, in which execution results of a previous command (the address of the found block in a data search, for example) can be used as parameters for the next command. This makes it possible to unload the host even when performing quite sophisticated data storage and retrieval procedures. True, far from all of these advanced features are actually used by operating systems and applications. But even without them, the ability of SCSI devices to work independently of each other gives SCSI unarguable advantages over ATA as an interface for high-end data storage systems.

The first version of the bus, later called SCSI-1, was standardized by ANSI in 1986 (X3.131-1986). It was an 8-bit parallel bus with a maximum switching frequency of 5 MT/sec[1], to which up to 8 devices could be attached. Data transfer was carried out at up to 5 MBps in the asynchronous mode. Later, in 1991, the SCSI-2 (X3.131-1994) specification appeared, expanding the capabilities of the bus. The Fast SCSI-2 bus has a switching frequency of up to 10 MT/sec, while the Ultra SCSI-2 reaches frequencies of up to 20 MT/sec. Bus width can be increased to 16 bits. The 16-bit version is called Wide SCSI-2; the 8-bit version is called Narrow SCSI-2. The SCSI-2 standard also defined a 32-bit version of the interface that has not yet been applied in practice. The synchronous data-transfer mode and a different version of the interface have also been introduced. The SCSI-2 specification defines a command set including the common one that all peripheral devices are required to support. It also defines specific command subsets to support peripheral devices of various classes. The standard completely describes the device-interaction protocol, including the structure of the transmitted information.

The SCSI-3 specification is a further development of the standard, aimed at increasing the number of attached devices, broadening the command set, and supporting plug-and-play technology. As an alternative to the parallel SPI (SCSI-3 Parallel Interface) interface, the possibility of employing serial interfaces, including fiber-optic interfaces with speeds of 100 MBps, has been made available. SCSI-3 is a plentiful collection of documents

---

[1] MT/sec: Mega Transfers/sec. It is incorrect to call it the clock rate, as there is no timing-clock signal on the bus.

defining separate aspects of the interface on the level of the physical connections, transport protocols, and command sets. On the transport level, various protocols that have the appropriate support for physical connections can be used:

❑ SCSI Parallel Interface (SPI) deals with the parallel interface (connectors, signals).

❑ SCSI-3 Interlocked Protocol (SIP) is a traditional interface exchange protocol implemented physically by the SPI interface.

❑ Fibre Channel Protocol (FCP) is a fiber channel protocol with the corresponding physical level of FC-PH and a data-transmission rate of 100 MBps.

❑ Serial Bus Protocol (SBP) is implemented by the 1394 (FireWire) interface.

❑ Generic Packetized Protocol (GPP) is a general-purpose packet protocol, implemented by any packet interface.

❑ Serial Storage Protocol (SSP) is implemented using Serial Storage Architecture (SSA).

The chronology of the development of the parallel interfaces in SCSI-3 is as follows:

❑ *The SPI standard* (1995) defines the SCSI-3 P-cable, a one-piece cable with 68-pin connectors for the wide bus. It also defines the Fast SCSI transfer rate (Fast Wide SCSI working at 20 MBps). Later, the supplementary Fast-20 specification, better known as Ultra SCSI, was adopted (Ultra Wide SCSI working at 40 MBps).

❑ *The SPI-2 standard* (1999) again doubled the switching frequency due to its use of the LVD interface. The Fast 40 SCSI interface is better known as Ultra2 SCSI (Wide Ultra2 SCSI with transfer speed of 80 MBps). It introduced the Single-Connector Attachment connector (SCA-2), which allows "hot-swap" connections, and the 68-contact Very High Density Cable Interface connector (VHDCI). SPI-2 includes both the SCSI-2 A-cable and the SPI P-cable. It is a complete document in itself, without reference to the preceding standards, and defines all the SCSI parallel interfaces, up to and including the Fast-40.

❑ *The SPI-3 standard* (2000) doubled the transfer frequency, but this time by making use of the Fast-80DT (DT means double transition) double-synchronization interface, known as Ultra3 SCSI or Ultra160. This mode utilizes only the wide (16-bit) version. The traditional (high-voltage) differential version was abolished, as was the 32-bit bus and the Q-cable. Only the LVD interface and synchronization using the positive and negative transitions of the REQ#/ACK# signals were considered. CRC transmission control, packetized commands and messaging, and quick arbitration were introduced. This standard is also a complete document in itself. It describes all the SCSI parallel interfaces and abolishes HVD, SCSI Configured AutoMatically (SCAM), and the 32-bit bus.

❏ *The SPI-4 standard* (2001) doubled the switching frequency producing the Fast-160DT interface, already known as the Ultra320 SCSI. It uses only the wide bus with transfer rate 320 MBps.

5.1. SCSI Parallel Interfaces

There are several versions of the SCSI parallel interface. They differ in bus widths and in their methods of signal transmission and synchronization. Physically, the narrow SCSI interface is a bus consisting of 18 signal and several power lines. In the wide version, the number of signal lines is greater. Each signal line has its own return wire to reduce noise interference. The contacts of the signal and return lines in the 2-row connectors are located opposite each other. This allows the use of both twisted-pair wires and flat ribbon cables in which the signal and return wires alternate.

SCSI is divided into two categories by the type of signal used: single-ended and differential. They use identical cables and connectors, but have devices that are not electrically compatible.

In the widely used single-ended version, each signal is sent by a TTL-level potential referenced to the common wire. Every signal must have a separate common (return) wire to reduce crosstalk interference. SCSI-1 uses open-collector transmitters and receivers built on bipolar transistors. Passive terminators are employed to keep the signal level high when transmitters are inactive (see *Section 5.1.4*). In SCSI-2, active-negation transmitters also started to be used. To remove the signal, an open-collector circuit "drops" the line, and its potential is returned to the initial state only by the terminators. When active negation is used, the output circuit of the transmitter briefly forces the line into passive-state potential, after which it "releases" the line. This creates the illusion that it is possible to operate without terminators. In SCSI-3, the SPI standard prescribes CMOS-interface integrated circuits.

The *differential version (Diff or HVD)* sends a paraphase signal on a wire pair. It uses the same special differential transceivers as the RS-485 interface, which allows significantly greater cable length while preserving the exchange rate. The differential interface is used in server-disk systems, but is not common in standard PCs. The HVD interface (under its old name of Diff) was introduced in SCSI-2, but SPI-3 (SCSI-3 in 1999) abolished it as it could not support the speeds of Ultra2 and higher.

The Low-Voltage Differential interface (LVD) allows Ultra2-, Ultra160-, and Ultra320-class devices to work at transfer frequencies of 40 MT/sec, 80 MT/sec, and 160 MT/sec on buses 80 feet long (8 devices) or 40 feet long (16 devices). LVD devices are compatible with single-ended devices because of their automatic-reconfiguration capability (Multimode LVD). LVD devices sense the voltage level on the DIFFSENS line and can switch from the LVD (differential) mode into the single-ended mode at low voltage levels. The connector contact, to which this line is attached, is grounded, so all devices attached to the bus automatically switch to the single-ended mode if there is even one single-ended device present on the bus.

Data-transfer rate is determined by signal-switching frequency (measured in MT/sec), bus width, and, in later versions, also by the method of synchronization (single- or double-transition clocking). The first SCSI buses were 8 bits wide (Narrow) and had switching frequencies of up to 5 MT/sec. The wide version of the bus is 16 bits wide. The combination of these parameters provides a broad throughput range (Table 5.1) reaching up to 320 MBps. The terminology used to indicate the throughput of various interfaces varies; in this book, I shall use the designations used by Western Digital in 2000. Fast SCSI means transmission frequency of 10 MT/sec; time diagrams for this mode are defined by SCSI-2. Fast-20 denotes Fast Wide SCSI (16-bit bus width, 10 MT/sec switching frequency). The Ultra SCSI mode indicates a transfer frequency of 20 MT/sec. It is defined for the parallel interface by the SCSI-3. Fast-40 corresponds to Wide Ultra SCSI (16-bit bus, 20 MT/sec switching frequency). Ultra2 SCSI indicates a switching frequency of 40 MT/sec. Fast-80 means Wide Ultra 2 SCSI (16-bit bus width, 40 MT/sec switching frequency). This mode, defined by SCSI-3, currently is the most widely used by new devices with parallel buses; it has been implemented only in the low-voltage differential version of the interface (LVD). The concept of Ultra3 SCSI in SCSI-3 is rather broad. Ultra160 SCSI indicates a speed of 160 MBps and exists only in the wide (16-bit) version. It uses double-transition clocking and employs CRC to control data integrity, which means it can "squeeze" the maximum transfer rate out of the cable (like the Ultra DMA ATA interface). In 2001, the Ultra320 SCSI interface came out, with speeds of 320 MBps.

Table 5.1. Data-Transfer Rates (MBps) in the Parallel SCSI Bus

Bus width (bits)	Version Regular	Fast	Fast-20 (Ultra)	Fast-40 (Ultra2)	Ultra160 (Ultra3)	Ultra320
8 (Narrow)	5	10	20	40	–	–
16 (Wide)	10	20	40	80	160	320

The most popular interface, Ultra2 SCSI, provides a good combination of bus throughput, length, device cost, and compatibility with traditional SCSI devices.

5.1.1. Bus Protocol

Table 5.2 shows the functions of parallel-bus signals. All signals are low-active: Low potential corresponds to the active state and to logical one, marked here by the # character. The reverse, or paraphase, circuits are marked by the + character.

Table 5.2. Functions of the SCSI Bus Signals

Signal	Function
BSY#	Busy: bus is busy
SEL#	Select: selection of a target device by the initiator (Select) or selection of the initiator by a target device (Reselect)
C/D#	Control/Data: control — low level, data — high level
I/O#	Input/Output: transmission direction relative to the initiating device. Low level corresponds to input into the initiating device. Used to differentiate between direct (Select) and reverse (Reselect) selection: low level corresponds to the selection phase.
MSG#	Message: sending message
DB[0:31]#	Data Bus: inverted data bus
DP[0:3]#	Data Parity: Inverted parity bits that augment byte parity to odd DP0# pertains to DB[0:7], ... DP3# pertains to DB[24:31]. Inoperative in the arbitration phase
TERMPWR	Terminator Power
ATN#	Attention. Indicates initiator's intention to send a message
REQ#	Request. Request from a target device to send data
ACK#	Acknowledge: transmission confirmation (answer to REQ#)
RST#	Reset
DIFFSENS	Indicator of the differential (LVD) interface: below 0.7 V — single ended 0.9 V to 1.9 V — differential LVD above 2.4 V — differential HVD

Every SCSI device connected to the bus must have a unique address, which is assigned to it when the device is configured. For the 8-bit bus, the address value range is from 0 to 7, while for the 16-bit bus it is from 0 to 15. The address is assigned by setting switches or jumpers. A host adapter can be configured using software. Addressing devices on the bus during the selection phase is carried out using the SCSI ID identifier, which presents the address in positional code. The device's address is defined by the number of the data-bus line that selects given device. A device with an address of zero is selected by the low level on line DB0# (SCSI ID=00000001); a device with an address of seven — by the low level on line DB7# (SCSI ID=10000000). The identifier value determines the device's priority in using the bus, and the device with the highest address has the highest priority. The address and identifier concepts are often confused, but they are simply two different ways of referring to the same parameter.

Only two devices can use the bus to exchange information at any one moment. The exchange process is set off by the exchange initiator and executed by the target device. The exchange initiator selects the target device by its identifier. In most cases, the devices' roles are fixed: The host adapter is the exchange initiator and a peripheral device is the target device. Combination devices, which function as both the exchange initiator and the target device, are also possible. In some cases, devices can switch their roles: Having completed the arbitration phase, the exchange initiator may perform reverse selection (Reselect) of the target device to continue the interrupted operation. When executing the Copy command, the exchange initiator directs the copying master device to perform data exchange that may also be performed with another target device, in which case the copying master device functions as the exchange initiator.

Information is transferred through the data bus, one byte (or word) at a time, asynchronously, employing request (REQ) acknowledge (ACK). Each byte is checked on odd parity (except at the arbitration phase), but this control may be disabled. The interface has the capability for synchronous data transfer, which increases the exchange rate. (SCSI-1 did not have the synchronous transfer feature).

The bus may be in one of the phases listed below. The functions of the signal sources between the exchange initiator and the target device are described in Table 5.3.

Table 5.3. SCSI Signal Sources

Bus phase	Signal BSY#	SEL#	REQ#, C/D#, I/O#, MSG#	ACK#, ATN#	DBx#, DBPx#
Bus Free	—	—	—	—	—
Arbitration	AA[1]	WA[2]	—	—	SID[3]
Selection	I[4], T[5]	I	—	I	I
Reselection	I, T	T	T	I	T
Command	T	—	T	I	I
Data IN	T	—	T	I	T
Data OUT	T	—	T	I	I
Status	T	—	T	I	T
Message IN	T	—	T	I	T
Message OUT	T	—	T	I	I

[1] AA: signal source is a device arbitrating for bus control.

[2] WA: signal source is the device that has won the arbitration.

[3] SID: each device controls only 1 data bit, which corresponds to the value of its SCSI ID.

[4] I: signal source is the exchange initiator.

[5] T: signal source is a target device.

In the Bus Free phase, the bus is inactive: No transfer processes are taking place, and it is ready for arbitration. This phase is indicated by the passive state of the BSY# and SEL# lines.

In the Arbitration phase, a device can obtain the right to control the bus. When the bus is free, a device asserts the BSY# signal and its SCSI ID identifier. If several devices assert their address lines at the same time, the device with the highest address receives the right to control the bus, and the rest of the devices disconnect until the next time the bus is free. The device that wins the arbitration asserts the SEL# signal and proceeds to the Selection or Reselection phase.

In the Selection phase, the exchange initiator that has won the arbitration performs a logical OR function on two identifiers — its own and that of the target device — then adds a parity bit to the result and places the final result on the data bus. By asserting the ATN# signal, the exchange initiator indicates that the following phase will be Message OUT. Next, the exchange initiator deasserts the BSY# signal. (The absence of an I/O# signal differentiates this phase from the Reselection phase.) The addressed target device responds with a BSY# signal if the parity is correct and there are only two identifiers on the data bus (its own and that of the exchange initiator). Devices do not react to wrong data. If during the predetermined time the target device does not answer, a time out is triggered and the exchange initiator releases the bus or asserts the reset signal RST#.

The Reselection phase is analogous to the Selection phase, but is initiated by a target device. This phase is introduced when a target device disconnects from the bus while a command is being executed. When the internal operation is completed, this device, having won the arbitration, will call the exchange initiator that initiated the operation. The target device deasserts the BSY# signal. (The active I/O# signal distinguishes this phase from the Selection phase.) The addressed exchange initiator responds by asserting the BSY# signal line. The response and time-out conditions are analogous to the previous phase.

During the Command, Data, Status, and Message phases, the bus is engaged in information transfer; the phases are identified by the MSG#, C/D#, and I/O# signals (Table 5.4), which are controlled by the target device. The exchange initiator may request to send a message (Message OUT phase) by asserting the ATN# signal line, and the target device may let go of the bus by deasserting the MSG#, C/D#, I/O#, and BSY# signals.

Table 5.4. SCSI Information Phases

Signal MSG#	C/D#	I/O#	Phase	Direction
0	0	0	Data OUT	I → T
0	0	1	Data IN	I ← T
0	1	0	Command	I → T

continues

Table 5.4 Continued

Signal MSG#	C/D#	I/O#	Phase	Direction
0	1	1	Status	I ← T
1	0	0	Reserved	
1	0	1	Reserved	
1	1	0	Message OUT	I → T
1	1	1	Message IN	I ← T

Fig. 5.1 shows time diagrams for asynchronous exchange. Here, the transmission of each byte is accompanied by an interclocked pair of REQ#/ACK# signals. The exchange initiator latches in the incoming data at the trailing edge of the REQ# signal. The target device considers the received data valid at the trailing edge of the ACK# signal. The asynchronous-transfer mode is supported by all devices during all information-transfer phases.

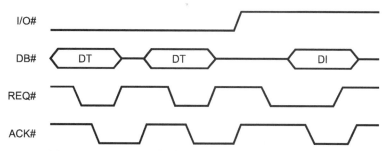

Fig. 5.1. Time diagrams for asynchronous transfer
(DI: data from exchange initiator, DT: data from target device)

If the devices agree, the data-transfer phases Data OUT and Data IN can also be carried out in the synchronous-transfer mode, time diagrams for which are shown in Fig. 5.2. During negotiation to the synchronous mode, the minimum lengths and periods of the ACK# and REQ# control signals are established, as is the permissible time lag between requests and acknowledgements (the REQ/ACK offset agreement). The target device sends a series of data accompanied by REQ# strobes (Fig. 5.2, *a*), at a rate bounded by the set timing parameters. The exchange initiator latches the input data at the negative edge of the REQ# signal, but can confirm the data by the ACK# signal only after some delay. As soon as the lag between the sent ACK# and received REQ# signals reaches the predetermined limit (2 in the present example), the target device will suspend the exchange until the arrival of the next ACK# confirmation. The operation is considered to have been completed when the number of received acknowledgements matches the number of sent requests. When data are received by the target device, the negotiation mechanism is the same, but data are latched at the negative edge of the ACK# signal (Fig. 5.2, *b*).

CAUTION

The SCSI-1 specification does not explicitly describe when the transmission is resumed after the lag has been eliminated. As a result, developers could assume that the next request (and data) could follow only after the end of the positive transition of an ACK# signal. A device constructed with this assumption can lose data, as the last REQ# signal appears unexpected to it (as do the data) and looks as though it exceeds the negotiated offset.

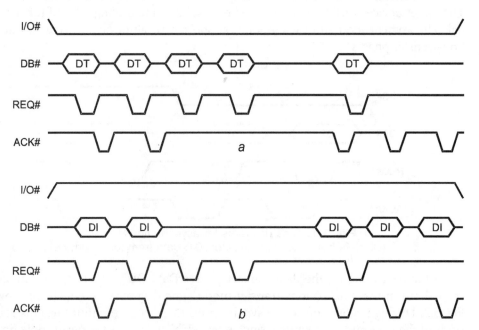

Fig. 5.2. Time diagrams for synchronous exchange: *a* — transmission; *b* — reception

16-bit exchange is done in a similar way. If not all bytes are used in the last data phase, the transmitter must set the correct parity for the unused bytes as well.

Time delays were not mentioned in the descriptions of data-transmission phases. The specification defines them in such a way that a potential "skew" — signals' not arriving at the same time because of delays caused by the electronic circuits or by different cable wires — will not affect the stability of the protocol. In the asynchronous mode, the data-transfer rate also is affected by the length of the cable, as changes in the transfer participants' states propagate along the cable at limited speed. If the wide bus consists of two cables (A and B, although this does not often happen in practice), then each of them has its own pair of control signals (REQ#/ACK# and REQB#/ACKB#) because the cables may be of different lengths.

During the Command phase, the target device requests a command from the exchange initiator. In the Status phase, the target device makes a request to send the exchange initiator information about its state. In the Data IN and Data OUT phases, the target device makes requests for transmitting data to and from the exchange initiator, respectively. The Message IN and Message OUT phases are used to send messages. The Message OUT phase is launched by the target device in response to the *Attention* condition, created by an ATN# signal from the exchange initiator when it needs to send a message to the target device. The Message IN phase is initiated by the target device when it needs to send a message to the exchange initiator.

The BSY#, SEL#, REQ#, and ACK# signals cannot change their states between data-transmission phases; only the C/D#, I/O#, MSG#, and the data-bus signals can change.

The ATN# and RST# signals can initiate the Attention and Reset conditions, respectively; moreover, they do this asynchronously with respect to the bus phases. These conditions may lead to a change in the predetermined sequence of phases. The ATN# signal is asserted by an exchange initiator at any phase, except in the Arbitration and Bus Free phases. The RST# signal may be asserted by any device, and all devices must release the bus upon Reset. Depending on the setup parameters adopted for all devices of the particular system, two reset versions are possible. The "hard" reset places devices into the state assumed when the power is turned on, clearing all current processes, queues, etc. With the "soft" reset, devices attempt to complete the operations in progress, preserving the current setup parameters, when the bus becomes available.

An input/output process consists of the following sequence of bus phases: from the Bus Free phase, a transition is made into the Selection or Reselection phase via the Arbitration phase. Then follow the Command, Data, Status, and Message information-transfer phases. The final phase is the Message IN phase, during which the Disconnect or Command Complete message is sent. The bus then goes into the inactive Bus Free phase.

The SCSI architecture allows each input/output process to save a set of three pointers (saved SCSI pointers): command, status, and data. The exchange initiator has the current set of pointers (only one), into which the saved set for the current process is copied. The current pointers point to the bytes of the next command, status, and data, which are going to be transferred between the exchange initiator and the target device. The saved command and status pointers always point to the start of the command and status descriptor blocks. The saved data pointer points to the beginning of the data block until the target device sends the Save Data Pointer message. Upon receiving it, the exchange initiator saves the current data pointer. When the target device disconnects from the bus, information about the current I/O process is contained in the saved set of pointers. When the process is resumed, the target device may send a Restore Pointers message, requesting the exchange initiator to copy the saved set into the current set and to continue executing the commands of the given I/O process.

Because the target device may modify the data pointer before the I/O operation is completed, determining the real amount of data transferred using the pointer does not produce reliable results.

CAUTION

5.1.2. Interface Control and Command Execution

The *Message System* — a system of message exchange between the exchange initiator and the target device — is employed to control the interface. Exchange takes place during the Message IN/OUT phases; several messages can be sent during one phase.

Synchronous-mode parameters and data width are negotiated using messages. The process of negotiating synchronous-exchange parameters is called *Synchronous Negotiation.* Devices requesting synchronous exchange send a Synchronous Data Transfer Request message indicating the acceptable cycle period and REQ/ACK lag. If the other exchange participant supports the synchronous mode, it will offer its parameters. Parameters that need to be negotiated are the maximum period and the minimum lag (zero lag is equivalent to asynchronous mode). The selected mode will be valid only for the phases of transmission between the given pair of devices. A rejected message is a request for the asynchronous mode. Because old host adapters did not support synchronous-mode negotiation, a target device may have its synchronous-mode request feature disabled. The host can determine whether synchronous-mode operation is possible by sending the Request Sense and Inquiry commands.

The width of transmissions is similarly negotiated, using the Wide Data Transfer Request. The negotiated modes will be valid until the devices are reset by the Bus Device Reset message or by a hard reset, which will cause the devices to switch into the default power-on mode. Transmission-mode negotiation should not be initiated in every process, since time expenditures on this procedure can nullify any productivity gains.

The *SCSI command system* includes common commands supported by all classes of devices, as well as commands specific to individual classes. Any SCSI device must support the mandatory commands of the common set and of its class, which provides a high level of compatibility. Commands are transmitted by an exchange initiator to a target device via the *command descriptor block* sent during the *Command* phase. Some commands are accompanied by a parameter block that follows the descriptor block during the *Data* phase. The block formats are standardized; block length determined by the operation code (the first byte in the block) may be 6, 10, or 12 bytes.

As an example, the SCSI bus process can be considered using a *single command*: Read. The exchange initiator has the active set of pointers and several saved sets, one for each of the permitted number of simultaneous contenting processes. The exchange initiator restores the process pointers to the active set and, having won the arbitration, selects a target device. As soon as the target device is selected, it takes control over the process. During the *Selection* phase, the exchange initiator asserts the ATN# signal, informing of its intention to send an *Identify* message that indicates the addressed logical device. The target device goes into the *Command* phase and receives the descriptor block of the *Read* command. Having interpreted the command, the target device goes into the Data IN phase and sends the requested data, then goes into the *Status* phase and sends the status *Good*. Then, in the *Message In* phase, the device sends a *Command Complete* message, after which it releases the bus (*Bus Free* phase). The process has been completed.

The same example can be considered with a disconnection from the bus in the process of the command execution. If a device that receives the *Read* command determines that it will take it a long time to prepare the requested data for transmission, it will release the bus by sending a *Disconnect* message. As soon as the target device has the requested data ready, it goes into arbitration. Having won it, the device will select the exchange initiator (during the *Reselect* phase), and during the *Message In* phase will send an *Identify* message to the exchange initiator. The exchange initiator will return the corresponding set of pointers to the active state and will continue executing the process as described earlier. If the target device wants to disconnect when a portion of data has already been transmitted (e.g., if a disk head has reached the end of the cylinder and needs to be repositioned), it sends a *Save Data Pointer* message followed by a *Disconnect* message. After reconnecting, transmission will resume from the point defined by the last saved pointer value. In case of an error or exception, the target device can repeat the data exchange by sending a *Restore Pointers* message or disconnecting without sending a *Save Data Pointers* message.

The process could also include a *chain of linked commands*. Upon successful completion of each command in the chain, the target device automatically begins executing the next one. All the commands in the chain are part of a single process. The commands are not completely independent: When relative addressing is employed, the block addressed by the last command is accessible to the next one. For example, by executing a *Search Data* command, the block of the disk containing the information that matches the search template will be found. By linking the *Read* command to the *Search Data* command, this block or a block with the specified offset relative to the found one can be read. When execution of the linked commands is complete, the target device sends a *Linked Command Complete* message (possibly with a flag), and the exchange initiator refreshes the set of the saved pointers so that they point to the next command in the chain. Commands in the chain are executed as being single but with the potential for relative addressing.

Commands may be executed *using queues*. Target devices can support tagged and untagged queues. Support of the tagged queues, which was defined as early as SCSI-1, allows any logical unit number or a target program executing a process from one exchange initiator to accept commands (launch a process) from other exchange initiators.

Tagged queues are defined in SCSI-2 for logical unit numbers. For each exchange initiator-target device-logical unit link, there is a queue up to 256 processes long. Each process employing tagged queues is identified by an I_T_L_Q link, where Q is a one-byte queue tag. Tags are assigned to the processes by the exchange initiator; their values do not affect the sequence, in which operations are executed.

Queue placement is done by a messaging mechanism. Moreover, the next process may be placed into the queue either "honestly" or may jump the line: A process placed into the queue with a Head of Queue Tag message will be executed immediately after the active process is completed. Processes placed into the queue with Simple Queue Tag messages are executed by the target device in the sequence that it considers to be optimal. A process placed into the queue with an Ordered Queue Tag message will be executed last. The exchange initiator can remove a process from the queue by referencing it by its tag. Changing the order, in which the target device executes commands, does not affect the command order in the chain, because the chain belongs to a single process; it is the processes that are placed into queues.

The various situations that can lead to deviations from the interface's normal event sequence are not considered here. These situations include erroneous connections by the exchange initiator, the selection of a non-existent logical unit number, unexpected exchange-initiator selections, parameter rounding, reaction to asynchronous events, etc.

5.1.3. Cables, Connectors, and Signals

Flat ribbon or round flexible cables are typical for parallel interfaces. Flat ribbon cables are used to connect internal devices. They can have several connectors. If necessary, cables can be linked using special matching connectors but only of the butt type. (T-connectors are not allowed, although it is possible to have a branch of less than 4 inches, including the length of cable from the branch to the input of the transceiver's integrated circuit.) Twisted-pair round cross-section cables are used to attach external devices. External peripheral devices usually have two connectors, allowing them to be connected in chain. The length of the cable depends on the interface version and the frequency (Table 5.5). When calculating the overall cable length, the possibility of employing one host adapter port simultaneously for external and internal connections must be considered. In this case the lengths of the external and the internal cables must be added up. Cable connectors are always connected one-to-one to contacts of similar circuits.

Table 5.5. Maximum Lengths of SCSI Cables

Interface type	Regular (5 MT/sec)	Fast (10 MT/sec)	Ultra (20 MT/sec)	Ultra 2 (40 MT/sec)	Ultra160 (80 MT/sec)	Ultra320 (160 MT/sec)
Single-ended	6 m	3 m	1.5 m (8 devices) 3 m (4 devices)	–	–	–
High-Voltage Differential (HVD)	25 m	12 m (16 devices) 25 m (8 devices)	6 m (16 devices) 25 m (8 devices)	–	–	–
Low-Voltage Differential (LVD)	–	–	–	12 m (16 devices) 25 m (8 devices)	12 m (16 devices) 25 m (8 devices)	12 m (16 devices) 25 m (8 devices)

The variety of connectors used in SCSI devices is now so diverse that matching adapters sometimes need to be used. Connectors vary in the number their contacts, as well as in the contacts' shape and size. Practically all connectors are of the two-row type, and the layout of the contacts is designed for the alternation of the signal and return wires. The exceptions are DB-25 connectors, which have fewer earth contacts than signal contacts, and three-row DB-50 connectors. Connector types are as follows:

❏ IDC-50 connectors (analogous to ATA 40-pin IDC-40 connectors) are used for connecting internal devices. They have square pins spaced 0.1 inch (2.54 mm) apart and plastic cases without additional casing or latches (Fig 5.3, *a*). Devices are fitted with plugs (IDC-50M); ribbon cables are fitted with sockets (IDC-50F).

❏ CX-50 are Centronics-type connectors, analogous to those used on printers, but with 50 contacts. They have flat contacts spaced 0.085 inches (2.16 mm) apart and have a metal casing (Fig. 5.3, *b*). X-50 connectors are used to attach external devices. Devices (and SCSI adapters) are equipped with sockets (CX-50F); cables are equipped with plugs (XC-50M). To secure connectors in place, female connectors have wire latches that snap into notches on male connectors. These connectors are often called SCSI-1 External.

❏ DB-25 are connectors with round pins enclosed in a D-shaped protective shell (like LPT port connectors). Devices are equipped with female connectors (DB-25F), cables are equipped with male connectors (DB-25M); connectors are secured in place by screws (Fig. 5.3, *c*). These connectors are used on some external devices, such as Zip drives).

❏ HD-50, or MiniD50, (Fig. 5.3, *d*), connectors have pins enclosed in a metal D-shell. They are high pin-density connectors, with pins 0.05 inch (1.27 mm) apart. Devices are equipped with *female* connectors (HD-50F), cables with *male* (HD-50M) connectors. Connectors are secured in place by a clip-type latch.

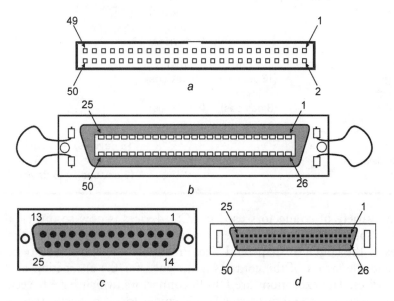

Fig. 5.3. Connectors for 8-bit SCSI devices:
a — IDC-50F; *b* — CX-50F; *c* — DB-25F; *d* — HD-50F

❏ HD-68HD-68, or Mini68, connectors are similar to HD-50, but have 68 contacts. Devices are equipped with female connectors (HD-68F or MiniD68F), cables are equipped with male connectors (HD-68M or MiniD68M). External connectors are secured in place by clips or screws, internal connectors are held in place only by friction. They are often called SCSI-3 connectors and now are most commonly used for the wide SCSI interface. Fig. 5.4 shows an external connector; the left part shows the clip type latch, the right part shows the screw bushing.

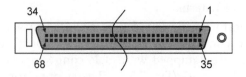

Fig. 5.4. HD-68F connector for a 16-bit SCSI device

❏ VHDCI-68 are very high density, Centronics-type external connectors with contacts spaced 0.8 mm apart. They are seldom used. Sometimes they are mistakenly referred to as SCSI-4 or SCSI-5 connectors.

❏ MCX (Micro-Centronics) are miniaturized versions of Centronics-style connectors. The most commonly used are MCX-68 and MCX-80 connectors, better known as SCA connectors.

❏ Single Connector Attachment (SCA) connectors are used to attach devices using only the connectors (i.e., using no cables). They are meant to connect internal disk drives with the possibility of hot-swap replacement (or at least easy replacement via the front panel). Currently, the prevalent is the SCA-2 specification implemented in MCX-80 connectors (Fig. 5.5). Devices are equipped with male connectors (MCX-80M), while female connectors (MCX-80F) are installed on computers. In addition to the regular interface signals, an SCA connector includes all the power and configuration signals needed by the device (identifier, modes, etc.). The side guides of the connector have additional contacts for the ground connection. Configuration jumpers are installed on the computer case or the adapter card, not on the device.

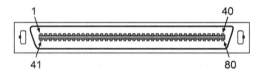

Fig. 5.5. SCA-80 connector for a hot-swap SCSI device

Narrow SCSI uses the connectors depicted in Fig. 5.3, while Wide SCSI uses those shown in Fig. 5.4. Miniature D-shape SCA-2 connectors accommodating all the power and signal circuits needed by a device are used to attach hot-swap devices.

SCSI also employs a broad variety of cables:

❏ *A-cable* is the standard cable for 8-bit interfaces. It has 25 wire pairs. Flat ribbon cable is used for connecting internal devices; round cable consisting of 25 twisted pairs enclosed in a common shield is used for attaching external devices.

  • Internal SCSI-1 and SCSI-2 A-cable has low contact-density IDC-50 female connectors (see Fig. 5.3, *a*).

  • External SCSI-1 A-cable has Centronics-type CX-50M male connectors (Fig. 5.3, *b*).

  • External SCSI-2 A-cable has MiniD50M (HD-50M) male connectors (Fig. 5.3, *c*).

❏ *B-cable* is a seldom-used 16- or 32-bit SCSI-2 expander.

❏ *P-cable* is a 34-wire-pair, 8- or 16-bit cable with improved, shielded miniature connectors. It is used in SCSI-2 and SCSI-3. Contacts 1–5, 31–39, and 65–68 are not used in the 8-bit version.

- Internal SCSI-3 P-cable has HD68M male connectors without latches.
- External SCSI-3 P-cable has MiniD68M male connectors with latches.
- External SCSI-2 SPI-2 P-cable has VHDCI-68M high contact-density male connectors. (It is sometimes mistakenly called a SCSI-4 or SCSI-5 cable).

❏ *Q-cable* is a 68-wire expansion to the 32-bit bus used in pair with the P-cable and has an analogous construction. Q-cable has never been used in practice, and the SCSI SPI-3 specification no longer recognizes it.

❏ *Mac SCSI* is an 8-bit cable with DB-25P connectors (Fig. 5.3, *d*). It is a standard cable for Macintosh computers, used to attach some external devices, such as Iomega Zip drives. If a 25-contact connector is installed on the host adapter, the cable has a different line layout.

There are also various types of matching adapters and cables, with different types of connectors. Adapters are produced as a printed circuit board or a monolithic construction with different types of connectors on opposite ends. Adapters that connect buses of different widths may have a high-order byte terminator, which must have a disconnect feature (see *Section 5.1.5*). Adapters for attaching SCA to a regular bus have standard power connectors, as well as a set of device-configuration jumpers.

Tables 5.6–5.10 list the functions of SCSI cable connectors' contacts. The contact numbering system, which is different for external and internal connectors, is inconvenient. However, the physical layout of the contacts on the connector and wires in the flat ribbon cable is the same. Signal lines alternate with return lines, which are grounded in single-ended devices.

Table 5.6. SCSI A-Cable Connector

Contact IDC-50/CX-50	Signal SE/Diff	Contact IDC-50/CX-50	Signal
1/1	GND/DB0+	2/26	DB0#
3/2	GND/DB1+	4/27	DB1#
5/3	GND/DB2+	6/28	DB2#
7/4	GND/DB3+	8/29	DB3#
9/5	GND/DB4+	10/30	DB4#

continues

Table 5.6 Continued

Contact IDC-50/CX-50	Signal SE/Diff	Contact IDC-50/CX-50	Signal
11/6	GND/DB5+	12/31	DB5#
13/7	GND/DB6+	14/32	DB6#
15/8	GND/DB7+	16/33	DB7#
17/9	GND/DBP0+	18/34	DBP0#
19/10	GND/GND	20/35	GND
21/11	GND/GND	22/36	GND
3/12	Reserved	24/37	Reserved
25/13	Not used	26/38	TERMPWR
27/14	Reserved	28/39	Reserved
29/15	GND	30/40	GND
31/16	GND/ATN+	32/41	ATN#
33/17	GND	34/42	GND
35/18	GND/BSY+	36/43	BSY#
37/19	GND/ACK+	38/44	ACK#
39/20	GND/RST+	40/45	RST#
41/21	GND/MSG+	42/46	MSG#
43/22	GND/SEL+	44/47	SEL#
45/23	GND/C/D+	46/48	C/D#
47/24	GND/REQ+	48/49	REQ#
49/25	GND/I/O+	50/50	I/O#

Table 5.7. SCSI B-Cable Connector

Contact internal/external	Signal SE/Diff	Contact internal/external	Signal
1/1	GND	2/35	GND
3/2	GND/DB8+	4/36	DB8#
5/3	GND/DB9+	6/37	DB9#

continues

Table 5.7 Continued

Contact internal/external	Signal SE/Diff	Contact internal/external	Signal
7/4	GND/DB10+	8/38	DB10#
9/5	GND/DB11+	10/39	DB11#
11/6	GND/DB12+	12/40	DB12#
13/7	GND/DB13+	14/41	DB13#
15/8	GND/DB14+	16/42	DB14#
17/9	GND/DB15+	18/43	DB15#
19/10	GND/DBP1+	20/44	DBP1#
21/11	GND/ACKB+	22/45	ACKB#
23/12	GND/GND	24/46	GND
25/13	GND/REQB+	26/47	REQB#
27/14	GND/DB16+	28/48	DB16#
29/15	GND/DB17+	30/49	DB17#
31/16	GND/DB18+	32/50	DB18#
33/17	TERMPWR	34/51	TERMPWR
35/18	TERMPWR	36/52	TERMPWR
37/19	GND/DB19+	38/53	DB19#
39/20	GND/DB20+	40/54	DB20#
41/21	GND/DB21+	42/55	DB21#
43/22	GND/DB22+	44/56	DB22#
45/23	GND/DB23+	46/57	DB23#
47/24	GND/DBP2+	48/58	DBP2#
49/25	GND/DB24+	50/59	DB24#
51/26	GND/DB25+	52/60	DB25#
53/27	GND/DB26+	54/61	DB26#
55/28	GND/DB27+	56/62	DB27#
57/29	GND/DB28+	58/63	DB28#
59/30	GND/DB29+	60/64	DB29#

continues

Table 5.7 Continued

Contact internal/external	Signal SE/Diff	Contact internal/external	Signal
61/31	GND/DB30+	62/65	DB30#
53/32	GND/DB31+	64/66	DB31#
65/33	GND/DBP2+	66/67	DBP2#
67/34	GND/GND	68/68	GND

Table 5.8. SCSI P-Cable Connector

Contact	Signal SE/Diff	Contact	Signal
1	GND/DB12+	35	DB12#
2	GND/DB13+	36	DB13#
3	GND/DB14+	37	DB14#
4	GND/DB15+	38	DB15#
5	GND/DBP1+	39	DBP1#
6	GND/DB0+	40	DB0#
7	GND/DB1+	41	DB1#
8	GND/DB2+	42	DB2#
9	GND/DB3+	43	DB3#
10	GND/DB4+	44	DB4#
11	GND/DB5+	45	DB5#
12	GND/DB6+	46	DB6#
13	GND/DB7+	47	DB7#
14	GND/DBP0+	48	DBP0#
15	GND	49	GND
16	DIFFSENS (GND)[1]	50	GND
17	TERMPWR	51	TERMPWR
18	TERMPWR	52	TERMPWR
19	Reserved	53	Reserved

continues

Table 5.8 Continued

Contact	Signal SE/Diff	Contact	Signal
20	GND	54	GND
21	GND/ATN+	55	ATN#
22	GND/GND	56	GND
23	GND/BSY+	57	BSY#
24	GND/ACK+	58	ACK#
25	GND/RST+	59	RST#
26	GND/MSG+	60	MSG#
27	GND/SEL+	61	SEL#
28	GND/C/D+	62	C/D#
29	GND/REQ+	63	REQ#
30	GND/I/O+	64	I/O#
31	GND/DB8+	65	DB8#
32	GND/DB9+	66	DB9#
33	GND/DB10+	67	DB10#
34	GND/DB11+	68	DB11#

[1] The DIFFSENS signal is defined only for the LVD interface.

Table 5.9. Mac SCSI Connector (DB-25)

Contact	Signal	Contact	Signal
1	REQ#	14	GND
2	MSG#	15	C/D#
3	I/O#	16	GND
4	RST#	17	ATN#
5	ACK#	18	GND
6	BSY#	19	SEL#
7	GND	20	DBP0#
8	DB0#	21	DB1#

continues

Table 5.9 Continued

Contact	Signal	Contact	Signal
9	GND	22	DB2#
10	DB3#	23	DB4#
11	DB5#	24	GND
12	DB6#	25	TERMPWR
13	DB7#		

Table 5.10. SCA-80 Connector

Contact	Signal	Contact	Signal SE/Diff
01	12 V Charge	41	12 V GND
02	12 V	42	12 V GND
03	12 V	43	12 V GND
04	12 V	44	Mated 1
05	Reserved	45	Reserved
06	Reserved	46	GND (DIFFSENS)
07	DB11#	47	GND/DB11+
08	DB10#	48	GND/DB10+
09	DB9#	49	GND/DB9+
10	DB8#	50	GND/DB8+
11	I/O#	51	GND/I/O+
12	REQ#	52	GND/REQ+
13	C/D#	53	GND/C/D+
14	SEL#	54	GND/SEL+
15	MSG#	55	GND/MSG+
16	RST#	56	GND/RST+
17	ACK#	57	GND/ACK+
18	BSY#	58	GND/BSY+
19	ATN#	59	GND/ATN+

continues

Table 5.10 Continued

Contact	Signal	Contact	Signal SE/Diff
20	DBP0#	60	GND/DBP0+
21	DB7#	61	GND/DB7+
22	DB6#	62	GND/DB6+
23	DB5#	63	GND/DB5+
24	DB4#	64	GND/DB4+
25	DB3#	65	GND/DB3+
26	DB2#	66	GND/DB2+
27	DB1#	67	GND/DB1+
28	DB0#	68	GND/DB0+
29	DBP1#	69	GND/DBP1+
30	DB15#	70	GND/DB15+
31	DB14#	71	GND/DB14+
32	DB13#	72	GND/DB13+
33	DB12#	73	GND/DB12+
34	5 V	74	Mated 2
35	5 V	75	5 V GND
36	5 V Charge	76	5 V GND
37	Reserved	77	Active LED Out
38	Auto Spin Up	78	Delayed Start
39	SCSI I D 0	79	SCSI I D 1
40	SCSI I D 2	80	SCSI I D 3

5.1.4. Terminators

All physical SCSI buses must have terminators installed on both ends. These terminators can be either internal (installed inside the controllers or peripheral SCSI devices) or external (small modules attached to the cable connector or to the auxiliary connector of the last device on the bus). SCSI-bus terminators must accomplish two objectives:

❏ Ridding the bus of the signals reflected from its ends
❏ Providing the necessary passive-line signal level

The first objective stems from the fact that SCSI cables can be long, and according to the theoretical basics of electrical engineering every signal line is a "long line." To stop reflecting electrical signals from the ends of the line, both ends of the line must be loaded with matching loads. ("Matching" means that the wave impedance of the line must match the dynamic impedance of the load. The wave impedance of SCSI ribbon cables usually lies between 85 ohms and 110 ohms.) If a line is not terminated (or if its impedance does not match that of the terminator), the "jingle" of reflected signals will cause interference on the bus.

The second task is necessitated by the specifics of the SCSI interface, where each signal line can be controlled by any of several devices attached to the bus. However, the sending device stipulates only the active level of the signal (low in non-differential SCSI versions), and the terminators are responsible for returning the line to the passive state. If there are no terminators at all, then the level on the lines "released" by the device will also return to passive state, under the influence of the input currents of the signal receivers, but it will happen much later. If a bus is long enough and has many devices attached, then this return will be severely delayed and may cause protocol malfunctions. High-speed devices employ an active-signal negation technique to return signals to the passive state, creating the illusion that a bus can work without terminators. However, stable operation with numerous devices (more than two, including the controller) on the line without terminators is problematic.

From this, it is clear when it is possible to neglect the rules for installing terminators: when the bus is not too long, there are not many devices attached to it (e.g., just a controller and a hard drive), and the exchange speed is low. However, more often, one SCSI bus has many devices attached, making the bus quite long. (Additionally, users try to operate devices at high transfer rates and with elevated reliability requirement.) In some cases, it would be better to use devices with a different interface. For data-storage devices, this would be the widely-used and inexpensive ATA interface.

There are different terminators for single-ended and LVD devices, which are the most popular. Many LVD interface devices are capable of working with a single-ended interface (but at low speeds), and are marked "LVD/SE." These devices are capable of determining the operating mode automatically: If all the devices on the bus (including the terminators) support the LVD mode, then this mode will be selected (if no device has been forced into the single-ended mode). If there is even one device on the bus capable of operating only in the single-ended mode, then the other devices will switch into this mode, reducing the maximum data-transfer speed. HVD (Diff) devices must not be included in the LVD/SE category.

The transmission methods and termination schemes are different for the single-ended and LVD transmission modes. Each SCSI-bus signal circuit consists of a pair of conductors: forward and reverse. In the single-ended mode, all the reverse conductors are grounded on each device, and the terminating circuits are connected only to the forward conductors. In the LVD mode, the signal is sent on a pair of wires in a differential paraphase form, while the terminating circuits are connected to the both wires of each pair. Fig. 5.6 shows possible terminator-circuit schematics for the single-ended and LVD transmission modes; load circuits are shown for one signal line. All terminators, not only those that are active, need to be powered. They are powered from special TERMPWR (+5 V) lines.

❑ Passive single-ended terminators (Fig. 5.6, *a*) have an impedance of 132 ohms, which is not a good match for the bus' ribbon cable. These terminators can be used only with a regular SCSI interface (transmission speeds up to 5 MBps to 10 MBps in the narrow/wide versions). They cannot be used with Fast SCSI, Ultra SCSI, or higher versions.

❑ Active single-ended terminators (Fig. 5.6, *b*) have an impedance of 110 ohms, which means they can be used at higher speeds in Fast SCSI. Their "active" mode consists only of having a +2.85 V reference-voltage source (RVS) powered from the same TERMPWR lines. The integrated circuits of the active terminators also have electronic keys connected serially into each line. The keys are controlled by a common signal that can turn the terminator on or off.

❑ Forced Perfect Terminators for SE (FPT SE) are an improved version of active terminators that have diode-surge limiters. They are used in high-speed single-ended interface versions.

❑ Terminators for LVD (Fig 5.6, *c*) have a differential impedance of 105 ohms (linear impedance of 150 ohms). Two base voltage sources provide a 112 mV offset between the forward and reverse conductors in the passive state.

❑ Universal LVD/SE terminators combine active single-ended terminators, differential LVD terminators, transmission-mode detection circuits, and circuits for switching every SCSI bus conductor (forward and reverse) to the corresponding terminating circuits.

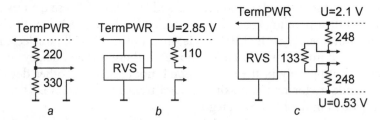

Fig. 5.6. SCSI terminators: *a* — SE passive, *b* — SE active, *c* — LVD

Universal LVD/SE terminators, like the other devices, detect the bus' operation mode using the DIFSENSE line. In older single-ended devices, the connector contact corresponding to this line was grounded. LVD devices attempt to put a 1.3 V potential on the line, while HVD devices are used to put a voltage potential greater than 2.1 V on it. The terminator has comparators that compare the signal on the line with the reference signal, and logic that switches the terminator's modes. (If HVD is detected, the terminator disconnects all its circuits). There are also integrated circuits produced specially for universal terminators (such as Dallas Semiconductor's DS2117M, DS2118M) that perform all the automatic termination functions for nine pairs of wires. To terminate a 16-bit data bus (Wide SCSI), three such integrated circuits are needed. Laser-adjusted precision resistors are used in these integrated circuits, a technology that is not cheap.

In terms of physical implementation, terminators may be either internal (located on the printed circuit board of a device) or external (mounted on the cable or devices connectors). Internal terminators in every device can be turned on and off. In older devices (SCSI-1), a group of jumpers had to be set or a resistor network installed into a special socket to turn a terminator on. Active terminators are turned on and off by repositioning one jumper, or even, by software when configuring the device, without using jumpers. A terminator can even be turned on automatically if the device supports this option and it was enabled when the device was configured. External terminators look like connectors with a small cover concealing the insides. Despite their outer simplicity, they are rather expensive (a terminator for Ultra-Wide SCSI costs from \$10 to \$15). External terminators can only be mounted and removed manually.

Practically all non-LVD interface devices have internal terminators, or at least a socket for their installation. As a rule, LVD interface devices do not have terminators for reasons of economy. When several devices are attached to the bus, a terminator is employed only as the last device in the chain. However, when connecting only one such device, the savings are insignificant, but the expense of purchasing an external terminator is not.

The absence of terminators on LVD devices does not mean that termination requirements may be ignored.

CAUTION

5.1.5. Configuring SCSI Devices

All devices attached to the bus must be properly configured. They must have the parameters listed below set up either by software or by using jumpers.

❐   The *device identifier* (SCSI ID) is a unique address from 0 to 7 (from 0 to 15 for Wide SCSI) for every device attached to the bus. The host adapter, which must have the highest priority, is usually assigned address 7 (15 for Wide SCSI if all devices are 16-bit). The positional code used for addressing provides addressing compatibility for 8- and 16-bit devices on the same bus. Some BIOS versions recognize as bootable only the device with SCSI ID = 0.

❏ *Parity control* (SCSI Parity). If even one device does not support parity checking, it must be disabled in all the devices attached to the bus. Parity control, especially for disk drives, is an essential means of ensuring data integrity during bus transfers.

❏ *Termination.* Modern devices use active terminators, which can be enabled by one jumper or by a software-controlled signal. Only the end devices in the chain are to have their terminators enabled. Modern host adapters have a feature allowing them to enable their terminators automatically if they are the last device on the chain, and to disable them if another device is attached to an internal or external bus connector. This allows external devices to be connected and disconnected without having to switch the terminators on the host-adapter card. Previously, to do this, it was necessary to open the case and move the jumpers for active termi- nators, or to install or remove passive terminators from their sockets. When there were no internal terminators, external ones, mounted on the cable, were necessary.

 It is very important to install terminators correctly: No or too many terminators may re- sult in unstable interface operation or in the interface being non-operational alto- gether.

CAUTION

❏ *Terminator power* must be connected by a jumper (or by software) to at least one device.

❏ *Synchronous-exchange speed negotiation.* The high-efficiency synchronous ex- change mode is enabled by agreement between devices. Disabling negotiation on the host adapter is recommended if even one device on the bus does not support it. If the exchange is initiated by a target device that supports synchronous mode, a regular host adapter will support this mode. Use of the synchronous-transfer mode request on a target device may be disabled by a special jumper, which may be called "Enable Target Initiated Synchronous Data Transfer Request Negotia- tion" (TI-SDTR).

❏ *Enable disconnection* — a parameter that allows devices to disconnect from the bus when there are no data during protracted operations with the data medium. This is quite effective in a multitasking mode with several peripheral devices attached to the bus. If there is just one device attached to the bus, disconnection only wastes time on reconnection.

❏ *Data-bus width negotiation* is also executed using the bus protocol, based on the capabilities of each participant in the exchange. The 16-bit-mode request may be disabled in the target device by a special jumper, which may be called "Enable Target Initiated Wide Data Transfer Request Negotiation" (TI-WDTR).

❏ *Disable wide* disables the 16-bit mode and allows a wide device to be attached to a narrow bus.

- *Force SE* is a forced switch into the single-ended mode. It allows an LVD device to be switched into the single-ended mode, regardless of the state of the DIFFSENS line.
- *Disabling double transition clocking* (Disable U160) allows a class Ultra3 SCSI device to be forced into the Ultra2 mode.
- *Start on command* or *Disable Auto Spin up*. When this parameter is enabled, the motor of a device can start only on a command from the host adapter. This allows the power-supply load peak to be reduced when powering up the system. The host will start devices' motors one by one.
- *Delayed Start*, when employed in conjunction with delay-selection jumpers, allows a device's motor to be started at a set interval after the power is turned on. (Each device is assigned a different delay period).

5.1.6. Connecting Devices to a SCSI Bus

Connecting devices to a SCSI bus is relatively simple, but there are certain peculiarities when mixing devices of different types on one bus. The throughput of the SCSI "mastered" by the computer is determined, naturally, by the potential of the host controller. SCSI buses provide good compatibility of parallel-interface devices of different generations — narrow and wide; but quite often, an older device can nullify the power of new devices that share the bus with it. The only compatible devices in interface terms are single-ended and LVD-mode devices.

CAUTION

LVD- and HVD-mode devices must not be attached to the same bus.

LVD devices can be mixed with single-ended devices on the same bus, but this will make all devices switch into the single-ended mode and the bus will not be able to operate in the Ultra2 mode intrinsic to LVD devices. The LVD interface, being differential, requires that every reverse wire (the + signal) come back to the input of its receiver; in the single-ended version, all reverse wires are bundled up together and connected to the bus ground. If there is even one single-ended device on a bus with LVD devices, the DIFFSENS line will be grounded, and all LVD devices will switch into the single-ended mode. At configuration, an LVD device can be forced into the single-ended mode by setting the Force SE jumper.

If there are Ultra160 and Ultra2 (or even lower) devices mixed on the bus, then the bus will work in the lowest of these modes. The Ultra160 mode can be forced into the Ultra2 mode by the Disable U160 jumper.

Attaching a narrow device to a narrow bus is the simplest task, as only two types of connectors are encountered (not counting Mac SCSI): external (Centronics type) and internal. Devices must be preconfigured and each must be assigned a unique (for the bus) SCSI ID identifier, nominally any number from 0 to 7. The length of the bus must not exceed the permissible limit; at both ends of the bus (and only at the ends), terminators must be mounted and turned on. The TERMPWR line must be supplied with power (usually from the host adapter), which can be checked by measuring voltage on the appropriate connector contacts.

Attaching a wide device to a wide bus may turn out to be a bit more complicated because of the greater variety of connectors involved. This may require using matching adapters for the connectors. Difficulties may also arise when connecting terminators, especially for LVD devices, which seldom have internal terminators. External terminators may require a separate connector. The devices' identifiers can be assigned numbers from 0 to 15.

Connecting a narrow device to the wide bus requires using a 68-pin-to-50-pin connector — matching adapter. The most significant byte in this adapter must not be terminated if the device being connected is not the last one on the bus. If the device is the last one on the bus, then the most significant byte in the adapter must have terminator ON, as well as the device itself. The decision on where on the bus to attach the device (in the middle or at the end) may be determined by the adapter on hand. Device identifiers between 0 and 7 must be assigned to all devices; otherwise, the arbitration procedure will not function properly because of the narrow devices' inability to see the identifiers from 8 to 15. Since all narrow devices are of the single-ended type, the DIFFSENS line will be grounded, and all LVD devices will switch into the single-ended mode. There are, however, bridging adapters that allow LVD devices to remain in LVD mode even when a single-ended device is connected to the bus. The mode can be determined by measuring voltage on the 16th contact of a 68-contact connector (the 46th contact of an 80-contact connector).

Connecting a wide device to the narrow bus also will require using a special adapter and installing the Disable Wide jumper on the wide device. Additionally, the most significant byte and its associated control lines may have to be terminated to secure a reliable passive state on them. ("Hanging" inputs are susceptible to interference). Some versions of the firmware allow devices to work without additional terminators. The identifiers of all the devices must be between 0 and 7, for the same reasons as in the preceding case.

There are various configurations for attaching devices to a SCSI controller (Fig. 5.7). The controller may be implemented on a PCI- or ISA-slot expansion card or built into the motherboard. Devices that are connected to it can be internal (various types of disk and tape devices) or external (the same devices, as well as scanners and other peripheral devices). Terminators are installed based on the specific conditions.

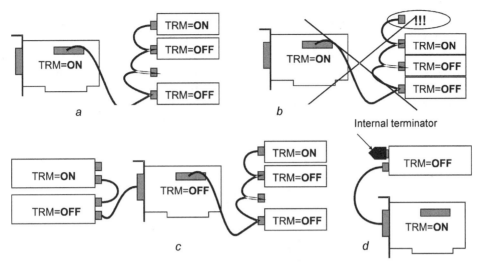

Fig. 5.7. Connecting devices to a SCSI controller card:
a, c, and *d* — correct; *b* — wrong

The connection rules are relatively simple:

❑ The ends of the ribbon cable must not hang in the air (Fig. 5.7, *b*).
❑ Devices attached to the ends of the cable must have their internal terminators turned on (marked as TRM=ON) or have external terminators mounted (Fig. 5.7, *d*).
❑ The devices attached in the middle of the bus must have their terminators turned off (marked as TRM=OFF).

If the SCSI controller is built on an expansion card, then the connector, to which external devices are attached, is located close enough to the internal connector, therefore there is no long line between them. In this case, terminating the external connector is no problem: If only the internal (Fig. 5.7, *a*) or only the external (Fig. 5.7, *d*) connection is used, then the terminator on the controller is turned on. If both the external and the internal connection are used (Fig. 5.7, *c*), then the terminator on the controller is turned off.

If the internal connection is used but the external devices are not connected at all the times, then it becomes necessary to switch the controller's terminator to correspond to the current configuration. In older controllers, it was necessary to open up the system block and rearrange the jumpers. If for some reason you do not want to switch the controller's terminator, you can turn it off permanently and use an external terminator mounted on the external connector (outside the computer case) when there are no external devices connected.

If the SCSI controller is built into the motherboard, it has only one connector, to which a ribbon cable is connected. If an internal-only or external-only connection is needed (Fig. 5.8, *a–b*), then the terminator on the controller is turned on. If both the internal and external connections are used, then the terminator on the controller is turned off. If a universal ribbon cable with internal and external connectors is used (Fig. 5.8, *c*) but no external devices are connected, then the terminator on the controller must be turned off, and the external connector must have an external terminator mounted on it.

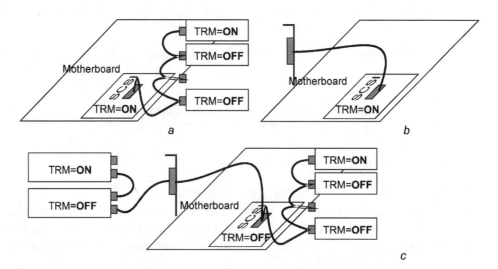

Fig. 5.8. Connecting devices to the integrated SCSI controller

Cables and connectors may be supplied with SCSI adapters and motherboards that have a built-in SCSI controller, or they may have to be purchased separately. The supplied items are not always suitable for a particular purpose. For example, in the kit supplied with the CT-6BTS motherboard, which has a built-in Ultra-Wide SCSI controller, a universal wide ribbon cable (similar to the one shown in Fig. 5.8, *c*, but with fewer internal connectors) and an internal narrow one are included. This kit is not sufficient for attaching internal Wide SCSI disk drives, as an external terminator is needed. A possible solution might be to cut off the part of the ribbon cable going from the controller to the external connector, but that would be a waste.

Wide SCSI controllers usually also have connectors for attaching regular (narrow) devices. As well as the 68-contact Wide SCSI connector, the CT-6BTS motherboard also has a regular, 50-contact connector for regular devices. The narrow (8-bit) interface may be considered as a subset of the wide (16-bit) that uses only the lower half of the data bus. Simple one-channel controllers (like the one on this card) have the contacts of their narrow connectors connected in parallel with a part of the contacts of the wide connector. This allows mixing of wide and narrow devices, for which the terminators on the controller are divided into two halves: Terminators of the least significant byte (TrmL) and those of the most significant byte (TrmH) can be controlled independently. Fig. 5.9, *a–b* shows the correct way to connect mixed devices (assuming that the devices at the ends of the ribbon cable have terminators). Fig 5.9, *c* shows the wrong way of connecting mixed devices: In this case, the LSB and the control-signal lines will have either three terminators (causing transmitter overload) or a loose end (causing reflections). It is not possible to connect mixed devices correctly using only the standard cables supplied with the motherboard (shown in Fig. 5.9).

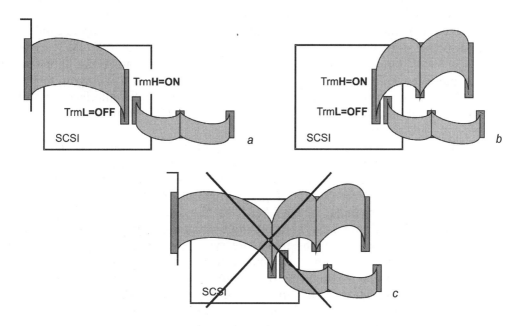

Fig. 5.9. Connecting narrow and wide SCSI devices: *a, b* — right; *c* — wrong

If these rules are followed (and neither the permissible cable length nor the number of connections is exceeded) then, provided all of the equipment is in good order, the SCSI bus will work reliably, as it is supposed to. If the rules are not followed, the consequences will vary. Certain models of controllers and terminators are more forgiving to some experimentation with terminators. (For example, they may forgive, or almost forgive, a loose unterminated cable-end, if it is not too long). These devices may work (the operating system will boot, drives will function) but, possibly with glitches that are not always visible. However, if the operating system being used is Windows NT, then looking into the event log will reveal a "bouquet", or red flashes having to do with SCSI devices. How big this bouquet is will depend on the seriousness of the transgressions and the "temper" of the used devices. The necessary measures for each specific case are probably left up to the installer: There simply may be not enough money for an "extra" terminator or a cable of different configuration.

5.2. Fibre Channel Interface

As well as the parallel interface, SCSI-3 also can use the serial Fibre Channel interface, or *Fibre Channel Arbitrated Loop* (FCAL), which occupies an intermediate position between peripheral-device interfaces (SCSI-3) and LAN technologies. This interface can be implemented using electrical (coaxial cable), as well as fiber-optic conductors. In both cases, a frequency of 1 GHz provides a data-transfer rate of 100 MBps. Copper cable allows a bus length of up to 100 feet, while optical cable can extend up to 6 miles. This interface employs a different protocol and physical levels, allowing up to 126 devices be attached to the bus (not just 8 or 16, like with parallel interfaces). Point-to-point connections can operate in the full-duplex mode (200 MBps), which is not possible with regular parallel buses.

Adaptec has put on the market an adapter capable of operating at 2 GHz (in optical and copper channels) that is backward compatible with regular 1 GHz adapters. In the full-duplex mode, an aggregate throughput of 400 MBps can be reached. Up to 126 nodes can be connected in the ring, the length of which may reach up to 6 miles. The ring structure is similar to the Fiber Distributed Data Interface (FDDI): All the nodes are assembled into a closed chain and translate incoming frames further along the ring. Transmitters in all the nodes are synchronized separately, and between-the-frames filler words — some of which can be periodically discarded or inserted during the transmission— are used to compensate for the synchronization-frequency divergence. To provide reliable communications, 8B/10B coding is used; to obtain a 100 MBps transmission rate with allowances for the frame service data overhead, a line capable of supporting speeds up to 1.0625 Gbps is needed.

The architectural model of the FCAL consists of five levels: FC-0 to FC-4. The lowest level (FC-0) defines the transmission medium (fiber optic or twin-axial cable) and the physical interface. The top level (FC-4) defines the data-representation protocols related to both the peripheral device interfaces (SCSI and some others) and networks (802.2 and IP). The information is sent along the ring in frames of size between 36 to 2,148 bytes. Data exchange between devices is possible both by establishing a connection and without one. Multiple connections can be open simultaneously; moreover, they may be of different protocols (e.g., SCSI and IP).

Fibre Channel equipment includes interface adapters, hubs, multiplexers, and routers. *Interface adapters* are computer expansion cards (for high-performance buses such as PCI). Data-storage devices (disk and tape devices, storage device arrays) are equipped with the FCAL interface. In theory, hubs are not needed for the FCAL, but they allow a ring to be organized based on the star topology and make it possible to bypass failed (disconnected) devices. Without them, a ring becomes vulnerable if a line or a device fails.

As in Ethernet technology, Fibre Channel switches allow one-to-one connections to be established for a group of devices that are effective if several servers are sharing several storage devices. *Routers*, or *bridges*, allow the FCAL to be connected to other data-transmission environments (such as standard SCSI interfaces or LANs). Currently, the FCAL is used to connect external data-storage devices to servers when high efficiency is needed and the devices are located at some distance from each other. In theory, the FCAL allows resource sharing to be organized, and also provides communications link redundancy, but so far there have been some difficulties in the operating-systems area.

5.3. SCSI Host-Adapter

The host-adapter is the most important part of the interface, defining the efficiency of SCSI systems. Its job is to transfer data between the host (a program being executed by the CPU) and other devices connected to the bus under the protocols of the physical interfaces described above. The structures of the data blocks to be transferred and device commands are standardized; the descriptions can be found in the technical literature. However, the architectures and the software models of adapters have not been standardized (unlike, for example, ATA adapters). A wide range of adapters exists. Only devices that are not critical to efficiency can be connected to the simplest ones. Such adapters may be included, for example, into the standard hardware kit supplied with a scanner, but it may be impossible to connect a hard drive to them.

High-end adapters are equipped with their own specialized processors and high-capacity buffer memory, and use high-performance bus-control methods to access the computer's memory. There are SCSI adapters for all types of expansion buses (ISA, EISA, MCA, PCI, VLB, PCMCIA, CardBus), for the USB and FireWire buses, and for the LPT port. Several types of motherboard have a built-in SCSI adapter that is connected to a local bus. The selection process for an interface to which the host-adapter is to be connected must take productivity into account: The interface must not become a bottleneck in the process of data exchange with high-efficiency SCSI devices. The most efficient models are host-adapters for the PCI bus. Of course, a high-efficiency server adapter is not cheap: Its price may be higher than the price of a regular desktop computer. Adapters with built-in RAID controllers, which have a powerful RISC processor and lots of local memory, are even more expensive.

In terms of SCSI buses, configuring host adapters is no different from configuring other devices. Modern adapters are configured by software instead of jumpers. A configuration utility is usually included with adapter's BIOS extension, and its prompt is displayed during POST.

Just like any other expansion card, a host adapter must be configured in terms of the expansion bus, to which it is connected. The system resources for an expansion-bus SCSI adapter include:

❏ ROM BIOS-extension memory area, which is needed to configure devices and to support disk functions. (If there are several host-adapters of the same type installed in the system, they all share the ROM BIOS of one of the adapters, but host adapters of different types cannot always do this).
❏ Shared buffer memory area.
❏ I/O ports area.
❏ Interrupt request (IRQ).
❏ Direct memory access (DMA) channels (for ISA/EISA buses), which is often used for bus mastering.

All SCSI devices, including the host adapter, require special drivers. A core driver for disk devices is included with the host adapter's BIOS; it usually emulates the three-dimensional addressing scheme for the Int 13h disk service. Extensions, such as Advanced SCSI Programming Interface (ASPI), are loaded separately. The productivity of SCSI devices depends heavily on the drivers. "Smart" software can efficiently assign the workload to devices, and sometimes even cut corners (e.g., by transferring data between devices without going to the system bus). Most preferable of all are drivers that are capable of operating in the bus-mastering mode. Their use allows all of the advantages of SCSI in multitask systems to be implemented.

Chapter 6: I/O Expansion Buses and Cards

Expansion buses are a system-level means of connection that allow adapters and controllers to use the computer's system resources — memory and I/O space, interrupts, DMA channels, and so on — directly. Devices connected to expansion buses can also control these buses themselves, obtaining access to the rest of the computer's resources (usually, memory space). This kind of direct control, known as "bus mastering," makes it possible to unload the CPU and to achieve high rates of data exchange. Physically, expansion buses are implemented as slot or pin connectors; they typically have short conductors, which allow high operating frequencies. Buses may not necessarily have external connectors mounted on them, but can be used to connect devices integrated onto motherboards.

Currently, the third generation of I/O expansion bus architecture is getting dominant; these buses include PCI Express (also known as 3GIO), Hyper Transport, and InfiniBand. The ISA bus, an asynchronous parallel bus with low bandwidth (less than 10 MBps) that does not provide exchange robustness or autoconfiguration, belongs to the first generation. The second generation started with the EISA and MCA buses, followed by the PCI bus and its PCI-X extension. This is a generation of synchronous, reliable buses that have autoconfiguration capabilities; some versions are capable of hot-swapping. Transfer rates measured in GBps can be reached. In order to connect a large number of devices, buses are connected into a hierarchical tree-like structure using bridges. For the third generation of buses, the transition from parallel buses to point-to-point connections with serial interface is characteristic; multiple clients are connected using so-called "switching fabric." In essence, the third generation of the I/O expansion approaches very local networks (within the limits of the motherboard).

The most commonly used expansion bus in modern computers is the PCI bus, supplemented by the AGP port. In desktop computers, the ISA bus is becoming less popular, but it has maintained its positions in industrial and embedded computers, both in its traditional slot version as well as the PC/104 "sandwich" type. In notebook computers, PCMCIA slots with PC Card and CardBus buses are extensively used. The LPC bus is a modern, inexpensive way to connect devices on the motherboard that are not resource-intensive. All these buses are considered in detail in this chapter. Information about the obsolete MCA, EISA, and VLB buses can be found in other books.

The characteristics of the standard PC expansion buses are given in Table 6.1.

Table 6.1. Characteristics of Expansion Buses

Bus	Peak Bandwidth (MBps)	DMA Channels	Bus Master	ACFG[1]	Data width (Bits)	Address width (Bits)	Frequency (MHz)
ISA-8	4	3	−	−	8	20	8
ISA-16	8	7	+	−	16	24	8
LPC	6.7	7	+	−	8/16/32	32	33
EISA	33.3	7	+	+	32	32	8,33
MCA-16	16	−	+	+	16	24	10
MCA-32	20	−	+	+	32	32	10
VLB	132	−	(+)	−	32/64	32	33−50(66)
PCI	133−533	−	+	+	32/64	32/64	33/66
PCI-X	533−4256	−	+	+	16/32/64	32/64	66−133
PCI Express	496−15872	−	+	+	1/2/4/8/ 12/16/32	32/64	2.5 GHz
AGP 1x/ 2x/4x/8x	266/533/ 1066/2132	−	+	+	32	32/64	66
PCMCIA	10/20	+	−	+	8/16	26	10
Card Bus	132	−	+	+	32	32	33

[1] Automatic configuration support. This is the latest add-on to the ISA bus, and is implemented by software and adapters.

6.1. PCI and PCI-X Buses

The Peripheral Component Interconnect (PCI) local bus is the principal expansion bus in modern computers. It was developed for the Pentium family processors, but it is also well suited to the 486 family processors, as well as to the modern processors.

Currently, the PCI is a well-standardized, highly efficient, reliable expansion bus supported by several computer platforms, including PC-compatible computers, PowerPC, and others. The specifications of the PCI bus are updated periodically. The given description covers all PCI and PCI-X bus standards, up to and including versions 2.3 and 2.0, respectively:

❑ PCI 1.0 (1992): general conception defined; signals and protocol of a 32-bit parallel synchronous bus with clock frequency of up to 33.3 MHz and peak bandwidth of 132 MBps.

❑ PCI 2.0 (1993): introduced specification for connectors and expansion cards with possible width extension to 64 bits (speed of up to 264 MBps); 5 V and 3.3 V power supplies provided for.

❑ Version 2.1 (1995): introduced 66 MHz clock frequency (3.3 V only), making it possible to provide peak bandwidth of up to 264 MBps in the 32-bit version and 528 MBps in the 64-bit version.

❑ Version PCI 2.2 (PCI Local Bus Specification. Revision 2.2 of 12/18/1998): specified and clarified some provisions of version 2.1. Also introduced a new interrupt signaling mechanism, MSI.

❑ Version PCI 2.3 (2002): defined bits for interrupts that facilitate identifying interrupt source; 5 V cards now obsolete (only 3.3 V and universal card left); low profile expansion card build introduced; supplementary SMBus and signals introduced. This version is described in the PCI Local Bus Specification; Revision 2.3 is the basis for the current expansions.

❑ Version PCI 3.0 obsoletes 5 V motherboards, leaving only universal and 3.3 V.

In 1999, the PCI-X expansion came out based on the PCI 2.3. It is intended to raise peak bus bandwidth significantly by using a higher transfer frequency, and to increase the operation efficiency by employing an improved protocol. The protocol also defines split transactions and attributes that allow the exchange parties to plan their actions. The extension provides for mechanical, electrical, and software compatibility of the PCI-X devices and motherboards with the regular PCI; however, naturally, all devices on the bus adjust to the slowest piece of equipment.

In the 3.3 V interface of PCI-X 1.0, the clock frequency was raised to 133 MHz, producing PCI-X66, PCI-X100, and PCI-X133. Peak bandwidth reaches up to 528 MBps in the 32-bit version, and over 1 GBps in the 64-bit version. PCI-X 1.0 is described in the PCI-X Addendum to the PCI Local Bus Specification, Revision 1.0b (2002).

PCI-X 2.0 introduced new clocking modes with doubled (PCI-X266) and quadrupled (PCI-X533) data transfer frequency relative to the base clock frequency of 133 MHz. This high frequency requires a low-voltage interface (1.5 V) and error-correction coding (ECC). In addition to the 32- and 64-bit version, a 16-bit version is specified for embedded computers. A new type of transaction — Device ID Messages (DIM) — was introduced: These are messages that address a device using its identifier. PCI-X 2.0 is described in two documents: PCI-X Protocol Addendum to the PCI Local Bus Specification, Revision 2.0 (PCI-X PT 2.0); and PCI-X Electrical and Mechanical Addendum to the PCI Local Bus Specification, Revision 2.0 (PCI-X EM 2.0).

In addition to the bus specification, there are several specifications for other components:

□ PCI to PCI Bridge Architecture Specification, Revision 1.1 (PCI Bridge 1.1), for bridges interconnecting PCI and other bus types
□ PCI BIOS specification, defining configuring of PCI devices and interrupt controllers
□ PCI Hot-Plug Specification, Revision 1.1 (PCI HP 1.1), providing for dynamic (hot) device connection and disconnection
□ PCI Power Management Interface Specification, Revision 1.1 (PCI PM 1.1), for controlling power consumption

Based on the PCI 2.0 bus, Intel developed the dedicated Accelerated Graphics Ports (AGP) interface for connecting a graphics accelerator (see *Section 6.2*).

PCI specifications are published and supported by the PCI Special Interest Group (PCI SIG, **www.pcisig.org**). The PCI bus exists in different build variations: Compact PCI (CPCI), Mini-PCI, PXI, Card Bus.

The PCI bus was first introduced as a mezzanine bus for the systems with the ISA bus, and later became the central bus. It is connected to the processor system bus by the high-performance north bridge that is a part of the motherboard chipset. The south bridge connects to the PCI bus the other I/O expansion buses and devices. These include the ISA/EISA and MCA buses, as well as the ISA-like X-BUS and the LPC interface to which the motherboard's integrated circuits (such as the ROM BIOS, interrupt, keyboard, DMA, COM and LPT ports, FDD, and so on) are connected. In modern motherboards that use hub architecture, the PCI bus has been taken out of the mainstream: The power of its CPU and RAM communication channel has not been reduced, but neither is it loaded up by transit traffic from the other buses' devices.

The bus is synchronous: All signals are latched at the rising edge of the CLK signal. The nominal synchronization frequency is 33 MHz, but this can be lowered if necessary (on machines with 486 CPUs, frequencies of 20–33 MHz were used). Often, the bus frequency can be overclocked to 41.5 MHz, or half the typical 83 MHz system bus frequency. From the PCI 2.1 revision, the bus frequency can be raised to 66 MHz provided that all devices connected to the bus support it.

The nominal bus width is 32 bits, although the specification also defines a 64-bit bus. At 33 MHz, the theoretical throughput capacity of the bus reaches 132 MB/sec for the 32-bit bus and 264 MB/sec for the 64-bit bus. At 66 MHz, it reaches 264 MB/sec and 528 MB/sec for the 32-bit and 64-bit buses, respectively. But these peak values are achieved only during burst transmissions. Because of the protocol overhead, the real average aggregate bus throughput is lower for all masters.

The CPU can interact with PCI devices by memory and I/O port commands addressed within the ranges allocated to each device at configuration. Devices may generate masked and nonmasked interrupt requests. There is no concept of the DMA channel number for the PCI bus, but a bus agent may play the role of master and maintain a high-performance exchange with the memory and other devices without using CPU resources. In this way, for example, DMA exchange with ATA devices connected to the PCI IDE controller can be implemented (see *Section 8.2.1*).

Operating in the Bus Master role is desirable for all devices that require extensive data exchange, as the device can generate quite lengthy packet transactions, for which the effective data transfer speed approaches the declared peak. Instead of I/O ports, memory-mapped I/O are recommended for controlling devices as far as possible.

Each PCI device has a standard set of configuration registers located in addressing space separate from the memory and I/O space. Using these registers, devices are identified and configured, and their characteristics are controlled.

The PCI specification requires a device to be capable of moving the resources it uses (the memory and I/O ranges) within the limits of the available address space. This allows conflict-free resource allocation for many devices and/or functions. A device can be configured in two different ways: mapping its registers either onto the memory space or onto the I/O space. The driver can determine its current settings by reading the contents of the device's base address register. The driver also can determine the interrupt request number used by the device.

6.1.1. Device Enumeration

For the PCI bus, a hierarchy of enumeration categories — bus, device, function — has been adopted: The *host* — the bus master — enumerates and configures all PCI devices. This role is usually played by the central processor, which is connected to the PCI bus by the host (main) bridge, relative to which bus addressing begins.

The *PCI bus* is a set of signal lines that directly connect the interface pins of a group of devices such as slots or devices integrated onto the motherboard. A system can have several PCI buses interconnected by *PCI bridges*. The bridges electrically isolate one bus' interface signals from another's while connecting them logically. The *host bridge* connects the main bus with the host: the CPU and RAM. Each bus has its own PCI *bus number*. Buses are numbered sequentially; the main bus is assigned number 0.

A *PCI device* is an integrated circuit or expansion card, connected to one of the PCI buses, that uses an IDSEL bus line allocated to it for identifying itself to access the configuration registers. A device can be multifunctional (i.e., consisting of so-called functions numbered from 0 to 7). Every function is allocated a 256-byte configuration space. Multifunctional devices can respond only to the configuration cycles of those function numbers, for which there is configuration space available. A device must always have function 0 (whether a device with the given number is present is determined by the results of accessing this function); other functions are assigned numbers as needed from 1 to 7 by the device vendor. Depending on their implementation, simple, one-function devices can respond to either any function number or only to function 0.

Enumeration categories are involved only when accessing configuration space registers (see *Section 6.1.12*). These registers are accessed during the configuration state, which involves enumerating the devices detected, allocating them nonconflicting resources (memory and I/O ranges), and assigning hardware interrupt numbers. In the course of further regular operation, the devices will respond to accesses to the memory and I/O addresses allocated to them, which have been conveyed to the software modules associated with them.

Each function is configured. The full function identifier consists of three parts: the bus number, device number, and function number. The short identification form (used in OS Unix messages, for example) is of the PCI0:1:2 type, meaning function 2 of device 1 is connected to the main (0) PCI bus. The configuration software must operate with a list of all functions of all devices that have been detected on the PCI buses of the given system.

The PCI bus employs *positional addressing*, meaning that the number assigned to a device is determined by where the device is connected to the bus. The *device number*, or *dev*, is determined by the AD bus line to which the IDSEL signal line of the given slot is connected: As a rule, adjacent PCI slots use adjacent device numbers; their numbering is determined by the manufacturer of the motherboard (or of the passive backplane for industrial computers). Very often, decreasing device numbers, beginning with 20 or 15, are used for the slots. Groups of adjacent slots may be connected to different buses; devices are numbered independently on each PCI bus (devices may have the same dev numbers, but their bus numbers will be different). PCI devices integrated into the motherboard use the same numbering system. Their numbers are hard-wired, whereas the numbers of expansion cards can be changed by moving them into different slots.

One *PCI card* can have only one device for the bus to which it is connected, because it is allocated only one EDSEL line for the slot into which it is installed. If a card contains several devices (a 4-port Ethernet card, for example), then it needs a bridge installed on it, as well as a PCI device, which is addressed by the EDSEL line allocated to the given card. This bridge creates on the card a supplementary PCI bus to which several devices can be connected. Each of these devices is assigned its own IDSEL line, but this line now is a part of the given card's supplementary PCI bus.

In terms of memory and I/O space addressing, the positional address (bus and device number) is not important within the limits of one bus. However, the device number determines the interrupt request line number that the given device can use. (See *Section 6.2.6* for more information on this subject; here, it is enough to note that devices on the same bus whose numbers differ by 4 will use the same interrupt request line. Assigning them different interrupt request line numbers may be possible only when they are located on different buses, but this depends on the motherboard.) In systems with several PCI buses, installing a device into slots of different buses may affect its productivity; this depends on the characteristics of a particular bus and how far away it is from the host bridge.

Figuring out device numbering and the system for assigning interrupt request line numbers system is simple. This can be done by installing a PCI card sequentially into each of the slots (remembering to turn the power off each time) and noting the messages about the PCI devices found that are displayed at the end of POST. PCI devices built into the motherboard and not disabled by the SMOS Setup will also appear in these messages. Although this may all seem to be very clear and simple, some operating systems — especially "smart" ones, such as Windows — are not content with the allocated interrupt request numbers, and change them as they deem fit; this does not affect line-sharing in any way.

All bus devices can be configured only from the host's side; this is the host's special role. No master on any PCI bus has access to the configuration registers of all devices; without this access, complete configuration cannot be done. Even from the main PCI bus, the registers of the host bridge are not accessible to a master; without access to these registers, address distribution between the host and the PCI devices cannot be programmed. Access possibilities to the configuration registers are even more modest from the other PCI buses (see *Section 6.1.6*).

6.1.2. Bus Protocol

Two devices are involved in every transaction, or bus exchange: the exchange initiator device (or bus master) and a target device (or bus slave). The rules for these devices' interactions are defined by the PCI bus protocol. A device can monitor the bus transactions without participating in them (i.e., without generating any signals); this mode is called Snooping. A Special Cycle happens to be of the broadcast type; in such cycle, the initiator does not interact with any of the devices using the protocol. The suite and functions of the bus interface signals are shown in Table 6.2.

Table 6.2. PCI Bus Signals

Signal	Description
AD[31:0]	Address/Data. A multiplexed address/data bus. The address is sent at the beginning of the transaction; data are sent in the following clock cycles.
C/BE[3:0]#	Bus Command/Byte Enable. A command that determines the next bus cycle type, defined by the 4-bit code in the address phase.
FRAME#	Frame. Driving the signal low indicates the start of a new bus transaction (address phase); driving it high indicates that the following data-transmission cycle will be the last one in this transaction.
DEVSEL#	Device Select. Driven low by the target device to indicate that it has detected its address on the PCI bus.
IRDY#	Initiator Ready. Indicates that the master is ready for data exchange.
TRDY#	Target Ready. Indicates that the target device is ready for data exchange.
STOP#	Request from the target device to the master device to terminate the current transaction.
LOCK#	Signal to lock the bus to ensure error-free completion of the operation. Used by a bridge device that requires several PCI transactions to complete one operation.
REQ#	Request from the master to use the bus.
GNT#	Grants bus control to the master.
PAR	Parity. Common parity bit for lines AD[31:0] and C/BE[3:0]#.
PERR#	Parity Error signal for all but the special cycles. Generated by any device that detects an error.
PME#	Power Management Event. Signals events that cause changes in the power consumption. An extra signal introduced in the PCI 2.2.
CLKRUN#	Clock running signal. Low means that the bus is working at the nominal synchronization speed. Driven high, it indicates lowering or stopping the synchronization clock for the purpose of lowering power consumption. Intended only for mobile applications.
PRSNT[1,2]#	Present signal. Indicates that a card is physically present and what its power requirements are. The card power requirements are coded by connecting one or both indicator lines to the bus ground, which is then accordingly interpreted by the motherboard.
RST#	Resets all registers to their initial state. Activated by the reset button or rebooting.

continues

Table 6.2 Continued

Signal	Description
IDSEL	Initialization Device Select. Used to select devices during the configuration read and write transactions. A device that detects a high-level signal on this line answers to these cycles.
SERR#	System Error signal. Indicates a special cycle data- or address-parity error or any other fatal error that a device has detected. Activated by any PCI device and generates a non-masked interrupt (NMI).
REQ64#	Request 64 bit. Indicates a request for 64-bit exchange. A 64-bit initiator asserts the signal. Its timing coincides with the timing of the FRAME# signal. At the end of reset by the RST# signal, it informs a 64-bit device that it is connected to the 64-bit bus. If the 64-bit device does not detect this signal, it must reconfigure to the 32-bit mode by disconnecting its buffers of AD[63:32].
ACK64#	64-bit exchange acknowledgement. Asserted simultaneously with the DEVSEL# signal by a 64-bit target device that has recognized its address. If the target device does not assert this signal, the initiating device will conduct the exchange in the 32-bit mode.
INTA#, INTB#, INTC#, INTD#	Interrupt A, B, C, and D lines. Asserted by devices to request attention from their drivers. They are level-sensitive. The active level is low, which allows interrupt lines sharing.
CLK	Bus clock. Must be between 20 and 33 MHz. PCI 2.1 allows up to 66 MHz; can be up to 100 or 133 MHz in PCI-X.
M66EN	66 MHz Enable signal. Allows synchronization frequency of up to 66 MHz (on 33 MHz cards is grounded, on 66 MHz cards not connected).
PCIXCAP	PCI-X capabilities. Grounded on PCI cards; connected to the ground via a 0.001 mcF capacitor on PCI-X133 cards; connected to the ground via a parallel RC chain of 10 K and 0.01 mcF, respectively, on PCI-X66 cards.
SDONE	Snoop Done signal. Indicates the status of the snoop cycle for the current transaction. Low level indicates that the memory and cache coherence snooping cycle has not been completed yet. Not a required signal; used only by devices that have a memory cache. Abolished from PCI 2.2
SBO#	Snoop Backoff signal. Low level indicates a hit into a modified cache line when referencing the current bus agent's memory. Not a required signal; used only by devices with a memory cache during writeback operations. Abolished from PCI 2.2.
SMBCLK	SMBus Clock (I2C interface). Introduced in PCI 2.3.
SMBDAT	SMBus Data (I2C interface). Introduced in PCI 2.3.

continues

Table 6.2 Continued

Signal	Description
TCK	Test Clock. Used to synchronize the JTAG testing interface.
TDI	Test Data Input. Provides data for the JTAG testing interface.
TDO	Test Data Output of the JTAG testing interface.
TMS	Test Mode Select for the JTAG testing interface.
TRST	Test Logic Reset.

The states of all signal lines are perceived at the positive transition of the CLK signal, and it is precisely these moments that in the further description are meant by "bus cycles" (marked by vertical dotted lines in the drawings). At different points in time, the same signal lines are controlled by different bus devices; for conflict-free handing over of the authority of the bus, some time is needed when no device controls the lines. On the timing diagrams, this event — known as turnaround — is marked by a pair of semicircular arrows. See Fig. 6.1.

At any given moment, the bus can be controlled by only one master device, which has received this right from the arbiter. Each master device has a REQ# signal to request control of the bus and a GNT# signal to acknowledge bus control having been granted. A device can begin a transaction (i.e., assert a FRAME# signal) only when it receives an active GNT# signal and having waited until the bus is in the idle state. While waiting for the bus to assume the idle state, the arbiter can change its mind and give bus control to another device with higher priority. Deactivating the GNT# signal stops the device from beginning next transaction, and under certain conditions, which are considered later in this chapter, forces it to terminate the transaction in progress. A special unit, which is a part of the bridge that connects the given bus to the computer core, handles the arbitration requests. The priority scheme (whether fixed, cyclic, or combined) is determined by the arbiter's programming.

Addresses and data are transmitted over common multiplexed AD lines. The four multiplexed lines C/BE[3:0] encode commands during the address phase and enable bytes during the data phase. In write transactions, the C/BE[3:0] lines enable bytes that are on the AD bus at the same time as their signals; in read transactions, they enable data in the following data phase. At the beginning of a transaction, the master device activates the FRAME# signal, sends the target device address over the AD bus, and sends the information about the transaction type, i.e., command, over the C/BE# lines. The addressed target device responds with a DEVSEL# signal. The master device indicates its readiness to exchange data by the IRDY# signal, which it also may assert before receiving the DEVSEL# signal. When the target device is also ready to exchange data, it will assert the TRDY# signal. Data are sent over the AD bus only when both signals, IRDY# and TRDY#, are asserted. The master and slave devices use these signals to coordinate their exchange rates by introducing wait cycles. If they asserted their ready signals at the end of the address phase and maintained them until the end of the transfer, then 32 bits of data would be sent after the address phase in each cycle. This would make it possible to reach the maximum exchange efficiency. In read transactions, an extra clock is required for the turnaround after the address phase, during which the initiator passes control over the AD line. The target device can take the AD bus only in the next clock. No turnaround is needed in a write transaction, because the data are sent by the initiator.

On the PCI bus, all transactions are of the burst type: Each transaction begins with the address phase, which may be followed by one or more data phases. The number of data phases in a burst is not indicated explicitly, but the master device releases the FRAME# signal before the last data phase, with the IRDY# signal still asserted. In single transactions, the FRAME# signal is active only for the duration of one cycle. If a device does not support burst transactions in the slave mode, then during the first data phase, it must request that the burst transaction be terminated by simultaneously asserting the STOP# and TRDY# signals. In response, the master device will complete the current transaction and will continue the exchange with the following transaction to the next address. After the last data phase, the master device releases the IRDY# signal and the bus goes into the *PCI idle state*, in which both the FRAME# and the IRDY# signals are inactive.

By asserting the FRAME# signal simultaneously with releasing the IRDY# signal, the initiator can begin the next transaction without going through the bus idle phase. Such *fast back-to-back transactions* may be directed to a target device. All PCI devices acting as targets support the first type of transactions. The second type, which is optional, is indicated by bit 7 of the status register. An initiator is allowed to use fast back-to-back transactions (by bit 9 of the command register if it is capable of doing so) with different target devices only if all bus agents are capable of fast transactions. When data exchange is conducted in the PCI-X mode, fast back-to-back transactions are not allowed.

The handshaking protocol makes the exchange reliable, as the master device will always receive information about the target device finishing the transaction. Using parity control makes the exchange more reliable and valid: The AD[31:0] and C/BE[3:0] lines are protected by the parity bit PAR line; the number of ones on these lines, including the PAR line, must be even. The actual value of PAR appears on the bus with a one-cycle delay with respect to the AD[31:0] and C/BE# lines. When a target device detects an error, it asserts the PERR# signal, shifting it one cycle after the valid parity-bit signal. When the parity is calculated during the data transfer, all bytes are taken into account, including invalid ones (marked by the high level C/BEx# signal). The bits' state, even in invalid data bytes, must remain stable during the data phase.

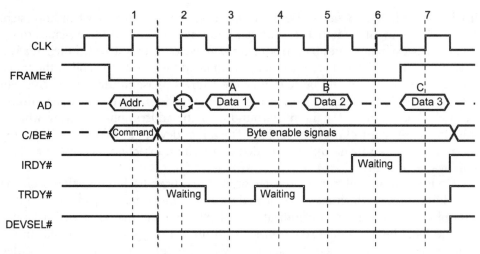

Fig. 6.1. A PCI bus exchange cycle

Each bus transaction must be completed as planned, or terminated with the bus assuming the bus idle state (the FRAME# and IRDY# signals going inactive). Both the master and the slave device may initiate a transaction conclusion.

A *master device* can conclude a transaction in one of the following ways:

❏ *Completion* is executed when the data exchange ends.
❏ A time-out occurs when the master device is deprived of control of the bus (by the GNT# signal being driven high) during a transaction and the time indicated in its Latency Time timer has expired. This may happen when the addressed target device turns out to be slower than expected, or the planned transaction is too long. Short transactions (of one or two data phases) complete normally even when the GNT# signal goes high and a time-out is triggered.
❏ A master-abort termination takes place when the master device does not receive a response from the target device (DEVSEL#) during the specified length of time.

A transaction may be terminated at the target device's initiative. The target device can do this by asserting the STOP# signal. Here, three types of termination are possible:

❏ *Retry*. The STOP# signal is asserted at the inactive TRDY# signal before the first data phase. This situation arises when the target device does not manage to present the first data within the allowed time period (16 cycles) because of being too busy. Retry is an instruction to the master device to execute the same transaction again.
❏ *Disconnect*. The STOP# signal is asserted during or after the first data phase. If the STOP# signal is asserted when the TRDY# signal of the current data phase is active, then these data are transmitted and the transaction is terminated.

If the STOP# signal is asserted when the TRDY# signal is inactive, then the transaction is terminated without transmitting the next phase's data. Disconnect is executed when a target device cannot send or receive the next portion of the burst's data in time. The disconnect is a directive to the master device to repeat the transaction but with the modified start address.

❏ Target-abort. The STOP# signal is asserted simultaneously with deactivation of the DEVSEL# signal. (In the preceding situations, the DEVSEL# signal was active when the STOP# signal was being asserted.) No data are sent after this termination. A target-abort is executed when a target device detects a fatal error or some other conditions (e.g., an unsupported command), because of which it will not be able to service the current request.

Using all three termination types is not mandatory for all target devices; however, any master device must be capable of terminating a transaction upon any of these reasons.

Terminations of the Retry type are used to organize *delayed transactions*. Delayed transactions are only used by slow target devices and also by PCI bridges when transferring transactions to another bus. When terminating (for the initiator) a transaction by a Retry condition, the target device executes the transaction internally. When the initiator repeats this transaction (issues the same command with the same address and set of the C/BE# signals in the data phase), the target device (or the bridge) will have the result ready (data for a read transaction or execution status for a write transaction), and will promptly return it to the initiator. The target device (or the bridge) must store the results of an executed delayed transaction until the time they are requested by the initiator. However, due to some abnormal situation, the initiator can "forget" to repeat the transaction. In order to keep the result storage buffer from overflowing, the device has to discard these results. This can be done without producing detrimental effects only if transactions with prefetchable memory were delayed. The other types of transactions cannot be discarded without the danger of data integrity violation. They can be discarded only if no repeat request is made within 2^{15} bus cycles (upon a Discard Timer timeout). Devices can inform their drivers (or the operating system) about this particular situation.

A transaction initiator may request exclusive use of the PCI bus during the whole exchange operation that requires several bus transactions. For example, if the central processor is executing an instruction that modifies the contents of a memory cell in a PCI device, it needs to read the data from the device, modify them in its ALU, and then return the data to the device. In order to prevent other initiators from intruding their transactions into this operation sequence (which is fraught with the danger of data integrity violation), the host bridge executes this operation as *locked*: I.e., keeps a LOCK# bus signal during of its execution. Regular PCI devices neither use nor generate this signal; only bridges use it to control arbitration.

PCI Bus Commands

PCI commands are defined by the transaction direction and type, as well as the address space to which they pertain. The PCI bus command set includes the following commands:

- [ ] The *I/O Read and Write commands* are used to access the I/O address space.
- [ ] *Memory Read and Write* commands are used to perform short, non-burst (as a rule) transactions. Their direct purpose is to access I/O devices that are mapped onto the memory space. For real memory, which allows prefetching, memory line read, memory line read multiple, and memory write and invalidate commands are used.
- [ ] *Memory Read Line* is employed when reading to the end of a cache line is planned. Separating this type of read allows increased memory exchange efficiency.
- [ ] *Multiple Memory Read* is used for transactions involving more than one cache line. Using this type of transaction allows the memory controller to prefetch lines, which gives an extra productivity increase.
- [ ] *Memory Write and Invalidate* is used to write an entire cache line; moreover, all bytes in all phases must be enabled. This operation saves time by forcing the cache controller to flush the "dirty" cache lines corresponding to the written area without unloading them from the main memory. The initiator that issues this command must know the cache line size in the given system (it has a special register for this purpose in the configuration area).
- [ ] The *Dual Address Cycle* (DAC) allows the 32-bit bus to be used to communicate with devices employing 64-bit addressing. In this case, the lower 32 address bits are sent in this cycle simultaneously with this command, after which follows a regular cycle setting the exchange type and carrying the higher 32 address bits. The PCI bus permits 64-bit I/O port addressing. (It is of no use for the x86 machines, but PCI also is used in other platforms.)
- [ ] The *Configuration Read and Write* commands address the configuration space of the devices. Only aligned double words are used to perform access; bits AD[1:0] are used to identify the cycle type. A special hardware/software mechanism is needed to generate these commands.
- [ ] The *Special Cycle* command is a broadcast type, which makes it different from all other commands. However, no bus agent responds to it, and the host bridge or another device that starts this cycle always terminates it with a master-abort. It takes 6 bus cycles to complete. The Special Cycle broadcasts messages that any "interested" bus agents can read. The message type is encoded in the contents of the AD[15:0] lines; the data sent in the message may be placed on the AD[31:16] lines. Regular devices ignore the address phase in this cycle, but bridges use the information to control how the message is broadcast. Messages with codes 0000h, 0001h, and 0002h are used to indicate Shutdown, processor Halt,

or the x86-specific functions pertaining to cache operations and tracing. The codes 0003–FFFFh are reserved. The same hardware/software mechanism that generates configuration cycles may generate the Special Cycle, but with the address having a specific meaning.

☐ The *Interrupt Acknowledge* command reads the interrupt vector. In protocol terms, it looks like a read command addressed to the interrupt controller (PIC or APIC). This command does not send any useful information over the AD bus in the address phase (BE[3:0]# sets the vector size), but its initiator — the host bridge — must ensure that the signal is stable and the parity is correct. In PC, an 8-bit vector in byte 0 is sent when the interrupt controller is ready (upon the TRDY# signal). Interrupts are acknowledged in one cycle; the bridge suppresses the first null cycle that x86 processors perform for reverse-compatibility reasons.

Commands are coded by the C/BE# bits in the address phase (see Table 6.3); PCI-X specific commands are considered in the following sections.

Table 6.3. PCI and PCI-X Bus Command Decoding

C/BE[3:0] code	PCI Command	PCI-X		
		Command	Length	Splitting capability
0000	Interrupt Acknowledge	Interrupt Acknowledge	DWORD	+
0001	Special Cycle	Special Cycle; broadcast type	DWORD	−
0010	I/O Read	I/O Read	DWORD	+
0011	I/O Write	I/O Write	DWORD	+
0100	Reserved	Reserved	−	−
0101	Reserved	Device ID Message (DIM), PCI-X v.2.0	Burst	−
0110	Memory Read	Memory Read DWORD	DWORD	+
0111	Memory Write	Memory Write	Burst	−
1000	Reserved	Alias to Memory Read Block	Burst	+
1001	Reserved	Alias to Memory Write Block	Burst	−
1010	Configuration Read	Configuration Read	DWORD	+

continues

Table 6.3 Continued

C/BE[3:0] code	PCI Command	PCI-X		
		Command	**Length**	**Splitting capability**
1011	Configuration Write	Configuration Write	DWORD	+
1100	Memory Read Multiple	Split Completion	Burst	−
1101	Dual Address Cycle	Dual Address Cycle	−	−
1110	Memory Read Line	Memory Read Block	Burst	+
1111	Memory Write and Invalidate	Memory Write Block	Burst	−

Each bus command contains the address of the data that pertain to the first data phase of the burst. The address for every subsequent data phase in the burst is incremented by 4 (the next double word), or by 8 (for 64-bit transfers), but the order may be different in memory-reference commands. The bytes of the AD bus that carry meaningful information are selected in data phases by the C/CB[3:0]# signals. Within a burst, these signals may arbitrarily change their states in different phases. Enabled bytes may not be adjacent on the data bus; data phases, in which not a single byte is enabled, are possible. Unlike the ISA bus, the PCI bus cannot change its width dynamically: All devices must connect to the bus in the 32- or 64-bit mode. If a PCI device uses a function circuit of different width (e.g., an 8255 integrated circuit, which has an 8-bit data bus and four registers, needs to be connected), then it becomes necessary to employ schematic conversions that map all registers to the 32-bit AD bus. The 16-bit connection capability appeared only in the second version of PCI-X.

Addressing is different for each of the three spaces — memory, I/O ports, and configuration registers; the address is ignored in the special cycles.

Memory Addressing

Physical memory space address is sent over the PCI bus; in x86 (and other) processors, it is derived from the logical addressing by table page translation done by the MMU block. In the *memory-access commands*, the address aligned at the double-word boundary is transmitted over the AD[31:2] lines; the AD[1:0] lines set the burst addressing modes:

❐   00 — Linear incrementing. The address of the next phase is obtained by incrementing the preceding address by the number of the bus-width bytes: 4 bytes for a 32-bit bus and 8 bytes for a 64-bit bus.

❏ 10 — Cacheline Wrap mode. In this mode, memory access addresses wrap around the end of the cacheline. In a transaction, each subsequent phase address is incremented until its value reaches the end of the cacheline, after which it wraps around to the beginning of this line and increments to the value preceding the starting-address value. If a transaction is longer than the cacheline, then it will continue in the next line from the offset, at which it started. Thus, with a 16-byte line and a 32-bit bus, the subsequent data phases of a transaction that began at the address xxxxxx08h will have the addresses xxxxxx0Ch, xxxxxx00h, xxxxxx04h; then in the next cacheline: xxxxxx18h, xxxxxx1Ch, xxxxxx10h, xxxxxx14h. The length of a cacheline is set in the configuration space of the device. If a device does not have the `Cacheline Size` register, then it must terminate the transaction after the first data phase because the order in which the addresses alternate turns out to be not indeterminate.

❏ 01 and 11 — These combinations are reserved. They may be used as a Disconnect direction after the first data phase.

If addresses over 4 GB need to be accessed, then a two-address cycle is used that carries the lower 32 bits of the 64-bit address for the following commands, along with which the higher bits of the address are sent. In regular commands, bits [63:32] are assumed to be having zero value.

A full memory address is sent in PCI-X using all `AD[31:0]` lines. In burst transactions, the address determines the exact location of the burst's starting byte, and the addresses are assumed to be incremented in a linear ascending order. All bytes are involved in packet transactions, starting from the specified starting byte and ending with the last as given in the byte counter. Individual bytes cannot be disabled in a PCI-X burst transaction as they can be in PCI. In single DWORD transactions, the `AD[1:0]` address bits determine the bytes that can be enabled by the `C/BE[3:0]#` signals. Thus, if:

❏ `AD[1:0]=00` then `C/BE[3:0]=xxxx`
❏ `AD[1:0]=01` then `C/BE[3:0]=xxx1`
❏ `AD[1:0]=10` then `C/BE[3:0]=xx11`
❏ `AD[1:0]=11` then `C/BE[3:0]=x111` (Only byte 3 is sent, or no bytes are enabled.)

I/O Addressing

In the I/O port-access addressing commands, all `AD[31:0]` lines are used (decoded) to address any byte. The `AD[31:2]` address bits point to the address of the double-word data being transmitted. The `AD[1:0]` address bits define the bytes that can be enabled by the `C/BE[3:0]#` signals. The rules for the PCI transactions are somewhat different here: When at least one byte is sent, the byte pointed to by the address also must be enabled. Thus, when:

❏ `AD[1:0]=00` then `C/BE[3:0]#=xxx0` or `1111`

❏ AD[1:0]=01 then C/BE[3:0]# = xx01 or 1111
❏ AD[1:0]=10 then C/BE[3:0]# = x011 or 1111
❏ AD[1:0]=11 then C/BE[3:0]# = 0111 (only byte 3 is sent)
                   or C/BE[3:0]# = 1111 (no bytes are enabled)

These cycles formally can also come in bursts, although this capability is seldom used in practice. All 32 address bits are available for I/O port addressing on the PCI bus, but x86 processors can use only the lower 16 bits.

The same interrelations between the C/BE[3:0]# and address signals for single DWORD memory transactions described in the previous paragraph extend to PCI-X I/O transactions. These transactions are always single DWORD.

Addressing Configurations Registers and Special Cycle

The configuration write/read commands have two address formats, each of which is used for specific situations. To access registers of a device located on the given bus, Type 0 configuration transactions are employed (Fig. 6.2, *a*). The device (an expansion card) is selected by an individual IDSEL signal generated by the bus' bridge based on the number of the device. The selected device sees the function number Fun in bits AD[10:8] and the configuration register number Reg in bits AD[7:2]; bits AD[1:0] are the Type 0 indicator. The AD[31:11] lines are used as the source of the IDSEL signals for the devices of the given bus. The bus specification defines the AD11 line as the IDSEL line for device 0, the AD12 line as the IDSEL line for device 1; the sequence continues in this order with the AD31 line being the IDSEL line for device 20. The bridge specification features a table in which only lines AD16 (device 0) through AD32 (device 15) are used.

PCI devices combined with a bridge (sharing the same microchip) can also use larger numbers, for which there are not enough AD lines. In PCI-X, the undecoded device number Dev is sent over the AD[15:11] lines: Devices use it as a part of their identifier in the transaction attributes. For devices operating in Mode 1, the AD[31:16] lines are used for IDSEL; only AD[23:16] lines are used in Mode 2, with seven being the largest device number. This allows the function's configuration space to be expanded to four kilobytes: The AD[27:24] lines are used as the higher bits of the configuration register number UReg (Fig. 6.2, *c*).

Type 1 configuration transactions are used to access devices on the other buses (Fig. 6.2, *d*). Here, the bus number Bus of the bus, on which the device being sought is located, is determined by the AD[23:16] bits; the device number Dev is determined by the AD[15:11] bits; bits AD[10:8] contain the function number Fun; bits AD[7:2] carry the register number Reg; the value 01 in bits AD[1:0] is the Type 1 indicator. In PCI-X Mode 2, the higher bits of the register number UReg are sent over the AD[27:24] lines.

31		11	10	8	7	2	1 0
IDSEL signal positional selection code (only one bit can have value 1)			Fun		Reg		00

a

31	16	15	11	10	8	7	2	1 0
IDSEL code		Dev		Fun		Reg		00

b

31	28	27	24	23	16	15	11	10	8	7	2	1 0
Reserved		UReg		IDSEL code		Dev		Fun		Reg		00

c

31	28	27	24	23	16	15	11	10	8	7	2	1 0
Reserved		UReg*		Bus		Dev		Fun		Reg		01

Fig. 6.2. Configuration cycle address format: *a* — PCI bus Type 0 cycle; *b* — PCI-X Mode 1 Type 0 cycle; *c* — PCI-X Mode 2 Type 0 cycle; *d* — Type 1 cycle (*reserved in PCI)

Because bits AD[1:0] are used only for identifying the transaction type, the configuration registers are accessed only by double words. The distinctions between the two configuration transaction types are used to construct the hierarchial PCI configuration system. Unlike in transactions conducted with the memory and I/O addresses, which arrive from the initiator to the target device no matter how they are mutually located, the configuration transactions propagate over the bus hierarchy only in one direction: downward, from the host (central processor) through the main bus to the subordinate buses. Consequently, only the host can configure all PCI devices (including bridges).

No information is sent over the AD bus in the address phase of the PCI broadcast command, called the special cycle. Any PCI bus agent can call a special cycle on any specifically indicated bus by using a Type 1 configuration write transaction and indicating the bus number in bits AD[23:16]. The device and function number fields (bits AD[15:8]) must be all set to one, while the register number field must be zeroed out. This transaction transits the buses independently of the mutual locations of the initiator and the target bus, and only the very last bridge converts it into the actual special cycle.

PCI-X Protocol Modification

In many respects, the PCI-X bus protocol is the same as described above: the same latching at the CLK transition, the same control signal functions. The changes in the protocol are aimed at raising the efficiency of bus cycle usage. For this purpose, additions were made to the protocol that allow devices to foresee upcoming events and to plan their actions accordingly.

In the regular PCI, all transactions begin in the same way (with the address phase) as burst transaction with their length unknown in advance. Here, in practice, the I/O transactions always have only one data phase; long bursts are efficient (and are used) only to access memory. In PCI-X, there are two transaction types in terms of length:

❑ Burst: All commands access memory except the Memory Read DWORD.
❑ Single double word size (DWORD): all other commands.

Each transaction has a new *attribute transmission phase* after the address phase. In this phase, the initiator presents its identifier (RBN — bus number, RDN — device number, and RFN — function number), a 5-bit tag, a 12-bit byte counter (only for burst transactions; UBC — higher bits, LBC — lower bits), and additional characteristics (RO and NS bits) of the memory area, to which the given transaction pertains. The attributes are sent over the AD[31:0] and BE[3:0]# bus lines (Fig. 6.3). The initiator identifier together with the tag defines the *Sequence*: one or more transactions that provide logical data transfer scheduled by the initiator. By using a 5-bit tag, each initiator can simultaneously execute up to 32 logical transfers (a tag can be reused for another logical transaction only after a previous transaction using the same tag value has been completed). A logical transfer (sequence) can be up to 4,096 bytes long (byte counter value 00 ... 01 corresponds to number 1, value 11 ... 11 corresponds to number 4,095,

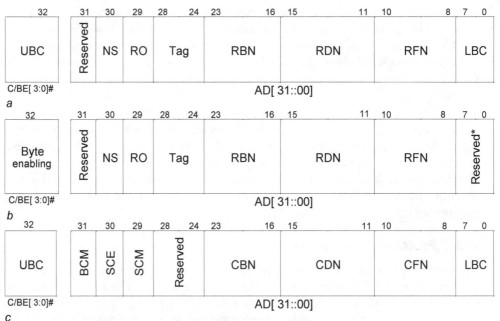

* Bits [7:0] contain the bus number in the configuration write cycle.

Fig. 6.3. Formats of PCI-X transaction attributes: *a* — burst transaction, *b* — single transaction (DWORD), *c* — split transaction completion

value 00 ... 00 corresponds to number 4,096); the number of bytes that must be transferred in the given sequence is indicated in the attributes for each transaction. The number of bytes to be transmitted in the given transaction is not determined in advance (either the initiator or the target device can stop a transaction). However, in order to raise efficiency, stringent requirements are applied to burst transactions.

If a transaction has more than one data phase, it can terminate either after all the bytes declared (in the byte counter in the attributes) have been transmitted or only on the cache line boundaries (on the 128-byte memory address boundaries). If the transaction participants are not ready to meet with these requirements, then one of them must stop the transaction after only the first data phase. Only the target device still has the right to emergency transaction termination at any moment; the initiator is strictly responsible for its actions.

The characteristics of the memory, to which a given transaction pertains, make it possible to select the optimal method to access it when processing the transaction. The characteristics are determined by the device that requests the particular sequence. How it learns the memory properties is something, with which its driver should be concerned. The attributes of the memory characteristics pertain only to burst access memory transactions (but not to MSI messages):

❑ The Relaxed Ordering (RO) flag means that the execution order of individual write or read transactions can be changed.

❑ The No Snoop (NS) flag means that the memory area, to which the given transaction pertains, is not cached anywhere.

In PCI-X, Delayed Transactions are replaced by Split Transactions. The target device can complete any transaction, with the exception of memory write transactions, either immediately (using the regular PCI method) or using the split transaction protocol. In the latter case, the target device issues a Split Response signal, executes the command internally, and afterwards initiates its own transaction (a Split Completion command) to send the data or inform the initiator of the completion of the initial (splitted) transaction. The target device must split the transaction if it cannot answer it before the initial latency period expires. The device that initiates a split transaction is called a *Requester*.

The device that completes a split transaction is called a *Completer*. To complete the transaction, the completer must request bus control from the arbiter; the requester will play the role of the target device in the completion phase. Even a device that is formally not a bus master (as indicated in its configuration space registers) can complete a transaction by the split method. A Split Completion transaction looks a lot like a burst write transaction, but differs from it in the addressing phase: Instead of the full memory or I/O address, the identifier of the sequence (with the requester's bus, device, and function numbers), to which this completion pertains, and only the lower six address bits are sent over the AD bus (Fig. 6.4). The completer obtains this identifier from the attributes of the transaction that it splits.

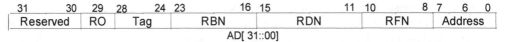

Fig. 6.4. Address format of a PCI-X split transaction completion

Using this identifier (the number of the requester's bus), the bridges convey the completion transaction to the requesting device. The completer's identifier (CBN — bus number, CDN — device number, and CFN — function number; see Fig 6.3, *c*) is sent in the attribute phase. The requester must recognize its sequence identifier and respond to the transaction in the regular way (immediately). The sequence may be processed in a series of completion transactions, until the byte counter is exhausted (or terminated by a time-out). The requester figures out itself, to which starting address each of the termination transactions belongs (it knows what it asked and how many bytes have already arrived). A completion transaction can carry either the requested read data or a Split Complete Message.

The requester must always be ready to receive the data of the sequence that it started; moreover, the data of different sequences may arrive in random order. The completer can generate completion transactions for several sequences also in random order. Within the limits of one sequence, the completions must, naturally, be arranged by addresses (which are not sent). The attributes of a completion transaction contain the bus, device, and function numbers and a byte counter. In addition, they contain three flags:

❒ Byte Count Modified (BCM): indicates that there will be fewer data bytes sent than the requester asked for (sent with the completion data).

❒ Split Completion Error (SCE): indicates a completion error; set when a completion message is sent as an early error indicator (before the message itself has been decoded).

❒ Split Completion Message (SCM): message indicator (distinguishes the message from data).

PCI-X 2.0 Data Transfer Distinctions

In addition to the above-described protocol changes, a new operating mode — Mode 2 — was introduced in PCI-X 2.0. The new mode allows faster memory block writes and uses ECC control, and can be used only with the low (1.5 V) power supply. It has the following features:

❒ The time for address decoding by the target device — the delay in its DEVSEL# response to the command directed to it — has been increased by 1 clock in all transactions.

This extra clock is needed for the ECC control to ascertain the validity of the address and command.

❏ In Memory Write Block transactions, data are transferred at two or four times the rate of the clocking frequency. In these transactions, the BEx# signals are used for synchronization from the data source (they are not used as intended, because it is assumed that all bytes must be enabled). Each data transfer (64, 32, or 16 bits) is strobed by the BEx# signals. The BE[1:0]# and BE[3:2] line pairs provide differential strobing signals for the AD[15:0] and AD[31:16] data lines. There can be two or four data subphases in one bus clock, which at the CLK frequency of 133 MHz provides the PCI-X266 and PCI-X533. Because all control signals are synchronized by the common signal CLK, the transfer granularity becomes two or four data subphases. For a 32-bit bus, this means that during transactions, data can be transferred (as well as transfers halted or suspended) in multiples of 8 or 16 bytes.

In the 64-bit version of the bus, the AD[63:32] lines are only used in data phases; only the 32-bit bus is used for the address (even 64-bit) and for the attributes.

Devices operating in Mode 2 have the option of using the 16-bit bus. In this case, the address and attribute phases take 2 clocks each, while the data phases always come in pairs (providing regular granularity). In the address/data bus, the AD[16:31] lines are used to send the information of bits [0:15] in the first phase of the pair, and of bits [16:31] in the second phase. The C/BE[0:1]# information is sent over lines C/BE[2:3]# in the first phase, and C/BE[2:3]# in the second phase. Lines ECC[2:5] are used for ECC control. Bits ECC[0,1,6] and the special E16 control bit are sent over these lines in the first phase, and ECC[2:5] in the second. The 16-bit bus is only intended for built-in applications (slots and expansion cards are not provided for).

Message Exchange Between Devices (DIM Command)

The ability to send information (messages) to a device addressing it using the identifier (bus, device, and function numbers) was introduced in PCI-X 2.0. The memory and I/O addressing spaces are not used to address and route these messages, which can be exchanged between any bus devices, including the host bridge. The messages are sent in sequences, in which Device ID Message (DIM) commands are used. This command has specific addresses and attributes. In the *address phase* (Fig. 6.5, *a*), the identifier of the message receiver (completer) is sent: the numbers of its bus, device, and function (CBN, CDN, and CFN, respectively). The Route Type (RT) bit indicates the routing type of the message: 0 — explicit addressing using the identifier mentioned above, 1 — implicit addressing to the host bridge (the identifier is not used in this case). The Silent Drop (SD) bit sets the error handling method when processing the given transaction: 0 — regular (as for a memory write), 1 — some types of errors are ignored (but not the parity or ECC errors). The Message Class field sets the message class, according to which the lower address byte is interpreted. A transaction can also use a two-address cycle. In this case, the DAC command code is sent over lines C/BE[3:0]# in the first address phase; the contents of bits AD[31:00] correspond to Fig. 6.5, *a*. The DIM command code is sent over the C/BE[3:0]# lines in the second address phase; bits AD[31:00] are interpreted depending on the message class. Having decoded the DIM command, a device that supports message exchange checks whether the receiver identifier field matches its own.

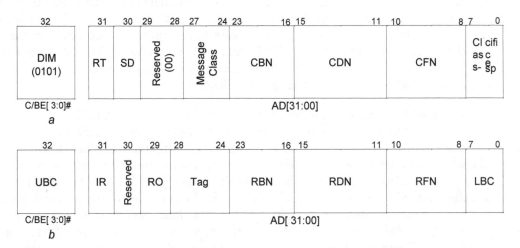

Fig. 6.5. DIM transaction formats: *a* — address, *b* — attributes

The message source identifier (RBN, RDN, and RFN), message tag (Tag), the 11-bit byte counter (UBC and LBC), and additional attribute bits are sent in the *attribute phase* (Fig. 6.5, *b*). The Initial Request (IR) bit is the start of message indicator; the message itself can be broken into parts by the initiator, receiver, or the intermediary bridges (the bit is set to zero in all the following parts). The Relaxed Ordering (RO) bit indicates that the given message can be delivered in any order relative to the other messages and memory writes that are propagated in the same direction (the order, in which the fragments of the given message are delivered, is always preserved).

The body of the message, which is sent in the data phase, can be up to 4,096 bytes long (this limit is due to the 12-bit byte counter). The contents of the body are determined by the message class; class 0 is used at the manufacturer's discretion.

Bridges transfer explicit routing messages using the bus number of the receiver. Problems with the transfer may only arise on the host bridges: If there is more than one host bridge, it may be very difficult to link them architecturally (using memory controller buses, for example). It is desirable to have the capability to transfer messages from one bus to another using host bridges (it is simpler than transferring transactions of all types), but it is not mandatory. If this method is supported, the user enjoys more freedom (the entire bus topology does not have to be considered when placing devices). Implicit routing messages are sent only in the direction of the host.

It is not mandatory for PCI-X devices to support DIM, but PCI-X Mode 2 devices are required to support it. If a DIM message is addressed to a device located on a bus operating in the standard PCI mode (or the path to it goes through the PCI), the bridge either cancels this message (if SD=1) or aborts the transactions (Target Abort, if SD=0).

Boundaries of Address Ranges and Transactions

The Base Address Registers (BAR) in the configuration space header describe the memory and I/O ranges taken by a device (or, more exactly, by a function). It is assumed that the range length is expressed by a 2^n number ($n = 0, 1, 2...$) and that the range is naturally aligned. In PCI, memory ranges are allocated in 2^n paragraphs (16 bytes; i.e., the minimal range size is 16 bytes). I/O ranges are allocated in 2^n double words. PCI to PCI bridges have maps of the memory addresses with granularity of 1 MB; maps of I/O addresses have granularity of 4 KB.

In the PCI, a burst transaction can be interrupted at the boundary of any double word (a quadruple word in the 64-bit transactions). In PCI-X, in order to optimize memory accesses, burst transactions can only be interrupted at the special point called the Allowable Disconnect Boundary (ADB). ADB points are located at intervals of 128 bytes: This is a whole number (1, 2, 4, or 8) of cache lines in modern processors. Of course, this limitation applies only to the transaction borders inside a sequence. If a sequence has been planned to complete not on an ADB boundary, then its last transaction will be completed not on a boundary. However, this type of situation is avoided by developing types of data structures that can be properly aligned (sometimes, even at the expense of being superfluous).

The term ADB Delimited Quantum (ADQ) is associated with the address boundaries; it denotes the part of a transaction or buffer memory (in bridges and devices) that lies between adjacent allowable disconnect boundaries. For example, a transaction crossing one allowable disconnect boundary consists of two data ADQs and occupies two ADQ buffers in the bridge.

In accordance with the allowable transaction boundaries, the memory areas that PCI-X devices occupy also must begin and end at ADBs: The memory is allocated in ADQ quanta. Consequently, the minimum memory area allocated to a PCI-X device cannot be less than 128 bytes and, taking into account the area description rules, it size is allowed to be 128×2^n bytes.

Transaction Execution Time, Timers, and Buffers

The PCI protocol regulates the time (number of clocks) allowed for different phases of a transaction. Bus operation is controlled by several timers, which do not allow bus cycles to be wasted and make it possible to plan bandwidth distribution.

Each target device must respond to the transaction addressed to it sufficiently rapidly. The reply from the addressed target device (the DEVSEL# signal) must come within 1–3 clocks after the address phase, depending on how fast the particular device is: 1 clock — fast, 2 clocks — medium, 3 clocks — slow decoding. If there is no answer, the next clock is allocated to transaction intercepting by a subtractive address decoding bridge.

Target initial latency (i.e., the delay in the appearance of the TRDY# signal with respect to the FRAME# signal), must not exceed 16 bus cycles. If, because of its technical characteristics, a device sometimes does not manage to complete its business during this interval, it must assert the STOP# signal, terminating the transaction. This will make the master device repeat the transaction, and chances are greater that this attempt will be successful. If a device is slow and often cannot manage to complete a transaction successfully within 16 bus cycles, then it must execute Delayed Transactions. Target devices are equipped with an incremental bus-cycle-duration tracking mechanism (Incremental Latency Mechanism) that does not allow the interval between the adjacent data phases in the burst (target subsequent latency) to exceed 8 bus cycles. If a target device cannot maintain this rate, it must terminate the transaction. It is desirable that a device inform about its "falling behind" as soon as possible, without waiting out the 16- or 8-cycle limits: This economizes on the bus' bandwidth.

The initiator must also not slow down the data flow. The permissible delay from the beginning of the FRAME# signal to the IRDY# signal (master data latency) and between data phases must not exceed 8 cycles. If a target device periodically rejects a memory write operation and requests a repeat (as may happen when writing to video memory, for example), then there is a time limit for the operation to be completed. The maximum complete time timer has a threshold of 10 μsec — 334 cycles at 33 MHz or 668 cycles at 66 MHz — during which the initiator must have an opportunity to push through at least one data phase. The timer begins to count from the moment the memory write operation repeat is requested, and is reset when a subsequent memory write transaction other than the requested repeat is completed. Devices that are not capable of complying with the limits on the maximum memory write time must provide the driver with a means of determining at what states sufficiently fast memory write operations are not possible with them. The driver, naturally, must take such states into consideration and not strain the bus and the device with fruitless write attempts.

Each master device capable of forming a burst of more than two data phases long must have its own programmable *Latency Timer*, which regulates its operation when it loses bus control. This timer actually sets the limitation on the length of a burst transaction and, consequently, on the portion of the bus bandwidth allotted to this device. The timer is set going every time the device asserts the FRAME# signal, and counts off bus cycles to the value specified in the configuration register of the same name. The actions of a master device when the timer reaches the threshold depend on the command type and the states of the FRAME# and GNT# signals at the moment the timer is triggered:

❏ If the master device deactivates the FRAME# signal before the timer is triggered, the transaction terminates normally.

❏ If the GNT# signal is deactivated and the command currently being executed is not a Memory Write and Invalidate command, then the initiator must curtail the transaction by deactivating the FRAME# signal. It is allowed to complete the current data phase and execute one more.

❏ If the GNT# signal is deasserted and a Memory Write and Invalidate command is being executed, then the initiator must complete the transaction in one of two ways. If the double word currently being transmitted is not the last in the cache line, the transaction is terminated at the end of the current cacheline. If the double word is the last in the current cacheline, the transaction is terminated at the end of the next cache line.

Arbitration latency is defined as the number of cycles that lapse from the time the initiator issues a bus-control request by the REQ# signal to the time it is granted this right by the GNT# signal. This latency depends on the activity of the other initiators, operating speeds of the other devices (the fewer wait cycles they introduce, the better), and how fast the arbiter itself is. Depending on the command being executed and the state of the signals, a master device must either curtail the transaction or continue it to the planned completion.

When master devices are configured, they declare their resource requirements, stating the maximum permissible *bus access grant delay* (Max_Lat) and the minimum time they must have *control over the bus* (Min_GNT). These requirements are functions of how fast a device is and how it has been designed. However, whether these requirements will actually be satisfied (the arbitrage strategy is supposed to be determined based on them) is not clear.

The arbitration latency is defined as the time that elapses from the moment the master's REQ# is asserted to the moment it receives a GNT# signal and the bus goes into the Idle state (only from that moment can the specific device begin a transaction). The total latency depends on how many master devices there are on the bus, how active they are, and on the values (in bus clocks) of their latency timers. The greater these values are, the more time other devices have to wait to be given control over the bus when it is considerably loaded.

The bus allows lower power consumption by the device at the price of decreased productivity, by using *address/data stepping* for the AD[31:0] and PAR lines:

❏ In continuous stepping, signals begin to be formed by low-current formers several cycles before asserting the valid-data acknowledgement signal (FRAME# in the address phase; IRDY# or TRDY# in the data phase). During these cycles, the signals will "crawl" to the required value using lower current.

❏ In discrete stepping, signal formers use regular currents, but instead of switching all at the same time switch in groups (e.g., by bytes), only one group switches during one cycle. This reduces surges of the current, as fewer formers are switched at the same time.

A device does not necessarily use these capabilities (see the description of the command register's bit 7 functions), but it must "understand" these cycles. If a device delays the FRAME# signal, it risks losing the right to access the bus if the arbiter receives a request from a device that has higher priority. For this reason, stepping was abolished in PCI 2.3 for all transactions except accesses to device configuration areas (type 0 configuration cycles). In these cycles, a device could have not enough time to recognize in the very first transaction cycle the IDSEL selection signal that arrives through a resistor from the corresponding ADx lines.

In PCI-X, the requirements on the number of cycles are more stringent:

❏ The initiator has no right to generate wait cycles. In write transactions, the initiator places the initial data (DATA0) on the bus two clocks after the attribute phase; if the transaction is of the burst type, the next data (DATA1) are placed two clocks after the device answers with a DEVSEL# signal. If the target device does not indicate that it is ready (by the TRDY# signal), the initiator must alternate DATA0 and DATA1 data in each clock, until the target device gives a ready signal (it is allowed to generate only an even number of wait cycles).

❏ The target device can introduce wait cycles only for the initial data phase of the transaction; no wait is allowed in the following data phases.

To take full advantage of the bus' capabilities, devices must have buffers to accumulate data for burst transmissions. It is recommended that devices with transmission speeds of up to 5 MB have buffers to hold at least 4 double words. For devices with higher speeds, it is recommended to have buffers to hold 32 double words. For memory exchange operations, transactions that operate with a whole cacheline are the most effective, which is also taken into account when the buffer size is determined. However, increasing the buffer size may cause difficulties when processing errors, and may also increase delays in delivering data: Until a device fills up the buffer to the predetermined level, it will not begin sending these data and the devices, for which they are intended, will be kept waiting.

The specification gives an example of a Fast Ethernet card design (transmission speed 10 MB/sec) that has a 64-byte buffer divided into two parts for each transmission direction (a ping pong buffer). While the adapter is filling up one half of the buffer with an incoming frame, it is outputting the accumulated contents of the second half into the memory, after which the two halves of the buffer swap places. It takes 8 data phases (approximately 0.25 μsec at 33 MHz) to output each half into the memory, which corresponds to the MIN_GNT=1 setting. When the speed of incoming data is 10 MBps, then it takes 3.2 μsec to fill up each half, which corresponds to the MAX_LAT=12 setting (in the MIN_GNT and MAX_LAT registers, the time is set in 0.25 μsec intervals).

Data Transfer Integrity Control and Error Handling

Parity checking of addresses and data is used to control data transfer integrity on the PCI bus; in PCI-X, ECC with correction of one-bit errors is employed. ECC is mandatory for PCI-X Mode 2 operations; it can also be used when operating in Mode 1. The data transfer integrity control method is communicated by the bridge in the initialization pattern after a hardware reset of the bus. The bridge selects the control method supported by all its bus clients (including itself). Errors are reported by the PERR# signals (protocol signaling between the devices) and SERR# (a fatal error signal that generates, as a rule, an unmasked system interrupt).

The PAR and PAR64 signals are used in parity checking; these signals provide even parity on the AD[31:0], C/BE[3:0]#, PAR, and AD[63:32], C/BE[7:4]#, PAR64 sets of lines. The parity signals PAR and PAR64 are generated by the device that controls the AD bus at the given moment (places a command and its address, attributes, or data). Parity signals are generated with a delay of one 1 clock with respect to the lines they control: AD and C/BE#. The rules are somewhat different for read operations in PCI-X: Parity bits in the N clock pertain to the data bits of the $N-1$ clock and the C/BE# signals of the $N-2$ clock. The PERR# and SERR# signals are generated by the information receiver in the clock that follows the clock, in which the wrong parity appeared.

With ECC, a 7-bit ECC on the ECC[6:0] lines is to check the AD[31:0] and C/BE#[3:0] lines in the 32-bit mode; in the 64-bit mode, an 8-bit code is employed with the ECC[7:0] signals; in the 16-bit mode, a somewhat modified ECC7+1 system is used. In all of the operating modes, the ECC control allows only single errors to be corrected and most errors with a larger repetitive factor to be detected. Error correction can be disabled by software (via the ECC control register); in this case, all parity errors with the repetition factor of 1, 2, or 3 are detected. In all cases, the diagnostic information is saved in the ECC registers. The ECC bits are placed on the bus following the same rules and with the same latency as the parity bits. However, the PERR# and SERR# signals are generated by the information receiver 1 clock after the valid ECC bits: An extra clock is given to ECC syndrome decoding and an attempt to correct the error.

A detected parity error (the same as an ECC error in more than one bit) is unrecoverable. Information integrity in the address phase, and for PCI-X in the attribute phase, is checked by the target device. If an unrecoverable error is detected in these phases, the target device issues a SERR# signal (one clock long) and sets bit 14 in its status register: Signaled System Error. In the data phase, data integrity is checked by the data receiver; if it detects an unrecoverable error, it issues a PERR# signal and sets bit 15 in its status register: Detected Parity Error.

In the status register of devices, bit 8 (Master Data Parity Error) reflects a transaction (sequence) execution failure because of a detected error. In PCI and PCI-X, the rules for setting it are different:

❒ In PCI, it is set only by the transaction initiator when it generates (when doing a read) or detects (when doing a write) a PERR# signal.
❒ In PCI-X, it is set by the transaction requester or a bridge: a read transaction initiator detects an error in data; a write transaction initiator detects the PERR# signal; a bridge as a target device receives completion data with an error or a completion message with a write transaction error from one of the devices.

When a data error is detected, a PCI-X device and its driver have two alternatives:

❒ Without attempting to undertake any actions to recover and continue working, issue a SERR# signal: This is an unrecoverable error signal that can be interpreted by the operating system as a reason to reboot. For PCI devices, this is the only option.
❒ Not issue a SERR# signal and attempt to handle the error by itself. This can be only done by software and taking into account all the potential side effects of the extra operations (a simple repeated read operation may, for example, cause data loss).

The alternative selected is determined by bit 0 (Unrecoverable Data Recovery Enable) in the PCI-X Command register. By default (after a reset), this bit is zeroed out, causing a SERR# signal to be generated in case of a data error. The other option must be selected by a driver that is capable of handling errors on its own.

A detected error in the address or attribute phase is always unrecoverable.

The initiator (requester) of a transaction must have the possibility of notifying the driver of the transaction if it is rejected upon a Master Abort (no answer from the target device) or Target Abort (transaction aborted by the target device) condition; this can be done by using interrupts or other suitable means. If such notification is not possible, the device must issue a SERR# signal.

6.1.3. Bus Bandwidth

In modern computers, the PCI bus is the fastest I/O bus; however, even its actual bus bandwidth is not that high. Here, the most common version of the bus — 32-bit wide, clocked at 33 MHz — will be considered. As previously mentioned, the peak data transfer rate within a burst cycle is 132 MB/sec, i.e., 4 bytes of data are sent over one bus clock ($33 \times 4 = 132$). However, burst cycles are used far from always. To communicate with PCI devices, the processor uses memory or I/O access instructions. It sends these instructions via the host bridge, which translates them into PCI bus transactions. Because the main registers of x86 processors are 32 bits wide, no more than four bytes of data can be transmitted in one PCI transaction produced by the processor instruction, which equals a single transmission (DWORD transaction). But if the address of the transmitted double word is not aligned on the corresponding boundary, then either two single cycles or one with two data phases will be produced. In either case, this access will take longer to execute than if the address were aligned.

However, when writing a data array to a PCI device (a sequentially incremented address transmission), the bridge may try to organize burst cycles. Modern processors, starting with the Pentium, have a 64-bit data bus and use buffers for writing, so two back-to-back 32-bit write requests may be combined into one 64-bit request. If this request is addressed to a 32-bit device, the bridge will try to send it by a burst with two data phases. An "advanced" bridge may also attempt to assemble consecutive requests into a burst, which may produce a burst of a considerable length. Burst write cycles may be observed, for example, when using the MOVSD string instruction with the repeat prefix REP to send a data array from the main memory to a PCI device. The same effect also produces a sequence of LODSW, STOSW, and other memory access instructions.

Because the kernel of modern processors executes instructions much faster than the bus is capable of outputting their results, the processors can execute several other operations between the instructions that produce assembled writes. However, if the data transfer is organized by a high-level-language instruction, which for the sake of versatility is much more complex than the above-mentioned primitive assembler instructions, the transactions will most likely be executed one at a time for one of two reasons: The first is that the processor's write buffers will not have enough "patience" to hold one 32-bit request until the next one appears; second, the processor's or bridge's write buffers will be forcedly cleared upon a write request (see *Section 6.2.10*).

Reading from a PCI device in the burst mode is more difficult. Naturally, processors do not buffer the data they read: A read operation may be considered completed only when actual data are received. Consequently, even string instructions will produce single cycles. However, modern processors can generate requests to read more than 4 bytes. For this purpose, instructions to load data into the MMX or XMM registers (8 and 16 bytes, respectively) may be used. From these registers, data then are unloaded to the RAM (which works much faster than any PCI device).

String I/O instructions (INSW, OUTSW with the REP repeat prefix) that are used for programmed input/output of data blocks (PIO) produce a series of single transactions because all the data in the block pertain to one PCI address.

It is easy to observe with an oscilloscope how a device is accessed: In single transactions, the FRAME# signal is asserted only for one clock; this is longer for burst transactions. The number of data phases in a burst is the same as the number of cycles during which both the IRDY# and TRDY# signals are asserted.

Trying to perform write transactions in the burst mode is advisable only when the PCI device supports burst transactions in the target mode. If it does not, then attempting to write data in the burst mode will even lead to a slight efficiency loss, because the transactions will be completed at the initiative of the slave device (by the STOP# signal) and not by the master device, thereby causing the loss of one bus cycle. Thus, for example, when writing an array into a PCI device memory using a high language instruction, a medium-speed device (one that introduces only 3 wait cycles) receives data every 7 cycles, which at 33 MHz gives speed of $33 \times 4/7 = 18.8$ MBps. Here, the active part of the transaction — from activation of the FRAME# signal to deactivation of the IRDY# signal — takes 4 cycles, and the pause takes 3 cycles. The same device using the MOVSD instruction receives data every eight bus cycles, giving a speed of $33 \times 4/8 = 16.5$ MBps.

These data were obtained by observing the operation of a PCI kernel implemented on the base of an Altera FPGA integrated circuit that does not support burst transactions in the slave mode. The same device works much slower when reading a PCI device memory: using the REP MOVSW instruction data could be obtained only once every 19–21 bus cycles, giving an average speed of $33 \times 4/20 = 6.6$ MBps. Here, the negative factors are the device's high latency (it presents data only 8 cycles after the FRAME# signal is activated) and the fact that the processor begins its next transmission only after receiving data from the previous one. In this case, despite losing a cycle (used by the target device to terminate the transaction), the trick of using the XMM register produces a positive effect. This happens because each processor's 64-bit request is executed by a consecutive pair of PCI transactions with only a two-cycle wait between them.

To determine the theoretical bus bandwidth limit, let's return to Fig. 6.1 to determine the minimal time (number of cycles) for executing a read or write transaction. In the read transaction, the current master of the AD bus changes after the initiator has issued the command and address (cycle 1). This turnaround takes cycle 2 to execute, which is due to the TRDY# signal being delayed by the target device. Then, if the target device is smart enough, a data phase may follow (cycle 3). After the last data phase, one more cycle is needed for the reverse turnaround of the AD bus (in this case, it is cycle 4). Thus, it takes at least 4 cycles of 30 nsec each (at 33 MHz) to read one double word (4 bytes). If these transactions follow each other immediately (if the initiator is capable of operating this way and the bus control is not taken away from it) then, for single transactions, maximum read speeds of 33 MBps can be reached. In write transactions, the initiator always controls the AD bus, so no time is lost on the turnarounds. With a smart target device, which does not insert extra wait cycles, write speeds of 66 MBps may be achieved.

Speeds comparable to the peak speeds may be achieved only when using burst transmissions, when three extra read cycles and one write cycle are added not to each data phase but to a burst of them. Thus, to read a burst with 4 data phases, 7 cycles are needed, producing the speed of $V=16/(7\times30)$ bytes/nsec = 76 MBps. Five cycles are needed to write such a burst, giving a speed of $V=16/(5\times30)$ bytes/nsec = 106.6 MBps. When the number of data phases equals 16, the read speed may reach 112 MBps, and the write speed may reach 125 MBps.

These calculations do not take into account time losses caused by the changes of the initiator. The initiator can begin a transaction at receiving the GNT# signal only after it ascertains that the bus is idle (i.e., that the FRAME# and IRDY# signals are deasserted); recognizing idle state takes another cycle. As can be seen, a single initiator can grab most of the bus' bandwidth by increasing the burst length. However, this will cause delays for other devices to obtain bus control, which is not always acceptable. It should also be noted that far from all devices can respond to transactions without inserting wait cycles, so the actual figures will be more modest.

Therefore, to achieve the maximum exchange efficiency, PCI devices themselves must be bus master devices and, moreover, be capable of operating in the burst mode. Far from all PCI devices support burst transmission mode, and those that do as a rule have substantial burst length limitations. It is possible to raise the bus' bandwidth radically by going over to a 66 MHz bus clock and a 64-bit bus, but this is not an inexpensive solution. For devices critical to data delivery timing (such as network adapters, audio and video devices, etc.) to be able to work normally on the bus, the bus' entire declared bandwidth should not be squeezed out of it, as overloading the bus may lead, for example, to losing packets because of data delivery timing errors. A Fast Ethernet adapter (100 MBps) operating in the half-duplex mode takes over about 13 MBps (10%) of a regular bus' declared bandwidth. Operating in the full-duplex mode, it takes 26 MBps. A Gigabit Ethernet adapter, even in the half-duplex mode, barely fits into a regular bus' declared bandwidth (it "survives" only because of its large internal buffers); a 64-bit bus operating at 66 MHz is more suitable for it. Switching to PCI-X, with its higher clock frequencies (PCI-X66, PCI-X100, PCI-X133) and fast memory write (PCI-X266 and PCI-X533), produces a substantial increase in peak speed and effective throughput capacity.

While on the subject of bus throughput and effective exchange rate with PCI devices, the overhead introduced by additional PCI to PCI bridges should be kept in mind. A device located on a distant bus receives less throughput than a device located immediately after the host bridge and to which the above discussion applies. This is due to the way in which the bridge operates: Transactions over the bridge are executed in several stages (see *Section 6.1.6*).

6.1.4. Interrupts: INTx#, PME#, MSI, and SERR#

PCI devices can signal asynchronous events using interrupts. There are four types of interrupts available on the PCI bus:

❑ Traditional wire signaling over the INTx lines
❑ Wire signaling for power management events over the PME# line
❑ Signaling using messages: MSI
❑ Signaling an unrecoverable error over the SERR# line

Hardware Interrupts in PC-Compatible Computers

Hardware interrupts provide a processor's reaction to the events that occur asynchronously relative to the program code being executed. As a reminder, hardware interrupts are divided into masked and nonmasked.

The processor always reacts to nonmasked interrupts (if it has already handled the previous NMI). These interrupts have the fixed vector 2. Nonmasked interrupts are used in PC to signal fatal errors. A signal comes on the NMI line from the parity check or ECC control circuits, from the ISA bus control lines (IOCHK) and from PCI bus (SERR#). The NMI signal is blocked from entering the processor by setting bit 7 in port 070h to one; individual sources are enabled and identified by the bits of port 061h:

❑ Bit 2 — ERP (R/W): enables main memory control and the PCI bus SERR# signal
❑ Bit 3 — EIC (R/W): enables ISA bus control
❑ Bit 6 — IOCHK (R): ISA bus control error (IOCHK# signal)
❑ Bit 7 — PCK (R): memory parity error or a SERR# signal on the PCI bus

The processor's reaction to masked interrupts can be delayed by resetting its internal IF flag (the CLI instruction enables interrupt; STI disables). When an event requiring the processor's attention arises, the adapter (controller) of the device generates an interrupt request that arrives to the input of the interrupt controller. The interrupt controller generates a general masked interrupt request to the processor; when the processor confirms this request, the controller communicates to the processor the interrupt vector pointing to the software interrupt handler. The interrupt handler must service the given device, including resetting its request so that subsequent events can be reacted to and sending a completion command to the interrupt controller. On calling the interrupt handler, the processor automatically saves all the flags in the stack and clears the IF flag, disabling masked interrupts.

Having returned from the interrupt handler procedure (by the IRET instruction), the processor restores the flags it had saved, including IF (previously set to one), which enables interrupts again. The interrupt handler must have an STI instruction if other (higher priority) interrupts need to be reacted to during handling of the current interrupt. This is especially important for long handlers; here, the STI instruction must be inserted as early as possible, right after the crucial section (not allowing interruptions). The interrupt controller will handle the following interrupts of the same or lower priority only after it has received an interrupt completion command EOI (End of Interrupt).

Masked interrupts are used to signal about device events. Interrupt request signals are handled by interrupt controllers that are software-compatible with a chained pair or 8259A interrupt controllers. The general principle of generating interrupt requests is depicted in Fig. 6.6.

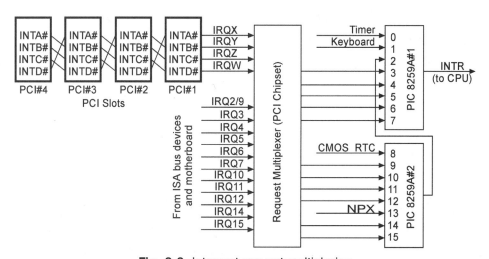

Fig. 6.6. Interrupt request multiplexing

The 8259A controller allows individual request inputs to be masked and requests from different inputs organized into a priority system. The 8253A#1 master controller services requests 0, 1, 3–7; its output is connected to the processor's interrupt request input. The 8259A#2 slave controller is connected, which services requests 8–15, to its input 2. Requests 8–15, with their descending priorities, are wedged between requests 1 and 3 of the master controller, whose request priorities also descend as the request numbers become larger.

Requests to the inputs of the interrupt controllers arrive from system devices (keyboard, system timer, CMOS timer, coprocessor), motherboard peripheral controllers, and expansion cards. Traditionally, all ISA/EISA bus slots have all request lines that are not taken by the above-listed devices. These lines are denoted as IRQx and have conventional functions (Table 6.4). Some of these lines are given over to the PCI bus. The table also shows interrupt priorities: Requests are located in order of decreasing priorities. The vector numbers corresponding to the controllers' request lines, the priority systems, and certain other parameters are set by software when the controllers are initialized. These main settings remain unchanged for purposes of software compatibility.

Table 6.4. Hardware Interrupts (in order of decreasing priority)

Name (number[1])	Vector	Controller/Mask	Description
NMI	02h		Channel control, parity (in XT — co-processor)
IRQ0	08h	#1/1h	Timer (8253/8254 channel 0)
IRQ1	09h	#1/2h	Keyboard
IRQ2	0Ah	#1/4h	XT — reserved; AT — not available (the second interrupt controller is connected, interrupts IRQ8–IRQ15)
IRQ8	70h	#2/1h	CMOS RTC: real-time clock
IRQ9	71h	#2/2h	Reserved
IRQ10	72h	#2/4h	Reserved
IRQ11	73h	#2/8h	Reserved
IRQ12	74h	#2/10h	PS/2 Mouse (reserved)
IRQ13	75h	#2/20h	Math coprocessor
IRQ14	76h	#2/40h	HDD controller
IRQ15	77h	#2/80h	Reserved
IRQ3	0Bh	#1/4h	COM2, COM4
IRQ4	0Ch	#1/10h	COM1, COM3
IRQ5	0Dh	#1/20h	XT — HDC, AT — LPT2, Sound (reserved)
IRQ6	0Eh	#1/40h	FDD controller
IRQ7	0Fh	#1/80h	LPT1 — printer

[1] Interrupt requests 0, 1, 8, and 13 are not brought out onto the expansion buses.

Each device requiring interrupts for its work must be assigned an interrupt number. The process of assigning interrupt numbers has two parts: First, the adapter that needs interrupts must be configured to use a specific interrupt line on the bus (by jumpers or software); second, the software support for the given adapter must be informed of the interrupt vector used. The Plug-and-Play system for the ISA or PCI buses can be engaged in the process of assigning interrupt numbers; special parameters in CMOS setup are used to allocate interrupt request lines between buses. Modern operating systems can change the request number allocation performed by SMOS Setup.

Traditional PCI Interrupts: INTx#

Four physical interrupt request lines are allocated to PCI devices: IRQX, IRQY, IRQZ, and IRQW. They are connected with the INTA#, INTB#, INTC#, and INTD# out of all PCI slots with cyclic line offset (see Fig. 6.6). The correspondence of INTx# lines to IRQ inputs for devices on any PCI bus is shown in Table 6.5. PCI bridges simply electrically connect the same-name INTx lines of their primary and secondary buses.

Table 6.5. Interrupt Request Routing for PCI devices

Slot contact	Input of the request router for device with number:			
	0, 4, 8, ..., 28	1, 5, 9, ..., 29	2, 6, 10, ..., 30	3, 7, 11, ..., 31
INTA#	IRQW	IRQX	IRQY	IRQZ
INTB#	IRQX	IRQY	IRQZ	IRQW
INTC#	IRQY	IRQZ	IRQW	IRQX
INTD#	IRQZ	IRQW	IRQX	IRQY

A PCI device activates the interrupt signal by placing a *low-level* (open collector or sink output) signal on the selected interrupt line: INTx#. This signal must remain asserted until the software driver summoned by the interrupt resets the interrupt request by addressing the device that has issued it. If the interrupt controller again detects a low level on the interrupt request line after this, it means that an interrupt request on the same line has been placed by another device that shares the line with the first one, and that it is also requesting to be serviced.

Propagation of an interrupt request signal is not synchronized with the associated data transfers. A situation is possible in which an active device, having completed data transfer to the memory, issues an interrupt notifying the processor of this event. However, the data transferred by the device may have been delayed in the bridges (if the bus is overloaded) and the processor will begin servicing the interrupt without having received the data yet. In order to guarantee data integrity, the Interrupt Service

Routine (ISR) program must read one of the registers of its device: Reading from behind the bridge will force all bridges to unload all their buffers of memory writes sent to them prior to the interrupt processing (see *Section 6.1.6*).

Interrupt request lines from the PCI slots and from the motherboard's PCI devices are assigned to the inputs of the interrupt controllers in a relatively arbitrary manner. Configuration software can identify and indicate the taken interrupt request lines and the interrupt controller's number by accessing the configuration space of the device (see *Section 6.2.12*). A software driver, having read the configuration registers, also can determine these parameters in order to provide the interrupt handler with the necessary vector and to reset the request line when servicing the interrupt.

Any PCI device function may enable its interrupt request line, but its interrupt request handler must be prepared to share it with other devices. If a device requires only one interrupt request line, then it should take the INTA# line; if it requires two interrupt request lines, then it should take the INTA# and INTB# lines; and so on. Taking into account the cyclic shift of the interrupt request lines, this rule makes it possible to install 4 simple devices into 4 adjacent slots, and each of them will take an individual interrupt request line. If a card requires two interrupt request lines, then the adjacent slot must be left unoccupied to preserve the monopolistic use of the interrupts. However, it must be remembered that the PCI devices built into the motherboard enable interrupts in the same manner (with the exception of the IDE controller, which, fortunately, is in class by itself). In terms of interrupts, the AGP port must be considered like any other PCI slot. Consequently, it may turn out that far from all slots have individual interrupt lines.

Modern motherboards are equipped with an advanced programmable interrupt controller (APIC), which can provide additional inputs (as a rule eight of them, numbered from 16 to 23). These inputs are used by integrated devices, and some of them can be allocated to the PCI slots, which somewhat alleviates the interrupt lines shortage.

Devices and/or functions are assigned interrupt lines by a POST procedure, and this process is only partially controlled by user. The interrupt request numbers available to the PCI bus are defined by the user in the CMOS Setup parameters (PCI/PNP Configuration). Depending on the BIOS version, this can be done in different ways: Either every INTA# ... INTD# line is explicitly assigned its own number, or a range of numbers is given to PCI and ISA plug-and-play devices (although not to the legacy ISA devices). In the end, POST determines, which INTx# line corresponds to which controller request number, and programs the interrupt request multiplexer accordingly. Depending on the user's actions, it may be that not every PCI bus interrupt request line gets its individual interrupt controller input assigned. If this is the case, then the multiplexer bundles up several PCI interrupt request lines to one controller input (i.e., even different PCI interrupt request lines will become shared). In the worst-case scenario, PCI devices do not receive any inputs on the interrupt controller. It is unlikely that BIOS will give interrupts 14 or 15 (which are given to the IDE controller) or interrupts 3 or 4 (which are given to the COM ports) to the PCI bus. New operating systems get involved into the hardware platform functions to such an extent that allow themselves (knowing the motherboard chipset or using PCI BIOS functions) to control the interrupt multiplexer. This capability can be enabled or disabled, for example, in Windows using the PCI Interrupt Steering flag in the PCI bus properties (Control Panel — System Devices — PCI Bus).

The driver (or other utility) that works with a PCI device determines the interrupt vector that the device (or, rather, the function) has been allocated by reading the `Interrupt Line` configuration register. This register shows the interrupt controller's input number (255 means that the number is not assigned) and the vector is determined by this number. The input number for each device is assigned by POST; it does this by reading the `Interrupt Pin` register of every function it detects and by the device address (read geographical address) determines, which of the INTA# ... INTD# lines (at the input of the interrupt multiplexer) is used. The rules, by which the correspondence between the `Interrupt Pin` and the interrupt request muliplexer input lines is defined on the motherboard, are not strictly set (dividing the device number by 4 is just a recommendation). However, the BIOS version of the motherboard in question knows them well. By this time, POST has already defined the lines-to-input-numbers correspondence table; using this table, it writes the required value to the `Interrupt Line` configuration register. To determine whether there are still any contenders for the same interrupt number is possible only by inspecting the configuration registers of the functions of all devices detected on the bus. This is not that difficult, and can be done using the PCI BIOS functions. The "delights" of shared interrupts are discussed in the following paragraph.

From version 2.1, PCI BIOS has functions for determining interrupt capabilities and their configuring. One function returns the data structure, in which information for each device (on each bus) is provided; this information concerns the interrupt controller inputs (IRQx), to which the device's INTx lines can be connected and exactly with which inputs these lines are currently connected. The physical number of the slot, into which the device is installed, is also indicated. In addition, a bit map is returned, showing which IRQx inputs are allocated exclusively to the PCI bus (and are not used by other bus clients). For the given device, the setup function links the selected INTx signals with the selected IRQx input of the interrupt controller (i.e., programs the multiplexer). This function is intended to be used only by the configuration software (BIOS, operating system), but not by device drivers. The software that uses it is itself responsible for avoiding potential conflicts, for proper programming of the interrupt controller (the selected input must respond to a low level of the signal and not to a positive transition), and for correcting the information in the configuration space of all devices involved (whose interrupt request lines are connected with the selected INTx line).

The Shared Interrupt Problem

Interrupt request lines are the scarcest resource in a computer inundated with peripheral devices; therefore, they have to be shared (i.e., one interrupt line is used by several devices). From the hardware point of view, the interrupt-sharing problem has been solved for the PCI bus: Here, the interrupt request is triggered by a low level, and the interrupt controller is sensitive to a level but not to a transition. Interrupts cannot be shared for the ISA bus, with its positive transition interrupt requests. The exception is motherboards and devices that support ISA Plug-and-Play, which can be made to work using the low level.

With the hardware solution of interrupt request line sharing successfully found, what remains is the task of identifying each interrupt source in order to launch a corresponding interrupt handler. It is desirable that this task be solved by the operating system and take minimal time.

Up to and including PCI 2.2, no commonly accepted method for indicating and disabling interrupts by software existed: For this purpose, each device used its specific bits of the operation registers pertaining to the memory or I/O spaces. In such a case, only the given device's interrupt handler, which is a part of its driver, can determine whether the given device is the interrupt source at the given moment. Therefore, the operating system has no other means of controlling shared interrupts other than to line up their interrupt handlers into a chain. The interrupt handler's developer is responsible for its correct and efficient functioning. In PCI 2.3, fixed bits in the status register and configuration control register of a device (function) finally appeared, so the operating system can use them to determine the source of a shared interrupt and summon only its interrupt handler. However, descriptions of devices and operating system often do not mention that they support the PCI 2.3.

Device interrupt handlers must act properly, taking into account the possibility of a shared interrupt getting into the chain of the interrupt handlers. When processing an interrupt, by reading the register of its device, the next interrupt handler in the chain must determine whether the interrupt was triggered by its device. If so, the interrupt handler must execute the necessary routine and clear the interrupt request from its device, handing over the control to the next handler in the chain thereafter; otherwise, it simply hands over the control to the next interrupt handler in the chain. Sometimes, the following typical interrupt handler error happens: Having read the status register of its device and not detected a request indicator, the driver clears all the request sources (or even the entire device), just in case. This error is caused by a heedless driver developer who does not consider the possibility of interrupts being shared and does not trust hardware developers. Seeing this unexpected situation during the debugging process, he or she "fixes" it by inserting the harmful code fragment. The harm lies in that from the moment the device status register is read (without producing a request indicator) to the moment this unnecessary clearing is executed, an interrupt request may arise in the device, which will be blindly cleared and, consequently, lost.

However, even when interrupt handlers lined up in a queue are correctly written, on the whole, shared interrupts for different type devices cannot be considered functional: It is possible that interrupts from devices that require rapid reaction can be lost. This may happen if the interrupt handler for such a device happens to be the last in the queue and the handlers in front of it turn out to be not fast enough (to detect that the interrupt is not theirs). How the system will behave in this case may be different depending on the order in which the drivers are loaded. For several same-type devices (network adapters based on the same chip, for example) that use one driver, shared interrupts work out just fine.

Interrupt conflicts can manifest themselves in various ways. A network adapter may not be able to receive frames from the network (while being able to send them). It may take an extremely long time to access mass storage devices (sometimes, it may take minutes for the file or catalog information to appear), or they may be impossible to access altogether. Audio cards may be silent or stutter, images on video players may be jerky, and so on. The interrupt conflict may also cause unexpected rebooting, for example, upon arrival of a frame from the network or a signal from the modem. The solution to the interrupt sharing problem can be moving cards around into a suitable slot, in which no conflicts are observed (which may not necessarily mean that there are none). However, sometimes a "present" can be encountered from integrated motherboard designers in which only one of several PCI slots has a nonshared interrupt line (or none of them has any at all). As a rule, this kind of disorder cannot be treated without an X-ecto knife and a soldering iron. A more drastic method is to switch to signaling interrupts using messages: MSI.

Power Management Event Signaling: PME#

The PME# line, introduced in the PCI 2.0, is used for signaling in the power management system: device state change, system wake up upon an event, etc. All PCI devices can electrically access this line; just like the INTx# lines, the PME# line is not processed by the bridges in any way but is only conveyed to all the clients. The signaling logic is analogous to the INTx#: The device signals an event by shorting the PME# to the ground; therefore, event signals are logically assembled according to the OR function logic. The interrupt handler of this interrupt can detect the device that has generated the interrupt by software access to the configuration registers of all devices that are capable of generating this signal. Devices (functions) capable of power management have a structure with the Capability ID=1 identifier and a set of registers in their configuration space. These registers and their functions are as follows:

❑ *Power Management Capabilities* (PMC): specification version, what states are supported, whether states are capable of PME# generation, whether the CLK signal is needed to generate a PME#, what is power consumption on the 3.3 V Aux.

❑ *Power Management Control/Status Register* (PMCSR): indicator of a PME# issuance, clearing, and enabling PM status; control of the data output via the Data register.

❑ *Data:* an optional register that can be used, for example, to output the power consumption information.

❑ *Bridge Support Extension* (PMSCR_BSE): indicator of bus support for secondary bridge control depending on the PM state; status of the secondary bus when switched into D3 (clock halt or depowering).

The details of PCI power management and the formats of the corresponding configuration registers can be found in the PCI PM 1.1 specification.

Message Signaled Interrupts: MSI

The PCI bus has a progressive asynchronous event-notification mechanism based on message signaling: Message Signaled Interrupts (MSI). Here, to signal an interrupt request, the device requests bus control and, having received it, sends a message. The message looks like a regular double word memory write; the address (32- or 64-bit) and the message template are written into the configuration registers of the device (or, to be more exact, of the function) during the configuration stage. The upper 16 bits of the message are always zeroes, while the lower 16 carry the information about the interrupt source. A device (function) may need to signal more than one type of request; according to the device's needs and its resources, the system tells the function how many different types of request it can generate.

Whether a function can use MSI is described in the configuration space by the MSI Capability structure (CAP_ID=05h), which must be in the space of each function that supports MSI. There are three or four registers in the structure (Fig. 6.7):

❑ *Message Address:* a 32-bit memory address to which the message is sent (bits [1:0]=00). If a 64-bit addressing is used (bit 7 in the Message Control register is set), then its upper part is located in the Message Upper Address register. The system software places values is the address registers during the configuration stage.

❑ *Message Data:* a 16-bit template for data that are sent in the message over the AD[15:0] lines. The system software writes the template during the configuration stage. The message sent by a function can have only a few lower bits (whose number is defined by the contents of the Multiple Message Enable field) modified in order to indicate different interrupt conditions. The rest of the message bits must comply with the template; bits [31:16] are always zeroed out.

❑ *Message Control:* 16 bit long. In bit 7, the function indicates its being able to generate a 64-bit address. In the Multiple Message Capable field of the function, its ability to generate differentiable interrupt conditions is set. In Multiple Message Enable, the system tells the function the allowable number of conditions. Here, the values 000–101 are the binary coded number of the lower template bits that the device can modify in order to identify the interrupt source: 000 — none (only one identifier is available to the device); 101 — five bits; during the write, the AD[4:0] lines identify the specific interrupt condition (one out of 32 available to the given function). Values 110 and 111 are reserved. The MSI_Enable bit enables MSI. MSI is disabled after a hardware reset. It can be enabled by software by setting the MSI_Enable bit (after the message address and template have been programmed), after which interrupt generation over the INTx# is disabled.

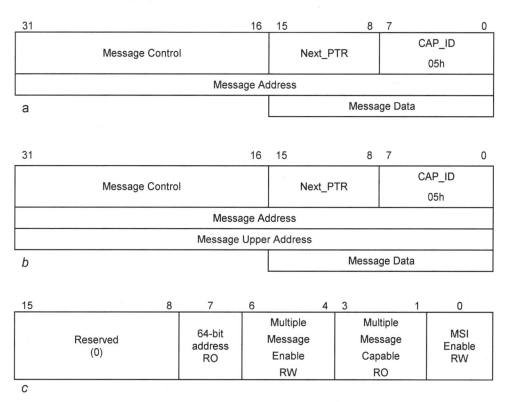

Fig. 6.7. MSI register formats: *a* — location of the registers in the 32-bit address MSI Capability structure; *b* — in the 64-bit address structure; *c* — Message_Control register

The system can interpret two or more identical fast back-to-back messages as one interrupt (because of the slow reaction). If each of them needs to be serviced, the interrupt handler must confirm to the device receiving a message, while the device must not send another message until it receives a confirmation that the previous one has been received. Different messages present no problems in this respect.

This mechanism can be used on motherboards that have an Advanced Peripheral Interrupt Controller (APIC). A message is sent by writing the request number into the corresponding APIC register. For example, for motherboards based on a chipset with the ICH2 82801 hub, this register is located at the memory address FEC00020h, and the interrupt number can be in the 0–23h range.

Interrupts using MSI make it possible to avoid the interrupt sharing problem arising from the scarcity of interrupt request lines in PCs. Moreover, they solve the data integrity problem: All data that the device writes prior to issuing an MSI are guaranteed to arrive to the recipient before the start of MSI processing. Interrupts using MSI by some devices can be used alongside the INTx interrupts by other devices in the same system. However, devices (functions) that use MSI must not use INTx interrupts.

6.1.5. Direct Memory Access, ISA DMA Emulation (PC/PCI, DDMA)

As mentioned previously, unlike the ISA bus with its 8237A controller, a PCI bus does not provide direct memory access using a centralized controller. To relieve the CPU of routine data transfers, PCI buses offer direct bus control by devices called PCI Bus Masters. The intelligence of these bus masters varies. The simplest ones transfer blocks of data to and from the system memory (or memory of other devices) under the CPU's control. By accessing the pertinent registers of the master device, the CPU sets the starting address, block length, and transfer direction, and then gives permission to begin the transmission. This done, the master device executes the transfer when it is ready and willing, without distracting the CPU. In this way, direct memory access is accomplished. A more sophisticated DMA controller can do coupled buffers reads, scattered writes, and other similar operations that are known from the advanced ISA/EISA DMA controllers. A more intelligent master device that, as a rule, has its own microcontroller does not limit itself to simply working under the CPU's control, but performs exchanges under its controller's program.

In order to keep PCI devices less complex and to make them compatible with the old PC-oriented software, Intel has developed the special *PC/PCI DMA protocol*. This protocol changes the functions of the REQi# *and* GNTi# signals of the bus agent specified in advance, and plays the role of a dedicated DMA conductor. The logic of this agent's signal pair DRQx# and DACKx# (external, in terms of the PCI bus) is analogous to the same-name ISA signals; the REQi# and GNTi# lines also have special uses when involved in a request for control of the bus. When the agent receives a DRQx request (one or several), it sends serially coded numbers of the active lines of the DRQx requests over the REQi# line using the CLK line for synchronization. In the first CLK cycle, the start bit is sent by low level on the REQi# line. In the second cycle, the activity of the DRQ0 request is sent, then of the DRQ1, and so on, up to the DRQ7, after which REQ# continues to be kept low. The arbiter will respond to this message by sending a message over the GNTi# line. This message also begins with a start bit, followed by the 3-bit code of the channel number that is getting the DACK# acknowledgement for data transmission in the transaction. The agent must inform the arbiter of all changes in the request lines, including request signal deactivations. The PC/PCI DMA mechanism can only be implemented in the motherboard chipset. An alternative solution — the Distributed DMA (DDMA) mechanism — makes it possible to disembody the standard controller and to emulate its individual channels by the resources of PCI cards. Both of these mechanisms can only be implemented as a part of the bridge between the primary PCI bus and the ISA bus; therefore, their support can (or cannot) be provided only on the motherboard and enabled in the CMOS Setup.

6.1.6. PCI and PCI-X Bridges

PCI Bridges are special hardware used to connect PCI buses to other buses and to each other. The Host Bridge is used to connect the main PCI bus (number 0) to the system bus (system RAM and the CPU). The honorable duty of the host bridge is to generate accesses to the configuration space under the control of the central processor; this allows the host (the central processor) to configure the entire subsystem of the PCI buses. There can be more than one host bridge in the system, which makes it possible to provide high-performance communications with the center for a large number of devices (there are limitations on how many devices can be placed on one bus). One of these buses is designated the main (bus 0).

Peer-to-peer PCI bridges are used to connect additional PCI buses. These bridges introduce an additional overhead to the data transfers, so the effective productivity of the exchange a device conducts with the center decreases with each bridge in the traffic's way.

To connect PCMCIA, CardBus, MCA, ISA/EISA, X-Bus, and LPC buses to a PCI bus, special bridges are used. These bridges may be either integral parts of the motherboard chipsets, or implemented as discrete PCI devices (microchips). The bridges interconvert the interfaces of the buses that they connect, and also synchronize and buffer data.

Each bridge must be programmed, or shown the memory and I/O address ranges allocated to the devices of the bus it services. If in the current transaction, the address of a target device connected to a bus on one side of the bridge belongs to the bus on the opposite side, the bridge redirects the transaction to the corresponding side and takes care of coordinating the protocols of the buses. If there is more than one host bridge in the system, then end-to-end routing between devices on different buses may not be possible: The host bridges will be connected with each other only via the memory controller buses. Supporting relaying of all types of PCI transactions via host bridges is too complicated in this case, and, consequently, is not among mandatory PCI requirements. Consequently, all active devices on all PCI buses can access the system memory, but their peer-to-peer communications may depend on the PCI bus on which they are located.

Using PCI bridges presents the following capabilities:

❐ Increasing the number of devices that can be connected to the bus by overcoming the electrical specifications of the bus.

❐ Dividing PCI devices into segments — PCI buses — that have different widths (32/64 bits), clock frequencies (33/66/100/133 MHz), and protocols (PCI, PCI-X, PCI-X Mode 1, PCI Express). On each bus, its devices keep pace with the weakest member; placing devices on buses properly makes it possible to use the capabilities of the devices and of the motherboard with maximum efficiency.

❐ Organizing segments with dynamic device connection/disconnection.

❐ Organizing simultaneous parallel transaction execution from initiators located on different buses.

Every PCI bridge connects two buses: the primary bus, which is closer to the top of the hierarchy, and the secondary bus. The interfaces that connect the bridge to these buses are correspondingly called the *primary* and *secondary*. Only the tree-type bus connection configuration is allowed (i.e., two buses are interconnected by only one bridge and there are no bridge loops). Buses connected to the secondary interface of a bridge are called *subordinate*. PCI bridges form a PCI bus hierarchy at whose apex is the main bus (number zero), which is connected to the host bridge. If there is more than one host bridge, then the bus assigned number zero will be the main one.

A bridge must perform a set of mandatory functions:

❐ To service the bus connected to its secondary interface. Namely:
  ● To perform arbitration: receiving REQx# request signals from master devices on the bus and granting them, by GNTx# signals, the right to control the bus.
  ● To park the bus: issuing a GNTx# signal to any device on the bus if none of the masters needs bus control.
  ● To generate type 0 bus configuration cycles with issuing individual IDSEL signals to the addressed PCI device.
  ● To pull the control signal to the high level.
  ● To determine the capabilities of the connected devices and select the bus operation mode that suits them (clock frequency, bus width, protocol).
  ● To generate a hardware reset (RST#) up a primary interface reset and at a command, informing of the selected mode by special signalization (see *Section 6.1.8*).

❐ To support maps of the resources located on the opposite sides on the bridge.

❏ To reply as a target device to transactions initiated by another master on one interface and directed to a resource located on another interface. To convey these transactions on the other interface playing role of a master device, and to convey the results of the transactions to the actual initiator.

Bridges that perform these functions are called *transparent*; no additional drivers are needed to work with devices that are located on such bridges. It is these bridges that are described in PCI Bridge 1.1; being PCI devices, they are assigned a special class (06). In the given case, the flat resource addressing model is assumed (resources being memory and I/O): Each device has its own addresses, unique within a given computer system (not overlapping with others).

There also are *nontransparent* bridges; these organize individual segments with their local address spaces. Nontransparent bridges convert addresses for transactions, in which the initiator and the target are located on the opposite sides of the bridge. Not all of resources of the opposite side (address ranges) may be reachable on such bridges. An example of nontransparent bridge use is when a computer has a separate intelligent I/O subsystem (I2O) with its own I/O processor and local address space.

Routing Functions of Transparent Bridges

The task of routing is to determine where in relation to the bridge the resources addressed in each transaction are located; this task is the first to perform when processing each transaction that a bridge sees on any of its interfaces. This task can be solved in two ways, because either a hierarchical PCI address (bus:device:function) or a flat memory or I/O address can be sent in the address phase.

Hierarchical Address Routing

Configuration write and read transactions, special cycle transactions, and (in PCI-X) also split transaction completions are addressed via bus and device numbers. The routing for these transactions is based on a bus-numbering system. When a system is configured, numbers are assigned to PCI buses strictly sequentially; bridge numbers correspond to the numbers of their secondary buses. Thus, the host bridge is assigned number zero. Numbers of the bridge's subordinate buses start with the number that follows the number of its secondary bus. Therefore, the system bus topology information that each bridge needs is described by a bus number list — three numerical parameters in its configuration space:

❏ Primary Bus Number
❏ Secondary Bus Number (also, the bridge number)
❏ Subordinate Bus Number — the maximal number of the subordinate bus

All buses with numbers in the range from the Secondary Bus Number to the Subordinate Bus Number inclusive lie on the secondary-interface side; all the other buses lie on the primary-interface side.

Knowing bus numbers allows bridges to relay accesses to the device configuration registers in the direction from the host to the subordinate buses, and to propagate special cycles in all directions. Bridges relay responses to split transactions (Split Complete) from one interface to another if they are addressed to a bus of the opposite bridge.

Bridges do not relay type 0 configuration cycles. Bridges process type 1 configuration transactions detected on the primary interface in the following way:

❑ If the bus number (AD[23:16]) corresponds to the secondary bus, bridges convert type 1 configuration transactions into type 0 configuration cycles or special cycles. During conversion to a type 0 cycle, the device number from the primary bus is decoded into a positional code on the secondary bus (see *Section 6.1.2.1*), the function and register numbers are relayed unchanged; the AD[1:0] bits on the secondary bus are zeroed out. In PCI-X, besides the positioned code, the secondary bus also receives the device number. A conversion into a special cycle (changing the command code) is used if all bits in the device and function number fields have values of one, while all bits in the register number field have values of zero.

❑ If the bus number corresponds to the number range of the subordinate buses, bridges pass the transaction from the primary interface to the secondary without changes.

❑ If the bus number lies outside the bus number range of the secondary interface side, bridges ignore the transaction.

Bridges only relay type 1 configuration cycles pertaining to special cycles (all bits in the device and function number fields are ones, while in the register number field, all bits are zeroes) from the secondary interface to the primary. If the bus number corresponds to the primary bus number, the bridge converts the transaction into a special cycle.

If none of the devices reacts to a configuration cycle, bridges can process this situation in two ways: by recording the absences of a device (Master Abort will be triggered) or executing dummy operations. However, in any case, reading a configuration register of a nonexisting device (function) must return a value of FFFFFFFFh (this is safe information, because it is an illegal device number).

Flat Address Routing

In order to manipulate memory and I/O access transactions, ports need address maps, on which memory ranges belonging to the secondary and subordinate bus devices are indicated. This is enough for the flat unique addressing system. For the indicated memory ranges, the bridge must respond to transactions it sees on the primary interface as a target device and initiate these transactions as a master on the secondary interface; the bridge ignores all other primary interface transactions. For addresses outside of the indicated address ranges, the bridge must act in reverse: Respond as a target device to transactions it sees on the secondary interface and initiate these transactions on the primary interface; the bridge ignores all other secondary interface transactions. How the bridge relays transactions is described in *Section 6.1.6.*

All PCI-to-PCI bridges have one descriptor for each of the three resource types: I/O, I/O mapped onto the memory, and the real memory (prefetchable). The descriptor shows the base address and the range size. Resources of the same type for all devices that are located over the bridge (on the secondary and all subordinate buses) must be gathered into one — if possible, compact — range.

The I/O address area is set by the 8-bit I/O Base and I/O Limit registers with granularity of 4 KB. By their high bits, these registers define only four high bits of the 16-bit address of the beginning and the end of the relayed range. The lower 12 bits for I/O Base are assumed to be 000h; for I/O Limit, they are assumed to be FFFh. If there are no I/O ports on the secondary side of the bridge, then a number smaller than that contained in I/O Base is written into I/O Limit. If the bridge does not support I/O address mapping, then both registers always return zeroes when read; this type of bridge does not relay I/O transactions from the primary to the secondary side. If the bridge supports only 16-bit I/O addressing, then zeroes are returned in the lower four bits of both registers when a read is performed. It is assumed that the high address bits AD[31:16]=0, but they also must be decoded. If the bridge supports 32-bit I/O addressing, then 0001 is returned in the lower four bits of both registers when a read is performed. The I/O Base Upper 16 Bits and I/O Limit Upper 16 Bits registers contain the upper 16 bits of the lower and upper boundaries.

The bridge relays I/O transactions for the indicated range from the primary interface to the secondary only if the I/O Space Enable bit in the command register is set. I/O transactions from the secondary interface to the primary are relayed only when the Bus Master Enable bit is set.

Memory mapped I/O can use the first 4 GB of addresses (the limit of the 32-bit addressing) with granularity of 1 MB. The relayed range is set by the Memory Base (starting address) and Memory Limit (end address) registers. Only the upper 12 address bits AD[31:20] are used in these registers; the lower AD[19:0] bits are assumed to be 0 for Memory Base and FFFFFh for Memory Limit. In addition, the VGA memory range can be relayed (see *Section 6.1.6*).

Real PCI device memory, which allows prefetching, can lie within both the 32-bit (4 GB) and the 64-bit addressing ranges with granularity of 1 MB. The relayed range is set by the Prefetchable Memory Base (starting address) and Prefetchable Memory Limit (end address) registers. A value of 0001 (not 0000) returned by a read operation in the lower bits ([3:0]) of these registers is a 64-bit addressing indicator. In this case, the upper part of the addresses is located in the Prefetchable Base Upper 32 Bits and Prefetchable Limit Upper 32 Bits registers. The bridge may not necessarily support prefetchable memory; in this case, the above-described registers return zero during read operations.

Bridges relay memory transactions of the indicated ranges from the primary interface to the secondary only if the `Memory Space Enable` bit in the command register is set. Memory transactions from the secondary interface to the primary are relayed only if the `Bus Master Enable` bit is set.

Concepts of positive and subtractive address decoding are connected with bridges. Ordinary PCI agents (devices and bridges) respond only to calls addressed within the ranges described in their configuration space (via the base addresses and the memory and I/O ranges). This decoding method is called *positive*. A bridge employing *positive decoding* lets through only calls belonging to a predetermined address list specified in its configuration registers. A *subtractive decoding* bridge lets through only calls not pertaining to other devices. Its transparency ranges are formed as if by subtraction (hence the name) from the total space of the ranges described in the configuration ranges of the other devices. Physically, devices (bridges) implement subtractive decoding in an easier way: The device monitors all bus transactions of the type that interests it (usually I/O or memory accesses); if it sees no response (a DEVSEL# signal in clocks 1–3 after the FRAME#) from any of the regular devices, it considers this transaction to be addressed to it and issues a DEVSEL# signal itself.

Only certain types of bridges possess subtractive decoding capability, which supplements positive decoding. Subtractive decoding has to be used for old devices (ISA, EISA), whose addresses are so scattered over the range that they cannot be gathered into an acceptably sized positive decoding range. Subtractive decoding is used for bridges that connect old expansion buses (ISA, EISA). Positive and subtractive decoding pertains only to the memory and I/O range accesses. Configuration accesses are routed using the bus number, which is sent in type 1 cycles (see *Section 6.2.11*): Each bridge knows the numbers of all surrounding buses. Only the specific class code 060401h found in the header of the bridge's configuration registers can indicate that the given bridge supports subtractive decoding.

ISA I/O Addressing Support

There are some peculiarities in I/O port addressing that are rooted in the ISA bus legacy. The 10-bit address decoding used in the ISA bus leads each of the addresses in the 0–3FFh range (the 10-bit addressing coverage limitation) to have 63 alias addresses, at which the same ISA device can be addressed when using 16-bit addressing. For example, addresses *x*778h, *x*B78h, and *x*F78h (where *x* is any hexadecimal digit) are aliases for the 0378h address. ISA address aliases are used for various purposes, in particular in ISA Plug and Play. The 0–FFh address range is reserved for system (not user) ISA devices, for which aliases are not used. Consequently, in each kilobyte of the I/O address space, the last 768 bytes (addresses 100–1FFh) can be aliases, but the first

256 bytes (addresses (0–0FFh) can not. There is an ISA Enable bit in the bus control register setting that will eliminate alias address ranges from the common address range described by the I/O Base and I/O Limit bridge registers.

This elimination is effective only for the first 64 KB of the address space (produced by 16-bit addressing). Bridges do not relay transactions that pertain to these eliminated ranges from the primary interface to the secondary. Conversely, transactions that do pertain to these ranges are relayed to the primary interface. This capability is needed to share the use of the small (64 KB) address range by the PCI and ISA devices, reconciling the cut-up ISA address map with the capability to set only one I/O address range for each bridge. It makes sense to set the ISA Enable bit for the bridges that do not have ISA devices on their downstream side. These bridges will relay downstream all I/O transactions addressed to the first 256 bytes of each 1 Kbyte of the address range described by the I/O Base and I/O Limit bridge registers. The configuration software can allocate these addresses to PCI devices that are below the given bridge (except the 0000h–00FFh addresses that belong to the motherboard devices).

Special VGA Support

Bridges may provide special support for a VGA graphics adapter that can be located on the secondary interface side. This support is initialized and enabled by the VGA Enable bit of the bridge configuration register. When the support is enabled, bridges relay VGA memory accesses in the 0A0000h–0BFFFFh address range; I/O register accesses are relayed in the 3B0h–3BBh and 3C0h–3DFh address ranges including all their aliases (the AD[15:10] address lines are not decoded). This special approach is explained by the need to provide compatibility with the most common graphics adapter and the impossibility to describe all the needed ranges in the positive decoding address range tables. Additionally, to support VGA, the palette registers, which are located at the 3C6h, 3C8h, and 3C9h addresses and their aliases (the AD[15:10] address lines are not decoded here either) require to be accessed in a special way.

Monitoring writing to the VGA palettte registers (VGA Palette Snooping) is an exception to the rule of the unique routing of memory and I/O accesses. In a computer with a PCI bus, the video card is usually installed into this bus slot or into the AGP slot, which is logically equivalent to installing it into the PCI bus slot. A VGA card has Palette Registers that are traditionally mapped onto the I/O space. Sometimes, the computer's graphic system will have an additional graphics card to mix the graphic adapter's signals with live-video signals by intercepting the binary information about the current pixel's color on the VESA Feature Connector bus before it reaches the palette registers. In this case, the color palette will be determined by the palette register of this additional graphic card. A situation arises in which a write operation to the palette registers must be executed simultaneously to the video adapter (in the PCI bus or AGP slot) and to the additional video expansion card, which may even be located on another bus (including an ISA). The CMOS Setup may have the PCI VGA Palette Snoop parameter. With this parameter enabled, an I/O write to the palette register address will initiate a transaction not only on the bus where the video adapter is installed, but also on other buses. A read transaction at this address will be performed only with the video adapter. If the VGA Enable bit is set, read transactions will also be relayed over the bridge, because the palette register addresses lie within the VGA port common address range. The implementation of the monitoring may be delegated to the PCI video adapter. To do this, the card latches the data while writing to the palette register, but does not generate the DEVSEL# and TRDY# negotiation signals. As a result of this, the bridge passes this unclaimed signal on to the ISA bus.

Transaction Relaying and Buffering

Transaction relaying is quite a difficult task for a bridge, and overall system efficiency depends on how it is solved. Exactly which transaction needs to be relayed from one interface to another is decided by the above-described part of the bridge that handles the routing. When relaying a transaction, the bridge, as a target PCI device, immediately replies to its initiator, regardless of what is taking place on its other side. This allows the bridge, like any other PCI device, to observe the limitations on the response time and transaction execution time. Further, the bridge requests control of the opposite side bus and, having received this control, executes the transaction as if it were its initiator. If a read transaction is being relayed, the bridge must receive its results in order to forward them to the real transaction initiator. This general scenario is implemented differently for different commands; however, with all the abundance of choices, there are only two ways, in which a PCI bridge can reply to the initiator:

❑ A *delayed transaction*: The bridge delays the transaction by answering with a Retry condition. This makes the initiator repeat the transaction some time later. During this time, the bridge must perform the ordered transaction on the other side of the interface.

❑ A *posted write*: The bridge pretends that the transaction has been successfully completed. This option is only possible for memory write operations. The real write is executed later, when the bridge obtains bus control on the other side of the interface.

Instead of posting transactions that are relayed from a bus operating in the PCI-X mode, PCI-X bridges must split them.

In order to speed up transaction execution arriving from the primary bus, it is practical for the bridge to park the secondary bus for itself; in this way, if the secondary bus is free, the bridge will not waste time for obtaining bus control when relaying transactions.

Delayed Transactions

PCI bridges execute delayed transactions for all accesses to the I/O and configuration registers, as well as for all types of memory reads. Delayed transactions are executed in three stages:

❏ Initiator requests a transaction (data exchange with the target device has not started yet).
❏ Transaction completed by the target device.
❏ Transaction completed by the initiator.

In order to execute a delayed transaction, the bridge must place a Delayed Request into the queue and issue a Retry conditions by a STOP# signal. This completes the first phase of the transaction. The request contains latched values of the address, command, enabled bytes, and parity lines (and the REQ64# line for 64-bit buses); for delayed write transactions, data also need to be saved. This information is sufficient for the bridge to initiate the transaction on the opposite interface: the second phase of the delayed transaction. Its result is the queued delayed request converted into a *delayed completion*: the delayed request information together with the completion status (and the requested read data).

Having received the Retry condition, the initial transaction initiator has to reissue the request some time later; moreover, the reissued request must be identical to the original, otherwise the bus will consider it a new request. If by this time the bridge has completed processing the given transaction, this reissued request will be completed in the regular way (or aborted if that is what the target device did). If the transaction has not been completed yet, the bridge will issue a Retry again; the initiator will have to keep reissuing its request until it is normally completed by the bridge. This is the third, final phase of the delayed transaction.

An initiator that receives a Retry condition must reissue exactly the same transaction request, otherwise the bridge will accumulate unclaimed answers. Of course, the bridge also must track the unclaimed transactions and some time later (2^{10} or 2^{15} bus clocks, depending on the value in the Bridge Control register) remove them from its queue, so as not to overfill it because of the initiator's forgetfulness.

Delaying transactions by bridges significantly increases the execution time of each of them (from the initiator's point of view); however, it allows multiple transactions queued by bridges to be processed. The result is an increase of the overall volume of the executed transactions on all PCI bridges over a unit of time (i.e., the bus throughput increases as a whole). In principle, bridges, being the custodians of the transaction queue, can execute two transactions simultaneously, each on its own interface. If transactions were not delayed but executed directly, the initiator would have to hold its bus until the destination bus became available (as well as all the intermediate buses, if the transaction transits more than one bridge). The resulting number of the useless wait cycles on all buses would be unacceptably large.

When relaying memory-read transactions (using delayed requests), in some cases, bridges can employ prefetching in order to speed-up memory operations. In doing prefetching, the bridge runs a risk of reading more data from the source than the initiator will take from it in the given transaction. The extra data in the buffer are best cancelled in the transaction completion phase, because their real source in the memory may well have been changed by the time they are requested again. More sophisticated bridges can track these changes and cancel only those data in the buffer that have been modified in the source. Regular Memory Read commands allow bridges to read only the exact amount of the requested data. In this case there are fewer opportunities to speed up transfers but neither are there side effects from reading extra data. Reading extra data is absolutely prohibited for memory mapped I/O registers. For example, reading control registers may change their state; an extra read (with unused results) of data registers may cause data loss. Bridges can do prefetching without any concerns when processing requests with Memory Read Line or Multiple Memory Read commands relayed in any direction. Masters that use these commands are responsible for ensuring that prefetching is allowed for the addressed ranges. If the bridge has registers describing prefetchable memory, then during the relaying, simple read command transactions from the primary interface addressed to the prefetchable memory on the secondary interface can be converted into Memory Read Line or Multiple Memory Read commands. The bridge may also assume that all memory transactions from the secondary interface have the main memory as the target device and, therefore, allow prefetching. However, the bridge must have a special bit that disables command conversion and prefetching that are based upon this assumption (blind prefetching can cause problems of software and hardware interaction).

Posted Writes

For memory-write transactions initiated on one side of the bridge and directed to the memory on the other side of the bridge, the bridge must perform posted writes. Here, the data are received in the bridge's buffers and the transaction will be terminated for the initiator before the data reach their actual destination. The bridge will deliver them when it is convenient for the recipient; moreover, this delivery can take more than one transaction, which this time is initiated by the bridge. Of course, if the bridge has no room in its posted write buffers (their size is limited), it will have to answer some of these memory-write transactions with a Retry condition. However, this is not a delayed transaction: Bridges do not queue memory write requests. Bridges have separate buffers for posted writes. In general, posted writes are used only with memory operations. Only the host bridge has the right to send writes to the I/O ports, and even then only for processor-initiated transactions. Posted writes cannot be used with the configuration memory space.

In order to optimize bus bandwidth and the efficiency of the entire system, bridges may convert memory-write transactions that they relay. For example, one long regular memory-write burst transaction (MW, Memory Write) of a block that is not aligned on the cacheline boundaries can be broken down into three transactions: MW from the start of the block to the nearest line boundary, MWI (Memory Write Invalidate) with one or more full cachelines, and another MW for the last cacheline boundary to the end of the block. Moreover, several consecutive write transactions can be combined into one burst transaction, in which extra writes can be blocked using the byte-enable signals. For example, a sequence of single double-word writes to the addresses 0h, 4h, and Ch can be write-combined into one burst with the starting address 0. During the third data phase, when the non-needed address 8h is accessed, all the C/BE[3:0]# signals are inactive. In some write transactions, individual bytes can be *merged* into one transaction; this is allowed for prefetchable memory.

For example, a sequence of byte writes to addresses 3, 1, 0, and 2 can be merged into one double-word write, as these bytes belong to the same addressed double word. Combining and merging can work independently (merged transactions can be combined), but these conversions do not change the order of the physical writes to the devices. These capabilities are not mandatory: Whether or not a bridge has them depends on how "skillful" it is. The purpose of these conversions is to reduce the number of individual transactions (each of which has at least one "extra" address phase) and, as far as possible, the number of data phases. However, the bridge has no right to collapse writes: If it receives two or more posted writes with the same starting address, it must process them all.

PCI devices must perform combined writes without any problems: If a device cannot do this, it has been improperly designed. If a device does not allow byte-merging, it must have the Prefetchable bit in its memory descriptor zeroed out.

PCI-X Bridge Distinctions

The PCI-X bus protocol enables more efficient bus operation. Knowing exactly the transaction length allows the bridge to plan its transfer more efficiently. Special requirements are applied to the bridge buffers: Buffers for each queue type must hold no fewer than two cache lines. Compared with PCI bridges, PCI-X bridges have the following distinctions:

❏ PIC-X bridge interfaces can work in the PCI mode as well as PCI-X Mode 1 or Mode 2. Bridges must determine the capabilities of the weakest device on their secondary interfaces and switch this bus (all the devices on it) into the appropriate mode (in terms of the protocol and clock frequency).

❏ When PCI and PCI-X buses are interconnected, the bridge has to convert some commands, as well as the protocol. When relaying transactions from a PCI bus to a PCI-X bus, the bridge has to generate transaction attributes. For these, the bus number is obtained from the bridge registers; the device and function number are set to zero. The bridge can "make up" the value of the memory access command byte counter based on the particular command (for cache line reads and writes, the length can be figured out from the line length) or address (to determine the prefetching availability).

❏ All single (DWORD) transactions, as well as all burst reads from a PCI-X bus addressed to the other side of the bridge, are completed by the bridge as split transactions (and not as delayed, as is done in the PCI). This makes for more efficient bus use, as the transaction initiator (requester) does not have to periodically reissue the request: The answer will come to the requester as it becomes available. All burst memory writes are processed as posted writes. Of course, if the bridge's request buffers are filled up, it will have to delay the transaction (by a Retry condition).

Transaction Execution Order and Synchronization

The posted write and delayed transaction mechanisms are aimed at providing, as far as possible, simultaneous execution of multiple exchange transactions in the PCI bus system. Each bridge has posted write and delayed transaction buffers and queues for commands that are relayed in both directions. The bridge can perform simultaneous data exchange on both of its interfaces, functioning both as the initiator and the target device. A question concerning the transaction order execution arises; moreover, it involves exactly the order of completions (phases in which the end target device is interacted with). Bridges follow the following main rules:

❏ Posted writes transiting the bridge in one direction are completed in the target device in the same order as on the initiator's bus.
❏ Write transactions transiting the bridge in opposite directions are not coordinated with each other in terms of order.
❏ A read transaction pushes out of the bridge all writes sent from the same side prior to its arrival. Before this transaction completes on its initiator's side (before the third delayed transaction phase), it also pushes out of the bridge all writes sent from the other side prior to completion of the given read by the end target device. In this way, the order or write and read transactions is preserved.
❏ As a target device, the bridge can never accept a memory-write transaction for posting until it has completed a non-locked transaction as a master device on the same bus.

Bridges by themselves do not undertake any measures to synchronize transactions or interrupt requests. While transactions are buffered (e.g., they may get stuck in the bridge queues), interrupt request signals (INTx) are transferred by the bridge absolutely transparently (the bridge simply connects electrically these lines on the primary and secondary interface). For software to work correctly, all the data sent prior to issuance of the interrupt signal must reach their destinations. For this, buffers of all the bridges located between the device that issued the interrupt request and its end partners in the transaction must be unloaded. This can be done easily by software by reading any register of the device: Reading over the bridge unloads the buffers. Another method also is possible: Prior to issuing the interrupt signal, the device reads the last data written by it. These matters are simpler with the MSI interrupts: An MSI message cannot overtake the data issued earlier by this device.

One of the specific applications for which the PCI bus and its bridge connections can be used is the true simultaneous multiple data-exchange transactions over non-intersecting pathways; this is known as Concurrent PCI Transferring or PCI Concurrency. For example, while the processor conducts data exchange with the memory, a master PCI device can exchange data with another PCI device. However, this example of simultaneity is more from the realm of theory, as a PCI master device exchanges data with the system memory as a rule. A more interesting example presents the exchange conducted between a video adapter connected to the AGP (a PCI relative; see *Section 6.3*) and the memory simultaneously with an exchange conducted between the processor and a PCI device. Another example would be a processor loading data into the graphic adapter at the same time as a PCI master device exchanges data with the system memory. Simultaneity requires quite complex logic to arbitrate requests from all system agents, as well as to resort to various tricks to buffer data. Not all chipsets are capable of simultaneity (this feature is always emphasized in the product description) and it can be disabled in the CMOS Setup settings.

6.1.7. Device Configuration

The automatic system resource configuration capability (memory and I/O spaces and interrupt request lines) is built into the PCI bus from the beginning. Automatic device configuration (selection of addresses and interrupt request lines) is supported by BIOS and the operating system and is oriented toward the plug-and-play technology. For every function, the PCI standard defines a configuration space of up to 256 8-bit registers that pertain neither to the memory nor the I/O addressing space. Access to these registers is implemented via special bus commands, *Configuration Read* and *Configuration Write,* which are generated by one of the previously described mechanisms. This addressing space has areas mandatory for all devices, as well as special-purpose areas. A specific device may not necessarily have registers at all addresses, but it has to support the normal termination of operations addressed to them. Reading nonexisting registers must return zeros while writing is done as a dummy operation.

A device configuration space begins with a standard header containing the vendor ID, the device ID, the device class ID, and a description of the required and allocated system resources. The header structure is standardized for regular devices (type 0), PCI/PCI bridges (type 1), and PCI/CardBus bridges (type 2). The header type determines the location of the common registers and the functions of their bits. Device-specific registers may follow the header. For standard device capabilities (such as power management), there are predefined-purpose register blocks. These blocks are linked in chains, with the first of these blocks referred to by a pointer in the standard header (CAP_PTR). The block's first register contains a pointer to the next block (or 0, if the given block is the last one). In this way, having examined the chain, the configuration software obtains a list of all available device capabilities and their locations in the function's configuration space. In PCI 2.3, the following identifiers CAP_ID are defined (partly considered in this book):

❏ 01 — power management
❏ 02 — AGP port
❏ 03 — VPD (Vital Product Data), the data that give a comprehensive description of the hardware (possibly, the software as well) properties of the devices
❏ 04 — numbering of slots and chassis
❏ 05 — MSI interrupts
❏ 06 — Hot Swap, the connection for Compact PCI
❏ 07 — PCI-X protocol extensions
❏ 08 — reserved for AMD
❏ 09 — at the manufacturer's discretion (Vendor Specific)
❏ 0Ah — Debug Port
❏ 0Bh — PCI Hot Plug, a standard support for "hot plugging"

The configuration space has been expanded to 1,204 bytes for PCI-X Mode 2 devices; this expanded space may contain expanded capabilities descriptions.

After a hardware reset or a power up, PCI devices do not respond to memory and I/O accesses, and are accessible only for configuration read and write operations. In these operations, devices are selected by the individual IDSEL signals, and provide information about their resource requirements and possible configuration options. After resources have been allocated by a configuration program (during POST or operating system booting), the configuration parameters (base addresses) are written into the configuration registers of a device. Only after this are the bits set in the devices (or, more precisely, in their functions) that enable them to respond to memory and I/O access commands, and also to control the bus themselves. In order to be able always to find a viable configuration, all the resources occupied by cards must be relocatable within their spaces. In the case of multifunctional cards, each function must have its own configuration space. A device can have the same registers mapped to either the memory or I/O space. In this case, its configuration register must contain both descriptors, but the driver must use only one access method (preferably, via the memory).

The configuration space header describes the device's needs of three types of addresses:

☐ *I/O Space registers.*

☐ *Memory Mapped I/O registers.* This is a memory area that must be accessed in strict compliance with the exchange-initiator requests. Accessing these registers can change the internal state of peripheral devices.

☐ *Prefetchable Memory.* Reading extra data out of this memory area does not cause side effects; all bytes are read regardless of the BE[3:0]# signals, and bridges can merge individual byte writes (i.e., this is pure memory).

Address requirements are indicated in the Base Address Registers (BAR). The configuration software can determine the sizes of the necessary areas, which it does as follows: after a hardware reset, it reads and saves the values of the base addresses (these will be the default addresses); then, it writes FFFFFFFFh into each register and reads their values again; in the obtained words, the type-decoding bits (bits [3:0] for memory spaces and bits [1:0] for I/O spaces) are zeroed out, and the resulting 32-bit word is inverted and incremented. (Bits [31:16] are ignored for ports.) These operations will produce the length of the address range. It is assumed that the range size is expressed by a 2^n number, and that the range is normally aligned. Up to six base address registers fit into a standard header; however, the number of described blocks decreases when the 64-bit addressing is used. Non-used registers must always return zeroes when read.

The PCI supports legacy devices (VGA, IDE); they declare themselves such by the class code in the header. Their traditional (fixed) port addresses are not declared in the configuration space, but as soon as the port access-enable bit is set, devices can answer to accesses to these addresses.

Configuration Space of Regular Devices (Type 0)

The header format is shown in Fig. 6.8. Fields mandatory for all devices are indicated in gray. Device specific registers can occupy configuration space addresses within the limits of 40–FFh.

The identifier fields listed below only can be read:

☐ Device ID — device identifier assigned by the vendor.

☐ Vendor ID — identifier of the PCI microchip manufacturer assigned by PCI SIG. Identifier FFFFh cannot be used; this value must be returned when an attempt to read the configuration space of a nonexisting device is made.

☐ Revision ID — product revision assigned by the vendor. Used as an expansion of the Device ID field.

☐ Header Type — bits [6:0] define the cell layout in the 10h–3Fh range. Bit 7 indicates a multifunctional device if set to 1. Fig. 6.8 shows a type 0 header format, which applies specifically to PCI devices. Type 01 applies to PCI-PCI bridges. Type 02 format applies to CardBus bridges.

☐ Class Code — defines the device's main function and sometimes its programming interface (see *Section 6.2.13*). The upper byte (address 0Bh) defines the base class, the middle byte defines the subclass, and the lower byte defines the programming interface (if it is standardized).

31	24 23	16	15	8 7	0	
Device ID			Vendor ID			00h
Status			Command			04h
Class code				Revision ID		08h
BIST	Header type		Latency timer	Cache line size		0Ch
						10h
Base address registers						....
						24h
CardBus CIS pointer						28h
Subsystem ID			Subsystem vendor ID			2Ch
Expansion ROM base address						30h
Reserved				Capabilities pointer		34h
Reserved						38h
Max_Lat	Min_Gnt		Interrupt pin	Interrupt line		3Ch

Fig. 6.8. PCI device configuration-space type 0 header format

The rest of the header fields are *device registers* that allow both read and write operations:

☐ Command (RW) — controls a PCI device's behavior. This register allows reading and writing. After a hardware reset, all the register bits, except specially stipulated exemptions, are zeroed out. The register bits' functions are as follows:

  ● Bit 0 — IO Space. Enables a device's response to I/O space accesses.
  ● Bit 1 — Memory Space. Enables a device's response to memory space accesses.
  ● Bit 2 — Bus Master. Enables a device to work as an initiator (bus master); ignored in PCI-X in completing split transaction.
  ● Bit 3 — Special Cycles. Enables a device's responses to Special Cycle operations.

- Bit 4 — `Memory Write and Invalidate` enable. Enables a device to use Memory Write and Invalidate commands when working as an initiator. If this bit is zeroed out, the device must use regular memory writes instead of write and invalidate. Ignored in PCI-X.

- Bit 5 — `VGA palette snoop`. Enables tracking writes to the palette registers.

- Bit 6 — `Parity Error Response`. When set, this bit enables normal reaction to a parity or ECC error, generating the `PERR#` signal. If the bit is zeroed out, then the device only has to record the error in the status register and can continue normal operation. When ECC is used, error information is written into the ECC registers.

- Bit 7 — `Stepping Control`. This bit controls the device's address/data stepping. If the device never does it, the bit must be hardwired to 0. If it always does it, then the bit must be hardwired to 1. Devices that have this capability set this bit to 1 after reset. In Version 2.3 and PCI-X, the bit is deallocated due to the abolition of stepping.

- Bit 8 — `SERR# Enable`. This bit enables generation of the error signal `SERR#`. An address parity error is reported if this bit and bit 6 equal 1.

- Bit 9 — `Fast Back-to-Back Enable` (optional, ignored in PCI-X). When set, it permits the master device to perform fast back-to-back transactions to different devices. When it is zeroed out, these transactions are allowed to only one device.

- Bit 10 — Interrupt Disable. Disables interrupt signal generation on the `INTx` lines (the bit is zeroed out and interrupts are enabled after a hardware reset and power up). Bit is defined starting with PCI 2.3; it was reserved before.

- Bits [11:15] — reserved.

☐ The `Status` register can be read from and written to. However, the writes can only zero out bits, not set them. Bits marked RO are read only. To zero out a register bit, its corresponding bit in the write data must be set to 1. The functions of the status register bits are as follows:

- Bits [0:2] — reserved.

- Bit 3 — `Interrupt Status`. Set to one prior to issuing a signal over an `INTx` line, regardless of the value of the `Interrupt Disable` bit. Not associated with MSI interrupts. The bit is defined starting from PCI 2.3; it was reserved before. It is mandatory in PCI-X 2.0.

- Bit 4 — `Capability List` (RO, optional). Shows whether the capabilities indicator is present (offset 34h in the header).

- Bit 5 — `66 MHz Capable` (RO, optional). Indication of device's 66 MHz operation capabilities.

- Bit 6 — reserved.

- Bit 7 — `Fast Back-to-Back Capable` (RO, optional). Indicates whether the device is capable of supporting fast back-to-back transactions to different devices.

- Bit 8 — Master Data Parity Error (bus masters only). Indicates that the transaction initiator (requester) has detected a non-recoverable error.
- Bits [10:9] — DEVSEL Timing. Sets the selection time: 00 — fast, 01 — medium, 10 — low. It defines the slowest reaction of the DEVSEL# signal to all commands except the Configuration Read and Configuration Write commands.
- Bit 11 — Signaled Target Abort. This bit is set by a target device when it terminates a transaction with Target-Abort command.
- Bit 12 — Received Target Abort. This bit is set by an initiator when it detects a rejected transaction.
- Bit 13 — Received Master Abort. This bit is set by the master device when it rejects a transaction (except for a Special Cycle transaction).
- Bit 14 — Signaled System Error. Set by the device that activates the SERR# signal.
- Bit 15 — Detected Parity Error. Set by the device that detects a parity error.

❏ Cache Line Size (RW) — cacheline length. Sets cacheline size of between 0 and 128 bytes. Allowable values are 2^n; others are treated as 0. The initiator uses this parameter to determine which read command to use: regular, line, or multiple. The target device uses this parameter to cross the line boundaries in burst memory accesses. After reset, this register is zeroed out.

❏ Latency Timer (RW). Indicates the value of the latency timer (see *Section 6.2.4*) in terms of the bus clocks. Some of the bits may not allow modifications. (The lower three bits do not usually change, so the timer is programmed in 8-clock increments.)

❏ BIST (RW) — built-in self-test register. The functions of its bits are as follows:
- Bit 7 — indicates whether the device is BIST-capable. 1 if yes, 0 if no.
- Bit 6 — test start. Writing a logical one into this bit initiates BIST. After the test is completed, the device sets the bit to 0. The test must take no longer than 2 sec to conclude.
- Bits [5:4] — reserved. Set to zero.
- Bits [3:0] — test results code. If set to zero, means that the test has been successful.

❏ CardBus CIS Pointer (optional). This register points to the CardBus descriptor structure for combination PCI+CardBus devices.

❏ Interrupt Line (RW). Holds the input number of the interrupt request controller for the utilized request line. Values in the 0–15 range indicate IRQ0–IRQ15 (in system with APIC, these values may be greater). Value 255 means the input number is not known or is not used.

❏ Interrupt Pin (RO). This register indicates the interrupt pin used by the device or device function. 0 is not used; a value of 1 means INTA#; a value of 2 means INTB#; a value of 3 means INTC#; a value of 4 means INTD#. Values 5–FFh are reserved.

- ☐ `Min_GNT` (RO). This register indicates the minimal time that a master device must be given for bus control in 0.25-μsec intervals at a bus clock frequency of 33 MHz.

- ☐ `Max_LAT` (RO). Indicates the maximum latency in providing the master device access to the bus in 0.25-μsec increments. A value of 0 means that the device has no special requirements.

- ☐ `Subsystem ID` (assigned by the vendor) and `Subsystem Vendor ID` (assigned to the vendor by PCI SIG). These registers make it possible to identify cards and devices precisely among several cards with matching `Device ID` and `Vendor ID` that may be installed in one system. The PCI card Vendor ID goes into the 2Ch field. It may match values with the 0 field if the company produces both microchips and cards.

- ☐ `Capability Pointer` (CAP_PTR). A pointer to the chain of the function's capabilities that are described in the configuration registers. Each capability has a set of registers that starts at a double word boundary (in the pointer bits `[1:0]`=0). Each list item starts with a capability type configuration byte (`CAP_ID`, defined by the PCI SIG), followed by the pointer to the next list item (a zero pointer indicates end of list), followed by the capability descriptor bytes proper. Using `CAP_PTR`, for example, the power management register (if it exists), AGP and other registers are located.

- ☐ `Base Address Registers` (BAR) of the memory and I/O ports. For memory spaces, bit 0 is set to logical zero. Bits `[2:1]` define the memory type. If they equal 00, the memory is 32-bit; if they equal 10, the memory is 64-bit (in this case, the register is expanded by the following 4-byte word; 64-bit addressing is mandatory for PCI-X). Values 01 and 11 are reserved. (In previous versions of the standard, 01 was used to indicate that the base register must be mapped onto the memory below 1 MB.) Bit 3 (`Prefetchable`) is set for the real memory allowing prefetching. Bits `[3:4]` are the base memory address; block size cannot exceed 2 GB. For I/O space, bit 0 = 1; bit 1 = 0 (reserved); bits `[31:2]` are the port block base address; the size of one range cannot exceed 256 bytes.

- ☐ `Expansion ROM Base Address`. For card software support. Bit 0 is used to enable accesses to the card's ROM. Bits [1:10] are reserved. Bits [11:31] hold the base address. The size of the ROM range is determined the same way as in the BAR. (See above.) ROM can be accessed only when memory use is enabled (i.e., bit 1 in the command register is set).

PCI-X Device Special Registers

PCI-X devices have additional register (Fig. 6.9) whose location is defined using the capabilities list (`Capability ID`=07). ECC registers appeared only in PCI-X 2.0.

The `PCI-X Command` register controls the new capabilities of the PCI-X protocol:

- ☐ Bit 0 (RW) — `Uncorrectable Data Error Recovery Enable`. If the bit is not set, a `SERR#` signal is formed when a parity error is detected.

❏ Bit 1 (RW) — Enable Relaxed Ordering in transaction attributes.
❏ Bits [3:2] (RW) — Maximum Memory Read Byte Count: 0 — 512 bytes, 1 — 1,024 bytes, 2 — 2,048 bytes, 3 — 4,096 bytes.
❏ Bits [6:4] (RW) — Maximum Outstanding Split Transactions: 0 through 7 — 1, 2, 3, 4, 8, 12, 16, 32 transactions, respectively.
❏ Bits [11:7] — reserved.
❏ Bits [13:12] (RO): PCI-X capabilities version (ECC support): 00 — ECC not supported; 01 — ECC only in Mode 2; 10 — ECC in Mode 1 and 2.
❏ Bits [15:14] — reserved.

31		16	15	8	7	0
PCI-X command			Pointer to next ID		PCI-X capability ID = 07	
PCI-X status						
ECC control and status						
ECC first address						
ECC second address						
ECC attribute						

Fig. 6.9. Additional PCI-X registers

The PCI-X Status register holds the function identifier (its address in the hierarchy of the configuration space); the device constantly monitors this address on the bus when executing configuration write operations. The device needs this identifier for presenting in the attribute phase. In addition, the register has device capability indicators and also split transaction error indicators. The functions of the PCI-X Status register's bits are as follows:

❏ Bits [2:0] (RO) — Function Number.
❏ Bits [7:3] (RO) — Device Number. The device learns this number from the value in AD[15:11] during the address phase of the configuration write directed to the given device; the device is selected by the IDSEL line. Set to 1Fh after a reset.
❏ Bits [15:8] (RO) — Bus Number. The device learns this number by the value in AD[7:0] during the attribute phase of the configuration write directed to the given device. Set to FFh after a reset.
❏ Bit 16 (RO) — 64-bit Device.
❏ Bit 17 (RO) — 133 MHz Capable (66 MHz otherwise).
❏ Bit 18 (RWC) — Split Completion Discarded (by the requester).

❏ Bit 19 (RWC) — Unexpected Split Completion.

❏ Bit 20 (RO) — Device Complexity (of a bridge).

❏ Bits [22:21] (RO) — Designed Maximum Memory Read Byte Count in the sequence initiated by the device: 0 — 512 bytes, 1 — 1,024 bytes, 2 — 2,048 bytes, 3 — 4, 096 bytes.

❏ Bits [25:23] (RO) — Designed Maximum Outstanding Split Transactions: 0 through 7 — 1, 2, 3, 4, 8, 12, 16, 32 transactions, respectively.

❏ Bits [28:26] (RO) — Designed Maximum Cumulative Read Size expected by the device (requests have been sent, the replies have not been received yet): 0 through 7 — 8, 16, 32 ... 1,024 ADQ.

❏ Bit 29 (RWC) — Received Split Completion Error Message.

❏ Bit 30 (RO) — PCI-X 266 Capable (Mode 2).

❏ Bit 31 (RO) — PCI-X 533 Capable (Mode 2).

The ECC registers are used for control and diagnostics purposes. The ECC Control, and Status Register is used to control ECC: to enable ECC in Mode 1 (in Mode 2 it is mandatory), to enable single-occurrence errors correction. The same register reports the indicators of error detection, command and bus phase in which the error was detected, and also the error syndrome value and the transaction attributes. The ECC First Address, ECC Second Address, and ECC Attribute registers hold the address accessing which the ECC error was detected and the attributes.

PCI-X Expanded Configuration Space

The PCI-X 2.0 specification expanded the configuration space of one function to 1,024 bytes. The standard 256-byte set of registers and the header format are preserved and the additional space is used for the device's needs, including holding the description of the additional capabilities. The expanded configuration space can be accessed by either using the expanded version of mechanism 1 (see further discussion) with sending additional 4 bits of the register number over AD[27:24] or by mapping the configuration registers onto the memory addresses. With memory mapping, the hierarchical configuration register addresses of all PCI devices is reflected in bits A[27:0]; the base address (A[63:28]) depends on how the system has been implemented and is communicated to the operating system. For memory mapping, all configuration registers of all devices of all PCI buses require a 256 MB memory area. The mapping scheme is simple and logical:

❏ A[27:20] — Bus number (8 bits)

❏ A[19:15] — Device number (5 bits)

❏ A[14:12] — Function number (3 bits)

❏ A[11:8] — Extended Register number (4 bits)

❏ A[7:0] — Register number (8 bits)

Devices must detect and process configuration accesses performed in any way. The device developer must keep in mind that only the first 256 bytes of the function's configuration space will be software-accessible if the device is placed on a regular PCI bus; therefore, only those registers not used in the standard PCI mode should be placed into the expanded area.

A new capability description format has also been introduced for the expanded configuration space that takes into account the long (10-bit) register address. The expanded capabilities list must begin at address 100h (or there must be a structure not allowing this fragment to be interpreted as the beginning of the chain). Each capability starts with a 32-bit identifier, followed by the registers that describe the given capability. The 32-bit expanded capability identifier has the following structure:

❏ Bits [15:0] — Capability ID
❏ Bits [19:16] — Capability Version Number
❏ Bits [31:20] — Next Capability Offset (relative to the number 0 register)

Configuration Space of PCI Bridges

The format of the configuration space of PCI-PCI bridges is shown in Fig. 6.10. The registers in the 00–17h address range fully coincide with the registers of a regular PCI device and describe the bridge's behavior and status on the primary bus. Bit 2 of the command register (Bus Master Enable) controls the bridge's capability to transfer transactions from the secondary bus to the primary. If this bit is zeroed out, the bridge must not respond as a target device on the secondary side in memory and I/O read/write transactions, because it will not be able to transfer these transactions to the primary bus. The BAR registers describe only the specific registers area (depending on the bridge's implementation); they are not involved in the routing.

The bridge's routing capabilities are defined by the following registers (see *Section 6.1.6* for details):

❏ Primary Bus Number register.
❏ Secondary Bus Number register (also the bridge number).
❏ Subordinate Bus Number register.
❏ I/O Base and I/O Limit. These registers set the starting and the ending I/O range addresses of devices located behind the bridge. They provide only the upper four bits of the 16-bit I/O address; consequently, the address allocation granularity is 4 KB.
❏ I/O Limit Upper 16 Bits and I/O Base Upper 16 Bits. These registers hold the upper part of the I/O address when 32-bit I/O addressing is used (indicated by a one in bits 0 of the I/O Base and I/O Limit registers).
❏ Memory Base and Memory Limit. These registers set the starting and ending addresses of the memory range, onto which the I/O registers of the devices located

behind the bridge are mapped. These register set only the upper 12 bits of the 32-bit address; consequently, the address allocation granularity is 1 MB.

☐ Prefetchable Memory Base and Prefetchable Memory Limit. These registers set the starting and the ending memory range addresses for devices located behind the bridge. They set only the upper 12 bits of the 32-bit memory address; consequently, the address allocation granularity is 1 MB.

☐ Prefetchable Base Upper 32 Bits and Prefetchable Limit Upper 32 Bits. These are the registers of the upper address part of "pure" memory when 64-bit addressing is used (indicated by the bits 0 in the Prefetchable Memory Base and Prefetchable Memory Limit registers being set to one).

31 24	23 16	15 8	7 0	
Device ID		Vendor ID		00h
Status		Command		04h
Class code			Revision ID	08h
BIST	Header type	Primary latency timer	Cacheline size	0Ch
Base address register 0				10h
Base address register 1				14h
Secondary latency timer	Subordinate bus number	Secondary bus number	Primary bus number	18h
Secondary status		I/O limit	I/O base	1Ch
Memory limit		Memory base		20h
Prefetchable memory limit		Prefetchable memory base		24h
Prefetchable base upper 32 bits				28h
Prefetchable limit upper 32 bits				2Ch
I/O limit upper 16 bits		I/O base upper 16 bits		30h
Reserved			Capabilities pointer	34h
Expansion ROM base address				38h
Bridge control		Interrupt pin	Interrupt line	3Ch

Fig. 6.10. Header format of a PCI-PCI bridge configuration space (Type 1 header)

The Secondary Status register is analogous to the regular Status register, but reflects the status of the secondary bus. The only difference is bit 14, which in the Secondary Status register indicates detecting the SERR# signal on the secondary interface, and not its issuance by the given device.

The `Expansion ROM Base Address` register, as with regular devices, sets the location of the BIOS expansion ROM (if the bridge has this ROM).

The `Interrupt Line` and `Interrupt Pin` registers pertain to the interrupts generated by the bridge (if they exist). These registers have no relation to the interrupts transferred by the bridge.

The `Bridge Control` register controls the bridge operation and indicates unclaimed completions of the delayed transactions. The functions of its bits are as follows:

☐ Bit 0: `Parity Error Response Enable`. Enables the bridge to signal address or data parity error detected on the secondary interface.

☐ Bit 1: `SERR# Enable`. Enables transferring the `SERR#` signal from the secondary interface to the primary (the same name bit must also be set in the command register).

☐ Bit 2: `ISA Enable`. Enables ISA bus I/O addressing support (excluding the last 768 bytes from each kilobyte of the data range set by the `I/O Base` and `I/O Limit` registers).

☐ Bit 4: reserved.

☐ Bit 5: `Master-Abort Mode`. Defines bridge behavior in case it does not receive a reply from the target device when transferring a transaction: 0 — ignore this situation, returning FF...FFh for reads and discarding write data; 1 — inform the transaction initiator by a Target-Abort condition or, if this is not possible (in case of a posted write), issue a `SERR#` signal.

☐ Bit 6: `Secondary Bus Reset`. Places a `RST#` signal on the secondary interface (when the bit is cleared, the `RST#` on the secondary interface is generated upon a `RST#` on the primary interface).

☐ Bit 7: `Fast Back-to-Back Enable` on the secondary interface.

☐ Bit 8: `Primary Discard Timer`. A discard timer for the results of the delayed transactions initiated by the master from the primary interface: 0 — wait 2^{15} bus clocks, 1 — wait 2^{10} bus clocks. The countdown starts when the result of a delayed transaction comes up to the top of the queue. If the master does not pick up the result (by a transaction repeat) within the set time, the result is discarded.

☐ Bit 9: `Secondary Discard Timer`. Analogous to bit 8, only for transactions initiated by the master from the secondary interface.

☐ `Discard Timer Status`. Indicator of delayed transaction discard on all interfaces.

☐ Bit 11: `Discard Timer SERR# Enable`. Enables `SERR#` signal generation on the primary interface upon the discard timer actuation.

☐ Bits `[12:15]`: reserved.

`Secondary Latency Timer` register controls bridge acting as the secondary bus master when it is deprived of bus control.

For a large system with expansion chassis, bridges can have slot and chassis numeration capability; for this, the bridge must have a capability with `Capabilities ID=0` (see Fig. 6.11).

31 24	23 16	15 8	7 0
Chassis number	Expansion slot	Pointer to next ID	Slot numbering capabilities ID = 04

Fig. 6.11. Chassis and slot numbering structure

The `Expansion Slot` register describes the status and the secondary bus of the bridge:

❑ Bits [4:0]: `Expansion Slots Provided` — number of slots on the secondary bus of the bridge.

❑ Bit 5: `First in Chassis`. Indicator of the first bridge in the expansion chassis. Also indicates that a chassis is present and, consequently, that the chassis register number is used. If the chassis has more than one bridge, the first one will be either the bridge with the lowest primary bus number (to which other bridges will be subordinate) or the lowest device number (other bridges will be of the same rank, but their secondary buses will have higher numbers).

❑ Bits [7:6]: reserved.

The `Chassis Number` register sets the number of the chassis in which the given bridge is located (0 — the chassis on which the host processor that carries out the configuration is located).

Software Access to the Configuration Space and Special Cycle Generation

Because the PCI configuration space is isolated, the host bridge must be equipped with a special mechanism to access it via commands from the processor whose instructions can only access memory and I/O. The same mechanism is used to generate special cycles. Two mechanisms have been stipulated for PC-compatible computers, of which the PCI 2.2 specification has left only the first one: Configuration Mechanism #1, which is more transparent. The number of the configuration mechanism used by a particular motherboard can be found out by calling PCI BIOS. These mechanisms cannot be used to access the expanded configuration space of PCI-X (it can be assessed only via direct memory mapping; see above).

Configuration cycles are addressed to the concrete device (a PCI microchip) located on the bus with a predetermined number. Bridges decode the bus and device numbers for the device, for which the `IDSEL` select signal has to be issued. The function number and the register address are decoded by the device itself.

Two 32-bit I/O ports are reserved on the host bridge for Configuration Mechanism #1. Their names and addresses are `CONFIG_ADDRESS` (0CF8h) and `CONFIG_DATA` (0CFCh).

Both can be written to and read from. To address the configuration space, a 32-bit address (decoded as shown in Fig. 6.12) is first written to the CONFIG_ADDRESS register. After this, the contents of the required configuration port can be read from or written to the CONFIG_DATA register. Bit 31 in the CONFIG_ADDRES enables configuration and the generation of special cycles. Depending on the bus number indicated in this register, the host bridge generates one of the two types of configuration cycle.

❏ To access a device located on bus number zero (i.e., connected to the host bridge) a type 0 cycle is used (see Fig. 6.2, *a*, *b*, and *c*). In the address phase of this cycle, the bridge places the device-selection positional code on the AD[31:11] lines, the function number on the AD[10:8] lines, the register address on the AD[7:2] lines; bits [1:0]=0 indicate a type 0 cycle. In the PCI-X address phase, the device number is placed on the AD[15:11] lines; the expanded configuration space cannot be accessed via this mechanism.

❏ To access a device that is not located on bus 0, a type 1 cycle is used. Here, the host bridge passes the address information from the CONFIG_ADDRESS register (bus, device, and function numbers and register address) to the main PCI bus, zeroing out the high-order bits [31:24] and setting the type 01 indicator in bits [1:0]. (See Fig. 6.2, *d*.)

31	30 24	23 16	15 11	10 8	7 2	1 0
1	0	Bus number	Device number	Function number	Register address	01

Fig. 6.12. CONFIG_ADDRESS register address format

The Special Cycle is generated by writing to the CONFIG_DATA register, with bits [15:8] in the CONFIG_ADDRESS register set to logical one and bits [7:0] of the same register zeroed out. The number of the bus on which the cycle is generated is given in bits [23:16] of the CONFIG_ADDRESS register. Since the Special Cycle is a broadcast type operation, no address information is sent in it, but its propagation can be controlled by setting the bus number. If the host generates a special cycle with the zero bus address, this cycle will be executed on the main bus only, and all the other bridges won't propagate this cycle. If the bus address is not zero, the host bridge will produce a cycle of Type 1 configuration write, which will be transformed into the special cycle by nothing else than the bridge of the destination bus. A special cycle generated by the master device of the bus is only active on the bus of this device, and does not propagate through the bridges. In case of necessity to generate this cycle at another bus, the master device may do this through writes to the CONGIG_ADDRESS and CONFIG_DATA registers.

Two 8-bit I/O ports are reserved on the host bridge for the outdated and cumbersome *Configuration Mechanism #2*. Their addresses are 0CF8h and 0CFAh. *Configuration Mechanism #2* maps the PCI devices configuration space onto the C000h–CFFFh range of the I/O space. Because this range (only 4 K ports) is not sufficient to map the configuration spaces of all the devices of all the PCI buses, the address is generated in a rather elaborate way. Bits `[7:4]` in the `Configuration Space Enable` (CSE) register located at 0CF8h are the key to enabling mapping, while bits `[3:1]` carry the number of the function to whose addressing space the accesses are addressed. When set to logical one, bit 0 (`SCE` — Special Cycle Enable) causes a special cycle to be generated instead of a configuration cycle. When the value of the key is zero, the C000–CFFFh port range remains a regular part of the I/O range; when the value is not zero, configuration spaces of a selected function of sixteen possible devices are mapped onto it.

When addressed to the configuration space of the bus 0's devices, reading or writing a double word into a port at the C000h–CFFCh generates a configuration cycle. In this cycle, bits `[2:7]` of the port address are placed on the `AD[2:7]` lines as the configuration space index, and bits `[11:8]` are decoded into a positional device-select code (`IDSEL` lines) on the `AD[31:16]` lines. The function number is placed on the `AD[10:8]` lines from the `CSE` register, while lines `AD[1:0]` are zeroed out. To address devices located on non-0 buses, the `Forward Register` (0CFAh) is used, into which the bus number is placed (this register is zeroed out upon a reset). If the bus number is not zero, then a type 1 cycle is generated; here, the function number comes from the `SCE` register, the lower four bits of the device number arrive from the address bits (`AD15=0`), and the bus number is taken from the Forward Register (bits `AD[1:0]=0` and `AD[31:24]=0` are hardware-generated).

To generate a Special Cycle using this mechanism, the `CSE` register is set to a non-0 key, the function number is assigned a value of 111, and `SCE = 1`, after which a write is done to port CF00h. Depending on the contents of the Forward Register, either a special cycle or a configuration cycle, which will be converted into a special cycle on the target bus, will be generated.

PCI Device Classes

An important part of the PCI specification is the classification of devices and indication of the class code in its configuration space (3 bytes of the Class Code). The upper byte identifies the *base class*, the middle byte identifies the *subclass*, while the lower byte identifies the *programming interface* (if it has been standardized). The class code makes it possible to detect presence of particular devices in the system, which can be done with PCI BIOS. For standardized devices (such as 01:01:80 — IDE controller, or 07:00:01 — 16450 serial port) a service program can find the necessary device and select the appropriate driver version. Classification codes are defined by PCI SIG; they are regularly updated on the organization's site, **www.pcisig.com**. As a rule, fields with 0 values give the most broad device descriptions. Subclass value 80h defines "other devices."

PCI BIOS

There are additional BIOS functions that can facilitate interaction with PCI devices. These functions can be accessed from both the real and protected processor operation modes. PCI BIOS functions are used only to locate and configure PCI devices, both procedures that require access to their configuration spaces. The functions need to be supported and used because configuration access cycles, like the special cycle, are executed in a specific way. Additionally, PCI BIOS allows controlling the PCI Interrupt Steering, hiding the specific software interface of an individual motherboard chipset.

The other types of interaction with devices using their memory and I/O spaces as well as interrupt servicing do not require BIOS support, because they are executed directly by processor commands and are independent of the platform (motherboard chipset). Regular operations with these devices are conducted using accesses to the device registers at the addresses received during the configuration and servicing the predefined interrupt requests from these devices. The PCI BIOS presence check function determines the configuration mechanisms available; knowing how they operate, calls to PCI BIOS may henceforth be dispensed with.

Using PCI BIOS functions, software can search for the devices it needs by their identifiers or class codes. If all the installed devices need to be reinventoried, this can be done by reading the configuration information of all functions of all devices on all buses; this is faster than going through all possible identifier or class code combinations. For the detected devices, the software must determine the actual settings by reading the configuration space registers, taking into account that resources can be moved over the whole space and even between different memory and I/O ranges.

For the 16-bit real mode, V86 mode, and 16-bit protected mode, PCI BIOS functions are called via the `Int 1Ah` interrupt; when making the call, the function number is provided in the `AX` register. Software interrupt emulation also is possible. This is done by a far call to the physical address 000FFE6Eh (the standard entry point for the `Int 1Ah` interrupt handler); the flag register is pushed on the stack prior to making this call.

For 32-bit protected mode calls, the same functions are called via the entry points found in the catalog of the 32-bit services, but the functions of the input and output registers and the carry flag (CF) are preserved. In order to use the 32-bit interface, its catalog needs to be found first and the presence of PCI BIOS services ascertained by the $PCI identifier (040435024h).

The calls require a deep stack (up to 1,024 bytes). The sign of normal completion is CF=0 and AH=0; if there has been an error, then CF=1 and AH contains the error code.

- ❏ 81h — unsupported function
- ❏ 83h — invalid vendor ID

❐ 86h — device not found

❐ 87h — invalid PCI register number

❐ 88h — installation failed

❐ 89h — not enough space in the data buffer

PCI BIOS functions are listed below:

❐ AX=B101h — PCI BIOS presence check. When PCI BIOS is present, CF=0, AH=0, and EDX=20494350h ("PCI" character string); all three conditions must be checked. The AL register holds the descriptor of the hardware access mechanism to configuration space and the special PCI cycle generation mechanism:

- Bit 0 — support of configuration space access mechanism #1
- Bit 1 — support of configuration space access mechanism #2
- Bits [2:3] — reserved
- Bit 4 — special cycle generation using mechanism #1 support
- Bit 5 — special cycle generation using mechanism #2 support
- Bits [6:7] — reserved

The BH and BL registers return the upper and lower version numbers (in BCD digits); the CL register returns the maximum PCI bus number present in the system (number of buses plus one, because their sequential numbering starts from zero). The EDI register may return the linear address on the entry point for the 32-bit BIOS services. Not all BIOS versions return this address (some BIOS do not modify the EDI). To check this, the EDI is zeroed out prior to making a call, and then the returned value is checked for zero.

❐ AX=B102h — device search by identifier. When making a call, the device ID, vendor ID, and device index (the sequential number) are indicated in the CX, DX, and SI registers, respectively. Upon a successful return, the bus, device, and function numbers are indicated in the BH, BL[7:3], and BL[2:0] registers, respectively. To find all devices with these identifiers, calls are made incrementing the SI sequentially from zero until the return code of 86h is received.

❐ AX=B103h — device search by the class code. When making a call, the class, subclass, interface, and device index are indicated in the ECX[23:16], ECX[15:8], ECX[7:0], and SI registers, respectively. Upon a successful return, the bus, device, and function numbers are indicated in the BH, BL[7:3], and BL[2:0] registers, respectively.

❐ AX=B106h — special PCI cycle generation. When making a call, the bus number is indicated in the BL register, and the EDX register carries the special cycle data.

❐ AX=B108h — reading a byte from a PCI device configuration space. When making a call, the bus, device, function, and register numbers(0–FFh) are held in the BH, BL[7:3], BL[2:0], and DI registers, respectively. Upon a successful return, the CL register holds the read byte.

❐ AX=B109h — reading a word from a PCI device configuration space. When making the call, the bus, device, function, and register numbers (0–FFh, even) are held in the BH, BL[7:3], BL[2:0], and DI registers, respectively. Upon a successful return, the CX register holds the read word.

❐ AX=B10Ah — reading a double word from a PCI device configuration space. When making the call, the bus, device, function, and register numbers (0–FFh, a multiple of four) are held in the BH, BL[7:3], BL[2:0], and DI registers, respectively. Upon a successful return, the ECX register holds the read double word.

❐ AX=B10Bh — writing a byte into a PCI device configuration space. When making the call, the bus, device, function, and register numbers (0–FFh) are held in the BH, BL[7:3], BL[2:0], and DI registers, respectively. The CL register holds the byte being written.

❐ AX=B10Ch — writing a word into a PCI device configuration space. When making the call, the bus, device, function, and register numbers (0–FFh, even) are held in the BH, BL[7:3], BL[2:0], and DI registers, respectively. The CX register holds the word being written.

❐ AX=B10Dh — writing a word into a PCI device configuration space. When making the call, the bus, device, function, and register numbers (0–FFh, a multiple of four) are held in the BH, BL[7:3], BL[2:0], and DI registers, respectively. The ECX register holds the double word being written.

❐ AX=B10E — determining interrupt allocation options (GET_IRQ_ROUTING_OPTIONS). When making the call, BX=0, ES:EDI point to the parameter structure of the buffer for storing the results; this structure consists of a word holding the buffer length, followed by the far pointer to the buffer's start address. In the 16-bit mode, the DS register points to the segment with the physical address F0000h; in the 32-bit mode, its contents are defined by the rules set out in the next subsection. Upon a successful return, the BX register holds a bit map of the IRQx requests. Bit values of one in this map mean that the given input of the interrupt controller is used exclusively by the PCI bus (see Table 6.6). The sequential set of structures describing the capabilities of and the interrupt allocation for each PCI device is placed into the buffer. Upon the return, the actual buffer length is held in the parameter structure. If a buffer size too small to hold the entire result was given when making the call, the error code 89h is set.

❐ AX=B10Fh — interrupt request line allocation (SET_PCI_IRQ). When making the call, the BH holds the bus number, bits [7:3] of the BL hold the device number, and bits [2:0] of the BL hold the function for which the request is being assigned. The output (0Ah — INTA#, ..., 0Dh — INTD#) is held in the CL; the desired IRQx number (0–0Fh; 0 corresponds to disconnecting INTx# from the controller's inputs) is placed into the CH register. If the ordered allocation is not possible, the 88h error code is set upon the return from the call. When using the given function, the attendant changes must be made in the configuration registers of all involved devices and their functions.

Table 6.6. Description of Interrupt Options for One PCI Device

Offset	Size	Function
0	Byte	PCI Bus number
1	Byte	PCI Device number
2	Byte	Allocated link for the INTA# line (0 — none, 1 — IRQ1, ..., 0Fh — IRQ15)
3	Word	Bit map of the possible allocation for INTA# (bit 0 — IRQ0, ..., bit 15 — IRQ15)
5	Byte	Allocated link for the INTB# line
6	Word	Bit map of the possible allocation for INTB#
8	Byte	Allocated link for the INTC# line
9	Word	Bit map of the possible allocation for INTC#
11	Byte	Allocated link for the INTD# line
12	Word	Bit map of the possible allocation for INTD#
14	Byte	Slot number (for physical identification of the card)
15	Byte	Reserved

32-Bit BIOS Services Search

The 32-bit BIOS32 services are searched using the 32-bit service catalog. The address of the catalog entry point is not known in advance. However, the way to find it is known: The signature string "_32_" (ASCCI code 325F5F33h) is sought at the beginnings of paragraphs in the memory address range 0E0000–0FFFFFh. The 32-bit physical address of the catalog entry point follows this string. The entry points to the services proper are also sought using the service catalog. The number, parameters, and results of the called functions are sent in the processor registers.

To search for a service in the catalog, a four-byte identifier string is placed into the EAX register, code 0 is placed (search function code in the catalog) into the EBX register and a far call is made to the catalog entry point address. The results of the search are returned in the registers: AL=00h — service found; in this case, EBX returns the base address of the service, ECX returns the service segment length, and EDX returns the offset of the entry point relative to the service's start (the EBX). A value of 81h returned in the AL register means that the service has not been found.

Prior to attempting to use the service catalog, it should be ascertained that the header is correct. This is done by inspecting its checksum: The accumulated sum of all header bytes must equal zero. The header length (in sections) is indicated in the byte at offset nine; the eighth byte holds the header version number. The checksum inspection is mandatory, as the four-byte signature may coincide with a fragment of the BIOS code (string "_32_" disassembles as POP DI; XOR SI, [BP+SI]).

The 32-bit services are called by far calls (CALL FAR). The base of the code segment (CS) must start at the beginning of a 4-kilobyte page that contains the entry point; the limit must encompass this and the following page[1]. The requirements for the data segment (DS) segment base are the same, and its limit must be no smaller than the CS limit. It should be remembered that the addresses are physical (obtained after page conversion of the linear addresses).

PCI Card Expansion ROM

The ROM BIOS in the microchip installed on the motherboard supports only the standard (in purpose and function) devices. Should it be necessary, additional devices installed into the expansion slots (ISA, PCI, PCMCIA) can have Additional ROM BIOS for their software support (it is also called Expansion ROM). This need arises when the device needs software support before the operating system and the application software have been loaded. This type of additional ROM modules can also contain all the software needed to support a specialized diskless PC-based controller. Expansion ROM BIOS is used in EGA/VGA/SVGA graphics adapters, some hard drive controllers, SCSI controllers, remote boot network adapters, and other peripheral devices.

The C8000h–F4000h range has been reserved in the memory space for the ISA bus expansion modules. The POST procedure scans this range in 2 KB steps looking for additional modules during its final stage (after the interrupt vectors have been loaded with the help of pointers to its own handlers). The additional BIOS module for graphics adapters (EGA, VGA, SVGA, etc.) has a fixed address, C000h, and is initialized earlier (during the video adapter initialization). A PCI bus device contains only an expansion module flag in its configuration space; the actual memory address is assigned to it by the POST procedure.

Additional ROM BIOS modules must have a header aligned at the 2 KB memory page boundary; the format of the header is shown in Table 6.7.

---

[1] The segment may also begin a few pages earlier.

Table 6.7. Additional ROM Module Header

Offset	Length	Function
0	2	Signature (start of module indicator): byte 0=55h, byte 1=AAh.
2	1	Length in 512-byte blocks.
3	3	The entry point of the initialization procedure. Usually, a three-byte JMP instruction is located at the entry point, pointing to the procedure's start. The procedure is called by a Far Call instruction during the POST and terminates with a far return (Ret Far).
6–17h		Reserved.
18h	2	Pointer to the PCI data structure (for PCI cards only).
1Ah	2	Pointer to the expanded header structure of ISA PnP cards.

In the traditional header, there were only the first three fields; the pointers to the PCI and ISA PnP structures were added later. A valid module starts with the AA55h flag and a zero sum (modulo 256) of all bytes in the declared range. The real module length can exceed the declared length, but the checksum byte, naturally, must be in the declared area.

If it finds a valid module, the POST executes a far call (Call Far) to the module's initialization procedure, which starts at the third address of the module's header. The module's designer is responsible for this procedure being correct. The procedure can reassign the vectors of interrupts serviced by the BIOS. If a procedure reassigns the Bootstrap (Int 19h) interrupt to itself, it obtains control over the operating system loading procedure; this feature is used, for example, to remotely boot computers in local area networks (Remote Boot Reset). If it is not necessary to continue the standard booting procedure, and the additional module is, for example, a control program for some equipment. Instead of the initialization procedure, the ROM can also contain the main program that does not return the control of the system loading sequence to the POST.

The initialization procedure and device-support software contained in the ROM must be written in such a way that the physical addresses, at which they are located in the memory space, do not matter to them. As a rule, the base address, and sometimes the ROM size of expansion cards, can be changed by hardware (jumpers or software-controlled switches). This feature makes it possible to allocate memory address ranges to ROM modules of several installed cards without conflicts.

For ROM BIOS expansions installed on PCI cards, a standard somewhat different from traditional ROM BIOS modules has been adopted. The ROM header is like the traditional one, but it has an additional pointer to the PCI data structure (Table 6.8). The vendor and device identifiers, as well as the class code, coincide with those described in the PCI device's configuration space. Because the PCI bus is used not only in PCs, the card's ROM can contain several modules. Each module starts with a data structure; the module proper follows the structure. The next module's data structure starts after the previous module (if the last module indicator is not set in the previous module), and so on. The platform (processor) type is indicated in the module header, and only the needed module is activated during the BIOS initialization. This mechanism allows, for example, the same graphics adapter to be installed either into an IBM PC or a Power PC.

Table 6.8. PCI Data Structure

Offset	Length (bytes)	Function
0	4	Signature, a "PCIR" string
4	2	Vendor ID
6	2	Device ID
8	2	Reserved[1]
Ah	2	Structure length, starting with the signature
Ch	1	Structure version (0 for the given version)
Dh	3	Class code
10h	2	Image length
12h	2	Code/Data version
14h	1	Code type: 0 — x86 for PC-AT, 2 — HP PA-RISC
15h	1	Indicator: 1 — the last module, 0 — otherwise
16h	2	Reserved

[1] Prior to the PCI 2.2 specification, a pointer to the Vital Product Data string was located here.

Additional PCI card ROM has three parameters pertaining to its size. The ROM size is determined by reading the configuration space. The size indicated in the second byte of the header shows the module's length during the initialization process. This module is loaded into the main memory by the POST procedure prior to calling the initialization procedure (the entry point with offset 3). The checksum, which is usually located at the end of the module, provides zero checksum for all bytes. The length of the image indicated in the PCI data structure (the word with offset 10h) describes the size of the area that must remain in the main memory during normal operation (this area can be smaller, as the initialization procedure code is no longer needed). This area is also protected by a checksum.

PCI card ROM modules are serviced in accordance with the DIMM model. The POST procedure determines ROM presence by the `Expansion ROM Base Address` field in the configuration space, and assigns it an address in the free memory area. Afterward, by programming the command register, the ROM is enabled for reading and the AA55h header signature string is looked for in it. When the signature is found, by using the code type, the POST procedure looks for the appropriate image (whose identifiers coincide with the detected PCI devices) and, having found it, loads it into the C0000–DFFFFh range in the main memory. After this, reading of the ROM is disabled (by a write to the `Expansion ROM Base Address` field) and the initialization procedure is called (from address 3). When calling the procedure, the POST communicates to it the bus number (in the `AH` register), the device number (in the `AL[7:3]` register), and the function number (in the `AL[2:0]` register), thus providing the initialization procedure with the exact coordinates of the hardware resources.

Afterward, the POST determines the size of the area that needs to be left in the main memory (by using byte 2, which can be modified by the initialization procedure) and disables writes to this area. If the initialization procedure cuts the occupied memory, it must take care that the checksum of the area described by byte 2 is valid. If no memory is needed (the procedure zeroes out byte 2), neither is, naturally, needed the checksum. The VGA extension (determined by the class code) is serviced in a special way: it is loaded to the C0000h address. The initialization procedure can determine presence of PnP BIOS in the system by inspecting the PnP control structure at the address indicated in the `ES:DI`, and execute it based on the system environment.

6.1.8. Electrical Interface and Constructs

The PCI bus is built on CMOS integrated circuits that may use either 5 V or 3.3 V power supplies. The direct current signal parameters are listed in Table 6.9. However, the rated power of the interface elements (gate transistors) was set lower than is actually necessary to switch high-frequency signals (33 or 66 MHz). This was possible because the signals, with which integrated circuits drive the bus lines, reflect off the unmatched ends of these lines, which for such high frequencies have the electrical characteristics of long lines. There are no terminators at the ends of the bus, therefore the arriving signal wave reflects off them with the same polarity and amplitude. In merging with the forward signal, the reflected wave provides the signal level required by the receiver. Therefore, the transmitter generates signals with levels between the switching levels until they merge with their reflected signals and reach the necessary level only after the arrival of the reflected wave. This imposes limitations on the physical bus length: The signal must reach the end and come back reflected in less than a third of the clock period (i.e., 10 nsec at 33 MHz, 5 nsec at 66 MHz).

Table 6.9. PCI DC Interface Signal Parameters

Parameter (V)	5 V	3.3 V
Low level input voltage	$-0.5 \le U_{IL} \le 0.8$	$-0.5 \le U_{IL} \le 0.3 \times V_{CC}$
High level input voltage	$2 \le U_{IH} \le V_{CC} + 0.5$	$V_{CC}/2 \le U_{IH} \le V_{CC} + 0.5$
Low level output voltage	$U_{OL} \le 0.55$	$U_{OL} \le 0.1 \times V_{CC}$
High level output voltage	$U_{OH} \ge 0.8$	$U_{OH} \ge 0.9 \times V_{CC}$
Power supply voltage V_{CC}	$4.75 \le U_{CC} \le 5.25$	$3.3 \le U_{CC} \le 3.6$

In order to avoid false responses when all bus agents are inactive, on the motherboard, the control line signals FRAME#, TRDY#, IRDY#, DEVSEL#, STOP#, SERR#, PERR#, LOCK#, INTA#, INTB#, INTC#, INTD#, REQ64#, and ACK64# are pulled up to the power rail by resistors (typically, 2.7 K for the 5 V bus version and 8.2 K for the 3.3 V bus version).

Electrical specifications provide for two versions of peak load limits: two PCI devices built into the motherboard plus four expansion slots or six built-in devices and two expansion slots. It is understood that one built-in PCI device sinks only a single CMOS load. Cards sinking only a single CMOS load may be installed into the expansion slots. If the characteristics of component and motherboard track routing surpass those required by the specification, other slot-device combinations are possible. For example, motherboards with five PCI slots can often be encountered. Strict restrictions are imposed on the conductor length, as well as on the expansion-card components and conductors placement. From the above, it becomes clear that producing homemade PCI cards based on medium-scale integrated circuits difficult, as could be done for ISA cards, is impossible.

The *clock rate of the bus* is determined by the capabilities of all bus agents including the bridges (as well as the host bridge, which is a part of the motherboard chipset). The clock frequency generator can set the high 66 MHz frequency only when line M66EN is high. Therefore, installing any card that does not support 66 MHz (with its contact B49 grounded) will lower the frequency down to 33 MHz. Server motherboards have several PCI buses and allow different bus clocks (66 MHz and 33 MHz) to be used on different buses. For example, the 66 MHz clock can be used on 64-bit buses, and the 33 MHz clock can be used on 32-bit buses. There are no hardware controls on overclocking the bus to 40–50 MHz, but doing this may cause expansion cards to operate with errors.

As per PCI specification, the devices must work without faults when the frequency drops from its nominal value (33 MHz) to zero. The frequency alteration during the devices' functioning is not prohibited, provided that the limitations on minimal duration of high and low levels of CLK signal are duly observed. The CLK signal must stop at a low level only. After the CLK pulses issuing is resumed, the devices have to resume their work as if there were no synchronization break. When operating at 66 MHz and higher frequencies, in order to lower the electromagnetic interference from the fixed frequency signal, the spread spectrum of the CLK signal can be employed: low-percentage frequency modulation with a modulation frequency of 30–33 KHz. If devices use phase-locked loop for synchronization, their speed ought to be sufficient to handle this modulation. In the PCI-X specification, the allowable clock frequency change ranges depend on the bus mode (see Table 6.12).

Standard PCI Slots and Cards

Standard PCI and PCI-X slots are slot-type connectors with contacts spaced 0.05 inches apart. Slots are located somewhat farther from the back panel than the ISA/EISA or MCA slots. PCI card components are placed on the card's left surface. Because of this, the last PCI slot usually shares the back panel opening with the neighboring ISA slot. This kind of slot is called *shared,* and either ISA or PCI cards can be installed into it.

PCI cards can use either 5 V or 3.3 V interface signal levels, or both. PCI slots' signal levels correspond to the power supply voltages of the integrated circuits of the motherboard's built-in PCI devices: either 5 V or 3.3 V. To avoid installing a card into a wrong slot, slots have keys determining their voltages. The role of keys is played by the rows of the missing contacts 12 and 13 and/or 50 and 51:

☐ The key (a rib) for the 5 V slots is located in place of contacts 50 and 51 (closer to the front panel); these slots are abolished in PCI 3.0.
☐ The key to the 3.3 V slots is in the place of contacts 12 and 13 (closer to the back panel).
☐ Universal slots have no key ribs.
☐ Edge connectors of the 5 V cards have matching notches only in the place of contacts 50 and 51; this type of card was abolished in PCI 2.3.
☐ The 3.3 V cards have key notches only in the place of contacts 12 and 13.
☐ Universal cards have both key notches.

The keys prevent installation of a card into a slot with a wrong power supply voltage. Cards and slots differ only in the buffer circuit power supply voltages that they receive off the +V I/O lines:

☐ 5 V slot is fed +5 V to its +V I/O line.
☐ 3.3 V slot is fed between +3.3 V and 3.6 V to its +V I/O line.
☐ 5 V card's buffer integrated circuits may only be powered from +5 V.

❏ 3.3 V card's buffer integrated circuits may be powered only from a +3.3 V to +3.6 V power supply.

❏ A universal card's buffer integrated circuits may be powered from either power supply and will generate and receive 5 V and 3.3 V specification signals without problems, depending on the type of slot in which it is installed (i.e., on the voltage on the +V I/O contacts).

Slots of both types have +3.3 V, +5 V, +12 V, and –12 V *power supplies* on the lines of the same names. The PCI 2.2 standard defines an additional 3.3Vaux power line; this provides a stand-by 3.3 V power supply for devices that generate PME# signal when the main power supply is turned off.

Motherboards are more commonly equipped with 5 V, 32-bit slots that terminate with the contacts A62/B62. 64-bit slots are encountered more seldom; they are longer and they end with the contacts A94/B94. Connector construction and the protocol allow 64-bit cards to be installed into 32-bit slots and vice versa, but the exchange will, naturally, be conducted in the 32-bit mode.

In terms of the mechanical keys, PCI-X cards and slots correspond to 3.3 V cards and slots; the +V I/O power supply voltage for PCI-X Mode 2 is set at 1.5 V.

Figure 6.13 shows a maximum-length 32-bit card (Long Card) with sizes given in millimeters. A Short Card is shorter, at 175 mm, but even shorter cards are very common. A PCI card has an ISA-card-style mounting bracket (previously, cards with IBM PS/2 MCA style mounting brackets could be encountered). There also are Low Profile cards; their brackets are also lower. These cards can be installed vertically into 19-inch cases of 2U height (about 9 cm).

The functions of the PCI/PCI-X card connector contacts are shown in Table 6.10.

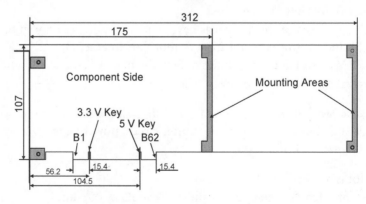

Fig. 6.13. PCI bus expansion card

Table 6.10. PCI Bus Connectors

Row B	Contact	Row A	Row B	Contact	Row A
−12 V	1	TRST#	GND/M66EN[1]	49	AD 9
TCK	2	+12 V	GND/ 5 V key/MODE 2	50	GND/5 V key
GND	3	TMS	GND/ 5 V key	51	GND/5 V key
TDO	4	TDI	AD 8	52	C/BE0#
+5 V	5	+5 V	AD 7	53	+3.3 V
+5 V	6	INTA#	+3.3 V	54	AD 6
INTB#	7	INTC#	AD 5	55	AD 4
INTD#	8	+5 V	AD 3	56	GND
PRSNT1#	9	ECC5[2]	GND	57	AD 2
ECC4[2]	10	+V I/O	AD 1	58	AD 0
PRSNT2#	11	ECC3[2]	+V I/O	59	+V I/O
GND/3.3 V key	12	GND/ 3.3 V key	ACK64#/ ECC1	60	REQ64#/ ECC6
GND/3.3 V key	13	GND/ 3.3 V key	+5 V	61	+5 V
ECC2[2]	14	3.3 Vaux[3]	+5 V	62	+5 V
GND	15	RST#	End of the 32-bit connector		
CLK	16	+V I/O	Reserved	63	GND
GND	17	GNT#	GND	64	C/BE7#
REQ#	18	GND	C/BE6#	65	C/BE5#
+V I/O	19	PME#[3]	C/BE4#	66	+V I/O
AD 31	20	AD 30	GND	67	PAR64/ ECC7[2]
AD 29	21	+3.3 V	AD 63	68	AD 62
GND	22	AD 28	AD 61	69	GND
AD 27	23	AD 26	+V I/O	70	AD 60
AD 25	24	GND	AD 59	71	AD 58
+3.3 V	25	AD 24	AD 57	72	GND
C/BE3#	26	IDSEL	GND	73	AD 56
AD 23	27	+3.3 V	AD 55	74	AD 54
GND	28	AD 22	AD 53	75	+V I/O
AD 21	29	AD 20	GND	76	AD 52

continues

Table 6.10 Continued

Row B	Contact	Row A	Row B	Contact	Row A
AD 19	30	GND	AD 51	77	AD 50
+3.3 V	31	AD 18	AD 49	78	GND
AD 17	32	AD 16	+V I/O	79	AD 48
C/BE2#	33	+3.3 V	AD 47	80	AD 46
GND	34	FRAME#	AD 45	81	GND
IRDY#	35	GND	GND	82	AD 44
+3.3 V	36	TRDY#	AD 43	83	AD 42
DEVSEL#	37	GND	AD 41	84	+V I/O
PCIXCAP[4]	38	STOP#	GND	85	AD 40
LOCK#	39	+3.3 V	AD 39	86	AD 38
PERR#	40	SMBCLK[5]	AD 37	87	GND
+3.3 V	41	SMBDAT[5]	+V I/O	88	AD 36
SERR#	42	GND	AD 35	89	AD 34
+3.3 V	43	PAR/ECC0	AD 33	90	GND
C/BE1#	44	AD 15	GND	91	AD 32
AD 14	45	+3.3 V	Reserved	92	Reserved
GND	46	AD 13	Reserved	93	GND
AD 12	47	AD 11	GND	94	Reserved
AD 10	48	GND	End of the 64-bit connector		

[1] In PCI 2.1, the M66EN signal is defined only for the 3.3 V slots.

[2] The signal was introduced in PCI_X 2.0. It was previously reserved.

[3] The signal was introduced in PCI 2.2. It was previously reserved.

[4] The signal was introduced in PCI-X (in PCI, it is GND).

[5] The signals were introduced in PCI 2.3. In PCI 2.0 and 2.1 contacts, A40 (SDONE#) and A41 (SBOFF#) were used to monitor cache; in PCI 2.2, they were left unconnected (for compatibility purposes, they are pulled to high level by 5 K resistors on the motherboard).

PCI slots have connectors to test adapters using the JTAG interface (TCK, TDI, TDO, TMS, and TRST# signals). These signals are not always present on the motherboard, but they can form a logical chain of the tested adapters, to which external testing equipment can be connected. In order for the chain to be uninterrupted on a card that does not use JTAG, there must be a TDI–TDO link.

Most PCI signals are connected under the pure bus topology (i.e., the same-name contacts of one PCI bus slots are electrically connected with each other). There are some exceptions to this rule:

❐ Each slot has individual REQ# and GNT# signal lines. They connect the slot with the arbiter (usually — the bridge connecting this bus to the upstream bus).
❐ Each slot's IDSEL signal is connected (via a resistor) to one of the AD[31:11] lines, thereby setting the device's number on the bus.
❐ The INTA, INTB, INTC, and INTD signal are cycled over the contacts (Fig. 6.6) distributing interrupt requests.
❐ The CLK signal is routed individually to each slot from its synchronization buffer output. The lengths of all individual feeding tracks are made equal, thus providing synchronous signal on all slots (the tolerance for the 33 MHz slots is ±2 nsec, for the 66 MHz slots it is ±1 nsec).

When a standard motherboard is used in a low profile case, a passive riser card can be installed into one of the PCI slots, and expansion cards installed into it. If more than one card is installed into the riser card, in order to implement the above-described exceptions, PCI extension connectors (small printed-circuitboard edge connectors) are used to bring the above-described signals from other, unoccupied, PCI slots on the motherboard. Moving these connectors around, the numbers of the devices installed in the riser card can be changed; however, the most important thing is that their interrupt-request line allocation can be changed. There is a weak link in this type of connection, though: the long (10–15 cm) ribbon cables that connect the riser card with the slots. All signals in such cables are sent over parallel nontwisted wires, which negatively affects the CLK signal: Its shape is distorted and a noticeable delay is introduced. This can result in sudden computer hangings without any diagnostic messages issued by the system. This situation can be helped by separating the CLK signal from the common ribbon and counter-coiling its excess (this reduces the conductor's inductivity). The other signals in the ribbon cable are not so crucial to the quality of the cable layout. The best solution is using low-profile PCI cards installed into the motherboard without using a riser card. There would be no problem with using a riser card if there were a clock source chip installed on it distributing the clock signal on all its slots. However, this requires using microchips with phase-locked loop that tie their output signal to the motherboard clock signal.

PCI-X Bus Initialization and Operating Mode Determination

Each PCI-X segment (a physical bus) must work in the most advanced mode available to all its clients, including the bus' host bridge. In the standard PCI bus, the level of advancement is defined only by the available clock frequency (33 or 66 MHz), and a card informs about its capabilities over contact B49 (M66EN, see above). In the PCI-X bus, new capabilities are available: support of the PCI-X protocol proper (Mode 1 in PCI-X 2.0 terminology) and fast transfers (Mode 2). The card informs the bridge of these capabilities over contact B38 (PCIXCAP), which can be connected to the GND rail via a resistor or not be connected at all (NC), as illustrated in Table 6.11. Resistors' nominal values are selected in such a way that the bridge can determine the capabilities of cards in multislot buses when the PCIXCAP circuits of all cards are connected in parallel (besides resistors, cards also have capacitors). The bridge that is the master of the given bus inspects the status of the M66EN and PCIXCAP lines at the start of a reset signal. It will select the operating mode of the bus according to the capabilities it sees on those lines (they will correspond to the weakest client's capabilities). This mode is communicated to all clients using the PCI-X Initialization Pattern: levels of the PERR#, DEVSEL#, STOP#, and TRDY# signals at the end of the RST# signal (at its rising edge). By this moment, the corresponding +V I/O voltage is already being supplied to the slots. Possible bus operation modes and their patterns are shown in Table 6.12.

Table 6.11. Communication of PCI/PCI-X Card Capabilities

B49 (M66EN)	B38 (PCIXCAP)	Expansion card capabilities
GND	GND	PCI 33 MHz
NC	GND	PCI 66 MHz
GND or NC	GND via R1	PCI-X 66
GND or NC	NC	PCI-X 133
GND or NC	GND via R2	PCI-X 266
GND or NC	GND via R3	PCI-X 533

Table 6.12. PCI/PCI-X Bus Modes and Initialization Patterns

PERR#	DEVSEL#	STOP#	TRDY#	Bus mode	Frequency	Error control
H	H	H	H	PCI	0–33	Parity
H	H	H	H	PCI	33–66	Parity
H	H	H	L	PCI-X Mode 1	50–66	Parity
H	H	L	H	PCI-X Mode 1	66–100	Parity
H	H	L	L	PCI-X Mode 1	100–133	Parity
H	L	H	H	PCI-X Mode 1	Reserved	ECC

continues

Table 6.12 Continued

PERR#	DEVSEL#	STOP#	TRDY#	Bus mode	Frequency	Error control
H	L	H	L	PCI-X Mode 1	50–66	ECC
H	L	L	H	PCI-X Mode 1	66–100	ECC
H	L	L	L	PCI-X Mode 1	100–133	ECC
L	H	H	H	PCI-X266 Mode 2	Reserved	ECC
L	H	H	L	PCI-X266 Mode 2	50–66	ECC
L	H	L	H	PCI-X266 Mode 2	66–100	ECC
L	H	L	L	PCI-X266 Mode 2	100–133	ECC
L	L	H	H	PCI-X533 Mode 2	Reserved	ECC
L	L	H	L	PCI-X533 Mode 2	50–66	ECC
L	L	L	H	PCI-X533 Mode 2	66–100	ECC
L	L	L	L	PCI-X533 Mode 2	100–133	ECC

Device Hot-Plugging

Hot-plugging PCI devices require a special Hot-Plug Controller in the system that controls the hot-plug slots, as well as appropriate software support: operating system, device, and controller drivers.

Hot-plug slots must be connected to the PCI bus via switching circuits that provide the following:

❏ Controlled switching (using electronic keys) of all PCI signal circuits
❏ Controlled power supply

The hot-plug controller must provide the following for each of its slots:

❏ Individual control of signal switching and the power supply.
❏ Individual control of the RST# signal.
❏ Individual detection of the PRSNT[1:2]# lines' status, regardless of the slot's state (connected or isolated).
❏ Individual detection of the M66EN line's status, regardless of the slot's state (connected or isolated).
❏ Individual indicator "Attention" signaling the status of the slot's power supply (can the card be pulled out or inserted). The flag is software-controlled, and also communicates to the user the problems detected by the system for the device in the given slot.

The user participates in the hot-plug process. He or she must install (and take out) the expansion card only into slots with their power supply disconnected (the slot's signals are also disconnected from the bus). After the module is installed, the power is supplied to it; and some time later, it is reset by a RST# signal and the device is initialized. Only after this does the controller connect the slot's signals lines to the bus. Further, the software must identify and configure the connected device. Additional difficulties arise if a 33 MHz device is connected to a 66 MHz bus. Because the bus clock can only be changed while the RST# signal is active, and the device being connected cannot work at the high frequency, the entire PCI bus needs to be reset (with the following initialization of all its devices). Before the slot is depowered, it is reset by an RST# signal and all its signal lines are disconnected from the bus.

Variants of PCI Bus Constructs

The PCI bus also has other constructs, specifications for which are available on the site **www.pcisig.org** (albeit, free of charge only to the members; others have to pay).

The Low-Profile PCI card has the conventional connector but a modified mounting bracket. These cards can be mounted vertically (without a riser card) even into low-profile cases (such as 19-inch-high 2U form factor). For these cards, only the 3.3 V power supply for interface circuits is specified (although, the 5 V power rail is preserved).

The PCI bus has dual use in notebook computers:

❒ Expansion cards that can be installed by the end user without opening up the computer (with hot-plug capability) use the CardBus PCMCIA construct (see *Section 6.5.1*).

❒ For internal component installation by the manufacturer (not available to the end user), various versions of Small PCI and Mini PCI constructs are used.

Small PCI (SPCI) is a miniaturized form factor of the PCI specification. It used to be called *Small Form-Factor PCI (SFF PCI)*. This specification is primarily intended for portable computers, and is logically compatible with the conventional 32 bits/33 MHz PCI bus. To the standard signal suite, a new signal has been added: CLKRUN. The host or devices can use this signal to control the bus clock for energy-saving reasons. The SPCI card's dimensions are the same as those of the PC Card or CardBus card, but special keys stop it from being wrongly connected. To connect a SPCI card to the motherboard, the latter is equipped with a two-row connector with 108 contact pins each spaced 2 mm apart. The card can be installed directly into this connector, or a special adapter with two-sided ribbon contacts spaced 0.8 mm apart can be used. The SPCI bus is internal (expansion cards are located inside the case, and are installed by the manufacturer with the power supply turned off). Therefore, it is not aimed at replacing the CardBus (a bus for hot-swap connection of external equipment). There are three types of the SPCI card, which have 5 V, 3.3 V, and universal power supplies, respectively. Thanks to the card's reduced dimensions, which entail reduced conductor lengths, its signal power requirements have been lowered. SPCI cards make it possible to take advantage of the modular assemblies (unloading the motherboard), while providing high exchange efficiency (which the CardBus does not).

The Mini PCI Specification is a miniature version of the PCI card (2.75" × 1.81" × 0.22"). Logically and electrically, it corresponds to the 32-bit PCI, and also uses the CLKRUN signal to lower the power consumption and does not have the JTAG signals. It also has additional signals to control audio and video applications.

The *Compact PCI* bus (cPCI) for industrial-purpose devices is based on the PCI 2.1 specification. The bus allows for quite great number of slots (up to 8) and supports 32-bit and 64-bit exchange. Constructively, Compact PCI circuit boards are Euro-card of 3U size (100 × 160 mm) with two connectors (J1 and J2) or of 6U size (233.35 × 160 mm) with 4 or 5 connectors (J1–J5).

The *PXI* bus (PCI eXtensions for Instrumentation) is developed by National Instruments based on the Compact PCI bus. PXI modules use the same constructs (Euro cards). In addition to the PCI signals' inputs, PXI connectors reserve place for the extra buses:

❑ Local buses coupling the neighbor modules
❑ Buses (*Trigger Bus*) for mutual synchronization of modules and radially propagated signals (Star Trigger)

Designing Custom PCI Devices

Having studied the PCI protocol, it becomes clear that designing custom PCI devices using small- and medium-scale integration chips is a thankless task. The protocol itself is not that complex, but implementing the requirements to the configuration registers is difficult. As a rule, production-run PCI devices are built on one chip: The interface and the functional parts of the device are placed in one package. The development of such microchips is quite expensive, and makes sense only when there is the promise of mass production. For making development models and low production-run devices, several companies produce various-purpose interface PCI microchips. On the PCI side, practically all these microchips support single-target transactions, while more sophisticated models also allow burst cycles. More complex integrated circuits function as bus mastering devices, setting up DMA channels for system memory data exchanges. Depending on the functional capabilities of the microchip, exchanges over these channels may be initiated by host software (host-initiated DMA), and by devices on the peripheral side of the microchip (target-initiated DMA). On the peripheral side, there are interfaces to connect peripheral microchips, microcontrollers, and universal microprocessors and microcontrollers of popular families. A quite extensive selection of microchips is presented on the site **www.plxtech.com**; other companies also work in this area.

Worth noting is the implementation of the PCI interface in Field Programmable Gate Array (FPGA) microchips. Here, the PCI kernel and the initiator and target device functions use from 10,000 to 15,000 gates, the exact number depending on the required functions (see **www.xilink.com**, **www.altera.com**). FPGA microchips are made with 20,000, 30,000 or 40,000 gates, so the other gates can be used for implementing the functional part of the device, FIFO buffers, etc.

ISA bus designs can be quickly converted to PCI using PCI-ISA microchip bridges (see, for example, **www.iss-us.com**).

6.2. AGP Interface

The Accelerated Graphics Port (AGP) was introduced to connect graphics adapters with 3D accelerators. This type of adapter comprises an *accelerator* (specialized graphics processor), local memory used as both the video memory and the local memory of the graphics processor, and control and configuration registers accessible by both the local and the central processors. The accelerator can access both the local memory and the main memory, in which it may store data that do not fit into the local memory (as a rule, large-volume textures). The main idea of the AGP lies in providing the accelerator with the quickest possible access to the system memory (it already has quick access to the local memory), with higher priority than for other devices.

The AGP is a 32-bit parallel synchronous interface with a 66 MHz bus clock; most of the signals have been borrowed from the PCI bus. However, unlike the PCI bus, the AGP is a two-point interface. Using the logic and data channels of the motherboard chipset, it connects the video adapter with memory and processor system bus directly, without getting into the bottleneck that is the PCI bus. Exchange via the port can be conducted using either the PCI or the AGP protocol. The distinctive features of the AGP are as follows:

❏ Pipelined memory access
❏ Multiplied (2x/4x/8x) data transfer rate (relative to the port clock frequency)
❏ Sideband command system (SBA) provided by the demultiplexed address and data buses

The concept of pipelined memory access is illustrated in Fig. 6.14, where the PCI and AGP memory accesses are compared. In the PCI, the bus does not work, but is not free, during the memory response to the access request. The pipelined AGP access allows the next-in-line access requests to be sent during this time, and then a stream of responses received.

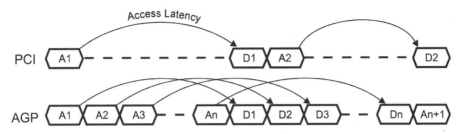

Fig. 6.14. PCI and AGP memory access cycles

Multiplying the data transfer rate of the 66 MHz bus clock provides bus bandwidth of up to 532 MBps (2x), 1,066 MBps (4x), and 2,132 MBps (8x).

The way the address and data buses are demultiplexed is somewhat unusual. In order to save on the number of the interface lines, the address and command bus in the demultiplexed AGP mode are implemented using only 8 SideBand Address (SBA) lines. The command and address, as well as the transfer-length indicator, are transmitted serially over several cycles. It was not mandatory for AGP 1.0 devices to support demultiplexed addressing, since there was an alternative way of supplying address using the AD bus. In AGP 2.0, this became mandatory; and in the AGP 3.0 version, it is the only addressing method.

Many of the AGP's advantages are only potential, and can only be implemented with the support of the video adapter's hardware and software. In real life, an AGP video adapter can act in different ways:

❑ Not use pipelining and use only PCI Fast Write
❑ Not work with textures located in the system memory, but exchange data between memory and the local buffer, which is faster

AGP has practically the entire suite of PCI bus signals, and additional AGP-specific signals. A device connected to the AGP may be intended solely for AGP operations, or it may be an AGP+PCI combination. The adapter's accelerator is an AGP master device; it can execute its requests in both the AGP and the PCI modes. In the AGP mode, the exchanges are carried out employing (or not) features such as sideband addressing (SBA) and 2x/4x/8x speeds. For transactions in the AGP mode, it can only access the main memory (but not the local memory of PCI devices). Moreover, the adapter is a target PCI device that in addition to regular PCI commands can support (or not) fast writes at 2x/4x/8x from the processor side. The adapter plays the role of the target device when its local memory, I/O or configuration space registers are accessed by the central processor.

It is mandatory that a device connected to AGP is able to perform functions of a master AGP device (otherwise, there is no sense in connecting it to the AGP) and functions of a slave PCI device with all its attributes (configuration registers, etc); additionally, it can be a master PCI device.

There are two models of AGP accelerator operation: DMA and DIME (DIrect Memory Execute). When performing calculations in DMA, the accelerator views the local memory as the primary memory, and when it runs low on it uses the main memory to swap the excess data into and out of the local memory. In DIME (or Execute), the accelerator views the local memory and the main memory as logically equivalent and located in one addressing space. In DMA operations, port traffic tends to be long block transfers; in DIME, the traffic is saturated with short random accesses.

The AGP specification was developed by Intel based on the 66 MHz PCI 2.1 bus. Currently, there are three main specification versions:

❑ AGP 1.0 (1996): A port with two alternative pipelined memory access methods defined: sideband (over the SBA bus) and in-band (using the PIPE# signal). Two transfer modes — 1x and 2x — defined. Power supply is 3.3 V.

❑ AGP 2.0 (1998): Fast Write capability in the PCI mode added, along with 4x operation mode with 1.5 V power supply.

❑ AGP 3.0 (2002; the project was called AGP8X): 8x operation mode added with 0.8 V power supply. 1x and 2x speeds are abolished; only one command method left: sideband (SBA); some AGP commands eliminated; isochronous exchange commands introduced; capability to select pages described in GART introduced; selective coherence support when accessing different pages within GART limits introduced.

Only an intelligent graphics adapter with a 3D accelerator (only one) can be connected to the AGP. AGP system logic has a sophisticated memory controller that performs deep buffering and services requests from the AGP (from the adapter) and other its clients (one or several central processors and the PCI bus) with high efficiency. The only way to connect more than one AGP adapter is to implement several AGPs on the motherboard, which is unlikely ever to be done.

AGP can use the entire memory bandwidth of a 64-bit modern computer system. Here, the memory can be accessed from both the processor and the PCI bus bridges sides. AGP support was first introduced by Intel in chipsets for P6 processors; its competitors use the AGP in motherboards for processors with the Pentium interface. Currently, practically all modern motherboards for PC-compatible computers and other platforms (even Macintosh) support AGP.

6.2.1. Transaction Protocols

In the PCI mode, transactions that are initiated by the accelerator begin with the activation of the FRAME# signal and are executed in the conventional PCI manner (see *Section 6.1*). Note that here, the AD bus is occupied for the entire duration of the transaction. Moreover, memory read transactions take more cycles to execute than write trans-actions do: After the address is issued, wait cycles are unavoidable while the memory is accessed. Writes are executed faster: The master sends the write data immediately after the address, and they "settle" in memory controller buffer while the memory is being ac-cessed. The memory controller makes it possible to complete the transaction and release the bus before the data are physically written to the memory. The adapter handles ac-cesses from the processor (or PCI bus masters), just like a regular PCI device does.

Only the accelerator can initiate *pipelined AGP transactions*. These are placed by the AGP logic into the process queue, and are executed in the order depending on their priorities, the order the requests come in, and availability of data. The accelerator may address these transactions only to the system memory. If an AGP device needs to access the local memory of a PCI device, then it must perform these transactions in the PCI mode. Transactions that are addressed to an AGP device are handled by this device as they are handled by a PCI slave device; however, they can be executed using a *fast write* to the local memory operation. In this operation, data are sent at the AGP speed (2x/4x/8x), and their flow control is more like the AGP protocol rather than the PCI. Fast-write transactions are usually initiated by the processor, and are intended to force "push" data into the accelerator's local memory.

Figure 6.15 illustrates the concept of the *AGP pipeline*. AGP can assume one of four states:

❏ *IDLE*
❏ *DATA* — transmitting data of the pipelined instructions
❏ *AGP* — placing an AGP command into the queue
❏ *PCI* — executing transaction in the PCI mode

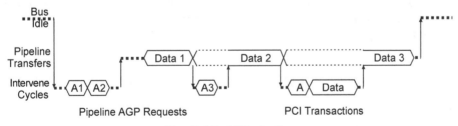

Fig. 6.15. AGP pipeline

The AGP *IDLE* state may be terminated by a PCI transaction request (from the ac-celerator or from the system side) or an AGP request (only from the accelerator). In the PCI state, a PCI transaction is executed completely, from the issuing of the ad-dress and command to the completion of data transfer. In the AGP state, the master device only transmits the command and the address for the transaction (upon the PIPE# signal or through the SBA port), which are placed into the queue; several requests may follow immediately each other. The port switches into the DATA state when it has an unserviced command ready for execution enqueued. Data for the enqueued commands are transmitted in this state. This state may be interrupted by intervening PCI requests (to execute a complete transaction) or AGP requests (to enqueue a new command); interrupts[1] are only possible on the boundary of the current AGP transactions, however. When AGP has serviced all commands, it returns into the idle state. All transitions are controlled by the AGP arbiter, which reacts to the incoming requests (REQ# from the accelerator and external accesses from the processor and other PCI devices) and to the memory controller's responses.

The AGP transactions differ from the PCI transactions in some details, which are as follows:

❑ The data phase is separated from the address phase, which is what makes pipelining possible.
❑ A custom set of commands is used.
❑ Transactions are addressed to the system memory only, and use physical address space (like the PCI bus). Transactions length in bytes can be only a multiple of 8, and can begin only on 8-byte boundaries. Read transactions with a length in bytes other than multiple of 8 must be executed only in the PCI mode; write transactions can use the C/BE[3:0]# signals to mask unneeded bytes.
❑ The transaction length is indicated explicitly in the request.
❑ Pipelined requests do not guarantee memory and cache coherence. For operations requiring coherence, PCI transactions must be used. In AGP 3.0, the memory areas may be specified, for which the coherence is ensured at pipeline transactions as well.

Two methods to issue AGP commands (enqueueing requests) are available, out of which one is chosen in the current configuration; the methods cannot be changed on the fly:

❑ Requests are issued on the AD[31:0] and C/BE[3:0] bus by the PIPE# signal. On each CLK edge, the master device transmits the next double word along with the command code.
❑ Commands are issued using the *sideband* SBA[7:0] address lines. Sideband means that these signals can be used regardless of whether or not the AD bus is busy. How the requests are clocked in depends on the mode (1x, 2x, 4x, or 8x).

When commands are issued over the AD bus and the PIPE# signal is active, the AGP command code (CCCC) is coded by the C/BE[3:0] signals. The starting address and

---

[1] Here, the term "interrupt" means the intrusion of the AGP commands and PCI transactions into the data flow; which has nothing to do with CPU interrupts.

the length n of the requested data block are placed on the AD bus address on lines AD[31:3] and AD[2:0], respectively. The following commands are defined:

- ❏ 0000 — Read. Reading $(n + 1)$ number of quadruple words from the memory starting from the specified address.
- ❏ 0001 — HP Read. High priority read. Abolished in AGP 3.0.
- ❏ 0100 — Write. Memory write.
- ❏ 0101 — HP Write. High priority memory write. Abolished in AGP 3.0.
- ❏ 1000 — Long Read. Reading $(n+1) \times 4$ number of quadruple words (up to 256 bytes of data).
- ❏ 1001 — HP Long Read. High priority long read. Abolished in AGP 3.0.
- ❏ 1010 — Flush. Flushes data of all previous write commands to their destination addresses (with AGP, it looks like a read that returns a random quadruple word as the acknowledgement of the execution; the address and length specified in the request have no meaning).
- ❏ 1100 — Fence. Creates boundaries that do not let reads pass over writes in a low-priority access stream.
- ❏ 1101 — Dual Address Cycle (DAC). This is a two-address cycle for 64-bit addressing. In the first cycle, the lower part of the address and the request length are sent over the AD lines. In the second cycle, the upper part of the address is sent over the AD lines and the actual command is sent over the C/BE[3:0] lines.

Special commands are set aside in AGP 3.0 for isochronous transfers (see *Section 6.2.3*).

In the *sideband mode*, commands are sent over the SBA[7:0] bus in four types of 16-bit packets. The type of packet is coded by the upper bits as follows:

- ❏ Type 1: 0AAA AAAA AAAA ALLL — length field (LLL) and the lower address bits (A[14:03])
- ❏ Type 2: 10CC CCRA AAAA AAAA — command code (CCCC) and the middle address bits (A[23:15])
- ❏ Type 3: 110R AAAA AAAA AAAA — upper address bits (A[35:24])
- ❏ Type 4: 1110 AAAA AAAA AAAA — additional upper address bits if 64-bit addressing is required

An all-ones packet is a no-operation command (NOP). This type of command is sent when the SBA bus is idle. Bits marked R are reserved. Type 2, 3, and 4 packets are *sticky*, meaning that their values are retained until a new packet of the same type has been sent. A command is enqueued by the type 1 packet that sets the transaction length and its lower addresses. The command code and the rest of the address must be specified by the previously sent type 2–4 packets. This method uses bus cycles very efficiently to issue commands when transferring arrays of data. Each two-byte packet is sent via the 8-bit SBA bus in two portions (upper byte first). Data on the SBA are synchronized depending on the port operation mode.

❑ In the 1x operating mode, each byte is sent at the CLK front edge. The start of the packet (the upper byte) is determined by the first received byte that is not 11111111h; the lower byte is sent at the trailing clock edge. The next command (a type 1 packet) may be enqueued every two CLK cycles (contingent on the command code and the upper address having already been issued by earlier packets). The full command input cycle takes 10 clocks.

❑ In the 2x operating mode, a separate strobe SB_STB is used for the SBA. The upper byte of a packet is sent at its negative transition, and the lower byte is sent at the next rising edge. The frequency of this strobe (but not the phase) coincides with the CLK frequency, so the next command can be enqueued in every CLK cycle.

❑ In the 4x operating mode, yet another, inverted, strobe is used: SB_STB#. The upper byte of a packet is latched at the negative transition of the SB_STB, and the lower byte is latched at the next negative transition of the SB_STB#. The frequency of the strobes is twice the CLK frequency, so two packets can be enqueued in each CLK cycle. However, the AGP master may issue no more than one type 1 packet in each clock (i.e. enqueue no more than one request).

❑ In 8x mode, the strobes have different names: SB_STBF and SB_STBS. Their frequency is four times the CLK frequency, so 4 packets fit into one clock. Nevertheless, the command enqueueing rate is still limited to one command per clock tick.

Responding to the received commands, the AGP executes data transmission. The AGP data phase is not tied to the command/address phase explicitly. The AGP will supply data phases when the system memory is ready for the requested exchange.

The AGP data are transmitted when the bus is in the *DATA* state. Data phases are supplied by the AGP (system logic), based on the order of the commands it receives from the accelerator. The accelerator is informed of the role that the AD bus will play in the next transaction by the ST[2:0] signals, which are valid only during the GNT# signal (codes 100–110 are reserved):

❑ 000 — Data of the previously enqueued low-priority read request (simple asynchronous read in AGP 3.0) will be sent to the master device (or buffers are flushed).

❑ 001 — Data of a high-priority read request will be sent to the master device. (Reserved in AGP 3.0).

❑ 010 — The master device will have to supply low-priority write request data (simple asynchronous write data in AGP 3.0).

❑ 011 — The master device will have to supply high-priority write request data. (Reserved in AGP 3.0.)

❏ 111 — The master device is permitted to enqueue an AGP command (by the `PIPE#` signal) or to begin a PCI transaction (by the `FRAME#` signal).
❏ 110 — Transceiver calibration cycle (for 8x speed in AGP 3.0).

The accelerator only finds out the type and priority of the command whose results are to follow in the current transaction. Exactly which enqueued command the port is to service is determined by the accelerator itself, as it did the command enqueueing itself (i.e., it knows their order). The AGP interface has nothing like the transaction tags that can be found in the system bus of the P6 processors or in the PCI-X bus. There are only four independent queues for each command type: low-priority read, high-priority read, low-priority write, high-priority write. Commands from different queues may be executed in an arbitrary order; the port has the right to execute them in the order that is most optimal in terms of efficiency. The actual order of command execution (memory reads and write) may also change. However, for every queue, the order, in which commands are executed, matches the order, in which they had been enqueued, and both the accelerator and the port know this. Queue priorities were abolished in AGP 3.0, but isochronous transaction capability was introduced.

The system logic arbiter assigns higher priority to high-priority AGP requests than to requests from the CPU or the PCI bus master devices. To low-priority AGP requests, it assigns lower priority than to requests from the CPU but higher than to requests from the other master devices. Although the adopted protocol in no way explicitly limits the queue depth, the AGP specification officially limits it to 256 requests. During the configuration stage, the plug-and-play system sets the actual limits in the accelerator's configuration register according to its own capabilities and those of the motherboard. Programs that work with the accelerator (executed by both the local and the central processors) may not exceed the limit of pending commands in the queue (they have all the information necessary for this).

When transferring AGP data, the control signals borrowed from the PCI have almost the same functions as in the PCI. Data transfer in the AGP 1x mode is very similar to the PCI cycles, but the handshaking procedure is a little simpler (as this is a dedicated port and the exchange is performed only with the fast system-memory controller). The 2x, 4x, and 8x modes use specific strobing:

❏ In the 1x mode, data (4 bytes on the `AD[31:0]`) are latched by the recipient at the rising edge of every `CLK` cycle, which provides a peak throughput of $66.6 \times 4 = 266$ MBps.
❏ In the 2x mode, two strobe signals are used: `AD_STB0` for the `AD[0:15]` lines and `AD_STB1` for the `AD[16:31]` lines. They are generated by the data source; the receiver latches data at both the rising and the falling edges of the strobe signals. The strobe frequency coincides with the `CLK` frequency, which provides a peak bandwidth of $66.6 \times 2 \times 4 = 533$ MBps.

❏ In the 4x mode, two additional inverted strobes are used: `AD_STB0#` and `AD_STB1#`. Data are clocked at the rising and falling edges of both the positive and inverted strobes (strobe pairs can be used either as two individual signals or as one differential signal). The strobe frequency is twice the `CLK` frequency, which provides a bandwidth of $66.6 \times 2 \times 2 \times 4 = 1,066$ MBps.

❏ In 8x mode, the strobe pairs were given new names: `AD_STBF[1:0]` (F — first) and `AD_STBS[1:0]` (S — second). The even parts of data are latched at the positive transition of the first strobe; the odd portions are latched at the positive transition of the second strobe. The switching frequency of each strobe is four times higher than the `CLK` frequency; the strobes are shifted half of the their period relative to each other, which is what provides the eightfold data strobing frequency on the `AD` lines. From this comes the peak bandwidth of $66.6 \times 4 \times 2 \times 4 = 2,132$ MBps.

The AGP must keep track of the accelerator buffers' readiness to receive and send data of the enqueued transactions. By the `RBF#` (Read Buffer Full) signal, the accelerator can inform the port of its not being ready to receive data of low-priority read transactions (it must always be ready to receive high-priority transactions). Using the `WBF#` (Write Buffer Full) signal, the accelerator informs the port that it is not ready to accept a new batch of fast-write data.

6.2.2. Address Translation: AGP Aperture and GART

The AGP provides translation of logical addresses used in accelerator requests to the system memory into physical addresses, thereby making compatible the views of the system memory as seen by the accelerator's software and the software running on the central processor. The translation is done on a page basis (the default page size is 4 KB) adopted in the virtual memory system with page swapping upon request as used in x86 and other modern processors. All accesses that fall within the AGP aperture must be translated. The *AGP aperture* is the physical address area that lies above the main memory boundary and, as a rule, is adjacent to the adapter's local memory (Fig. 6.16).

Therefore, when working in DIME, the accelerator has continuous memory area available, part of which comprises the adapter's local memory. The rest of the memory that it addresses is mapped onto the system memory via the aperture using the Graphics Address Remapping Table (GART). Each element of this table describes its own page in the aperture area. A validity flag indicates the validity of each GART element; the valid elements specify the address of the physical memory page, onto which the corresponding aperture area is mapped. Physically, the GART is located in the system memory, it is aligned at 4 KB page boundary, and the AGP configuration registers point to its beginning.

The size of the AGP aperture (which also determines the size of the GART) is set by programming the chipset registers. By adjusting the CMOS Setup parameters or using external utilities, it can be set to 8, 16, 32, ..., 256, or more megabytes. The optimal aperture size depends on the size of the memory and the programs running, but is recommended to be half of the main memory size. Setting the aperture size does not mean that the entire volume will be made unavailable to the system: This is simply the maximum memory size that the operating system will allocate to the accelerator upon request. While its own memory is sufficient for the accelerator, it will not ask for additional memory from the system memory resources. Only when the local memory is not enough for its needs will it dynamically ask for additional memory, and these requests will be satisfied within the set aperture limits. As the accelerator's needs for additional memory decrease, it will be dynamically released for the regular needs of the operating system. However, if the graphics accelerator has no local memory at all (as in cheap integrated adapters), then a portion of memory (at least for the screen buffer) will be statically expropriated from the system memory. It can be seen by the lessened memory size, which the POST shows at the beginning of the system boot.

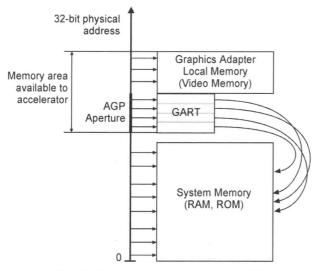

Fig. 6.16. Memory addressing in AGP

The port logic ensures the coherence of all system cache memories for AGP accesses outside the aperture address range. A selective coherence enabling capability for accesses inside the aperture was introduced in AGP 3.0. Previous versions simply assumed that the memory area inside the aperture must be uncacheable. Because this memory was intended to use to store textures, which are rather static, this simplification is quite acceptable.

6.2.3. AGP 3.0 Isochronous Transactions

To support isochronous transactions in AGP 3.0, new command and status codes were introduced, as well as configuration registers controlling the isochronous connection. Isochronous transfers can be performed by the AGP master only via the AGP aperture; moreover, it can do this only with those memory areas that have no coherence support (in order to avoid unpredicted delays due to the flushing of dirty lines). Isochronous transactions are available only at 8x. An agreement for an isochronous transfer is described by the following parameter set:

❏ N — the number of read or write transactions over time T
❏ Y — isochronous transaction data block size
❏ L — maximum data delivery latency from the moment a command was issued (in T periods)

The bandwidth $BW=N \times Y/T$; a T interval of 1 mcsec is adopted. The block size Y can be 32, 64, 128, or 256 bytes; for read transactions, which can have the same lengths, the asynchronous block is transferred in one transaction. Write transactions can be 32 or 64 bytes long, so 1, 2, or 4 transactions can be transferred in one block. Depending on the memory subsystem size, the AGP can support isochronous traffic sufficient for the following applications:

❏ Video capture (in desktop PCs): 128 MBps, $N = 2$, $L = 2$, $Y = 64$
❏ Video editing: 320 MBps, $N = 5$, $L = 2$, $Y = 64$
❏ One HDTV channel stream: 384 MBps, $N = 3$, $L = 10$, $Y = 128$
❏ Two HDTV channel streams (in powerful workstations): 640 MBps, $N = 5$, $L = 10$, $Y = 128$

The new AGP commands for isochronous transactions include the following:

❏ 0111 (ISOCH Read): isochronous read. The LLL field holds the transaction length code: 000 — 32 bytes, 001 — 64 bytes, 010 — 128 bytes, 011 — 256 bytes.
❏ 0110 (ISOCH Write/Unfenced): isochronous write with out-of-order completion. The LLL field holds the transaction length code: 000 — 32 bytes, 001 — 64 bytes.
❏ 0111 (ISOCH Write/Fenced): isochronous write with ordered completions. The LLL field holds the transaction length code: 000 — 32 bytes, 001 — 64 bytes.
❏ 1110 (ISOCH Align): reading the time offset relative to the isochronous period.

The new AGP status codes include the following:

❏ 100: isochronous data read
❏ 101: isochronous data write

6.2.4. AGP Configuration Registers

AGP interface devices are configured the same way as the regular PCI devices, by accessing their configuration space registers (see Section 6.2.12). However, AGP devices do not require the external IDSEL line: Their external configuration registers enable signal is connected to the AD16 line so that AGP configuration registers can be accessed when AD16=1.

During the initialization, POST allocates only system resources, but AGP operations remain disabled. The loaded operating system sets the required AGP parameters — the exchange mode, fast-write support, over 4 GB addressing, enqueueing method, and the queue length — and then enables AGP operations. To set the device requirements, their parameters are read from the AGP status register, and the negotiated parameters are written to the AGP command register that is located in the configuration space. Port parameters are set via the motherboard chipset's host bridge-configuration registers.

Two functions and their configuration spaces are involved in configuring an AGP system:

❑ The AGP proper (core logic), which is the target device in AGP transactions
❑ The graphics adapter, which is the AGP transaction initiator

The purposes of the specific configuration registers of these functions partially coincide (Fig. 6.17). The registers of importance to the port only are marked in gray; optional registers are marked by an asterisk.

The APBASELO register (port only) sets the location of the AGP aperture:

❑ Bits [31:32] set the address.
❑ Bits [21:4] are always zeroes (aperture size cannot be less than 4 MB).
❑ Bit 3 = 1 indicates prefetching capability.
❑ Bits [2:1] set the address width: 00 — 32 bits, 10 — 64 bits (the APBASEHI register is also used).

The location of the rest of the registers is defined by the value of CAP_PTR.
The NCAPID register (in port or card) contains the AGP specification version.

❑ Bits [31:24] — reserved
❑ Bits [23:20] — the higher digit
❑ Bits [19:16] — the lower digit
❑ Bits [15:8] — NEXT_PTR: a pointer to the next capabilities list (or zero)
❑ Bits [7:0] — CAP_ID: AGP identifier (02).

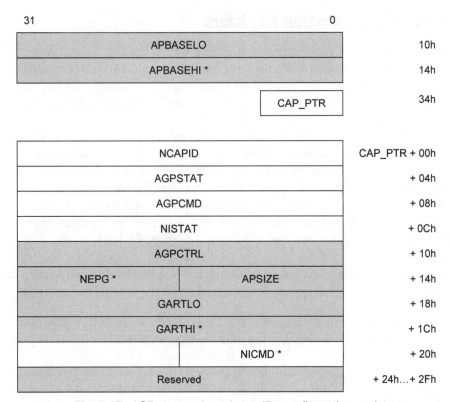

Fig 6.17. AGP port and card specific configuration registers

The AGP status register, AGPSTAT (in port or card), indicates the main AGP capabilities: the allowable number of enqueued requests, sideband addressing support, over 4GB addressing support, 1x, 2x, 4x, or 8x modes:

❏ Bits [31:24] — RQ (port only), the allowable total number of enqueued requests: 0 — 1 request, 255 — 256 requests.
❏ Bits [23:18] — reserved (0).
❏ Bit 17 — ISOCH SUPPORT: isochronous transfer support (AGP 3.0).
❏ Bit 16 — reserved.
❏ Bits [15:13] — ARQSZ (port only): indication of the optimal size of a request to the graphics adapter; $Opt\_Rq\_Size = 2^{(ARQSZ+4)}$. Introduced in AGP 3.0.
❏ Bits [12:10] — Cal_Cycle (AGP 3.0 only), calibration period: 000 — 4 msec, 001 — 16 msec, 010 — 64 msec, 011 — 256 msec, 111 — no calibration needed; other values are reserved.
❏ Bit 9 — SBA, sideband command support (reserved in AGP 3.0).

❏ Bit 8 — ITA_COH, providing coherence when accessing the accelerator via the aperture (with the coherence bit set in the corresponding GART entry).

❏ Bit 7 — GART64B, 64-bit GART element support.

❏ Bit 6 — HTRANS# (AGP 3.0 only), translation of the host requests via the aperture: 0 — when the host access is within the aperture range, the address is translated via the GART, 1 — the host does not send requests within the aperture range.

❏ Bit 5 — Over4G memory addressing support.

❏ Bit 4 — FW, fast write support.

❏ Bit 3 — AGP3.0_MODE: 0 — AGP 1.0/2.0, 1 — AGP 3.0.

❏ Bits [2:0] — RATE, exchange rates supported over AD and SBA. In AGP 1.0/2.0 mode: bit 0 — 1x, bit 1 — 2x, bit 2 — 4x. In AGP 3.0 mode: bit 0 — 4x, bit 1 — 8x.

The AGP command register, AGPCMD (card and port), is used to enable the above capabilities, and contains the following fields:

❏ Bits [31:24] — RQ_DEPTH, setting the depth of the command queue.

❏ Bits [23:16] — reserved (0).

❏ Bits [15:13] — PARQSZ (AGP 3.0 only), setting the optimal request size that the AGP master must attempt to attain; $Opt\_Rq\_Size=2^{(PARQSZ+4)}$.

❏ Bits [12:10] — PCAL_Cycle (AGP 3.0 only), setting the calibration cycle period.

❏ Bit 9 — SBA_ENABLE, setting the sideband command issuance.

❏ Bit 8 — AGP_ENABLE.

❏ Bit 7 — GART64B, enabling 64-bit GART elements.

❏ Bit 6 — reserved.

❏ Bit 5 — 4G, enabling over 4G memory addressing (two-address cycles and type 4 parcels over the SBA).

❏ Bit 4 — FW_Enable, fast write enable.

❏ Bit 3 — reserved.

❏ Bits [2:0] — DATA_RATE, setting the exchange mode (only one bit can be set). In AGP 2.0: bit 0 — 1x, bit 1 — 2x, bit 2 — 4x. In AGP 3.0: bit 0 — 4x, bit 1 — 8x, bit 3 — reserved.

The NISTAT register (port and card) defines isochronous transfer capabilities (AGP 3.0 only):

❏ Bits [31:24] — reserved (0).

❏ Bits [23:16] — MAXBW, the maximum device bandwidth (total for the asynchronous and isochronous transfers) in 32-byte units per 1 μsec (μsec).

❏ Bits [15:8] — ISOCH_N, maximum number of isochronous transactions over a 1 μsec period.

- Bits [7:6] — ISOCH_Y, supported isochronous transfer sizes: 00 — 32, 64, 128, and 256 bytes; 10 — 128, 256, and more bytes; 11 — 256 bytes.
- Bits [5:3] — ISOCH_L, maximum isochronous transfer latency in μsec (1–5).
- Bit 2 — reserved.
- Bits [1:0] — Isoch-ErrorCode, isochronous exchange error code (00 — no errors). For the port: 01 — isochronous request queue overflow. For cards: 01 — read buffer underflow, 10 — read buffer overflow.

The NICMD register (port and card) controls isochronous transfers (AGP 3.0 only):

- Bits [15:8] — PISOCH_N, the maximum number of isochronous transaction per 1 μsec period (for cards)
- Bits [7:6] — PISOCH_Y, isochronous transfer size: 00 — 32, 64, 128, 256 bytes; 01 — 64, 128, 256 bytes; 10 — 128, 256 bytes and more; 11 — 256 bytes
- Bits [5:0] — reserved

The AGPCTRL register controls the AGP port proper:

- Bits [3:10] — reserved
- Bit 9 — CAL_CYCLE_DIS, disabling calibration cycles
- Bit 8 — APERENB, enabling aperture operations
- Bit 7 — GTLBEN, enabling TLB buffer operation (if the port has them)
- Bits [6:0] — reserved

The APSIZE register (port) sets the aperture size:

- Bits [15:12] — reserved.
- Bits [11:8, 5:0] — APSIZE: 111…111 — 4 MB, 111 … 110 — 8 MB, 11110 … 0 — 256 MB, 000 … 000 — 4,096 MB
- Bits [7:6] = 0

The NEPG register (in AGP 3.0 ports) sets the size of the page described in the GART from the list of supported sizes:

- Bits [15:12] — SEL, selected page size ($2^{(SEL+12)}$).
- Bits [11:0] — different page size support bit map. A one in bit N indicates that a page size ($2^{(N+12)}$) is supported. Bit 6 is always set to one: All ports are required to support 4 KB pages.

The GARTLO[31:12] and GARTHI (port) registers set the starting address of the GART.

6.2.5. AGP Slots and Cards

The AGP graphics controller may be built into the motherboard or implemented on an expansion card and installed into the *AGP slot*. External AGP cards are similar to PCI cards (Fig. 6.18), but they use a high-density connector with a two-level (EISA-style) contact-pad arrangement. The connector itself is located farther from the back panel than the PCI connector.

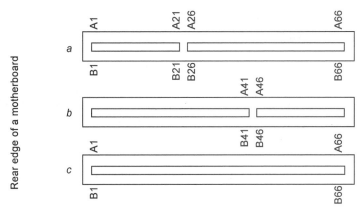

Fig. 6.18. AGP slots: *a* — 3.3 V, *b* — 1.5 V, *c* — universal

AGP interface circuits can be powered by power supplies of three different voltages (V_{ddq}): 3.3 V (for 1x and 2x), 1.5 V (for 2x and 4x), and 0.8 V (for 8x). The RST# and CLK signals are always 3 V. In order to prevent installing a card into a wrong slot, both have mechanical keys.

❑ AGP 1.0 slots and card use 3.3 V; they have keys in place of contacts 22–25: a rib in the slot and a notch in the card (Fig. 6.18, *a*).

❑ AGP 2.0 slots and card use 1.5 V. They have the keys in place of contacts 42–45.

❑ The universal AGP 2.0 slot (3.3 V/1.5 V) has no ribs, while the universal card has both notches. The universal motherboard determines the voltage, on which the installed card operates by the TYPEDET# signal: If this signal's contact is not connected to anywhere, the card is of 3.3 V type; if this contact is grounded, then the card is either of 1.5 V or universal type. The universal card detects the buffer power-supply nominal by the voltage level on the contacts V_{ddq} (3.3 V or 1.5 V). In this way, cards are matched with proper ports.

❑ AGP 3.0 slots and cards use 0.8 V power supply, but their keys are the same as the keys for the 1.5 V card (in place of contacts 42–45). The card recognizes the AGP 3.0 port by the grounded MB-DET# line (in AGP 2.0 ports, this line is not connected).

❏ The universal AGP 3.0 slot can work with both 8x (0.8 V power supply) and AGP 2.0 4x (1.5 V power supply) cards. The 0.8 V power supply voltage and the 8x mode are selected by the port logic.

To operate in the 2x/4x/8x modes, receivers need a reference voltage V_{ref}. Its nominal for 3.3 V is $0.4 \times V_{ddq}$, $0.5 \times V_{ddq}$ for 1.5 V, and $0.233 \times V_{ddq}$ for 0.8 V. The receiver reference voltage is generated on the transmitters' side. The graphics device places the signal for the port on contact A66 (Vrefgc); the port (chipset) supplies the signal for the AGP device on contact B66 (Vrefcg).

When transferring data in the 8x mode, the data on the AD bus are dynamically inverted. The DBI_LO signal indicates inversion on lines AD[15:0]; the DBI_HI signal indicates inversion on lines AD[31:0]. The decision on changing the inversion state is made by comparing the output information with the information of the previous cycle: If the number of switched lines in the corresponding half of the AD bus is greater than eight, the corresponding DBI_xx signal changes its state to the opposite. Consequently, on each half of the AD bus, no more than eight signal lines are switched, which allows surges of the current to be lowered. Automatic transceiver calibration is used in the 8x mode; it allows their parameters to be matched with those of the line and the partner. The calibration is done either statically (during the initial launch) or dynamically (during the operation), in order to compensate the parameter drift due to temperature changes.

Table 6.13 shows the functions of AGP slot contacts for AGP 3.0; functions of AGP 1.0 and 2.0 contacts are shown in parentheses. Because two contacts for a V_{cc} 3.3 power supply on the AGP 2.0 universal cards are lost to the keys, leaving only four of them, the card's consumption current is limited (the maximum allowable current for each contact is 1 A). The auxiliary power supply line, 3.3 V_{aux}, which is used to feed the PME# signal generation circuits in the "sleep" mode, is also missing on the universal cards.

Table 6.13. Functions of AGP Contacts

Row B	Contact	Row A	Row B	Contact	Row A
OVRCNT#	1	12 V	V_{ddq}	34	V_{ddq}
5.0 V	2	TYPEDET#	AD21	35	AD22
5.0 V	3	Reserved	AD19	36	AD20
USB+	4	USB−	GND	37	GND
GND	5	GND	AD17	38	AD18

continues

Table 6.13 Continued

Row B	Contact	Row A	Row B	Contact	Row A
INTB#	6	INTA#	C/BE2#	39	AD16
CLK	7	RST#	V_{ddq}	40	V_{ddq}
REQ#	8	GNT#	IRDY#	41	FRAME#
VCC3.3	9	VCC3.3	1.5 V key (3.3 V_{aux})	42	1.5 V key (Reserved)
ST0	10	ST1	1.5 V key (GND)	43	1.5 V key (GND)
ST2	11	MB_DET#[3]	1.5 V key (Reserved)	44	1.5 V key (Reserved)
RBF#	12	DBI_HI (PIPE#)	1.5 V key (VCC3.3)	45	1.5 V key (VCC3.3)
GND	13	GND	DEVSEL#	46	TRDY#
DBI_LO[3]	14	WBF#	V_{ddq}	47	STOP#
SBA0	15	SBA1	PERR#	48	PME#
VCC3.3	16	VCC3.3	GND	49	GND
SBA2	17	SBA3	SERR#	50	PAR
SB_STBF (SB_STB)	18	SB_STBS (SB_STB#[1])	C/BE1#	51	AD15
GND	19	GND	V_{ddq}	52	V_{ddq}
SBA4	20	SBA5	AD14	53	AD13
SBA6	21	SBA7	AD12	54	AD11
Reserved (3.3 V key)	22	Reserved (3.3 V key)	GND	55	GND
GND (3.3 V key)	23	GND (3.3 V key)	AD10	56	AD9
3.3 Vaux (3.3 V key)	24	Reserved (3.3 V key)	AD8	57	C/BE0#
VCC3.3 (3.3 V key)	25	VCC3.3 (3.3 V key)	V_{ddq}	58	V_{ddq}
AD31	26	AD30	AD_STBF0 (AD_STB0)	59	AD_STBS0 (AD_STB0#[1])

continues

Table 6.13 Continued

Row B	Contact	Row A	Row B	Contact	Row A
AD29	27	AD28	AD7	60	AD6
VCC3.3	28	VCC3.3	GND	61	GND
AD27	29	AD26	AD5	62	AD4
AD25	30	AD24	AD3	63	AD2
GND	31	GND	V_{ddq}	64	V_{ddq}
AD_STBF1 (AD_STB1)	32	AD_STBS1 (AD_STB1#[1])	AD1	65	AD0
AD23	33	C/BE3#	V_{refcg}[2]	66	V_{refgc}[2]

[1] 3.3 V type cards and slots do not have inverted strobes (i.e., do not support the 4x/8x modes).

[2] 1x cards and slots do not need a reference voltage.

[3] AGP 3.0 only.

In addition to the AGP signals proper, AGP provides for USB bus signals. This bus is used to send USB data and control signals to peripheral devices, usually a USB capable video monitor. The lines are USB+, USB−, and the OVRCNT# signal that indicates current overload on the power rail supplying +5 V to the monitor.

The PME# signal pertains to the Power Management Interface. When there is a supplementary 3.3 V_{aux} power supply, the card can use this signal to initiate "wake up."

The AGP Pro specification defines a more powerful connector, which allows a fourfold increase in the power supplied to the graphics controller. In this case, one-way compatibility is preserved: AGP cards can be installed into AGP Pro slot, but not vice versa. Currently, the AGP Pro connector has been abolished, and a supplementary cable is used to supply power to the graphics card.

The AGP Pro connector has additional contact banks at each end of the regular AGP connector for the GND and 3.3 V and 12 V power lines. These contacts' functions are given in Table 6.14. In order not to install a regular AGP card into it improperly, the additional part of the AGP Pro connector, which is closer to the back panel, is covered by a removable plastic cover. An AGP Pro card can also use one or two neighboring PCI slots in several ways. They can be used simply mechanically or as a support point; their power supply connectors can be recruited to supply additional power; and their functional PCI connectors can also be used.

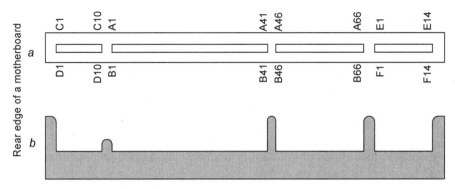

Fig. 6.19. AGP Pro card connector (a 1.5 V card key is shown):
a — view from above, *b* — keys' profile

Table 6.14. Additional Contacts of the AGP Pro Connector

Circuit	Contact
VCC3.3	C1, C3, D1...D8
GND	C2, C4...C8, E3...E14
VCC12	F3...F14
PRSNT1#	D10
PRSNT2#	D9
Reserved	C9, C10, E1, E2, F1, F2

In total, an AGP Pro card can consume up to 110 W of power, which it takes off the 3.3 V (up to 7.6 A) and 12 V (up 9.2 A) lines of the main AGP connector, the supplementary AGP Pro power supply connector, and one or two PCI connectors. High-power AGP Pro cards (50–110 W) take up two PCI slots; low-power cards (25–50 W) take up one PCI slot. Accordingly, their rear-panel mounting bracket is two or three times wider than usual. Additionally, cards have front-panel mounting hardware. In the supplementary connector, the PRSNT1# contact indicates card's presence when it is grounded. The PRSNT2# contact indicates the card's power consumption: up to 50 W when not connected, and up to 110 W when grounded.

6.3. PCI Express

The PCI Express is a new component-interconnect architecture introduced under the auspices of PCI SIG; it is also known as 3rd Generation Input-Output (3GIO). Here, connection of devices using parallel buses is replaced with point-to-point serial connections using switches. Many PCI bus software features are preserved in this architecture, which provides smooth migration from the PCI to PCI Express. The interface introduced new capabilities such as control over the quality of service (QoS) and the usage and budgeting of connections. The PCI Express protocol's characteristic features are low overheads and delay times.

The PCI Express is positioned as a universal I/O architecture for computers of different classes, telecommunications devices, and embedded computer systems. High bandwidth is achieved at a price comparable with the PCI, or even lower. Its application area ranges from on-board microchip interconnections to intercard plug-in and cable connections. The high throughput per each connection contact allows the number of connection contacts to be minimized. A small number of signal lines makes it possible to use compact constructs. The interface's versatility makes it possible to use one software model for all form factors.

A *PCI Express Link* is a pair of opposite simplex channels connecting two components. Over these channels, packets carrying commands and transaction data, messages, and control transfers are transmitted. All PCI read and write transactions in the split version are implemented in the PCI Express using a packet protocol. Consequently, a transaction *requester* and *completer* perform the transfers. There are *four addressing spaces* in the PCI Express: memory, I/O, configuration, and messages. The new (compared with the PCI) message space is used to transfer packetized sideband PCI signals: the INTx line interrupts, power consumption control signals, etc. In this way, virtual wires are implemented. A *PCI Express port* contains a transmitter, receiver, and components necessary to assemble and disassemble packets.

An example of the I/O topology illustrating the PCI Express architecture is shown in Fig. 6.20. The *root complex* is the central item of the architecture; it connects the I/O hierarchy with the core: the processor(s) and the memory. The root complex can have one and more PCI Express ports; each of these ports defines its own hierarchy domain. Each domain consists of one endpoint or a *sub-hierarchy*: several endpoints connected by switches. The capability of direct peer-to-peer communications between members of different domains is not mandatory, but can be present in specific situations. To provide transparent peer-to-peer communications, switches must be located in the root complex. The central processor must be able to communicate with any device of the domain, and all devices must be able to access the memory. The root complex must generate requests to the configuration space: Its role is analogous to the PCI host bridge. The root complex can generate I/O requests as a requester; it can also generate locked requests, which must be executed as atomic operation. The root complex must not support locked requests as a completer, in order to prevent I/O deadlock.

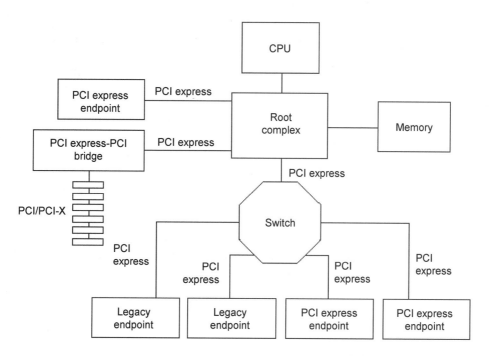

Fig. 6.20. PCI Express Fabric Topology

An *endpoint* is a device capable of initializing and/or executing PCI Express transactions on its own behalf, or on behalf of a non-PCI Express device (a USB host controller, for example). An endpoint must be visible in one of the hierarchy's domains. An endpoint must have a type 0 configuration space header (see *Section 6.1.7*) and respond as an executor to all configuration requests. All endpoints use the MSI mechanism to signal interrupts. There are two types of endpoints in the PCI Express: legacy endpoints, and endpoints built according to the PCI Express principles. Legacy endpoints are given more leeway:

❏ They are not required to support more than 4 GB addressing space.
❏ The I/O does not have to be absolutely relocatable using the base address registers (BAR), so I/O access transactions may be needed (memory access transactions are preferable).
❏ The range of occupied addresses must be no less than 128 bytes (the boundary requirements were formed rigidly in the PCI-X).

❑ The configuration space does not have to be expanded (it can remain 256 bytes).

❑ The software model may request using a locked request to the device (but not from it).

A *switch* has several PCI Express ports. In terms of logic, a switch is a set of several virtual PCI-PCI bridges that connect the switch's ports to its own internal local bus. A virtual PCI bridge is described by configuration registers with a type 1 header (see *Section 6.1.7*). The port that opens to the top of the hierarchy is called the upstream port; through it, the switch is configured as a set of PCI bridges. The switch transfers packets of all types between the ports using the address information relevant for the given type packet. The switch does not propagate locked requests from its downstream ports. The arbitration between the switch's ports can consider virtual channels and, accordingly, make fair bandwidth distribution depending on devices' demand. The switch cannot split packets into smaller parts (many PCI bridges can do analogs of this operation).

A *PCI Express-PCI bridge* connects the PCI/PCI-X bus hierarchy to the I/O fabric.

The fabric is configured using configuration mechanism 100% compatible with the PCI 2.3 or the expanded configuration space. Using virtual bridges, each PCI Express link is presented as a logical PCI bus with a unique number. Logical devices are reflected in the configuration space as PCI devices, each of which can have from one to eight functions with a set of configuration registers each.

The PCI Express architecture is divided into three layers:

❑ The *transaction layer* is the uppermost layer, responsible for assembling and disassembling of Transaction Layer Packets (TLP). These packets are used for read and write transactions, and also for signaling certain conditions. Each TLP has a unique identifier that allows a response packet be sent to its sender. Various forms of addressing are used for TLPs, depending on the transaction type. Packets can have carry coherence control disabling (No Snoop) or Relaxed Ordering attributes. Each transaction that requires an answer is split for execution (see section on PCI-X). The transaction layer is responsible for flow control, which is implemented on the basis of a credit mechanism.

❑ The *data link layer* is the middle layer in the stack. It is responsible for controlling the link, detecting errors, and organizing repeat transfers until they succeed or the link is declared to have failed. The data link layer adds packet numbers and control codes to the packets it receives from the transaction layer. The data link layer itself generates and receives Data Link Layer Packets (DLLP), which are used to control the link.

❑ The *physical layer* isolates the data link layer from all the details of signal transmission. It is made up of two parts. During transmission, the logic sub-block performs data distribution over the lines, scrambling the data, 8B/10B coding, framing, and converting them into serial code. The actions are repeated in reverse order when receiving data. Additional 8B/10B coding characters are used for control signaling. The *logic sub-block* is also responsible for negotiating the link's parameters, its initialization, etc. The *electrical sub-block* is responsible for matching electrical parameters, synchronization, receiver detection, etc. The layered model adopted in the PCI Express allows the physical layer or its sub-blocks be replaced with more effective coding and signaling schemes when such appear, without disturbing the other layers. The interface between the physical and data link layers depends on their implementation, and is decided by the manufacturer. The physical layer interface is clearly defined, and allows devices of different origin to be interconnected. The interface's transmitters and receivers are decoupled with respect to the direct current, which makes the interface matching independent on the technology used in the components' manufacturing. In order to test a PCI Express device for compliance with the electrical characteristic requirements, it is sufficient to connect it to a special tester.

The PCI Express supports differentiated classes by the quality of service (QoS), providing the following capabilities:

❑ Link resource allocation for each stream class (virtual channels)
❑ Policy configuration by QoS for individual components
❑ Specification of QoS for each packet
❑ Creation of isochronous links

To support QoS, each TLP is tagged with a three-bit *traffic class descriptor*. This allows the transferred data to be separated by types, and differentiated conditions for different classes of traffic transfers to be created. Transaction execution order is kept within class boundaries, but not in different classes. To differentiate the transfer conditions for different types of traffic, virtual channels can be created in the PCI Express switching elements. A *virtual channel* consists of physically dedicated sets of buffers and packet-routing mechanisms that are occupied only by processing the traffic of their virtual channel. When input packets are routed, arbitration is performed based on the virtual channel numbers and their priorities. Each port that supports virtual channels maps specific classes of packets onto the corresponding virtual channels. Any number of classes can be mapped to one channel. By default, all traffic is tagged as class 0 (TC0) and is sent over the default channel 0 (VC0). Virtual channels are created as required.

The main method to signal interrupts in the PCI Express is by sending messages (MSI) using 64-bit addressing (32-bit addressing is only allowed for legacy devices). However, in order to provide software compatibility, a device can emulate INTx# interrupts by sending these requests using special packets. As a rule, the interrupt controller, which is located in the root complex, receives both `MSI` and `INTx#` emulated interrupts. The `TC0` packets are used for the `INTx#` interrupt emulation signaling. When virtual channels are used, the `MSI` interrupts must employ the traffic class corresponding to the data traffic class, to which the given interrupts pertain. Otherwise, synchronization could be lost because of the relative disorder of the various classes of traffic. Synchronization can be supported by the same means as in the PCI/PCI-X: by reads (even of zero length) over the switch (bridge). Resorting to this technique is unavoidable if the interrupts belong to data of different classes (virtual channels).

Advanced Power Management and budgeting (PM) means being able to perform the following:

❏ To identify each function's PM capability
❏ To switch a function into the necessary power consumption state
❏ To obtain information about the current power consumption state of the function
❏ To generate a wake up request with the main power supply turned off
❏ To power up devices sequentially

Power management event signaling can be implemented in two ways: First, by packet emulation of the `PME#` signal (analogous to the `INTx#` signal emulation); second, by using the native PCI Express signaling using appropriate messages. When using the `PME#` emulation, the signal source is identified by sequential reading of the configuration registers of the devices capable of generating this signal. The native signaling is much more practical: The identifier of the interrupt source is contained in the message.

Devices can be hot-plugged and hot-swapped using either the existing mechanisms (PCI Hot-Plug and Hot-Swap) or the PCI Express native mechanisms, without requiring additional signals. The standard hot-plug model involves the following elements:

❏ A slot power supply indicator, which forbids insertion or extraction of the card (blinking indicates the transition process into the depowered state).
❏ An attention indicator, which signals problems with the device installed into the given slot (blinking facilitates locating the problem slot).
❏ A manually operated card latch.
❏ A manual latch status sensor, which allows the system software to detect an unlocked latch.
❏ An electromechanical blocking mechanism, preventing extraction of a card with the power on. There is no special blocking-control mechanism; if blocking is present, it must operate directly from the port's power lines.
❏ An "Attention" button to request a hot-plug connection.
❏ A software user interface for requesting a hot-plug connection.
❏ A slot numbering system allowing the required slot to be found visually.

A CRC control of all transactions and control packets is employed to provide transaction reliability and data integrity. The requester considers a transaction executed when it receives a confirmation message from the executor (only posted writes to the main memory do not require confirmations). The minimal error-handling capabilities are analogous to the PCI; the detected errors are indicated in the function's configuration registers (status register). Expanded error handling capabilities provide primary information to the advanced error isolation and recovery procedures, as well as to the error monitoring and logging procedures. Errors are divided into three categories; this allows adequate recovery procedures to be used. The categories are as follows:

❏ *Correctable errors:* automatically call the hardware recovery (repeat) procedure and do not require software intervention for a normal execution of the transaction.
❏ *Fatal errors:* require a reset for reliable resumption of operation. Some transactions having nothing to do with the error can suffer damages from this reset.
❏ *Non-fatal errors:* do not require a reset to resume operation. These errors may cause loss of only some transactions directly involved with the error.

The software model of the PCI Express is compatible with the PCI in the following aspects:

❏ PCI Express devices are detected, enumerated, and configured using the same configuration software as in the PCI (PCI-X 2.0).
❏ Existing operating systems do not need to be modified in any way.
❏ Drivers of existing devices are supported without any modifications.
❏ New PCI Express functional capabilities are configured and enabled following the general concept of PCI device configuration.

A *basic link* consists of two low-voltage differential signal pairs: transmitting and receiving. Data are transmitted using self-clocking coding, which makes high transfer speeds attainable. The basic speed is 2.5 GB of raw data (after 8B/10B coding) in each direction; higher speeds are planned in the future. Signal pairs (lanes) can be aggregated symmetrically in each direction to scale up the throughput. The specification allows the links to be configured in 1, 2, 4, 8, 12, 16, and 32 lane widths, with the transferred data distributed among them in bytes. In this way, speeds of up to 80 Gbps can be reached, which approximately corresponds to the peak speed of 8 GBps. When the hardware is initialized, the number of lanes and the transfer speed is negotiated for each link; the negotiation is conducted purely on the hardware level, without any software involvement. The negotiated link parameters remain in effect for the entire duration of the subsequent operation.

6.3.1. PCI Express Transactions and Packet Formats

All PCI Express traffic is conducted in packets. Of these, the transaction layer packets (TLP) present practical interest. Each TLP packet starts with a header, which may be followed by a data field and an optional trailer known as a digest: a 32-bit CRC. The length of all packet fields is a multiple of a double word (DW, 32 bits). The packet header contains the following mandatory fields:

❐ Fmt[1:0] — format field defining the packet type: bit 0 — header length (0 — 3 DW, 1 — 4 DW); bit 1 — data field presence (0 — no data field).

❐ Type[4:0] — type field, defining the packet (transaction) type (*Table 6.15*).

❐ TC[2:0] — traffic class field.

❐ TD — digest flag. A value of one indicates using a 32-bit CRC at the end of the packet; this CRC protects all the packet's fields, which do not change in the process of the packet's traveling via the PCI Express switches. This extra control is used for important transactions; for regular transactions, a channel level CRC control is employed.

❐ EP — error flag. Indicates that an error occurred during reading of the transferred data and the data may be invalid (poisoned data).

❐ Length[9:0] — data field length in double words: 000 ... 01 — 1; 111 ... 111 — 1,023; 000 ... 000 — 1,024.

Table 6.15. PCI Express Transaction Packets

Mnemonics	Fmt [1:0]	Type [4:0]	Function
MRd	00 01	0 0000	Memory Read Request.
MRdLk	00 01	0 0001	Memory Read Request Locked.
MWr	10 11	0 0000	Memory Write Request (with data).
IORd	00	0 0010	I/O Read Request.
IOWr	10	0 0010	I/O Write Request (with data).
CfgRd0	00	0 0100	Configuration Read Type 0.
CfgWr0	10	0 0100	Configuration Write Type 0.

continues

Table 6.15 Continued

Mnemonics	Fmt [1:0]	Type [4:0]	Function
CfgRd1	00	0 0101	Configuration Read Type 1.
CfgWr1	10	0 0101	Configuration Write Type 1.
Msg	01	1 0 *rrr*	Message Request without data. *rrr* defines the routing mechanism.
MsgD	11	1 0 *rrr*	Message Request with data payload. *rrr* defines the routing mechanism.
Cpl	00	0 1010	Completions without data. Used in response to IOWr and CfgWr, and also with any non-locked read completion with an error.
CplD	10	0 1010	Completion with data. Used in response to read requests.
CplLk	00	0 1011	Completion for Locked Memory Read without data.
CplDLk	10	0 1011	Completion for Locked Memory Read.

A *transaction identifier* is the identifier of the requester combined with an 8-bit tag; a *transaction descriptor* contains transaction attributes (RO and NS), as well as the traffic class TC. The tag is used only for transactions requiring packet completion. By default, the requester can hold uncompleted up to 32 transactions, so only five of the tag's 8 bits are used. However, the tag can be enabled into the expanded mode, in which all 8 bits are used (up to 256 uncompleted requests).

Depending on the transaction type, different address and routing formats are used in packets. The address is set accurate within an aligned double word (bits [1:0]=00). For all data-carrying transactions (except messages), one of the header's bytes carries bits that enable bytes in the first and the last double words of the data field (all bytes in between are assumed to be enabled). Consequently, a packet can carry an arbitrary number of adjacent bytes starting from an arbitrary address.

Memory transactions can use either short (32-bits) or long (64-bits) addresses. The combined transaction address and length must not cause the transaction to cross the 4 KB page boundaries. Memory write transactions are executed as posted writes, and do not require confirmations.

I/O transactions have been left in the PCI Express for reasons of compatibility with the PCI/PCI-X and old software, but it is planned to abolish them. A 32-bit address is used in these transactions, and only one double word of data is transferred.

Configuration transactions are addressed and routed using the device identifier; these transactions use 32-bit addressing, and transfer only one double word of data. The format of the device identifier is the same as used in the PCI: an 8-bit bus number field, a 5-bit device number field, and a 3-bit function number field.

Message transactions are routed depending on the value of the *rrr* field: 000 — toward the root complex; 001 — by address; 010 — by identifier; 011 — broadcast from the root complex; 100 — local message (comes no further than the receiver); 101 — assembled and routed toward the root complex. One byte in the message is given over to the message code; some messages do not use the data field. Messages with *rrr*=100 only change the receiver status (this way, for example, virtual INTx# wires are implemented). Messages with *rrr*=101 are used for one of the power management message types: A switch forwards this message to the upstream port only if it receives this type of message from all downstream ports. Message are used to emulate wire interrupts, signal power management events and errors, and also for interdevice communications.

To emulate INTx# interrupts (four virtual wires), eight message codes are employed (four for setting and four for clearing each signal). The switches (and the root complex) must monitor the status of the virtual wires on each of the downstream ports, considering message arrivals from the corresponding devices (the PCI-specific cyclic INTx# line alternation is preserved). According to these statuses, the status of the virtual wires of the upstream port is generated using an OR function, and corresponding messages are generated upon changes in the virtual wires' status changes. The root complex performs an analogous task, and conveys the virtual signal to the real interrupt controller. In this way, message packets make it possible to "connect" the logical INTx# wires of devices on all logical buses.

6.3.2. Packet Transfer and Connection Bandwidth

TLPs, which are used to perform transactions, arrive to the data link layer. The main task of the data link layer is to provide reliable delivery of TLPs. For this purpose, the data link layer frames a TLP with its header consisting of a 12-bit serial TLP number and a 32-bit LCRC field (link level CRC). Consequently, the data link level adds 6 bytes of overhead to each TLP. To each TLP, the receiver must receive a positive acknowledgement: a data link layer packet (DLLP) named Ack. If there is no acknowledgement, the timeout mechanism forces the transmitter to resend the packet. A negative acknowledgment mechanism is also provided for; it causes a repeat transfer without the timeout wait.

DLLPs are 6 bytes long: the information part is four bytes long and the CRC is 16 bits (two bytes) long. Besides confirming TLPs, DLLPs are used for flow control, and also to control the link's power consumption.

The physical layer adds its framing to the transferred packets: A special STP (for a TLP) or SDP (for a DLLP) code is sent in front of each packet. Each packet is terminated by an END code. These special codes are different from the codes representing 8B/10B encoded data.

The packet structure having been considered, the useful bandwidth of a basic PCI Express link can be evaluated (1 bit wide, 2.5 Gbps overall bandwidth). The shortest transaction — a double word I/O write — will be considered. The corresponding TLP is 4 double words long (three for the header and one for the data), or 16 bytes; the data link layer adds six more bytes to it, so 22 bytes arrive for 8B/10B coding. The physical layer adds two bytes of its framing to them, bringing the total to 24. 240 bits (24×10) will be sent into the line, which at 2.5 Gbps will take 96 nsec of the forward channel time to transmit. I/O port write transactions require an acknowledgement: an oncoming three-DW (12-byte) TLP that, after the data link and physical layers add their framings, will expand to 20 bytes and to 200 bits after going through the 8B/10B encoding. These will take 80 nsec of the reverse channel time to transmit. Now the data link layer acknowledgements of each TLP — the 6-byte Ack — need to be added, which with the 2-byte physical layer framing turn into 8 bytes, and after the 8B/10B encoding into 80 bits. These will take 32 nsec in each channel. Altogether, an I/O port write transaction takes $96 + 32 = 128$ nsec (0.128 msec) in the forward channel, and $80 + 32 = 112$ nsec in the reverse. The maximum transfer speed of continuous port writes is $V = 4/0.128 = 31.25$ MBps. The reverse channel is also occupied with a load factor of 112/128=0.875. The useful data transfer speed results are similar to the standard PCI bus (32 bits, 33 MHz) capabilities, which takes four bus cycles to execute this type of transaction. A PCI Express I/O read transaction produces the same results (the PCI results will be worse because of the extra clock needed for the turnaround).

Now, the most favorable type of transaction for efficiency comparison purposes will be considered: writing a packet of 1,024 double words into the memory (using the 32-bit addressing). Only one TLP is needed for this (a completing transaction is not required). The length of the packet is 3DW + 1,024DW = 4,108 bytes. The data link and physical layers add $6 + 2 = 8$ bytes to this number producing 4,116 bytes, which after going through 8B/10B encoding grows to 41,160 bits or 16.5 mcs of transmission time. The data transfer speed is $4,046/16.5 \approx 248$ MBps: the PCI (32 bits/66 MHz) efficiency level at long burst transfers. The loading of the reverse channel by the data link layer acknowledgements is negligibly small in this case. The speed of reading from the memory is somewhat lower, because each read transaction consists of two TLPs: a read request (three or four DWs) and a completion packet with the data (2 + N) DWs long. With a large packet length, the proportion of the additional three double words is small.

If the reverse channel were fully loaded with useful traffic, then the PCI Express bandwidth could be considered doubled thanks to the full-duplex operation capability. However, no such doubling is possible in the I/O port write example, because the reverse channel is loaded rather heavily with the acknowledgements. Calculating the useful speed per one signal connector contact, a speed of $248 \times 2/4 = 124$ MBps per contact is obtained in the most favorable full-duplex operation mode. For the purposes of comparison, the PCI-X533 can be considered. It provides peak write speed approaching $533 \times 4 = 2,132$ MBps. Its results of memory read operations are much more modest: The peak speed is only 533 MBps. With about 50 signal contacts employed (not counting many ground lines), this gives about 10–40 MBps per contact. The AGP uses even more lines to produce the same peak speed, so the claims of high contact efficiency for the PCI Express are based on solid ground. Neither the PCI/PCI-X nor the AGP can provide full duplex operation.

The above calculations are for a basic link; by increasing the width to 32 bits, a maximum memory write speed of $248 \times 32 = 7,936$ MBps can be obtained. And if the total load of a full duplex link is considered, the PCI Express can provide a total bandwidth potential of 15,872 MBps. Therefore, in its most efficient version, the PCI Express leaves the AGP with its 2,132 MBps peak speed far behind. However, a low contact count cannot be talked about here: A 32x PCI Express link requires $2 \times 2 \times 32 = 128$ signal contacts (the AGP has fewer).

6.4. LPC Interface

The Low Pin Count (LPC) interface is employed to connect local devices — FDD controllers, serial and parallel ports, keyboards, audio codecs, BIOS, etc. — that were previously connected via the X-Bus or ISA bus. The new interface has been introduced to replace the clumsy asynchronous ISA bus, with its numerous signals, which is rapidly becoming obsolete if it is not already. The interface provides the same access cycles as the ISA: memory and I/O read and write, DMA, and bus mastering. Devices can generate interrupt requests. Unlike the 24-bit address ISA/X-Bus buses, which allow only the lower 16 MB memory to be addressed, the LPC interface has 32-bit memory addressing, which provides access to 4 GB of memory. Employing 16-bit port addressing provides access to 64 KB of port addressing space. The interface is synchronized with the PCI bus, but devices can issue an unlimited number of wait cycles. The interface is software-transparent — like for the ISA/X-Bus — and does not require any drivers. The controller of the LPC interface is a PCI bridge device. The interface's bandwidth is practically the same as that of ISA buses. The LPC 1.0 specification provides bandwidth calculations of the interface and devices that use it. With FIFO buffers, the interface can be used most efficiently in the DMA mode. In this case, the main user is the LPT port: At a transfer rate of 2 MBps, it will take 47% of the bandwidth. Next comes the infrared port: 4 Mbps(11.4%). The rest of the devices (FDD controller, COM ports, audiocodecs) need even smaller shares; as a result, they take up to 75% of the bandwidth if they are all working together. Consequently, switching these devices from the ISA/X-Bus to the LPC should not cause bigger bandwidth-use problems than those in the older buses.

The interface has only seven mandatory signals:

❒ LAD[3:0] — bidirectional multiplexed data bus
❒ LFRAME# —host-controlled indicator of the beginning and the end of cycle
❒ LRESET# — reset signal, the same as the RST# signal on the PCI bus
❒ LCLK — synchronization signal (33 MHz), the same as the CLK signal on the PCI bus

Supplementary LPC interface signals are as follows:

❒ LDRQ# — Encoded DMA/Bus Master request from peripheral devices.
❒ SERIRQ — serially encoded interrupt request line. Used if there are no standard ISA-style interrupt request lines.
❒ CLKRUN# —used to halt the bus (in mobile systems). Required only for devices that need DMA or Bus mastering in systems capable of halting the PCI bus.
❒ PME# — Power Management Event. May be activated by peripheral devices, as in the PCI.
❒ LPCPD# — Power Down. Used by the host to indicate peripherals to prepare for the power cut-off.
❒ LSMI# — an SMI# interrupt request to repeat an I/O instruction.

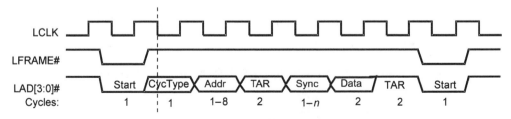

Fig. 6.21. LPC protocol

The LFRAME# and LAD[3:0] signals are synchronized by the front of the LCLK signal. During each clock tick of the exchange cycle, fields of the protocol elements are sent over the LAD[3:0] bus. A general timing diagram of the LPC exchange cycle is shown in Fig. 6.21. The host starts each exchange cycle by asserting the LFRAME# line, and placing the START field on the LAD[3:0] lines. Upon the LFRAME# signal, all peripheral devices must release the LAD[3:0] bus; the START field indicates that a bus cycle is to follow. In the next clock cycle, the host deasserts the FRAME# signal, and places the exchange-cycle-type code CYCTYPE on the LAD[3:0] bus. The LFRAME# signal may remain asserted longer than one clock cycle, but the exchange cycle starts (START field is considered valid) at the last clock cycle, in which the LFRAME# signal is asserted.

The host uses the LFRAME# signal to abort the exchange cycle (in case of a time-out error, for example) by placing corresponding code on the AD[3:0] lines.

The START field can have the following codes:

- ❐ 0000 — start of a device addressing by the host cycle
- ❐ 0010 — granting access for master device 0
- ❐ 0011— granting access for master device 1
- ❐ 1111 — forced cycle termination (abort)

The rest of the codes are reserved.

The CYCTYPE field sets the type and direction of the transfer. Bit 0 sets the direction: 0 — read, 1 — write. Bits [2:1] set the access type: 00 — I/O, 01 — memory, 10 — DMA, 11 — reserved. Bit 3 is reserved and is set to 0.

The TAR (Turn ARound) field is used to change the "owner" of the LAD[3:0] bus; it takes two clock ticks to complete. In the first clock tick, the previous owner places the 1111 code on the LAD[3:0] lines; in the second, it switches the buffers into the high-impedance state.

The ADDR field is used to send the address. In the memory cycle, it takes 8 clock ticks (32 bits); in the I/O cycle, it takes 4 clock ticks. The upper bits are transmitted first (to get the address decoder working earlier).

Data are sent in the DATA field. Sending each byte requires 2 clock ticks; the lower nibble is sent first. In multiple byte transmissions, the lower byte is sent first.

The SYNC field is used by the addressed device to add wait states. It may contain the following codes:

- ❐ 0000 — ready (without errors). For DMA, indicates request deassertion for the given channel.
- ❐ 0101 — short wait (a few clocks).
- ❐ 0110 — long wait.
- ❐ 1001 — ready and a DMA channel request is present (not allowed for other types of access).
- ❐ 1010 — error: Data have been transmitted but conditions have arisen that would generate the SERR# or IOCHK# signals on the PCI or ISA buses (for DMA, also means the request signal deassertion).

The rest of the codes are reserved.

The synchronization field controls the transmission, wait-cycle introduction, and time-out mechanism. Having begun the cycle, the host reads the synchronization field. If the device being addressed does not answer within three clocks, the host considers that there is no such device on the bus and terminates the transaction. If the host receives a short wait code, it waits until the code changes to the ready or error signal, but after 8 clocks it will terminate the transaction on a time-out. There is no time-out limit for the long wait code; it is the addressed device's responsibility not to hang the bus. When the host controls the SYNC, the target device must wait as long as needed until the host is ready without asserting any time-outs. In the fastest execution, the SYNC field takes one clock cycle.

Fig. 6.22 shows the sequence of cycles for the *host to access memory* or I/O (fields supplied by the device are marked in gray). In all of these accesses, 1 byte is sent. A memory read, assuming 5 SYNC field clocks and EPROM access of 120 nsec, will require 21 clocks (0.63 μsec), which gives a memory bandwidth of 1.59 MBps. If the memory is pipelined, then the following accesses will be executed faster. For a memory write, the SYNC field takes 1 clock and the entire cycle will take 17 clock ticks (0.51 μsec), giving a memory-write throughput of 1.96 MBps. hen addressing I/O, the addressing is shorter; there is one SYNC clock and no wait clocks. Consequently, these cycles take 13 clock ticks to execute (0.39 μsec), giving an I/O read/write throughput of 2.56 MBps.

a	START	CYCTYPE	ADDR	TAR	SYNC	DATA	TAR

b	START	CYCTYPE	ADDR	DATA	TAR	SYNC	TAR

Fig. 6.22. Memory and I/O access: *a* — read, *b* — write

To set up DMA exchange and bus mastering, the host must have one LDRQ# input line for each connected device that uses these functions. Over this line, the device sends serially encoded information about the status of DMA channel requests (Fig. 6.23.) Transmission of a packet begins with sending the start bit, followed by the channel number code and the request bit ACT: 1 (high level) means the request is active, 0 means the request is passive. Channel 4 code (100) is reserved for bus-mastering requests, and corresponds to the traditionally unavailable DMA channel. A packet is sent every time the request-status changes. Usually, a request is only asserted this way; deassertion of a request is signaled by the SYNC field.

The execution of DMA data transfer (Fig. 6.24) is controlled by the host, but it differs somewhat from the regular memory and I/O accesses. Here, new fields have been introduced:

❏ The SIZE field defines the length of the transmission. Code 0000 means 1 byte, code 0001 means 2 bytes, code 0011 means 4 bytes. The rest of the codes are reserved.

❏ The CHANNEL field is used by the host to send the DMA channel number — bits [2:0] — and the end of cycle indicator — TC, bit 3.

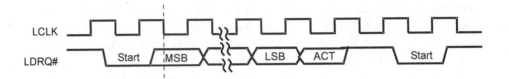

Fig. 6.23. Sending a DMA or bus mastering request

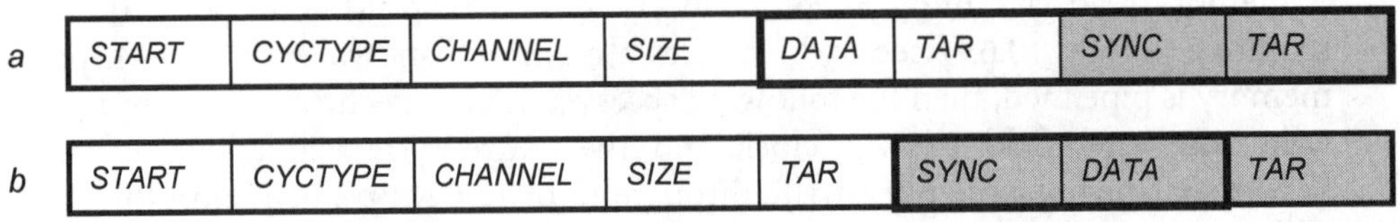

a | START | CYCTYPE | CHANNEL | SIZE | DATA | TAR | SYNC | TAR |

b | START | CYCTYPE | CHANNEL | SIZE | TAR | SYNC | DATA | TAR |

Fig. 6.24. DMA access: *a* — reading, *b* — writing

The length of memory access cycles may be 1, 2, or 4 bytes long. There are no wait states, as they are concealed by the DMA controller. Depending on the length of access, memory read cycles take 11, 18, or 32 clock ticks (0.33, 0.54, or 0.96 μsec). This gives bus bandwidths of 3.03 MBps, 3.7 MBps, or 4.17 MBps, respectively. Write cycles take 11, 14, or 20 clock ticks (0.33, 0.42, or 0.60 μsec), giving throughputs of 3.03 MBps, 4.76 MBps, or 6.67 MBps, respectively. The field sequence that is repeated when transmitting 2 or 4 bytes is outlined in bold.

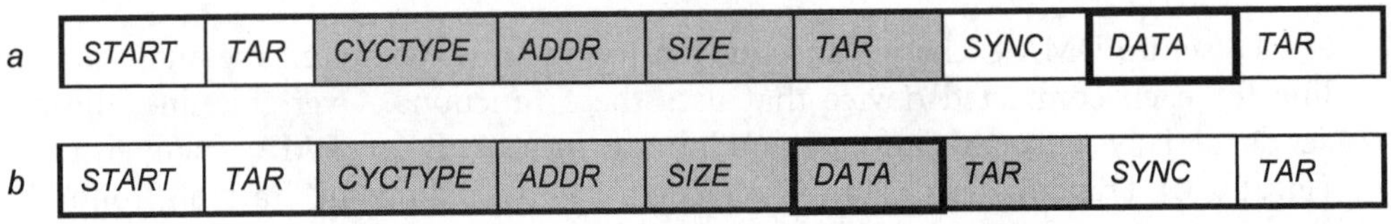

a | START | TAR | CYCTYPE | ADDR | SIZE | TAR | SYNC | DATA | TAR |

b | START | TAR | CYCTYPE | ADDR | SIZE | DATA | TAR | SYNC | TAR |

Fig. 6.25. A bus master access by a peripheral device:
a — memory or I/O read, *b* — memory or I/O write

A master device requests *bus-master access* the same way as direct memory access, but indicating the reserved channel number 4 (100). In granting access, the host in the START field sets the number of the master that will later establish the type of the cycle (Fig. 6.25.) Bus mastering implies access to the resources of the host — system memory, PCI device, etc. Data follow each other without interruption in 2- and 4-byte packets. However, there always will be wait states in the memory and I/O read cycles because of the extra time required to arbitrate for the PCI bus or access memory controller. Assuming the SYNC field is six clock ticks long (it is unlikely it can be shorter; it is more possible it may be longer), memory access cycles (read as well as write) will require 25, 27, or 31 clock ticks (0.75, 0.81, or 0.93 μsec), giving a throughput of 1.33 MBps,

2.47 MBps, or 4.30 MBps, respectively. Because port addressing is shorter, their accessing is shorter too: 21, 23, or 27 clock ticks (0.63, 0.69, or 0.81 μsec), with throughputs of 1.59 MBps, 2.90 MBps, or 4.94 MBps, respectively.

The electrical interface for the LAD[3:0], LFRAME#, LDRQ#, and SERIRQ signals corresponds to the PCI 2.1 specification for the 3.3 V version. Depending on the motherboard, the other signals may be either 5 V or 3.3 V.

Configuring LPC devices does not require using PCI or ISA plug-and-play protocols, as the system BIOS knows all the LPC devices a priori. To access an LPC device, the host must decode its address, and redirect accesses to this address to the LPC controller.

6.5. Notebook PC Expansion Buses and Cards

Originally, portable and notebook PCs were built without any attempts to standardize or provide component compatibility. The situation has changed over time, however, and today there are several interfaces and form factors for expansion devices. The most popular are listed in Table 6.16.

Table 6.16. Form Factors and Interfaces of Portable PC Peripheral Devices

	PC Card	Small PC Card
Length	85.6 mm	45.0 mm
Width	54.0 mm	42.8 mm
Height	3.3/5.0/10.5 mm	3.3/5.0/10.5 mm
Connector type	Pins	Pins
Number of contacts	68	68
Interfaces	Memory, I/O/ CardBus	Memory, I/O

The first standard for expansion cards was PCMCIA, which was later renamed PC Card. In addition to expansion bus slots, notebook and pocket PCs may have slots for connecting memory cards (see *Section 8.3*).

A desktop PC can be equipped with PC Card slots using a special adapter-bridge card that is installed into a PCI or ISA slot. The slots themselves (one or two) are enclosed into a 3" case and mounted into the PC's front panel. Bridge card is connected to this case via a ribbon cable.

6.5.1. PCMCIA, PC Card, and CardBus Interfaces

At the beginning of 1990s, the Personal Computer Memory Card International Association (PCMCIA) began work on standardizing notebook-computer expansion buses, with primary emphasis on memory expansion buses. The first to appear, in June 1990, was the PCMCIA Standard Release 1.0/JEIDA 4.0 standard. This standard described a 68-contact interface and two form factor types: Type I and Type II PC Card. At first, the standard applied only to the electrical and physical requirements of memory cards. The Card Information Structure (CIS) metaformat, which described card's characteristics and capabilities and was the key element in providing for cards' interchangeability and the plug-and-play mechanism, was also introduced.

The next version, PCMCIA 2.0, which was released in 1991, defined an I/O operation interface, dual power supplies for memory cards, and testing methods. The specifications for the connector were left unchanged. Version 2.01 added the PC Card ATA specification, a new form factor, Type III, the Auto-Indexing Mass Storage (AIMS) specification, and the initial version of the Card Services Specification (CSS). Version 2.1, which came out in 1994, expanded the Card and Socket Services Specification (CSSS) and developed the Card Information Structure.

The PC Card standard, adopted in 1995, is the continuation of the previous standards. This standard introduced additional requirements directed at improving compatibility, as well as new capabilities, including a 3.3 V power supply, DMA, and 32-bit CardBus bus mastering. Later, specifications of other additional capabilities were added to the standard.

All PCMCIA and PC Card cards have a 68-contact connector. The functions of its contacts vary depending on the type of the interface card. The type of interface is "ordered" by the card when it is installed into the slot, which, naturally, must support the required interface. The *memory interface* provides 8- and 16-bit accesses with a minimal cycle time of 100 nsec, giving a maximum throughput of 10 MBps and 20 MBps, respectively. The I/O interface has a 255-nsec minimum cycle length, which corresponds to 3.92 MBps and 7.84 MBps throughputs for the 8- and 16-bit accesses, respectively. The *CardBus interface* supports practically the same exchange protocol as the PCI, but is somewhat simplified. Its 33 MHz clock and 32-bit data bus provide peak bandwidth of up to 132 MBps in the burst cycle. Cards have bus-mastering capability. They use the same automatic configuring system as the PCI (using the configuration space registers). The interface has supplementary capabilities incorporated to transfer digital audio signal, which can be done using both the traditional pulse-code modulation (PCM) and the new pulse-width modulation (PWM), which is actually a revival of a forgotten old method.

There is a special interface specification for PC Card ATA disk devices.

There are four different PC Card varieties: Known as types, they all have the same height and width — 54 mm × 85.5 mm — but different thickness. Thinner adapters fit into slots for thicker cards. The four types are as follows:

❏   PC Card Type I — 3.3 mm — memory cards
❏   PC Card Type II — 5 mm — I/O device cards, modems, LAN adapters

❏ PC Card Type III — 10.5 mm — disk storage devices

❏ PC Card Type IV — 16 mm (no mention of this type could be found at the time of writing on the site **www.pc-card.com**)

There are also compact Small PC Card cards. These are 45 mm long by 42.8 mm wide, but have the same connector and thickness as the standard cards.

PCMCIA also maintains the Miniature Card standard (see *Section 9.3.4*) for memory cards (dynamic, static, ROM, and flash EPROM).

The functions of the connector contacts for different types of the interface are given in Table 6.17. The functions of the signals for memory and I/O interface cards are given in Table 6.18. Signal names for CardBus card are prefixed by letter C, which is followed by the PCI bus signal name. (See *Section 6.2.2*.)

Table 6.17. PC Card Connector

Pin #	Interface type			Pin #	Interface type		
	16-bit		32-bits CardBus		16-bit		32-bit CardBus
	Mem	I/O+Mem			Mem	I/O+Mem	
1	GND	GND	GND	35	GND	GND	GND
2	D3	D3	CAD0	36	CD1#	CD1#	CCD1#
3	D4	D4	CAD1	37	D11	D11	CAD2
4	D5	D5	CAD3	38	D12	D12	CAD4
5	D6	D6	CAD5	39	D13	D13	CAD6
6	D7	D7	CAD7	40	D14	D14	Reserved
7	CE1#	CE1#	CCBE0#	41	D15	D15	CAD8
8	A10	A10	CAD9	42	CE2#	CE2#	CAD10
9	OE#	OE#	CAD11	43	VS1#	VS1#	CVS1
10	A11	A11	CAD12	44	Reserved	IORD#	CAD13
11	A9	A9	CAD14	45	Reserved	IOWR#	CAD15
12	A8	A8	CCBE1#	46	A17	A17	CAD16
13	A13	A13	CPAR	47	A18	A18	Reserved
14	A14	A14	CPERR#	48	A19	A19	CBLOCK#
15	WE#	WE#	CGNT#	49	A20	A20	CSTOP#
16	READY	IREQ#	CINT#	50	A21	A21	CDEVSEL#

continues

Table 6.17 Continued

Pin #	Interface type			Pin #	Interface type		
	16-bit		32-bits CardBus		16-bit		32-bit CardBus
	Mem	I/O+Mem			Mem	I/O+Mem	
17	Vcc	Vcc	Vcc	51	Vcc	Vcc	Vcc
18	Vpp1	Vpp1	Vpp1	52	Vpp2	Vpp2	Vpp2
19	A16	A16	CCLK	53	A22	A22	CTRDY#
20	A15	A15	CIRDY#	54	A23	A23	CFRAME#
21	A12	A12	CCBE2#	55	A24	A24	CAD17
22	A7	A7	CAD18	56	A25	A25	CAD19
23	A6	A6	CAD20	57	VS2#	VS2#	CVS2
24	A5	A5	CAD21	58	RESET	RESET	CRST#
25	A4	A4	CAD22	59	WAIT#	WAIT#	CSERR#
26	A3	A3	CAD23	60	Reserved	INPACK#	CREQ#
27	A2	A2	CAD24	61	REG#	REG#	CCBE3#
28	A1	A1	CAD25	62	BVD2	SPKR#	CAUDIO
29	A0	A0	CAD26	63	BVD1	STSCHG#	CSTSCHG
30	D0	D0	CAD27	64	D8	D8	CAD28
31	D1	D1	CAD29	65	D9	D9	CAD30
32	D2	D2	Reserved	66	D10	D10	CAD31
33	WP	IOIS16#	CCLKRUN#	67	CD2#	CD2#	CCD2#
34	GND	GND	GND	68	GND	GND	GND

Table 6.18. Signal Functions of Memory and I/O Cards

Signal	I/O	Function
A[10:0]	I	Address bus lines.
BVD1, BVD2	I/O	Battery Volt Detection
STSCHG#	I/O	(IO) Signals to the host of the change in the RDY/BSY# and Write Protect signals. This signal is controlled by the Card Config and Status Register.

continues

Table 6.18 Continued

Signal	I/O	Function
SPKR#	O	(IO) Digital audio output (to loudspeaker).
CD1#, CD2#	O	Card Detect. Connected to the ground on the card. Used by the host to detect whether the card is completely inserted.
CE1#, CE2#	I	(IO, Mem) Card Enable and determining transmission width. The CE2# signal always pertains to the odd byte. Depending on the state of the A0 and CE2# signals, the CE#1 signal can pertain to either even or odd byte. Using these bytes an 8-bit host can conduct exchange with 16-bit cards over the D[7:0] lines.
D[15:0]	I/O	Data bus (8-bit signals do not use D[15:8] bits).
INPACK#	O	(IO) Input Acknowledge. Card's response to the IORD# signal by which the host opens its data buffers.
IORD#	I	I/O read command strobe.
IOWR#	I	I/O write command strobe (data must be latched at the rising clock edge).
OE#	I	Reading memory, configuration registers, and the CIS.
RDY/BSY#	I	High level indicates card's readiness to exchange data.
IREQ#	O	Low level indicates an interrupt request.
INTRQ	O	High level indicates an interrupt request.
REG#	I	Attribute memory select (Mem). For IO cards, the signal must be active in the I/O command cycles. In the IDE mode, the signal is inactive (connected to the Vcc on the host's side).
RESET	I	Reset (by high level).
VS1#, VS2#	O	Voltage Sense. Grounded VS1# indicates that card can read at 3.3 V power supply.
WAIT#	O	Request (by low level) to extend the access cycle.
WE#	I	Memory and configuration register write strobe (it is not used in the IDE mode and is connected by the host to Vcc).

continues

Table 6.18 Continued

Signal	I/O	Function
WP	O	Write Protect (for memory cards). Memory writing is enabled when low.
IOCS16#	O	16-bit exchange enable.

The interface of the memory and I/O cards is simple — practically the same as the asynchronous static memory interface. The card is selected by the CE# signal, which is asserted simultaneously with the address. The memory and configuration registers are read by the OE# signal; they are written to by the WE# signal. The REG# signal, activated simultaneously with the CE# signal and the address, differentiates between memory accesses and accesses to configuration registers. Separate IORD# and IOWR# signals, acting in tandem with an active REG# signal, are used to access I/O ports. During port accessing, the card can indicate if it is capable of 16-bit access by asserting the IOSC16# signal (as in the ISA bus). A device must acknowledge port reading by the INPACK# signal, which it asserts and deasserts on the CE# signal. This signal allows the host to be certain that it is not reading an empty slot.

PC Card slots may also provide DMA capability. Implementing DMA is the most cost-effective way to unload the CPU, but only simple ISA-bus-based hosts possess this capability. For PCI-bus systems, bus mastering of the CardBus is more usual. However, implementing bus mastering in cards is not a cheap option.

Multimedia cards can switch into the special Zoomed Video Port mode. In this mode, a separate two-point data transfer interface between the card and the host system is set up. Conceptually, the interface is similar to the VESA Feature Connector (VFC) for graphics cards: It has a dedicated bus for transferring video data that is not connected with other buses (and does not load them), but uses a different protocol. In the Zoomed Video Port mode, the A[25:4] address lines and the BVD2/SPKP#, INPACK#, and IOIS16# lines are assigned different functions, and used to send video data and four digital audio channels. There are only four address lines left for the regular interface, which makes it possible to address 16 bytes of system memory and card attributes.

The Zoomed Video Port interface matches the CCIR601 timing diagrams, which allows the NTSC decoder to deliver video data from the card into the VGA display buffer in real time. The card may receive video data from either an external video input or an MPEG decoder.

Cards have specially designated attribute memory space, in which the card's configuration and control registers used for auto-configuration are located. The standard describes the Card Information Structure (CIS) format. Cards may be multifunctional (a modem/network adapter combination, for example). The Multiple Function PC Cards (MFPC) specification provides separate configuration registers and defines the interrupt request line-sharing rules for each function.

For external memory devices, the standard describes MS-DOS FAT-compatible data-storage formats and also formats oriented to flash memory as the main information-carrying medium. For direct execution of the programs stored in the card's memory, there is the eXecute In Place (XIP) specification. This describes the software interface for executing these programs without loading them into the main system memory.

The standard describes the software-implemented *Card Services interface*, which standardizes interaction between its clients (drivers, application software, and utilities) with devices. There also is the *Socket Services interface*, which is used to detect cards' connections and disconnections, identify them, and to configure the power supplies and the hardware interface.

There are two extensions of the standard, specific to the two groups that maintain the PC Card standard.

❏ PCMCIA describes Auto-Indexed Mass Storage (AIMS), which is used for storing large volumes of data, such as images or multimedia data on block-oriented mass storage devices. It also contains specifications for a 15-pin shielded connector for modem I/O and LAN adapters. Another connector described is a 7-pin Modem I/O connector.

❏ The JEIDA extension contains the Small Block Flash Format specification that simplifies the file structure of flash memory cards. The Still Image, Sound, and Related Information Format (SISRIF) is directed at recording images and sound to memory cards. There also is a specification for DRAM-Type memory cards.

Most of the adapters support plug-and-play technology, and can be hot-swapped: installed and taken out without turning off the computer. For this, the card's power line contacts are longer than the rest and, therefore, are connected first and disconnect last. Two card-presence-detection contacts — CD1# and CD2# (Card Detect) — are shorter than the rest. When they connect with the slot's contacts, it signals to the host that the card has been completely inserted into the slot. Even though cards can be dynamically configured, sometimes it is necessary to reboot the system after changing configuration.

Initially, cards and host-systems used +5 V signaling voltage. With the addition of low-voltage signaling (+3.3 V), a mechanical key preventing the insertion of a 3.3 V card into a 5 V slot was introduced. Additionally, contacts 43 (VS1#) and 47 (VS2#) were defined for power-supply voltage selection. On the 5 V cards, they are not connected; on the 3.3 V cards, the VS1# contact is grounded and the VS2# contact is unconnected. A host that allows both power-supply voltages uses these lines to determine the installed card's requirements, and provides the appropriate voltage. If the host cannot provide the necessary voltage, it must not provide any and issue a connection error message instead. Cards usually support Advanced Power Management (APM), which is an important feature for battery-operated computers.

A diverse range of devices — including memory, storage devices, communications devices, interface ports, game adapters, multimedia devices, and so on — are produced under the PC Card standard. However, they are all significantly more expensive than their full-size counterparts. Via the PC Card slot, portable computers can be connected to dock stations that can be equipped with standard peripheral equipment. However, manufacturers not adhering strictly enough to the standard sometimes causes compatibility problems.

PC Card slots are connected to a portable PC system bus via a bridge. This will be the PCI-PC Card bridge for computers with an internal PCI bus. Notebook PCs may also have Small PCI slots (SPCI), but they are not accessible without opening the case, and do not allow devices to be hot-swapped.

Chapter 7: Specialized Interfaces for Peripheral Devices

This chapter describes the interfaces for connecting peripheral devices, from the most essential (e.g., keyboard, monitor, mouse, and printer) and multimedia (video and audio devices) to those used for entertainment purposes (the joystick and its relatives).

7.1. Keyboard Interface

A traditional PC keyboard is a standardized input device that has a standard connector and serial communication interface with the motherboard. Currently, so-called *enhanced AT* or *PS/2 keyboards*, which have over 100 keys, are used. They have supplanted the first AT keyboards, not to mention XT keyboards. XT and AT keyboards have interfaces that are electrically identical, except that the AT's is bidirectional, which allows commands to be received from the motherboard. However, the keyboards are incompatible in terms of the logical interface (sometimes, an AT keyboard has an XT/AT mode switch). The PS/2 keyboard differs from the AT keyboard only in its connector; an adapter may be used to connect a PS/2 keyboard to an AT connector.

All keyboards have an embedded microcontroller that registers the keys being pressed and released; moreover, the next key is registered even if several keys pressed previously have not been released. When a key is pressed, the keyboard sends a *scan code*, which identifies the location of the key, to its controller. When a key is released, the keyboard sends this key's scan code that indicates the releasing. After a key has been pressed for a certain period of time, the keyboard starts autorepeating the scan code of this key. The delay between the key is pressed and the autorepeat starts is called the *typematic delay*; the rate at which the scan code of the pressed key is autore-peated is called the *typematic rate*; both can be programmed in AT keyboards. The expanded keyboard has three sets of scan codes, one of which can be active.

As the USB bus has become more widely used, keyboards using this interface have appeared; they also have a built-in hub to connect, for example, a mouse. The USB keyboard is powered from the bus. The USB keyboard needs support from BIOS of a motherboard; modern motherboards provide this function.

7.1.1. AT and PS/2 Keyboard Interfaces

Keyboards are connected using a serial synchronous bidirectional interface that consists of two mandatory signals: `KB-Data` and `KB-Clock`. Both lines are pulled by resistors to the +5 V rail on the motherboard bus. The low level of output signals is formed at the both ends of the interface by open-collector (drain) type gates; the lines' status can be examined via the controllers' input lines. Keyboard connectors on a PC's back panel and their pinouts are shown in Fig. 7.1. There are two versions of the physical connector: the regular 5-contact DIN socket for the AT keyboard, and the mini-DIN socket for PS/2. The keyboard's +5 V power supply is routed to this connector via a fuse. The mini-DIN connector may also have PS/2 mouse signals (for built-in trackballs).

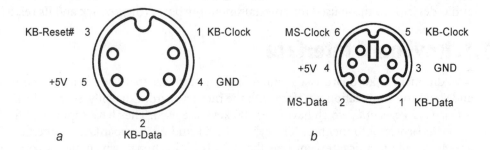

Fig. 7.1. Connectors for connecting keyboards:
a — AT and *b* — PS/2 (view from the front)

CAUTION

Devices like external data storage devices or LAN adapters that are connected to the parallel port often use the keyboard connector power supply line. The fuse installed on the motherboard may not be able to handle the current surge generated by these devices. This will also disable the keyboard: its indicators will not even blink when the system is powered up.

The processor communicates with the keyboard through the *keyboard interface controller* — an 8042 microcontroller (or one that is software-compatible with it) installed on the motherboard. Information exchange is conducted mainly through port 60h, from which scan codes are received. The controller alerts the processors of the necessity to read a scan code via the IRQ1 hardware interrupt. This interrupt is generated every time a keyboard event happens (i.e., a key is pressed or released). Commands sent to this port also set the typematic delay and rate, select scan code tables, control the keyboard's LED indicators, manage key matrix scanning, and perform diagnostic tests. The controller translates commands into code messages and sends them to the keyboard.

Fig. 7.2, *a* illustrates how a bidirectional interface works; signals generated by the controller are shown in gray; those generated by the keyboard are shown in black. In the initial state, both lines are held in the high-level state by the output gate circuits. The keyboard can begin sending data at any moment when the interface is idle. The keyboard places a start bit (low level) on the KB-Data line, and by issuing the first KB-Clock impulse notifies the controller that it must begin receiving data. After the KB-Clock goes high, the keyboard places data bit 0 on the KB-Data line, followed by the next KB-Clock pulse. The controller must latch the received data bit at the fall of the KB-Clock. In this way, all 8 data bits and the odd parity bit are sent. After it latches the parity bit, the *keyboard controller* must generate a KB-Clock impulse (Ack) acknowledging the recept of the byte. If the controller does not receive the byte, including the parity bit, within 2 msec, it stops receiving the current byte and records a time-out error.

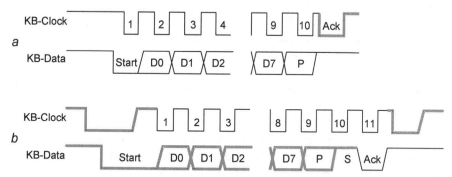

Fig. 7.2. Keyboard interface timing diagrams: *a* — receiving a scan code message from the keyboard; *b* — sending a command to the keyboard

The reverse transmission — sending a command from the controller to the keyboard — is somewhat more complex (Fig. 7.2, *b*). From the idle state, the controller drives the KB-Clock line low for 250 μsec, and generates a start bit by driving the KB-Data line low. This is the signal for the keyboard to start receiving commands.

The keyboard must answer it with a series of 11 KB-Clock pulses. At the fall of the next clock, the controller places the next data bit, and the keyboard latches it at the rise of a clock pulse that it now generates itself. In this way, all eight data bits, the ninth (parity) bit, and the tenth (stop) bit of a command are sent. At the 11th pulse, the keyboard generates an acknowledgement bit (Ack; low level). After this, the controller requests the keyboard's response by generating a 60-msec-long KB-Clock pulse. If the controller does not receive a response to this request within 20 msec, it generates a time-out error. An error also will be recorded if the keyboard does not generate the first clock pulse within 15 msec of the request being issued, or if the controller does not receive the data, including the stop bit, within 2 msec of the start of the clock pulse 0.

There was no 8042 controller on the PC/XT motherboard, and the keyboard interface was implemented by hardware logic; specifically, by a shift register whose parallel input was connected to the inputs of the port A of the i8255 system interface. Each time a byte was received from the keyboard, the hardware interrupt IRQ1 is generated and the interrupt handler could read the received byte out of port 60h. Bits 7 and 6 of port 61h could be used to block and reset the keyboard by software, respectively. The XT keyboard could be reset by zeroing out the KB-Clock line.

7.1.2. 8042/8242 Keyboard and Mouse Controller

The programmable i8042 keyboard microcontroller is an intermediary between the keyboard, to which it is connected by the interface described above, and the central processor, to which it is connected by the parallel interface. The microcontroller continuously executes an internal microprogram monitoring signals from the keyboard and commands from the central processors. This microprogram (keyboard controller BIOS) is stored in the controller's internal masked ROM; it is not externally accessible, and the controller may be considered as a set property device. Because the controller's operating logic is software-implemented, it reacts to the processor's commands and the interface's signals relatively slowly: the response time is measured in tens of microseconds. In addition to controlling the keyboard, the software-controlled and read lines of the controller's external ports are used to generate the Gate A20 control signals and the hardware reset signals; they are also used to read the signals from the motherboard configuration jumpers. In addition to the keyboard interface, the i8242 controller supports analogous interface for another device: the PS/2 mouse. Upon initialization (hardware reset), the controller assumes either the PS/2 or AT mode, depending on the state of the microchip's specific pin. In the AT mode, the controller does not support mouse functions, and ignores all mouse commands. The mode is selected by the appropriate setting in BIOS Setup.

The controller communicates with the central processors via the 8-bit parallel data bus. The controller is selected by the CS# signal of the address decoder, triggered by addresses 0060h and 0064h. The controller's internal registers are selected by the system address bus' SA2 line. The IORD# and IOWR# signals control reading and writing; they are generated when the central processor executes instructions IN and OUT, respectively. Subsequently, the controller occupies addresses 60h (data register) and 64h (command and status register) in the CPU I/O address space. The functions of the controller's registers are listed in Table 7.1. Data received over the interfaces from the keyboard and mouse, and data that the controller sends in response to the commands issued to it, are read out of the data register. The data register is written to in order to issue both commands and data addressed to the keyboard and mouse, as well as data addressed to the controller. Commands addressed to the controller are written into the command register. The controller's operating mode (keyboard and mouse interface and interrupt enabling, scan code transmission, and other parameters) is set by the *command byte* that is sent to the controller by a special command. Before anything is written to the controller, its availability must be ascertained. Bit 1 of the status register (port 064h) indicates controller's being ready/busy state.

Table 7.1. Keyboard Controller Register Functions

Port, R/W	Function
060 RW	8042 Data Register
064 R	8042 Status Register (Read Only). The functions of its bits are as follows:
	bit 7 — parity error in the last keyboard exchange
	bit 6 — receiver time-out/general time-out[1]
	bit 5 — transmitter time-out/ mouse buffer full (Mouse_OBF)[1]
	bit 4 — 1 = keyboard active, 0 = keyboard locked
	bit 3 — 1 = the last write was a command, 0 = the last write was data
	bit 2 — system flag, set to 0 upon system powering up; set to 1 by software to show that the system reset has been successfully completed
	bit 1 — 1 = keyboard input buffer full
	bit 1 — 1 = keyboard output buffer full (OBF)
064 W	8042 Command Register

[1] Bit's second function pertains to the i8242B controller, which has a supplementary interface for connecting a PS/2 mouse.

The controller has two external ports, which are used to implement the serial interfaces and to control GateA20. They also are used to control the processor reset signal and to read the signals from the motherboard configuration jumpers and the keyboard lock key. These ports are not mapped to the PC's I/O space, but are accessed using the controller commands. In addition to these two ports, the controller has two special inputs: T0 and T1. The controller's program can read these inputs and use them as the internal interrupt source (they are not CPU interrupts). Each of the bidirectional KB-Data, KB-Clock, MS-Data, and MS-Clock lines is implemented by an output port bit and by an input bit. In the PS/2 mode, inputs T0 and T1 are used to read the KB-Clock and MS-Clock lines; in the AT mode, the T1 input is used for the KB-Data line.

The P1 input port is accessed by the C0h command; in the PS/2 mode, its bits have the following functions:

❏ Bit 7 — KeyLock. 0 = the keyboard is locked.
❏ Bit 6 — video mode setting jumper. 0 = color; 1 = mono.
❏ Bit 5 — system jumper. 0 = closed.
❏ Bit 4 — RAM size jumper. 0 = 256 KB; 1 = 512 KB and over.
❏ Bits 3 and 2 — not used.
❏ Bit 1 — MS-Data line.
❏ Bit 0 — KB-Data line.

Modern PCs use only bits 0, 1, and 7; in the AT mode, bits 0 and 1 are not used.

The P2 output port can be read from and written to by the D1h and D0h commands, respectively. The functions of its bits are as follows:

❏ Bit 7 — KB-Data line.
❏ Bit 6 — KB-Clock line.
❏ Bit 5 — mouse interrupt request (IRQ12); not used in the AT mode.
❏ Bit 4 — keyboard interrupt request (IRQ1).
❏ Bit 3 — MS-Clock line; not used in the AT mode.
❏ Bit 2 — MS-Data line; not used in the AT mode.
❏ Bit 1 — the A20 address line gate (Gate A20, see Section 12.3). 0 = A20 is zeroed out; 1 = A20 is controlled by the processor.
❏ Bit 0 — alternative CPU reset (without system reboot).

Having received a byte from the keyboard, the controller internally converts the scan code (if it is not forbidden by a control byte) and sets the status register bit 1 (OBF) to 1, which triggers generation of the IRQ1 interrupt request (if is not forbidden by a control byte). In response, the host must read the data (converted scan codes, prefixes, etc.) from the data register (60h). Conversion serves to make the scan codes sent to port 60h by the XT and AT keyboards software-compatible. Bytes received from the mouse are not converted by the controller; it only sets the register status bit

`Mouse_OBF` to 1 and triggers an interrupt request IRQ12 (if it is not forbidden by a command byte). At this signal, the host must read the mouse data from the same port 60h. The same thing happens when a byte is written into the keyboard or mouse output buffers by software (codes D2h and D3h, respectively) with the corresponding status bits set and interrupt requests `IRQ1` or `IRQ12` generated.

Having received a command, in response to which the controller must return data, it sets the status register bit `OBF=1`, which triggers the interrupt request `IRQ1` (if it is not forbidden by the command byte). Then, the data must be read out of the data register (at address 60h). If the command returns several data bytes, interrupts are generated for each byte.

Communication with the controller is carried out by issuing commands to it (i.e., by writing into the command register at address 064h). Before a command is sent, it is necessary to ascertain that the controller is ready to receive it: Port 64h bit 1 must be logical zero. Keyboard controllers have different versions of the built-in software; therefore, changing one controller for another with a different software version (KBC BIOS) may cause problems: The motherboard BIOS microchip must know the keyboard controller's characteristics.

7.1.3. System Support and Software Interface

Keyboard events and functions — pressing and releasing keys, providing services to input the symbols, controlling its parameters (typematic delay and rate) and indicators — are supported at the BIOS level. Codes received from the keyboard by the controller are read and handled by the hardware interrupt `IRQ1` handler (vector 09h). The result is placed into the keyboard buffer, from where it can be extracted considerably later by the software interrupt `Int 16h` for further processing. The codes of the "system" key combination <Ctrl>+<Alt>+<Del>, the <Print Screen> (<Sys Rq>) key and some other keys are not placed into the keyboard buffer, but evoke special procedures. An application program that needs to use the keyboard in a nonstandard way (as a music keyboard, for example) will have to handle the `IRQ1` hardware interrupt by itself by intercepting and redirecting the hardware interrupt `Int 09h`. This interrupt needs to be intercepted to call some TSR program function using a hotkey combination.

POST initializes the keyboard and its controller and launches a diagnostic test. During this test, all of the keyboard's LED indicators flash momentarily, after which only the `NumLock` LED may remain on (depending on the BIOS settings). If there is a keyboard error, a message containing a possible scan code for the stuck key will be displayed on the monitor, and the user is usually prompted to press the `F1` key to continue. The same thing will happen if POST does not detect the keyboard (because of an unplugged connector or a burnt-out fuse, for example), but in this case pressing the `F1` key will not suffice. Connecting an XT keyboard to an AT computer will also produce a diagnostic error message; the reverse connection is not viable either. If for some reason it is desirable to continue POST even with a keyboard error, the keyboard testing may be disabled in BIOS setup.

The following RAM cells from the BIOS Data Area are used for the keyboard services:

❏ 0:0417, 0:0418 — keyboard status flags
❏ 0:0419 — the Alt key accumulator, 1 byte long
❏ 0:041A — Buffer Head pointer, 2 bytes long (modified on pushing a character into the buffer)
❏ 0:041C — Buffer Tail pointer, 2 bytes long (modified on popping a character out of the buffer)
❏ 0:041E–0:042D — keyboard buffer, 16 words long

7.2. Mouse Interface

A mouse is a device for inputting coordinates and issuing commands. A mouse interface can be used in any physical implementation of the device (mouse, trackball, etc.). In terms of the computer interface, three principal types of mouse are distinguished: bus mouse, serial mouse, and PS/2 mouse. Mice with a USB interface have come out too, but they have not yet received wide acceptance; nor has the USB keyboard, to the hub of which a USB mouse can be conveniently connected.

Serial and PS/2 mouse interfaces are not compatible. Even though they are both serial, there are significant differences in their signal levels, clocking methods, frequencies, and formats of sending signals.

❏ The PS/2 interface uses unipolar TTL-level signals; the mouse's power supply is unipolar +5 V with respect to the GND rail. The RS-232 interface used by serial mice employs a bipolar signal (see *Section 2.1*) with thresholds of +3 V and –3 V and requires a bipolar (with respect to the GND rail) power supply.
❏ The PS/2 interface uses two separate signal lines; one to send data and the other for clock signals. The serial mouse interface transmits data asynchronously only over one line.

Even without taking into consideration the frequency and format of the signals, it becomes obvious that direct compatibility between these interfaces is impossible. Nevertheless, passive (!) adapters intended to select the method to connect the mouse are produced and sold. These adapters are intended only for universal mice whose built-in controller can recognize the interface, to which it has been connected by the power supply voltage, and set the appropriate output interface. Universal mice are not that widely used, so quite often complaints can be heard about unsuccessful attempts to use these adapters with a regular serial mouse or PS/2 mouse.

Additional confusion is created by Macintosh mice that have a connector that outwardly resembles the PS/2 connector. However, upon closer examination and after an unsuccessful attempt to plug it into a PC, it becomes clear that these are different connectors; moreover, the interface is entirely different.

7.2.1. Serial Mice: MS Mouse and PC Mouse

Serial mouse has a serial interface connected to the PC through the 9- or 25-contact COM port connector (Table 7.2). This mouse has a built-in microcontroller that processes signals from the coordinate sensors and the buttons. Each event — mouse move or a button press or release — are sent in binary code over the RS-232 interface. Data are sent asynchronously; the bipolar power supply required by the RS-232 protocol is supplied by the interface control lines. A shortcoming of the serial mouse is that it takes a COM port and monopolizes its regular interrupt line (IRQ4 for COM1 and IRQ3 for COM2). Of course, the fact that in order to service the mouse, the COM1 port needs precisely the IRQ4 interrupt is a shortcoming not of the mouse itself, but of its driver, but for a user who is not into mouse drivers, only the fact of the shortcoming itself matters. The two main mouse types — Microsoft Mouse (MS Mouse) and PC Mouse — require different drivers; many mice have MS/PC switches. These two types of mice use the same 1,200 bps transfer rate, one stop bit, and no parity, but the formats of their signals are different:

❑ MS Mouse uses 7 data bits and a 3-byte packet (in the "classic" version). Movements to the right along the X-coordinate and down along the Y-coordinate are considered positive. For 3-button mice, another byte is added to the packet that is sent only when the status of the third button changes. In 3-D mice, this byte performs a different function.

❑ PC Mouse uses 8 data bits and a 5-byte packet. Movements to the right along the X-coordinate and up along the Y-coordinate are considered positive.

From considering these formats, it is clear why the mouse cursor moves about the screen chaotically when a matching driver for the given mouse has not been loaded. This incompatibility may manifest itself in even more unpleasant way: When loading (or being installed), Windows 95 does not recognize a mouse operating in the PC Mouse mode (it does not "like" the identifier this mouse presents when initialized). When the OS has loaded, switching mouse modes only leads to the cursor jumping unpredictably around the screen and the buttons not working properly.

Table 7.2. Serial Mouse Connectors

Mouse signal	DB9 connector	DB25 connector	COM port signal
Data	2	3	RxD
GND	5	7	GND
+V (power)	7, (4)	4, (20)	RTS, (DTR)
−V (power)	3	2	TxD

On the system level, the serial mouse is supported only on the operating system level (services are called via Int 33h); mouse drivers are either installable or built into the operating system's driver library. BIOS does not support a mouse even if it uses it to navigate in the BIOS Setup. To stress one more time: A mouse requires a hardware interrupt line to operate — IRQ4 or IRQ3 for serial mice installed to ports COM1 or COM2, respectively.

7.2.2. PS/2 Mouse

The PS/2 mouse was introduced with the PS/2 computers. Its interface and the 6-pin mini-DIN connector is the same as the keyboard connector (Fig. 7.1), and as a rule is serviced by the same 8242 keyboard controller (see *Section 7.1.2*). Many modern motherboards are equipped with PS/2 mouse adapters and connectors (Fig. 7.3). A PS/2 mouse controller may also be implemented on an ISA expansion card. In this case, it will occupy I/O address space addresses. Communication with a PS/2 mouse is bidirectional: The processor can send special commands to the 8242 controller; however, unlike in the keyboard interface, before a "mouse" byte is written to port 60h (a command and its parameters), code D4h must be written to port 64h.

Fig. 7.3. PS/2 Mouse Connector

The PS/2 mouse can operate in one of two modes. In the *stream mode*, the mouse sends data upon any change in its state; in the *remote mode*, it sends data only when requested by the processor. There also is the diagnostic *wrap mode*, in which the mouse returns data sent to it by the controller. When the controller receives a packet from the mouse, it sets the `Mouse_OBF` flag and generates the `IRQ2` interrupt request, if it is not disabled by the 8242 command byte.

Setting PS/2 mouse parameters by sending to it the above-described commands is supported at the BIOS level. The mouse driver itself (`IRQ12` interrupt handler at vector 74h) that services its data transmissions is a part of the operating system to be loaded separately. Mouse support is enabled via functions `C200h`–`C209h` of the BIOS `Int 15h`.

7.2.3. Bus Mouse

The bus mouse was one of the first versions of the mouse. The mouse itself contains only sensors and buttons. The controller to process signals from the mouse is located on a separate adapter, usually of ISA type. The mouse has nine-wire cable with a special connector (Fig. 7.4) that at first glance resembles the PS/2 Mouse connector. The major shortcoming of this system is that the adapter needs to be allocated system resources such as a bus slot, I/O space addresses, and an interrupt request line. Some vendors used to offer Multiport ISA cards (COM, LPT, and GAME ports) with a bus mouse adapter. Because Microsoft was one of the first to offer this type of mouse and the mouse had its logo, the MS Mouse is sometimes associated with the bus mouse. However, the MS Mouse can operate under any of the three interfaces.

Fig. 7.4. Bus mouse connector

7.3. Printer and Plotter Interfaces

Modern high-resolution graphics (including text in graphics mode) printers demand a high-rate external data-transfer interface. Most printers use either the traditions parallel Centronics or more efficient IEEE 1284 interface. The latter allows transmission speeds of 0.15 MBps–2 MBps, depending on the computer's efficiency and the selected transfer mode. Plotters use the same interfaces.

Various modifications of the LPT port are used to connect a parallel interface printer, from the traditional SPP to the today's standard efficient IEEE 1284 (see *Section 1.3*).

Originally, all parallel interface printers necessarily supported the Centronics interface, and the more advanced could even work in the ECP mode supporting the IEEE 1284 negotiation sequence. Their installers tried to install drivers that supported the advanced modes if the operating system and the LPT port capabilities allowed this. The situation has changed, and now there are printers that do not support the Centronics interface. During installation, they request to be connected using the bidirectional IEEE 1284 interface (usually, in the ECP mode) and refuse to work with the LPT port in the SPP mode. These printers require special drivers to be used with MS-DOS operating system.

Some printers use serial interfaces, such as RS-232C, RS-422, or the current loop. However, the theoretical transfer-rate limit of these interfaces is about 115 Kbps, and the actual transfer rate barely reaches 9,600 bps. These printers can be connected to a COM port directly, or by using a signal-level converting adapter.

Lately, the USB is being used more and more often to connect printers, but this switch over is not exactly trouble-free, since not all operating systems support USB. Old applications (the possibility of switching over to new ones does not always exist) that work with the printer using the BIOS Int 17h functions or directly with the LPT port registers (to prompt inserting a blank sheet of paper, for example) cannot work with a USB printer, even if the operating system fully supports USB. In terms of the data transfer rate, the USB 1.0, at 12 Mbps, is far from reaching speeds of 1.5 MB/sec (12:8) because of the bus overhead alone. The USB 2.0 offers peak speeds of up to 50 KBps (the bus speed is 480 Mbps), which for a printer is more than enough for the time being. However, in this case the printer and the computer have to support USB 2.0 and there must not be old (USB 1.0) hubs between them.

Printer may use the SCSI interface, but this is not common. They also may be connected not to a computer but to a local network using the Ethernet protocol (10 or 100 Mbps). It is convenient to connect shared printers in this way, and with a properly set-up network it serves users without problems. The FireWire bus has had some very limited use for connecting printers so far.

7.3.1. Centronics and IEEE 1284 Parallel Interfaces

The Centronics parallel interface is oriented at transmitting a data stream to the printer and receiving printer status data. This interface is supported by all LPT ports. The term "Centronics" is used to describe both the signal suite and interaction protocol and the 36-contact printer connector. The functions of this interface's signals are listed in Table 7.3. Printer exchange timing diagrams are shown in Fig. 7.5.

Table 7.3. Centronics Interface Signals

Signal	I/O[1]	Contact	Function
Strobe#	I	1	Data strobe. Data are latched at the signal's low level.
Data [0:7]	I	2–9	Data lines. Data 0 (contact 2) is the lowest bit.
Ack#	O	10	Acknowledgement of receiving a byte (request to receive another). May be used to generate an interrupt request.
Busy	O	11	Data can be received only when it is low.
PaperEnd	O	12	High level indicates the printer is out of paper.
Select	O	13	Indicates that printer is on. (Usually connected through a resistor with the printer's +5 V rail.)
Auto LF#	I	14	Automatic line feed. With this signal low, when the printer receives a *CR* (Carriage Return) signal, it automatically executes the *LF* (Line Feed) operation.
Error#	O	32	Out of paper, offline, or internal printer error.
Init#	I	31	Initialization: reset to the default settings, advance to the beginning of the line and top of the page.
Select In#	I	36	Low level selects printer. When high, the printer does not recognize other interface signals.
GND	–	19–30, 33	Common wire.

[1] I/O sets the direction (in or out) with respect to the printer.

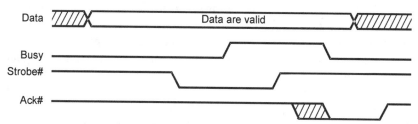

Fig. 7.5. Data transmission using the Centronics protocol

Data transmission starts with checking the status of the Busy line to establish whether the printer is ready. The data strobe may be fractions of a microsecond long, and the port finishes forming it regardless of the Busy signal state. During the strobe, the data must be valid. The Ack# signal confirms receiving a byte. It is generated an indeterminate interval after the printer receives the strobe. (During this time, the printer may perform some lengthy operation, such as paper feed.) By sending an Ack# pulse, the printer requests the next byte to be sent; this pulse is used to generate a printer port interrupt request. If interrupts are not used, the Ack# signal is ignored, and the data exchange is controlled by the Strobe# and Busy signals. The printer may inform the port of its status over the Select, Error#, and PaperEnd lines, which indicate whether the printer is turned on, in working order, and not out of paper, respectively. The printer may be reset by pulsing the Init# line; this will also clear its data buffer. The automatic line feed mode is not normally used, and the AutoLF# is set high. The SelectIn# signal logically disconnects printer from the interface.

The Centronics protocol can be implemented over the parallel port purely by software using the *SPP* mode; speeds of up to 150 KBps at full processor load can be reached. Thanks to the advanced port modes, the protocol can be hardware-implemented (*Fast Centronics*), reaching speeds of up to 2 MBps at a lower processor load.

Most modern parallel interface printers also support the IEEE 1284 standard, in which the optimal transfer mode is the ECP. (See *Section 1.3.4.*)

A Centronics cable, suitable for any parallel interface mode, is used to connect the printer. The simplest version of the cable — 18-wire with non-twisted pairs — can be used for the *SPP* mode. If the cable is over 2 m long, it is desirable that at least the Strobe# and Busy lines be intertwisted with individual common wires. For the high-speed modes, this cable may not be adequate, and may cause intermittent errors occurring only when certain code sequences are sent. There are Centronics cables that do not have contact 17 on the PC connector connected to contact 36 on the printer connector. Attempting to connect the printer operating under the 1284 standard using this cable will produce a system message to the effect that a "bidirectional cable" needs to be used. The printer cannot inform the system that it supports the expanded modes as the printer driver expects. Another manifestation of the missing contact 17–36 link is that the printer hangs after finishing a Windows printing job. This missing-link problem can be solved by soldering an extra wire between these two contacts, or simply replacing the cable with one where these contacts are connected.

The electrical properties of ribbon cables, with their alternating signal and common wires, are not too bad. But these cables are not practical for external use: Just one insulation layer makes them rather vulnerable to physical damage. Besides, they do not fit well with considerations of interior design: Round cables look better.

The ideal solution is shielded cables with a twisted wire pair for each signal, as this requires the IEEE 1248 standard. These cables are guaranteed to deliver speeds of up to 2 MBps at distances of up to 10 meters.

Table 7.4 shows the wiring of a printer connection cable to the X1 Type A (DB25-P) connector on the computer side and to the X2 Type B (Centronics-26) or Type C (miniature) connectors on the printer side. Whether the common GND wires are used depends on the quality of the cable. In the simplest (18-wire) cable, all ground signals are brought into one wire. Quality cables require a separate return wire for each signal line; however, Type A and B connectors do not have enough contacts to comply with this requirement (Table 7.4 shows in parentheses Type A connector contacts that have return wires). The Type C connector has a return (GND) wire for each signal wire; contacts 19–36 are the corresponding ground contacts for the signal contacts 1–17.

Table 7.4. Printer Connection Cable

X1, Type A PC connector	Signal	X2, Type B printer connector	X2, Type C printer connector
1	Strobe#	1	15
2	Data0	2	6
3	Data1	3	7
4	Data2	4	8
5	Data3	5	9
6	Data4	6	10
7	Data5	7	11
8	Data6	8	12
9	Data7	9	13
10	Ack#	10	3
11	Busy	11	1
12	PaperEnd	12	5
13	Select	13	2
14	Auto LF#	14	17
15	Error#	32	4
16	Init#	31	14
17	Select In#	36	16
18	GND (1)	19	33
19	GND (2 3)	20 21	24 25
20	GND (4 5)	22 23	26 27
21	GND (6 7)	24 25	28 29
22	GND (8 9)	26 27	30 31
23	GND (11 15)	29	19 22
24	GND (10 12 13)	28	20 21 23
25	GND (14 16 17)	30	32 34 35

7.3.2. Serial Interfaces for the Printers

The RS-232C is the most commonly used serial interface to connect printers to the COM port. Printers with the current loop or RS-422 serial interfaces can be encountered. They are connected to the COM port using special converting adapters. Printers always use asynchronous transfer protocols and, as a rule, allow the configuration of the serial interface to be adjusted. Parameters such as the transfer rate, packet format (number of data, start and stop bits, parity bit), and the flow control protocol (software XON/XOFF or hardware RTS/CTS) can be set. Printers and plotters are connected to the COM port using a cable that corresponds to the selected protocol. Cable wirings are shown in Figs. 7.6–7.7. A hardware protocol is preferable, as it is exactly this driver that the standard COM port driver uses. Naturally, printer interface parameters must correspond to the parameters' set for the COM port being used. The port can be configured by a DOS MODE command, among others. When printing from DOS (using COPY or PRINT commands), port interrupts are not used.

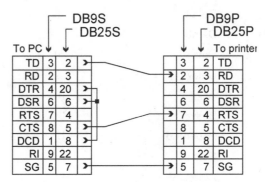

Fig. 7.6. Cable for connecting RTS-CTS protocol printers

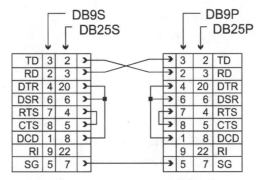

Fig. 7.7. Cable for connecting XON/XOFF protocol printers

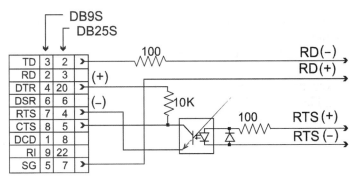

Fig. 7.8. Connecting a printer with the 20 mA current loop interface to COM port

If the printer has the current loop interface, it will require a signal converter; simple schematics of such signal converter is shown in Fig. 7.8. Here, the printer is connected to a COM port using hardware flow control. The bipolar signal required for COM ports is taken off the interface power supply lines.

7.3.3. System Printer Support

Output to the printer via the LPT port operating in the standard mode (SPP) under the Centronics interface is supported at the BIOS level. All the other operating modes of the port are supported only by means of additional drivers or the operating system. The BIOS Int 17h services initialize the printer, perform byte output, and query the printer status. Intercepting interrupt Int 17h is a convenient way for installing custom printer drivers. They may be needed when, for example, the printer's character set needs to be substituted.

The Print Screen function is supported by the BIOS Int 05h. Its interrupt handler outputs, character by character, the contents of the video memory in the text mode to the LPT1 port. The interrupt handler uses memory cell 0050:0000 to indicate its current status: 00 — inactive, 01 — printing in progress, FF — there has been an I/O error during the last call. The Int 05h interrupt is called by the keyboard hardware interrupt handler (Int 09h) when the PrintScreen (PrtSc) key is pressed.

7.4. Graphics Adapter Interfaces

Special interfaces are used for connecting a monitor to the computer's graphics adapter. Information about the instantaneous intensities of the primary colors (RGB) and the line and frame synchronization signals are transmitted over these interfaces. The transmission method has already made its first spiral of development, from the digital interface of the first adapters (MDA, CGA, EGA) through the analog VGA interface, and back to the digital interfaces (DVI, P&D, DFP). Most of the monitor interfaces have been standardized by VESA (**www.vesa.org**).

Video interfaces are used to output information to regular television sets and computer monitors, as well as to input data to the computer. Digital video data can be transferred over the FireWire and USB 2.0 buses.

Many graphic adapters have an internal VFC or VAFC connector. This is a parallel bus for exchanging pixel information with supplementary video cards.

A graphic adapter is connected to the processor and main memory via one of the expansion buses: AGP, PCI, or ISA, the interfaces of which are described in *Chapter 6*.

7.4.1. RGB TTL Discrete Interface

The discrete TTL level interface — RGB TTL — was used in monitors connected via MDA, HGC (Hercules), CGA, and EGA graphic adapters. This interface requires a DB-9 connector (female on the adapter); its signals are listed in Table 7.5. Monochrome displays use only two signals: Video (beam on/on) and Intens (beam intensity). Color Display class monitors for CGA adapters use one signal to control each color beam and one common beam intensity control signal; this allowed 16 colors to be specified. The Enhanced Color Display (ECD) for the EGA adapter requires two control signals for each primary color: One for the higher bit and the other for the lower bit of the primary colors — RED, GREEN, BLUE and Red, Green, Blue. In this way, 64 colors can be specified.

The H.Sync and V.Sync signals control the monitor's line and frame sweep, respectively. High resolution (720×350 pixels) monochrome MDA and HGC adapters employ a high frequency sweep. The CGA adapter works at low frequencies; its sweep frequencies are close to those of television. EGA adapters and monitors can work with any of these frequencies. The V.Sync is used to facilitate switching the monitor's sweep generator modes: The polarity of the pulses determines the current mode's sweep frequency range.

Table 7.5. Discrete Monitor Interface (RGB TTL)

Contact		Monitor	
	Mono	Color	Enhanced Color/Mono
1	GND	GND	GND
2	GND	GND	Red
3	–	RED	RED
4	–	GREEN	GREEN

continues

Table 7.5 Continued

Contact	Monitor		
	Mono	**Color**	**Enhanced Color/Mono**
5	–	BLUE	BLUE
6	Intens.	Intens.	Green/Intens.
7	Video	Reserved	Blue/Video
8	+H.Sync.	+H.Sync.	+H.Sync.
9	–V.Sync.	+V.Sync.	–(+)V.Sync.

7.4.2. Analog RGB Interfaces

The RGB Analog interface employs an analog method to transmit primary-color signals, which allows a nominally indefinite number of hues to be transmitted. In modern adapters, primary-color signals are generated by 8-bit DACs, allowing 16.7 million hues (True Color) to be represented. In order to reduce interference, these signals are sent over twisted wire pairs, each of which has its own Return wire. Inside the monitor, each signal pair is loaded by a resistor in order to match the cable impedance. Black is represented by zero potential on all color lines, full brightness is represented by +0.7 V (not all graphic adapters support full signal amplitude). Control, status, and synchronization signals are sent by TTL levels. RGB interface timing diagrams (also applicable to the RGB TTL) are shown in Fig. 7.9. The R, G, and B signals are shown symbolically; depicted are the time intervals during which the signals illuminate screen dots (the visible part of the image is in the area where the line scan and frame refresh signals overlap; the rest of the time, the beam is turned off). Only the main timing parameters of the signals are shown in the illustration. The VESA DMT (Discrete Monitor Timing, 1994–1998) standard specifies a discrete series of parameter sets for various display resolution modes. A later standard, VESA GTF (Generalized Timing Formula), provides formulas for determining all synchronization parameters. The source data for the calculations are as follows:

❑ Display resolution in pixels (800 × 600, for example)
❑ Overscan border requirements
❑ Non-interlaced or interlaced line sweep
❑ One of the frequencies: frame, line, or pixels

Because there are many standards, the same set of parameters used by different graphic adapters and their drivers will have slightly differing signal timing parameters.

These variations have to be compensated by adjusting the monitor (image size and vertical and horizontal positions). Table 7.6 shows some examples of line sweep synchronization parameters. For line sweep, synchronization parameters are given in μsec, and for the frame refresh they are given in the number of lines during this time.

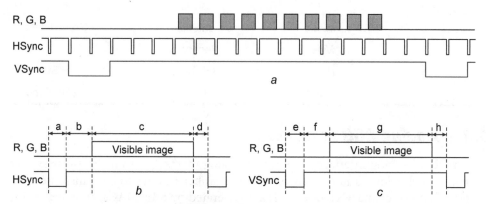

Fig. 7.9. RGB interface timing diagrams:
a — overall picture, *b* — line sweep, *c* — frame sweep

Table 7.6. Synchronization Parameters

VESA mode	Frames frequency (Hz)	Line frequency (KHz)	Pixel frequency (MHz)	Line sweep (μsec)				Frame sweep (lines)			
	Fv	Fh	Fp	A	b	c	d	e	f	g	h
640 × 480 VGA (60 Hz)	59.9	31.5	25.2	3.8	1.9	25.4	0.6	2	33	480	10
640 × 480 VGA (72 Hz)	72.8	37.9	31.5	1.3	3.8	20.3	1.0	3	28	480	9
640 × 480 VGA (85 Hz)	85.0	43.3	35.9	1.6	2.2	17.8	1.6	3	25	480	1
800 × 600 SVGA (60 Hz)	60.3	37.9	40.0	3.2	2.2	20.0	1.0	4	23	600	1
800 × 600 SVGA (85 Hz)	85.1	53.7	56.3	1.1	2.7	14.2	0.6	3	27	600	1

continues

Table 7.6 Continued

VESA mode	Frames frequency (Hz)	Line frequency (KHz)	Pixel frequency (MHz)	Line sweep (μsec)				Frame sweep (lines)			
	Fv	Fh	Fp	A	b	c	d	e	f	g	h
1024 × 768 XGA (60 Hz)	60.0	48.4	64.8	2.1	2.5	15.8	0.4	6	29	768	3
1024 × 768 XGA (75 Hz)	85.0	68.7	94.8	1.0	2.2	10.8	0.5	3	36	768	1
1152 × 864 (85 Hz)	85.0	77.5									
1280 × 1024 SXGA (60 Hz)	60.0	64.0	107.6	1.0	2.3	11.9	0.4	3	38	1024	1
1280 × 1024 SXGA (75 Hz)	75.0	79.9	135								
1280 × 1024 SXGA (85 Hz)	85.0	91.1									
1600 × 1024 (60 Hz)	60.0	63.6									
1600 × 1024 (85 Hz)	85.0	91.4									
1600 × 1200 (85 Hz)	85.0	106.3									
1920 × 1200 (60 Hz)	60.0	74.5									
1920 × 1200 (85 Hz)	85.0	107.1									
2048 × 1536 (75 Hz)	75.0	120.2									
2304 × 1440 (80 Hz)	80.0	120.6									

An analog interface was used for the first time by IBM in its PGA adapter, which employs a 9-pin DB-9S connector (Table 7.7). Later, starting with the VGA adapters, a 15-contact compact connector of the same size was employed (Table 7.8). For the most part, the signal functions of these interfaces are identical; there even are 15- to 9-contact connectors adapter cables (Table 7.9). Line and frame synchronizations in PGA adapters are done by one composite (H+V) Sync signal. This mode is called Composite Sync and is supported by many modern monitors.

Table 7.7. PGA Monitor Analog Interface (DB-9S Connector)

Contact	Signal
1	Red
2	Green
3	Blue
4	(H+V)Sync
5	Mode Control
6	Red Return
7	Green Return
8	Blue Return
9	GND

Table 7.8. VGA Monitor Analog Interface (RGB Analog)

Contact	Video adapter	Monitor	
DB-15	MCGA/VGA/SVGA/XGA	Mono	Color
1	Red	—	Red
2	Green	Video	Green
3	Blue	—	Blue
4	ID2	—	—
5	GND/DDC Return[1]	SelfTest/DDC Return	SelfTest/DDC Return
6	Red Return	Key	Red Return
7	Green Return	Video Return	Green Return
8	Blue Return	—	Blue Return
9	Key (no contact)[1]	—[1]	—[1]
10	GND (Sync Return)	GND (Sync Return)	GND (Sync Return)
11	ID0	—	GND
12	ID1/SDA[1]	— /SDA[1]	GND/SDA[1]

continues

Table 7.8 Continued

Contact	Video adapter	Monitor	
DB-15	MCGA/VGA/SVGA/XGA	Mono	Color
13	H.Sync/(H+V)Sync^2	H.Sync/(H+V)Sync^2	H.Sync/(H+V)Sync^2
14	V.Sync	V.Sync	V.Sync
15	ID3/SCL[1]	ID3/SCL[1]	ID3/SCL[1]

[1] DDC signals Return, SDA, and SCL can be used only with DDC support. In this case, contact 9 can be used to supply power to the DDC logic (+5 V).

[2] The (H+V)Sync signal is used with the Composite Sync.

Table 7.9. Nine-to-15 Monitor Interface Connector Adapter

DB9 connector contact	Signal	DB 15 connector contact
1	Red	1
2	Green	2
3	Blue	3
4	H.Sync	13
5	V.Sync	14
6	Red Return	6
7	Green Return	7
8	Blue Return	8
9	GND	10, 11

Even though the 15-contact connectors have a physical key — the D-case — quite often users manage to insert them in reverse. When this happens, one of the middle row contacts bends and eventually breaks off (pins on 15-pin connectors are thinner and more fragile then on 9-pin ones). Naturally, a monitor connected in this way will not work.

Macintosh computers, which are compatible with the VGA standard, have a DB-15P connector, the same as the PC's game port connector. The functions of its contacts are given in Table 7.10.

Table 7.10. Macintosh VGA Connector

Contact	Signal
1	Red Return
2	Red
3	Comp.Sync
4	ID0
5	Green
6	Green Return
7	ID1
8	Not used
9	Blue
10	ID2
11	Sync. GND
12	V.Sync
13	Blue Return
14	H.Sync GND
15	H.Sync

In addition to the image, the information necessary to automate the computer and monitor parameter matching is sent over the interface. The computer's "interests" are represented by the display adapter to which the monitor is connected. The adapter performs monitor identification that is necessary to provide Plug and Play support and to control the monitor's power consumption.

To perform the simplest identification, four logical signals ID0-ID3 were added to the interface. Using these signals, the adapter could identify the IBM monitor connected. On the monitor side, these lines were either connected to the ground or left unconnected. However, in this identification system, only the ID1 signal was employed, used to indicate the fact that a monochrome monitor was connected. The adapter can identify a monochrome adapter in another way, namely, by the absence of load on the Red and Blue lines.

The parallel monitor identification method was replaced with the serial method using the VESA DDC (Display Data Channel) digital interface channel. This channel is implemented using either the I2C (DDC2B) or ACCESS.Bus (DDC2AB) interfaces, which require only two TTL signals: SCL and SDA. The DDC1 interface is unidirectional: The monitor sends to the adapter a block of its parameters over the SDA line (contact 12); this transmission is synchronized by the v.Sync signal (contact 14). While it is receiving this parameter block, the adapter may raise the frequency up to 25 KHz (the vertical-scanning generator cannot be synchronized at such high frequency). The DDC2 interface is bidirectional, using the dedicated SCL signal (contact 15). The DDC2AB interface differs in that it allows peripheral devices that do not require high transfer exchange rates be connected to the computer over the ACCESS.Bus serial bus (see *Section 11.1.2.*)

The Extended Display Modification (*EDID*) parameter block has the same structure for any type of DDC implementation (Table 7.11).

Table 7.11. EDID Block Layout

Offset (bytes)	Length (bytes)	Function
0	8	Header (EDID flow start indicator)
8	10	Device code (vendor assigned)
18	2	EDID version
20	15	Display's main characteristics and capabilities
35	19	Set synchronization parameters
54	72	Synchronization parameters descriptors (bytes 4–18)
126	1	Expansion bytes
127	1	Checksum

To control the monitor's power consumption, the v.Sync and H.Sync frame and line synchronization signals are used in accordance with the VESA DPMS (Display Power Management Signaling) standard (Table 7.12.)

Table 7.12. Controlling Monitor Power Consumption (VESA DPMS)

Mode	H.Sync	V.Sync
On	Active	Active
Standby	Inactive	Active
Suspend	Active	Inactive
Off	Inactive	Inactive

Connectors used in modern adapters and SVGA monitors are not designed to transmit high-frequency signals. Their upper limit is approximately 150 MHz, which is not enough for high resolution and high refresh rate. Therefore, large, high-resolution, high synchronization frequency professional monitors and their corresponding adapters are equipped with BNC connectors for connecting via a coaxial cable. Monitors equipped with coaxial cable connectors can be connected to graphic adapters equipped with DB-15 connectors using special matching cable adapters. These cables can have three to five 75-ohm coaxial BNC connectors:

❑ Three connectors — primary-color signals; composite sync is sent over the green color channel.
❑ Four connectors — composite sync is sent over a separate cable.
❑ Five connectors — vertical and horizontal are transmitted over separate cables.

Using coaxial cables, the monitor may be located up to 10–15 meters from the computer and retain the quality of the image.

To expand the frequency range (and taking into account the tendency to use serial buses like USB and FireWire), in 1995 VESA put forward a new type of connector — Enhanced Video Connector (EVC) — to connect peripheral devices to the system block. In 1998, a new edition of this standard was accepted introducing minor modifications related to reserved contacts and charging device power lines. The connector also was renamed as Plug&Display-Analog (P&D-A). In addition to the regular analog RGB interface and the DDC2 channel, the P&D-A (EVC) connector has contacts for video input, incoming and outgoing stereo audio signals, USB and FireWire buses, as well as direct current power supply lines to charge the batteries in a portable PC. The connector is divided into two parts: a high-frequency section for connecting four coaxial cables, and a low-frequency 30-contact section (Fig. 7.10 and Table 7.13). Even though the high-frequency section contacts are not of the coaxial kind, they allow signals with frequencies of up to 2 GHz to be sent. Cables' shields are connected to the cross-like contact divider. When using 75-ohm coaxial cables, the level of signal bounce and crosstalk at 500 MHz is guaranteed to be no higher than 2%. The high-frequency section — contacts C1–C4 and C5 (shield) — is used to transmit the RGB color signals and the PX Clock pixel synchronization signal. The pixel synchronization signal is used by digital matrix displays; using it makes it possible to reduce the video information transmission error rate. This signal's frequency equals either the pixel scan frequency or half of it. (High frequency requires double synchronization, at the rising and falling edges, which evens out the bandwidth requirements for the color data lines and the pixel synchronization lines.)

Table 7.13. P&D-A (EVC) Connector

Contact	Signal	Contact	Signal	Contact	Signal
1	Audio Output, Right	11	Charging power input, +	21	Audio input, left
2	Audio Output, Left	12	Charging power input, −	22	Audio input, right
3	Audio Output, Return	13	Video input, Y or composite in	23	Audio input, return
4	Sync Return	14	Video input, return	24	Stereo sync (TTL)
5	Horizontal Sync (TTL)	15	Video input, C in	25	DDC return
6	Vertical Sync (TTL)	16	USB Data +	26	DDC Data (SDA)
7	Reserved	17	USB Data −	27	DDC Clock (SCL)
8	Reserved	18	USB/1394 common mode shield	28	+5 V
9	1394 TPA−	19	1394 VG	29	1394 TPB+
10	1394 TPA+	20	1394 VP	30	1394 TPB−
C1	R (analog)			C3	PX Clock
C2	G (analog)	C5	GND (for R, G, B)	C4	B (analog)

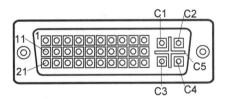

Fig. 7.10. P&D (EVC) connector (female)

The connector is divided into two compact areas for each signal group, although the USB and 1394 buses use a common shield contact. The functions of the video input contacts (S-Video or composite, PAL or NTSC) can be programmed over the DDC2 channel.

The standard defines three implementation levels: basic, multimedia, and full. The basic level only contains video signals and the DDC; the multimedia level must have audio signals. When all connector capabilities are used, the monitor turns into a switchboard connected by one cable to the computer, and the rest of the peripheral devices (including the keyboard, mouse, printer, etc.) are connected to the monitor. The connector may be used to connect a portable PC to the docking station. The EVC collects signals from various subsystems: graphic, video, audio, serial bus, and power supply. This common connector is mounted on the system block case; various expansion cards can be connected to it by internal cables with matching connectors. This connector should not be confused with the similarly looking and named P&D-A/D connector, which is described in the following section. EVC connectors are not very often encountered in PCs, and not only because of their high price. It is inconvenient to install an EVC connector on a graphic adapter card, as it sprouts superfluous interface cables; integrated motherboards seldom have high-quality adapters requiring an EVC connector.

7.4.4. Digital Interfaces P&D, DVI, and DFP

The widespread migration to digital technologies has not passed monitors by. The traditional analog video signal transmission channel has become the video system's bottleneck. On its way from the DAC to the monitor's input video amplifiers, the signal has to pass through a pair of connectors and a cable. A mismatch of the components' characteristics, causing signal "jitter" and irregular frequency characteristics, distorts the shape of the color signals, which becomes especially noticeable when operating in the high resolution and high refresh frequency rate modes. The image quality can be improved by placing the DAC device right into the monitor, on the video amplifier board, and feeding the digital signals into them. Flat-screen displays (built using thin-film transistor (TFT) technology) are implemented on the basis of digital technology, and have to convert incoming analog signals back into digital. All these reasons have led to the development of a digital interface for transmitting information to the monitor. This interface is required to provide an enormous bandwidth: for example, to operate at a pixel frequency of 150 MHz and 24-bit pixel coding (True Color) a bandwidth of 3.6 Gbps (450 MBps) is required.

To connect flat-screen displays, the special PaneLink interface was developed; in 1996, its specification — FPDI-2 — was approved by VESA. The interface's schematic is shown in Fig. 7.11. The interface has three data transmission channels (Data[0:2]) and a clocking channel Clock. Signals are transmitted using the Transition Minimized Differential Signaling (T.M.D.S.) protocol. Each data channel consists of a coder, which is located on the video adapter, and a decoder, which is located in the monitor. The 8-bit primary color intensity code of the current pixel is input into each coder. In addition to these data, the line and frame synchronization signals are input into the channel 0 coder and supplementary control signals CTL[0:3], a pair for each channel, are input into the channel 1 and 2 coders. The coders convert data into a serial code. In order to minimize switching, the 8 input bits are coded into a 10-bit symbol that is sent over the channel serially. Depending on the status of the input data-enabling signal, the decoders transmit either color channel data or synchronizing signals and control bits. On the receiving side, signals are decoded and restored to the same state in which they arrived at the coders' inputs. Pixel frequency may reach 165 MHz; the interface provides maximum resolution of 1280 × 1024 (24 bits per pixel).

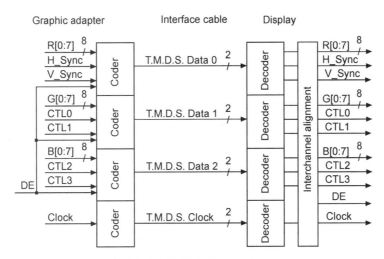

Fig. 7.11. Digital interface schematics

Physical lines are implemented using shielded twister pairs. The transmitters are differential switched 12-milliampere current sources; inputs of the differential receivers are pulled up to a +3.3 V power supply by load resistors; the signal amplitude is 500 millivolts. The coding method can be used to transmit signals over a fiber channel (the signal does not have a zero frequency component), but so far, the specification defines only the electrical interface.

The protocol described above is used in the P&D, DVI, and DFP interfaces. The most commonly used protocols are the DVI, as the most powerful and universal, and the DFP, as the cheapest specialized. Many graphics adapters with two outputs are equipped with connectors for these interfaces. The rarely encountered P&D interface may be considered a combination of cut-down versions of the EVC and DVI protocols. Because the signals (T.M.D.S.) are standardized, if the monitor and the video card are equipped with different connectors, they can be matched by passive adapters.

The VP&D (VESA Plug-and-Display, 1997), or P&D, interface uses the same connector as the EVC protocol (Fig. 7.10). It does not have analog audio signal circuits and video input; these contacts are given over to the digital signal transmission channels.

There are two versions of the interface: combined and purely digital. The combined P&D-A/D connector also has contacts for analog signals (RGB and synchronization), which makes it possible to connect digital as well as the traditional analog monitors. The strictly digital P&D version does not have analog signal contacts; an analog monitor (with an EVC or P&D-A connector) will not work with it (the connector's construction will not even allow it to be connected). Similarly, a purely digital monitor with a P&D input connector cannot be connected to an R&D-A (EVC) output connector.

Table 7.14. P&D-A/D Connector

Contact	Signal	Contact	Signal	Contact	Signal
1	Data 2+	11	Data 1+	21	Data 0−
2	Data 2−	12	Data 1−	22	Data 0+
3	Screen 2	13	Screen 1	23	Shield 0
4	Sync Rtn	14	Clock+	24	Stereo Sync TTL
5	H.Sync TTL	15	Clock-	25	DDC Return
6	V.Sync TTL	16	USB Data+	26	DDC Data
7	Shield Clock	17	USB Data-	27	DDC Clock
8	CHRG+	18	1394 Shield/CHRG−	28	+5 V
9	1394 TPA−	19	1394 VG	29	1394 TPB+, CLOCK+
10	1394 TPA+	20	1394 VP	30	1394 TPB−, CLOCK−
C1	R (analog)			C3	PX Clock
C2	G (analog)	C5	GND (for R, G, B)	C4	B (analog)

The *Digital Flat Panel* (DFP, 1999, **www.dfp-group.org**) interface uses an inexpensive MDR type (mini-D ribbon) connector with ribbon contacts (Fig. 7.12). On this connector, there are only three pairs of signals for digital data channels, a pair of signals for the digital synchronization channel, +5 V power supply lines, the DDC2 channel (Table 7.15), and the Hot Plug Detect signal (HPD). The pixel frequency may reach 85 MHz (flat monitors do not need a very high sweep frequency). The interface supports resolutions up to 1280 × 1024 (24 bits per pixel).

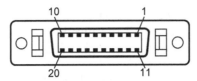

Fig. 7.12. DFP connector

Table 7.15. DFP Connector

Contact	Signal	Contact	Signal
1	TX1+	11	TX2+
2	TX1−	12	TX2−
3	SHLD1	13	SHLD2
4	SHLDC	14	SHLD0
5	TXC+	15	TX0+
6	TXC−	16	TX0−
7	GND	17	NC
8	+5 V	18	HPD
9	NC	19	DDC_DAT
10	NC	20	DDC_CLK

The *Digital Visual Interface* (DVI) was developed by the Digital Display Working Group (DDWG, **www.ddwg.org**) in 1999. It is aimed at connecting any type of displays (CRT and LCD) to the computer, and there are two versions of the interface and its connectors: a purely digital and a combination of digital with the traditional analog signals. In the latter case, a regular analog VGA interface monitor can be connected to a DVI connector with the help of a passive adapter.

A minimal capability digital interface version consists of a synchronization channel and three data channels (Data 0–2). This version is almost the same as the analog: Only the location of the DAC is changed and data are transferred digitally. However, the interface makes provisions for increasing the bandwidth by using time more efficiently. In traditional CRT monitors, the line and frame beam back travel takes a rather considerable amount of time, during which the screen pixels are naturally not updated and the interface is, therefore, idle. Matrix displays do not require these pauses; therefore, the same pixel information volume can be sent over a longer time, practically over the entire frame period. Consequently, either the pixel transmission frequency can be lowered (without changing the resolution or the sweep frequency) or the resolution and/or sweep frequency raised at the same pixel transmission frequency (its upper limit). The DVI specification implies extending data transmission for the duration of the entire frame in digital displays by using conventional CRTs and also by employing internal buffering.

In a monitor equipped with screen buffers, other improvements are possible: Instead of refreshing the screen continuously, which is what traditional video adapters are occupied in doing, it is possible to send data only when the image changes. This is, however, only a possible development. The full version of the DVI interface has three additional digital channels (Data 3–5); the information load must be distributed evenly between the channel pairs. Thus, even pixels will be sent over channels 0 (R), 1 (G), and 2 (B); accordingly, the odd pixels will be sent over channels 3, 4, and 5. The interface allows the transmission of pixels at frequencies up to 330 MHz (165 × 2). Provisions have been made for alternative use of the channels: When eight bits may not seem enough to encode the primary colors, channels 3, 4, and 5 may supplement (as lower bits) data of channels 0, 1, and 2 (upper bits).

In addition to the T.M.D.S. signals, the DVI interface contains VESA DDC2 interface signals, DDC Data, and DDC Clock, as well as the +5 V power supply lines, which allows the configuration information to be exchanged even when the monitor is turned off. The configuration information allows the system to determine the monitor's capabilities and to configure the available data channels properly, matching the capabilities of the video card and the display. There also is a HPD signal, which the system uses to keep track of the monitor's connections and disconnections. The connectors are physically constructed in such a way as to support hot connection by ensuring the proper sequence of different contact groups' connection or disconnection. Therefore, DVI displays provide all the functions necessary to implement Plug and Play standards. The DVI interface and displays must provide standard (VESA) graphic modes, starting from 640 × 480/60 Hz (22.175 MHz pixel frequency). Its upper limit is 2048 × 1536 pixels (330 MHz pixel frequency). The interface supports Display Power Management Signaling (DPMS).

Fig. 7.13 shows DVI connectors; their pinouts are given in Table 7.16.

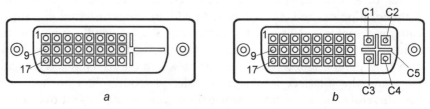

Fig. 7.13. DVI connectors (receptacles):
a — digital only, *b* — digital and analog combined

Table 7.16. DVI Connector

Contact	Signal	Contact	Signal	Contact	Signal
1	Data2−	9	Data1−	17	Data0−
2	Data2+	10	Data1+	18	Data0+
3	Shield	11	Shield	19	Shield
4	Data4−	12	Data3−	20	Data5−
5	Data4+	13	Data3+	21	Data5+
6	DDC Clock	14	+5 V	22	Shield Clock
7	DDC Data	15	GND (for +5 V, H.Sync and V.Sync)	23	Clock+
8	VSync (TTL)	16	HPD	24	Clock−
C1	R (analog)			C3	B (analog)
C2	G (analog)	C5	GND (for R, G, B)	C4	H.Sync (TTL)

7.4.5. Internal Digital Interfaces

In order to expand a digital adapter's capabilities, mainly in the area of video image processing, many graphics adapters are equipped with an internal interface to transmit pixel information synchronously with screen refreshing. This interface is employed to link graphic adapters with overlay cards (videoblasters) and MPEG decoders. The graphics adapter connector is linked to the same connector on the video card by a ribbon cable.

VGA adapters used to have a 26-contact edge VGA Auxiliary Video Connector with contact pads spaced 0.1 inch apart. Later, the VESA Feature Connector (VFC) (Table 7.17) was standardized; its signal suite is practically the same, but a two-row pin connector is used. This VGA and SVGA graphic adapter connector makes it possible to receive the flow of data bytes of the scanned pixels with the adapter operating in modes of up to 640 × 480 × 8 bits. Usually, the interface outputs data and is clocked by the graphics adapter clock. However, by setting the `Data Enable` signal low, the video card can force the graphics adapter to receive pixels; the `Sync Enable` signal switches the graphic adapter into receiving the line and frame synchronization signals; the `PCLK Enable` signal switches the graphic adapter into operating from the external pixel synchronization signal.

Table 7.17. VFC Connector

Signal	Contact	Contact	Signal
GND	2	1	Data 0
GND	4	3	Data 1
GND	6	5	Data 2
Data enable	8	7	Data 3
Sync. enable	10	9	Data 4
PCLK enable	12	11	Data 5
(Vcc)	14	13	Data 6
GND	16	15	Data 7
GND	18	17	PCLK
GND	20	19	BLANK
GND	22	21	HSYNC
(Vcc)	24	23	VSYNC
(GND)	26	25	GND

The VESA Advanced Feature Connector (VAFC) (Table 7.18) is designed to be used in up to 1024 × 768 High Color (16 bit) and True Color (24 or 32 bits) operating modes. It has two rows of contacts spaced 0.05 inch apart, with 0.1 inch between the rows. It is 16/32 bits wide, and at the maximum dot frequency of 37.5 MHz provides data flow speed of 150 MBps. The 16-bit VAFC version uses the first 56 contacts; the 32-bit version uses all 80 contacts. The maximum ribbon cable length is 7 inches. In this interface, the GRDY and VRDY signal indicate that the graphic adapter and the video system, respectively, are ready to generate pixel data. The EVID# signal controls the directions of the data transfer.

Table 7.18. VAFC Connector

Contact	Signal	Function	Contact	Signal	Function
1	RSRV0	Reserved	41	GND	Ground
2	RSRV1	Reserved	42	GND	Ground
3	GENCLK	Genclock input	43	GND	Ground

continues

Table 7.18 Continued

Contact	Signal	Function	Contact	Signal	Function
4	OFFSET0	Pixel offset 2	44	GND	Ground
5	OFFSET1	Pixel offset 1	45	GND	Ground
6	FSTAT	FIFO buffer status	46	GND	Ground
7	VRDY	Video ready	47	GND	Ground
8	GRDY	Graphics ready	48	GND	Ground
9	BLANK#	Blanking	49	GND	Ground
10	VSYNC	Vertical sync	50	GND	Ground
11	HSYNC	Horizontal sync	51	GND	Ground
12	EGEN#	Enable gen-clock	52	GND	Ground
13	VCLK	Graphics data clock	53	GND	Ground
14	RSRV2	Reserved	54	GND	Ground
15	DCLK (PCLK)	Video data (Pixel) clock	55	GND	Ground
16	EVIDEO#	Video data direction control	56	GND	Ground
17	P0	Video data 0	57	P1	Video data 1
18	GND	Ground	58	P2	Video data 2
19	P3	Video data 3	59	GND	Ground
20	P4	Video data 4	60	P5	Video data 5
21	GND	Ground	61	P6	Video data 6
22	P7	Video data 7	62	GND	Ground
23	P8	Video data 8	63	P9	Video data 9
24	GND	Ground	64	P10	Video data 10
25	P11	Video data 11	65	GND	Ground
26	P12	Video data 12	66	P13	Video data 13

continues

Table 7.18 Continued

Contact	Signal	Function	Contact	Signal	Function
27	GND	Ground	67	P14	Video data 14
28	P15	Video data 15	68	GND	Ground
29	P16	Video data 16	69	P17	Video data 17
30	GND	Ground	70	P18	Video data 18
31	P19	Video data 19	71	GND	Ground
32	P20	Video data 20	72	P21	Video data 21
33	GND	Ground	73	P22	Video data 22
34	P23	Video data 23	74	GND	Ground
35	P24	Video data 24	75	P25	Video data 25
36	GND	Ground	76	P26	Video data 26
37	P27	Video data 27	77	GND	Ground
38	P28	Video data 28	78	P29	Video data 29
39	GND	Ground	79	P30	Video data 30
40	P31	Video data 31	80	GND	Ground

In addition to these standards, there also is a special internal 32-bit-wide bus — the VESA Media Channel (VM Channel) — for exchanging data between multimedia devices. This bus (channel) unlike the ones described above is oriented at broadband data transmission among several parties.

7.4.6. Video Interfaces

In traditional color television broadcasting equipment, information about the instantaneous luminance value is carried along with the negative polarity sync pulses directly in the video signal. The color information is sent modulated on supplementary frequencies. In this way, the compatibility of black-and-white receivers, which ignore the color information, with the transmitting color channel is ensured. However, color information is coded differently in the PAL, SECAM, and NTSC systems; their sweep frequencies also are different. Various low-frequency interfaces are used in video equipment (radio-frequency channels are not considered in this book).

In the *Composite Video* interface, a complete video signal of about 1.5 V amplitude is sent over 75-ohm coaxial cable. Coaxial RCA connectors are used to connect cable to devices. This interface is typical of domestic video recorders, analog TV cameras, televisions, etc. In PCs, this interface is used as a graphics card's auxiliary output interface, and as an input interface in video signal capture devices.

The *S-Video* (Separate Video) interface uses separate signal lines: Y for the luminance and synchronization channels, and C for the color signal. Over the C line, the subcarrier frequency modulated by the chroma signal (burst signal) is transmitted. The amplitude of the Y signal is 1 V. The C signal has different amplitudes in different television standards: In the NTSC standard, it is 0.286 V; in the PAL/SECAM standard, it is 0.3 V. Both lines must be loaded with a 75-ohm terminator. The standard four-contact mini-DIN S-Video connector (Fig. 7.14, *a*) is used for interface in high-quality video systems; it is also called *S_VHS* or *Y/C*. In PCs, this interface may also be used as the main input or as auxiliary output. It provides better quality video transmission. Sometimes, seven-contact mini-DIN connectors also are used. Their four external contacts have the same functions, and the three internal contacts are used for various purposes (including for the composite signal). The S-Video output signal can easily be converted into a composite input signal (Fig. 7.14, *b*.) This schematics does not provide proper impedance matching, but the image quality is acceptable. The reverse conversion using the same schematics provides much lower quality, because the luminance signal will be affected by the color signal.

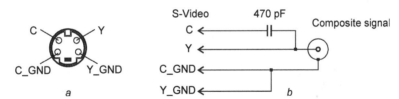

Fig. 7.14. S-Video interface: *a* — connector, *b* — conversion to composite signal

The YUV professional studio interface, which uses three signal lines, provides the best transmission quality: its U and V chroma signals are transmitted unmodulated.

7.5. Audio Interfaces

Audio cards can have a set of connectors for connecting external audio signals, analog and digital, as well as a MIDI interface for linking electronic musical instruments. Digital audio data can also be sent over the universal USB and FireWire buses. (See *Section 4.2.*)

7.5.1. Analog Interfaces

Analog interfaces allow consumer electronics devices, microphones, analog output CD-ROMs and the like to be connected to a computer. Most mass-produced analog signal cards employ 3.5 mm miniature jack connectors, mono and stereo. These are the universal connectors used in domestic electronic equipment, but they have rather low contact quality: They cause interference (rustling and crackling), and also sometimes simply fail to provide connection. Their full-size 6-mm "relatives," characteristic of the professional equipment, have quite high quality, but because of their large size are not used in audio cards. In some high quality audio cards, line inputs and outputs are brought onto RCA connectors, which provide very good connection, especially gold-plated ones.

The layout of the mini-jacks' contacts is standardized: The left channel is routed to the inside post, the ground is connected to the outer cylinder, and the right channel is linked to the middle band. If a stereo jack is plugged into a mono socket or vice versa, the signal will only go over the left channel. All connections in stereo systems are done by "straight" cables; connector contacts connect "one-to-one." There is no universal method to connect the middle and low-frequency channels in a six-speaker audio system, and a crossover cable may be needed. If the channels have been connected incorrectly, it will be noticeable by the squeaks from the subwoofer and thumping from the middle speaker.

Connecting devices to the sound card using external connectors does not usually cause any problems, as they are standardized, and all that is needed is to know the meaning of connector labeling:

❏ *Line In* — line input for tape player, tuner, record player, synthesizer and the like. Sensitivity about 0.1–0.3 V.
❏ *Line Out* — line output to the external amplifier or tape recorder; signal level about 0.1–0.3 V.
❏ *Speaker Out* — output to acoustic system or headphones. It is advisable to connect an external amplifier to this output, as its signal distortions are higher than on the line output.
❏ *Mic In* — microphone input (sensitivity 3–10 mV). Usually, it's mono; sometimes, it uses a 3-pin connector (like with stereo). An extra pin (in place of the left channel) is allotted to power up the electrete mircophone.

Connecting internal devices to analog outputs may produce some problems. Here, four-pin connectors differing both in their contact spacing and functions are employed. Often, two or even three connectors are placed next to each other and their contacts joined in parallel to connect a CD-ROM, but even this may not help if the cable's connector contact layout is different. The solution may be to switch the places of the contacts on the cable's connector. To do this, the contact's locking shoulder is pressed by a needle into its notch, and the contact is then pulled by the cable out of its hole and placed into the proper position. Naturally, if its new place is occupied by another contact, that contact will also have to be pulled out and the contacts' places switched. An external view and possible arrangements of audio signal input contacts are shown in Fig. 7.15, *b.* To complete the picture, it must be said that sometimes (because of an assembly error on the internal standard) the connector may have the key on the wrong side. This does not make connection a hopeless task, as only two signal contacts need to switch places; the common wire contacts can be determined as they are connected to the ground bus on the card and to the shield on the cable. Where the left and right audio CD channels are located does not really matter.

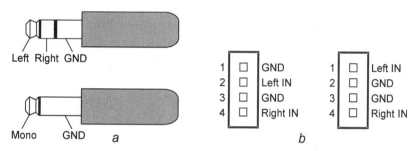

Fig. 7.15. Audio signals connectors

7.5.2. Digital Interfaces

The *Sony/Philips Digital Interface Format* (S/PDIF) is employed to exchange audio signals between pieces of domestic audio equipment (DAT, CD-ROM, and the like). This is a simplified version of the AES/EBU (Audio Engineers Society/European Broadcast Union) studio interface. The AES/EBU interface uses a symmetrical two-wire shielded 110-ohm impedance cable with XLR connectors; the signal level is 3 V to 10 V, cable length can be up to 12 meters.

The S/PDIF interface employs a 75-ohm coaxial cable and RCA or BNC connectors; the signal level is 0.5 V to 1 V, cable length is up to 2 meters. The connectors on the sound cards are simpler: They are just a pair of pins (like those used for jumpers) on the card to which the matching cable connector is attached. The same simplified connecters are used on new CD-ROM drives that have an S/PDIF output. The regular S/PDIF transmitter has a 1:1 pulse transformer, which galvanically decouples joined devices. Simplified versions without an isolating transformer may also be encountered. Connecting non-standard interface devices may cause problems stemming from mismatched signal levels. In this case, the signal may be unstable (the sound will be intermittent) or not received at all. These problems may be solved by installing additional signal drivers.

In addition to the electrical version of the S/PDIF interface, there is an optical version — Toslink, standard EIAJ CP-1201 — with infrared 660-nanometer emitters. Using optics makes it possible to decouple devices galvanically, which is necessary to reduce the level of crosstalk. Plastic fiber (POF) cable cannot exceed 1.5 meters in length; glass fiber cable can be no longer than 3 meters. Several interface conversion schematics — one of which is shown in Fig. 7.16 — are available on the Internet. Here, because of the feedback circuit, the first inverter is brought into the linear part of the transmission characteristic, thanks to which a low power input signal can switch it. A six-inverter HCT74U04 integrated circuit is used in the schematics. Instead of the light-emitting diode, a company's Toslink transceiver can be used; it should be connected without a loading 220-ohm resistor directly to the inverter's output (there is an internal loading resistor in the transceiver).

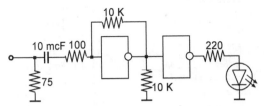

Fig. 7.16. S/PDIF electrical interface to optical (Toslink) converter schematics

Information is sent over the S/PDIF interface frame-by-frame in serial code, providing synchronization and controlling data validity using Reed-Solomon codes. Frames contain a data format indicator (i.e., whether it is pulse-code modulated or not), which allows packed digital data (such ad MPEG for AC-3) be sent over the interface. There also is a copy protection bit, a pre-distortion attribute, and some other service data. In the pulse-code modulation mode, each channel can be sampled at 16, 20, or 24 bits; the digital signal frequency is determined by the sample rate. An S/PDIF receiver can itself determine the sample rate by the received signal; the most frequently used frequencies are 32 KHz, 44.1 KHz, and 48 KHz.

In addition to these interfaces, the ADAT and TDIF interfaces are used in studio equipment. These are expensive interfaces, and are only used in professional audio cards.

To exchange data with DVD drives, the I2S digital serial interface is used.

7.5.3. MIDI Interface

The *Musical Instrument Digital Interface* (MIDI) is a serial asynchronous 31.25 Kbps interface that was developed in 1983. It has become the de-facto standard for linking computers, synthesizers, recording and reproducing equipment, mixers, special effect devices, and other electronic musical equipment. Currently, both expensive synthesizers and cheap musical keyboards that can be used as computer input devices are equipped with a MIDI interface. One interface may contain up to 16 channels, each of which can control its own instrument.

The physical interface uses a 5–10 milliampere current loop with a galvanically (optically) decoupled input circuit. Current flow corresponds to logical zero; the absence of current flow corresponds to logical one (in the classic communications current loop, the signals are reversed).

The interface defines three types of ports: MIDI-In, MIDI-Out, and MIDI-Thru.

The input MIDI-In port is of the current loop type, galvanically decoupled from the receiver by an optron with an operating speed of no less than 2 μsec. The device tracks the information stream at this input and reacts to the commands and data addressed to it.

The output MIDI-Out port is a current source output that is galvanically coupled with the device circuitry. Limiting resistors protects output circuits from damage when short-circuited to the ground or +5 V. The information stream from the current device is sent to the output. If a device is properly set-up, the output stream may contain the relayed input stream, but this operating mode is not typical.

The MIDI-Thru transit port is only used to relay the input stream; its electrical characteristics are analogous to the output port. It is not a mandatory port for all devices.

The connectors used are 5-contact DIN connectors, commonly utilized in the domestic audio equipment; a connecting cable schematics is shown in Fig. 7.17.

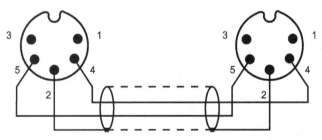

Fig. 7.17. MIDI connecting cables

The external MIDI port (with TTL signals) is usually routed to the unused contacts (12 and 15) of the game adapter connector (DB-15S). To connect standard MIDI devices to this connector, a matching current loop-to-TTL adapter is needed, since the game card connector has TTL interface. A matching adapter is usually built into a special cable, one version of which is shown in Fig. 7.18. Some PCs have built-in adapters and standard 5-pin MIDI connectors.

In terms of software, the MIDI port is compatible with the MPU-401 UART. (The "MPU" stands for "MIDI Processing Unit".) The Roland MPU-401 was the first MIDI interface PC expansion card to gain wide acceptance. In addition to the asynchronous serial port (UART) implementing the physical MIDI interface, this controller had well-developed hardware means to use the PC as a sequencer. The MPU-401 controller supported a simple operating mode, the UART mode, in which only the bidirectional asynchronous port was used; modern audio cards are compatible with the MPU-401 only in this mode.

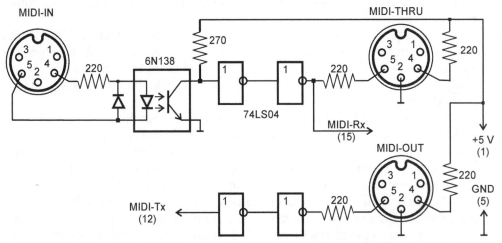

Fig. 7.18. Version of a MIDI matching cable schematics

In the I/O addressing space, the MPU-401 occupies two adjacent addresses: MPU (usually 330h) and MPU+1.

❏ The DATA port (address MPU+0) is used to read and write bytes transmitted and received via the MIDI interface. In the smart mode, auxiliary data not related to the MIDI stream are also read via this port.

❏ The STATUS/COMMAND port (address MPU+1) is used to read the status and write commands (writing can only be done in the smart mode). The following bits are defined in the status byte:

  ● Bit 7 — DSR (Data Set Ready). Received data are ready to be read when DSR=0. When all the data have been read out of the register, this bit is set to 1.

  ● Bit 6 — DRR (Data Read Ready). The UART is ready to write to the data or port register when DRR=0. If there is an unread data byte in the receiver, the ready condition cannot be set.

When powered up, a "true" MPU-401 card goes into the smart mode, from which it can be switched into the UART mode by the 3Fh command. The MPU-401 is reset (into the smart mode) by the RESET command (code FFh). The MPU-401 may confirm this command by generating an acknowledgement byte Ack (FEh). The acknowledge byte is extracted from the data register; until the MPU receives this byte, it will not accept following commands. The MPU does not acknowledge the 3Fh command (switch into the UART mode), although some emulators also confirm this command.

Data input can be implemented either by software polling the DSR bit, or by interrupts. In the UART mode, the MPU generates hardware interrupts upon receiving a byte. The interrupt handler must read out all the input data and terminates only upon ascertaining that DSR=1 (otherwise, some received bytes may be lost).

Data output is enabled by the DRR bit; no interrupt to send ready output data is generated.

MPU-401 compatibility, which most of the modern MIDI interface audio cards possess, means that a card must have a transceiver that is software compatible with MIDI in the UART mode; smart-mode functions are usually not supported.

In some motherboards, large-scale integration interface-controller microchips are used; these circuits' UART mode, used for the COM port, can be switched into the MIDI port mode in BIOS Setup.

USB can be used to connect multiple MIDI devices to a PC. For this purpose, Roland, among others, produces a 64-channel S-MPU64 processor block that, in addition to the USB, has four input and four output MIDI ports. Software support allows up to four blocks to be joined on one USB bus, which increases the number of channels to 256.

7.5.4. Daughterboard Interface

Several audio card models have an internal daughterboard connector for connecting a daughterboard with MIDI synthesizer. The MIDI port signal (TTL level, as for joystick connector) and the synthesizer hardware reset signal are routed from the main card to this connector (Table 7.19). The analog stereo signal is input from the daughterboard to this connector, to be farther relayed to the main card mixer. In the power supply circuits, the analog ground (AG) rail is separated from the digital ground (DG) rail. The MIDI input may also be used. The connector may be also be called a WT (Wavetable, Waveblaster) connector.

Table 7.19. Daughterboard Connector Contact Functions

Contact	Signal	Contact	Signal
1	DG	2	—
3	DG	4	MIDI_Out#
5	DG	6	+5 V
7	DG	8	MIDI_In# (not required)
9	DG	10	+5 V
11	DG	12	—
13		14	+5 V

continues

Table 7.19 Continued

Contact	Signal	Contact	Signal
15	AG	16	—
17	AG	18	+12 V
19	AG	20	Audio (R)
21	AG	22	−12 V
23	AG	24	Audio (L)
25	AG	26	Reset#

Connecting a daughterboard is equivalent to connecting an external synthesizer to an audio card's MIDI output. If the audio card does not have a daughterboard connector, the daughterboard can be connected to the external joystick/MIDI connector and to the audio card's analog inputs. Of course, the power supply and reset must also be supplied to the daughterboard.

7.6. Game Port Interface

Gaming devices — joysticks, automobile steering wheels and pedals, and others — generate analog and digital signals that can be input to a computer. The game adapter interface (*Game port*), to which two joysticks or other devices could be connected, was introduced and virtually standardized in the first IBM PCs. Altogether, four coordinate variable-resistor sensors are available (X1, X2, Y1, and Y2) and four discrete control button inputs. The coordinate sensors' roles depend on the particular game and the manipulator's construction. In aircraft simulators, the X1 sensor may be responsible for tracking up/down movements of the control lever, the Y1 sensor for right/left movements, the X2 sensor for pressing the left or right pedal, and the Y2 sensor for the throttle lever. In automobile games, the X1 sensor tracks the steering wheel, the Y1 sensor the throttle pedal, and the X2 sensor the brake pedal (the throttle and the brake pedals may share the Y1 sensor). As well as entertainment purposes, the port may also be used to connect "serious" sensors.

Modern game devices have their own "brains" — a microcontroller — and are connected to the computer via a digital interface (either the USB bus or the COM port). Their functional capabilities are broader, and they allow the introduction of mechanical feedback to the player.

The Game port adapter has one register in the I/O address range. Its address is 201h, and its bits reflect the status of the buttons and analog signal comparators when read. How discrete button signals are input is obvious, and does not need to be explained. A simplified schematics of one analog input channel is shown in Fig. 7.19. At the beginning of the conversion, the capacitor discharges on the key, after which it starts charging. The rate of charging is determined by the value of the sensor's resistance: The higher the resistance, the slower the charge. The voltage on the capacitor is controlled by the comparator, which is triggered upon reaching some certain threshold. The comparator outputs for all four conversion channels, as well as the discrete inputs, are collected into the register (see below) that can be read by software. The conversion is done purely by software, and begins when any byte has been output to the adapter register (201h); bits 0–3 are set to logical 1 at the beginning of this operation. Further, the program cyclically reads the adapter register and measures the time it takes bits 0–3 (which correspond to the four analog channels) to return to logical 0. If an analog input shorts to ground or a measured circuit is broken, the corresponding bit will not be zeroed out. Therefore, time-out provisions must be made in the conversion program. For resistors measured in the 0–100 K range, the time is calculated using the formula $T(ms) = 24.2 + 11 \times R(Kohm)$.

The precision and linearity of the conversion is not high, and the conversion itself is slow (taking up to 1.12 msec) and puts a heavy load on the processor. However, in contrast to "real" analog-to-digital converters, this one costs nothing: A game adapter is a part of practically all combined boards of parallel and serial ports and audio cards.

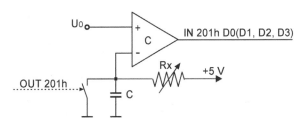

Fig. 7.19. Analog input channel

The port has a DB-15S female connector. The functions of the outputs and their corresponding register bits are shown in Table 7.20. The resistors are connected to the +5 V rail; the buttons are connected to the GND rail (Fig. 7.20.) Zeroes in bits 5–7 correspond to the closed button positions. The analog channels can be used to input discrete signals by connecting their inputs to buttons that link them to the GND rail, and to resistors that pull them up to +5 V. Two joysticks — A and B — can be connected using a Y-adapter. In audio cards, the game connector can be used along with joysticks to connect external MIDI devices by employing a special adapting cable that galvanically decouples the incoming signal and limits the incoming current (Fig. 7.18). The MIDI interface uses contacts 12 and 15, which used to be taken by GND and +5 V. This makes it safe to connect a MIDI adapter to a "pure" game port, and a usual joystick to a game port with MIDI signals.

Table 7.20. Game Adapter and MIDI Interface

Bit	Function	Contact
7	Joystick B button #2	14
6	Joystick B button #1	10
5	Joystick A button #2	7
4	Joystick A button #1	2
3	Joystick B Y-coordinate (Y2)	13
2	Joystick B X-coordinate (X2)	11
1	Joystick A Y-coordinate (Y1)	6
0	Joystick A X-coordinate (X1)	3
–	GND	4, 5, (12)
–	+5 V	1, 8, 9, (15)
–	MIDI In (Rx) — input (in audio card)	15
–	MIDI Out (Tx) — output (in audio card)	12

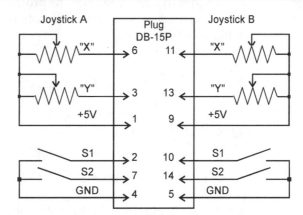

Fig. 7.20. Connecting sensors to a game adapter

Joystick system support is provided by the BIOS Int 15h service function 84h (AH=84h). When it is called, the subfunction number is loaded in the processor's DX register:

❑ DX=0 — button monitoring. Returns button status into the AL[7:4] register (corresponds to port 201h bits).

❑ DX=1 — reading X, Y coordinates of the joystick A into the registers AX and BX and of the joystick B into the registers CX and DX.

When a wrong code is placed into the DX register, the CF is set to logical 1. The standard joystick is also supported by Windows.

Chapter 8: Data Storage Device Interfaces

Data storage devices — removable and nonremovable hard and floppy disk drives, CD and DVD optical disks, streamers, solid disks, etc. — are connected to computers in various ways. The first PC data storage devices — floppy disk drives (FDD) — were connected by an interface ribbon cable to the controller, which was separated from the drive itself. This specialized interface has survived to the present day, and is used to connect disk drives that only require transfer speeds of 500 Kbps (about 60 KBps). The speeds of 1,000 Kbps needed for the 2.88 MB floppy drives, which were not as widely accepted as had been expected, has not been utilized. Old streamers (very low-speed ones) used to be connected to the disk drive interface. The similar interface was also used to connect MFM and RLL hard drives; raw, albeit amplified, data were sent over it to and from the disk heads.

Later, data storage devices were given some "brains," and for a short time the ESDI disk interface — which provided whopping transfer speeds of 1 MBps — appeared. However, soon the controller was moved to the drive itself and, moreover, was provided with its own buffers (at first holding only one sector, but subsequently growing rapidly), and everything that had to do with magnetic data recording and reproducing was taken out of the external interface. Thus developed were ATA interface devices, which first appeared in 1988 and now are the most commonly used type of data storage devices. For devices that are logically different from hard disks — optical, magneto-optical, tape, and any others — the ATAPI specification was accepted in 1996. This is a packet expansion of the interface that makes it possible to send command information blocks whose structure has been modeled on the SCSI to a device over the ATA bus. The ATA speed ceiling is 133 MBps in Ultra DMA Mode 6. The ATA interface has an addressing limit of about 137 GB, which is now being overstepped; the ATAPI interface employs 32-bit addressing, which allows up to 2 TB to be addressed (using 512 byte blocks). The next step in the development of the interface is the Serial ATA. In this interface, issues such as increasing the exchange speed, simultaneous work with multiple devices, and expanding the addressing limits are addressed. The same addressing has been introduced in the latest version of the parallel ATA.

Universal interfaces also are employed for storage devices. The SCSI bus is the ATA's first challenger in both the parallel and serial (FCAL) versions. Providing approximately the same exchange rates, the SCSI allows operation of multiple devices on the bus. The bus itself is available for use by other devices when it is executing a command with a long data wait time. In contrast to the purely internal ATA bus, the SCSI bus allows external devices to be connected to it. For connecting external storage devices, the USB and, less frequently, FireWire buses are employed; the LPT port can also be enlisted for this purpose.

8.1. FDD Interface

Floppy disk drives are connected to the controller using a special standard interface. The major control functions, as well as data coding/decoding, are performed by the controller, which is built into the overwhelming majority of modern motherboards. In the past, the controller was often built on a special expansion card along with floppy drive interface. The printed circuit board that is located on the floppy case contains only the motor controlling circuitry, the read and write signal amplifiers and generators, respectively, and sensor signal-drivers.

8.1.1. Hardware Interface

All FDD interface signals are active low logical TTL levels. The output signal drivers have the open collector type output. The interface presupposes terminators — load resistors — for each signal line of the device. Theoretically, they are supposed to be turned on only on the last drive in the chain, but in practice they are always on. Modern 3-inch drives employ "distributed terminators," relatively high value (1K–1.5K) resistors that permanently link the interface input lines with the +5 V rail. Because the interface operates at low frequencies, the problem of precisely matching the impedance of the ribbon cable and the terminator's resistors does not arise. However, if only old 5-inch floppy drives with their terminators removed are connected to the ribbon cable, they may not operate reliably (the open collector output lines will have no loads).

In terms of logic, the interface is quite simple. To set the drive into work, it needs to be selected by the Drive Sel signal and start the motor spindle with the Motor On signal. There are four signals for selecting a floppy drive (DS0 ... DS3), but a particular drive responds to only one, which is determined by its jumper settings. The selected drive responds to the controller's signals and sends its signals to the controller. The fact of a drive having been selected is indicated by a lit LED on its front panel.

To move the heads one step, the controller must issue the Step pulse; the direction is determined by the Direction signal level: the move is toward the center of the disk (track number increases) when the signal is active (low). The controller locates the zero track by moving the heads from the center toward the edge until the Track00 signal is sensed. The head number is selected by the Side1 signal. The drive marks the beginning of a track by the Index pulse that is generated when the index hole of the revolving disk passes under the sensor. The data that are read are MFM coded, amplified, converted to a TTL signal, and output over the Read Data line. The write mode is enabled by the Write Gate signal; encoded digital data are input from the controller over the Write Data line. If the diskette is write-protected, the drive will generate a Write Protect signal. To obtain the lower write current needed when double or quadruple density diskettes are used in a high density drive, the Reduce Write signal is employed. This signal is also called Low Current or FDHDIN. To switch the heads into the "vertical write" mode used for 2.88 MB diskettes, the FDEDIN signal is used. Both of these signals are generated by the controller, but for the drive itself they are duplicated by signals from the diskette type sensors. (The FDEDIN signal is not required; the drive itself will switch the mode at the sensor signal.)

Some disk drives allow the described diskette type sensor operating method, which is used in the PC compatible computers, to be modified: They may be disconnected or provide information to the controller. However, practically all controllers themselves control the interface lines that correspond to the sensor signals. In doing this, they take into consideration the disk drive type defined in the SMOS Setup and the requested diskette type. The controller generates the low-level Reduce Write signal at any time it accesses the drive described in the CMOS as high density (1.2 MB or 1.44 MB) for working with double or quadruple density diskettes (360 KB or 720 KB, respectively). Some controllers only generated this signal when they were set to the 300 Kbps operating speed (360/720 KB diskette in a 1.2 MB disk drive). This type of controller can format and write 720 KB diskettes in a 1.44 MB drive only when the drive is equipped with a high density sensor and the latter is properly configured; otherwise, it will write all 3.5 inch diskettes with high write current, which cannot be done for quadruple density diskettes.

High density drives assert the Disk Changed signal when a diskette has been changed; it is deasserted after the drive has been accessed. This signal deserves special attention; only high density and extra high density (the rare 2.88 MB) drives have it. The function of this signal is determined by setting the drive's jumpers. In PCs, the corresponding jumper is set to the DC (Disk Change) position. The alternative function of this line — device ready, which may be called RY, RDY, or SR — cannot be used in PC-compatible computers.

There are no signals in the interface that directly inform the controller of the drive being ready (i.e., a diskette having been inserted). The controller can determine this only after selecting the drive and starting its motor. Then, the absence of Index pulses will mean that the drive is not ready: either there is no diskette inserted, or it is not fixed on the spindle, or the drive's interface or power cables are not connected. The controller may determine whether the drive is present by issuing the recalibration command; the drive should respond with the Track00 signal when it is executed.

Regardless of their type and capacity, all floppy disk drives used in PCs employ the same interface and standardized 34-contact connectors of two types: two-sided PCB connectors used for 5.25 inch drives, and the other with two rows of pin connectors used for 3.5 inch devices. The ribbon cable used to connect floppy drives in PCs has wires 10–16 twisted around (Fig. 8.1). This twist allows two floppy drives to be connected to the controller by one ribbon cable. A drive's address is determined by its location of the ribbon cable: The B drive is connected by the straight cable, the A drive is connected to the connector on the twisted part of the ribbon cable. The universal ribbon cable with five connectors (shown in the drawing) allows a pair of any type of drives to be connected; they must be connected to the different parts of the cable. Some connectors may be absent, and this will limit the drive's configuration flexibility. Table 8.1 describes interface cable signals that arrive to different drives. Signal direction (I/O — input/output) is shown with respect to the controller.

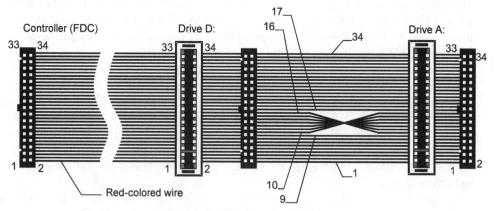

Fig. 8.1. FDD interface cable

Table 8.1. FDD Interface Cable Signals

Controller		I/O	Drive B:		Drive A:	
Contact[1]	Signal		Contact[1]	Signal	Contact[1]	Signal
2	FDHDIN (Reduce Write)	O	2	Low Current	2	Low Current
4	Reserved	–	4	Reserved	4	Reserved
6	FDEDEIN	–	6	FDEDIN (DS3)	6	FDEDIN (DS3)
8	Index	I	8	Index	8	Index
10	Motor On A	O	10	DS0	16	Motor[2]
12	Drive Sel 1	O	12	DS1[2]	14	DS2
14	Drive Sel 0	O	14	DS2	12	DS1[2]
16	Motor On B	O	16	Motor[2]	10	DS0
18	Direction	O	18	Direction	18	Direction
20	Step	O	20	Step	20	Step
22	Write Data	O	22	WData	22	Wdata
24	Write Gate	O	24	WGate	24	Wgate
26	Track 00	I	26	TR 00	26	TR 00
28	Write Protect	I	28	WProt	28	WProt
30	Read Data	I	30	RData	30	Rdata
32	Side 1	O	32	Side 1	32	Side 1
34[3]	Disk Changed	I	34[3]	DC	34[3]	DC

[1] Odd contacts 1–33 are grounded. For 5.25-inch drives, the key is between contacts 4–5 and 6–7.

[2] The signal pair that selects the FDD. (Motor On A and Drive Sel 0 for the A: drive and Motor On B and Drive Sel 1 for the B: drive.)

[3] Contact 34 is not used in XT.

The floppy drive controller and the interface cable employed in PCs allow one of the two drives be addressed and its motor turned on. The `Drive Sel 0` and `Motor On A` signals are used for the A: drive, and the `Drive Sel 1` and `Motor On B` signals are used for the B: drive. The jumpers on both drives are set so that they both respond to the DS1 signal (connector contact 12). Usually, the jumpers are labeled DA0/DS1/ DS2/DS3; in this case, the DS1 jumper must be set. If the jumpers are named as DS1/DS2/DS3/DS4, which is not encountered often, then the DS2 jumper must be installed. The adopted drive selection system allows all the drives to be configured the same way and their addresses to be set by their location on the ribbon cable. Certain PC clones employ a different drive selection system and a "straight" ribbon cable. In this case, a device is selected by the DS0 signal. However, using this line for selecting drives is not supported by some drives; consequently changing drives in these proprietary machines may turn out to be very troublesome, especially if the technical manual is not available.

8.1.2. FDD Controller

Software interacts with floppy disk drives via the *Floppy Drive Controller*, enlisting, as a rule, the DMA controller and interrupts. Programming the FDD controller to work with diskettes is a troublesome task. All functions necessary for using FDD for storing data are implemented in the BIOS Int 13h services and the operating system. Ignoring the BIOS services and even the operating system is justified mainly when implementing non-trivial tasks such as working with key diskettes and the like.

All controllers used in IBM PCs are compatible with the historical NEC PD765 controller microchip, an analog of the i8272 microchip. The AT floppy drive controller supports two drives and several data transfer speeds: 250 Kbps (for single, double, and quadruple density diskettes for old 5.25-inch drives), 500 Kbps for high density diskettes (1.2 MB and 1.44 MB), and also 300 Kbps for working with single, double, and quadruple density diskettes in high density 5.25-inch drives. Modern controllers that support extra-high density drives (2.88 MB) must provide transfer rates of 1,000 Kbps. The controller's modes that correspond to speeds of 250/300 Kbps, 500 Kbps, and 1,000 Kbps are named 1M, 2M, and 4M, respectively. In the 1M mode, one track holds nine 512-byte sectors, which requires a transfer rate of 250 Kbps at a rotational speed of 300 rpm and 300 Kbps at 360 rpm. In the 2M mode at 300 rpm (3.5-inch high-density drives), one track holds 18 sectors, and at 360 rpm (5.25-inch high-density drives), one track holds 15 sectors. The 4M mode appears to have been left unused. The selected speed determines the write and format synchronization frequency, and also adjusts the frequency locked loop circuitry of the controller's data separator. The data separator can reliably extract data and sync signal from the signal received from the reading head only when deviations in speed are within ±10% of the nominal; therefore, the speed for all disk data exchange operations must be selected correctly.

In the AT resource map, an area for two floppy disk controllers is allocated:

❑ AT#1 FDC (standard or main) is allocated ports 3F0h–3F7h (the same as the XT FDC).

❑ AT#2 FDC (supplementary) is allocated ports 370h–377h.

Upon completing execution of an internal operation, controllers generate the hardware interrupt request IRQ6 (BIOS Int OEh). The DMA2 channel can be used for data exchange. The functions of the controller's registers are listed in Table 8.2.

The FDC status register address 3F7h (377h) coincides with the address of HDC register (long not used), which makes separate operation of FDC and HDC located on different boards problematic. In the standard (not diagnostic) mode, only bit 7 — media change indicator — is of any interest.

Table 8.2. FDD Controller Registers

Address	Function (R — read, W — write)
3F2h (372h)	DOR — Digital Output Register (RW). Bits[4:7] —ON status of the A, B, C, and D motors: 1 — ON; bit 3: 1 — DMA2 and IRQ6 enable; bit 2: 0 — reset, 1 — controller enable; bits [1:0] — selected drive number 0–3. In AT, bits 1, 6, and 7 are not used.
3F3h (373h)	TDR — Tape Drive Register (RW): streamer register. Bits [1:0] — number of the device corresponding to the streamer. Set to 00 upon reset, but this means that there is no streamer (a streamer cannot be installed in place of drive A:).
3F4h (374h)	MSR — Main Status Register (R). Bit 7 (DQM) — request: 1 — ready to receive/send a byte; bit 6 (DIO) — data direction: 1 — FDC → CPU; bit 5 (NON DMA) — DMA use: 1 — DMA not used; bit 4 (CMD BSY): 1 — controller is busy executing command; bits [0:3] — drive A:, B:, C:, D: is busy (in AT, only bits 0 and 1 are used).
3F4h (374h)[1]	DSR — Data rate Select Register (W). Bit 7: 1 — controller reset (zeroed out automatically); bit 6: 1 — turning off controller's power; bit 5: 1 — external phase locked loop enabled (must be 0); bits [4:2]: write precompensation time select (000 — default precompensation); bits [1:0]: exchange rate (00 — 500 Kbps, 01 — 300 Kbps, 10 — 250 Kbps, 11 — 1 Mbps).
3F5h (375h)	DR — Data/Command Register (RW).
3F7h (377h)	CCR — Configuration Control Register (for AT) (W). Bits [7:2]: not used; bits [1:0]: exchange rate (00 — 500 Kbps, 01 — 300 Kbps, 10 — 250 Kbps, 11 — 1 Mbps).
3F7h (377h)	DIR — Digital Input Register (AT only) (R). Bit 7: 1 — media change (reading inverted DC line); bits [6:0] — not used; not placed on the data bus when read.

[1] The DSR register is compatible with the i8272 controller. In modern FDD controllers, the CCR is used instead of this register, as only the speed needs to be set.

An FDD controller can also be used to work with streamers. Especially for this purpose, it is equipped with the tape drive register TDR. The two lower bits of this register set the number of the device corresponding to the streamer. (The data separator phase locked loop circuitry is adjusted differently for streamers).

All operations with diskettes are done by commands sent by the host to the DR (3F5h) according to the status of the MSR (3F4h) bits. A command or data byte can only be written to the DR when MSR=10xxxxxxb; writing is allowed when MSR=11xxxxxxb. To read/write this register, separate subroutines need to be used that not only wait for the MSR enabling values, but also can exit upon an emergency time-out. The host also writes to the DOR (3F2h) to start/stop the drive, as well as to the CCR (3F7h) or DSR (3F4h) to set the data transfer rate. The DMA controller is usually involved in the diskette data exchange operations and it has to be initialized in due time. The TC signal (DMA cycle completion) is used to indicate the end of the data phase. The overall data exchange procedure consists of the following steps:

1. Disk selection and motor start (by writing to the DOR).
2. Setting the speed (by writing to the CCR).
3. Executing a recalibration command.
4. Waiting for the motor to spin up (if it has been on for less than 0.5 sec).
5. Positioning the head on the necessary cylinder.
6. Initializing the DMA controller.
7. Sending a read/write command.
8. Waiting for an interrupt from the controller. An interrupt will be generated upon completion of the controller/host data exchange phase execution. If no interrupt is forthcoming within the specified time period, a time-out access error is recorded.
9. After the controller issues an interrupt, the resulting bytes are read and if they are correct, the process terminates. If the data contain errors, then the DMA initialization and the read/write command sending steps are repeated. If the data still contain errors after three attempts, then another recalibration command is executed and steps 6–7 repeated. If after several recalibration attempts the data still contain errors, an abnormal exchange termination is performed.

In addition to the mechanism described, there is a mechanism to automatically turn off the FDD motor if it has not been accessed for a prolonged period of time. For this purpose, cell 0:0440h in the BIOS Data Area contains the FDD motor timer and cell 0:043Fh contains the address of the drive whose motor is currently ON. Every time diskette access is attempted, BIOS places the default time-out motor off value (25h, or about 2 seconds) into this cell. During each timer hardware interrupt IRQ0 (BIOS Int 08h), which occurs about every 55 msec, the value in this byte is decremented by 1. When it finally reaches 0, the drive motor is shut off. Therefore, if no accesses to diskette are made during the set interval, the motor automatically switches off. Of course, this works only when BIOS services the hardware timer interrupts, so the drive motor not shutting off may be an indirect indication that the computer has hung.

Execution of each command is broken into three phases:

1. The *command phase.* The controller sets bits DQM=1 and DIO=0, which is an invitation to input a command. A command byte is sent to the DR, followed by the parameter bytes in a strictly defined order. The controller respond to each received byte by zeroing out the DQM bit for the duration of the byte processing. After receiving the last required byte, the DQM bit remains zeroed out and the controller proceeds to the execution phase. The parameters involved are: the cylinder number C, the head number H, the sector number R, the size code N or the sector data field length DTL, the number of the last sector on the track EOT, the number or sectors SC, the gap length GPL, and some other data.

2. The *execution phase* requires the transfer of data from the host to the controller or vice versa. The transfer can be conducted in both the DMA mode and in the *Programmed Input/Output* (PIO) mode. In the DMA mode, the transfer is performed by the DRQ and DACK# signals of the channel being used. If the DMA mode is not used, then the transmission request is done by the DQM bit and the interrupt request signal. After the phase is terminated, the interrupt request signal is generated (and its flag is set in the ST0 register), and the controller advances to the result phase.

3. In the *result phase* DQM=1 and DIO=1, the host must read the result bytes from the DR, after which these bits change to DQM=0 and DIO=0, which corresponds to moving to the command reception phase.

From the moment a command is received and until the result phase terminates, the CMD BSY bit in the MSR remains set to logical 1. The controller can always be reset (i.e., moved to the beginning of the command phase) by writing to the DOR or DSR. If the controller receives a command it does not support, it sets DQM=1 and DIO=1, which means that the DR needs to be read. The host then must read the status code out of the DR; this code will be 80h (invalid command).

Modern FDD controllers employ a 16-byte-deep FIFO buffer to transfer data (but not commands or parameters) through the DR. The "historical" i8272 controller did not have this FIFO buffer. The logic to communicate with the DR remains the same. The buffer must be serviced in a timely manner so that it does not overflow or underflow. The buffer logic fashions data requests in such a way as not to bother the host unnecessarily. When reading the DR, the request is sent when there are *16-minus-threshold* bytes in the buffer, or when the last byte of the sector has been read off. When writing to the DR, at first the request is set and held until the buffer gets filled up, thereafter it is set when *threshold* bytes are left in the buffer. The advance to the result phase happens when the host concludes the exchange with the DR and the buffer empties. Communication with the DR when writing commands or parameters must be done according to the values of the high bits of the MSR (the FIFO buffer is not used in these communications).

8.2. ATA/ATAPI (IDE) Interface

The ATA (AT Attachment for Disk Drives) was developed during 1986–1990 to connect hard disk drives to IBM PC AT computers built around the ISA bus. The standard, which was developed by the X3T10 committee, defines a set of device registers and functions of the 40-contact interface connector signals. The interface came about as a result of moving the standard (for PC/AT) hard drive controller on the drive itself (i.e., creating a device with a built-in controller: IDE (Integrated Drive Electronics)). The standard AT controller allowed up to two hard drives to be connected, which in the ATA interface means connecting individual controllers of two devices in parallel. The ATA specification defines the following components:

❏ A *host-adapter* is a means to couple the ATA interface with the computer bus. In this book, the host is called a computer equipped with an ATA interface host-adapter. A host-controller is a more advanced version of a host-adapter.
❏ A *master* device in the ATA specification is officially called Device-0.
❏ A *slave* device in the ATA specification is officially called Device-1.

The host-adapter and devices are connected by a ribbon cable that connects the like contacts of the interface connectors in parallel. The registers of both controllers turn out to occupy the same area of the I/O address space. To select the device executing the current command, the DEV drive select bit in the drive/head register is used. If DEV=0, then the master device is selected; if DEV=1, then the slave device is selected. Writing to this register is sensed by both the master and the slave, but only the selected device reacts to access to the other registers. A fairly universal signal set allows the connection of any device that can support the device select method using the above-mentioned bit and that has a built-in controller for whose I/O operations the available register set is sufficient. The adopted system of commands and registers, which is a part of the ATA specification, is oriented at block data exchange with direct access devices. For other devices, there is the ATAPI specification, which is based on the same hardware resources but allows control of the information package to be exchanged (PI — Package Interface). Packets' structure and contents are borrowed from the universal SCSI interface. The packet interface makes it possible to expand the boundaries of ATA applications.

The ATA addressing has "disk roots": originally, so-called *tri-dimensional CHS addressing* was used for disk drives, in which the addresses of the cylinder, head, and sector were specified. At first, this addressing corresponded exactly to real spatial geometry: Physically, the sector was actually located at the given address. Later, due to many factors, ATA disks began to be described using logical geometry that differed from the actual internal disk structure. (Thus, for example, different areas on tracks have a different number of sectors; moreover, some of the sectors may be reserved for future replacement of defective sectors.) Virtual addresses are converted into real ones by the device's built-in controller. Using the CHS system, an ATA device may address up to 267,386,880 (65,536 × 16 × 255) sectors (clusters), which, assuming sector size is 512 bytes, gives 136,902,082,560 bytes (or about 137 GB). Later, *Logical Block Addressing* (LBA) began to be employed. In this method, the sector address is specified by a 28-bit number, which allows up to 268,435,455 (2^{28}) sectors to be addressed (a little more than using the CHS system). For ATA devices that support both CHS and LBA, the addressing mode for each command is determined by the L bit (bit 6) of the D/H register; the modes can alternate in random order. ATAPI devices use a 32-bit logical addressing method like the one used in the SCSI; this allows up to 2 TB be addressed (using 512-byte cluster size).

If only one device is connected to the ATA interface, it must be designated the master. If two devices are connected, one of them must be designated the master and the other the slave. Devices are configured as master or slave by setting their configuration jumpers. If the "cable selection" method is used (see below), the device's role is determined by its location on the special ribbon cable. Both devices perceive commands from the host-adapters at the same time; however, only the selected device will respond. Only the selected device has the right to output signals to the ATA bus. This type of system implies that once the host-adapter has begun an exchange operation with one of the devices, it cannot switch to servicing another until it has completed the operation in progress. Only devices connected to different ATA channels can work in parallel. The ATA-4 specification defines a method to get around this limitation, but this capability is seldom used.

Several versions of the interfaces exist for IDE devices. They are as follows:

❏ ATA, or AT-BUS — a 16-bit interface for connecting devices to an AT computer bus. This is the most common 40-wire signal and four-wire power interface for connecting disk drives to AT computers. For miniature (2.5-inch and smaller) drives, 44-wire cable incorporating the power supply lines is used.

❏ PC Card ATA — a 16-bit interface using a 68-contact PC Card (PCMCIA) connector for connecting devices to notebook PCs.

❏ XT IDE (8-bit), or XT-BUS — a 40-wire interface similar to the AT, but incompatible with it.

❑ MCA IDE (16-bit) — a 72-wire interface designed especially for the PS/2 bus and disk drives.

❑ ATA-2 — an extension to the ATA specification. It supports two channels, four devices, PIO Mode 3, Multiword DAM Mode 1, Block mode, disk size of up to 8 GB, and LBA and CHS.

❑ Fast ATA-2 allows the Multiword DMA Mode 2 (13.3 MBps) and PIO Mode 4 to be used.

❑ ATA-3 — an extension to ATA-2. It provides password protection, improved power management, and a self test with advanced failure warning (Self-Monitoring Analysis and Report Technology (SMART)).

❑ ATA/ATAPI-4 is an extension to ATA-3 that includes Ultra DMA (with transfer rates of up to 33 MBps) and the ATAPI packet interface. It also supports command queues and protocol overlap.

❑ ATA/ATAPI-5 — a revision of ATA-4/ATAPI-4. Outdated commands and bits are removed, new protection capabilities and power management are added. Includes Ultra DMA mode (transfer rates of up to 66 MBps).

❑ ATA/ATAPI-6 — a supplement to the ATA-5/ATAPI-5. Contains audio and video streaming for multimedia application, hard disk noise reduction, Acoustic Management, and Ultra DMA mode with transfer throughput of up to 100 MBps.

❑ Serial ATA.

❑ E-IDE (Enhanced IDE) — expanded interface introduced by Western Digital. It is implemented in adapters for the PCI and VLB buses. The interface allows up to four devices, including CD-ROM and streamers (ATAPI) be connected (to two channels). PIO Mode 3, Multiword DMA Mode 1, and LBA and CHS drives of up to 8 GB are supported. Hardware-wise, it conforms almost completely to the ATA-2 specification.

ATA IDE, E-IDE, ATA-2, Fast ATA-2, ATA-3, ATA/ATAPI-4, ATA/ATAPI-5, and ATA/ATAPI-6 devices are electrically compatible. The degree of logical compatibility is quite high: All basic functions are available. However, in order to implement all the extensions fully, the specifications of the devices must match up to the host-adapter and its software.

The ATA/ATAPI specifications are developed by the T13 technical committee of the International Committee for Information Technology Standards (INCITS). The specifications they develop are approved and published by the American National Standards Institute (ANSI). The ATA/ATAPI-6 specification has been declared the last parallel ATA version; it is followed by the Serial ATA serial interface.

8.2.1. ATA Parallel Interface

The ATA parallel interface is a bus with standard TTL logic signals:

❑ Output signal high level is no lower than 2.4 V (at up to 40 microampere current, the DMARQ signal is up to 50 microampere); low level is no higher than 0.5 V (at 4 milliampere current; current on the DASP line is 12 milliampere for compatibility with old devices).

❑ Input signal high level is not lower than 2.0 V; low level is no higher than 0.8 V.

All the interface's information signals are sent over a 40-contact connector. To ensure correct connection, the connector has a key: removed are a pin on the plug and a hole on the socket in the place of contact 20. The standard does not approve the use of a notch on the plug case and a protrusion on the socket as keys. Devices are connected using multiple-wire ribbon cable. Its length must not exceed 18 inches (0.46 meters); allowable conductor capacitance is no more than 35 picofarads. Terminators for the cable are not required by the standard (each device and the host-adapter are equipped with them). However, if a three-connector cable is used to connect one device, then it is recommended to connect the device and the host-adapter to the end connectors. The ATA interface signal set is shown in Table 8.3; the cable is shown in Fig. 8.2. In most connectors, the like contacts of all connectors are connected in parallel and all the connectors are equal. However, sometimes (not very often), ribbon cables adapted to select devices are encountered. These cables have their wire 28 cut (Fig. 8.2); consequently, contact 28 (SCEL) of the master device is grounded at the host-adapter and the slave device has this contact unconnected. This type of device selection is called *cable select*. Cable used must correspond to the addressing system selected for both devices.

Table 8.3. ATA (IDE) Interface

Signal	Type[1]	Contact	Contact	Type[1]	Signal
RESET#	I	1	2	–	GND
DD7	I/O TS	3	4	I/O TS	DD8
DD6	I/O TS	5	6	I/O TS	DD9
DD5	I/O TS	7	8	I/O TS	DD10
DD4	I/O TS	9	10	I/O TS	DD11
DD3	I/O TS	11	12	I/O TS	DD12

continues

Table 8.3 Continued

Signal	Type[1]	Contact	Contact	Type[1]	Signal
DD2	I/O TS	13	14	I/O TS	DD13
DD1	I/O TS	15	16	I/O TS	DD14
DD0	I/O TS	17	18	I/O TS	DD15
GND	–	19	20	–	Key (pin is missing)
DMARQ	O TS[2]	21	22	–	GND
DIOW#/STOP[3]	I	23	24	–	GND
DIOR#/HDMARDY#/ HSTROBE[3]	I	25	26	–	GND
IORDY/DDMARDY#/ DSTROBE[3]	O TS[2]	27	28	I/O	SPSYNC/CSEL[7]
DMACK#	I	29	30	–	GND
INTRQ	O TS[2]	31	32	O OC	IOCS16#[8]
DA1	I	33	34	I, O[4]	PDIAG#/CBLID[3]
DA0	I	35	36	I	DA2
CS0#	I	37	38	I	CS1#
DASP#	I/O OC[5]	39	40	–	GND
+5 V (Logic)	–	41[6]	42[6]	–	+5 V (Motor)
GND	–	43[6]	44[6]	–	Reserved

[1] Signal type for a device: I — input, O — output, I/O — bidirectional, TS — tristate, OC — open collector. For host-adapter, meanings of I and O are reversed.

[2] In old devices, signal may be of the OC type (different type signals on one bus may create a bus conflict).

[3] Signals listed after the / signs are only used in the Ultra DMA (ATA-4) mode.

[4] Input for the master device, output for the slave device.

[5] Output only for the slave device.

[6] Contacts 41–44 are only used for miniature disks.

[7] Starting with ATA-3 — only SCEL.

[8] Starting with ATA-3 — reserved.

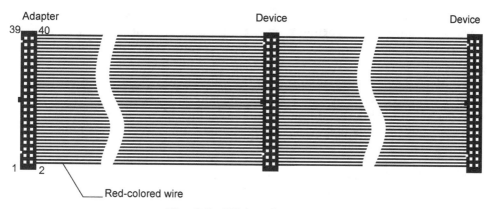

Fig. 8.2. ATA interface cable

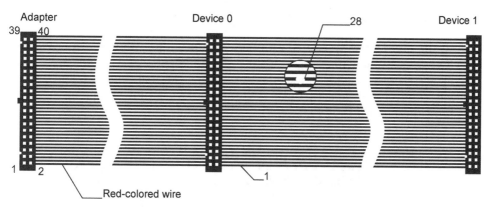

Fig. 8.3. ATA cable-select interface ribbon cable

Starting from ATA/ATAPI-4, cable-select ribbon cables were approved and the middle connector was designated for connecting device 1. In this cable, contact 28 is either not connected to the wire or is simply missing. Naturally, when using cable-select ribbon cables, the host-adapter cannot be connected to the middle connector (nor to the right connector in Fig. 8.3). If a device is assigned a number by a jumper, then devices and the host-adapter can be connected to any connector on the 40-wire ribbon cable; however, it is desirable to avoid loose ends.

For stable operations in the Ultra DMA mode, 80-wire cables with alternating signal and ground wires are recommended. These cables are required for Ultra DMA modes higher than 2 (transfer rates greater than 33 MBps). These cables are connected to special connectors whose pinout is the same as the regular 40-contact connectors.

All ground wires are connected to the special jack-in contacts. Either all even or all odd wires are grounded, depending on the type of the connectors used (they must be marked EVN GND or ODD GND). Different types of connectors cannot be mounted on one cable (in this case, all 80 wires will be connected together). On the 80-wire cable, contact 34 on the host-adapter connector is connected to the GND rail but not to the cable wire; this serves to identify the type of cable used (CBLID). The cable wire connects contacts 34 of the device connectors, allowing the PDIAG# signal pass from the master to slave. Because the cable select system is used, connectors' roles on the 80-wire cable are position-specific:

❑ The *host-controller* connector is located at one and of the cable; its contact 34 is grounded and not connected to the cable. It must be colored blue.

❑ The *device 0* (master) connecter is located on the opposite end of the ribbon cable; all of its contacts are connected to the cable. It must be colored black.

❑ The *device 1* (slave) connector (optional) is located in the middle of the cable; its contact 28 is not connected to the cable. It must be colored gray.

If the cable-select system is not used, devices 0 and 1 can be connected to any of the two device connectors.

The ATA specification allows both the 40-contact signal connector and the 4-contact power connector (Fig. 8.4), but for compact devices power can be supplied over 44-wire interface cable.

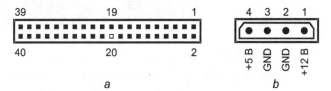

Fig. 8.4. ATA interface connectors (plugs on devices):
a — interface, *b* — power supply

Most devices are connected using a 40-contact connector with the contacts spaced 0.1 inch (2.54 mm) apart. Additional contacts employed for device configuration, diagnostic, and other service operations using the serial interface may be located next to the main contact group. The ATA/ATAPI specification defines two versions of supplementary contact group connectors (Fig. 8.5, *a* and *b*). In these drawings, unshaded squares indicate missing contacts taken by the keys; contacts 1–40 are used for the interface signals (Table 8.3), and contacts A–H are used to set jumpers (Table 8.4) and for the servicing signals. Compact devices are connected using a 50-contact connector with contacts 2 mm apart (Fig. 8.5, *c*) whose contacts correspond to Table 8.3

and contacts A–D correspond to Table 8.4. (Contacts A–D are used for configuration, and the missing pair of contacts serve as an additional key). In the 50-contact connectors, contacts A-D are usually assigned functions like those of the IBM Thinkpad/Travelstar drive outputs:

- Contact A is connected by a 10 K resistor to the +5 V rail.
- Contact B sets the device's role: low level — device 0, high level — device 1.
- Contact C sets the device mode on powering up: low level — Standby, high level — Idle.
- Contact D is connected to contact 28 (CSEL) and through a 10 K resistor to the +5 V power rail.

These contact functions, allowing both device selection and power consumption mode to be configured, are used not in all devices. In Toshiba drives, contacts A and B may be employed as serial interface input and output (B is pulled to the +5 V power rail through a 47 K resistor), contact C is connected to the GND rail, and contact D sets the device role (low level for device 1).

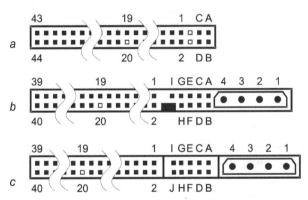

Fig. 8.5. ATA interface connectors supplementary contacts:
a — SFF8057, *b* — SFF8058, *c* — SFF8212 (a 50-contact connector)

Table 8.4. Functions of Supplementary Contacts

Select	SFF8057	SFF8058	SFF8212	Toshiba (1996)
Contacts used	E–H	A–F	A–D	A–D
Cable select	E–F	A–B	B–D	B–D
Master	G–H	E–F	–	–
Master with Slave present	G–H, E–F	E–F	–	–
Slave	–	C–D	A–B	C–D

For compact external drives, a quite common HP 36 connector is used, but it is not covered by the ATA/ATAPI specification. Flash memory storage devices use connectors conforming to the CompactFlash Association specification.

Device documentation may name signals somewhat differently. The ATA/ATAPI-4 standard signal names are given below:

❑   RESET# — Device Reset. A signal of no shorter than 25 μsec is generated after the power supply voltages have settled. The signal resets the interface into the initial state and sets the default parameters.

❑   DA[2:0] — Device Address. Three lower system address bus bits used to select device registers.

❑   DD[15:0] — Device Data. Biderectional 16-bit data bus between the adapter and devices. In 8-bit exchanges, only the lower D[7:0] bits are used. There must be no pull-up resistor on the device's DD7 line: on the host-controller, this is line connected by a 10 K resistor to the GND rail. This allows the host to determine whether there is no device on the bus right after a hardware reset: When an attempt to read the status register of a non-existing device is made, the BSY bit would seem as being reset, which is impossible for ATA/ATAPI.

❑   DIOR# — Device I/O Read. I/O read strobe. Data are latched at the positive signal transition.

❑   DIOW# — Device I/O Write. I/O write strobe. Data are latched at the positive signal transition.

❑   IORDY — I/O Channel Ready. Device is ready to complete the exchange cycle. By driving this signal low during the exchange cycle, a device can insert bus wait cycles. The signal is needed when performing exchanges in the PIO Mode 3 or higher. On the host-controller, this line must be pulled up to the power rail by a 1 K resistor.

❑   IOCS16# — 16-bit Operation Enable. All registers, except the data register, are always accessed in the 8-bit mode. In the PIO Modes 0, 1, and 2, when this signal is active (low), the access is 16 bits; when the signal is inactive (high), the access is 8 bits. In the PIO Modes 3 and 4 and DMA, all exchanges are 16 bits, with the exception of supplementary bytes (those extending past the 512-byte sector boundary) of the long read and write operations. Not used starting from ATA/ATAPI-3.

❑   DMARQ — DMA Request (optional). When the exchange is enabled, the high level signal is asserted by the device when it is ready to perform exchange. Having asserted the DMARQ signal, the device must wait until it receives the DMACK# acknowledgement signal from the host-adapter, after which it can deassert the DMARQ signal. The request must be asserted for next transmission. In the Multiword MDA mode, the signal may be held asserted for the duration of the transmission of all the data. The signal must have the tristate output; during DMA mode operations, only the selected device can hold it in an active state (either 0 or 1). In ATA-1, this signal could use both the tristate and the regular TTL outputs. Having two devices with different types of the DMARQ outputs on one bus may cause conflicts. On the host-controller, the line must be connected to the GND rail by a 5.6 K resistor.

☐ DMACK# — DMA Acknowledge. The signal is generated by the host-controller as a confirmation of the transmission cycle. Transmission of a data byte is controlled by the DIOR# or DIOW# signals. During exchange over a DMA channel, the IOCS16#, CS0#, and CS1# signals are not used; exchange is always conducted in 16-bit words.

☐ INTRQ — Interrupt Request. The output must be tristate. Only the selected device generates the active signal (logical one) when it has an unserviced interrupt request under the condition that it is not disabled by the nIEN bit in the Device Control register. The request is cleared by the RESET# signal, by setting the SRST bit in the Device Control register, by writing to the command register, or by reading the status register. In PIO exchanges, the request is set at the beginning of the transmission of each block (a sector or a group of sectors in multi-sector operations). The Format Track, Write Sector(S), Write Buffer, and Write Long commands at the beginning of the transmission of the first data block are exceptions and do not generate an interrupt request. In DMA exchanges, the interrupt request is generated only upon completion of the operation. On the host-controller, this line must be pulled up to the GND rail by a 10 K resistor.

☐ CS0# — Chip Select 0. A Command Block Register select signal. For channel 1, it is generated when there is an I/O port address in the 1F0h–1F7h range on the system bus. The signal is also called CS1FX#.

☐ CS1# — Chip Select 1. A Control Block Register select signal. For channel 1, it is generated when there is an I/O port address in the 3F6h–3F7h range on the system bus. This signal is also often called CS3FX#.

☐ PDIAG# — Passed Diagnostics. The master device monitors this signal, which the slave device must generate in response to a reset signal or a diagnostics command. If a slave device has been detected (by its DASP# signal), the master device waits for this signal 31 seconds after reset and 6 seconds after a diagnostics command. If during this time the signal does not come, the master device records this by setting bit 7 in the error register. If a slave device has not been detected, the master device zeroes out the slave device status register and informs the system of its own status immediately after completing its own self-diagnostics. The signal is only used for communicating between the two devices, and is not used by the host-adapter. (In ATA-4, this contact is used for the CBLID# signal.)

☐ CBLID# — Cable Assembly Type Identifier. In the 80-wire cable, contact 34 on the host-adapter connector is connected to the GND rail; contacts 34 of the device connectors are connected to each other but not to the host-adapter connector. On devices, this line must be pulled to the power rail by a 10 K resistor. After reset and when the PDIAG# signal is deasserted, a low level of signal informs the host that the 80-wire cable is present.

❒ DASP# — Device Active/Slave Present dual-purpose signal. Devices' outputs are of the open collector type and are connected by 10 K load resistors to the +5 V rail. Within 1 msec after a RESET# signal, or when initializing upon being powered up, both devices must deactivate this signal; afterward, the slave device asserts it no later than within 400 msec to inform the system of its presence. The master device does not activate this signal for 450 msec. The slave device deactivates this signal after it receives a command or automatically after 31 seconds, whichever happens first. Any device can then assert this signal to indicate its readiness. The host-adapter uses this signal to operate the HDD access LED indicator.

❒ SPSYNC/CSEL — Spindle Synchronization/Cable Select. A dual function signal. The function selected must be the same for the both devices. The SPSYNC allows spindles of devices to be synchronized, which is important for RAID systems. It is used at the user's discretion; since ATA/ATAPI-3, this signal has been removed from the specification. The CSEL signal allows devices to determine their addresses by their location on the special cable with wire 28 between the two devices cut (the seldom used cable select method). On the host-adapter, this line is grounded; the master device gets the grounded line and the slave device gets the unconnected line. On the device side, the line is pulled to the high level by a 10 K resistor. If the signal is controlled by the host-adapter, it must hold it for at least 31 seconds after the RESET# signal.

When the Ultra DMA mode is used, four signal lines get new functions:

❒ STOP — Stop Ultra DMA burst.
❒ DDMARDY# — Device Ultra DMA ready when receiving an Ultra DMA packet (flow control).
❒ DSTROBE — Host Ultra DMA data strobe from device when sending a burst to the host. Data are sent at both transitions of the DSTROBE signal.
❒ HDMARDY# — Host Ultra DMA ready when receiving a burst (flow control).
❒ HSTROBE — Host Ultra DMA data strobe when sending a packet to a device. Data are sent at both transitions of the HSTROBE signal.

For notebook PCs, the standard has a version of the IDE interface using the 68-contact PCMCIA connector (PC Card) shown in Table 8.5. This version of the standard has several specific signals.

❒ SELATA# — Select 68-pin ATA. This is a signal that the host uses to identify the mode in which the connector is used: in the PC Card mode, the signal is deasserted (high), in the ATA mode, the signal is asserted (low). The host must set this signal before the power is applied to the connector. For 19 msec after the power is applied, the device ignores all interface signals but this one. If this signal is active (low), the device must configure itself for ATA mode operation. If the signal is inactive, the device must configure itself for the PC Card mode or not answer to other signals from the host.

❑ CD1# and CD2# — Card Detect signals; grounded on the device. By these signals, the host determines whether a device is present.

❑ CS1# — Device Chip Select 1. Applied by the host to both contacts (11 and 42), but the device recognizes only one of them.

❑ DMARQ, DMACK#, and IORDY — optional signals.

❑ M/S# — Master/Slave. Inversion of the CSEL signal. The host issues the M/S# and CSEL signals before the power is applied; the device only recognizes one of them.

To provide for hot swap connection, the GND contact mates first when connecting a device and disconnects last when disconnecting it. The device's CS0#, CS1#, RESET#, and SELATA# signals are pulled to inactive (high) level.

Table 8.5. 68-Contact ATA PC Card (PCMCIA) Interface

Contact	Signal	Contact	Signal
1	GND	35	GND
2	DD3	36	CD1#
3	DD4	37	DD11
4	DD5	38	DD12
5	DD6	39	DD13
6	DD7	40	DD14
7	CS0#	41	DD15
8	–	42	CS1#
9	SELATA#	43	–
10	–	44	DIOR#
11	CS1#	45	DIOW#
12	–	46	–
13	–	47	–
14	–	48	–
15	–	49	–

continues

Table 8.5 Continued

Contact	Signal	Contact	Signal
16	INTRQ	50	–
17	+5 V	51	+5 V
18	–	52	–
19	–	53	–
20	–	54	–
21	–	55	M/S#
22	–	56	CSEL
23	–	57	–
24	–	58	RESET#
25	–	59	IORDY#
26	–	60	DMARQ
27	DA2	61	DMACK#
28	DA1	62	DASP#
29	DA0	63	PDIAG#
30	DD0	64	DD8
31	DD1	65	DD9
32	DD2	66	DD10
33	–	67	CD2#
34	GND	68	GND

There is an 8-bit version of the interface — called XT-IDE or, less frequently, XT-Bus — for XT class computers. Like the ATA interface, this interface is implemented by a 40-wire cable, and many of its signals match the 16-bit ATA bus signals. The XT-IDE interface may be considered as a subset of the ATA interface, although they are not directly compatible. Some ATA type devices have a jumper for selecting the XT/AT mode (in Seagate drives, this is indicated by the suffix AX in the model's name).

Device Registers

All ATA devices have a standard set of registers that are addressed by signals from the host-adapter (CS0#, CS1#, DA1, DA0, DIOR#, and DIOW#). The register set (Table 8.6) consists of two blocks that are selected by the CS0# and CS1# signals, of which only one may be active (asserted low). The table lists register addresses for the first and second ATA channels in the I/O space of an IBM PC compatible computer. When the registers are accessed, the DMACK# signal must be inactive (high). The *command block registers* serve to send commands to a device and read information about its status. The *control block registers* are used to control the device and to obtain more detailed information about its status. A zero value of the BSY bit in the status register indicates that the contents of the command block registers and of the alternative status register are valid. Except in separately stipulated cases, registers can be written to only when BSY=0 and DRQ=0. If the device supports power management control, in the sleeping mode the contents of these registers are invalid and a write to them is ignored, except in separately stipulated cases.

Table 8.6. ATA Device Controller Registers

Address for channel		Addressing signals (0 — low level, 1 — high level)					Function (R — read, W — write)
1	2	CS0#	CS1#	DA2	DA1	DA0	
		1	1	x	x	x	No access (bus is in the high impedance state)
		0	0	x	x	x	Invalid address (bus is in the high impedance state)
3FX	37X	*Control Block Registers*					
3F0– 3F5	370– 375	1 1	0 0	1 0	0 x	x x	Not used (bus is in the high impedance state)
3F6	376	1	0	1	1	0	AS: Alternate Status register (R)
3F6	376	1	0	1	1	0	DC: Device Control register (W)
3F7	377	1	0	1	1	1	DA: Drive Address register (R) (not used)[1]
1FX	17X	*Command Block Registers*					
1F0	170	0	1	0	0	0	DR: Data Register (R/W)
1F1	171	0	1	0	0	1	ER: Error Register (R)
1F1	171	0	1	0	0	1	FR: Features Register (W)

continues

Table 8.6 Continued

Address for channel		Addressing signals (0 — low level, 1 — high level)					Function (R — read, W — write)
1	2	CS0#	CS1#	DA2	DA1	DA0	
1F2	172	0	1	0	1	0	SC: Sector Count register (R/W)
1F3	173	0	1	0	1	1	SN: Sector Number register/LBA [7:0] (R/W)^2
1F4	174	0	1	1	0	0	CL: Cylinder Low byte register/LBA[15:8] (R/W)^2
1F5	175	0	1	1	0	1	CH: Cylinder High byte register/LBA [23:16] (R/W)^2
1F6	176	0	1	1	1	0	D/H: Device/Head register/LBA[27:24] (R/W)^2
1F7	177	0	1	1	1	1	SR: Status Register (R)
1F7	177	0	1	1	1	1	CR: Command Register (W)

[1] Recommended that the device not answer read signals at this address.

[2] Sector, cylinder, and head registers in the LBA mode contain the logical address bits shown.

The *alternative status register* AS (the address for channel 1 is 3F6h, for channel 2 it is 376h) has the same bits as the main register, but reading it does not change the device status in any way.

The *device control register* DC (3F6h, 376h,) is used to reset both devices simultaneously by software and to control interrupt enable of the selected device. This register can be written to at any time. Software reset using the DC register must also function in the Sleep mode.

DC register bit functions are as follows:

❏ Bits [7:3] — reserved.
❏ Bit 2 — SRST: Software Reset. Active all the time while the bit is not cleared (both devices on the bus sense the software reset simultaneously).
❏ Bit 1 — nIEN: Interrupt Enable. Inverted interrupt enable bit (when the bit has the zero value, the selected device can generate the INTRQ signal on the tristate output).
❏ Bit 0. Set to 0.

The *device address register* DA (3F7h, 377h) was only used in the first version of ATA in order to provide compatibility with old controllers; by reading this register, the addressed drive and head could be determined. The register drops out of the block (it coincides with the FDD controller status diagnostic register) and it is recommended that an ATA device not respond to reading this register. If the device does respond to a register reading, then it must not control the DD7 bit, in order to avoid a conflict with the FDD controller, which uses this line for the media change signaling. Not observing this rule may cause problems when the ATA adapter and the FDD controller are located on separate cards.

The functions of the DA register bits are as follows:

❒ Bit 7 — HiZ: Tristate. Not placed on the bus when read.
❒ Bit 6 — nWTG: inverted write indicator. During the physical write operation to the medium, the bit has zero value.
❒ Bits [5:2] — nHS[3:0]: head number (inverted bits).
❒ Bits [1:0] — nDS[1:0]: device select (inverted bits). 10 — device 0 selected; 01 — device 1 selected.

The *data register* DR (1F0h, 170h) can be used in the 8- or 16-bit mode depending on the type of data being transferred in the current command. This register is accessed in the PIO exchange mode (when the DMACK# signal is inactive (high)). When executing transmissions under the PO (PIO Out) protocol, the host writes to this register; when doing PI (PIO In) operations, the hosts reads the register. In the DMA mode, data exchange is carried via the data port; during this operation, the DMARQ and DMACK# signals are active and the CS0# and CS1# signals are inactive.

The *error register* ER (1F1h, 171h) stores the results of executing the last operation or a diagnostic code. After the operation terminates, the status register ERR bit indicates if there has been an error.

The functions of the ER register bits are as follows:

❒ Bit 7 — reserved.
❒ Bit 6 — UNC: Uncorrectable Data Error.
❒ Bit 5 — MC: Media Changed. After media is changed, the first access command is rejected and the bit is set; after the bit is cleared, subsequent commands will be executed normally.
❒ Bit 4 — IDNF: ID Not Found. Indicates that the sector ID has not been found.
❒ Bit 3 — MCR: Media Change Requested. Media change request indicator. After the media change request is detected, the Door Lock command will return the ERR error bit and the MCR bit. The MCR bit is cleared by the Door Unlock and Media Eject commands or by a hardware reset signal.

❏ Bit 2 — ABRT: Aborted Command. Set if a command is rejected as invalid or if some other error occurs.

❏ Bit 1 — TK0NF: Track 0 Not Found. Indicates that the Recalibrate command could not find track 0.

❏ Bit 0 — AMNF: Address Mark Not Found. Data address marker in the sector header not found.

After execution of any type of reset or after the Execute Device Diagnostic, the error register contains a diagnostic code. With the exception of bit 2 (ABRT), the meaning of the bits varies depending on the command that has been executed.

The use of the *features register* FR (1F1h, 171h) depends on the current command. In the Set Features command, this register is used to set the subcommand code. Some old devices may ignore a write to this register. Prior to accepting the ATA-2 specification, the value of the recommended cylinder number for write precompensation was placed into this register.

The *sector count register* SC (1F2h, 172h) holds the number of sectors involved in the exchange. The host initializes this register prior to issuing the command (zero value corresponds to 256 sectors). After a successful termination of a data access operation, the register must be zeroed out. If the command terminates with an error, the register will contain the number of sectors that must be transferred to complete the previous request successfully. The Initialize Device Parameters or Write Same commands may redefine the function of this register. In some commands, the register is used to send other parameters.

The *sector number* SN (1F3h, 173h) and *cylinder number* registers — low CL (1F4h, 174h) and high CH (1F5h, 175h) bytes — have dual functions depending on the addressing system being used (CHS or LBA). They are initialized by the host-adapter. If a device encounters an error during execution of a command, it places the address, at which the error occurred, into this register.

The *device and head number register* D/H (1F6h, 176h), in addition to storing part of the address information, is used to select the master or slave device and the addressing method.

The functions of the D/H register bits are as follows:

❏ Bits 7 and 5 in the ATA standards up to ATA-3 had to have values of logical 1. In ATA/ATAPI-4, these bits were declared obsolete.

❏ Bit 6 — L. Logical 1 indicates the LBA addressing mode; logical 0 indicates that the CHS mode is used.

❏ Bit 4 — DEV: Device select. When DEV=0, the master device is selected; when DEV=1, the slave device is selected.

❐ Bits [3:0] have dual functions depending on the addressing system being used. In the CHS mode, they hold the head number; in the LBA mode, they contain the higher bits of the logical address.

Like the SN, CH, and CL registers, the *address register* D/H is initialized by the host-adapter and a device places into it the address, at which it encountered an error during execution of the operation. Prior to accepting the ATA-2 specification, it was assumed that the address registers should also be modified after an operation terminated successfully to reflect the current medium address.

The *status register* SR (1F7h, 177h) reflects the current device command execution status: busy, ready, the presence of errors, etc. Reading the status register allows its bits to be subsequently changed and clears the hardware interrupt request.

The functions of the SR bits are as follows:

❐ Bit 7 — BSY: Busy. Indicates that the device is busy; this bit is always valid. When BSY=1, the device ignores attempts to write to the command block registers, and reading these registers produces indeterminate results. When BSY=0, the command block registers are accessible; the device cannot set the DRQ bit or change the values of the ERR bits or other registers' contents at this time (only the values of bits IDX, DRDY, DF, DSC, and CORR may change). The bit may be set for a fleeting period of time so the host may not notice it. The bit is set when one of the following events happens:

- Device reset.
- A command is received and the DRQ is not set.
- Between PIO mode data block transfers and afterward until the DRQ is zeroed out.
- During DMA mode data transfers.

❐ Bit 6 — DRDY: Device Ready. Indicates that the device is ready to receive any commands. If the bit's status has changed, it cannot be returned to its previous state until the status register has been read. When DRDY=0, the device only recognizes the Execute Device Diagnostic and Initialize Device Parameters commands, terminating execution of the current command and indicating this by setting the ABRT flag in the error register and the ERR flag in the status register. Other commands produce unpredictable results. An ATA device sets the bit when it is ready to execute any command. An ATAPI device sets the bit prior to terminating command execution, except for the Device Reset and Execute Device Diagnostic commands.

❐ Bit 5 — DF: Device Fault indicator.

❐ Bit 4 — DSC: Device Seek Complete. In commands that allow overlapping, the bit is called SERV (Service Required) by the device.

❐ Bit 3 — DRQ: Data Request. Indicates that the device is ready to exchange a word or byte of data.

❐ Bit 2 — CORR: Corrected Data Error indicator.

❐ Bit 1 — IDX: Index. Treated at individual vendor's discretion.

❐ Bit 0 — ERR: Error executing last command. Additional information is contained in the error register. If the ERR bit is set, the device will change neither it nor the error, sector count, sector number, cylinder, and head registers until it receives the next command, or until its hardware or software reset is executed. For the Packet and Service commands, the bit is called CHK and indicates an exception condition.

In the ATA/ATAPI-4 standard, bits 4 and 5 may have different functions in some commands and bits 1 and 2 are declared obsolete.

The *function of the command register* CR (1F7h, 177h) is obvious from its name. The device begins executing a command as soon as its code is written to this register. The Device Reset command is executed by an ATAPI device regardless of the status of the BSY and DRQ bits; it is even executed in the *Sleep* mode.

The 8-bit register formats described above allow only 28 bits of a logical block address to be stored (137 GB), and no more than 256 blocks to be transferred by one command. The 137-GB limitation has been overcome in the ATA/ATAPI by increasing the width of the SC, SN, SL, and CH registers to 16 bits. At the same time, the functions of their lower bytes have been preserved. The addresses of these registers in the I/O space have not changed, which is somewhat unexpected for 16-bit registers (by conventional logic, they ought to have even addresses). These registers are now "double-bottomed": The first 8-bit access to each of them pertains to the lower byte, while the following 8-bit access pertains to the upper byte. In the LBA mode, the upper bytes of the SN, CL, and CH registers carry bits [24:31], [32:39], and [40:47] of the logical address, respectively, which provides addressing of up to 2^{48} blocks (2^{47} KB). The 16-bit SC register allows transmission of up to 65,536 blocks to be ordered by one command. Serial ATA block addressing is expanded in a similar way.

Data Transfer Protocols and Modes

A program communicates with ATA devices that employ registers by using the IN and OUT I/O instructions. To transfer data at maximum speed, the PIO software method is used to access the data register by the INSW/OUTSW instructions or to exchange over the DMA channel. It is mandatory that all devices support the PIO access method; the DMA access method is optional. Table 8.7 lists parameters for various exchange modes.

Table 8.7. Transfer Mode Parameters

Transfer mode	Minimal cycle length (nsec)	Transfer rate (MBps)	Interface
PIO mode 0	600	3.3	ATA
PIO mode 1	383	5.2	ATA
PIO mode 2	240	8.3	ATA
PIO mode 3	180	11.1	E-IDE, ATA-2 (IORDY is used)
PIO mode 4	120	16.6	E-IDE, Fast ATA-2 (IORDY is used)
Singleword DMA Mode 0	960	2.08	ATA
Singleword DMA Mode 1	480	4.16	ATA
Singleword DMA Mode 2	240	8.33	ATA
Multiword DMA Mode 0	480	4.12	ATA
Multiword DMA Mode 1	150	13.3	ATA-2
Multiword DMA Mode 2	120	16.6	Fast ATA-2
Ultra DMA Mode 0	120[1]	16.6	ATA/ATAPI-4
Ultra DMA Mode 1	80[1]	25	ATA/ATAPI-4
Ultra DMA Mode 2	60[1]	33	ATA/ATAPI-4
Ultra DMA Mode 3	45[1]	44.4	ATA/ATAPI-5
Ultra DMA Mode 4	30[1]	66.6	ATA/ATAPI-5
Ultra DMA Mode 5	20[1]	100	ATA/ATAPI-6
Ultra DMA Mode 6	15[1]	133	ATA/ATAPI-6

[1] In the Ultra DMA mode burst, two data words are sent in each clock cycle: one at the positive transition of the clock, the other at the negative. The period of the sync signals equals double the cycle time.

Programmed Input/Output (PIO) is implemented as a series of read/write operations executed at the data register address in the I/O space. Before a block is transmitted, the device readiness is checked, after which the host performs a series of operations at a set rate, which is determined by the PIO Mode selected (0–4). Each mode has the allowable exchange cycle timing parameters defined. The PIO exchange is implemented by software using processor line I/O instructions REP INS or REP OUTS with the CX register containing the number of words (or bytes) in the transmitted block. These instructions provide the maximum possible exchange rate for the particular processor and system bus. To slow down the processor according to the chosen mode is a task of ATA adapter, which uses the bus ready signal (IOCHRDY for ISA) to extend the cycle. The traditional modes 0, 1, and 2 have timing parameters to which only the host-adapter responds. The advanced ATA-2 (PIO Mode3 and higher) modes a device can slow down the exchange using the IORDY ready signals. Software exchange occupies both the processor and the system bus during the whole time a block is being transmitted.

Exchange over a DMA channel only occupies the I/O and memory buses. All the processor needs to do is to initialize the channel, after which it disengages until the device requests its services by an interrupt at the end of the block transmission (multitask systems can take advantage of this method). ISA bus standard DMA channels are not used for the ATA interface because of their low throughput. High-efficiency ATA adapters have their own, more productive controllers. There are *Singleword* and *Multiword* DMA exchange modes. In the Singleword mode, the device generates a DMARQ request signal and clears it at the DMACK# signal that confirms the exchange cycle. In the Multiword mode, the host answers the DMARQ signal with a stream of cycles accompanied by DMACK# signals. If the device cannot handle the cycle, it can suspend it by clearing the DMARQ signal and setting it again when it is ready to resume. The Multiword mode makes it possible to achieve higher transfer rates.

A new mode — Ultra DMA — introduced in the ATA/ATAPI-4 specification makes it possible to exceed the 16.6 MBps barrier that had been specific to the traditional modes and cables. It also provides for controlling the validity of data transmitted over the bus, which was not done in the PIO or in the standard DMA mode (although it should have been!). The ATA-4 standard defined three Ultra DMA modes (0, 1, and 2); other modes were added later. A particular mode is selected by the Set Features command. In the Ultra DMA mode, the DMARQ and DMACK# signals have the same functions, but the meanings of the DIOR#, DIOW# and IORDY# signals change significantly during transmission of an Ultra DMA burst. Burst data on the bus are accompanied by a strobe that is generated by the data source; moreover, both strobe signal transitions are used to clock the data. This makes it possible to increase the bus bandwidth to 33 MBps without increasing the signal switching frequency over 8.33×10^6 sec^{-1} (this limit for regular cable is reached in PIO Mode 4 and Multiword DMA Mode 2). Each transmitted word is used in calculating the CRC code, which the host-controller sends at the end of the burst. The calculation is performed by both the data source and receiver. If the code received by the device is not what it expected, a transmission error is recorded and the receiver indicates this at the end of the command execution. Burst transmission may be suspended if the receiver clears the ready signal (DDMARDY# or HDMARDY#). Burst transmission may be terminated by the device (by clearing the DMARQ signal) or by the host (by the STOP signal). The opposite side must confirm the end of the cycle by the STOP or DMARQ signal, respectively.

A transmission-error reporting method depends on the type of command that caused the error. For the READ DMA, WRITE DMA, READ DMA QUEUED, or WRITE DMA QUEUED commands, bit 7 (ICRC) and bit 2 (ABRT) are set in the error register ER. For the burst command REQUEST SENSE, bit 0 (CHK) is set in the status register SR and value 0Bh (command rejected) is reported in the Sense key in case of an error. Errors caused by all other burst commands set the CHK bit and report status code 04h (hardware error); in the following REQUEST SENSE commands, values 08h/03h are reported for the ASC/ASCQ (a CRC error when communicating with a logical device). If the host receives an error message, it must re-execute the command. If frequent errors occur, the host must lower the transfer speed (exiting the Ultra DMA mode if necessary).

The exchange mode is determined by the capabilities of the host-adapter (and its driver), devices, and cable; for each device, it will be limited by the lowest maximum capabilities of all these devices. As a rule, the mode is set automatically by the system, but the user is allowed to customize the controller's settings from the BIOS setup. For operations in the Ultra DMA Mode 3 and higher, an 80-wire cable is needed. Its presence must be determined by software prior to enabling one of these exchange modes. However, the specification allows a 40-wire cable without the middle connector to be used in modes 3 and 4 for a two-point connection (controller-device). The system must not allow the user to enable the high-speed mode using regular cable; in this case, it is desirable that it inform the user about the detected non-compliance. The type of cable can be determined in several ways.

❑ The type of cable is detected by the host controller. For this, the host-controller must have a receiver for the CBLID# signal. Upon powering up or after a hardware reset, the host waits until the reset protocol completes and then issues the Identify (Packet) Device command to device 1. After a reset, an ATA-3 or higher device must deassert the PDIAG#/CBLID# signal no later than upon arrival of the first command. If an old device is detected, the protocol for identifying the cable by the host will not work (but with an old device on the cable, the high-speed mode should not be enabled anyway). A modern device will deassert the signal, and the host-adapter will be able to detect an 80-wire cable by the low-level signal on the CBLID# line. A faulty device may continue asserting the signal at low level; in this case, a 40-wire cable will be mistakenly identified as an 80-wire one.

❑ The type of cable is determined by the device. This method does not require an additional receiver in the controller: the PDIAG#/CBLID# line on the host-controller is grounded through a 0.047±20% microfarad capacitor. The receiver of the cable identification signal is located in the device. To determine the cable type, the host sends an Identify (Packet) Device command to device 1 (slave) ordering it to release the line (deassert the PDIAG# signal). An identification command is then sent to device 0. Approximately 30 μsec after it receives the command, the device briefly zeroes out this line and then releases it; 20–30 μsec later, the device reads the line's status and reports it in bit 13 of word 93. In the devices, the line is pulled by 10 K resistors to the +5 V rail. If a 40-wire cable is used, then the capacitor in the host-adapter will not have enough time to recharge, and the device will report logical zero value for the bit. With an 80-wire cable, the capacitor will be disconnected from the PDIAG#/CBLID# line in the master device, which will report logical one value for the bit. If the host-controller does not have a capacitor installed, then even a 40-wire cable will be identified as an 80-wire one, which does not bode well for data transfers. If a faulty slave device does not release the line in time, then even an 80-wire cable will appear to be a 40-wire one.

❏ The combined cable type identification method presupposes both a CBLID# signal receiver and a capacitor on the host-controller (they do not interfere with each other). The decision that an 80-wire cable is present is made only if both identification methods confirm it. A possible identification error will be harmless: if there is a faulty device 1 present, the high-speed mode will not be enabled on an 80-wire cable (which is, perhaps, for the better).

A correctly selected exchange mode makes data transfer reliable and efficient. All devices support PIO Mode 0, in which a parameter identification block is read. The block contains fields that describe the default exchange mode and the most efficient exchange mode supported by the device. The exchange mode parameters can be changed by the Set Features command. Sometimes, a drive will not provide reliable data transfer in the declared high-speed mode. If data begin to get lost, the first thing to do is to lower the exchange mode.

BIOS defines the exchange mode for each device, taking into account the restrictions set during Setup. Old drives that do not provide information about their parameters may not work with the new PIO modes. The specification allows two devices supporting different exchange modes to be put on one ribbon cable (ATA channel). In real life, however, hardware and software limitations may arise. Some chipsets do not allow the exchange mode to be programmed separately for each device in the channel. In this case, if two different mode devices (for example, PIO Mode 1 and PIO Mode 3) are connected on one cable, exchange with both devices will be conducted at the lower mode device speed (in this case, PIO Mode 1). Therefore, it is not recommended to connect a fast hard drive and a slow CD-ROM to one ATA channel (IDE port). Sometimes, the restricted exchange mode selection of two devices is caused by the limited choice of parameters in the BIOS configuration. Only operating system drivers support fast multiple DMA exchange modes. A "dumb" driver may attempt to force a slow exchange mode on both devices, so this is another reason not to mix different devices on one channel.

Using the PIO exchange protocol only is suitable for single task operating systems. For a multitask operating system, exchange using the DMA protocol presents more interest; that is, of course, if the supported mode provides an acceptable exchange rate. For the driver, only the type of the exchange mode matters (i.e., whether it is PIO, DMA, or UltraDMA); hardware variations of modes within a type only affect the transfer rate. The UltraDMA mode differs significantly from regular DMA in that it has to service potential errors that occur during transmissions over the bus; if transmission errors are a constant occurrence, then the drive must switch into a lower UltraDMA mode, or move to the regular exchange modes if necessary.

The host/device interaction protocol looks as follows:

1. The host reads the device's status register, waiting for the BSY bit's zero value. If there are two devices, the host addresses them randomly: The status information will be provided by the device selected last.

2. When a device becomes available, the host writes a byte whose DEV bit points to the addressed device into the D/H register.

3. The host reads the main or alternative status register of the addressed device, waiting for the ready status indicator DRDY=1.

4. The host enters the required parameters into the command block registers.

5. The host writes the command code to the command register.

6. The device sets the BSY bit and begins executing the command.

What happens next depends on the data transfer protocol specified by the command.

Commands that do not need to transmit data terminate in the next step (step 7). Having completed execution of the command, the device clears the BSY bit and asserts the interrupt request (if it has been enabled). By this time, the status and error registers contain the information about the results of the command execution. Between steps 6 and 7, the BSY bit may go low so fast that the host will not even notice it going high; however, to indicate that a command or a part of it has been executed, the interrupt request is employed.

Commands that need to *read data in the PIO mode* continue execution the following way:

7. With the first block of data ready for transmission over the ATA bus, the device sets the DRQ bit. If there has been an error, it is recorded in the status and error registers. The device then clears the BSY bit and sets the interrupt request (if it has not been disabled).

8. Having detected that the BSY bit has been zeroed out (or reacting to an interrupt), the host reads the status register, which resets the interrupt from the device.

9. If the host detects that DRQ=1, then it reads the first data block in the PIO mode, addressing the data register. If an error has been detected, the data that have been

read may turn out to be invalid. One of the following actions is possible when transmitting a block of data:

- If no mistake has been discovered in step 8 and the next block needs to be transmitted, the device sets the BSY bit and steps 7 to 9 are repeated.
- If an error has been made or the last data block has been transmitted, the device clears the DRQ bit and the execution of the command terminates.

For data write operations, the active phase of writing to the medium begins after step 6, which is marked by setting the BSY bit.

For commands that need to *write data in the PIO mode*, the procedure after step 6 continues as follows:

7. When it is ready to receive the first data block over the ATA bus, the device sets the DRQ bit (if no errors have been detected) and clears the BSY bit. If there has been an error, it is recorded.
8. Having detected that the BSY bit has been zeroed out, the host reads the status register.
9. If the host has detected that DRQ=1, it writes the first data block in the PIO mode to the address in the data register.
10. After the data block has been transmitted, one of the following happens:
    - If an error has been detected, the device clears the DRQ bit, sets an interrupt request, and terminates execution of the command; the data that have been transmitted over the bus are not processed by the device (not written to the medium).
    - If no error has been detected, the device sets the BSY bit and moves on to the next step.
11. The device processes the received data block and then does one of the following:
    - If there have been no errors and the processed block is the last one, the device clears the BSY bit and sets an interrupt request; the command has been successfully executed.
    - If an error has been detected, execution of the command completes in the same way but the error bits are set.
    - If there have been no errors and another block needs to be transmitted, the procedure continues.
12. When it is ready to receive the next block, the device sets the DRQ bit, clears the BSY bit and sets an interrupt request.
13. When the BSY bit is zeroed out or reacting to the interrupt, the host reads the status register.
14. Having detected that DRQ=1, the host writes the next block to the data register and the sequence is repeated starting from step 11.

Commands transmitting data in the DMA mode are executed similarly but with certain differences:

❑ Direct memory access is used instead of PIO. The host must initialize the DMA channel before the code is written to the command register so that the exchange can start when the DMARQ signal appears.
❑ Even in multisector transmissions, the interrupt request is set only once, upon completion of the command execution.

ATA Bus Adapters and Controllers

The simplest ATA adapter consists only of bus signal buffers and address range decoders. All controller registers and the coding circuitry are located in the IDE device itself. The ATA bus requires some system resources — two I/O areas and an interrupt line — to be allocated to it; a DMA channel may also be needed. The first channel ATA interface was allocated resources that used to be utilized by the HDD controller. The second channel was allocated resources that used to belong to the alternative HDD controller. Later, resources for two more channels were allocated (Table 8.8). The traditional HDD controller used to be assigned the DMA3 channel; however, it is 8 bits wide, whereas the ATA bus requires a 16-bit DMA channel. The throughput of the standard DMA channels is obviously not sufficient for the ATA bus.

Table 8.8. System Resources of the ATA Channels

Channel	CS0	CS1	IRQ
1	1F0h–1F7h	3F6h–3F7h	14
2	170h–177h	376h–377h	15 or 10
3	1E8h–1Efh	3Eeh–3Efh	12 or 11
4	168h–16Fh	36Eh–36Fh	10 or 9

Typical for PCI bus motherboards is a two-channel adapter, which is allocated the resources of channels 1 and 2. In the ideal case, the buses of two-channel controllers are totally isolated from each other by means of buffer and logic circuitry. In the cheapest case, they use common buffers for data and control signal lines and separate buffers only for especially exclusive signals. There is nothing wrong with this approach in terms of logic, but the load-carrying capacity (influence of stray parameters) must be kept in mind: The total length of both ribbon cables must not exceed 46 centimeters, and the total capacity of each line with all its devices must not exceed 35 picofarads. If these requirements are not met, data may get corrupted when transmitted in high transfer rate modes. The ATA/ATAPI-6 standard mandates the following:

☐ The recommended configuration option is that each channel have its own drivers of the DIOR# and DIOW# control signals and an IORDY signal receiver. The other option is that there must be separate drivers for the CS0# and CS1# signals. This is a more logical option, but is more susceptible to interferences. This configuration supports all exchange modes, with the exception of Ultra DMA.

☐ In order to provide support for Ultra DMA modes 0, 1, and 2 (up to 33 MBps), these requirements are supplemented with a requirement for a separate driver for the DMACK# signal.

☐ To provide support for Ultra DMA 3 and higher (44–100 MBps), all lines must have individual transceivers. The only shared signals may be the RESET#, INTRQ, DA(2:0), CS0#, CS1#, and DASP# signals, but the standard does not recommend this arrangement.

Because the speed of software-controlled exchange is set by the host-adapter, programming individual PIO modes for each channel/device may be problematic. Several chipsets do not allow this, and set a common minimum mode when initialized. As a result, connecting a slow device will drag down the exchange rate of its faster bus neighbor.

Modern motherboards are equipped with high efficiency ATA bus controllers that support PCI *bus mastering* when conducting an exchange with a device in the DMA and Ultra DMA modes. Bus mastering raises overall efficiency in computers with multitask and multithreaded operating systems. By themselves, DMA modes do not provide any gains in the ATA bus exchange rate: only Ultra DMA Mode 1 and higher surpass PIO Mode 4 in speed (see Table 8.7). However, conducting exchange in a DMA mode places a significantly lighter load on the processor, so the latter may process other threads (tasks) in parallel with conducting the disk exchange. In single-task (and single-thread) systems, the processor does not have anything else to do when conducting a disk exchange, so the PIO Mode is sufficient for it. For bus mastering to be actually used, a special Bus Master driver for the ATA controller (usually built into the motherboard) needs to be installed. The standard PCI IDE controller is described below. MS-DOS does not support DMA or bus mastering. Bus master drivers may be included into the installation distributives of multitask operating systems (such as Windows 9x/NT/2000, OS/2, Unix, Linux, NetWare, etc.) or they may be included with the motherboard utilities software supplied by the vendors. Finally, the connected devices must support the DMA mode. Practically all modern devices support Ultra DMA (or Multiword DMA), but if an old device not supporting this mode is connected to the controller in pair with a modern device, then the advanced modes may turn out to be unavailable (through the chipset's or driver's fault) to the new device as well.

CAUTION

The Ultra DMA mode is attractive not only because of its speed and light processor loads, but also because of its ATA bus transfer data validity control (although this control does not work correctly with all drivers).

Because ATA controllers are connected to the 32-bit PCI bus, they have been made capable of addressing the ATA data register using double words. In this way, two 16-bit words are sent over the ATA bus serially in one 32-bit processor and PCI bus operation. 32-bit access to the data register can be controlled by the BIOS Setup IDE `32-bit Transfer` (`Enable/Disable`) parameter.

More advanced controllers (on separate expansion cards) may have their own cache memory and a processor. They have hardware capabilities to support "mirror" disks and to organize RAID structures of ATA disks. Some adapters make it possible to merge several physical disks into one logical disk on the BIOS calls level.

In the past, ATA controllers often used to be placed on audio cards (to connect CD-ROMs). By default, they are allocated the resources of channel 3 or 4. Hard drives can be connected to these channels, but whether BIOS will look for them there during POST is questionable. Modern versions of BIOS allow configuration parameters of four drives to be stored, older versions store only two. Four ATA channels allow up to four physical storage devices to be connected, but their use is limited to software capabilities.

There are hybrid adapters to connect ATA HDDs to XT or MCA buses or, for example, to the LPT port. Recently, matching adapters that allow ATA/ATAPI devices to be connected to the USB bus have been gaining ground. USB 2.0 combines ease of connecting external devices with a high data transfer rate.

PCI IDE Controller

There is a standard version of the IDE controller interface for the PCI bus. (It is not appropriate to use the term ATA here, as it is oriented at the ISA-like bus.) The PCI IDE Controller Specification came out back in 1994, and described implementation of the ATA interface compatible controller. Compared with the regular controller, this one has only one address in the control block registers (the obsolete address register is unavailable). A little later, the Programming Interface for Bus Master IDE Controller specification was published; it described operating devices in DMA mode using bus mastering. A two-channel controller is considered as one PCI function; a four-channel controller is considered a multifunctional PCI device. Two resource allocation modes are defined for the controller:

❑ The *compatibility mode*, in which channels are allocated the traditional I/O address areas and interrupt lines.

❏ The *native PCI mode*, in which base addresses of the register blocks and interrupt lines are assigned in the configuration space registers and can be relocated to any area unrestrictedly.

Table 8.9 shows controller resource allocation. In the compatibility mode, the controller can only work on the primary PCI bus because the PCI-PCI bridge will not relay standard address accesses to the other bus. A controller operating in the native PCI mode can be located on either bus. A specific controller may support mode changes or one of the modes. A controller that operates in the compatibility mode is by default "transparent" to the software: Its operation is the same as the traditional ATA controller. The current mode and whether it can be changed is indicated in the software interface byte that is the last item in the device class identifier. The functions of the bits of this byte are as follows:

❏ Bit 7 — bus mastering capability.
❏ Bits [6:4] — 000. Indicates standard interface, corresponding to the PCI IDE Controller Specification.
❏ Bit 3 — indicates whether the channel 2 mode can be programmed (i.e., bit 2 changed).
❏ Bit 2 — channel 2 operating mode. 0 — compatible with the standard ATA IDE controller; 1 — PCI IDE.
❏ Bit 1 — indicates whether the channel 1 mode can be programmed (i.e., bit 0 changed).
❏ Bit 0 — channel 1 operating mode. 0 — compatible with the standard ATA IDE controller, 1 — PCI IDE.

Table 8.9. PCI IDE Controller Resources

Resource	Compatibility mode: channel resources		Native PCI mode: channel base address (configuration space offset)	
	1	2	1	2
Command Block registers	1F0h–1F7h	170h–177h	10h	14h
Control Block registers	3F6h	376h	18h	1Ch
Interrupt	14	15	–	–

A typical controller has the 01:01:80h class and is implemented in the chipsets of most modern motherboards. The controller is an extension of the standard ATA controller that provides access to ATA/ATAPI devices at fixed addresses. The extension concerns the PCI bus mastering that allows exchanging data with devices in the DMA mode.

The controller allows all PIO exchange modes available to it (3.3–16.6 MBps), 8237A controller style DMA modes (2–16.6 MBps), and UltraDMA modes (16.6–133 MBps) to be utilized. All timing parameters are set using the PCI configuration registers; their make up may be specific for individual controllers. However, only POST must work with these registers to set optimal PIO and DMA/UltraDMA modes for each detected ATA/ATAPI device. The user can get involved into the process of adjusting these parameters by setting some restrictions in the BIOS Setup. As a result, after POST configuration, only PIO and DMA (if the device supports DMA) will be available to software when accessing devices. To conduct exchange in the PIO mode, no special operations are needed. The program simply reads from and writes to the data register using the REP INS/OUTS commands. In order to conduct DMA exchange, the bus master controller needs to be "loaded" and started; this procedure is discussed next.

A two-channel controller has a 16-byte block of registers located in the I/O address space. The base address of the block is stored in the device's configuration space at offset 20h (the lower 16 bits of the double word are used). The registers' location within the block is shown in Table 8.10. Registers' names have prefix BMI (Bus Master IDE) and suffixes P (Primary) for channel 1, and S (Secondary) for channel 2. In the description, an "x" stands in place of the suffixes to mean any channel.

Table 8.10. PCI IDE Controller Register Block

Channel offset		Length in bytes	First/second channel register
1	2		
0	8	1	BMICP/BMICS (RW) — *command register:* bit 0: 1 — start, 0 — stop; bit 3 — direction: 0 — memory read, 1 — memory write; bits 1–2, 3–7 — reserved (0)
1	9	1	Reserved (0)
2	0Ah	1	BMISP/BMISS — status register: bit 0 (R/O) — channel activity; bit 1 (RWC) — PCI exchange error; bit 2 (RWC) — interrupt request from a device; bits 3–4 — reserved (0); bit 5 (RW) — device 0 supports DMA; bit 6 (RW) — device 1 supports DMA; bit 7 — simplex mode indicator (1, if both channels cannot work simultaneously)
3	0Bh	1	Reserved (0)
4	0Ch	4	BMIDPTP/BMIDPTS (RW) — address of the descriptor table

A read/write *command register* BMICx is used to start the controller and set the transfer direction. The controller is started when bit 0 changes from logical 0 to logical 1;

a command execution cannot be resumed following stop in the current session. The controller is usually halted (the bit cleared) by an interrupt when the ATA/ATAPI command has been executed. Halting the controller prematurely will cause a command execution error accompanied by a corresponding error message. The transfer direction must be set prior to starting the controller; it cannot be changed on the fly.

The BMISx status register's bits 1 and 2 are set by hardware and cleared when a byte with 1s in the corresponding bits is written. After the interrupt request bit has been cleared, it can be set again only by the next front edge of an interrupt signal from the device. Bits 5 and 6 are set by software, usually when POST determines the capabilities of the connected devices and programs the controller's modes. The status register must be read after a command completion to determine whether the PCI bus operations have been successful.

The BMIODPTx register is used to store the address of the *descriptor table of the memory region* with which the data exchange is conducted. When performing a memory read operation, the controller can assemble a data stream from any number of regions (gathered read), and in doing a write operation it can spread the stream to these areas (scatter write). This capability existed way back in EISA systems; it made it possible to cross the page boundaries intrinsic to the standard DMA controllers and the page memory mapping of the x86 processors. Each descriptor requires 8 bytes:

❏ Bytes 0–3 (double word) — physical address of the memory region start (even)
❏ Bytes 4–5 (word) — byte counter (even, 0000 corresponds to 65,536)
❏ Bytes 6–7 (word) — end of table indicator (bit 15), bits 0–14 are not used (set to 0)

Each region can be located at any memory space area (except the area mapped onto the ISA bus) and be of any size, but it cannot cross 64 KB page boundaries. The descriptor page must be aligned at the double word boundary, and must not cross the 64 KB page boundaries. There are no restrictions on the number of descriptors in the table; the last one must contain the end of table indicator. The exchange begins from the region described in the first descriptor, followed by the next descriptor, and so on until the end. The controller will halt when the counter in the last descriptor reaches zero, or at the device's initiative if not all data need to be transferred. If the device runs short of data, it will point out the error when completing command execution. After the controller has been started, the second and zero bits of the status register indicate the following conditions:

❏ 0, 1 — memory exchange is in progress; there has been no end of operation interrupt yet.
❏ 1, 0 — exchange completed; the transferred volume corresponds to the volume of the described buffers (normal termination).

❏ 1, 1 — the device terminated the exchange, but fewer data have been sent on the ATA command than described in the tables (allowable termination).

❏ 0, 0 — bus error (bit 1) or fewer data are described in the table than in the ATA command.

ATA Device Configuring

Before an ATA device can be connected to the bus, it must be properly configured. Configuring means selecting the interface type and determining the device's address. The interface type — XT or AT — is determined by the model of the storage device. In Seagate devices, for example, the interface type is indicated by the last letter in the model code: A — ATA (16 bit), X — XT (8 bit), AX — AT or XT can be selected using a jumper.

There are two ways to set the device's address: cable select or by explicitly setting the address on each device. The cable select is enabled by the CS jumper. In this case, both devices on the bus are configured identically into the CS mode, and the address of each device is determined by its physical location on the special ribbon cable (see Fig. 8.3). The cable select method will work if it is supported by and enabled on all devices in the channel, including the host-adapter, which provides grounding of contact 28. When this device selection method is used, the devices' motors cannot be synchronized using the contact 28 wire, which is relevant for old RAID structures. The cable select method is seldom used. Its main advantage is that device configuration is standardized, but its disadvantage is that a device's role is tied to its physical location on the cable: The master device must be connected to the connector closer to the adapter and the slave device to the one further away. It is possible to connect the host-adapter to the middle connector and the devices to the end connectors, but it is not always convenient.

The more often employed method is to assign addresses to devices explicitly using regular straight cable (Fig. 8.2). In this case, the CS jumper is not installed and a device is assigned its address by setting various jumper combinations. Basically, a device only needs to be shown its own number; but in pre-ATA standard devices, the master device had to be "told" of a slave device's presence (in the ATA interface, the master detects the slave by the DASP# signal). Jumper combinations that can be encountered on IDE devices are listed below:

❏ M/S (Master/Slave) — address switch. If there is only one device on the cable, it must be configured as the master. If there are two devices on the cable, one must be assigned as master, the other assigned as slave. Sometimes, the jumper is marked as C/D (disk C:/disk D:) but this name is not right for the second IDE channel. When the first 1 GB IDE drives came out, some models could be configured as two devices (0 and 1) each of half capacity, in order to get over the 504 MB barrier.

When configured like this, another physical device cannot be connected to their IDE ribbon cable.

☐ SP (Slave Present), DSP (Drive Slave Present), Master but Slave is not ATA-compatible or Master but Slave uses only PDIAG-signal — is set on the master device to indicate that a slave device is present. If the jumper is set but a slave device is not connected, POST will issue an error message. The jumper is used on a disk not utilizing the DASP# signal.

☐ Single Drive — this jumper is set on the device if it is the only one on the cable (some Western Digital drives have this jumper). The device will be designated as master.

☐ ACT (Drive Active) — this jumper connects the DASP# line with the device state indicator signal. Set on device 0; seldom encountered.

☐ HSP — this jumper grounds the DASP# line (the HSP and ACT settings are mutually exclusive). It is set on device 1 to indicate its presence. Seldom encountered.

Fully ATA-compatible correctly configured devices are identified automatically. Modern ATA controllers allow even one device to be connected as slave: The controller handles the interface functions of the master.

It is difficult to figure out the functions of the jumpers on old drives without technical manuals; however, the help file of the Disk Manager utility contains an extensive database on various drive models. Unnecessary jumpers have been removed from modern devices, and those that are left are explained in the label. If the jumpers are placed next to the interface connector, their positions probably correspond to the ATA standard (Fig. 8.5).

After jumpers have been reset, their new settings become effective only after the device is powered up. Moreover, it is often impossible to connect two different type devices to one ribbon cable unless they are ATA devices.

CAUTION

8.2.2. Serial ATA Interface

The parallel ATA interface exhausted its bandwidth resources in reaching 133 MBps in UltraDMA Mode 6. In order to increase the bandwidth of the interface (but, of course, not of the storage devices themselves, whose internal exchange rates with the medium are much lower), a decision was made to switch to serial interface. The objective of the move was to improve and reduce the price of cables and connectors, and to improve the cooling conditions inside the system block by getting rid of wide interface cables, providing possibilities for developing compact devices and making devices' configuring easier for the user. At the same time, the number of blocks that can be addressed has been increased (the ATA addressing limit was 137 GB). Serial ATA revision 1.0 was published in 2001 and is available on the Internet at **www.serialata.org**. Work in now in progress on the Serial ATA II specification that has greater bandwidth and special features for supporting network storage devices.

The serial ATA interface is host-centered: It defines only interactions between the host and each of the connected devices; interactions between the master and slave devices, as is the case with the traditional ATA interface, are not needed. The interface offers the capability of emulating a pair of devices (master and slave) on one channel should such a need arise. Software interaction with Serial ATA devices practically matches the parallel ATA; the command set corresponds to the ATA/ATAPI-5 command set. At the same time, the hardware implementation of the Serial ATA host-adapter differs greatly from the primitive ATA interface (in the initial version). The parallel ATA host-adapter is a simple means of providing software access to the registers located on the connected devices themselves. The situation is different in Serial ATA: The host-adapter is equipped with blocks of so-called Shadow Registers whose functions match the functions of the regular ATA devices. Each connected device has its set of registers. Accessing these shadow registers sets off the processes of the host's interaction with the connected devices and command execution.

The standard describes a multilevel host/device interaction model in which exchanging commands, status information, and stored data make up the application layer. At the physical layer, information between the controller and devices is transferred over two pairs of wires. Data are transferred in frames; the transport layer forms and checks the integrity of the Frame Information Structure (FIS). To facilitate high-speed transmission at the channel layer, data are coded using the 8B/10B scheme (8 data bits are coded into a 10-bit character), scrambled, and then are sent over the physical line using the simplest NRZ method (the level of the signal corresponds to the transmitted bit). Between the channel and the application layers lies the transport layer, which is responsible for frame delivery. Each layer has its own data validity and integrity controls.

In Generation 1 Serial ATA, data are sent via a cable at a rate of 1,500 Mbps, which, with compensation for the 8B/10B, provides speed of 150 MBps (without taking into account the upper layer protocols' overheads). In the future, increases of the transfer rate are planned; consequently, a speed negotiation capability for each interface according to the host's and device's capabilities and the channel quality is built into the interface standard. The host-adapter has facilities to control connections; these facilities can be accessed by software via the special Serial ATA registers.

The standard provides for controlling power consumption by interfaces. In addition to the active state, each interface can enter the decreased power consumption *PARTIAL* or *SLUMBER* states; it takes a noticeable 10 msec to exit these states.

Commands requiring data transfers can be executed in various exchange modes. Accesses in the PIO mode and the legacy DMA exchanges are executed analogously to the regular ATA interface. However, the protocol for internal exchange between the host adapter and devices makes it possible to transfer different types of information (the FIS structures are defined not only for commands, status, and the stored data proper). The specification's Appendix D describes quite an original DMA transfer method — so-called first-party DMA — that is considered a primary one for Serial ATA devices. The traditional ATA adapter's DMA controller has a buffer for each channel into which descriptors of memory blocks involved in the exchange are loaded prior to the exchange operation (see *Section 8.2.1*). The first-party DMA method presupposes that the address information pertaining to the system memory of the host computer is presented to a storage device connected to the Serial ATA adapter. This information is unloaded from the storage device to the DMA controller of the host adapter during execution of transfer commands, and is used by the controller to generate the address for the current transaction. The reasons behind and the usefulness of this innovation are not quite clear; the price that has to be paid for some simplification of the host-adapter (especially of a multichannel one) is complication of the protocol and expansion of the functions that the storage device must perform. More customary is the traditional division of roles, in which the storage device's responsibility is to store data without worrying where in the computer's system memory they have to be during the exchange operation.

Serial ATA Physical Interface

The Serial ATA interface, like its parallel predecessor, is intended to connect devices internally. Cable length does not exceed 1 m, and each device is connected to the host adapter by a separate cable. The standard provides for direct hot swap connection of devices to motherboard connectors. The standard defines a new two-segment connector with mechanical keys that prevent devices being connected wrongly. The signal segment of the connector has seven contacts (S1–S7), the power segment has 15 contacts (P1–P15); all contacts are placed in one row 1.27 mm (0.5 inch) apart. Table 8.11 lists the functions of the contacts. The connector's small dimensions (its full length is about 36 mm) and a small number of signal circuits facilitate the layout of motherboards and expansion cards. The power segment of the connector may be absent and the device powered from a regular four-contact ATA connector. Fig. 8.6 shows serial ATA connectors. To provide hot swap capability, connector contacts have different lengths. First the P4 and P12 ground contacts mate, then the other ground contacts and the P3, P7, and P13 power circuit capacitor precharge contacts (to reduce the surge of the current), and finally the main power- and signal-circuit contacts are mated.

Table 8.11. Serial ATA Connector

Contact	Signal	Function
S1	GND	Shield
S2	A+	Differential signal pair A
S3	A–	Differential signal pair A
S4	GND	Shield
S5	B–	Differential signal pair B
S6	B+	Differential signal pair B
S7	GND	Shield
Key and free space		
P1	V33	3.3 V power
P2	V33	3.3 V power
P3	V33	3.3 V precharge power
P4	GND	Common
P5	GND	Common
P6	GND	Common
P7	V5	3.3 V precharge power
P8	V5	5 V power
P9	V5	5 V power

continues

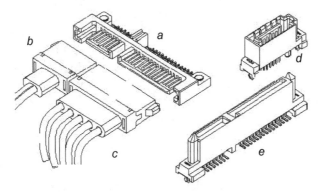

Fig. 8.6. Serial ATA connectors: *a* — device two-segment connector, *b* — signal segment of the cable connector, *c* — power segment of the cable connector, *d* — signal segment of the host connector, *e* — direct device mating host connector

Table 8.11 Continued

Contact	Signal	Function
P10	GND	Common
P11	Reserved	–
P12	GND	Common
P13	V12	12 V precharge power
P14	V12	12 V power
P15	V12	12 V power

Serial ATA Registers

Each device connected to the Serial ATA adapter is represented by three blocks of register; two of these register blocks correspond to the traditional ATA registers (see *Section 8.2.1*) and are called shadow registers; the third block is new. How the blocks' addresses are tied to the host's address space is not regulated by the standard. Blocks for the PCI controller are specified by the configuration space registers, and the shadow registers can be located at the standard ATA addresses.

As in the ATA, only one register is used in the control register block (AS for reads, DC for writes). The SC, SN, CL, and CH command block registers have been widened to 16 bits; the functions of the lower bytes have remained the same. In the LBA mode, the high byte of the SN, CL, and CH registers contain the logical address bits [24:32], [32:39], and [40:47] respectively. In the D/H register, bit DEV is ignored (when a pair of devices are emulated on one channel, bit DEV is used to select a device). The specification is not quite clear as to whether the lower bits of the D/H register are used to set the LBA[27:24] bits, as the same bits appear in the SN register's high byte.

The new register block SCR — Serial ATA Status and Control registers — consists of 16 adjacent 32-bit registers SCR0-SCR15, of which three have been assigned specific functions, with the other thirteen currently being reserved.

The *SStatus Register* (SCR0) indicates current state of the interface and the host adapter; it is read-only register. The functions of its bits are as follows:

□ Bits [3:0] — the DET field. Its value indicates the interface device detection:
  - 0000 — No device detected and physical communication not established.
  - 0001 — Device presence detected but physical communication not established.
  - 0011 — Device presence detected and physical communication established.
  - 0100 — Device is disconnected (disabled by the interface or running an internal test).

❐ Bits [7:4] — the SPD field. Conveys the negotiated communication speed:
- 0000 — Speed has not been negotiated (device not present or communication not established).
- 0001 — First-generation speed has been negotiated.

❐ Bits [11:8] — the IPM field. Indicates the interface power consumption:
- 0000 — No device detected or no physical communication.
- 0001 — Interface in active state.
- 0010 — Interface in *PARTIAL* state.
- 0110 — Interface in *SLUMBER* state.

The rest of the bits and fields are reserved.

The *SError Register* (SCR1) conveys interface diagnostic information. The register holds errors that accumulate since the last time the register was cleared. The register is cleared by a reset operation; individual bits are cleared by writing 1s to the corresponding register bits. The functions of its bits are as follows:

❐ Bits [15:0] — the ERR field. Contains errors serviced by the host's standard software:
- Bit 9 — C — non-recovered persistent communication error or data integrity violation. May be caused by a faulty connection, device failure, or device removal.
- Bit 11 – E — internal error discovered by the host adapter. If the error persists after reset, it may indicate that the host adapter and the device are incompatible.
- Bit 0 — I — recovered data integrity error (does not require software actions but may be considered, for example, when deciding to reduce speed).
- Bit 1 — M — recovered communication error (may arise when a device is temporarily disconnected or temporary loss of synchronization occurs; does not require any action from the host software).
- Bit 10 — P — protocol error; requires interface reset and the operation to be repeated (if persistent, may be an indication of device/adapter incompatibility).
- Bit 8 — T — non-recovered data integrity error; requires operation to be repeated.

❐ Bits [31:16] — the DIAG field; used by diagnostic software.
- Bit 19 — B — 10B/8B decoding error.
- Bit 21 — C — channel level CRC error.
- Bit 20 — D — Disparity: data blocks parity error.
- Bit 26 — F — unrecognized FIS type (error discovered in the transport layer with the CRC code being correct).
- Bit 17 — I — interface physical layer internal error.

- Bit 16 — N — physical ready signal has changed state.
- Bit 22 — H — frame handshake error (may be the result of the B, C, or D errors).
- Bit 23 — S — channel level state sequence error.
- Bit 24 — T — transport layer error.
- Bit 18 — W — *Comm Wake* signal has been detected.

The rest of the bits are reserved.

The *SControl Register* (SCR2) is a read/write interface control register. The functions of its bits are as follows:

❑ Bits [3:0] — the DET field. Controls device detection and interface initialization:
- 0000 — no action requested.
- 0001 — communication initialization and establishment (equivalent to hardware reset).
- 0100 — disables the interface and puts the physical level into the Offline mode.

❑ Bits [7:4] — the SPD field. Sets speed limits when negotiating communications:
- 0000 — no speed limit.
- 0001 — speeds higher than first generation not allowed.

❑ Bits [11:8] — the IPM field. Interface power management.
- 0000 — no restrictions.
- 0001 — transition to *PARTIAL* state is disabled.
- 0010 — transition to *SLUMBER* state is disabled.
- 0011 — transitions to both *PARTIAL* and *SLUMBER* states is disabled.

The rest of the bits and fields are reserved.

8.3. Interfaces and Constructions of Solid-State Mass-Storage Devices

Solid-state mass-storage devices have found application in miniature computers and in computerized digital consumer electronics devices, such as cameras, players, GPS receivers, musical instruments, etc. The majority of these devices are based on flash memory microchips, with the most advanced using NAND structure memory. This type of flash memory can be read from and written to quickly and erased in small (256- or 512-byte) blocks, which is convenient for writing files. True random reading is done rather slowly in this type of memory and writing an individual byte is altogether impossible, but the applications, in which these cards are used, have no need of such capabilities anyway because they are block-exchange oriented. Flash memory devices are power-source independent (do not need to be powered while in the storage mode), economical in terms of power consumption (especially when only read from), adequately efficient, but unfortunately not inexpensive. Writing to this media has its peculiarities: It is done fastest to an erased block (disk sector); also, overwriting requires that the previous contents be erased, which is a relatively lengthy process. Moreover, flash memory has a large (in the order of 10^5) but nevertheless limited number of erase/write cycles. As strange as it may seem, movable media storage devices have no such limitation. Storage devices are usually a combination of memory chips proper and a microcontroller that handles the external interface functions. In this, they are different from linear-access memory cards, such as Miniature Card, which contain only memory chips and do not need a built-in controller.

There are other solid-state storage devices, such as ferroelectric memory (FRAM), but they are not widely used so far. In less than a decade, flash-memory-based storage devices have come a long way from electronic 3-inch "disks" to the modern postage-stamp size devices. The interfaces of solid-state storage devices — external memory cards — are highly dependent on their constructs. Table 8.12 lists the characteristics of the most common cards.

Table 8.12. Main Characteristics of External Memory Cards

	CompactFlash	SmartMedia Card	MultiMedia Card	Sequre Digital	Miniature Card
Length (mm)	36.0	45.0	32.0	32.0	33.0
Width (mm)	43.0	37.0	24.0	24.0	38.0
Thickness (mm)	3.3/5.0	0.76	1.4	2.1	3.5
Connector	Pin	Printed pads	Printed pads	Printed pads	Conducting elastomer
Number of contacts	50	22	7	9	60

The above listed cards can also be connected to regular computers. For this purpose, there are various adapters for PC Card slots (for notebook PCs), for the USB bus (for all kinds of PCs), and for other external interfaces. With the help of these adapters, the computer "sees" the connected card as a regular removable medium (disk). Of course, general purpose computers have no need of such memory, as their own is larger and cheaper. The main purpose of connecting a card to a PC is to transfer application data from a consumer-electronics device (such as photographs, music, etc.) or to transfer (or store) other information between computers (using cards instead of diskettes) quickly.

Solid-state mass-storage devices can use the standard ATA as their interface. There are DOM (Disk On Module) devices that are connected to the regular 40-contact ATA connector that any modern motherboard has. However, the characteristics of this "hard drive" are not that very great: Its capacity is 4–256 MB, average data transfer speed is 1.6 MBps, and the cost of storage is about \$1.5/MB. Inside, the module has NAND-type flash memory and a controller that emulates ATA command system. These modules' main application is to store software in embedded computers, but then can also be used as removable mass-storage devices.

8.3.1. CompactFlash

CompactFlash cards (Fig. 8.7), which are supported by the Compact Flash Association (CFA), are extensively used in the most diverse electronic devices: digital cameras, photo printers, MP3 players, digital dictaphones, personal communicators, and, of course, computers — desktop, pocket, and mobile. The card's dimensions are $42.8 \times 36.4 \times 3.3$ mm (4 mm counting the raised part); they have a 50-contact connector (socket on the cards; two-row pin — with pins 1.27 mm apart — connector plug on the slot). The functions of the contacts are listed in Table 8.13. Using a 50-to-68-contact connector adapter, cards can be installed into the PC Card Type II or III slot, which almost all notebook PCs have. The cards' memory size ranges from 4 MB to 1 GB; their power supply voltage is from 3.3 V to 5 V. Cards can operate in one of three modes: memory card, PC Card I/O, and "pure" IDE (ATA) mode. In the first two modes, cards use the same interface signals as the PC Card. In the IDE mode, the electrical interface and the command system are fully compatible with the ATA specification (see *Section 8.2.1*), but data can only be exchanged in the PIO mode. The IDE mode is selected by grounding the ATA_SEL# signal on the host's side. Only the A[2:0] lines of the address bus are used; the rest are grounded by the host. The data bus is 8 bits wide when used to access ATA registers, and 16 bits wide when used to transmit data. The CS0# and CS1# signals are used to select the command and control block registers respectively. The PDIAG#, DASP#, CSEL#, RESET#, and IORDY signals conform to the ATA specification. The CSEL# signal selects the card's role: grounded signal corresponds to device 0 (master); not connected signal corresponds to device 1 (slave). The device's role may also be assigned by cable select system. The REG# and WE# signals should be connected to the V_{cc} power rail. The CD1# and CD2# signals play the role of card presence indicators; their contacts are mated last and are grounded on the card. Table 8.14 describes a purely passive matching adapter that allows a Compact Flash card to be connected to the regular ATA (IDE) port, which is present on every modern motherboard.

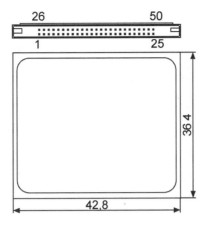

Fig. 8.7. CompactFlash Cards

Table 8.13. CompactFlash Card Contact Functions

Contact	Mem	I/O	IDE	Contact	Mem	I/O	IDE
1	GND	GND	GND	26	CD1#	CD1#	CD1#
2	D03	D03	D03	27	D11	D11	D11
3	D04	D04	D04	28	D12	D12	D12
4	D05	D05	D05	29	D13	D13	D13
5	D06	D06	D06	30	D14	D14	D14
6	D07	D07	D07	31	D15	D15	D15
7	CE1#	CE1#	CS0#	32	CE2#	CE2#	CS1#
8	A10	A10	A10	33	VS1#	VS1#	VS1#
9	OE#	OE#	ATA_SEL#	34	IORD#	IORD#	IORD#
10	A09	A09	A09	35	IOWR#	IOWR#	IOWR#
11	A08	A08	A08	36	WE#	WE#	WE#
12	A07	A07	A07	37	RDY/BSY	IREQ	INTRQ
13	VCC	VCC	VCC	38	VCC	VCC	VCC
14	A06	A06	A06	39	CSEL#	CSEL#	CSEL#

continues

Table 8.13 Continued

Contact	Mem	I/O	IDE	Contact	Mem	I/O	IDE
15	A05	A05	A05	40	VS2#	VS2#	VS2#
16	A04	A04	A04	41	RESET	RESET	RESET#
17	A03	A03	A03	42	WAIT#	WAIT#	IORDY
18	A02	A02	A02	43	INPACK#	INPACK#	INPACK#
19	A01	A01	A01	44	REG#	REG#	REG#
20	A00	A00	A00	45	BVD2	SPKR#	DASP#
21	D00	D00	D00	46	BVD1	STSCHG#	PDIAG#
22	D01	D01	D01	47	D08	D08	D08
23	D02	D02	D02	48	D09	D09	D09
24	WP	IOIS16#	IOCS16#	49	D10	D10	D10
25	CD2#	CD2#	CD2#	50	GND	GND	GND

Table 8.14. CompactFlash Card-to-ATA Adapter

ATA contact	Signal	CFC contact	CFC contact	Signal	ATA contact
2	GND	1	26	CD1#	—
11	D03	2	27	D11	10
9	D04	3	28	D12	12
7	D05	4	29	D13	14
5	D06	5	30	D14	16
3	D07	6	31	D15	18
37	CS0#	7	32	CS1#	38
GND[1]	A10	8	33	VS1#	—
GND[1]	ATA_SEL#	9	34	IORD#	25
GND[1]	A09	10	35	IOWR#	23
GND[1]	A08	11	36	WE#	+5 V[2]
GND[1]	A07	12	37	INTRQ	31

continues

Table 8.14 Continued

ATA contact	Signal	CFC contact	CFC contact	Signal	ATA contact
$+5V^2$	VCC	13	38	VCC	$+5\ V^2$
GND^1	A06	14	39	CSEL#	28^3
GND^1	A05	15	40	VS2#	–
GND^1	A04	16	41	RESET#	1
GND^1	A03	17	42	IORDY	27
36	A02	18	43	INPACK#	–
33	A01	19	44	REG#	$+5\ V^2$
35	A00	20	45	DASP#	39
17	D00	21	46	PDIAG#	34
15	D01	22	47	D08	4
13	D02	23	48	D09	6
32	IOCS16#	24	49	D10	8
–	CD2#	25	50	GND	GND^1

[1] Contacts 2, 19, 22, 24, 26, 30, and 40 of the ATA connector, as well as the power supply connector contact, must be connected to the GND rail.

[2] +5 V to the adapter is supplied from the supplementary connector.

[3] Can be connected not to the ATA connector but to the GND rail using a jumper: connected — master, not connected — slave.

8.3.2. SmartMedia Card

Cards of the SmartMedia Card type, which are supported by the PCMCIA, are intended for roughly the same range of applications as the CompactFlash. They are very thin, their printed connector is more robust and has fewer contacts (only 22), and they are not just water-resistant but waterproof. The cards are based on NAND flash memory microchips. Their average data transmission speed is 2 MBps, the peak rate is up to 10 MBps. The card's physical appearance is shown in Fig. 8.8; the functions of its contacts are described in Table 8.15. There are 16 Mbit and 32 Mbit (2 MB and 4 MB) 5 V cards. The 3 V cards are made in 16, 32, or 64 Mbit (2 MB, 4 MB, or 8 MB) sizes; their contact 17 is connected with V_{CC}. Simple PC Card Type II slot matching adapters are made for SmartMedia cards, and there are even FlashPath™ devices for reading them in regular 1.44 MB drives.

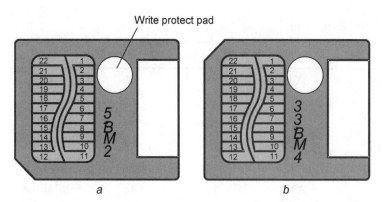

Fig. 8.8. SmartMedia Cards: *a* — 5 V power, *b* — 3.3 V power

Table 8.15. SmartMedia Card Contact Functions

Conctact #	Signal	Contact #	Signal
22	V_{cc} (5 B)	1	V_{ss}
21	CE#	2	CLE
20	RE#	3	ALE
19	R/B	4	WE#
18	GND	5	WP#
17	Power Detect	6	I/O1
16	I/O8	7	I/O2
15	I/O7	8	I/O3
14	I/O6	9	I/O4
13	I/O5	10	V_{ss}
12	V_{cc}	11	V_{ss}

8.3.3. MultiMediaCard and Secure Digital Cards

The MultiMediaCard (MMC) and Secure Digital (SD) cards are even more compact: they measure only 32 mm long and 24 mm wide; the MMC cards are 1.4 mm thick, and the SD cards are 2.1 mm thick. These cards have a printed edge connector with seven contacts for the MMC and nine contacts for the SD. The MMC cards have the power, control signal, clock signal, and 2-bit data bus lines routed to the edge connector. The data bus of the SD cards has been expanded to 4 bits, which makes it possible to increase the exchange rate. The SD cards are constructed in such a way that devices that use them can physically work with MMCs, but not vice versa (the narrower MMC slot cannot accept the thicker SD card anyway). Logical compatibility must be provided by the host's software (the device, into which the card is inserted). The MMC and SD cards are intended for approximately the same range of devices as the CompactFlash cards; to this list, electronic books (eBooks) need to be added. However, these cards serve different purposes: MMC are aimed at distribution of voluminous data (music, games, electronic books) and are fairly inexpensive information media; the SD cards are aimed at secure (in the sense of confidential) data distribution, and are substantially more expensive.

The SD card has been developed by a consortium of three companies: Toshiba, Matsushita (better known by its trade name, Panasonic), and SanDisk. These companies organized the Secure Digital Association (SDA) issuing specifications that hundreds of companies all over the world have already accepted. Membership of the association is paid — and expensive. For obvious reasons, the SD card's technical details are not commonly available (otherwise, their proclaimed security would not be worth much).

The SD cards (Fig. 8.9) have dimensions of 32 × 24 × 2.1 mm. The write protect switch that protects the card from accidental erasure can be seen on the right side of the card. The SD card has NAND flash memory chips, an SD controller, and an auxiliary component mounted on its printed circuit board. Contacts 1–7 of the nine-contact SD card connector (Table 8.16) match the MMC cards. SD cards can be hot swapped. The connector has been designed to last 10,000 insert/remove cycles. Cards can withstand up to 200,000–300,000 write cycles to each flash memory block, and a 3-meter drop. They are heat and cold resistant. The first SD cards had a data transfer rate of 2 MBps, and could store 8–512 MB. Around 2002, the transfer rate was raised to 10 MBps and the size to 1GB; in 2004, increases to 20 MBps and 4 GB in speed and size, respectively, are planned. The starting price per megabyte is high ($3.00), but it should go down gradually to $1.00 per megabyte (which is still high!) and lower.

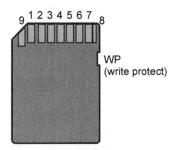

Fig. 8.9. SD Memory Card (Back View)

A three-layered format specification has been developed (and is continuing to be developed) for the SD cards. They are as follows:

❏ The physical layer describes SD-Rewritable cards and SD-Read Only nonvolatile memory cards.

❏ The file system layer uses the ISO 9293 standard.

❏ The application layer takes into account the specific characteristics of various content types: music — SD-Audio, images — SD-Picture, voice — SD-Voice, video — SD-video, etc.

Table 8.16. MMC and SD Cards Contact Functions

Contact	Signal	Contact	Signal
1	Command	6	Data 0
2	Vss	7	Data 1
3	Vdd	8	Data 2
4	Clock	9	Data 3
5	Vss		

Security features, which are SD's main strength, are employed at all layers. To provide these features, the Content Protection for Recordable Media technology of the coding and certification/authentication standard developed by IBM, Intel, Matsushita (Panasonic), and Toshiba is used. SD-Audio cards meet the Secure Digital Music Initiative (SDMI[1]) requirements for portable devices.

The SD card has three storage areas with various access levels: the coding and authentication key storage area, confidential data area, and common data area. Confidential data are stored and transferred encoded; they are encoded/decoded by the host (the device into which the card is inserted). In order to establish a confidential data exchange channel, the host and the card must mutually authenticate each other: the host must recognize the card, and the card must recognize the host. In this way, data exchange with the protected area of the card is possible only on authentic company devices (until hackers get their hands on the coding algorithms and keys).

SD cards are sold already formatted; should the need arise, they can be reformatted in a special equipment or a SD host that has formatting capabilities. Formatting them in equipment not intended for this purpose may render the card unusable: The protection may work out as a locked door, the only key to which has been left inside.

---

[1] SDMI is a coalition of audio equipment manufacturers (Recording Industry Association of America (RIAA) and recording industry companies (including leading companies such as UMG, BMG, EMI, WMG, SME) whose objective is to protect music copyright.

The compatibility between SD and MMC cards is rather limited. SD card hosts are compatible with MMC cards at the physical layer. MMC and SD cards both use the same FAT structure, which also provides compatibility at the file read/write layer. However, at the application layer, the internal software specifications of these cards may differ. For example, MMC cards cannot be used with SD MP3 players, as they use different data formats. Common data (not confidential) may be transferred from MMC to SD cards, but hosts will not allow the transfer of confidential data (if the host is not a computer running a cracked program). MMC card hosts are not compatible with SD cards even on purely physical level: SD cards are too thick for the MMC host slot.

In addition to SD memory cards, plans for SD I/O cards are being made. The Bluetooth interface is the first interface among those being considered. It allows devices with SD slots to quickly synchronize their data with each other and with devices that already have this interface, and without having to use wires.

8.3.4. Miniature Card

Cards of the Miniature Card standard are intended for use in inexpensive consumer electronics devices as removable flash memory and also as expansion to the dynamic memory (Fig. 8.10). The card's interface employs linear random memory access and can address up to 64 MB. Cards use a 16-bit nonmultiplexed data bus and can transfer data in burst mode. They can also work with an 8-bit host (the high and low bytes are merged in parallel, and the BS8# line is grounded). The host interface in these cards is configured to work in DRAM or flash memory mode; cards are equipped with a nonvolatile memory identification chip that operates using the I2C interface. Cards have key notches to ensure correct installation and a hot swap connector (even for DRAM!). When being installed, the connector's edge is inserted into the slot first, mating GND, VCC, and CINS# (the contact that is grounded), i.e., the connectors of primary importance. The card is then inserted deeper into the slot, and the contacts of the main conductive elastomer connector are mated and the detection contact CD# is bridged.

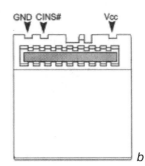

a   b

Fig. 8.10. Minituare Card card: *a* — overall view, *b* — bottom view

Card can use 5 V or 3.3 V power supplies; voltage level is identified by the VS1# and VS2# signals. Using a matching adapter, Miniature Card cards can be installed into PC Card type II slots.

The address lines A[12:0] and control signals RAS#, CASH#, and CASL# (the latter two are high and low byte strobes, respectively), and also the WE# signal are used when operating using the DRAM interface. Cards have separate V_{ccr} line for refreshing when the main power supply is turned off.

When operating using a flash memory interface, the A[24:0] address lines and the OE# (read), WE# (write), and CEH# and CEL# (high and low byte select) signals are used.

8.4. System Support of Storage Devices

Disk drives have standardized support on the BIOS and operating system levels. BIOS support for disk drives consists of providing disk sector read/write and track formatting services to the higher software levels, as well as performing auxiliary services. These capabilities are made available by calling Int 13h of the BIOS disk service. BIOS disk service is intended to isolate high-level software — operating systems and application programs — from the nitty-gritty details of disk system implementation.

Disk service Int 13h works at the physical device level, also called the physical drives level. The traditional disk service has a software interface that dates back to the IBM PC/XT and allows work with disks up to 528 MB. When larger disks appeared, the traditional interface was expanded using conversion algorithms that allowed this barrier to be crossed and, theoretically, to work with disks up to 8.4 GB. To work with large disks, new BIOS Int 13h services have been added whose interface is nothing like the traditional one at all.

The operating system furnishes application programs with services more sophisticated than BIOS functions, providing access to the disk's file system. The lowest level access allowable by the operating system deals with the sectors of logical drives that are associated with the device name (A:, B:, C:, ... Z:). One physical hard disk can have several logical disks. The physical disk may contain system areas (master boot record and reserved sectors) that cannot be accessed using the operating system.

Utilities and applications are provided with several disk service levels.

❏ The disk controller can be accessed on the register level by specifying the block address and number of sectors. This is the most effective method of exchange, but it requires knowledge of how disk partitions and the file system are organized, as well as the command set of the disk controller. Access is provided to all elements, with the exception of the areas blocked by the Set Max Address command (for ATA drives). When this method is used, the geometry-translation phase (done, in general, at the BIOS discretion) is bypassed.

❏ BIOS Int 13h services also allow unlimited disk access, but if they use the traditional calls (functions lower than 40h), then only disk with volumes below 8.4 GB (using geometry translation) or up to 528 MB (without geometry translation) are

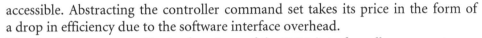

accessible. Abstracting the controller command set takes its price in the form of a drop in efficiency due to the software interface overhead.

❑ The absolute sector read/write functions of the DOS interface allow access to any logical disk sector by only stating its logical name. However, when using these functions, the first accessible sector (logical address 0) is the boot sector of the logical disk, and the partition table sectors and those sectors that are not included into the logical disk partitions become inaccessible. Knowledge of FAT and catalog structures is required to access disk data intelligibly, and the risk of making a serious blunder, including complete data loss, is quite considerable.

❑ Finally, the operating system file interface makes it possible to create, search, and delete files and directories, read and write whole or partial files, and perform other auxiliary functions. Using this interface hides from the user all FAT and catalog subtleties, not to mention all low level intricacies.

Application programs and utilities isolate the user from all these details, allowing him or her to concentrate on solving logical problems. The level at which a program accesses the disk is chosen by the software developer based on considerations of minimal sufficiency: the higher the service level, the easier it is to achieve compatibility with the rest of the software (fewer chances of making a mistake). The lower the service level, the more knowledge must be applied to develop a program that will interact with the disk without breaking some common rules.

Because CD-ROM data organization (file system) is substantially different from traditional disks (hard or floppy), special software is needed to provide applications with "transparent" access to the files on CD-ROM. Although it is possible to load an operating system from a CD-ROM supported by modern BIOS, nevertheless these BIOS do not provide full access to CD-ROMs (as they do to hard disks). Applications can access a CD-ROM only using operating system services, either built into the operating system or loaded separately (drivers).

For loading an operating system from a CD-ROM, Phoenix and IBM issued the El Torito Bootable CD-ROM Format Specification; version 1.0 was published in January 1995. The specification's objective is to make it possible to load an operating system and applications from CD-ROM by BIOS (on a bare machine). The specification provides the following capabilities:

❑ Selection of the operating system to load from the Boot Catalog located on the CD-ROM.

❑ Selecting whether to configure the CD-ROM as a hard drive or as a floppy drive.

❑ Renaming the installed drives (if necessary).

❑ Using the existing BIOS technology (LBA mode access) to access code and data.

❑ Compatibility with DOS and Windows applications that use `Int 13h` functions.

The specification expands the traditional BIOS functions set, and is aimed at ATAPI and SCSI interface drives.

Chapter 9: Computer Network Interfaces

Computer networks are categorized into local (covering a building or a group of buildings) and global. The Ethernet technology is currently almost totally dominant in the local network field. It offers three bandwidth rates — 10, 100, and 1,000 Mbps — and 10 Gbps is not far off. Other technologies — local ARCNet, Token ring, 100VG-AnyLAN, as well as wireless and global — will not be considered.

9.1. Ethernet Standards and Interfaces

The Ethernet technology allows various transmission media to be used. Each of these media has a standard name of the type *XBaseY*, where *X* is the transmission speed in Mbps (10, 100, 1,000...), *Base* is a key word, which means unmodulated transmission, and *Y* is a conventional designation of the transmission media and the communication range. All modern Ethernet versions use twisted-pair or fiber optic cable and star-connected topology. The *central unit* in a star topology network is a repeater (also known as a hub) or a network switch. A network can also consist of two units connected in a point-to-point scheme. Old versions of networks implemented on coaxial cable were typically connected using bus topology, whose main shortcoming was low network reliability. There also is an exotic version of the passive optical bus 10BaseFP. Sometimes *media converters* are used in networks, which convert one type of interface to another. Most often, twisted-pair-to-optic converters are used, but one-mode-to-multi-mode fiber optic converters are also used.

The following standards exist for 10 Mbps Ethernet:

❏ *10Base5* is a bus topology network utilizing thick 50-ohm RG-8 coaxial cable; the maximum length of a cable segment is 500 meters. An adapter is connected to the network cable via a transceiver using the Media Attached Unit Interface (AUI; four shielded twisted-pair patch cables). It is not used for new networks as it is too expensive, bulky, inefficient, and has no future.

❏ *10Base2* is a bus topology network utilizing thick 50-ohm RG-8 coaxial cable; the maximum length of a cable segment is 185 meters. A network adapter is connected using an interface BNC connector (or AUI with a transceiver). This is the most inexpensive version of the network (in terms of equipment); it also has no future.

❏ *10BaseT* network is built using category 3 and higher 2-pair twisted-pair cable; the length of a segment is up to 100 meters. (When using category 5 cables, the segment length may reach 500 meters, but it is not recommended.) A network adapter is connected via a RJ-45 connector (or AUI with a transceiver). This is a practical option for an entry-level network that allows the bandwidth be expanded by replacing hubs with switches. Speeds of up to 100 and even 1,000 Mbps can be achieved using category 5 and higher cables (with cards and hubs replaced).

❏ *10BaseF* and *FOIRL* is a network built on 2-fiber fiber-optic cable. An adapter is connected via the AUI interface equipped with an optical transceiver. Inexpensive multimode transceivers with 850 nanometers wavelength and a transmission range of up to 1 kilometer are used. For long-distance transmissions — tens of kilometers using one-mode fiber — single-mode 1,310 nm transceivers are used; they can also work on multimode fiber cable over distances of up to 2 kilometers.

The following standards exist for 100 Mbps Fast Ethernet networks:

❏ *100BaseTX* is a network built on a category 5 and higher 2-pair twisted-pair cable with segment length of up to 100 meters. The network adapter is connected via a RJ-45 connector. This is a popular and optimal option (in terms of value for the money) to connect nodes to a network. It allows up to 1,000 Mbps speed provided quality cabling and appropriate cards and hub replacements are used.

❏ *100BaseT4* is built on 4-pair category 3 and higher twisted-pair cable with segment length of up to 100 meters. Adapters are connected using RJ-45 connectors. This is a seldom-used version for networks.

❏ *100BaseFX* uses 2-fiber fiber-optic cable. Single-mode 1,310 nm transceivers are used, which can also work with multimode optical fiber at distances of up to 2 kilometers. The communication range operating in the full-duplex mode is tens of kilometers.

❏ *100BaseSX* is built on fiber-optic cable and uses inexpensive 850 nm transceivers; the transmission range is up to 300 m. It is compatible with the 10BaseF network and supports mode and speed negotiation (10/100).

The following standards exist for 1,000 Mbps Gigabit Ethernet networks:

❏ 1000BaseCX. Active equipment is connected using short (up to 25 meters) shielded twisted-pair (STP) or twinaxial cable.

❏ 1000BaseT. Equipment is connected using 4-pair category 5 or higher twisted-pair cable over distances of up to 100 meters; RJ-45 connectors are used.

❏ 1000BaseSX. Equipment is connected using multimode fiber cable; communication range is from 200 to 500 meters, depending on the quality of the fiber.

❏ 1000BaseLX. Equipment is connected using a pair of single-mode fibers; communication range is up to 50 kilometers, depending on the transceivers' characteristics.

The length limitations for each physical connection in a network were described above; however, to ensure network operability (i.e., reliable functioning of the collision resolution protocol), certain conditions must be met. The task of reducing the diameter of the collision domain is solved by using switches, while the collision restrictions on the length of each connection are overcome by moving to the full-duplex communications mode (in which collisions as such do not exist). The following requirements must be complied with in 10 Mbps Ethernet networks:

❏ For coaxial networks, the 5-4-3 rule must be obeyed: No more than five segments may connect no more than four repeaters; stations (adapters) may be connected in no more than three segments.

❏ For twisted-pair and fiber-optic networks, no more than four hubs can be between any pair of nodes.

❏ For any type of network, the diameter of the collision domain — the greatest distance (electrical length of cables between two nodes) — must not exceed 5 kilometers.

❏ The number of nodes within a collision domain must be no greater than 1,024 (and in reality, there should be no more than 30–50 of them).

The limitations are stricter for Fast Ethernet networks:

❏ The diameter of the collision domain must not exceed 205 meters.

❏ The number of class II repeaters within the collision domain must be no greater than two, those of class 1 no greater than one.

Only switches are used in Gigabit Ethernet, so limitations apply only to the length of connections.

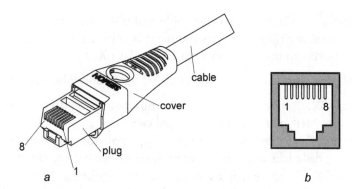

Fig. 9.1. RJ-45 connector: *a* — plug, *b* — socket

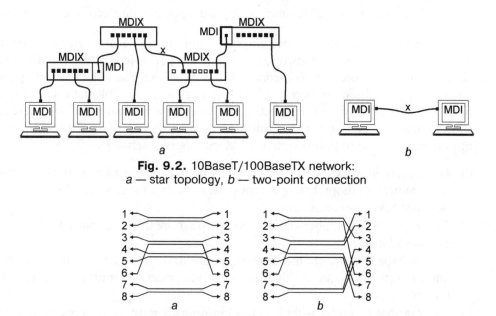

Fig. 9.2. 10BaseT/100BaseTX network:
a — star topology, *b* — two-point connection

Fig. 9.3. Ethernet interface cables: *a* — straight, *b* — crossover

Various connectors (ST, SC, MT-RJ, and others) are used for optical connections. Coaxial connectors for thick and thin cables are different: N and BNC series, respectively. Each coaxial segment must end with 50-ohm terminators and be grounded at one point. The computer's circuit ground is not galvanically coupled with the shield of the coaxial connector, so care must be taken not to accidentally touch the BNC connector to the computer case's metal parts. Coaxial networks must be properly grounded; disregarding these rules is fraught with the danger of adapter burn-up.

For twisted-pair cables, RJ-45 connectors are used (Fig. 9.1); the functions of the net adapter connector contacts (port MDI) are listed in Table 9.1. Ports of the 10BaseT, 100BaseTX and 100BaseT4 hubs are of the MDIX type; their TX and RX signals are switched over. To connect terminal nodes to active equipment ports (MDI-MDIX connection ports, Fig. 9.2, *a*), straight cable is used (Fig. 9.3, *a*), while for direct connection of adapters (MDI-MID, Fig. 9.2, *b*) or two communications devices (MDIX-MDIX), a crossover cable is used (Fig. 9.3, *b*). As a rule, one of the ports in communications devices is equipped with either an MDI-MDIX switch or an additional connector.

Table 9.1. Ethernet Adapter RJ-45 Connector

Contact	10BaseT/100BaseTX	100BaseT4	1000BaseTX
1	Tx+	Tx_D1 +	BI_D1+
2	Tx–	Tx_D1–	BI_D1–
3	Rx+	Rx_D2+	BI_D2+
4	Not connected	BI_D3+	BI_D3+
5	Not connected	BI_D3–	BI_D3–
6	Rx–	Rx_D2–	BI_D2–
7	Not connected	BI_D4+	BI_D4+
8	Not connected	BI_D4–	BI_D4–

Local networks are usually built using stationary cables fitted with sockets at the ends, and patching cables. The contacts of the stationary cable sockets are connected directly. Patching cables can be straight and crossover. Only 100BaseT4 and 1000BaseTX networks need to have contacts 4, 5, 7, and 8 connected, but these connections do not interfere with 10BaseT and 100BaseTX networks, so all these networks can share the same cabling.

Only straight cables are used in Gigabit Ethernet 1000BaseTX. Universal ports are compatible with Fast Ethernet (i.e., they support auto negotiation). If two Gigabit Ethernet ports are connected using a crossover cable, they will negotiate to a 100BaseTX mode connection.

The twisted-pair Ethernet implementations mentioned above employ the *mode autonegotiation protocol*, which is executed every time when establishing a link after physical connection was made or after port initialization. The protocol is based on exchanging service impulses, which differ from the transmitted information. This protocol allows the ports that are being connected to choose the most effective mode available to both ports. The mode priorities, in descending order, are as follows: 1000BaseT, 100BaseTX full duplex, 100BaseT4, 100BaseTX half duplex, 10BaseT full duplex, and 10BaseT half duplex. The autonegotiation protocol may be disabled (or not implemented); in this case, the operating mode is forced when configuring the port. Ports' ability to switch modes is reflected in their names (e.g., Fast Ethernet 10/100); the 100BaseT4 mode is not frequently supported.

An autonegotiation protocol for optical versions has also been developed, but its capabilities are limited by the possibility of mismatching the wavelengths employed in different modes. In fact, autonegotiation is not really needed here, as there are much fewer optical connections, they are designed carefully, and they are not reconfigured very often.

The Ethernet standard (10 Mbps) defines the Attachment Unit Interface (AUI) that is used to connect a transceiver for any transmission medium to the adapter. The transceiver contains the terminal circuits of the transmitter and receiver and the collision detector. The functions of the AUI contacts are shown in Table 9.2; the DB-15 connector is used (plug on the adapter, socket on the transceiver).

Table 9.2. Ethernet AUI Connector

Contact	Signal
1	Collision (shield)
2	Collision +
3	Transmit +
4	Receive (shield)
5	Receive +
6	DC Power GND
7	Not connected
8	Not connected
9	Collision −
10	Transmit −
11	Transmit (shield)
12	Receive −
13	DC Power (+12 V)
14	DC Power (shield)
15	Not connected

The Fast Ethernet standard contains the Media Independent Interface (MII). Using this interface, data for the receiver and transmitter are sent uncoded over 4-bit parallel buses (at 2.5 or 25 MHz clock speed for 10 or 100 Mbps, respectively) or serially encoded (for 10 Mbps). The interface has synchronization, receiver and transmitter control, and line status (carrier presence, collision) signals, as well as the System Management Interface (SMI) serial control interface (see *Section 11.2*), which is used to communicate with the transceiver's control registers. A 40-contact, 2-row physical connector for connecting plug-in modules also is defined, but it is practically not used in PCs.

9.2. Network Adapters

PCs are interfaced to a network using *network adapters* or *Network Interface Cards* (NIC). Adapters have transmitting and receiving sections that must be independent from each other if full duplex support is required. Having received a data block and the transmission destination address from the central processor, the transmitting section must obtain access to the transmission medium and form, and transmit the frame (add the preamble and the CRC code), repeating the transmission attempt if a collision has been detected. The adapter must inform the processor whether the transmission has been successful or has failed. The receiving section scans the headers of all the frames going through the line and pulls the frames addressed to this node out of the flow in the unique, broadcasting, or group mode. The adapter can be programmed into the promiscuous mode, in which it will receive all frames regardless of their destination addresses. Frames are received into a buffer and are checked for errors (frame length, correct CRC). The processor is informed when a correct frame has been received and the frame is transferred from the local buffer to the computer's system memory. Error frames, as a rule, are ignored, although the adapter may maintain statistics on their frequency. In practice, there are adapters that do not detect errors in damaged frames. It is not easy to perform diagnostics of a network containing such an adapter.

Network adapters for PC are produced for the ISA, EISA, MCA, VLB, PCI, and PC Card buses. There are adapters that are connected to the PC's standard LPT port: Their advantage is that they do not require system resources (ports, interrupts, etc.), and are easy to connect (without opening up the system block). But they also have shortcomings: They load the processor significantly, and their transmission rates are low (10 Mbps is the ceiling). Adapters for the USB also exist. Some motherboards have network adapters integrated into them.

The effective network data exchange speed depends greatly on the architecture of the network adapters and, all else being equal, on the speed at which data are transferred between the adapter's local memory and the computer's system memory, as well as on whether the parallel execution of several operations is available. DMA channels, programmed I/O, or bus mastering are employed as the delivery vehicles for data exchange between the adapter and the computer memory. The standard 8-bit ISA DMA channels can reach speeds of up to 2 MBps; 16-bit channels can reach speeds of up to 4 MBps. A maximum length frame is sent over these channels in approximately 1.3 and 2.6 ms, respectively. Compared with the 12 ms needed to send a frame in the Ethernet environment, this is relatively little time.

However, for the Fast Ethernet environment, where the same frame is sent in 1.2 ms in the media, this transportation is too slow. The PIO mode provides higher exchange speed with the adapter's buffer, but it completely loads the processor during the transmission. Smart ISA/EISA adapters with bus mastering are more efficient and provide relatively high speeds (up to 8 MBps for 16-bit ISA and up to 33 MBps for EISA). However, ISA bus throughput is not sufficient for speeds of 100 Mbps. Currently, PCI bus adapters are widely used; their throughput reaches up to 132 MBps for 32-bit interface at 33 MHz. However, even this is barely enough for Gigabit Ethernet. The PCI, though, has some reserves, namely going over to 66 MHz and 64-bit width; not all motherboards have these capabilities, however. Especially effective are active adapters for PCI bus that have their own processors: They execute the transfer at the PCI's full speed, putting practically no load on the processor.

This property is especially important for servers. Parallel operation execution means full-duplex support: complete independence of the receiving and transmitting sections, as well as being able to simultaneously perform receiving a frame into the buffer, transmitting another frame, and exchanging data between the adapter's buffer memory and the computer's main memory. The efficiency of an ISA/EISA adapter is also affected by the size of the buffer memory: When the bus throughput is limited (comparing to the line speed), up to 64 KB of buffer memory is used, which is divided between the transmitter and receiver either evenly or with the transmitter getting the larger share. PCI bus adapters with efficient deliver methods (smart bus mastering) do not need buffers for speeds below 100 Mbps: 2 KB for both the receiver and transmitter is enough. However, Gigabit Ethernet adapters are again equipped with a substantial size buffer (256 KB).

Adapters can be divided into two categories: adapters for workstations and adapters for servers. The division is relative: Workstation adapters may have server features. It is not worth trying to use regular adapters in servers: They may become the network's bottleneck and devour the processor's resources.

Workstation adapters are simpler and cheaper: They do not require speeds over 100 Mbps (at least for the time being), full duplex is seldom encountered in them, and they do not make especially severe demands on the use of the processor time. Adapters that are software compatible with the NE2000 cards — 16-bit unintelligent ISA bus cards from Novell-Eagle — have been used for many years. A series of PCI bus cards also are compatible with this model. The most handy and popular are the two-speed 10/100 Mbps cards: An optimal place for their connection can be easily found in modern networks. The cards usually have a socket for installing Boot ROM; modern cards also provide remote LAN wake-up and support the DMI and ACPI interfaces. For this, they have a special 3-wire interface: a cable with a connector that is connected to the motherboard. Over this cable, the ATX motherboard supplies stand-by power ($+5 V_{SB}$) even when the main power is not supplied to the motherboard and other devices. This line feeds power to the stand-by receiver circuit, which is tuned up to receive a special format frame — Magic Packet — over the network interface. When the network adapter receives this frame, it sends the wake-up PME signal to the motherboard over this cable, and the motherboard issues a signal to turn the power supply on; the computer powers up and the operating system with the DMI support loads. Now, the network administrator can perform the planned work and when the work is finished, the computer's operating system will turn the computer off.

Server adapters must have a high-efficiency bus. Currently, the PCI 32/64-bit bus at 33/66 MHz is used; earlier, the EISA or MCA bus was used. When engaged in data exchange, CPU loading is crucial to the server cards; therefore, they are equipped with smart capabilities to support bus mastering and parallel work of the adapter's components. Full-duplex adapters must support flow control under the 802.3x specification. A series of advanced models support traffic prioritization under the 802.1p specification, multiaddress traffic filtration, tagged VLAN, Fast IP, and hardware IP packet checksum calculation. Tagged VLAN support allows the server connected to the switch by one line to be a member of several VLANs defined for the entire local network. In order to increase their reliability, server cards can support Resilient Links, in which a spare adapter and a communication line replace the main channel if it fails. The spare adapter is assigned the same MAC address as the main one, so that the network does not notice the switch. Resilient Links must be supported by software drivers, so that the switch will be also executed transparently for server applications. Self-Healing Drivers can automatically reset and reinitialize the adapter if an operational error is detected (hanging). As a rule, servers do not need remote boot and LAN wake-up. Adapters (together with drivers) can support the Simple Network Management Protocol (SNMP) and Remote MONitoring (RMON). Multiple port adapters (as a rule, with four ports) are also produced for servers; they are configured both for separate independent use, and for backing each other up. This type of card allows PCI slots to be saved (the slot economizing problem was not acute for the EISA bus). Today, typical server card speed is 100 Mbps; Gigabit Ethernet capabilities may be only required for the most powerful servers.

An adapter can have one or several interface connectors:

❑ BNC — a coaxial connector for connecting to a segment of the 10Base2 network

❑ AUI — a DB-15 socket for connecting external 10Base5, 10Base2, 10BaseT, 10BaseF, and FOIRL adapters (transceivers)

❏ RJ-45 — an 8-contact socket for connecting 10BaseT, 100BaseTX, 100BaseT, 100BaseT4, 1000BaseT concentrators (hubs or switches) using twisted-pair cable

❏ SC (a pair), sometimes ST — optical connectors for connecting 100BaseFX, 1000BaseSX, 1000BaseLX concentrators

For 10 Mb adapters, combinations of BNC+AUI or RJ-45+AUI connectors are typical; the most universal, known as "Combos", have the entire 10-Mb set of BNC/AUI/RJ45 connectors. First model cards for 10 and 100 Mbps had a pair of RJ-45 sockets, one for each speed. Even if adapter has different connectors (a BNC and a RJ-45, for example), they are not used simultaneously: The adapter cannot work as a repeater. Most modern adapters have one RJ-45 socket and support standards: 10BaseT, 100BaseTX, and more powerful 1000BaseT. Multiport server cards have several independent adapters, each having its own interface.

Interface cards use the following computer system resources:

❏ *I/O space* — as a rule, four to 32 adjacent addresses from the area addressed by a 10-bit (for ISA bus) or 16-bit (EISA, PCI·buses) address. It is used to access the adapter's registers during initialization, current operation control, status querying, and data transmission.

❏ *Interrupt request* — one line (IRQ 3, 5, 7, 9, 10, 11, 12, or 15) triggered by receiving a frame addressed to a particular node, and also when a frame has been transmitted (successfully or unsuccessfully, depending on collisions). Network adapters cannot work without interrupts, and with incorrectly assigned interrupts adapters hang when accessing the network.

❏ *DMA channel* — used in some ISA/EISA cards; only 16-bit channels 5–7 can be used for ISA bus mastering.

❏ *Adapter shared RAM* — buffer for transmitted and received frames — for ISA cards, usually mapped onto the upper memory area in the A0000h–FFFFFh range. PCI cards can be located in any area of the address space not occupied by the computer main memory. Not all cards use shared memory.

❏ *Adapter ROM* — an address area for ROM BIOS expansion modules — occupies 4/8/16/32 KB in the C0000-DFFFFh range. It is used for Boot ROM and antivirus protection.

The *adapter configuration* consists of allocating PC system resources and selecting the transmission medium. Depending on the type of card, configuration can be done in different ways:

❏ Using jumpers that are installed on the card. This method is employed on adapters of the first generation ISA bus. All resources, as well as the transmission medium, are selected by its own group of jumpers.

❏ Using nonvolatile configuration memory (NVRAM, EEPROM) installed on ISA bus cards. This type of cards are jumperless, but still are configured manually. A small utility specific to the concrete card model (family) is needed to configure these cards.

❏ Using nonvolatile configuration memory installed on EISA or MCA bus cards and the system device configuration memory (ESCD for EISA). Resources are configured with the help of a special ESIA Configuration Utility (ECU).

❏ Automatically using Plug and Play for ISA and PCI buses. Resources are allocated during the operating system loading stage.

The transmission media and speed can be selected manually (via software) or automatically. In some cases, it is sensible to assign resources explicitly, in order to avoid the surprises of the excessive automation. These surprises, as a rule, stem from insufficient coordination between adapters and their drivers. In such situations, the driver cannot correctly recognize the mode that has been set, and make use of its advantageous features. The automatic configuration inserts additional delays into the initialization process during the loading of the operating system, and may not work properly with some network equipment. Some cards with the 10Base2 interface (BNC connector) can be programmed into the extended mode, which increases the communication range to 305 meters from the regular 185 meters. If long segments are needed, this mode can be resorted to, but on the condition that it is available and enabled on all cards of the particular segment. Configuration utilities can offer other adjustments: client and server optimization, modem support, and some others. Their settings must conform to concrete applications.

Chapter 10: Auxiliary Serial Interfaces and Buses

The interfaces considered in this chapter are mainly intended for computer-internal use. In this capacity, the I2C bus is used to identify DIMM modules, information about which is stored in low capacity nonvolatile memory chips. Several models of modern motherboards are equipped with the SMBus, which is based on the same I2C interface. This bus is used to read the identification information from memory modules, as well as to access the memory identifiers and the thermocontrol services of the Xeon processors; it is also a part of the CNR slot signal set for configuring audio and communications equipment. Modern monitors exchange configuration and control information with the graphic adapter (and via it, with the central processor) over the I2C interface, which is a part of the VESA DDC1/2B interface. The DDC channel is a part of the regular 15-contact VGA analog interface; its developments are the EVC and the P&D, DVI, and DFP interfaces. If the graphics adapter and the monitor support the DDC1/2AB interface, the user can theoretically connect external equipment via the ACCESS.Bus using the connector mounted on the monitor (in practice, this type of monitor is seldom encountered). This equipment may be positioning devices (e.g., digitizers and mice), card readers, bar-code readers, etc. The serial ACCESS.Bus was developed by DEC to allow the computer to interact with its accessories (e.g., with a VESA DDC channel monitor, Smart Battery power supply, etc.). The I2C interface can be used to load firmware into the nonvolatile (flash) memory of a series of popular microcontrollers. The I2C interface provides data transmission rates of up to 100 Kbps and even 400 Kbps, while being much simpler and cheaper than the RS232C interface, which has a limit of 115.2 Kbps; it also allows several devices to be connected and supports hot-plugging and the plug-and-play technology. Recently, a high transmission speed — up to 3.4 Mbps — has been added to the I2C, but only new microchips with hardware support for the interface can work at this speed.

The SMI interface in its pure form is not often used in PCs. It originates from the Fast Ethernet communication equipment, where it is widely used to control physical level modules (including exchangeable concentrator modules).

The SPI and JTAG interfaces are used in equipment based on microcontrollers and configurable logic; most often, they are used to store configuration information and program codes. Other 3- and 4-wire interfaces are used for the same purposes, but in this book their description will be limited to just mentioning their existence.

10.1. Serial Buses Based on I2C

The I2C serial bus interface, introduced by Philips as a simple and inexpensive means of interfacing consumer electronics microchips, has become the de facto standard for equipment of various purposes. It is very practical for small data exchange applications (e.g., for configuring various devices). The I2C bus specification defines a two-way data transmission protocol over two signal lines. This protocol is used in a diverse range of applications, with the information content depending on the particular application. The ACCESS.Bus and SMBus are based on the I2C specification. These two buses will be considered in further sections.

10.1.1. I2C Bus

The *Inter IC Bus*, or I2C for short, is a synchronous serial bus providing bidirectional data transfer between connected devices. The bus is directed at 8-bit transfers. Data may be transmitted in both the one-address mode to a selected device and in the broadcast mode. Signal levels are standard, and compatible with the commonly used TTL, CMOS, and N-MOS logic of both the +5 V and +3.3 V (and lower) types. The protocol functions of the I2C microchips are usually supported by hardware. The protocol allows interaction on one bus between devices with different interface speeds. The requirements to the signal timing parameters are quite liberal; therefore, computers and microcontrollers without hardware support for the I2C bus can implement its protocol purely by software.

The I2C bus has been in use for a long time; the official Version 1.0 came out in 1992. The option to specify the address of the slave device by software that existed in the previous (draft) versions has been eliminated as too complicated and unused. The Low Speed mode, which is a special case of the *Standard Mode* (S) with a speed of 0–100 Kbps, has also been eliminated. Version 1.0 introduced the definition of the *Fast Mode* (F), with a speed of 0–400 Kbps and related changes in the requirements to the signal slope control and the interference filtration. The 10-bit device-addressing mode was also introduced in Version 1.0. Version 2.0 was introduced in 1998, when the I2C interface became the de facto standard of the industry, and used in a great number of different integrated circuits. In this version, a new *High speed* (Hs) mode appeared with transmission speeds of up to 3.4 Mbps. In terms of logic, the F and S modes function similarly and are designated by a common term, F/S. Version 2.0 revised the requirements for the level and shape of the signal, taking into account the high speeds and a possibility of connecting 2 V and lower devices. Version 2.1 (2000) clarified some points in the Hs mode timings. The information presented here is based on the specification for the Version 2.1 of the I2C bus, available on the site **www.philips.com.** The parameters of the I2C interface signals are given in *Section 10.1.4*, where they are compared with the SMBus and ACCESS.Bus requirements.

The I2C interface uses 3 wires: GND and two signal lines — the SDA (Serial Data) line and the SCL (Serial Clock) line. Two devices are involved in the exchange process: a master and a slave. The master and the slave devices can play role of both the transmitter and receiver of data. The protocol allows presence of several master devices on the bus, and has a simple collision-detection and arbitration mechanism.

The exchange protocol for regular F/S devices is shown in Fig. 10.1. Both signal lines are connected to a positive power supply voltage via pull-up resistors. A device has an open-collector (open-drain) transmitter and a receiver connected to each line; the slave device does not have to have a transmitter on the SCL line. All transmitters with the same name are connected to the line, forming a wired-AND circuit: The line level will be high if all transmitters are inactive, and low if even one of the transmitters has its output transistor open. In the Idle state, all transmitters are inactive. The synchronization is set by the master device, but the slave device can slow down the data exchange if it cannot keep up with the transmission speed.

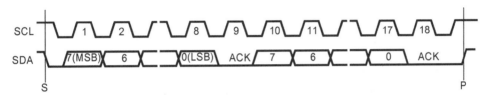

Fig. 10.1. I2C data transfer protocol

Transmissions are initiated by the master by generating the *Start* condition after it ascertains that the bus is available (i.e., when the SCL and SDA signals are high). The Start condition, represented by the s symbol on timing diagrams, is a high to low transition of the SDA signal while the SCL signal is high. The operation is completed by the *Stop* condition: a low to high transition of the SDA signal while the SCL signal is high. This condition is also always initiated by the master device and is represented by the P symbol on timing diagrams. While the data are being transmitted, the SDA line can change its state only at the low SCL signal; data bits are considered valid during the high level SCL signal. The master device can begin the next transmission right after the current without generating the Stop condition; this is called *repeated Start* and is represented by Sr on timing diagrams. The s and Sr conditions are almost equivalent. Each data transmission consists of 8 bits generated by the transmitter (the MSB is transmitted first). After transmitting each byte, the transmitter releases the line for one clock in order to receive the acknowledgement. During this ninth clock, the receiver generates the Ack acknowledge bit, which is used by the transmitter to ascertain that it has been "heard." After transmitting the Ack bit, the slave device may hold up the transmission of the next byte by holding the SCL line low. In the F/S modes, the slave device can delay bus transmissions at the bit level by holding the SCL signal low after the master releases it. Therefore, the master device must not generate the SCL signal haphazardly, but after first analyzing the SCL line: Having released this signal, it can generate a new one (opening the transmitter's key) only after ascertaining that it has returned into the inactive state (high level). Otherwise, the timing will get out of sync. The SCL signal may be held in the low state by another device that is trying to obtain bus control simultaneously. The SCL clocking signal does not necessarily have to be uniform: How long it is held low is determined by the maximum time that the slowest device engaged in the exchange decides to hold it, even if there is a conflict among the devices involved in the exchange. How long the SCL is held high is determined by the fastest of the conflicting master devices.

A *bus collision* (conflict) may arise when two or more devices, being ascertained that the bus is free, simultaneously, or almost simultaneously, initiate data exchange. They all control the SCL and SDA lines and watch them. If a device sending a 1 (high level) senses a 0 (low level) on the SDA line at the instant clock, it must admit that it has lost the arbitration and relinquish the SCL and SDA lines. (However, it may continue to control the SCL line until the current byte has been transmitted). The winning device will not even notice the losing contenders, and will continue working. The arbitration may terminate at any point during the transfer generated by the master device. Information transmitted by the device that has won the arbitration does not become corrupted (a pleasant difference from Ethernet network collisions). If the master device that loses the arbitration can also function as a slave, it must switch into the slave mode, because the conflict may be caused by the winning master device trying to address it.

The ACK acknowledge bit generated at the end of each received byte by the receiving device performs several functions. When the transmitter is the master device, the receiver (slave) must generate a logical zero ACK bit confirming successful reception of the immediate byte. A logical one ACK bit (not acknowledge) generated in response to the issued address means that the addressed slave device either is not present on the bus or that it is busy executing some real-time task. If a slave does not acknowledge a data byte, it means that it is busy. If the master device does not receive an acknowledge bit, it must generate the Stop condition to free the bus. When the master device acts as a receiver, it must generate a logical zero ACK bit after each byte it receives except for the last byte, when a logical one ACK bit is generated. This serves to inform the slave device that the transmission has been completed and that it must release the SDA and SCL lines now so that the master device can generate a P or Sr condition.

The data exchange protocol over the I2C bus is constructed on the above-described physical base. Each slave device has its own unique bus address. At the beginning of each transmission, after generating a S or Sr condition, the master device sends the address of a slave device or a special address (Table 10.1). The slave device that recognizes its address after the Start condition becomes *selected*; it must acknowledge the receipt of the address and the following bytes transmitted by the master until a P or Sr condition is generated. In the original version of the interface, the device address width was 7 bits; later, a 10-bit addressing mode that was compatible with the 7-bit mode was introduced. Devices with 7- and 10-bit addressing modes can share the same bus.

When operating in the 7-bit addressing mode, in the first byte after the S (Sr), the master device sends 7 address bits (A[6:0] in bits [7:1]) and the operation indicator RW in bit 0 (RW = 1 — read, RW = 0 — write). The addresses of the slave devices must differ from special addresses shown in Table 10.1. The address ranges for devices of various types are issued monopolistically to the microchip manufacturers by Philips. For example, for memory microchips, the 7-bit address consists of two parts: the high 4 bits A[6:3] carry the information about the device type (e.g., EEPROM — 1010), while the low 3 bits A[0:2] define the number of the given-type device on the bus. Microchips with the I2C interface have three address inputs, which are set to logical one or logical zero to specify the number to which a device responds; the device type is wired into it by the manufacturer.

When the master device sends data, in the first transmitted byte it sends the address of the slave device with the RW bit set to 0. The selected device responds with an acknowledgement (ACK = 0), after which the master device sends one or several data bytes, each of which the slave device must acknowledge.

When the master device receives data, in the first byte it sends the address of the slave device with the RW bit set to 1. The selected device responds with an acknowledgement (ACK = 0), after which the transfer direction changes and the slave device sends data. The master device acknowledges each received byte except for the last one.

These transmissions may be terminated by the master device issuing the P condition, after which any master device can obtain bus control. Mixed transmission is also possible; in it, the master device does not relinquish the bus after completing a transfer, but generates a repeated Start condition (Sr), after which it accesses either the same or a different device.

The I2C specification does not specify the rules for modification of the microchip-internal data address during serial access: They are determined by the designer of the device according to its functions. Address autoincrement is normally used for memory chip addressing, which simplifies serial accesses. Register-oriented devices usually do not need autoincrement.

Table 10.1. I2C Special Addresses

Bits [7:1]	Bit 0 (RW)	Function
0000 000	0	General call address
0000 000	1	Start — beginning of active exchange
0000 001	X	Address of a CBUS device (for compatibility)
0000 010	X	Address for devices with other buses
0000 011	X	Reserved
0000 1XX	X	Code of Hs mode master device
1111 1XX	X	Reserved
1111 0XX	X	10-bit addressing indicator

The special codes listed in Table 10.1 are interpreted as follows:

❏ General call is of the broadcast type; only devices supporting appropriate functions must respond to it.

❏ The Start byte serves to make the software implementation of the I2C protocol easier (for functions of slave devices that do not have fully hardware-implemented protocol). All devices must not answer the Start byte. The generated SDA signal (Fig. 10.2) can be used as a hardware interrupt request, on which the processor will begin servicing the I2C signals in earnest. Until it receives this byte, the processor (microcontroller) does not have to bother monitoring the interface signals.

❏ I2C devices are not allowed to respond to CBUS (a 3-wire "relative" of the I2C bus) devices or devices built on other buses.

❏ When 10-bit addressing is employed, bits [2:1] contain the upper part of the address; the formats of transmissions using 10-bit addressing are considered further on in this section.

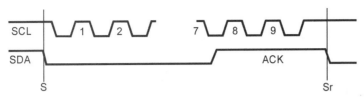

Fig. 10.2. Timing diagram of the Start byte

Sending a general call pursues one of two goals. These goals are defined in the second byte, whose least significant bit (bit 0) is called B. When B=0, devices that have accepted the general call must either reset (if the second byte holds 00000110b) or not (if the second byte holds 00000100b) and then read the programmable part of their hardware address. Device must ignore other values in the second byte. How the address is programmed depends on the device (it is stated in its data sheet). When B =1, the general call is used for *broadcast data transmission*. In this case, the master device generates its address (the same one that it responds when acting as a slave) in the higher seven bits of the second byte, and then sends the bytes that it needs to deliver to the unknown recipient. The receiver (as a rule, an intelligent device) must acknowledge each byte it receives, starting with the general call byte, followed by the master device address and then the data bytes.

Broadcast transmission can be resorted to, for example, by hardware keyboard controllers, which do not know to what address their asynchronous messages are to be sent. Another scheme also is possible: Upon powering up (or resetting), this device becomes a slave receiver, to which the master device (the system controller) will communicate the address of the information recipient for further targeted transmissions, in which this device itself will be the master.

Ten-bit addressing has solved the problem of the address shortage: whereas there are only 112 addresses available in the 7-bit addressing mode, taking into account reserved combinations, the 10-bit addressing mode makes further 1024 addresses available. Data transmission by a 10-bit addressing master device is simple: Bits [2:1] of the first byte after the S (Sr) carry the upper address bits with bit 0 (the RW indicator) set to 0; the second byte carries the lower eight address bits, while the following bytes are the transmitted data. The receiver acknowledges the received bytes in the usual way. Data receiving by a master device is somewhat more complex, because the RW indicator explicitly indicates the transmission direction change after the first byte, and the master device cannot now send the lower part of the address. To get around this stumbling block, the master device begins reception of a 10-bit address as a dummy transmission: It sends the 10-bit write indicator and the two address bits in the first byte, with the rest of the address sent in the second byte. The master device then generates the Sr condition and sends a 10-bit read indicator (RW = 1) with the two upper bits of the same address. After the slave transmitter receives the same two upper address bits as before the sr, it responds with an acknowledgement and starts transmitting data to the master device. This process continues and terminates the same way as 7-bit addressing. Combination exchanges also are possible in which a master device executes an actual transmission to a 10-bit device, generates an sr condition, and then reads the same device. Combination 7- and 10-bit accesses to different devices are also possible employing the sr condition. Broadcasting using 10-bit addressing is the same as in 7-bit, except that the address of the master device is sent in two bytes (the lower eight address bits are sent instead of the first data byte).

The high-speed Hs mode makes it possible to exchange data at speeds of up to 3.4 Mbps; at this speed, Hs devices are compatible with fast and standard devices (F/S). In order to make exchanges at such high speeds possible, the output and input buffers of the microchips must switch into a special operating mode in which the sent and received signals have different characteristics. Signals of high-speed devices are designated as SDAH and SCLH; in combined systems, they must be separated from the SDA and SCL lines of regular devices by special bridges in order to work in the Hs mode, as the behavior of F/S devices at these speeds is unpredictable. Arbitration is not possible in the Hs mode as it is carried out at the F/S mode speed; neither is it possible to have synchronization at each bit (slave device delaying the transmission); the master device sets a rigid ratio of the low and high levels of the SCLH signal duration (2 to 1). The slave device can slow down the exchange only after the acknowledgement bits.

To switch into the Hs mode, the master device uses in the first byte after the s condition the reserved value of 00001xxx, where xxx is the code of the master device. During the transmission of this byte (at the F/S speed) arbitration is performed: If several devices are attempting to begin exchanges simultaneously, only the winning master device will be able to proceed. In the Hs mode, a master device is assigned code during configuration, and all Hs master devices on the bus must have different codes (code 000 is reserved); this provides for completion of the arbitration during the transmission of the first byte. A master device can switch into the Hs mode only if it has won the arbitration and received the logical one acknowledgement bit. In this event, it readjusts its input/output buffers to the Hs parameters and generates a repeated start condition (sr). Thereafter, the exchange is conducted exactly the same as in the F/S mode, only at high speed. The Hs mode can extend to several successive transmission separated by sr conditions; the Hs operation is terminated by a P condition, at which the buffers will revert to the F/S parameters.

10.1.2. ACCESS.Bus

The serial Accessory Bus (ACCESS.Bus) was developed by DEC as a standardized inexpensive interface for interaction between a computer and external devices such as keyboards, pointer devices, character-processing devices (e.g., printers or bar-code readers), and monitors (in terms of exchanging control and configuration information over the VESA DCC). The history of ACCESS.Bus began in 1991; later, additional specifications for interaction with internal devices (such as Smart Battery, etc.) were added. As System Management devices belong to the internal device class, the specification has a contact point with the SMBus, which is based on the same I2C interface. The bus allows the system to control and communicate with up to 125 devices (the limit of the adopted addressing system). Above the ACCESS.Bus' I2C hardware protocol lies a basic software protocol with which protocols of the specific connected devices interact. The protocols allow devices to be connected and disconnected without rebooting the operating system, as well as dynamic address allocation. The latest version, ACCESS.Bus Specification Version 3.0, was published by the ACCESS.Bus Industry Group in 1995; the following description is based on this version.

On the hardware level, the bus is logically identical to I2C bus in terms of its standard speed (up to 100 Kbps) and 7-bit addressing of slave devices. The same synchronization and arbitration mechanisms are employed. However, out of all possible data transfer modes, the main one in the ACCESS.Bus is data transmission by a master device and reception by a slave device: This is the simplest method, in which there is no transmission direction change in any transaction. From this, it follows that in order to conduct a bidirectional data exchange, all the devices must support the master (transmitter) and slave (receiver) device modes. To provide compatibility with the SMBus, a master device is allowed to read data, and combination transfers using the `Sr` mode are possible.

There are two electrical signal specifications, one for external (*off-board*) devices and one for internal (*on-board*).

The Off-board ACCESS.Bus specification, which is the main specification for the bus, defines the use of a 4-contact shielded modular connector (MOLEX SEMCONN or AMP SDL); the functions of this connector's contacts are given in Table 10.2. The host computer must provide 5 V at 50–1,000 mA power supply. Each device (and cable) is defined in terms of the current I (mA) it draws and the capacitance C (pF) introduced by the signal conductors. The maximum number of devices that can be connected is limited by the total introduced capacitance (not to exceed 1,000 pF) and the current drawn. In practice, the addressing limit of 125 devices is never reached. The maximum total cable length (without repeaters) cannot exceed 10 meters. As compared with the I2C, the load current of the SDA and SCL lines has been increased to 6 mA (low level output current). To improve the pulse form and provide protection against static electricity, it is recommended to connect devices to the SDA and SCL lines via serial 51-Ohm protection resistors. It is also recommended to protect the microchips' inputs by diodes connected to the GND and +5 V rails.

VESA offers a different 5-contact ACCESS.Bus connector for routing the external ACCESS.Bus on the outside of monitor cases. The functions of its contacts are listed in Table 10.3.

Table 10.2. Functions of the ACCESS.Bus External Connector Contacts

Contact	Function	Wire color
1	GND	Black
2	SDA	Green
3	+5 V (device power supply)	Red
4	SCL	White

Table 10.3. ACCESS.Bus Connector (VESA)

Contact	Function
1	GND
2	Key
3	SDA
4	+5 V (device power supply)
5	SCL

The On-board ACCESS.Bus specification is designed for lower load currents (350 mA) and allows serial resistors of greater values. The restriction on the introduced capacitance has been replaced by the requirements to the positive and negative signal transitions. This specification was only introduced in 1995. It aims at being compatible with SMBus devices, so supplementary restrictions on the maximum duration of various phases corresponding to SMBus have been added.

The ACCESS.bus 3.0 base protocol consists of two subsets: the PA protocol for programmable address devices and FA protocol for fixed address devices. Either or both of these protocols can be implemented in either an external or internal device. The previous version of the specification described only external PA devices; internal FA devices are called SM-devices (System Management) in it. The FA protocol is practically identical to the SMBus (described in *Section 10.1.3*) but without such not vitally important features as the Packet Error Code (PEC) and dynamic address allocation. SM-devices can communicate with the host using the Write Word protocol. The PA base protocol is based on transmitting unidirectional messages. The ACCESS.bus is host-centered: Messages are sent from a device to the host and from the host to a device; the only exception is when an attempt is made to reset a device's double (a device with the same address). Upon power up, devices must respond only to the default address 0110 111; each device is allocated an individual address during configuration. In the operation mode, the bus allows new devices to be detected and configured without rebooting.

Messages are sent in packets whose format is given in Fig. 10.3. The DestAddr destination address is perceived by the receiver on the hardware level (this is the address of the I2C slave device). The SrcAddr source address allows the receiver to identify the data source (and to determine where to send the answer). The protocol flag P makes it possible to determine the purpose of the packet's body: P = 0 — Device Data Stream, P = 1 — control/status. The Length field determines the packet's length in bytes; the Body itself is contained in the following bytes. The CheckSum byte is a result of performing an XOR operation on all the preceding bytes of the packet, starting with the receiver's address. A zero result of this operation for all the packet's bytes, including the checksum byte, indicates the packet's integrity. Only packets with a correct checksum byte are to be processed. The minimum packet length is 4 bytes, the maximum length is formally 131 bytes (127 bytes body and 4 bytes framing). However, the maximum packet length is limited by the time allowed to the device for transmitting a packet.

Each device is assigned its own address, to which it must respond with acknowledgment bits when receiving a message. The address is a one-byte number; it is always even, because in the I2C, a 7-bit address is supplemented by the least significant bit RW, whose value is 0 in the ACCESS.bus. Address 50h is always assigned to the host computer; address 10h is reserved for the host of system management devices. Address 6Eh is the default address to which only devices without an assigned individual address answer. Devices are assigned individual addresses from the address ranges 02–4Eh, 52–6Ch, and 70–FEh. A total of 125 addresses is available, but some of them are reserved for the fixed addresses of SM devices and monitors.

Bit/Byte	7	6		1	0
1	DestAddr — Receiver Address				0
2	SrcAddr — Source Address				0
3	P	length			
4	Body — Package Body				
	...				
Length + 4	CheckSum — Checksum Byte				

Fig. 10.3. ACCESS.bus message packet format

There are nine protocol messages (P flag equals 1) defined for the ACCESS.bus that are mandatory for implementing the bus' interface functions (autoconfiguration). Only devices that have been configured can exchange useful application messages, and then only after the exchange has been explicitly permitted.

Messages from the host to devices are listed below:

❐ Reset — forces a device to the power-up state and assigns it the default address. The body consists of one-byte code F0h. A device that has detected a double on the bus can also send this message. By sending this message to its own address, the device will force its double to switch to the default address.

☐ Identification Request — asks device for its identification string. The body consists of one-byte code F1h.

☐ Assign Address — assigns a new address to a device that has a matching identification string. The body (30 bytes long) begins with code F2h, followed by the 28-byte device identifier, and concludes with a one-byte new address.

☐ Capabilities Request — requests a device to send a fragment of its capability information. In the message body, the starting byte F3h is followed by a 16-bit parameter indicating the offset of the required data relative to the start of the device's capability structure. In order to simplify the device logic, the parameter is limited to the values providing for the first (null offset), next, and last transmitted fragment to be requested.

☐ Enable Application Report — enables a device to send application data. The code F5h is followed by a one-byte operation code: 00h — disable, 01h — enable.

☐ Presence Check — checks whether there is a device on the bus at the specified address. The code F7h is followed by a zero-value byte (which is reserved for future needs).

Messages from devices to the host are listed below:

☐ Attention — a configuration request (device has powered up and completed autoinitialization). The body consists of one-byte operation code E0h.

☐ Identification Reply — a reply to the identification string request. The body (29 bytes long) starts with the operation code E1h followed by a 28-byte identification string.

☐ Capabilities Reply — a reply to the request to a device to send a fragment of its capability information. The body (3–35 bytes long) begins with the operation code E3h, followed by a 16-bit offset (see Capabilities Request) and then the data itself (0 to 32 bytes). The host assembles fragments using the offset.

The specification also defines supplementary protocol messages used to control power consumption and resource distribution, and for other purposes (the P flag of these messages also is 1).

☐ Resource Request — resource request from a device to the host. The operation code E5h is followed by a one-byte resource designator and optional data. The command allows the following requests to be made: for an address for private use and to relinquish it; for the current time; for the host to store a block of data or to give it back; for the host to continue to power the bus so that the device can complete internal operations; and for additional bandwidth.

☐ Resource Grant — host's reply to a Resource Request from a device. The operation code F4h is followed by the resource descriptor and then optional data.

❒ `Application Hardware Signal` — a request from a device to the host to generate a high priority hardware signal. The operation code A0h is followed by a one-byte code of on the following signals:

- 1 — `Reset`: attempt a soft reset of the computer
- 2 — `Halt`: call a debugger
- 3 — `Attention`: call the computer's attention

❒ `Application Test` — command from the host to a device to execute an application test (code B1h).

❒ `Application Test Reply` — device report of the test results. The operation code A1h is followed by a one-byte test result code (0 — success, non-zero — failure), then by 0–30 bytes of additional test information.

❒ `Application Status Message` — device informing of its application-specific status change. The operation code A2h is followed by a zero byte, then a status byte, and then two bytes of specific data. The status byte has the following meanings:

- 00 — device ready
- 01 — device not ready
- 02 — device capabilities have changed
- 03 — device has lost its internal state
- 04 — device has lost application data (most likely because of buffer overflow)

❒ `Device Power Management Command`. The operation code F6h is followed by one-byte mode code:

- 00 — run
- 01 — standby
- 02 — suspend
- 03 — shutdown
- 04 — power off advisory
- 05 — restart
- 06 — query power

The rest of the protocol message codes are assigned by the vendor according a device specific purpose. Application data are sent with $P = 0$.

The 28-byte ACCESS.bus *device identification string* consists of a series of character fields structured as follows: a one-byte protocol revision, a 7-byte module revision, an 8-byte vendor name, an 8-byte module name, and a 32-bit unique device number. This number can be either fixed (i.e., the vendor implements unique numbers, which is not cheap) or a random number generated upon powering up for the duration of the work session. System software must not use the device identification string to identify the device for the purpose of installing drivers. Instead, it must use the device capability string fields. (The structure of these fields depends on the device type.)

The autoconfiguration mechanism is based on the uniqueness of the identifier: all devices, which have not been assigned their unique numbers yet, respond to the identifier request made to the default address. However, in the arbitration process, only one of these devices gets to the end of the message, and the host assigns this device its own unique number. In the next round of the general identifier querying, another device will come up a winner, and so on, until all devices have been assigned their unique numbers. The host finds out about this by the absence of response to the general call. A newly connected device will inform the host of its arrival by issuing an Attention message, in response to which the host will execute the above-described device identification and address assignment procedure.

The ACCESS.bus specification defines the structure of the host's software environment. The central element of the software environment is the ACCESS.bus Manager: a software driver that manages all operations with devices connected to the bus. On one side, this driver communicates with the hardware resources of the host through the Mini Port Driver (MPD); on the other side, device drivers communicate with it. Application software makes calls to the drivers of the necessary devices or to the bus manager, but in no event directly to the host. The bus manager initializes the bus and controls it thereafter, identifying devices being connected to and disconnected from the bus. It links device drivers (or application software) with the devices themselves, checks the incoming messages, and works as a bidirectional data switch reformatting and buffering incoming and outgoing messages. The MPD separates the bus manager from the host's specific hardware. *Device drivers* are bidirectional interfaces between application programs and specific devices. The ACCESS.bus specification describes software driver interfaces (Device Driver, MPD), as well as the protocols for keyboards, positioning devices (Locator), monitors, batteries, and character processing devices.

10.1.3. SMBus

The System Management Bus (SMBus) is a two-wire interface that provides data exchange between microchips of the various system components of the computer, as well as linking them with the computer itself. The main purpose of the interface is to control the power supply subsystem and the attendant subsystems. Initially, the bus was being developed for smart batteries and charging devices, and the first SMBus specifications were named Smart Battery System Specifications. A Smart Battery System consists of the batteries proper and charging devices that can exchange information between themselves and with the host system to which it supplies power. This exchange allows the batteries to communicate their parameters (current and expected values) and to switch into the operation (powering the host system) or charging mode. Some control functions are carried out with the host's participation, while others are performed autonomously. The first SMBus specification came out in 1995, and Version 1.1 was issued in 1998. Version 2.0 came out in 2000; batteries are no longer mentioned in its name. The current description is based on the System Management Bus (SMBus) Specification Version 2.0, which was issued by a forum of smart battery systems developers (SMS, **www.sbs-forum.org**) that counts among its members many battery manufacturers, as well as Intel. The specification covers the three lower layers of the open system interface (OSI) model, from the physical to the network.

The SMBus is based on the principles of the I2C, and everything said in *Section 10.1.1* applies to it. A dynamic reconfiguration (connecting and disconnecting devices during operation) and automatic device address assignment capability were added to the bus. Compared with the I2C, the requirements to the signals' upper and lower level limits and their timing parameters have been somewhat changed in the SMBus (see *Section 10.1.4*), but in general, the signals are similar for the two buses. The SMBus is supported at the BIOS level. The distinguishing feature of the SMBus, connected to its role in controlling system power supply, is its autonomous operation capability: Devices connected with its help can exchange information even when the central processor (or other subsystems) is not powered up. Of course, any interaction in this state between the bus devices via BIOS is out of question, because BIOS is still sleeping.

At the physical layer (the lowest OSI layer), the specification defines the electrical and timing parameters of the signals. In terms of signal levels (and load-carrying capacity), there are two different specifications. The *low power* specification is for the SMBus' native battery powered applications in which low currents are typical. The *high power* specification is intended for SMBus clients working in a high interference environment (on a PCI card, for example). Low and high power devices cannot work on one bus at the same time, but this is not needed. Should it become necessary to use different class devices together on the bus, they can be placed on separate bus segments joined by a bridge.

The specifications of timing parameters incorporate measures aimed at decreasing the response time and preventing bus hanging. The clock signal has been restricted to 10 KHz from below and to 100 KHz from above. Restrictions on the maximum high and low clock signal duration have been introduced, along with restrictions on the maximum cumulative time of bit interval stretching per byte. A time-out mechanism is also provided for, by which the devices that detect bus hanging must immediately terminate the exchange and reinitialize. The I2C does not have these provisions.

The following supplementary hardware signals can be used on the SMBus:

❑ The SMBSUS# active signal indicates that the bus and devices have entered the suspend mode. This signal is generated by the power supply controller; when it is active (low), devices do not react to the regular SDA and SCL signals. These signals can be used, however, to provide specifics of the suspend mode.

❑ A slave-only device uses the SMBALERT# signal to inform the master device that it needs to conduct an exchange. This signal is assembled into a wired-AND circuit from all devices. Having received this signal, the master device must issue a byte read command to the 0001 1000 address, which only the device that issued the alert signal can answer by sending a byte containing its address (a device may also answer with a Packet Error Code (PEC) byte).

The same data transmission rules are defined at the data link layer (the next lowest OSI layer) like in the I2C: the S, P, and Sr conditions; acknowledgement bytes; 7-bit addressing and the RW indicator in the first byte following the S (Sr) condition. Like in the I2C, the master device can both read from and write to a slave device; combination transactions using the Sr condition are also used. Acknowledgement generation in the SMBus has its pecularities. A device must always answer its address with an acknowledgment bit ACK even if it is busy performing internal operations. This rule provides a mechanism to detect a particular device's presence on the bus. A slave device can generate an NACK bit in response to any non-address byte if it is busy or if the data requested by the command are unavailable. It the latter case, it can also delay the sync signal at the low level (within the allowable limits). A slave device must generate an NACK bit in response to invalid commands or data codes. An NACK response forces the master device to terminate the transaction (generate the P condition). A master device acting as a receiver uses the NACK response to inform the transmitter that it has received the last expected byte.

SMBus Network Layer

The network layer (the third-lowest OSI layer) defines the nature of the SMBus and warrants more detailed consideration.

Besides master and slave devices, the SMBus has a concept of a host device. A host is a bus client that performs coordinating and configuration functions; it is also a master device that must also perform some slave functions and handle notification messages.

Each slave device has a unique address. Within the 7-bit address range, several values are set aside (Table 10.4); there are slightly more of them than in the I2C. Ten-bit addressing is not considered in the current version. Device addresses are broken into several types. Specific types of devices are allocated purpose-assigned addresses. For example, Smart Battery devices have address 0001 011, their charging devices have address 0001 001. Devices assigned these addresses must meet the SMBus requirements for this class of devices. A series of systems within SMBus detect and use these devices based on their address. Other systems may not rely solely on the address, and may determine the type of present devices in a different way. Multiple purpose devices, as well as devices not fully compliant with the specification for their class, are assigned other addresses by their manufacturers; these addresses are listed on the SMBus site, **www.smbus.org**. Addresses of prototype devices are used for experimental and developing purposes and must not be used in production devices. The SMBus 2.0 specification introduced an automatic dynamic address assigning capability, which will be considered further on.

Table 10.4. SMBus Special Addresses

Bits [7:1]	Bit 0 (RW)	Function
0000 000	0	General call address
0000 000	1	Start. Beginning active exchange
0000 001	X	CBUS device address (for compatibility)
0000 010	X	Address reserved for devices of different bus formats
0000 011	X	Reserved
0000 1XX	X	Reserved
0101 000	X	ACCESS.bus host
0110 111	X	ACCESS.bus default address
1111 0XX	X	10-bit addressing indicator
1111 1XX	X	Reserved
0001 000	X	SMBus host
0001 100	X	SMBus alert response address
1100 001	X	SMBus default address
1001 0XX	X	Addresses for prototype devices

Every SMBus device supports a fixed set of commands for interaction (controlled, status polled, exchanged data). The command code consists of 1 byte sent after the transaction's address byte. Commands can use one of the 11 protocols defined in the SMBus. There also are simplified commands, which do not have command's code byte as such (Quick Command, Send Byte, and Receive Byte). Which of the protocols to use in a transaction is decided on by its initiator (knowing the characteristics of the addressed device). The addressed device properly interprets and correctly responds only to the commands and protocols it supports (responses to unsupported commands are undetermined).

A Packet Error-Checking (PEC) feature was introduced in the SMBus Specification Version 1.1. The PEC mechanism is based on adding a CRC code to the end of each transmitted packet that is calculated using all the preceding packet's bytes, including the address byte. Almost all protocols can have two versions: with PEC or without it. Devices that support PEC and those that do not can be mixed on one bus. The receiver answers the PEC byte with an acknowledgement byte, but this can be interpreted by the transmitter in various ways. If the transmitter receives an NACK byte in response to PEC byte, it means that the receiver does not confirm receiving the packet without errors. However, an ACK response does not mean that the receiver acknowledges receiving correct data: It may not understand the PEC and reply to it as to a regular data byte; the receiver may also not perform real time checking of the input data flow. A more reliable data validity check can only be performed by enlisting higher layer protocols. For example, to control writing valid data to a device, the same data can be read using PEC code, and the master device will determine whether the operation was successful or not by analyzing the entire received packet.

The SMBus bus protocols are based on the following 7-bit addressing I2C transactions.

❏   *Quick Command.* Sending an address byte; command action is determined by the RW bit of the address byte.

❏   *Send Byte.* Master device sends one byte following the address byte (RW = 0). Two bytes are sent in the PEC version: The first is data, the second is the PEC.

❏   *Receive Byte.* The master device receives one data byte following the address byte (RW = 1). Two bytes are received in the PEC version: The first is data, the second is the PEC.

❏   *Write Byte, Write Word.* After the address byte (RW = 0), the master device sends one command byte followed by 1 or 2 data bytes; the low byte is transmitted first. In the PEC version, a check byte is added at the end.

❏   *Read Byte, Read Word.* Combined transactions: First, the address byte (RW = 0) is sent, followed by the command code. Next, using an S condition, another address byte with the same device address but with RW = 1 is sent, followed by receiving 1 or 2 data bytes. In the PEC version, a check byte is expected at the end of the reception.

❏   *Block Write.* Following an address byte in which RW = 0, the master device sends one command byte followed by a byte-count byte indicating the number of bytes to follow; finally, the data proper are sent. In the PEC version, a check byte is added at the end. The PEC byte is not included into the byte-count field, which itself cannot be 0. Up to 32 data bytes can be sent by one block command.

❏   *Block Read.* A combined transaction: First, the address byte (RW = 0) is sent, followed by the command code. Further, using the S condition, another address byte with the same device number but with RW = 1 is sent, followed by receiving the byte-count byte followed by the data proper.

❏ *Process Call.* A combination of a Write Word command with receiving a word (two byte) from the device with the same address. The command is called a process call because the data it expects depends on the code and data byte it sends. In the PEC version, the check byte is expected only at the very end, following the last data byte received.

❏ *Block Write — Block Read Process Call.* A combination of block write with a following block read at the same device address. In the PEC version, the control byte is expected only at the very end, after the last byte of the received data.

If a regular device (not the host) is going to act as a master device, it must use the SMBus host notification protocol: The device sends a byte with its own address to the host's address (RW = 0), followed by a word of the message proper. The host must be able to understand these messages; an optional SMBALERT# alert signal can also be used here.

Automatic Address Assignment

Dynamic SMBus reconfiguration — or "hot" connecting and disconnecting — is based on the basic principles of the I2C protocol. The automatic address assignment capability introduced in Version 2.0 also uses Packet Error Check (PEC) bytes. The task of automatic address assignment consists of detecting a device being connected or disconnected and providing it with a nonconflicting address. Detecting new connected devices can be done in two ways. Upon connecting (after initialization upon power up), a device that can work as a master can send to the host a message containing its address. The other detection method is periodical polling by the master device in charge of inventorying devices on the bus.

The *Address Resolution Protocol* (ARP) is used to dynamically assign devices unique nonconflicting addresses. Address assignment is based on the standard SMBus (and I2C) arbitration mechanism. A device remembers the address it has been assigned for the whole time it is powered up. There also are so-called Persistent Slave Address (PSA) devices, which remember their previously assigned address upon power resumption. After a device has been assigned an address, data exchange with it is conducted exactly the same as with a device with a fixed address. Any SMBus master device can assign addresses.

To be assigned an address, a device needs to be isolated: The enumerator device must be able to conduct dialog with each device being assigned an address without interference from other devices (a typical Plug-and-Play system configuration task). The isolation procedure is based on the Unique Device IDentifier (UDID): a 128-bit structure containing device capability description, its version, identifiers of the vendor, device, and subsystem, as well as device-specific information. The identifier begins with the Device Capabilities byte, whose two upper bits carry information about the device's dynamic addressing capabilities, and lower bit indicates whether PEC is supported. The master device uses the block-read protocol to read the identifiers at the SMBus default address. All devices without assigned addresses respond to this call, and devices are isolated during the arbitration process of this operation. The first byte read (byte count) is the same for all devices and causes no conflicts. Next, the devices send their identifiers, and those devices whose data bits will have zero value first will have priority. Taking this into consideration, the following device class coding by the first two upper bits of the identifier byte has been adopted:

❏   00 — devices with fixed addresses; identified first
❏   01 — Persistent Slave Address devices
❏   10 — dynamically changing (volatile) address devices
❏   11 — random address devices; identified last

The least significant bit of the identifier byte indicates PEC support and all the capabilities based on the identifier. When this byte equals zero, nothing certain can be said about PEC support.

The last element of the UDID is a 32-bit device identifier that plays an important role in recognizing similar devices. This can be either a number assigned by the device manufacturer (who is responsible for its being unique) or a random number generated and remembered by the device every time upon power up or reset.

A device that supports ARP must have the following flags:

❏   AR (Address Resolved) — The particular device has been assigned an address by the ARP procedure.
❏   AV (Address Valid) — The device has a valid unique address to which it responds in regular transactions (when AV = 0, the device must ignore all addresses except the bus default address).

When AV = AR = 0, the device has no unique number and must go through the ARP process (answer the general call of the enumerator device). When AV = 1 and AR = 0, the device has a unique address, but still must go through ARP. When AV = AR = 1, the device has a unique address but does not have to respond to the general call of the enumerator. However, it must process the address assigning command addressed to it (and use the newly-assigned address thereafter). The combination AV = 0 and AR = 1 is inadmissible.

The following special commands have been created for the ARP:

❏   Get UDID (general) — general call of the enumerator: a block read command with address 1100 001 and command code 3. Devices supporting ARP reply to this command by sending a 17-byte block followed by a PEC. The first 16 bytes of the block are UDID; the 17th byte is the device's address (with 1 in the least significant bit). If the device's AV flag equals 0, it returns code 1111 111 instead of the address. The command does not affect the AV or AR flags.

☐ Assign address — a 17-byte long data block write command with address 1100 001 and command code 4, followed by a PEC byte. The first 16 bytes are the UDID; the 17th byte is the device address being assigned (the least significant bit is ignored). The device that detects that the UDID matches its own identifier exactly sets the AV and AR flags to 1 and sets the assigned address for utself.

☐ Get UDID (directed) — a directed request by the enumerator. A data block read command with address 1100 001. The address of the relevant device is contained in the code field of the command, with the least significant bit set to 1. Only devices that recognize their address in the command field respond to this command, and send a 17-byte long block followed by PEC. The first 16 bytes of the block are the UDID; the 17th byte is the address of the devices (with 1 in the least significant bit). The command does not affect the AV or AR flags.

☐ Reset device (general) — sends a code 2 command byte to address 1100 001, followed by a PEC byte. At this command, all devices initialize and zero out their AR and AV flags (PSA devices do not change their AV flags).

☐ Reset device ARP (directed) — sends a byte containing the address of the target device (with the least significant bit set to 0) to address 1100 001, followed by a PEC byte. At this command, the selected device initializes and zeroes out the AR and AV flags (the AV flag of a PSA device is not zeroed out).

☐ Notify ARP master — sends to address 0001 000 a byte with the default address 1100 0010, followed by two zero bytes. The device can send this notification of the need to perform ARP upon power up, and also when it detects a collision while providing data to a read command that accessed the device by its unique address.

A device that supports the ARP protocol acknowledges every command byte of ARP. Absence of acknowledgements is interpreted by the ARP master device as absence of ARP devices on the bus.

In brief, the reinventory and address assignment procedure works as follows: the ARP master device generates a general request of identifier and receives the UDID and possibly the address of the first winner in the arbitration. Further, this winner is assigned a unique address that is the same one it already had or not, at the discretion of the ARP master device, after which it no longer participates in the general call arbitration. The ARP master device records the information about this device and its address into the device table. Then, this general request and address assignment are repeated until all ARP devices have been assigned addresses. This will be indicated by the absence of acknowledgements of the general call commands.

SMBus Support in BIOS and ACPI

Unlike the ACCESS.bus, the SMBus' support on the BIOS level was given immediate specification. Later, specifications allowing SMBus devices to be integrated into the ACPI system were issued.

In 1995, the System Management Bus BIOS Interface Specification, a brief description of the main concepts of which is given below, was published. The interface allows the upper software levels to disengage from the host adapter hardware. BIOS support is provided for all three processor operation modes: real (and V86), protected 16-bit, and protected 32-bit. Functions are called either via the BIOS Int 15h (in the real and V86 modes) or via the entry point received when connecting in the corresponding mode. BIOS Int 15h service is also used for connecting and disconnecting; after connecting, access via Int 15h is blocked (until disconnection). In the protected mode, interface functions can be called only via the entry point received when connecting. The entry point method is optional for the real mode.

The SMBus BIOS specification provides host-centered access to the bus clients: At the initiative of the calling program, the host-controller sends a command to the device to which the device may be required to react immediately. However, devices can send messages to the host at their own initiative, using the Write Word protocol. The host can place the received messages in a short queue, from which they are extracted by calling function 7 (the program must periodically execute this call to check whether there are any messages in the queue). Each message in the queue consists of one-byte source address and a two-byte message body.

The SMBus is closely associated with the equipment that controls the power supply, and is involved in generating and handling System Management Interrupt (SMI) requests. This required a special mechanism to be introduced into BIOS that makes it possible to detect interrupt processing by the SMI during transaction execution and at other times. This is necessary because the SMI handler, working in the SMM mode, is totally invisible to the application program and the results of its work can significantly affect operation of the program calling SMBus BIOS.

The functions of general calls to the SMBus are as follows:

❏ SMBus Installation Check (01h) — ascertaining the function's presence
❏ SMBus Real Mode Connect (02h) — real mode connection
❏ SMBus 16-Bit Connect — 16-bit protected mode connection
❏ SMBus 32-Bit Connect (04h) — 32-bit protected mode connection
❏ SMBus Disconnect (05h) — disconnecting from the service

❏ SMBus Device Address (06h) — receiving SMBus device address list

❏ SMBus Critical Messages (07h) — reading messages sent to the host by the devices

There is a set of functions for interaction with specific SMBus devices that makes it possible to generate SMBus protocol commands and receive the results of their execution. The functions for issuing requests are separated from those for receiving replies, which makes it possible not to take up CPU time during the execution and transmission of rather lengthy commands. Most protocol commands are issued within one BIOS call; the exception is the block write command, data of which are sent in one or more successive requests. The results of most commands are also received within one call; results of a block read are received within several continuation calls.

The SMBus protocol command calls are as follows:

❏ SMBus Request (10h) — command request to a device

❏ SMBus Request Continuation (11h) — continuing block write request

❏ SMBus Request Abort (12h) — aborting a previously sent request

❏ SMBus Request Data and Status (13h)

The SMBus is one of the main communication means in the ACPI. The SMBus interface for ACPI is defined in the System Management Bus Control Method Interface (SMBus CMI) Specification Version 1.0, which was published at the end of 1999. This interface makes using all SMBus capabilities easy, regardless of the nature of the equipment and the peculiarities of its implementation. The main aims of the specification are as follows:

❏ To provide an effective and reliable ACPI interface for the host-controller's hardware, independent of its implementation (with or without a built-in microcontroller)

❏ To provide system-wide synchronization for access to all SMBus resources

❏ To guarantee interface compliance with the SMBus Specification Versions 1.0 and 1.1, and to ensure that it can easily be extended to support new functions anticipated in future versions

For the system to function successfully, it needs to be supported by the appropriate operating system drivers. For controlling power supply, the Smart Battery System Implementers Forum (SBS-IF) has developed specification for Windows9*x*/2000 drivers, which can be found at **www.sbs-forum.org/smbus**.

Considering the CMI is beyond the scope of this book. It will only be noted that the codes of the SMBus protocol used in the CMI are different from those used in the SMBus BIOS. The same protocols, but with a PEC byte, are encoded with a 1 in the most significant bit (the value is increased by 80h).

10.1.4. Comparison of the I2C, ACCESS, and SMBus

As can be seen from the above descriptions, all three buses are close relatives; however, they have a series of electrical, constructive, and protocol differences.

The electrical interfaces of the buses (Table 10.5) are similar and no compatibility problems arise when powering circuits off the regular (5 V) power supply (V_{dd} — power supply voltage).

Table 10.5. Electrical Characteristics of I2C, ACCESS.bus, and SMBus

Characteristic	I2C	ACCESS.bus external	ACCESS.bus internal	SMBus high power	SMBus low power
Input level of logical zero, no higher than	1.5 V or 0.3 V_{dd}	0.3 V_{dd}	0.3 V_{dd}	0.8 V	0.8 V
Input level of logical one, no lower than	3.0 V or 0.7 V_{dd}	0.7 V_{dd}	0.7 V_{dd}	2.1 V	2.1 V
Output level of logical zero, no higher than	0.4 V or 0.2 V_{dd} or $V_{dd} < 2$ V	0.6 V	0.6 V	0.4 V	0.4 V
Output current of logical zero (mA)	3	6	0.35	4	0.35
Maximum capacitance of the bus (pF)	400	1000	$-^1$	400	400
Frequency (KHz)	0–100, 0–400, 0–3,400	0–100	0–100	10–100	10–100

[1] Instead of capacitance, the permissible duration of the positive and negative transitions are indicated.

In terms of physical implementation, the external ACCESS.Bus stands apart from the others: It has connectors and cables defined, as well as being able to power devices from the bus (5 V); the other buses do not have this.

Protocol differences are more substantial; only the following will be noted:

❑ Only data transmission by the master device is defined in the ACCESS.Bus; in other buses, the master device can also receive data.

❑ The master device in ACCESS.bus and SMBus cannot take over the bus again earlier than 50 μsec after beginning transmission. The SCL signal can be kept at the low level no longer than 2 msec in this bus. There are no such restrictions in the I2C bus.

❏ In the SMBus, a master device expects an immediate reply from the slave device, whereas in the ACCESS.bus the response arrives independently, but is expected after no more than 40 msec. In the SMBus, both the master and the slave devices can delay the exchange at the bit reception level, which allows them to fit into their timing requirements (to wake up in time, service interrupts, etc.).

10.2. MII Interface SMI Control Bus

In 1995, the Media Independent Interface (MII) was introduced into the IEEE802.3u specification of the Ethernet technology, making it possible to separate specific physical level devices (PHY) from the higher levels. In addition to the interface for transmitting useful network data, the Serial Management Interface (SMI), which allows access to the internal PHY registers, is a part of the MII. The internal PHY device registers make it possible to monitor the PHY device state and control it, and in particular, to control the negotiation of the network port modes. The specification describes registers mandatory for devices, and also provides space for the specific registers used at the developer's discretion. The SMI interface is a serial synchronous 3-wire bus (the MDC and MDIO signals and the GND rail) that provides read and write access to 16-bit device registers. The bus protocol provides 5-bit addressing of the connected devices, which allows up to 32 devices be connected to one bus.

Each device can have up to 32 registers. The bus is host-centered: It is controlled by one controller that initiates transactions, whereas the rest of the connected devices are slaves. The controller generates the clocking pulses on the unidirectional MDC line, using the MDIO line to generate command and data bits (when writing) and to receive read data. A device that recognizes its address must execute the command addressed to it. Signal levels are regular TTL and CMOS logic levels; for the MDIO line, open collector (drain) signal drivers are normally used along with resistors pulling the passive line up to the power supply voltage level (+5 V or +3.3 V). The frequency of MDC pulses, not necessarily constant, must not exceed 2.5 MHz, which allows controller functions to be implemented purely by software. Timing diagrams for write and read transactions are shown in Fig. 10.4. Devices must latch bits at the positive transitions of the MDC signal; the controller latches bits at the negative transitions. Addresses and data are transmitted beginning with the most significant bits.

In general, each transaction is preceded by a preamble Pre, in which the MDIO signal is held high for no fewer than 32 clocks. The transaction proper is started by the Start condition: a 2-bit sequence 01 generated by the controller, followed by a 2-bit Cmd command, where 10 means read, 01 — write. Then, the controller transmits a 5-bit device address (PhyAd) followed by a 5-bit register address (RegAd). After this follows a 2-bit turnaround `TA` to switch to data transmission. When a write operation is executed, the 2-bit turnaround sequence is 10, after which the controller sends 16 data bits (`WData`) to be written to the register. When a read operation is executed, the controller relinquishes the `MDIO` line when starting sending the turnaround sequence, and during its second bit the responding addressed device sets this line to zero, which serves as an acknowledgement. During the next 16 clocks, the device sends read off data (`RData`) to the controller.

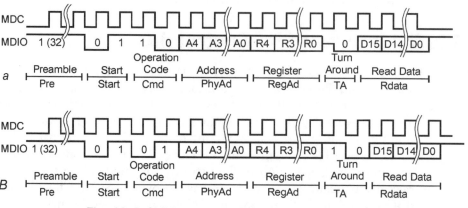

Fig. 10.4. SMI bus transactions: *a* — write, *b* — read

The preamble is only needed to initialize the device (after a power up); if the power supply has not been interrupted, the following transactions can be executed without preambles. The turnaround also has its peculiarity: For some devices, its second bit is one too many — it offsets data synchronization by one clock.

10.3. SPI Interface

The *Serial Peripheral Interface* (SPI), also known as Microwire, is a 4-wire synchronous interface with separate lines for the input and output data. It is used to provide communications between controllers and peripheral and memory microchips. It is used to program many types of programmable logic microchips (such as Altera's FPGA) used in various PC modules and peripheral devices. Compared with the I2C, the SPI provides a higher data transmission rate. The clock frequency may reach 5 MHz (depending on the connected devices); moreover, during each synchronization clock, a data bit can be transmitted and received simultaneously. The main use version presupposes that the interface connects one master device with one or several slave devices. The interface can also be used to conduct exchange among several microcontrollers, allowing several master devices on the bus, but the protocol to grant access is not standardized. Further interface operation with one master device is considered. The interface has 3 mandatory signals (the fourth wire is GND):

❑ SCK (Serial Clock) — sync signal by which the master device strobes each data bit
❑ MOSI (Master Output Slave Input) — master device output and slave device input data
❑ MISO (Master Input Slave Output) — master device input and slave device output data

Additionally, the SS# (Slave Select) or CS# (Chip Select) signals can be used: The slave device must react to the interface signals and place output data on the MISO line only when this signal is low; when it is high, the MISO output must be placed into the high-impedance state. Using the SS# signals that are generated by the master device separately for each slave device, the master can select one of the slaves for a partner in the transaction. This results in a hybrid bus topology: With respect to the SCK, MOSI, and MISO signals, the topology is of the bus type; while with respect to the SS# signal, the topology is of the star type, with the master being the center.

Another, purely bus topology way of the master device communicating with several slaves also is possible. In it, the SS# signal is not used to select a device, but the slave devices constantly listen to the bus, expecting a special address message at the beginning of the transaction. Having recognized its address, a device services the successive protocol messages and is allowed to place data on the MISO line until the end of the current transaction. However, this method requires complex logic on the part of the slave device.

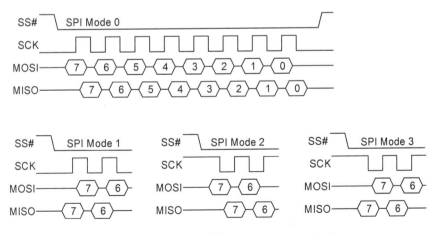

Fig. 10.5. Formats of SPI interface transmissions

Data are transmitted starting with the most significant bit. Devices from different manufacturers can use different exchange modes (SPI Mode 0 . . . SPI Mode 3), which differ by the phase and polarity of the sync signals. Fig. 10.5 illustrates transmission and reception of a byte in different modes. In any of the modes, the input and output data are strobed by different sync pulse transitions. Moreover, the SS# signal can be used in different ways. In the first case (shown in Fig. 10.5), the indication of the transaction start for the slave device is the fall of the SS# signal, while the indication of the transaction end is its rise. In the second case, transaction start is determined by the first rise (fall) of the SCK signal, and the SS# signal must be held low at all times. The second version is sometimes preferred for two-point synchronization. As a rule, microcontrollers with a hardware SPI port can select the mode using software. Transaction formats depend on the particular device, but the common idea is that the master device sends the operation code and the address information to the device over the MOSI line followed by the data. In the write operation, data are sent by the master over the same line, while in the read operation, the slave device sends them over the MISO line. The master device keeps the SS# line active for the duration of the entire transaction; the number of necessary sync clocks depends on the format of the command.

10.4. JTAG Interface

The Joint Test Action Group (JTAG) interface is aimed at testing complex logical circuits installed in the device. This interface is described in the IEEE1149.1 Boundary Scan Architecture standard and is of synchronous parallel type; however, because of its specific objective, it differs substantially from the interfaces described above, which are primarily oriented at data transfer. The JTAG interface is controlled by only one controller device (most often, this is a PC with an appropriate interface adapter), to which several devices being tested can be connected. Below are listed JTAG interface signals:

❐ TCK (Test Clock) — controller-generated serial data synchronization signal. Its frequency may reach 16 MHz.
❐ TMS (Test Mode Select) — controller-generated.
❐ TDI (Test Data Input) — input data received by the device in a serial binary code (the least significant bit first).
❐ TDO (Test Data Output) — output data transmitted by the device in a serial binary code.
❐ TRST (Test Logic Reset) — a controller-generated optional interface port logic reset signal.

These regular logical level signals (all unidirectional) form the *Test Access Port* (TAP), via which the device being tested is connected to the test equipment (the controller). The task of the test equipment consists of generating test signals in accordance with the test program defined by the developer of the device being tested, and comparing the obtained results with the template signals. The same controller and port can be used to test any number of devices that support JTAG. For this, the devices are connected in chain by their TAPs (Fig. 10.6). The standardized logic format allows the controller to communicate independently with each device in the chain (for this, they must have working JTAG cells, of course).

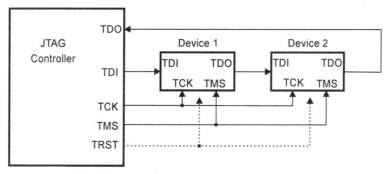

Fig. 10.6. A chain of JTAG interface devices

The principle of testing any digital circuit is illustrated in Fig. 10.7, which shows a symbolic digital circuit that has input, output (possibly high-impedance capable), and bidirectional signals. The B/S test cells are inserted between the actual external outputs of the device and the logical device proper (i.e., are located on the logical boundary of the device). A TAP controller can scan the cells (i.e., control them and read information from them), hence the name: *Boundary Scan*. When the test mode is on, the TAP controller can logically disconnect signals from the external outputs, set input actions, and read out the results: Basically, this is all that is necessary to test serial circuits (automatons with memory). The lovely part of the JTAG is that regardless of how complex a device may be, only four signals are used to test it: All the complexities are hidden in the relatively simple cells enveloping its signal outputs.

The testing logic built into a JTAG supporting device consists of the following elements:

❐ Test Access Port (TAP) (four interface signals).
❐ TAP register controller.
❐ Instruction Register (IR). Accepts the incoming serial code from the TDI input (the instruction code is used to select the test operation to perform or a test data register to which the access is made).
❐ Test Data Registers. A device must have three mandatory registers: BPR (Bypass Register), DID (Device Identification Register), and BSR (Boundary Scan Register).

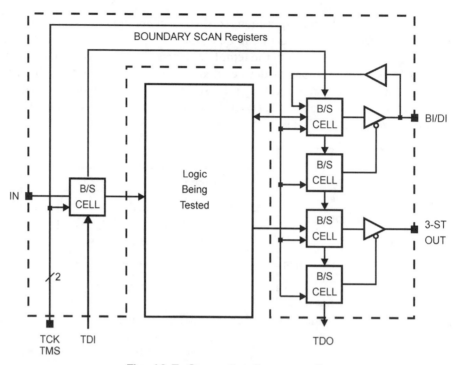

Fig. 10.7. Connecting the scan sells

The instruction and data registers are separate shift registers connected in parallel. The TDI signal is placed on their inputs and the TDO signal is taken off their outputs. Data are moved one bit for each positive transition.

The BPR register is 1 bit long. It is used as the shortest bypass for the serial data when the rest of the registers are not engaged in the exchange.

The BSR register is a long shift register whose bits are boundary cells placed at each input and output signal of the processor. For bidirectional signal (or their groups), there are control cells that set the operation mode of the information cells, in addition to the register information cells proper corresponding to the external signals. For example, the BSR register for P6 processors is 159 bits long.

The 32-bit DID register holds the manufacturer identifier, device code, and the version number, by which the TAP controller can determine the device, with which it is dealing.

The IR register is used to store the executed test instruction. Its length depends on the device being tested. The instructions BYPASS, IDCODE, SAMPLE, and EXTEST are mandatory for all devices.

The BYPASS instruction (all code bits are 1) is intended for connecting a 1-bit bypass register, providing data the fastest path through the device; at this, the device does not react to the transiting data flow. The TDI line is usually pulled by a resistor to the high level, so that breaking a JTAG chain will connect the bypass registers in all devices after the break point. This excludes potentially unpredictable device behavior in case of a chain break.

The IDCODE identification instruction (two least significant bits of the code are set to 10) connects the DID register to the interface, making it possible to read its contents (incoming input data cannot change its value).

The SAMPLE/PRELOAD instruction (two least significant code bits are 01) has two functions. When the TAP controller is in the Capture-DR state, this instruction allows a snapshot of all external signals to be taken without affecting the device's operation. Signals' values are latched at the positive TCK transition. In the Update-DR state, this instruction loads data into the output cells of the test port (but not to the device's outputs yet), from where they will be subsequently placed onto the processor's outputs by the EXTEST instruction. Data are loaded at the negative transition of the TCK signal.

The EXTEST instruction (two least significant bits of its code are 00) is used to test external (with respect to the device being tested) circuits. In this operation, signals written in advance to the BSR register are placed on the outputs, while the state of the input signals is latched in these registers. Bidirectional signals are configured beforehand by their corresponding bits of the BSR cells.

The 1149.1 standard also provides the INTEST instruction for testing internal logic of devices, but not all devices support it.

The TAP controller is a synchronous finite automaton that changes its state at the positive transition of the TCK signal and upon power up. Change of states is controlled by the TMS (Test Mode State) signal, which is clocked by the positive transition of the TCK signal. A flow chart of the TAP controller's states and transitions is shown in Fig. 10.8. Values of the TMS signal at the rise of the TCK signal are shown near the transition arrows.

The controller returns to the initial Test-Logic-Reset state automatically upon power up. From any other state, it can be returned to the initial state by the high-level TMS signal held for at least five TCK cycles. Sometimes, the controller can also be placed into the initial state by the optional TRST signal. In this state, the test logic is disabled, and the device works in the regular mode.

The Run-Test/Idle state is an intermediate state between test operation executions. In this state, the registers' values do not change.

While in the Capture-DR state, during execution of the EXTEST and SAMPLE/PRELOAD instructions, the scanning register only latches data on the input lines.

In the Shift-DR state, data from the TDI move via the connected shift register to the TDO output.

In the Pause-DR state, the controller temporarily disables data movement via the shift register.

In the Update-DR state, signals from the shift register are latched on the outputs of the test cells at the TCK fall.

In the Capture-IR state, the controller loads the code of the SAMPLE instruction into the shift register.

In the Shift-IR state, an instruction shift register is inserted into the chain between the TDI and TDO, but the previous instruction is still being executed.

In the Pause-IR state, the controller temporarily disables data movement through the instruction shift register.

In the Update-IR state, a new instruction to be executed is latched at the fall of the TCK signal and its corresponding register is inserted into the TDI–TDO chain.

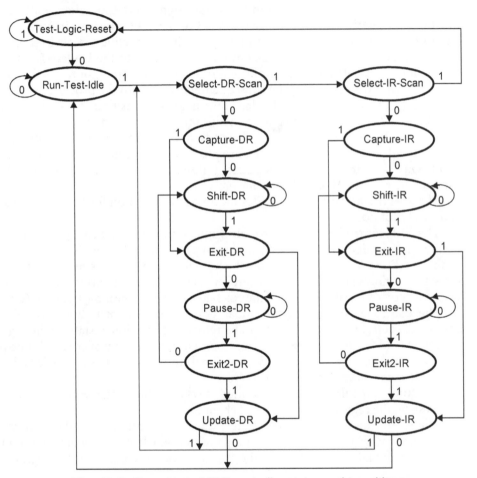

Fig. 10.8. Flow chart of TAP controller states and transitions

In addition to these main controller states, which determine the actions of the test equipment, there also are temporary intermediate states necessary to implement automaton's transitions. To these belong the Select-DR-Scan, Exit1-DR, Exit2-DR, Select-DR-Scan, Exit1-IR, and Exit2-IR states.

A special Boundary Scan Description Language (BSDL) has been developed for the JTAG interface to describe devices. The make-up and sequence order of the information and control cells in the data shift register is specific to each device (that's what the identification register is for), and is provided by the device's developers.

The JTAG interface is used not only for testing but also for programming various devices, including nonvolatile microcontroller memory. The PCI bus has contacts for the JTAG signals. However, their usage is not uniform: They are either left unused or are chained up. Modern processors are equipped with the JTAG interface, making it possible not only to test the processor itself (which operation has no application interest) but also to organize probe-mode debugging. The probe mode is a powerful means of system software debugging; a usual processor linked with a test controller by the JTAG interface turns into an in-circuit emulator — every system-software developer's dream.

10.5. Software-Controlled Implementation of Serial Interfaces

The interfaces considered above — I2C, SMBus, SMI, SPI, and JTAG — have one thing in common: They are controlled and synchronized by a controller and do not require a fixed synchronization frequency. This allows many applications to be implemented by software on any computer or microcontroller. Fig. 10.9 shows a schematic for a simple I2C, SMBus, or SMI interface adapter for the LPT port. Here, the SCL (or MDC in the SMI) signal is generated directly off the output Strobe line; it is enough to write zeroes (high level) and ones (low level) to bit 0 of the control register (port address LPT_BASE+2) to switch its states. The bidirectional SDA (MDIO in SMI) signal is a little more difficult to implement: A logical one is written to bit 1 of the control register (LPT_BASE+2) to send a 0; a logical zero is written to send a 1. This bit must contain zero during a read operation (so that the output is at the high level); the inverted data are read from bit 7 of the status register (LPT_BASE+1). The adapter must use a low direct voltage drop diode. Germanium mesa diodes are best suited to this purpose; silicon diodes, even with Schottky barriers, do not work as well here, as too high level of the logical zero is possible.

Software implementation of the protocols in the DOS and Windows $9x$ environments does not cause any particular difficulties, as the programmer can access the port registers directly. Operating systems with more protection (UNIX, Linux, Windows NT/2000) require API calls to access the LPT port.

When using these adapters, attention must be paid to the issue of protection from interference. Signals can be sent directly from the adapter only over short distances (tens of centimeters). To transmit signals over longer distances, an adapter from TTL to RS-422 and backwards can be used. In this case, the adapter is made out of two sections connected by a cable: One section is connected to the LPT port; the other one connects the device.

COM-port adapters for these interfaces are somewhat more complex. Here, the DTR and RTS signals can be generated and the state of the CTS, DSR, DCD, and RI signals read by software. The problem lies in having to use RS-232C-to-TTL signal level converters (there are several microchips that can be used for this purpose, such as those from Maxim or Sypex).

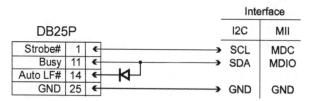

Fig. 10.9. LPT port adapter for 3-wire interfaces

For the SPI and JTAG interfaces, the LPT port can also be used; it is not even necessary to provide bidirectional lines. The SCK and MOSI signals (in SPI) and the TCK, TMS, TDO, or TRST signals (in JTAG) can be connected to any output lines of the port; the MISO (in SPI) and the TDI (in JTAG) signals can be connected to any input line. The simplest adapter is made up only of serial 100–150 ohm resistors placed into the signal lines to debounce and to reduce cable influence on the circuit. However, this type of adapter can only work reliably over short distances (20–30 centimeters), which is not always convenient. More reliable and practical is a circuit with buffers that can switch into the high-impedance state (such as 74HC244). This type of adapter can be connected to the LPT port by quite a long cable; the device is connected to the adapter by a short cable. The software-controlled switching of the buffer's output signals into the high-impedance state makes it possible to disconnect the adapter logically from the circuit being programmed, which is especially convenient when debugging programmable devices. This is exactly the way the popular ByteBlaster adapter, used to program programmable logic devices from Altera and other companies, is constructed. Jointly with software, the adapter can provide the SPI (to act as a master device in the two-point topology), JTAG, and its own programming protocols "Serial Passive" for programming some devices. Circuit schematics and software for them can be easily found on the Internet.

Software implementation of serial protocols limits their data transfer speeds to 50–150 Kbps with the LPT port working in the standard mode. In the EPP or ECP modes, speeds of up to 1–2 Mbps can be reached, but the adapter schematics becomes more complex here (because data needs to be simultaneously sent and received in these interfaces). The efficiency problem can be solved along with expanding the functional capabilities by using a specialized interface adapter for PCI and ISA buses; these are manufactured by several companies. However, such adapters and devices cost significantly more than a simple adapter that a user could make by him or herself.

Index